## Praise for *Where Peachtree Meets Sweet Auburn*

"*Peachtree* should stand as the definitive history of Atlanta's turmoil and triumph from the Civil War until now."
—*USA Today*

"*Where Peachtree Meets Sweet Auburn* is more than a political and social history of Atlanta. It is a story of the South and the twentieth century. . . . It is a genuine American story that any reader would find fascinating."
—*St. Louis Post-Dispatch*

"Pomerantz has done a remarkable job of digging through the historical record—delving into archives and stomping across graveyards—to chronicle these two intriguing clans . . . Pomerantz's dual family approach . . . provides a window on both the black and white communities through the city's most racially tense days."
—*Chicago Tribune*

"A valuable distillation of a larger drama, the birth of a New South."
—*The Washington Post Book World*

"As a rich blend of dense research and fluid, engaging storytelling, this book is a remarkable achievement. Pomerantz, in the tradition of J. Anthony Lukas' *Common Ground* and Nicholas Lemann's *The Promised Land*, tells a sweeping, complex history through the lives of families with triumphs and tragedies of their own. In the balance between grand stories and small, he conveys a portrait of a city and a region that lives very much at the center of the South's, and the nation's, conscience."
—*Star-Ledger*

"A finely drawn, epic history of Atlanta . . . Pomerantz has accumulated a formidable amount of research and deploys it expertly, rarely losing sight of his characters as they play out their unique destinies against the backdrop of history. An engrossing genealogical window on a remarkable city."
—*Kirkus Reviews*

"It's a work in love with history: carefully researched, powerfully written, rich with the pathos, tension, victories and bitterness of Atlanta's actual past. . . . Atlanta is not just a city of half-fake triumphalism. It's also a place of subtleties and intelligence, of honesty and good sense, of sadness and grace—like Pomerantz's book about it."
—*The Atlanta Journal-Constitution*

"A remarkably coherent view of the lives and times of the leaders whose actions and interactions, fraught with drama and peril, changed the face of the South and of the nation."
—*Entertainment Weekly*

"For Southern white readers of a certain age, the book may contain—perhaps not surprises, but recognitions: that black people can be as class conscious as whites; that even when we were young, educated and affluent black people likely lived not so far away from us—something our parents could not then have admitted; that the black aristocracy is distinguished indeed. . . . [A] fine and rewarding book."
—*The Raleigh News & Observer*

"Pomerantz is at his best in describing the strange and sometimes murderous relations between black and white in this century. . . . This is a book worth any Yankee's dollar."
—*The Hartford Courant*

"American history at its most accessible and readable—a rich and singularly human story."
—David Halberstam

"This book is a must-read. It tells the remarkable story of two families—one black and one white. It depicts their almost unbelievable struggle. In their stories, you can see the dying of the Old South and the birth of the New South."
—United States Representative John Lewis, 5th District, Georgia

"Impeccably researched and compassionately told."
—*BookPage*

"A powerful and splendidly written story, impressively researched and energetically told. Pomerantz is sensitive to the remarkable family histories he's uncovered, yet fair and tough-minded in his insider's portrait of the making of modern Atlanta."
—David J. Garrow, author of the Pulitzer Prize–winning *Bearing the Cross: Martin Luther King, Jr., and the Southern Christian Leadership Conference*

"It is the best book about a city that I have ever read."
—Pat Conroy

"There's powerful history here and much humanity, too. This book is a flat-out joy to read."
—*The Calgary Herald*

PENGUIN BOOKS

## WHERE PEACHTREE MEETS SWEET AUBURN

Gary M. Pomerantz is a writer for *The Atlanta Journal-Constitution*. Previously, he spent six years as a reporter for *The Washington Post*. A graduate of the University of California, Berkeley, with a bachelor's degree in history, he later served as a journalism fellow at the University of Michigan in Ann Arbor. He is married to the former Carrie Schwab. They have three children and live in Atlanta. This is his first book.

# WHERE PEACHTREE MEETS SWEET AUBURN

## A SAGA OF RACE AND FAMILY

## GARY M. POMERANTZ

PENGUIN BOOKS

*For Carrie,*
*naturally,*
*and for Ross and Win,*
*our Atlantans*

PENGUIN BOOKS
Published by the Penguin Group
Penguin Group (USA) Inc., 375 Hudson Street, New York, New York 10014, U.S.A.
Penguin Group (Canada), 90 Eglinton Avenue East, Suite 700, Toronto,
Ontario, Canada M4P 2Y3 (a division of Pearson Penguin Canada Inc.)
Penguin Books Ltd, 80 Strand, London WC2R 0RL, England
Penguin Ireland, 25 St Stephen's Green, Dublin 2, Ireland (a division of Penguin Books Ltd)
Penguin Group (Australia), 250 Camberwell Road, Camberwell,
Victoria 3124, Australia (a division of Pearson Australia Group Pty Ltd)
Penguin Books India Pvt Ltd, 11 Community Centre, Panchsheel Park,
New Delhi – 110 017, India
Penguin Group (NZ), 67 Apollo Drive, Rosedale, North Shore 0632, New Zealand
(a division of Pearson New Zealand Ltd)
Penguin Books (South Africa) (Pty) Ltd, 24 Sturdee Avenue,
Rosebank, Johannesburg 2196, South Africa

Penguin Books Ltd, Registered Offices: 80 Strand, London WC2R 0RL, England

First published in the United States of America by Scribner,
an imprint of Simon & Schuster, Inc. 1996
Published in Penguin Books 1997

7   9   10   8

Copyright © Gary M. Pomerantz, 1996
All rights reserved

THE LIBRARY OF CONGRESS HAS CATALOGUED THE HARDCOVER AS FOLLOWS:
Pomerantz, Gary.
Where Peachtree meets Sweet Auburn: the saga of two families
and the making of Atlanta/Gary M. Pomerantz.
p.   cm.
ISBN 0-684-80717-3 (hc.)
ISBN 978-0-14-026509-5 (pbk.)
"A Lisa Drew Book."
Includes bibliographical references (p.) and index.
1. Atlanta (Ga.)—Biography.   2. Dobbs family.   3. Allen family.   4. Afro-Americans—
Georgia—History—20th century.   5. Atlanta (Ga.)—Race relations.
6. Atlanta (Ga.)—History.
F294.A853A28   1996
920.0758'231—dc20        96–10399

Printed in the United States of America
Set in New Caledonia
Designed by Erich Hobbing

In the spring of 1856, a free person of color named Mary Combs paid $250 for a tract of land that today is marked precisely where Peachtree meets Sweet Auburn. She sold it six years later for $500 and used the money to emancipate her enslaved husband.

An Atlanta pioneer, Mary Combs knew how to make a profit. She also knew about freedom.

# Contents

➤◄

# THE ALLENS: DIRECT LINE OF DESCENT

**Daniel Allen**
b 1791 in Greene County, TN
d 1857 in Greene County, TN
Farmer (brother of Sam Allen)
Ran family plantation; owned 4,500 acres in
1850; at death, 23 slaves kept in family.

**Mary "Polly" Baker Allen**
b 1793
d Jan 19, 1865, in Greene County, TN
Homemaker
Married March 1, 1813; had 12 children;
died several months before the end of Civil War.

**Isaac A. Allen**
b Oct 21, 1820, in Greene County, TN
d Oct 21, 1884, in Greene County, TN
Farmer/livestock trader
Prosperous early, went bankrupt in 1866
from speculation in Confederate notes;
died insolvent.

**Sarah Earnest Allen**
b 1822 in Greene County, TN
d Feb 1, 1852, in Greene County, TN
Homemaker
From elite Greene County family;
had 3 children, then died in childbirth;
Isaac Allen remarried, had 7 more children.

**Daniel "Earnest" Allen**
b Dec 19, 1847, in Greene County, TN
d Sep 14, 1879, in Greene County, TN
Merchant in Dalton, GA (filed bankruptcy)
Enlisted Confederacy in 1862 at age 14; died
of dyspepsia at 31; buried in Dalton, GA.

**Susan Harris Allen**
b Feb 6, 1859, in UNKNOWN
d Mar 6, 1936, in Dalton, GA
Homemaker
Had 3 children; changed name of son Isaac
to Ivan after reading Russian novel.

**Ivan Earnest Allen, Sr.**
b Mar 1, 1876, in Dalton, GA
d Oct 16, 1968, in Atlanta, GA
Owned business: Ivan Allen office supplies;
Arrived in Atlanta in 1895; prominent civic
leader, aristocrat, state senator, booster.

**Irene Beaumont Allen**
b Apr 25, 1890, in Atlanta, GA
d Feb 27, 1972, in Atlanta, GA
Homemaker
Honeymooned in Cuba; had 1 child; lived
at 2600 Peachtree Road for nearly 50 years.

**Ivan Allen, Jr.**
b Mar 15, 1911, in Atlanta, GA

President, Ivan Allen Company
Atlanta mayor, 1962–70; championed civil
rights; lured pro sports, built skyline.

**Louise Richardson Allen**
b Jan 12, 1917, in Atlanta, GA

Homemaker/civic fund-raiser.
Descended from Inmans, elite Atlanta family;
president of Jr. League; met Clark Gable
at *GWTW* affair.

**Ivan Allen III**
b Oct 4, 1938, in Atlanta, GA
d May 17, 1992, in Franklin, GA
President, Ivan Allen Company
Civic leader; Atlanta Chamber
president, 1975; raised the city's
Olympic bid funds; son, Ivan IV.

**Beaumont Allen**
b Mar 3, 1951

Businessman: real estate
Married, 2 children; UGA graduate, former radio station producer in Atlanta.

**H. Inman Allen**
b May 9, 1941, in Atlanta, GA

Businessman; became chairman
Ivan Allen Company in 1995;
married, 3 children; chair of
Egleston Children's Hospital.

# The Dobbses: Direct Line of Descent

**Wesley Dobbs**
b 1819 in UNKNOWN
d Feb 5, 1897, in Kennesaw, GA
Slave farm hand/sharecropper
Owned by Josiah Dobbs; as slave, valued at
$800 in 1851. Married: 14 children; Baptist.

**Judie Dobbs**
b UNKNOWN
d Aug 21, 1925, in Kennesaw, GA
Freed slave/homemaker
Octoroon fathered by slavemaster; as child
beaten by master's wife; lived past 90 years.

**Will Dobbs**
b 1847 in Kennesaw, GA
d UNKNOWN
Artisan
At 29, married 14-year-old Minnie; played
fiddle. Divorced in 1882, later remarried.

**Minnie McAfee Hendricks Dobbs**
b Jan 1862, in Woodstock, GA
d May 26, 1937, in Atlanta, GA
Seamstress. Slavemaster/father, Dr. John
McAfee, let her live in Big House. With
2 children, moved to Atlanta in 1897. Later
remarried.

**John Wesley Dobbs**
b Mar 6, 1882, in Kennesaw, GA
d Aug 30, 1961, in Atlanta, GA
Railway mail clerk
Led Atlanta Negro Voters League & Georgia
Prince Hall Masons. Named "Sweet Auburn"
Avenue. Noted orator.

**Irene Thompson Dobbs**
b Apr 28, 1885, in Columbus, MS
d Jul 22, 1972, in Durham, NC
Homemaker
Had 6 daughters, all Spelman graduates.
Their married names: Irene Dobbs Jackson,
Willie Dobbs Blackburn, Millicent Dobbs
Jordan, Josephine Dobbs Clement,
Mattiwilda Dobbs Janzon, June Dobbs Butts.

**Irene Dobbs Jackson**
b Feb 16, 1908, in Atlanta, GA

College professor/homemaker
Spelman valedictorian. Earned doctorate
in France. Had 6 children. Integrated Atlanta
Public Library.

**Rev. Maynard H. Jackson, Sr.**
b May 3, 1894, in New Orleans, LA
d Jun 27, 1953, in Rusk, TX
Pastor, Atlanta Friendship Baptist Church.
Grandson/son of pastors; Morehouse
Endowment secretary; founded Negro
Voters League.

**Maynard H. Jackson, Jr.**
b Mar 23, 1938, in Dallas, TX

Three-term mayor of Atlanta/bond attorney.
Morehouse graduate; elected the South's
first black big-city mayor in 1973; 5 children;
2nd wife, Valerie.

**Valerie Richardson Jackson**
b Apr 3, 1949, in Richmond, VA

Homemaker/civic roles in education and Girl
Scouts. Master's degree Wharton School of
Finance; former advertising account execu-
tive; 2 children.

# Historic Time Line

><-

**1843** Named Terminus by the Western & Atlantic Railroad only five years before, city renamed Marthasville to honor daughter of Georgia Gov. Wilson Lumpkin.

**1845** City renamed Atlanta—feminine of Atlantic—by J. Edgar Thomson, Pennsylvania-born chief engineer of the Georgia Railroad.

**1851** Farmer Josiah Dobbs dies near Kennesaw, Georgia, 25 miles north of Atlanta. Among his inventory are 13 slaves. The most valuable, a black field hand named Wesley, appraised at $800.

**1864** Gen. William T. Sherman's Union forces destroy the city, signaling the death knell for the Old South. Five churches are saved by the pleading of Father Thomas O'Reilly.

**1867** Congress passes Reconstruction Act, making Atlanta headquarters of the Third Military District.

**1895** At the Cotton States and International Exposition in Piedmont Park, Booker T. Washington delivers a historic racial doctrine. Known by critics as the "Atlanta Compromise," he says, "In all things that are purely social, we can be as separate as the fingers, yet one as the hand in all things essential to mutual progress."

**1906** Fanned by sensationalized local reports of black men raping white women, mobs of whites erupt in a race riot. About two dozen blacks, and several whites, die. A white mob drops the bodies of two blacks at the foot of the Henry Grady statue.

**1915** Vigilantes seize Leo Frank, a Jewish businessman convicted of murdering factory girl Mary Phagan, from his cell in Milledgeville and drive him to Marietta. There, they hang him from a tree.

**1926** The Forward Atlanta campaign, spurred by civic leader Ivan Allen, Sr., lures to Atlanta, over a four-year period, 679 new factories, warehouses and sales offices with nearly 17,000 employees.

**1939** *Gone With the Wind* premieres at the Loew's Grand theater on Peachtree Street. Atlanta author Margaret Mitchell attends.

**1947** The death of governor-elect Eugene Talmadge in Atlanta in December 1946 leads to a scramble for a replacement. With the state constitution unclear about succession, three men lay claim to being Georgia's governor. One, Herman Talmadge, son of the governor-elect, storms the statehouse office, and his men change the locks. He serves 63 days before the courts declare Lt. Gov. M. E. Thompson as governor.

1948  Mayor William Hartsfield installs the city's first eight black policemen; their lockers are at the Butler Street YMCA, apart from the downtown police precinct.

1949  John Wesley Dobbs and A. T. Walden, powerhouses along Auburn Avenue as leaders of the black Republicans and black Democrats in Atlanta, co-found the Atlanta Negro Voters League.

1958  A bomb rips through the Temple, a Jewish synagogue, on Peachtree Street. The bomb causes substantial structural damage, but no one is hurt.

1960  Authorities jail the Rev. Martin Luther King, Jr., who joins Atlanta University Center students in protest at Rich's department store.

1961  Ivan Allen, Jr., president of the Atlanta Chamber of Commerce, successfully negotiates a plan with black leaders to desegregate the city's lunch counters in concert with school desegregation.

1961  On the day of John Wesley Dobbs's death, Atlanta schools are desegregated peacefully.

1964  Brandishing a pistol, Lester Maddox chases three blacks from his Pickrick restaurant near Georgia Tech, in defiance of the new Civil Rights Act. An all-white jury later clears Maddox on charges of disorderly conduct, requiring only 44 minutes of deliberation.

1966  Mayor Ivan Allen, Jr., quiets a Summerhill riot stirred by Stokely Carmichael, leader of the Student Non-Violent Coordinating Committee (SNCC). As Allen stands atop a car to address the crowd, blacks rock it side to side and he topples to the ground.

1968  More than 150,000 people march through the streets of the city behind a mule-drawn cart that carries the bier of the slain Rev. Martin Luther King, Jr. A memorial service is held at Morehouse College.

1973  Maynard Holbrook Jackson, Jr., a 35-year-old Atlanta attorney and grandson of John Wesley Dobbs, becomes the first black mayor of a major southern city.

1980  Hartsfield Atlanta International Airport, physically the largest in the nation, opens its new midfield terminal, constructed using Mayor Maynard Jackson's controversial "joint-venture" program. This program aims to award 25 percent of all municipal contracts to minorities.

1982  A jury convicts Wayne B. Williams, an unemployed 23-year-old

black music promoter, of two murders. Authorities implicate
Williams in 22 other murders of young blacks, ending Atlanta's
Missing & Murdered case.

1990 Atlanta wins the bid to host the 1996 Summer Olympics, the centennial celebration of the modern Games.

# PREFACE

><

My research for this book has taught me what the people of Atlanta have known for a century and more: there are two Atlantas.

The old-line southern families, white and wealthy, lived in an Atlanta that developed along its most famous thoroughfare, Peachtree Street.

The other Atlanta existed as if a parallel universe. It was home to blacks learning to be free. The center of their Atlanta was Auburn Avenue. Hungry to share in the fruits of the city, they built a commercial district that became known as Sweet Auburn.

Where Peachtree meets Sweet Auburn, then, is more than a mere intersection on a city street map. It is the meeting of two worlds.

To understand these distinct worlds and their people, I have studied two Old Atlanta families, the Allens and the Dobbses. Ivan Allen, Sr., son of an ex-Confederate cavalryman, arrived in 1895. He aimed to create wealth. Over time the Allens became model white patricians, millionaires living by a meadow. John Wesley Dobbs, son of Georgia freedmen, came to the city in 1897, seeking education. He brought with him energy, intellect and an orator's special gift. Over time, the Dobbses became solidly established among the city's black elite.

I was drawn to these families because their stories are instructive of the personal, business and political complexities in their worlds. Each family produced a major political figure—in fact, the two most significant mayors of the New South—whose work helped shape the Atlanta that ascended from the ashes of the Civil War to stand on the world stage as host to the 1996 Olympic Games.

The 1864 razing of the city by U.S. Gen. William T. Sherman's invading army has not been forgotten. It serves yet as a cautionary tale. The city burned to the ground during a war in which race was a central issue, and the people of Atlanta have worked mightily the past 132 years to make certain it didn't burn again. The city's black and white worlds came together for that purpose.

I asked two of the centerpiece figures in this book, Ivan Allen, Jr., and Maynard Jackson, Jr., to show me the Atlanta that shaped them. Only when these two mayors drove me to their old haunts did I gain a full appreciation of the gulf of geography and culture that separated the two Atlantas.

Ivan Allen drove me through the leafy streets of an elite enclave decorated by mansions, magnolias and honeysuckle. How time has changed his town. All but shouting: "Northside Drive is a racetrack now!" "My Lord! Look at that skyline!" He dropped names of old friends familiar to the white elites: the legendary golfer Bob Jones, the banker/mayor Robert F. Maddox, the Frank Inmans, the Mell Wilkinsons and Mrs. J. M. High. "These were some of the best old families in Atlanta, yes," Ivan Jr. said. "Peachtree Street was Peachtree Street."

Maynard Jackson, grandson of John Wesley Dobbs, stopped at a corner near his grandparents' old neighborhood. Once stately, the Dobbs home had fallen from grace. No leafy enclave or honeysuckle here. Jackson pointed to a street sign and said, "What's it say? 'Glen Iris.' " Across the street the sign said "Randolph." "You know why? Racial living patterns. Whites didn't want to live on the same street as blacks. So blacks lived on 'Randolph Street' and whites lived on 'Glen Iris.' "

Allen searched for an old brick building that once was his school. "Quite a number of my friends and later well-to-do Atlanta people were in the same class," he said. We drove past a grand Presbyterian church, his family's. We drove past a fancy social club where the young Ivan Jr. played tennis and swam. "As we grew up, for many of the social affairs, we'd go to the Piedmont Driving Club. The Driving Club was always the epitome of society in Atlanta."

Jackson remembered roller skates on a city street. "On Christmas day, this street, Jones Avenue, N.W., was packed with skaters. You're talking about styling—on skates. The brothers were super *baaaad!*" At his father's first home, he remembered eating figs year-round. He also remembered the twenty-seven steps up to the front door. "We were very crowded. We had four children and three bedrooms. The church had promised my father a parsonage, then all of a sudden it didn't happen."

At 2600 Peachtree, Allen stopped. He had grown up at that address. "Daddy built here at about the time I got out of Boys High School and went to Tech. It was a beautiful English Tudor home, limestone facing, a select brick. Nice home, very much the order of those days. You didn't hear ambulances runnin' up and down Peachtree in those days. It was very quiet."

Jackson looked up the twenty-seven steps to the house at 451 Ashby Street, N.W. He remembered the family's white collie, Lady White. "One time my sister, Carol Ann, who got confused by the name, stood on top of here at rush hour," he said. "The collie had disappeared and instead of calling, 'Lady White, Lady White,' she called, 'White Lady! White Lady!' Traffic was stopping all up and down the street."

Any understanding of the co-existence of the two Atlantas must begin with an understanding of the people who built the city. With only a nominal presence of European ethnic groups, Atlanta is not a New York City shaped by waves of immigrants arriving at Ellis Island. Nor is Atlanta, like the great cities of the Northeast and Midwest, created by broad-shouldered industries. For generations the South has remained an agrarian society and Atlanta its transportation hub, initially by rail, later by air. Even today the relationship of the British planter and his African slave remains at the heart of Atlanta's character.

The city's character is best revealed in answer to the question: How can blacks truly be free within a white southern society? It is a moral question that Atlanta has answered not with morality but with pragmatism. The answer has been a truce between white and black leaders. If not a full and just peace, the truce at least has been a fruitful cessation of hostilities. It did not eliminate the prejudice of the white southerner; it only kept it out of view. It did not guarantee blacks a better life; it made such a life seem possible. Though blacks and whites gained from such a truce, the gains were small in terms of tolerance and understanding. They were gains of profit in business and politics. Whatever trickled down from that profit, in terms of human relations, was a bonus.

Atlanta's emergence as a symbol of the New South has been as much an exercise in public relations as in morality, for it is hard to imagine a city that has more carefully managed and manipulated its image as a hospitable place of racial moderation. The wonder truly is that the image was projected with such vigor for so long as to become, in many ways, the reality.

The reality: America burned in the 1960s. Watts burned in riot. So did Washington, D.C., Cleveland and Detroit. Boston seethed in racial fury. Fire hoses and police dogs were turned against black men, women and children in Birmingham. Provocateurs spoke of a race war. In Atlanta, meanwhile, a city's racial conscience was tested as never before. The racial détente that had been established held up against the rage. Instead of burning again, the city came of age.

It became the city imagined by the Allens and Dobbses. Ivan Jr. was the son of a Babbitt-like businessman/booster who believed that whatever was good for business was good for Atlanta. The elder Allen liked to be called "Senator" (he had served two years in the Georgia General Assembly) and imagined himself as governor of Georgia. When business duties precluded politics, the Senator hoped that one day his son, Ivan Jr., would be governor.

Because John Wesley Dobbs and his wife, Irene, had six daughters and no sons, the Dobbs name, as the locals like to say, "went to girls." Even without the name, Maynard Jackson, Jr., carried the Dobbs fire and passion. As John Wesley Dobbs's firstborn grandson, he was so closely identified with the patriarch that even in 1995 aged members of the black community in suburban Atlanta referred to him as "one of the Kennesaw Dobbses," a phrase born in the days of slavery at the foot of nearby Kennesaw Mountain.

No accidental politicians, both Ivan Allen, Jr., and Maynard Jackson, Jr., came to the game eagerly, even with the idea of office beyond a mayor's. They came from patrician families that had built dynasties of power and influence in their parallel worlds. They came from families shaped by the tumultuous racial dynamic that changed Atlanta even as it changed America. They came from families whose stories speak of triumph and tragedy.

In these family stories is the story of a city.

GARY M. POMERANTZ
Atlanta, Georgia
Fall 1995

# PART I

# OLD SOUTH

| | |
|---|---|
| *Record for:* | Kate Bowie. |
| *Date of Application:* | January 8, 1870. |
| *Where born:* | 3 miles out of Atlanta. |
| *Where brought up:* | In Atlanta. Sold when 14 to Alabama. |
| *Residence:* | Gilmon St. this side Ricks mill. |
| *Age:* | 27. |
| *Complexion:* | Light Brown. Her mother raised her Emeline. Her name was changed by Jack Jones, who bought her at sheriff sale. |
| *Husband:* | Robert. |
| *Father:* | John Welch in Jacksonville, Fla. |
| *Mother:* | Agnes Nelson, sold away. |
| *Brothers:* | Anderson, sold away & Thomas in Texas. Henry & Willard sold away. |
| *Sisters:* | Sarah, wife of Peter Pitman at Cotton Hill, Clay Co., Ga. & Narcissa & Caroline both sold away & Mary Janes & Mary both dead. |

—Depositor's application No. 34, the Freedmen's Savings & Trust Company branch office in Atlanta

# CHAPTER 1

➤◄

In the upper chain of the Great Smokies along the Appalachian range, where a heavy limestone base makes the soil fertile for livestock farming, the father, grandfather and great-grandfather of Ivan Allen, Sr., were born and flourished. The patriarch of these east Tennessee Allens, Ivan's great-great-grandfather, Robert Allen, was nearly sixty years old when he left Chester County, Pennsylvania, after the Revolution to come to the virgin mountain territory, then still part of North Carolina. By 1786, the year Davy Crockett was born ten miles away, Robert Allen had settled on the undulating north bank of the Nolichucky River.

There, seven miles south of Greeneville, he built a log home with portholes that were used to defend against the Cherokees still roaming the river. The 'Chucky flows from western North Carolina through Greene County and snakes to the west, finally depositing into the French Broad above Newport, Tennessee. The Cherokees once looked to the snow-capped Smokies, rising to a daunting six thousand feet, and called them "the Unakas," which translates to "white." They named each of the small tributaries with a purpose—Lick Creek was near the salt licks, Horse Creek was where they hid their stolen horses, and Camp Creek sliced through the Cherokee campgrounds. The farm fields filled with Indian corn, wheat and grazing livestock. In the springtime, the valley burst with wild aster and goldenrod and the grasses grew long and lush. Local farmers boasted that these grasses bred the finest mules known to the South.

Nearly a century and a half after the antebellum Allens' years of glory, their legacy, and sense of industry, remains spread across these mountains. Allen's Bridge spans the Nolichucky; Highway 70 to North Carolina cuts through a mountain pass known as Allen's Gap; and just inside the North Carolina line, a traveler will notice Allenstand, which the Allens created to serve farmers as they drove their livestock between the two states. The enduring portrait of Greene County from this period is of livestock traders driving mules and cattle toward Asheville, North Carolina.

As the architect of the family prosperity, Daniel Allen, Robert's son, was more than a farmer. He built toll roads, bridges, had his own saw mill and grist mill and often played the role of personal banker, loaning money to local farmers at hefty rates. He had married Mary "Polly" Baker in the Presbyterian church in 1813 and they had twelve children, five of them boys, the most enterprising being Isaac and James. A dour and irascible man, Daniel Allen's most endearing trait was his affection for his children. He sent Isaac and James to the nearby Tusculum Academy. When his daughter Nancy married James M. Lowry he built a fine brick home on Irish Street in Greeneville for them. He thought the finished product insufficient and subsequently built the newlyweds an even more elaborate house in the country surrounded by ash and cedar trees; his slaves fired the bricks at the site. As proof of his enduring strength and legacy, the two homes built for his daughter still stand.

During the 1830s, Daniel and his younger brother Sam, who lived on the adjoining plantation, often ventured into Greeneville. It was a small, peaceful village of manicured gardens and brick homes with about five hundred residents. The Allen brothers shopped at the log cabin tailor business on Main Street owned by the Greeneville alderman Andrew Johnson. Andy Johnson, as he was known, later would serve as Abraham Lincoln's vice president and assume the presidency upon Lincoln's death.

"Sam Alens coat $4.66" reads one entry in Andrew Johnson's tailoring logbook from June 1832. An entry from December 1836 reads: "To the account of Daniel Alens $6.50."

In a frontier period when disputes between neighbors often were resolved with fists or rifles, Daniel Allen used a more civilized form of conflict resolution. It proved every bit as devastating. He sued his foes. While also capable of more immediate, if crude, action—in October 1838, he pleaded no contest to a charge of assaulting his neighbor with a stone, a case in which Andrew Johnson served as grand jury foreman—he was among the county's most litigious citizens. He could be petty and defiant: in 1843, he prompted a lawsuit by closing a ford that for decades had been the safest crossing of the Nolichucky and had deposited travelers to a road that passed within yards of the Allen home. Charged with obstruction by his neighbor Jacob Dyche, Daniel Allen was found not guilty by a jury. Soon after the suit, he planted orchards in the open space, presumably to be used for the blending of whiskey. This was typical of the way Daniel Allen conducted business. It's no wonder that he was widely known in Greene County for his imperious and pecuniary ways.

In the autumn of 1838, under the cover of darkness, a slave named Cain broke into a storehouse near Greeneville, Tennessee. He fumbled through the inner sanctum of a white man's store and stole only what he needed: $100, enough to buy his way into the North; and a pair of shoes.

These he would need, for he would run in the moonlight as fast as the Lord and new shoes would carry him. He would run from Sam Allen, the master of the only plantation he had ever known.

The crime detected, word went out the next day to slave patrols. Store owner Andrew Kennedy warned Sam Allen that unless he received total compensation for his loss he would prosecute Cain to the full extent of the law. In Tennessee, burglary by a slave was punishable by death. Kennedy allowed that if Cain was apprehended Allen could sell him to ease his financial loss, but he demanded the sale be done outside of Tennessee, to avoid a recurrence of the theft.

About twenty years old and strong, Cain moved quickly and surreptitiously to elude slave patrols at the Kentucky state line. He moved through the darkness of November nights.

Freedom eluded him. Spotted just south of Danville, Kentucky, more than 185 miles from Sam Allen's whip, Cain was placed in the Rockcastle County jail in Lancaster. In the runaway slave's possession the jailer found $100.

News of Cain's capture reached Sam Allen several days later; it pleased him. Allen was forty-two years old, a farmer and a Presbyterian. Together with his brother Daniel, he was building a small county empire. The Allen brothers lived among commonsense people: mountain farmers, Democrats and Scotch-Irish, many of whose families had arrived, like their own, soon after the American Revolution. The typical Greene County farmer of the period owned a hundred acres and perhaps one or two slaves, producing enough for self-sufficiency and small amounts for the market. Far removed from the cotton and rice plantations of the Deep South, ownership of slaves in east Tennessee was a sign of stature rather than a matter of necessity. By 1830, Daniel already owned eleven hundred acres; in another decade he owned nineteen slaves as well, among the largest totals in the county. Sam had ten slaves of his own. The Allens' attitudes toward the family slaves tended to be financially pragmatic and paternalistic; when their slaves required medical attention they sent for the family physician, Dr. Joseph Bell. One local legend, about the troublesome slave on the adjacent Johnston plantation who was nailed into a barrel and thrown into the river where he drifted downstream, presumably to his death, could not have happened at the Allens', according to one Greene County historian: "A good slave would cost $500 and the Allens would never roll $500 into the river."

In the case of Cain, Sam Allen dispatched a local man to Lancaster to confirm the slave's identity. Mistakes often were made and he could not afford the lost time.

Once he received confirmation, he set out on horseback on November 26, 1838, to retrieve his property. "The Negro is the same as land," his half-brother James Allen once had said. Sam Allen agreed: valuable property needed to be protected. He ferried across the Holston and Clinch rivers, then passed through the Cumberland turnpike. But when he arrived at the jail he heard startling news: Cain had escaped and his whereabouts were unknown.

Sam Allen was furious. Now the stakes grew: loss of time, loss of money and, if Cain were not retrieved, loss of the Allen reputation among local farmers. The unspoken gentleman's code among masters was that slaves were to be kept in line. Later, Sam Allen would file suit against jailer George Proctor, charging negligence in allowing the escape. (Though the jury would find for Proctor, Allen sought, and was granted, a new trial. He waited four terms for his case to be called but Proctor died in the interim. His attempt at retribution would add an additional $200 to the cost of his adventure.)

Sensing no alternative, he mounted his horse in Lancaster and began anew the chase for his runaway. He rode north to Lexington where coffles of slaves, manacled together and driven to markets, were a common sight. Then he rode on to Louisville, his anger rising, and then into the free state of Indiana. Finally, he gave up the chase and returned home, arriving the week before Christmas, having ridden about six hundred miles over twenty-one days. Cain, he thought, was gone forever.

Four weeks passed before the postmaster in Greeneville sent a surprising message. Cain had been captured by a bounty hunter in Ohio and was being held in a jail in northwestern Kentucky. Sam Allen wasted no time. Again on horseback, he retraced his path. He ferried across the Rockcastle and Kentucky rivers, passed through the "stamping grounds" and entered Gallatin County, where the only remaining obstacle to freedom for slaves on the run was the Ohio River. Sam Allen covered as many as forty miles per day.

In another dozen years Sam Allen would dictate his will from his deathbed and his wishes would reflect a belief that slaves were property and, as such, possessed only nominal human rights. Apart from his favorite black mare, Nig, which he would leave to his wife, he ordered the sale of his six slaves, "except my old Negro Etta and my mulatto girl Lize." Most likely Lize had been fathered by Sam Allen himself.

But now, in the winter of 1839, Sam Allen was on the chase. He wanted Cain back. And this time he knew he had him.

He arrived at the jail in Gallatin County on January 24, 1839. To the young bounty hunter, David E. Gibson, he paid $90. Now, with Cain in his possession, Allen was in control again. In another year, Kentucky's largest slaveholder, Robert Wickcliffe, a man known fondly as Old Duke, would tell the state legislature that six thousand slaves were being sold annually in Kentucky to southern markets, a traffic he abhorred and wanted stopped. "Generally speaking, slaves are treated with more humanity in Kentucky than any other state in the Union," Wickcliffe would say.

To return Cain to Tennessee, Allen knew, was to risk exposing him to the death penalty. So he made a swift decision that must have conveyed a powerful message about the price of disobedience to his slaves back on the plantation.

There in Kentucky, he sold Cain. To whom he was sold is unknown, though to have sold Cain to a much-dreaded Deep South cotton plantation would have been consistent with Daniel and Sam Allen's sense of fair play and retribution.

What is clear is that, in exchange for Cain, Sam Allen received $900, most of which he accepted in personal notes.

The remainder he took in the form of a horse, which he brought with him on the long and satisfying trip home.

The disposal of Cain lingered for a decade in the mind of Sam's half-sister Frances Allen Farnsworth. In July 1848, following the death of the aged family matriarch, Martha Allen, Frances wanted accountability. She sued Sam for her rightful share not only to the sold-off Cain but also to a block of ten of Martha Allen's slaves still in his possession.

What emerged in the chancery court in Greeneville was a messy family dispute that illustrates how the Allens treated blacks as property—to be divided into one-fifth shares and ceded in wills, like a team of horses or chest of drawers. Naturally, Daniel Allen gave supporting testimony for his brother.

The dispute was traced to 1811 when Robert Allen—father of Sam and Daniel and of Frances—was too weak to write his own will and dictated his wishes to a friend. He divided his five-hundred-acre plantation evenly between his young sons, Daniel and Sam, both born of his second marriage. He also gave one slave to each, and to two of his daughters. To his second wife, Martha, Robert Allen bequeathed two black women, Letty and Pris; they would become the source of the later dispute.

When Reuben Allen, one of Robert's five children from his first marriage, read the paper reputed to be his father's will, he was enraged by its contents and burned it. When a copy was produced, Reuben contested it. The court ruled the will legitimate in 1812 but his lawsuit proved an omen.

By willing the slave women to his second wife, Robert Allen also passed on rights to any slave children they would bear. He further stipulated that upon his wife's death, all such rights would transfer to the five children from his first marriage: Reuben, Frances, Polly, James and Robert.

By 1849, Frances reckoned her share of the estate amounted to one-fifth interest in Letty and nine other slaves that represented Letty's and Pris's "increase"—as well as a share from the sale of Pris's son Cain.

Sam Allen, who before his senile mother's death had taken control of her estate, told the court he was willing to sell the ten slaves at issue and divide the proceeds among his half-siblings.

But it would be no simple matter. Nothing with the Allens was simple when it came to litigation.

Even as he said he was willing to sell his slaves and split the proceeds, Sam Allen also informed the court that he had purchased from family members a two-fifths share in the ten slaves. If forced to sell, Sam said he wanted two-fifths of the proceeds in addition to being reimbursed for expenses in chasing down Cain. Further, if the court said he must pay Frances a sum equal to the value of labor performed by the ten slaves in the months since Martha Allen's death, he wanted repayment for feeding and clothing the slaves during that time.

A chancery court ruling came on May 18, 1849. Sam Allen would have to expose the ten slaves for sale at the Greeneville courthouse door, with Frances Allen Farnsworth receiving one-fifth of the proceeds. At the same time, the court ruled that Sam was due two-fifths.

On May 22, David Sevier, clerk of the court, nailed the following notice on the courthouse door:

NOTICE. Chancery Sale of Negroes. Pursuant to a decree, rendered at May term, 1849, of the Chancery Court held at Greeneville, Tennessee, in the suit of Henry Farnsworth and wife, complainants against Sam Allen and others, Respondents; I will offer a public sale, to the highest bidder, at the Court-House door in Greeneville, on Saturday, the 16th day of June next, a family of ten valuable Negroes, to-wit:

> **Letty, Eliza, Becca, Prisey [sic], David,**
> **Nancy, Tyler, Gibson, Harriet and**
> **Margarett [sic].**

A credit of twelve months will be given the purchaser on his giving bond with approved security for the purchase money. Said Negroes are, for the most part, young and healthy, and persons desiring to purchase valuable servants may do well to attend.

D. Sevier, Clerk & Master.

On that Saturday, the Allens' slaves were paraded up the courthouse steps on Main Street. At street level stood a crowd of prospective buyers and the usual curious onlookers. Daniel and Sam Allen were among the crowd as was Daniel's son James. By consent of the Allen family members involved in the suit, the two slave mothers were to be sold in tandem with their infants.

Typically, the auctioneer offered a quick analysis of each slave and then the bidding began, loud and lively. Letty, forty-eight years old, often sick and "not worth her victuals and clothes," according to court testimony, was sold for $161. Four-year-old Gibson and two-year-old Harriet brought $279 and $220.

Sam Allen bought back three of his slaves, the thirty-one-year-old Eliza plus Prissy and her infant Margaret. He spent $1,211.

Daniel Allen paid $380 for the boy David; his son James bought Tyler for $325.

In all, the ten slaves brought $3,263. The Allens repurchased seven, including the pair bought by Henry A. Farnsworth, whose parents had initiated the suit. Two prominent local men, Dr. William West and Thomas Weems, purchased the remaining three.

Even with his two-fifths share, Sam Allen lost seven slaves and $253.08 in the transaction.

Ten years later, Cain, wherever he was, was still costing him money.

Some of the neighbors watched in 1926 when Daniel and Sam Allen's plantation homes were submerged beneath the muddy waters of the 'Chucky. The East Tennessee Electric Company built a dam across the river to generate electricity for the area. The Allen plantation homes, and slave cabins, were among the necessary losses. As part of the process, workers scaled the knoll above the river and dug up the caskets of five generations of Allens. Those who bore witness saw water pour from the saturated boxes that held the remains of Daniel and Sam Allen and their kin. The caskets were loaded onto wagons and taken to the Oak Grove Cemetery several miles away for reburial.

Of Daniel Allen's sons, Isaac had been the favorite. Isaac's marriage in 1843 to Sarah Ruth Earnest must have greatly pleased his father. The Earnests, living five miles upriver, were a prominent east Tennessee family—Daniel Allen's kind of people. One tale passed down through the generations in Greene County suggests that Daniel Allen often loaned one of his male slaves to Nicholas Earnest for breeding purposes. The slave, according to the tale, later became deeply religious and, rather than defy Allen by refusing to perform, jumped in the 'Chucky and drowned.

Though probably apocryphal, the tale reflects the cold, miserly legend left by Daniel Allen. Isaac was a more carefree spirit than his father and became a livestock trader. His speculative habits, however, created problems. Isaac pleaded guilty to charges that he had bet on an election in 1844, the year Tennessee's James Polk, a Jacksonian promising the annexation of Texas, defeated Henry Clay for the presidency.

Isaac's devotion to his father was plain to see. When his first son was born in December 1847, he was named Daniel Earnest Allen. Named for the family patriarch, Ivan Allen's father would be known throughout his life as "Earnest" Allen, a blending of two of east Tennessee's finer families.

Soon, Isaac would assume the Allen mantle. In the summer of 1851, family physician Dr. Joseph Bell had rushed to Sam Allen's plantation. Hoping to restore his fading health, Bell attempted to "electrify" him with shock treatment, to no avail. Sam Allen died that fall.

An era ended six years later, in 1857, when Daniel Allen died at the age of sixty-six. His nephew, attorney Robert A. Crawford, drew up the papers. By the end of his life, Daniel Allen's empire was worth in excess of $100,000. He owned more than 4,500 acres in Greene County and twenty-three slaves. His children gathered with their widowed mother at the old plantation home on September 2 and divided his possessions, including furniture, livestock and slaves. James took seven of his father's slaves and Isaac four, including a black woman Sarah and her mulatto infant Nancy. The list of personal notes due Daniel Allen exceeded $13,000. Some insolvent notes dated back more than twenty years.

Isaac moved into the old Daniel Allen home by the river. Isaac was more tolerant and optimistic than his father. His eyes were a magnetic blue; he had light brown hair and a beard, which waved in the wind as he rode. During these years, he suffered personal losses. His wife, Sarah Earnest, died in childbirth in 1852, leaving him with three children. Four years later, he married nineteen-year-old Laura Haygood at her family's Baptist church in Sandy Level, South Carolina. They would have seven children.

Isaac traveled the South, buying and selling livestock. From him, his son Earnest developed an appreciation for riding and driving fine horses. In time it would become apparent that Isaac took too many speculative risks. But in 1860, his good fortune seemed as certain and eternal as the flowing waters of the Nolichucky.

# Chapter 2

➤❮

In November 1851, Dr. John Miller McAfee drove a carriage from his plantation in Woodstock, Georgia, more than seven miles along Noonday Creek to the farm of Josiah Dobbs.

A small, imperturbable man who cast long and impressive shadows across his community, McAfee for years had been a country doctor, riding horseback across the rolling hills of north Georgia with his bag of liniments, elixirs and crude medical instruments. He had accepted livestock from patients too poor to pay. But now, near his fiftieth birthday, he had retired from medicine and settled down to farming.

Few men in the upper Piedmont of Georgia were as rich as Dr. McAfee. He lived on a seven-hundred-acre plantation near Rubes Creek in Cherokee County, owned an additional four hundred acres on the Little River and several other large parcels of land in Lumpkin, Hall and Floyd counties. Like his penned signature, his plantation home reflected great style and flourish with a fanciful array of chandeliers, portraits, looking glasses and a grand piano. McAfee kept forty-two slaves on his plantation, many of whom worked fields brimming at harvest with Indian corn, wheat, sweet potatoes and cotton. Some of his slaves worked the syrup mill or the cotton gin and threshing machine; others he hired out. McAfee had enough slaves that he could spare eight to live with his mother-in-law in Jackson County.

On this day, McAfee walked along the Dobbs farm in the Big Shanty district of Cobb County, twenty-five miles north of Atlanta, canvassing the available plows, farm tools, furniture and livestock. He was among several dozen farmers who arrived from nearby Marietta and the settlements at Smyrna and Kennesaw stations. These farmers were well acquainted with one another: the Roberts brothers (Willis and Thomas), the McAfees (the doctor and his brother Bob) and the Dobbs brothers (Asa, David and Josiah) were among the wealthier men in these parts; there had been several marriages between their families. The Dobbs brothers had settled in Cobb more than a decade before, moving from their native Elbert County.

Josiah Dobbs, a widower and member of the Noonday Baptist Church, had died that summer. His brothers, Asa and David, administrated his will. They also became guardians to four of their brother's children.

From the Josiah Dobbs estate, John McAfee purchased three hoes, five axes, a handsaw, one lot of tools and a hammer. He paid $5.55. His brother, Bob, bought a blanket and one lot of dry peaches. Among the Roberts brothers' purchases were a bell, several plows, a stack of fodder and fifteen sheep.

Cobb County was in a period of enormous prosperity and Josiah Dobbs had shared in it. At his death he had owned thirteen slaves, among the county's largest totals. As part of the administration of Josiah Dobbs's estate a county assessor had appraised their value. Nine of Josiah Dobbs's slaves were children and three were women. Only one was a man, a dark-complexioned field hand, about thirty-two years of age. He was the most valuable in the group.

Assessing the worth of John Wesley Dobbs's grandfather, the county appraiser wrote:

WESLEY, a negro man valued at———$800.00.

The scant availability of documentation relating to the white Dobbses suggests a tangled web of family connections, typical of the times. Though it is unclear who assumed ownership of the slave Wesley in 1851, Josiah Dobbs wished for all of his slaves to remain in the family and almost certainly his wish was not violated.

What is important is that Wesley is the point from which the lineage of the black Dobbses of Atlanta may be traced.

The irony is that this same lineage may be traced from the white physician, Dr. John Miller McAfee, who, from his position in the shaded eminence of the Old South, is also the great-great-grandfather of Atlanta's first black mayor.

On a night of blood lust and terror in August 1831 that sent shivers down the spine of every southern slave-owner, a slave named Nat Turner and several dozen black compatriots went on a killing spree in southern Virginia, stabbing, shooting and hacking to pieces more than fifty whites, including several masters and many women and children. Turner eluded authorities for two months. His capture and hanging did not diminish the specter of his deed. One Virginia legislator in 1832 bemoaned "the suspicion that a Nat Turner might be in every family."

Two years after the rebellion, in 1833, when the reign of the Cherokee was nearly at an end in north Georgia, Dr. John Miller McAfee was among four men elected to the Georgia House of Representatives from Hall County. He was a Jacksonian Democrat who opposed the Whigs and States' Rights men who would have certain federal laws nullified in Georgia. At a July 4 dinner in Gainesville in 1833, Dr. McAfee made two toasts. "To George Washington, the father of our Independence; Andrew Jackson the protector," he said. Then he saluted Jackson alone: "The President, the protector and preserver of our Government, may he never be forgotten by the American people." Raised by tent revival Methodists in Rutherfordton, North Carolina, McAfee was only thirty-one years old. He had married Malinda Hemphill of Jackson County in 1826. With seventeen slaves on his farm, already he was on the brink of planter status. Politics seemed a natural course in the McAfee family. Robert McAfee, a prosperous farmer and the father of eight, including the doctor, had been elected in 1831 to the North Carolina House of Representatives. Robert McAfee served one term, then moved to Pinck-neyville in Gwinnett County, Georgia. When he applied in 1834 to build a toll bridge across the Chattahoochee River, he found ample support in the Georgia legislature: not only from his son, Rep. John McAfee of Hall, but from another son, Sen. James Taliaferro McAfee of Cobb County. Naturally, he was allowed to build his bridge.

Like Dr. McAfee, many Georgia legislators during these years were slave-owners. Some policies enacted were designed to limit the possibil-ities of a Turner-like rebellion. An 1833 law prohibited slaves from preach-ing before more than seven slaves unless the preacher had received letters from three ordained white ministers; the letters were to set forth the colored preacher's moral character and pious deportment. Another law, passed in 1835, was designed to allay a master's fear of poisoning by his slaves. It forbade any person of color from compounding or dispensing medicine in a drugstore; white pharmacists who failed to obey were to be fined $100 for the first offense, $500 for each offense thereafter.

The French writer Alexis de Tocqueville traveled the South during these years and offered a quick study of racial tensions: "The danger of conflict between the white and the black inhabitants of the Southern states of the Union (a danger which, however remote it may be, is inevitable) perpetually haunts the imagination of the Americans, like a painful dream." De Tocqueville understood the white master's reaction to the rising cry of the abolitionist. "The more the utility of slavery is contested," he wrote, "the more firmly it is established in laws."

In 1835, the Georgia legislature passed a resolution that warned those who would abolish slavery: "The perpetuity of this glorious Union, which has shed such blessings on us as a people, is only to be insured by a strict adherence to the letter of the Constitution, which has guaranteed to us certain rights, with which we will suffer no power on earth to interfere; that it is deeply incumbent on the people of the North to crush the traitorous designs of the abolitionists. . . ."

Each winter the sleepy capital city of Milledgeville, Georgia, sprang to life when legislators returned. Dr. John McAfee traveled from Woodstock to the capital in December 1836 when railroads were the central issue. The local newspaper, *The Southern Recorder,* reported that the city's annual Christmas ball would be held at Mr. Horton's hotel near the statehouse; that an itinerant dentist was available for consultation in an office on Jefferson Street and that General Wool, commander of the troops in the Cherokee lands of north Georgia, had spoken harshly against the selling of liquor to the Indians.

All across the South the rush for expansion was on. The South Carolina statesman John C. Calhoun promoted a railroad that would connect Charleston with Louisville and Cincinnati on the Ohio River. In Georgia, the former governor Wilson Lumpkin, realizing that his state was among those that would benefit most by tapping into Calhoun's rail project, warned legislators that "the apathy of Georgia is pregnant with the most fatal consequences." But Georgia was slow to react and was excluded from the new rail line. In November 1836, Georgians held their own railroad convention in Macon. Thirty-eight counties and officials from two railroad companies proposed the creation of a state-funded rail line that would connect the commercial centers in Georgia with the Tennessee River. That line would cover about 120 miles from southeast Tennessee to a spot along the Chattahoochee in north Georgia; it would unite Georgia's inland commerce centers of Athens, Milledgeville, Madison, Forsyth and Columbus.

Legislative voting records indicate that Dr. John McAfee of Hall County favored the rail line but did not want the state to foot the majority of the bill. Neither did he feel Lumpkin's sense of urgency about the issue. McAfee was among a group that voted to table the railroad bill for the remainder of the session.

The debate in the House was animated on both sides. Rep. Alexander Stephens of Taliaferro County, the future vice president of the Confederacy, spoke in favor of the bill. Though it passed, Representative McAfee and his Hall County colleagues opposed it, apparently for reasons related to funding.

Eleven days later, on December 21, 1836, Gov. William Schley signed into law the new state-funded Western & Atlantic Railroad of Georgia.

The following autumn surveyors chose a site in De Kalb County as the crossing point of the Chattahoochee. The future city of Atlanta was born as a small railroad settlement in a spot later described by Lumpkin as being "in a perfect state of nature—a wild unmolested forest, not a fence or cabin to be seen anywhere in sight."

To locals, the new settlement was known as Terminus.

In 1839, in the old Cherokee lands of Dahlonega, Georgia, where gold first was spotted a decade before, the Bank of Darien appointed Dr. John Miller McAfee as cashier in its branch office. His job was to buy gold from speculators on behalf of the bank. Not only was he well-compensated by the bank during the short-lived rush, but also by his patients, some of whom paid him in gold. His stature in the sparsely populated Lumpkin County was evidenced in 1840 when he was elected state senator; he served a pair of two-year terms.

Returning to Milledgeville on Christmas Eve, 1842, Senator McAfee witnessed the effects of the vote he had opposed six years earlier when the Western & Atlantic Railroad opened a small terminal. On that day, the first excursion from Terminus to the new station in Marietta—only a few miles from the plantation of Josiah Dobbs—was made amidst great celebration.

Now that the locomotive had arrived, railroad officials determined that the settlement required a name more respectable than Terminus. The surveyors of the line wanted to honor their great advocate, former governor Lumpkin, but he deferred, reminding them that Lumpkin County already carried his name. So the railroad men opted to honor Lumpkin's daughter, Martha.

Sen. John Miller McAfee of Lumpkin County, progenitor of Atlanta's first black mayor, sat in the chamber of the Georgia Senate in Milledgeville on that December day in 1843 when, according to the *Senate Journal*, "The Senate took up the report of the Committee of the Whole, on the bill of the House of Representatives, to incorporate the town of 'Marthasville,' in the county of DeKalb, and to appoint commissioners for the same, and for other purpose therein mentioned.

"The report was agreed to; the bill was read the third time and passed."

By the time the first Georgia Railroad train from Augusta arrived in 1845, Marthasville was a burgeoning settlement. When the president of the Georgia line, Judge John P. King, made his first trip into Marthasville, he stepped off the train and into an open well being dug at the depot. Speculators came in legions and soon Marthasville took on the air of a rowdy western town. Railroad agents complained that "Marthasville" was too long to print on tickets. The chief engineer of the Georgia Railroad, J. Edgar

Thomson, was asked by Supt. Richard Peters to create a more suitable name for Marthasville. His response was: "Atlanta, the terminus of the Western and Atlantic Railroad—Atlantic masculine, Atlanta feminine—a coined word, and if you think it will suit, adopt it." The Georgia Railroad began to distribute circulars in Georgia and Tennessee, promoting "Atlanta," and on December 26, 1845, the name was signed into law.

Years later, Wilson Lumpkin wrote to his daughter, "You may always remember that one of the most distinguished towns in Georgia was located by your father, and by its original and first proprietor named in honor of yourself 'Marthasville.' The name being stolen from you will never change the facts appertaining to the case."

What is known of the black Dobbses from antebellum days comes in pieces from beneath the shroud of slavery. There is an inherent difficulty in chronicling the daily human experiences of slaves, who, as property, were cited in the official records of southern states not by name, only by gender, estimated age and color (black or mulatto). That difficulty is compounded in Cobb County because virtually all of its records were burned by federal soldiers in 1864.

Yet, like so many others, the descendants of the slave Wesley and his wife, Judie, have maintained a rich oral tradition. Tales of their slave experiences have been passed down through the generations. However imperfect the documentation of these tales, they have been accepted by the family as truth and therefore carry the force of truth, fortifying and guiding the next generations.

Judie would live about one hundred years. Her parentage and date of birth remain a mystery, though it is believed that she was born in about 1824. Her eyes were blue, her hair long and flowing. One existing photograph of her shows a middle-aged woman with soft eyes and an expression that suggests both superiority and indifference. She told her descendants that her slave mother was one-fourth black and her father a white master, which made her, in the term of the times, an octoroon (one-eighth black).

By all accounts, she looked white. "She was as white as people get to be but she was considered black," one great-granddaughter recalled. Another would remember only a small and fragile elderly woman, "that looked like Whistler's Mother."

As a young girl, Judie said, she had cared for her father's invalid wife. She had served her meals and combed her hair. The wife had been less than appreciative, for she had known of the girl's origins and was bitterly resentful. Occasionally she beat or scratched the slave girl; other times she cursed her for her mere existence. Later, Judie hoped to marry a light-skinned slave for whom she had an amorous eye, but was paired instead with a dark, African-looking man, so that there would be no mistaking her children for anything other than what they were, slaves.

With Josiah Dobbs's field hand, Wesley, she would have fourteen children, the first, a son Will, in 1847. By the time their last child, Jesse, was born in 1874, Judie Dobbs was about fifty. Neither Judie nor Wil was listed among Josiah Dobbs's slaves in his 1851 inventory; the probability is that they were living on a nearby plantation in Cobb County.

Judie Dobbs was proud of her light complexion. In one private moment, she called out to a great-granddaughter, "Come here, sister. I want to show you something." Then she drew back several layers of petticoats to expose her pure-white thigh. "See, sister," said she, "that's my real color!"

In death, the mystery of her life was recorded in a sad though honest sequence. Her bachelor son George filled out her death certificate in Marietta as follows:

> Name of Father: *"Don't Know."*
> Maiden Name of Mother: *"Don't Know."*
> Date of Birth: *"Don't Know."*

Of at least one fact about his mother's life, George Dobbs was certain.

> Race: *"Colored."*

Seeking to maximize his profits, John McAfee hired out one of his slaves, Peter, to the Western & Atlantic Railroad for the year 1857. Through an agent, Dr. McAfee contracted for Peter to work at the freight depot in Atlanta.

It would prove a galling and costly experience.

Peter was twenty-four and, as the Atlanta stationmaster George W. Lee said, "He was the most trusty Negro I ever saw. . . . His size was 160 pounds and in his disposition was easily controlled and obedient. . . . His qualities were extraordinary."

McAfee understood that Peter would work only on the loading platform, assisting in the shipment of goods. Yet, unknown to him, Peter was soon put to work on a passenger train, making the round-trip to Chattanooga either as a brakeman or as servant to white passengers. Peter was also permitted to make trips to Marietta at least once a week to visit his wife.

On those days when he was scheduled to work at the loading depot, Peter typically rode the train from the passenger terminal for nearly a half mile, then leaped from the steps of the platform just before the train reached the first switch on a downgrade. It was faster than walking and saved a few minutes.

But on May 1 the conductor was unaware that the slave was on board. The train was said to be traveling more than twenty-five miles per hour when Peter jumped from the steps of the platform of the second car. His body fell across the tracks and was run over by the passenger cars.

His injuries were severe. A physician called to the scene amputated one leg below the knee and a portion of his other foot.

Within twenty-four hours, John Miller McAfee's valuable slave was dead. When McAfee learned of the accident he filed a claim with the W&A. The rail line refused his settlement overtures. McAfee responded by filing suit in Fulton County Superior Court in March 1859, charging negligence. In his suit McAfee contended that Peter had been used in a manner other than that for which he had been contracted. He also maintained that the law of the road required that when a slave hand, who belonged to one train, rode upon another, a written pass from the superintendent was required. Peter had not been given a pass. Further, McAfee contended that the train was traveling in excess of the ten-miles-per-hour limit.

The trial was held during the court term of October 1860. The jury found for Dr. McAfee. He was awarded $1,500 plus legal expenses. The W&A appealed, but the Georgia Supreme Court affirmed the verdict.

"The rule of law on this subject is, that if the thing [hired] is used for a different purpose from that which was intended by the parties," the court asserted, ". . . the hirer is not only responsible for all damages but if a loss occurs, although by inevitable casualty, he will generally be responsible therefor."

The court added: "Had the negro been put to the service for which he was employed, and that only, this accident could not have happened."

In the Illinois U.S. Senate race of 1858, candidate Abraham Lincoln said the incumbent Stephen Douglas was "horrified at the thought of mixing blood by the white and black races."

Lincoln then twisted Douglas's pro-slavery logic inside out.

"In 1850, there were in the United States 405,523 mulattoes. Very few of these are the offspring of whites and free blacks; nearly all have sprung from black slaves and white masters," Lincoln said, in a declaration that should not be accepted as fact. (Most historians disregard his contention that "nearly all" mulatto slaves were the children of masters; in fact, the majority were products of mulatto parentage.) Lincoln added, "Could we have had our way, the chances of these black girls, ever mixing their blood with that of white people, would have been diminished at least to the extent that it could not have been done without their consent.

"But Judge Douglas is delighted to have them decided to be slaves."

Douglas won reelection, though Lincoln's oratorical polish and his prophecy during this Senate race that "A house divided against itself cannot stand" elevated him into a figure of national import and promise.

In January 1862, when both Lincoln's political promise and prophecy had been fulfilled to epic proportions—he was President of the United States and the nation was immersed in Civil War, the slave states against the free states—a mulatto child was born on the McAfee plantation in Woodstock. The child was named Minnie, common for a slave girl, and in a distant day she would marry Will Dobbs, son of Josiah Dobbs's slave Wesley.

Already, Dr. John Miller McAfee owned eighty-seven slaves. But Minnie was different: the overwhelming preponderance of evidence suggests that McAfee not only was her master but her father as well. At the age of fifty-nine, Dr. McAfee had impregnated a slave not yet twenty.

The oral tradition of the black Dobbs family is vibrant and colorful and, when put to the test of available documentation, proves accurate almost without exception. Minnie Dobbs would tell her granddaughters that her father was "a white physician of Scottish descent," her mother one of his slaves, and that she had been born in Woodstock, Georgia, a tiny community that, the 1860 U.S. Census reveals, had only a few doctors. She explained that her father's wife was unable to bear children, and that both she and the physician treated her with devotion and affection. Not surprisingly, her white father's name was not transferred to the passing generations when the Dobbs family's ambition was to move beyond the ignominy of slavery.

But when Minnie Dobbs died in 1937, her daughter-in-law, Irene T. Dobbs, signed the death certificate and, in the space allotted for Minnie Dobbs's "Mother's Maiden Name," she wrote, in revealing fashion, "Martha McAfee."

For years, Minnie Dobbs kept a photograph of her mother, Martha, on the living room wall in her east Atlanta home. To her granddaughters, she described her mother as "a Madagascar type." In the picture they saw a woman with emboldened black features and flowing black hair.

As a child, the mulatto Minnie McAfee lived in her father's Big House, a position slave-owners viewed as superior. With the Civil War raging, the young mulatto seemed much like the nation itself: a house divided, half slave, half free.

# CHAPTER 3

At the beginning of the Civil War, Atlanta bustled with the sounds of industry. Its radius was approximately one mile in all directions, and its streets, wide and spacious, converged at the railroad depot. Train whistles interrupted the peace of morning. From Augusta, the Georgia Railroad arrived at 5:53. The Macon and Western pulled in next at 7:15. Three hours later the Atlanta & West Point and the Western & Atlantic departed for West Point and Chattanooga. For years Atlanta had failed to register to visitors as a city in its own right—they regarded it only as a place to stop en route to somewhere else—but by 1861 that had begun to change. The city was developing its own sense of place with several fine hotels, a courthouse, churches and a commercial district that featured brick buildings with New Orleans–style fronts, most prominently on Whitehall Street. Among its foundries, the Atlanta Rolling Mill was among the most extensive of its kind in the South. Even as the "cracker" farmers arrived driving their ox-drawn wagons and cracking their whips, the city seemed an unlikely symbol of an old agricultural empire. It was an upcountry town, devoid of the planter's influence. Everything about it seemed fresh and new, if dusty. It was becoming a commercial center, a window to the region's industrial future. Virgin forest land fifteen years earlier, the place had given rise to a city with a population of more than 9,500. Whereas in coastal cities, such as Charleston and Savannah, the number of slaves ranged as high as 40 percent of the total population, in Atlanta slaves constituted only about 20 percent. Several slave marts were located next to the Atlanta depot, though. SLAVE AUCTION ROOMS, read one sign. And another: SLAVES BOUGHT AND SOLD HERE. The local merchant Samuel P. Richards had bemoaned Abraham Lincoln's victory in the 1860 presidential election. "Disunion seems imminent," Richards fretted in his diary, "and . . . will prove ruinous to business."

Lincoln's blockade of the southern states was not yet a week old on April 23, 1861, when Atlanta's Mechanic Fire Company, No. 2, offered to form a home guard unit. "We will teach Mr. Lincoln, and his cohorts, before this war is over," Atlanta mayor Jared Whitaker wrote, in accepting the fire company's offer, "that the South never surrenders, and that the people of the South will never be satisfied until the Capitol, at Washington, is rescued and our Flag raised upon it." The fire company's history in fighting "the devouring and destructive flames of fire," Whitaker wrote, "is a sufficient guarantee that you will ever prove successful in protecting and defending, if need be, the lives and property of the good people of Atlanta."

The South was awash in optimism and enthusiasm. No one expected a long war. Across Georgia men and boys rushed to enter the fray, cloaking their units in nicknames such as the Bartow Yankee Killers, the Chattahoochee Beauregards, the Flint Hill Grays and the Calhoun Rifles. In a time for high-minded rhetoric, Gov. Joseph Brown vowed that rather than submit to federal guns in Georgia he would make like the biblical Samson and "die a glorious death beneath the crumbling ruins of the temple of Southern freedom."

On April 25, near Greeneville, Tennessee, Isaac Allen, a forty-one-year-old trader, responded to the emerging conflict by forming a partnership with his friend John Pogue in a stock speculation firm. To Allen, war was the same as peace—a business proposition. They immediately began a buying spree that soon put them, and their firm, $14,000 in debt.

On May 1, Asa A. Dobbs, twenty-seven-year-old son of the late Josiah Dobbs, mustered into a Confederate regiment in Cartersville, Georgia, eighteen miles northwest of Marietta. By the following spring his younger brothers Nathaniel, Thomas and William also had joined the Southern Cause.

In Atlanta, war began, as crusades often do, with a display of righteousness: June 13, 1861, was set aside for fasting and prayer in the city in response to a proclamation by Confederate States president Jefferson Davis.

The high stakes of war soon became apparent to Atlantans. City Council members gathered at the train depot on August 11 to greet William Watkins, who was returning from Manassas, Virginia, with the city's first casualty, his son, killed in the Confederate victory at Bull Run.

Feeling a patriotic imperative, Mayor Whitaker soon resigned to become commissary general of the Confederate Army of Georgia.

In the mountains of east Tennessee, where pro-Union sentiment was strong, the Greeneville Convention of June 1861 was called to circumvent Tennessee's recent vote to secede. Two out of every three voters in the area had opposed secession, and the purpose of the convention was to forge a separate state of east Tennessee that would remain neutral during the war. Some of Greene County's most notable leaders took part, including slaveholders such as former U.S. congressman Thomas D. Arnold, Benjamin and Nick Earnest and Dr. William West. "The little batch of disaffected traitors who hover around the noxious atmosphere of Andrew Johnson's home" is how *The Memphis Appeal,* a pro-South organ, characterized the participants at the convention. Though it received wide notice, the Greeneville Convention produced little more than a statement of objectives.

None of the Allens took part in the four-day convention. They were firmly on the side of the Confederacy, as were most of the farming families along the Nolichucky. Living in the comfort of his father's old plantation home, Isaac Allen would spend most of the war years on the move, either en route to Fairfield County, South Carolina, where his wife's family lived, or on a speculative journey, buying and selling across the upper South. Each time he left, he placed the plantation, and his twelve slaves, in the hands of his overseer, a white man named Moore. At least three times during 1863, and in three different locations, he supplied the Confederacy with stock. In May, he sold three horses in Greeneville for $750 in Confederate notes. At Spartanburg, South Carolina, in September, he sold to a Confederate regiment a dozen cattle, weighing more than ten thousand pounds, for $1,836. In November, he joined his brother James on a trip to Bristol, Tennessee, where he was paid, according to Confederate quartermaster records, for "services as agent in collecting stock." His young cousin Samuel was paid $16 on this trip for tending to the cattle while the Confederates staged a local raid. Once during the war, according to Allen family lore, Isaac Allen was on another speculative trip and awoke to the sound of a young voice calling out for him. Frantically, he rode all night for home. Upon arriving the next morning he saw a freshly dug grave in the family cemetery above the Nolichucky. His daughter Margaret Luana, just twenty months old, had died during the night.

There was little fighting in Greeneville during the war, though the sounds of conflict could be heard coming from Bull's Gap and Big Creek, near Rogersville. Greeneville was occupied alternately by the southern and federal armies, changing hands several times. Soldiers on both sides foraged through the countryside and theft of food, clothing and weapons was rampant. In his diary, Dr. Joseph Bell, the Allen family physician, who lived in Meadow Creek about five miles from the Allen plantation, wrote often of bushwhackers. His victimization was an experience undoubtedly shared by the Allens. "Springhouse robbed," Bell wrote in January 1862; and the following month: "Thieves took nearly all widow Cutshaw's bacon and her horse." On March 11, 1862, three men, wearing long overcoats and goatees, entered Bell's home about one A.M. "Are you a Southern man?" they asked. "No, a submissionist," replied Bell, a slaveholder who remained neutral during the war. The men asked for a telescope, "to spy out the Yankees," but Bell said he had none. They left quietly and Bell penned in his diary: "William Ricker had just been robbed of $30.00 by 3 men—probably the same men."

The family story that would ring in Ivan Allen's ears as a young boy in Dalton concerned that summer day in 1862 when his father, Earnest, along with cousin James (Sam Allen's second son) rode into Greeneville to muster into the Confederate cavalry. Earnest Allen was only fourteen, an impressionable age. The call sounded by Confederate leaders in town on June 28, 1862, was emotional. Only recently had the federals, under Adm. David Farragut, taken New Orleans. "Come boys, if you want to go into a good company," Greeneville's newspaper, the *Tri-Weekly Banner,* wrote, "and to show your patriotism, now is the time." Together, Earnest and James Allen joined the Tennessee 12th Cavalry Battalion, B Company, a unit later known as the Independent Partisan Rangers. When asked his age that day Earnest Allen lied, saying he was seventeen, the same as James, the minimum for enlisting. Other river families, including the Johnstons and Dyches, made contributions to the 12th, as well.

The extent of Earnest Allen's duty with the 12th is unclear, for his entire service record is limited to his muster card. In this battalion of seventy-two men, age seems not to have mattered, for it featured a fifty-four-year-old first corporal, a forty-four-year-old bugler and a nineteen-year-old captain, the rapacious John Quincy Arnold, son of the former congressman and Union man. J. Q. Arnold was a fiery leader, though at times his fire was misdirected. He shot and killed his superior, Maj. T. J. Adrian, as he crossed a street in Kingston, Tennessee, in the fall of 1862. A military court sentenced him "to be shot to death by musketry," but because military law remanded capital crimes to civil courts during the war, Arnold's sentence was effectively suspended. Though court-martialed in May 1863, Arnold returned to his unit in time to lead the 12th and 16th cavalries in a blood-soaked Confederate victory at Chickamauga; by the end of that battle in September 1863, Gen. Braxton Bragg and his Confederates, with help from Gen. James Longstreet, had driven the federal forces of Gen. William Rosecrans into Chattanooga, leaving behind a combined thirty-five thousand casualties. Not only was Captain Arnold badly wounded at Chickamauga (he was later praised by superior officers for his gallantry in battle) but James Allen was killed; he was the only Allen family member to die in battle.

Soon southern hopes, like Confederate currency, were on the wane. Watching Gen. Ambrose Burnside's spirited federal troops pass through Greeneville that autumn, a small boy named H. G. Robertson noted the brightness of their new uniforms and the gleam from their guns as they marched out of town "by fours in almost endless stream, it was a sight never to be forgotten." When Longstreet's Confederates marched in, Robertson, who hailed from a family of Confederate sympathizers, sadly noted, "the uniforms showed wear and tear."

In September, the darkness of the times was apparent in Dr. Joseph Bell's diary. A slave had set fire to a pine field and then blamed it on soldiers, Bell wrote. The bushwhacking continued at a relentless pace. "Now what has secession done?" Bell asked in September 1863. His answer: "Ruined the country."

The courage and fading glory of the Confederate States Army was personified by the fate of the late Josiah Dobbs's four sons: Asa, Nathaniel, Thomas and William. Two were wounded, one captured and one killed.

*September 1862.* With superior forces, Gen. George McClellan's federals attacked Gen. Robert E. Lee alongside the Antietam Creek in Maryland. Lee staved off Union advances. Included in the bloodbath of more than thirteen thousand Confederate casualties was William Dobbs, who suffered an unspecified injury while fighting with Phillips Legion, a unit of Cobb County boys. Dispatched to Richmond, he spent three weeks recuperating at Chimborazo Hospital, then was furloughed home. He returned to the Georgia state troops in the fall of 1863, whereupon he contracted chronic diarrhea, or dysentery, from which he would suffer severely for the rest of his life.

*May 1863.* Having risen to the rank of second sergeant in the 14th Georgia Infantry, Nathaniel J. Dobbs spent October and December 1862 in Richmond as a telegraph operator before joining Lee's Army of Northern Virginia. On the night of May 2, 1863—the last night of Nathaniel Dobbs's life—a Confederate unit near Chancellorsville, Virginia, in a moment of confusion, began firing at moving figures in a wooded area. "Cease firing, you are firing into your own men!" came a shout. A North Carolina major replied, "It's a lie! Pour it into them, boys!" Twenty paces away, Confederate men and horses fell, their bodies ripped and torn by bullets. Among the fallen was Gen. Thomas "Stonewall" Jackson, the most revered hero of the South, shot three times, in the hand, forearm and shoulder. Jackson's left arm was amputated by surgeons in a field tent as he lapsed from consciousness. Days later, with Jackson near death, General Lee bemoaned his loss. On the night Jackson was shot, Nathaniel

Dobbs heard "the shrieks and groans of the wounded and dying," a fellow Georgia infantryman recalled, which "displayed all the horrors of war and put feelings and imaginations through the mind that I never wish to experience again." The next day, Nathaniel Dobbs was killed, one of nearly thirteen thousand Confederate casualties in a four-day battle that would be most remembered for the mortal wounding of Jackson. Indeed, just as the Battle of Chancellorsville would elevate to mythic status both Lee and Jackson (who finally died on May 10), so would it virtually ignore the gallantry of common soldiers.

*July 1863.* On the Fourth of July, the nation's eighty-seventh birthday, Vicksburg, Mississippi, fell and Thomas Dobbs was among the twenty-nine thousand Confederates captured and forced to sign a loyalty oath: "I will not take up arms against the United States, nor serve in any military, police, or constabulary force in any Fort, Garrison or field work, held by the Confederate States of America." Once signed, Thomas Dobbs was paroled. The Union oath meant nothing to him. Like the vast majority of Confederates paroled at Vicksburg, Dobbs soon was back in the Confederate service. Within weeks, he returned to the Georgia 41st Infantry; by the fall he was in Decatur, Georgia, near Atlanta, signing Confederate requisition papers for two frying pans, seven mess pans, five pairs of shoes and two wash buckets.

*June 1864.* As the vise began to close on the Confederacy, Gens. Ulysses Grant and George Meade led the federal Army of the Potomac against Lee on the flat lowlands of the Chickahominy, near the village of Cold Harbor, nine miles east of Richmond. Lee knew that a defeat would signal the end of the Confederacy in the Virginia campaign. During one hour on June 3 in the Battle of Cold Harbor nearly seven thousand Union soldiers were killed, an average of more than 115 per minute. At Cold Harbor, Asa Dobbs, who had been fighting for nearly three years and already had spent time at Chimborazo Hospital with an acute case of rheumatism, suffered a wound to his arm. Soon, he, too, was furloughed to Georgia.

Back home in Cartersville, Georgia, that June, there were bigger troubles. William T. Sherman's federal forces already had passed through Bartow County. His invaders were within twenty-five miles of Atlanta.

The problem for Jefferson Davis was that he had only one Robert E. Lee.

The proud Mississippian had placed the Army of Tennessee, his primary military force in the west, in the hands of Gen. Joseph E. Johnston.

With this army went the fate of Georgia. It was a decision that Davis had not enjoyed making, for Joe Johnston was not his kind of leader. Davis had graduated from West Point in 1828, one class before Johnston and Lee. Davis was a leader who, if need be, would carry his convictions to his grave. Once, in the Mexican War, Davis had offered to take an enemy stronghold even though his fifty men were armed only with knives. To Davis, Johnston possessed certain narrow qualities that limited his value as a general: Davis felt the aristocratic Virginian was secretive, cautious to a fault and too willing to retreat.

Johnston had assumed command in Dalton, about ninety miles north of Atlanta, on December 27, 1863. By spring 1864, most Georgians believed that any federal advance from Tennessee would be repelled by Johnston. On April 19, Dr. John Miller McAfee, taking no chances, rode from his plantation into Marietta to reaffirm the terms of his will written ten years earlier.

A clear pattern of the Atlanta Campaign emerged by mid-May: Johnston entrenched in well-fortified, defensive hill positions and Sherman using a series of flanking maneuvers.

His hand forced by Sherman, Johnston evacuated Dalton and retreated south to Resaca. There, he engaged in heavy fighting with Sherman on May 14 and 15. Further engagements followed at New Hope Church, Pickett's Mill and Dallas. Suddenly, it was June, and though Johnston had suffered relatively few casualties and received significant reinforcements, he had retreated more than sixty miles deep into Georgia. Atlanta was twenty-five miles away with only one river, the Chattahoochee, to serve as a protective barrier.

Johnston settled into the mountains of Kennesaw, which provided one of the finest defensive positions in Georgia. Atlantans braced for the worst. On June 1, the City Council sought providential guidance. "Whereas the Lincoln government has concentrated two of the largest armies ever seen on this continent," a City Council resolution began, "the one under the leadership of Gen'l Grant to besiege Richmond, the Seat of Government, and the other under Gen'l Sherman to invade Georgia and capture Atlanta 'The Citadel of the Confederacy' as they term it, and have left nothing in their power undone to accomplish their design . . . it becomes us as Christian people to humble ourselves before the Mercy Seat."

Years later, Judie Dobbs would tell her descendants that she watched Sherman's soldiers arrive in Cobb County. Union soldiers foraged for supplies, and as a result, she recalled, "we were scuffling for food." Though not in Sherman's line of march, Dr. McAfee is believed to have hastened south from Woodstock in early June, before the federal forces appeared. Most of Marietta's wealthy landowners also fled, leaving their homes and slaves behind. "It must have cost the citizens many a pang to tear themselves away from the grateful shade and quiet comfort of the luxurious homes of Marietta, to wander in the Saharas of Southern Georgia at the present hot and dusty season," the correspondent for *The New York Tribune,* traveling with Sherman's forces, wrote on July 16, 1864. "The town is a perfect grotto of shade. The best estates are owned by Ed. Denmead, John H. Glover . . . Dix Fletcher, the Rev. John Hunt, Col. David Dobbs, one of the oldest citizens. . . ." Though it is not certain where the slave Wesley Dobbs spent the war years, most likely he was owned by David Dobbs, brother of the late Josiah and Asa. The number of slaves owned by David Dobbs had escalated to sixty-two in 1860, up from forty-one a decade earlier.

Living only a couple miles from Kennesaw, Bob McAfee and his family had sought refuge south of Atlanta, though not until his wife, Eliza, had hidden the family silver beneath manure in the barn. Across the fields of his vacated plantation on June 20 the Battle of McAfee's Crossroads was fought, replete with charging steeds and swinging sabers; both sides claimed victory. Brig. Gen. Kenner Garrard turned Bob McAfee's home into a Union hospital.

Heavy rains continued to fall on north Georgia. On June 23, Sherman wrote to Gen. Henry Halleck, Lincoln's chief of staff, in Washington, "The whole country is one vast fort, and Johnston must have at least fifty miles of connected trenches, with abatis and finished batteries." The Union assault at Kennesaw Mountain began on the morning of June 27 and for at least one brutal thirty-minute period Joe Johnston's defensive posture paid dividends. Sherman's forces charged the Confederate mountain positions from multiple angles. The assault was a disaster for Sherman. Confederates poured rounds of hot lead into the charging Union men. As far away as Atlanta the sounds of cannons were heard. Sherman estimated his losses at twenty-five hundred, including his former law partner, Daniel McCook; Johnston claimed about eight hundred casualties. As the summer heat rose, the stench from decaying bodies, fallen in clumps below the Confederate breastworks, became ghastly and prompted a truce two days later to allow for burials.

Sherman's flanking maneuvers began anew. Georgia governor Joseph Brown pleaded with Davis for more troops. From Atlanta on June 28, Brown wrote, "I need not call your attention to the fact that this place is to the Confederacy almost as important as the heart is to the human body. We must hold it." Brown suggested that Gen. Nathan Bedford Forrest or the renegade raider Gen. John Hunt Morgan cut Sherman's supply lines to the rear. But before Davis could respond, Johnston evacuated his positions at Kennesaw on the night of July 2. Before retreating to nearby Smyrna, the Confederates tore up the W&A lines from the base of Kennesaw to Marietta and destroyed four miles of telegraph. On July 4, Davis, in Richmond, wrote Brown that he was not inclined to change the disposition of his forces. That night, Johnston fell back once more, this time to fortifications on the north side of the Chattahoochee. Four days later, Union forces went upstream to cross the Chattahoochee, near Roswell, and met little resistance.

Joe Johnston retreated to the south side of the river. Nature offered him no other barriers. Atlanta was less than nine miles away.

Johnston was standing on the Marietta Road, three miles outside of Atlanta, on July 17 when he was handed a telegram from Richmond: "As you have failed to arrest the advance of the enemy to the vicinity of Atlanta," the telegram read, ". . . you are hereby relieved from the command of the Army and Department of Tennessee, which you will immediately turn over to General Hood."

Jefferson Davis was fed up with retreat.

Gen. John Bell Hood was a fighter, and in the summer of 1864 his body bore the proof. His left arm hung limp as a result of shrapnel at Gettysburg. His right leg was a four-and-a-half-inch stump, the remainder left in a surgeon's tent at Chickamauga. Everywhere he had been—Manassas, Antietam, Gettysburg, Chickamauga—Hood had attacked. What Joe Johnston was to entrenchments, John B. Hood was to frontal charges. This was the spirit that Jefferson Davis believed the Confederacy must have.

Three times during an eight-day period in late July, Hood lashed out from inside Atlanta at various points in Sherman's line. But attacks from Peachtree Creek, Decatur and Ezra Church failed at a cost of fourteen thousand Confederate casualties. As August arrived, Davis's hope was that Hood would hold out in Atlanta long enough to subvert Lincoln's reelection bid in November.

For weeks, Sherman pulverized the fortifications in Atlanta. Of the Atlantans who remained in the city, many hid in muddy dug-out shelters beneath their gardens. Sherman telegraphed Lincoln's chief of staff Halleck on August 7: "One thing is certain, whether we get inside Atlanta or not, it will be a used up community by the time we are done with it." Many of Hood's soldiers were recent additions, including Lemuel McAfee, John McAfee's forty-nine-year-old younger brother, who had enlisted in the Georgia Reserves in May. Paroled from Vicksburg, Thomas Dobbs had returned to Confederate service as well and was in Atlanta, with Hood and Lemuel McAfee, on August 29. Two days later, Hood made his final attack in the Battle of Jonesboro, south of Atlanta. He aimed to protect his line of supplies and communications to Macon, but federal forces repulsed the attack, in short order. Seizing the opportunity, Gen. John McAllister Schofield's federal Army of the Ohio then cut the Macon and Western Railroad between Jonesboro and Atlanta.

Even John Bell Hood, the consummate fighter, had no alternative: he evacuated Atlanta the next day. Before leaving, his forces destroyed the munitions, magazines and railroad supplies. The explosions lit up the sky over Atlanta early on September 2 and, to the south, Sherman wondered if a battle was being waged in the city.

Atlanta mayor James Calhoun, with several citizens by his side, walked out on Marietta Street, beyond the elaborate Confederate earthworks, to surrender the city later that day. News of Atlanta's capture was received with great joy by Lincoln, whose reelection was now assured. Gleefully, *The New York Times* reported, "Atlanta is at the centre of a network of towns and villages which have furnished forth half its war material to the entire Confederacy from the Rappahannock to the Rio Grande. This valuable region is now all ours." In South Bend, Indiana, citizens gathered in the moonlight beneath a hotel window as bands serenaded the wife of the conquering commander. "I became a hero myself," Ellen Sherman wrote to her husband in Atlanta, "in the light of your reflected glory."

Lincoln telegraphed Sherman that he had rendered the Atlanta campaign "famous in the annals of war" and "entitled those who have participated therein to the applause and thanks of the nation."

A more intimate form of congratulations came on September 7 when Sherman himself finally arrived in Atlanta. An old black man, suddenly emancipated, said, "Lord, massa, is dat General Sherman? I'se glad I'se seen him . . . I just wanted to see de man what made old massa run."

Sherman transformed Atlanta into a military garrison. He ordered the departure of all citizens who remained in the city: 446 families, totaling 1,565 people, were transported south, and 79 blacks, a small minority of the total, chose to go with them rather than begin an uncertain freedom. Mayor Calhoun pleaded with Sherman to reconsider this order on behalf of the city's pregnant women. Sherman replied: "You might as well appeal against the thunderstorm as against these terrible hardships of war. . . . The use of Atlanta for warlike purposes is inconsistent with its character as a home for families. . . . We don't want your negroes, or your horses, or your houses, or your lands, or any thing that you have, but we do want and will have a just obedience to the laws of the United States." From the field, an infuriated General Hood wrote Sherman that his order "transcends, in studied and ingenious cruelty, all acts ever before brought to my attention in the dark history of war." Three days later, Hood fumed: "We will fight you to the death! Better to die a thousand deaths than to submit to live under you or your Government, and your Negro allies!"

That William Tecumseh Sherman became a military conqueror was a remarkable reversal of fate. Stress and overwork in the fall of 1861 had made Sherman conjure images of impossibly large Confederate armies poised to strike his undermanned federal troops in Louisville. Sherman had demanded more soldiers from the War Department: 200,000 would be needed to go on the offensive, he suggested. Newspapers termed him crazy, insane. In November 1861, he had been relieved from command. He returned home to Lancaster, Ohio, with a shattered reputation, and his suggested new assignment would do little to repair it—to rest his mind for twenty days.

But in the fall of 1864, Halleck found his old friend Sherman to be the only commanding officer whose heart was cold enough to prosecute war as it needed to be prosecuted. "I would destroy every mill and factory within reach which I do not want for my own use," Halleck wrote to Sherman in Atlanta on September 28. "I have endeavored to impress these views upon our commanders for the last two years.

"You are almost the only one who has properly applied them."

Atlanta had been christened only nineteen years before, which made the city younger even than some of the raw-boned Union boys from Illinois, Ohio and Indiana. From the earliest days of Atlanta came the shrill sound of a people who wanted their city to be important. "The Chinese once believed that China was the center of the universe," the newspaper in Milledgeville, the Georgia capital, mocked in 1854, adding, "It has lately been discovered that Atlanta is." Certainly, the city had become the operational center of the Confederate universe. In Atlanta, percussion caps, canteens, bullets and other munitions were made, then transported, to wage the battle against the Lincoln government. "We have been fighting Atlanta all the time, in the past: have been capturing guns, wagons . . . marked 'Atlanta,' " Sherman told an aide during his two months inside the city. "Now since they have been doing so much to destroy us, and our Government, we have to destroy them, at least enough to prevent any more of that."

Early on the evening of November 14, 1864, Col. O. M. Poe, Sherman's chief engineer, was engaged in the special task of destroying Atlanta. Union soldiers looted storefronts for clothes and whiskey. Not since the tea party in Boston Harbor ninety-one years before had destruction in America raged with such symbolism, though this time destruction was waged not in the name of rebellion but in the name of ending rebellion. The razing of the city would have the dramatic effect of dividing southern history, much like the biblical testaments, into the Old and the New. Atlanta's burning represents the end of the Old South.

The Georgia Railroad depot had been leveled with a battering ram earlier in the day. Then a torch had been applied to the wreck. Soon the commercial district on Whitehall Street became a sheet of flames. Metal sizzled and the air became loaded with black particles. Washington Hall and the Trout House hotel burned as a pall rose above Peachtree Street. Flames leaped from the slave marts to the dry-goods stores. Sherman's special order called for the destruction of all things in the city that were of potential military value to the Confederacy; though private residences were to be spared, many were lost to the spreading flames.

The morning of November 16 broke cloudy and cool. Sherman began his legendary march into history by heading east, toward the sea. In front of him were the cotton lands that stretched to Savannah. Behind him, black smoke billowed above Atlanta. He rode out Decatur Road, the 14th Corps and his staff by his side. A band struck "John Brown's body lies a-moldering in the grave . . . Glory, glory Hallelujah!" and Sherman later commented that never before had he heard the song performed with "more spirit, or in better harmony of time and place." The infantrymen, uncertain of their destination, called out to Sherman in singsong fashion, "Uncle Billy, I guess Grant is waiting for us at Richmond!"

Sherman would remember: "We turned our horses' heads to the east. Atlanta was soon lost behind the screen of trees and became a thing of the past."

Five months later, the Civil War ended with Lee's signature at Appomattox. Lincoln would savor the Union victory for only five days. His murder in April 1865 by a southern loyalist promoted Andrew Johnson, once Daniel and Sam Allen's tailor, to the presidency.

When emancipation came to Woodstock, Georgia, Dr. John McAfee and his wife dressed his slave daughter Minnie in pink wool, with a cape collar and a matching hat. They sent Minnie and her mother, Martha, out into the countryside. A driver took them in a carriage through the front gates of the McAfee plantation. They shared a picnic lunch and Martha

McAfee told her three-year-old daughter, "This is freedom!" They had no intention to leave yet. The carriage returned them to the plantation where they would live for several more years. When Minnie Dobbs retold this story seventy years later, one of her grandchildren asked about that first taste of freedom. "Why didn't you make a break and go north?" The old woman shook her head and shrugged. "To what? That was our home."

Because he yet owned more than $20,000 worth of property, McAfee was not included in Andrew Johnson's amnesty proclamation for former Confederates; he was made to file a personal application. On September 19, 1865, he rode into Marietta and wrote, "Applicant admits that in common with almost the entire population of his State, so far as feelings and inclinations were concerned, he did participate in the rebellion and that while there was any hope at all his sympathies were with the so-called Confederate States." McAfee noted that he had not spent even a single day in the Confederate service. He also signed, in Canton, Georgia, a loyalty oath to the United States, promising to emancipate his slaves.

In Greeneville, Tennessee, creditors swarmed Isaac Allen. Like many speculators, he had borrowed too often, including $2,000 in Confederate notes from his brother James in September 1863. To repay loans from his sister Margaret Allen Noel, Isaac Allen gave to her their father's home on the river, a loss softened perhaps only by the fact that it would remain in the family. Even his former brother-in-law, Nick Earnest, sought collection in May 1866 on a $250 note Isaac Allen had signed with Nick Earnest's father five years earlier. The court made numerous attachments on Isaac Allen's lands, most of which he subsequently gave up. He moved his young family about twelve miles away, to a clapboard home overlooking the rich bottomlands of Lick Creek, near Mosheim.

All of the Allen slaves were freed. According to Greene County legend, the slave Moses had been told in 1855 by Daniel Allen that if he cut a path through the mountain at Paint Creek wide enough for a wagon to gain passage, freedom would be his reward. Moses labored for nine years, past Daniel Allen's death. He was nearly finished when the war ended and Daniel Jr. told him he was free.

Following the path of hordes of other ex-Confederates in east Tennessee, Earnest Allen decided to leave his native state rather than face the wrath of returning Union men. With his uncles James Lowry and Tolbert Eason, he moved to Dalton, Georgia, and worked in the dry-goods business. In 1870, he married Susie Harris, from a prominent Dalton family, in the Presbyterian church. The ravages of war were apparent throughout the region. In May 1875, Earnest Allen paid $3,000, deeding his home on

Hawthorne Street to secure payment, to buy goods from the widow of a local merchant; then, he opened his own shop. Already his uncles Lowry and Eason were in debt and had sold their homes to raise money. An R. G. Dun & Company official surmised that Eason and Lowry had been extravagant in the purchases, lacking in good judgment, and had granted "too much indulgence to their customers." Earnest Allen was a young married man who was known in Dalton "as honest and energetic," according to the Dun & Company official, though "in our opinion, is honest but too sanguine—risks too much." This assessment proved true. In November 1875, Allen and Lowry both filed for voluntary bankruptcy. Only days before they had borrowed money from widows and poor men, conduct that R. G. Dun & Company termed "very questionable. Their failure is a very serious affair in the community." From Tennessee, Isaac Allen paid 25 percent of his son's creditors.

Across the South, the planter's power would begin to shift to the manufacturer and merchant in the growing urban areas. Atlanta rebuilt from the ashes with a renewed fervor: 150 stores were back in operation by the end of 1865 and real estate values in the city in 1870 were triple those of 1860. Meanwhile, city leaders lured the state capital away from Milledgeville in 1868 by promising to build, free of charge for ten years, any state government building required, much to the chagrin of *The Southern Recorder.* "The people are not such a set of asses as to listen to such an idea," the Milledgeville newspaper suggested in March 1868. Later, the *Recorder* offered an alternative: "Atlanta may have the penitentiary if she wants it; as it is an institution that will not come amiss to many of her population."

The freedmen rushed to Atlanta, many to flee brutal treatment in rural areas. C. C. Sibley, director of the Freedmen's Bureau in Georgia, a federal program to aid emancipated slaves, reported from Atlanta in 1867 that "the spirit of oppression is to be found almost everywhere." Whites were perpetrating serious outrages against the freedmen. In Jefferson County, Georgia, Sibley reported, a black man accused of raping a white woman was burned alive by whites. Within twenty miles of Atlanta, two freedmen were tied and whipped by whites and another was abused and had his home burned; in some cases, freedmen defended themselves and killed white predators.

Having taken the surname of his former master, Wesley Dobbs, with his wife, Judie, and their large brood, remained in Cobb County during Reconstruction. For him, freedom had its costs. Never was he able to rise above hardscrabble living. In 1895, two years before his death, seventy-six-year-old Wesley Dobbs needed to borrow $75 to purchase a black mule. As one of freedom's spoils, though, he registered to vote for the first time as an American citizen on July 29, 1867. Though unable to read or write, Wesley Dobbs signed his name with an X. On that same day, ex-Confederate Thomas Dobbs, Josiah's third son, registered at the same location.

The Old South was peeling away. In the spring of 1868, Dr. John Miller McAfee died reportedly from tuberculosis and was buried in the Marietta cemetery beneath an ornate nearly fifteen-foot obelisk on which the McAfee family crest was engraved. McAfee's epitaph reads, "Boast not thyself of tomorrow for death is everywhere." Sixty-four freedmen living on or near his plantation in Woodstock assumed the McAfee name, according to the 1870 Census. Soon, Martha and Minnie McAfee would pass through the plantation's front gates again, this time not to turn back but to start their lives anew.

By 1879 even General Sherman was ready to close the wounds of war. As his train pulled into Atlanta, one man playfully called out, "Ring the fire bells! The town will be gone in forty minutes!" Clark Howell, a young reporter for the *Constitution*, asked Sherman that day why he had burned the city fifteen years earlier. The retired general took Howell's hand in his own. "Young man, when I got to Atlanta what was left of the Confederacy could roughly be compared to your hand. Atlanta was the palm and by destroying it I spared myself much further fighting," Sherman explained. He hastened to add, "But remember, the same reason which caused me to destroy Atlanta will make it a great city in the future."

In the fall of that year, a gravely ill Earnest Allen and his wife returned to east Tennessee. Their hope was that the familiarity of Greene County and a gentle wash of family affection would restore him to health. Though thirty-one, Earnest Allen looked much older. One portrait of him reveals a slump-shouldered man with a receding hairline and goatee. Already, he had done a lifetime's worth of living—and losing. His father, Isaac, would only live five more years; on his deathbed in 1884, Isaac would call his family to his bedside and then die with the name of Jesus on his lips. "Few Tennesseans were better acquainted in the Southern markets than he," the Greeneville newspaper reported upon his death. Yet the magnitude of the Allens' fall from antebellum grace was spelled out in the sparse inventory of Isaac Allen's personal holdings at the time of his death: a mowing machine, two wagons, one cart, seven calves, six horses, six steer, one red cow and a half interest in a bull. His brothers James and Robert would die insolvent as well.

As the sun set behind Bays Mountain on September 14, 1879, beyond the fertile lands of Lick Creek, Earnest Allen died in his father's home.

Susie Allen placed her husband's body in a pine box and carried it back to Georgia on a wagon. She buried him in the family plot in Dalton, on a knoll overlooking a Confederate burial ground.

To honor her husband, she decided to change the name of their four-year-old son. Instead of bearing his grandfather's name of Isaac Anderson Allen, he would now be known as Ivan Earnest Allen. The story later passed down through the family was that Susie Allen had discovered the name Ivan while reading a Russian novel.

# PART II

# THE PATRIARCHS ARRIVE

"If Atlanta could suck as hard as it blows it would be a sea-
port city!"

—Favored barb of Savannah leaders, 1900

# CHAPTER 4

➤◄

Typewriters brought the first Ivan Allen to Atlanta. He could sell 'em. In the big city, he reckoned, he could sell lots of 'em. He came to town from Dalton, full of ambition.

Atlanta was like no place the country boy had ever seen: the columned mansions that lined Peachtree Street, the eight-story Equitable Building at Five Points, the energy of the people.

Henry Grady also brought him here. Grady, the late editor of *The Atlanta Constitution* and eminent New South spokesman, had led to Atlanta, virtually by the hand, thousands of white southerners. He promised a golden tomorrow. In December 1886, the month after the Statue of Liberty opened in New York, Grady told the New England Society in New York, and its guest, retired general William T. Sherman, "From the ashes he left us in 1864, we have raised a brave and beautiful city; somehow or other we have caught the sunshine in the bricks and mortar of our homes, and have builded therein not one ignoble prejudice or memory."

Grady spoke a booster's language. No greater lie could be told than Grady's on Atlanta's purity from prejudice. Ivan Allen's parents hated the Yankees, as he would say in his final years, "wouldn't sell them the boxwood out of the yard no matter how much we needed the money." In the Civil War, Allen's family—his mother's and his father's—lost not only their slaves and much of their land but, in a few cases, their lives. His uncle William C. Harris was shot dead on the Confederate retreat from Petersburg, Virginia, three days before the surrender. His father's cousin James Allen died on the field at Chickamauga. In their hallowed memory young Ivan's world took shape. Raised without a father, he worshipped his schoolmaster, Gen. Bryan Thomas, who had fought at Murfreesboro and later was taken prisoner at the Battle of Mobile. Known to his students as "Cotton Top," the general thought his students ought to forget about books by Jules Verne and his flying machines ("He said that was too visionary and we should be spending our time on mathematics") but to remember always the glorious men of the Cause. Young Ivan's widowed mother, Susie Allen, a dignified southern lady, became a charter member of the United Daughters of the Confederacy, formed to remember those "in the sanguinary struggle for the Lost Cause, fought not for a sentiment but for a principle."

Ivan Allen could forgive Henry Grady for the elasticity of his spoken truths. He knew about sales pitches and, in Atlanta, the sales pitch was working like magic. Between 1880 and 1910, the tired, poor and huddled masses across the vanquished South—the plowman and the freedman, the broken former master and his rootless former slave—poured into Atlanta, nearly quadrupling its population, to more than 150,000. With them came the carpetbaggers from the North, seeking to exploit their own new freedoms.

Allen had arrived at a historic moment. The Cotton States and International Exposition was being held at Atlanta's Piedmont Park. Its bold mission was to portray the New South as a prosperous and industrializing region with Atlanta as its vibrant commercial hub. The Exposition lasted about one hundred days and drew more than 800,000 visitors, including Ivan Allen. Yet it almost never happened. In May 1894, a group of Exposition officials from Atlanta had appeared before the House Committee on Appropriations in Washington, hoping to land $200,000 in federal funding. "How many states grow cotton?" one northern congressman asked. "Ten or twelve," replied Charles Collier, chairman of the Atlanta Exposition. "Do you mean to say that the whole nation should spend its money for something that benefits only a few states?" another congressman asked. Only then did L. F. Livingston, a congressman from Atlanta, save the day with a vintage sales pitch: "Mr. Chairman, this exposition is for the benefit of all those who grow cotton *and all those who wear cotton.*" Booker T. Washington, the black educator from the Tuskegee Normal and Industrial Institute in Alabama, spoke on behalf of the Exposition that day. He told congressmen that he had long avoided politics, and now was urging blacks to do the same. Washington said that the best way for the black to obtain political rights was through practical and industrial pursuits: raising crops, remaining free of debt and purchasing property. His tone soothed and impressed his white listeners. The federal funds were granted to the Exposition, though with one caveat: organizers had to place a Negro exhibit in a separate building and not, as proposed, inside the government building on the park grounds.

What would resonate most powerfully from the 1895 Atlanta Exposition was Booker T. Washington's speech on the Opening Program. Many whites on the organizing committee had expressed grave concerns about inviting a black to speak for fear that the mere appearance of equal status would alienate, perhaps even enrage, southern whites. Yet, as he called for self-help among blacks, and accommodation with whites, Booker Washington was the sort of black spokesman whites willingly would embrace. Only months before, Frederick Douglass, a symbol of black hope and racial pride, had died. Now, Washington called out that the time had come to heal divisions between the races, and between North and South. On September 18, the ex-carpetbag governor Rufus Bullock, who in 1868 had become the only Republican governor in Georgia history (and later was forced to resign under pressure in the days of Radical Reconstruction), introduced Washington by saying, "We have with us today a representative of Negro enterprise and Negro civilization." As Washington rose from his chair, correspondent James Creelman of *The New York World* took notice and later wrote of how "a Negro Moses stood before a great audience of white people and delivered an oration that marks a new epoch in the history of the South."

In what became known as his "Atlanta Compromise" speech, Washington spoke of a racial bargain in which southern blacks would concede social and political rights already lost to white supremacy in hopes that southern whites would remove obstacles to economic progress, particularly in the areas of small business, industrial education and the trades. To southern whites that day, Washington said:

> As we have proved our loyalty to you in the past in nursing your children, watching by the sick bed of your mothers and fathers, and often following them with tear-dimmed eyes to their graves, so in the future, in our humble way, shall we stand by you with a devotion that no foreigner can approach, ready to lay down our lives if need be, in defence of yours, interlacing our industrial, commercial, civil and religious life with yours in a way that shall make the interests of both races one. In all things that are purely social, we can be as separate as the fingers, yet one as the hand in all things essential to mutual progress.

When Washington finished, whites in the audience threw their hats into the air and waved handkerchiefs. Bullock raced across the platform to shake Washington's hand. Clark Howell, successor to Grady as publisher of *The Atlanta Constitution*, told Creelman, "That man's speech is the beginning of a moral revolution in America." Creelman wrote that even the legendary Gladstone could not have "pleaded a cause with more consummate power than did this angular Negro, standing in a nimbus of sunshine, surrounded by the men who once fought to keep his race in bondage." President Grover Cleveland, after reading Washington's speech, sent his congratulations. The *Constitution* glowed that "his effort was most happy." Certainly, Washington's words pleased southern whites: *Separate as the fingers, yet one as the hand.* It was pure New South dogma, Gradyesque. ("What God hath separated let no man join together," Grady had said in 1887. "The white race must dominate forever in the South, because it is the white race.") The call to retain a strict separation of the races would be affirmed one year later in 1896 by the U.S. Supreme Court in the Plessy doctrine. Though it is uncertain whether Ivan Allen attended Booker Washington's address that day, he, as a young man with traditional southern views on race, certainly agreed with its spirit and would have thrown his hat at least as high, and waved his handkerchief at least as happily, as any of the cheering listeners.

In Atlanta, at the firm of Fielder & Mower, Allen began at a salary of $40 per month. He was a smooth talker, self-confident, a salesman to the core. Soon, he sold Yost typewriters to ex-governor William J. Northern, the rural statesman Tom Watson and Asa Candler, who recently had purchased the Coca-Cola Company. In short order, he was earning $60 per month, enough to send some home to his mother, "Mumpsie." Years earlier, Mumpsie had prodded him to study law in Dalton, and he had, in the office of Colonel Starr. He had prepared the papers for local farmers whose cows had been killed along the railroads. "The Cow Coroner" was how he was known at the Whitfield County courthouse. But now, with his wavy brown hair parted cleanly in the middle, young Ivan wore tailor-made suits, top-of-the-line derbies and pointed shoes with high-buttoned tops. More than merely a ladies' man, the salesman was becoming an Atlanta man.

In 1899, he lived in a boardinghouse, near Peachtree Street, around the corner from the Capital City Club where he sometimes spotted local luminaries such as Candler, Howell, Samuel Inman, John Grant and Robert F. Maddox. As Atlanta's leading men, they were his role models. With money in his pocket and big dreams in his head, Ivan Allen's address was 6 West Ellis Street.

In June 1897, less than two years after the salesman had arrived, another train pulled into Atlanta, this one from Savannah. Sitting in the Jim Crow car was a precocious fifteen-year-old black named John Wesley Dobbs. A boy on the brink of manhood, already he knew the hard costs of freedom for his race. Raised without a father by freed slaves who had seen Sherman march through north Georgia toward Atlanta, Dobbs heard them sing their spirituals and felt the profoundness of their odyssey.

Decades later, he would stand before a mirror in his fine Atlanta home, button his vest, knot his tie and smack cologne onto his smooth ebony face, which, with high cheekbones, hinted vaguely at Indian ancestry. Then he would throw out his chest and jab his index finger into the air in front of his gathered grandchildren who stood at the foot of the man the way the man, as a boy, once had stood at the foot of Kennesaw Mountain. "It wasn't always like this!" he would remind his flock. His grandchildren thought him Herculean in every way, loving, respecting and, at times, fearing him. In a distant day one grandson nervously would drive behind Dobbs's car, as commanded, and even followed Dobbs as he made an illegal left-hand turn. "I'd rather face the judge than Grandpa," the grandson explained later.

The poverty of Dobbs's youth, on the farm in Kennesaw, twenty-five miles north of Five Points, was severe. He ran barefoot in the fields and collected spent shells that remained from the battle on Kennesaw Mountain. The daily monotony of farm life occasionally was broken by passing trains. There were days when the only white faces John Wesley Dobbs saw were those peering from the club cars with what he took to be curiosity and pity. At almost any moment, Dobbs could put his ear to the red clay and hear the thrumming and feel the rumble of the locomotive in the distance. Sometimes, workers in the dining cars tossed out banana peels. Not knowing better, Dobbs ate the lining inside the peels, a story he would tell with gusto to his children and grandchildren so they would understand he had never forgotten his humble beginnings. From these early years Dobbs developed the principles that would guide him throughout his life in Atlanta: the importance of family, and the need to rectify the sufferings of his race.

His mother, Minnie Dobbs, his safety net as a child, was only fourteen years old in 1876 when she had married Will Dobbs, a twenty-nine-year-old freedman. Their marriage produced a daughter, then a son, but broke up after eight years. A tempestuous and aristocratic mulatto seamstress, Minnie Dobbs acted as if her light complexion made her superior to darker-skinned blacks. In 1884, she left for Savannah to work for a white family; Will Dobbs went in a different direction to marry another teenager and to have more children. For the next seven years, John Wesley and his older sister Willie were cared for by their grandparents, Wesley and Judie Dobbs. The Dobbses had fourteen children of their own, with too many grandchildren to count. A horde of Dobbs family members lived with them in Kennesaw in their two log cabins, each with three rooms and a hall, reminiscent of the old slave cottages. John Wesley Dobbs's uncle Jesse, only eight years older, became like a brother during these years. His grandfather demanded that John Wesley have the wagon ready on time each Sunday for the trip to the Noonday Baptist Church for blacks. His grandmother, whose complexion was as white as chalk, the result of a white master imposing his will on a slave, made their clothes by hand and baked ashcakes in the open hearth.

Minnie Dobbs promised her children that she would return to Kennesaw, and she did, visiting once or twice a year, sometimes bringing clothes for them.

Fearing abandonment, John Wesley Dobbs cried each time she departed: "Mama, don't go! Please don't go!" She left with his whimpers echoing in her ear.

Not until 1891, when Dobbs was nine, did his mother fulfill her promise to bring him and his sister back to Savannah to live with her.

Only now did his education begin in earnest. Instead of attending a school for blacks only three months each year, as he had in Kennesaw, he attended the West Broad Street School in Savannah for the full term. Yet due to unyielding poverty his mother wanted to remove him from the fifth grade. She could not afford to buy him clothes and shoes. A white woman intervened. When she offered him a job so that he could continue his schooling, young Dobbs cried again—this time for joy. He vowed never to stop working. He shined shoes at a Savannah barbershop. He delivered *The Savannah Evening Press* and did it so well he won a contest, the prize a watch. It was the first watch he ever owned. Suddenly, at the age of twelve, he had earned enough money to buy his own clothes and shoes. He shopped at B.H. Levy and Company on Broughton Street, paying one dollar down on every purchase. "Then I would pay one dollar until I got them out," Dobbs recalled years later. He finished grammar school in 1897, a time of mounting racial tensions, when the number of lynchings in the South increased to 123 from 78 the previous year.

He came to Atlanta because of his mother. According to one family legend, Minnie Dobbs had moved first, in pursuit of a love interest. As much as he wanted to be with his mother again, John Wesley also knew that Atlanta offered him more than Savannah ever could: namely, education. The brilliant social scientist W. E. B. Du Bois taught at Atlanta University, a school for blacks. Atlanta University's faculty included a number of Yale-trained whites; living on or near campus, they created the only nominally integrated area of Atlanta. A west side seminary for blacks founded by northern missionaries recently had changed its name to Atlanta Baptist College. Here, at the future Morehouse College, where Confederate earthworks had remained until only a few years before (Rebel skulls were said to have been dug up when the seminary began clearing the land), thirty-year-old blacks sat in the same classroom with fourteen-year-olds; all came in search of a new beginning. The college president, George Sale, dismissed northern arguments that blacks were too poorly equipped for geometry, Greek, logic or church history. "If these studies have educational value for the white students," Sale inquired, "why should they not have the same value for Negroes?"

Dobbs saw an Atlanta that Ivan Allen never saw. Most blacks lived on the east side of town, in shanties. Darktown and Niggertown and Shermantown (in honor of the Union general) were slang names used by whites for the poor black districts. Nevertheless, Dobbs also discovered black culture and enterprise: black druggists, grocers, undertakers and educators. A colored aristocracy arose in Atlanta, predominantly light-skinned, the children of freed mulatto house servants. These aristocrats built lives around the First Congregational Church, social clubs and the black colleges. Atlanta's preeminent black man, the freed slave Alonzo Herndon, owned an elegant barbershop for whites. Herndon added a life insurance company for blacks. Soon, he became the city's first black millionaire, proof that in Atlanta anything was possible, even for blacks.

Dobbs worked barefoot on a farm in the summer of 1897, picking peaches and chopping cotton. He planned to attend the Atlanta Baptist College's academy that fall. Minnie Dobbs became ill, though, and her son's earnings went to her care. Rev. E. J. Fisher of the Mount Olive Baptist Church took Dobbs to the Baptist academy, with his own children, and paid his tuition. Dobbs secured a job with the school's black physician, Dr. James McDougall, working at his drugstore at the corner of Piedmont and Houston streets. He opened the store at six o'clock every morning, worked two hours, then sprinted on his bicycle to school, about two miles. In years to come, he often told the drugstore/bicycle story by way of illustrating the glories of hard work and ambition. Every time he told the story, the young John Wesley pedaled that bicycle with greater fury.

"They'd liiiiiiiiiiine up to waaatch me!" he always said, his body twisting, his hands sweeping in broad arcs. "And I'd come down that Fair Street Hill and I'd sliiiiiiiiiide in to class just before that morning bell!"

In 1900, Minnie Dobbs, her two children and her daughter's four-year-old son, Joseph Eaves, moved into a boardinghouse at 226 East Ellis Street where their neighbors were black waiters, mail carriers and blacksmiths. On that street, seven blocks to the west, Ivan Allen had boarded the year before. In 1900, Allen lived in a boardinghouse at 84 West Peachtree Street, joined there by his older brother, Will, recently moved from Dalton.

Like virtually all rural southerners rushing into the city, Ivan Allen and John Wesley Dobbs saw in Atlanta their own family hardship transformed into hope: a ruined city, burned to the ground, now rebuilding, robust and alive.

At the dawn of the twentieth century Allen and Dobbs lived in parallel universes that would intersect in time and in ways they could not imagine.

# PART III

# New South Capital

>+<

"Shall we permit ourselves to go down in history as a nation of traders simply like the Phoenicians and the Carthaginians, or shall we aspire to something like the measure of Athens and Rome?"

> —"Important Steps for Atlanta's Future Progress,"
> WILLIAM J. SAYWARD, architect, 1918

"I grew up in Plains during the Depression. To make a trip to Atlanta was like—I don't know how to describe it—it was like going to Moscow or Beijing. It was a totally different world. . . . My father and my uncle were avid supporters of the Class D Georgia-Florida League, which had a team in Americus. Our main excursion to Atlanta was on the weekends when there was a doubleheader. . . . We lived off Sears-Roebuck, buying stuff that wasn't sold in Plains. A highlight of going to the games [in Atlanta] was going across the street to Sears-Roebuck. The remarkable thing was that you could place your order on the first floor and thirty minutes later you could pick it up. It was like a dream!"

> —JIMMY CARTER,
> former President of the United States

# CHAPTER 5

➤◄

John Wesley Dobbs had known little stability or order in his life. His aim was to break free as no one in his family ever had. He thought he had laid the foundation in the fall of 1901. Upon graduating from the academy, he enrolled at the Atlanta Baptist College. But several months later, when Minnie Dobbs again took sick, he had little choice but to drop out of school and get a job.

To get the job he wanted, he studied intensely for the civil service examination, even with a sense of gravity, and passed. In September 1903, he began his career as a railway mail clerk for the Nashville & Atlanta, Railway Postal Office (RPO). His salary of $800 per year allowed him to support his mother and to hold on to his dreams. He sorted envelopes into complicated schemes inside the mail car and heard the hissing of air from the steam locomotive as it moved through the mountain cuts and alongside the rivers and streams of north Georgia and middle Tennessee. It was a job he would keep for thirty-two years.

Dobbs's choice of the United States government as his employer was no fluke. The economic panics of the 1890s and the 1900s made the security of federal jobs alluring, particularly to blacks whose economic opportunities were limited by segregation. A federal job allowed a black to buy a home, educate his children and achieve a status within his community that was comparable to that of the professionals. His government-issue Colt revolver elevated Dobbs's status even further.

In these early years, Wes Dobbs, loud and brash, and just returned to Atlanta from his train run, strode down Auburn Avenue, passing the shoeshine stands, churches and small groceries. He wore a white shirt and khakis, a silver-plated badge with his government number, a long brass chain with keys for mail locks and the Colt revolver, unseen, holstered on his hip or carried inside his satchel. He had smooth facial features and brown eyes perpetually alight with curiosity. Handsome, of average height and build, about five foot ten, he projected as a much bigger man. His voice had not yet developed its husky texture of later years; still, its volume was such he might be trying to be heard over the roar of the train. Already Dobbs had developed that forward lean to his walk that suggested a man of supreme self-confidence, certain that he was on the rise and someone to behold. His satchel was heavy with books: Shakespeare, Francis Bacon, Frederick Douglass. Though his formal education had ended forever, he read at a pace that would have impressed even a college professor. He borrowed the books from Fisk University in Nashville, a black institution, because the Atlanta Public Library prohibited blacks from taking books home. (Blacks were permitted only to read in a room reserved in the basement.)

Early in 1905, Dobbs sat in a barber's chair on Auburn Avenue and noticed two women passing on the street. In a story he would tell many times over the years, he rose from the barber's chair.

"Great God A'mighty!" he bellowed, pointing through the barbershop window. *"Who is that?"*

A man in the shop said it was the wife of Ed Wright, a tailor who lived on Auburn. "No it's not," said another. "That's Ed Wright's wife's sister. That's Wright's wife with her."

"Well," Dobbs said, shaking his head and sitting back in his chair, "I got to find out."

Irene Ophelia Thompson, a twenty-year-old from Columbus, Mississippi, was visiting her sister, Carolyn, Ed Wright's wife. She was well-raised and carried herself with a quiet dignity. Fair in complexion, she looked to her daughter Renie almost like a bright-toned Indian.

Dobbs began his pursuit of her almost at once. Their courtship blossomed in what W. E. B. Du Bois would term "the Black World beyond the Veil." From his desk at Atlanta University, Du Bois was at work on a social study of the black condition in America that would total several thousand pages when completed and was unparalleled for its time. Admired by northern intellectuals for his challenge to Booker T. Washington's supremacy as spokesman for the race, Du Bois was fully ignored by white Atlanta. That summer three of Du Bois's closest friends in Atlanta's elite light-skinned colored society—educators John Hope and George Towns and businessman Alonzo Herndon—joined him and twenty-five other national black leaders at the Niagara Conference in Ontario, Canada, where they produced a controversial declaration against racial injustice.

In the marriages of many successful black families, an ambitious dark-skinned man often married a woman of light complexion, usually better educated and from a more established family. Such a marriage amounted to a social asset for the black man eager to climb the economic ladder; light-skinned black women, knowing this equation, often chose the suitor with the greatest promise. Soon Wesley Dobbs and Irene Thompson were locked arm-in-arm as they took walks along Auburn Avenue. She called him Wesley. He called her Miss Thompson. She had an elegance and understated respectability that Minnie Dobbs could only dream of.

In a letter written past midnight in April 1905, John Wesley Dobbs put his emotions into words:

> Dear Irene, I hope you will forgive me for addressing you in this manner, but the name sounds so good to me that although I could not muster courage to call you by it I have dared to write it. . . . It is past bedtime but I feel as if I could sit here till morning trying to tell you how I feel and what is buried in the recesses of my heart. But day would break and still I would not have finished. . . . Really and truly I feel that I am unworthy of the love of one so good and true as I know that you are. This thought nearly drives me mad. But still God in His Omnipotence has ordained that I should love only you. . . . If you should tell me that you love another or that you could not love me, although you may think well of me, I should think none the less of you, but should love you always and say, "Thy will be done." . . . [Then, apologizing for quoting Washington Irving, he wrote] "Your heart has become my world; it is there my ambition strives for empire, it is there my avarice seeks for hidden treasures; I send forth my sympathies on adventure, I embark my whole soul in the traffic of affection, and if ship-wrecked my case is hopeless—for t'will be a bankruptcy of the heart." . . . Sincerely Yours, Wesley.

She had been raised a Methodist, he a Baptist, and together they attended the First Congregational Church on Houston Street, a church established in 1867 by white missionaries. At First Congregational, elite blacks of Atlanta prayed in the rigid New England tradition. Pictured in the stained-glass windows were the likenesses of Jesus Christ and Abraham Lincoln. Sunday sermons at First Congregational were not intended as emotional cloudbursts. Members expected sermons to be rational and principled. According to good-humored lore, a preacher at First Congregational could be fired if his noun and verb did not agree. Wesley and Irene Dobbs were married in this church by the Rev. Henry Hugh Proctor on June 6, 1906. Dobbs had joined the church out of deference to his new wife, though one attraction was Proctor, a Yale-educated minister and friend to Booker T. Washington who in 1894 became the first black pastor of First Congregational after a long line of whites. An eloquent race leader, Proctor brought a new prestige to the church so that when President-elect William Howard Taft and former President Theodore Roosevelt visited Atlanta both stopped by First

Congregational. ("When you can get the best types of both races, then all friction will disappear," Roosevelt said during his 1910 visit.)

John Wesley and Irene Dobbs spent their honeymoon in Kennesaw, a place that warmed Dobbs's heart like few others. His uncle Jesse Dobbs, with whom he had spent much of his childhood, picked up the newly-weds at the Kennesaw train station and drove them by wagon back to the small farm where he and his brother, George Dobbs, had worked as sharecroppers for the past six years. Known as the Butler Place, it was owned by a white railroad engineer named Jesse Butler; Butler blew the whistle each time his train passed and Jesse Dobbs, in the darkness, waved a lantern or lit a match in response. The farm featured a weather-worn L-shaped farmhouse where the Dobbs brothers lived with the family matriarch, Judie Dobbs, then in her eighties. The house had been designed without plan, additions made haphazardly. White clean-swept dirt surrounded the farmhouse on all sides except in front where a few blades of grass sprouted. A wooden bucket and gourd hung from the nearby spring well. Hams cured in the smokehouse. Wooden washtubs and rub boards were set beneath the trees. The Dobbses used a heavy paddle and battling block to pound stubborn soil from their handmade clothes before the scrub, boil and blue rinse. A few cattle drank from a trough. A sweet potato patch covered the hundred yards that led to the N.C. & Saint L. tracks.

Far removed from the fray, John Wesley and Irene shared quiet moments in the soft summer moonlight of Kennesaw. With Jesse Dobbs and his wife, Lizzie, they laughed about stories from their youth—the many nights in which they had sneaked outside and sat atop the chicken coop to play the card game 5 Up, which Judie Dobbs had forbidden, and the sly execution of their favorite prank of sticking cotton between the other's toes while he slept, then setting a match to the cotton. A hot foot, they called it.

With a federal job and a young, beautiful wife, the pieces of Dobbs's dreams began to fall into place. He and Irene planned on having children and buying their own home, though for now they would live with Ed and Carolyn Wright at 446 Auburn Avenue.

Nowhere else in the South in 1906, Dobbs believed, could a black man have managed all of this.

Only in Atlanta.

At this moment, a racial conflict brewed in Atlanta, a product of an acrimonious gubernatorial race in which the candidates attempted to use negrophobia in Georgia to their favor.

The leading gubernatorial candidates were Hoke Smith and Clark Howell, two of Atlanta's most prosperous citizens. Howell published *The Atlanta Constitution;* his father, Evan P. Howell, once a Confederate infantry captain under Gen. Joseph Johnston and later Atlanta's mayor, was one of the city's most admired men. Smith, a lawyer, had sold his interest in *The Atlanta Journal* in 1900 for a handsome profit. In his *Journal* columns, he had advocated the presidential bid of Grover Cleveland; Cleveland rewarded Smith by naming him secretary of the interior. Both Smith and Howell were champions of white supremacy. During the campaign, *The Journal* fell in stride with Smith, mocking Howell by suggesting he "appears to be unable to understand why it is that we wish the legal disfranchisement of the 223,000 male negroes of voting age in Georgia. . . . Because we are the superior race and do not intend to be ruled by our semi-barbaric inferiors." As Howell's mouthpiece, the *Constitution* charged Smith with appointing blacks to federal positions while a member of Cleveland's cabinet, an accusation he denied. Smith lobbied intensely for the support of Tom Watson, the south Georgia demagogue, support he later earned. With a fear of black domination sweeping the southern states, Watson wrote in *Tom Watson's Magazine,* "What does Civilization owe to the negro? Nothing! *Nothing!* NOTHING!" Viewing Smith's inevitable victory with resignation, Negro leader Benjamin J. Davis, a Republican National Committee member and publisher of *The Atlanta Independent,* a black weekly, wrote, "It matters not with him whether his scheme of disfranchisement disfranchises every decent and helpful negro citizen and enfranchises every venal and vicious white thug." In August, Hoke Smith easily defeated Howell and several others in the Democratic primary en route to the governorship.

Into this hostile environment one month later came the newspaper extras.

On Saturday, September 22, 1906, the shrill sound of newsboys pierced Five Points:

"*Extra! Third Assault on White Woman by a Negro Brute!*"

"*Extra! Bold Negro Kisses White Girl's Hand!*"

"*Extra! Bright Mulatto Insults White Girls!*"

Atlanta newspapers had been publishing sensationalized accounts of black vice for a week. One day earlier Atlanta police had swept dives frequented by blacks along Decatur Street and removed photographs of nude white women from the walls of one parlor. *The Georgian* suggested that eleven assaults had been made by blacks against white women during the past seven weeks alone. The accounts were lurid and dramatic, including one in *The Evening News:* "With his yellow lips forming insulting phrases, Luther Frazier, a young negro, attacked Miss Orrie Bryan, the pretty 18-year-old daughter of Thomas L. Bryan, in her home." *The Evening News* sent out an emotional call in that same edition: "Men of Fulton, what will you do to stop these outrages against the women? . . . Shall these black devils be permitted to assault and almost kill our women, and go unpunished?"

Four more assaults against white women reportedly had been made that afternoon. Liquored up on a Saturday night, a mob of whites gathered in the city's streets. A colored bootblack from Alonzo Herndon's barbershop at 66 Peachtree was chased down and beaten to death with fists and clubs. A voice then cried out, "There goes another nigger!" The mob set off in a new direction. By nine o'clock, frenzied whites near Decatur Street shouted, "Save our women!" "Kill the Niggers!" Wild rumors of an impending black uprising spread across the city. In black communities, horrifying tales were told of widespread lynchings. Mayor James Woodward tried to calm the whites: "The honor of Atlanta before the world is in your hands tonight." But he and James English, head of the police commission, were met with cries of "Nigger lover!" A black messenger was assaulted. Gunshots rang out. An occasional rebel yell was heard. Woodward called for police and fire units. Fire hoses were turned on the white mob, with little effect. Several hundred blacks, seeking strength in numbers, congregated near Decatur Street and they, too, faced the fire hoses. What followed was a scene of terror: several thousand white men, with an assortment of weapons, attacked the group of blacks. The blacks attempted to fight back, fists against clubs, but quickly turned and ran. Sketches of this scene were displayed in newspapers across the world, beneath the headline: "Race Riot in Atlanta."

Soon the white mobs ruled the streets of Atlanta. Policemen did little to stop the carnage; in several instances they aided the rioters, who stalked blacks past midnight. Streetcar lines were cut and several blacks were dragged from the cars on Peachtree and clubbed to death. A black woman was said to have "fought like a wildcat," using her umbrella as both lance and shield. The mobs moved past Ivan Allen's office supplies store at 61 Peachtree, a few doors down from Herndon's. Along Decatur Street, the mob shattered plate-glass windows of black restaurants, clubs and dives. In the darkness, black maids, draymen and messengers fled the city. Presidents of Clark University and the Gammon Theological Seminary for blacks collected frightened black women and children and gave them refuge on campus. Reacting with patrician instincts, many white families in the city offered shelter to their colored servants. The Aragon Hotel and Silverman's restaurant locked up their black workers overnight to keep them from harm. On the street, a black tailor was beaten with iron bars. Another black man was trapped by two large mobs and murdered with hatchets and knives; souvenir hunters are said to have sliced off his toes and fingers and paraded through the streets, holding high the blood-smeared digits. A couple of black bodies were dropped on Marietta Street at the foot of the Henry Grady monument, a symbolic punctuation mark to his New South credo. Frank Smith, a black messenger for Western Union, made it to the Forsyth Street bridge but not a step beyond. "A mob of poor white crackers caught our friend Frank Smith . . . and stoned him to death," a grieving friend, J. L. Black, wrote the following week in a letter published in *The Atlanta Independent.* "It was said in one of the white papers that he was a self-important 'colored gentleman' meaning he thought more of himself than anyone thought of him, but it was only a mistake. . . . We do not know a single person who would or could say Frank ever did them harm."

Sporadic violence broke out in the city over the next three nights. Because of the sensationalized reports, a precise count of casualties remains difficult to discern, though several whites and about two dozen blacks are believed to have been killed while hundreds more were injured. "Some times I doubt if there is any spot in this country where one with Negro blood can plant a home free from prejudice and scorn & molestation," Adrienne McNeil Herndon, the wife of Alonzo Herndon, later wrote to Booker T. Washington. After the riot, Mrs. Herndon left the city for several months, taking her son Norris to a school in Philadelphia. She added, "I should like to hide from the eyes of the white man, or any rate the Southern white man the things I, as a Negro woman hold most sacred for fear they pause & look to jeer and ridicule." The future author Margaret Mitchell was only five years old and spent that night with her father, Eugene, at their home on Jackson Street, about a mile east of Five Points. She would recall hearing neighbor John Slaton, the future governor, warn everyone to ready their guns. Since he did not own a gun, Eugene Mitchell stood inside his front door, holding an ax and an iron water key. To young Margaret, "No sight has ever been so sweet to these eyes," as the appearance of the state militia marching up the street.

Hearing the news of the riot, Du Bois rushed home to Atlanta by train from Alabama, where he was on a research assignment. He armed himself with a shotgun and sat on the steps of South Hall at Atlanta University, protecting his wife and daughter. Walter White had a similar experience. The future executive secretary of the NAACP, White, then thirteen years old, was handed a gun by his father, a postal carrier, as a white mob approached the family home on Houston Street. "Son, don't shoot until the first man puts his foot on the lawn and then—don't you miss!" A black neighbor fired first, though, causing the mob to scatter. A member of First Congregational, Walter White was affected profoundly by the experience: "I knew then who I was."

Several blocks away, John Wesley Dobbs sat, in a fright, inside the bolted front door of 446 Auburn Avenue, gripping his Colt revolver. His ammunition was set neatly on the floor next to him. Dobbs often practiced his marksmanship at a local shooting range, as was the custom among railway mail clerks. He had been issued the gun to protect the U.S. mail, though now he would not hesitate to use it to protect his family.

The white mob swept down Auburn Avenue, marauders searching for blacks to abuse, silhouetted in the dim orange and blue glow cast by their torch lights. Dobbs peered out the front window, watching and waiting, his heart pounding. When the mob turned from the deserted street before reaching the Wright home, between Randolph and Boulevard, he breathed a sigh of relief. He spent the next several nights in the same spot, in his role as family sentinel, just to be safe.

In black Atlanta, the scars were deep. In the days that followed the riot, more than three thousand white families were without black servants too fearful to return. More than one thousand blacks are said to have left the city, not to come back. Atlanta's streets emptied for several days. Business at the Herndon barbershop on Peachtree, which averaged about $30 per day, plummeted to $4.75 on the Monday that followed the riot. Blacks gained small solace when white leaders admitted later that newspaper reports of black assaults on women had been exaggerated three- or fourfold. Booker T. Washington, who participated in the negotiations between the races after the riot (along with Reverend Proctor and Alonzo Herndon), maintained that never before had he seen the leading white men of a city gathered "at the mourner's bench to the extent that these people are." The riot prompted many small black-owned businesses to relocate from the central business district to the security of their own race on Auburn Avenue.

Over time, memories in Atlanta would prove segregated, too. The unspeakable horror of the 1906 race riot lurked in the recesses of black families in Atlanta for generations, passed on, as in the Dobbs family, with a spellbinding definition that time could not reduce. If white families in the city retained any memories of the riot—and few seem to—it typically centered on how some paternalistic whites had saved black servants from the mob, or how the riot had prompted a new cooperation between the races. "There has been no more hopeful or courageous movement in the South since the war," Ray Stannard Baker wrote in

*American Magazine* in April 1907, "than this effort of the good men of Atlanta to get hold of the monumentally complex negro problem in a new way." His optimistic conclusion was unwarranted.

The lingering fear in black Atlanta was reflected in a proposal by the city editor of the *Independent,* who, shortly after the riot, called for a city ordinance to prohibit whites from riding on elevators designated for blacks. (Oftentimes, whites who were too impatient to wait for crowded elevators designated for whites instead boarded black elevators.) "Suppose, accidentally some colored man should stumble and fall against some white lady while getting on or off the car, what would be the outcome?" the editor wrote. In the *Independent,* Benjamin J. Davis asked "the proud Caucasian for a square deal and such opportunities under the law as a child race just verging from slavery deserves and ought to have in the light of Christianity."

"What is the ultimate end?" John Temple Graves of *The Georgian* asked, rhetorically.

"Separation of the races—the only possible logical, inevitable solution. These two opposite antagonistic races can never live together in the same government under equal laws—never. Help us to separate."

The tone of race relations in Atlanta was set for the next fifty years.

As a precaution, John Wesley Dobbs kept guns and bullets hidden in his house for decades to come.

As Dobbs's family grew, he reveled in its growth. The first child, a namesake daughter, Irene, was born in the Wright home on Auburn Avenue in the winter of 1908; to distinguish from his wife, Dobbs called her Renie (pronounced Ree-knee). Two more daughters, Willie and Millicent, followed in 1910 and 1911. Irene gave birth thrice more: to a fourth daughter, Josephine, in 1918, and to Mattiwilda and June in 1925 and 1928. Six children spread across twenty years—all girls. Their names were full of harmony—Irene Carolyn, Willie Juliet, Millicent Doris, Josephine Ophelia, Mattiwilda and June Selena—though by household nickname they became Renie, Willie, Millie, Josie, Geekie and June. Named for her maternal grandmother (Mattie Wilda Sykes), Mattiwilda's nickname was coined when her younger sister, June, unable to pronounce Wilda, called her Weekie, which soon became Geekie, a playful name that stuck. The wide range of ages—Renie was a Spelman College junior when June was born—made the Dobbses seem almost like two families. Renie didn't even know her mother was pregnant, until she opened her skirt to show her rapidly expanding waistline. "People are all saying we're gonna have another Spelman girl," Irene Dobbs told her eldest daughter. "We've decided to make one last try to have a son to go with you five girls." Among the elite black families in town, the only couple to exceed the Dobbses was Henry and Annie Long Rucker—he, the former collector of internal revenues in Georgia (appointed by President William McKinley) and she the daughter of Jefferson Long, Georgia's first colored congressman during Reconstruction. They had six daughters and two sons.

A son of his own remained one of John Wesley Dobbs's unfulfilled dreams. "We kept thinking the next one would be a boy," Dobbs wrote a friend years later. "I guess that is why we have so many girls."

He adored his daughters. Before he departed for his train run the older girls lined up at the front door. "The Dobbs Goodbye" became a family tradition. Pronounced and genuine, their hugs and kisses seemed to last forever.

"Remember," Dobbs often said before leaving, "you girls are pretty but none of you are as beautiful as your mother, right, Babe?"

Each time, Irene blushed and rolled her eyes. "Oh, Wes . . ."

With bursting pride, Dobbs purchased a fine home at 400 Houston Street (later renumbered 540). To a German woman named Bertha Steinechen he paid $2,767 in 1909 for a home that featured ornate plaster and terra-cotta molding throughout, including lacy fairies dancing beneath the mantel next to the fireplace. So stylish was the molding that one of Dobbs's daughters later would liken the home to a New York museum; friends wanted to come inside just to see it. The transition in the old Fourth Ward neighborhood, from German-Jewish to black, was nearly completed and the changing disposition was manifest in the prevailing architectural style of the street, a hybrid mishmash that hinted at Victorian. The Dobbs home had three bedrooms, a large back porch where the smell of oven-baked cornbread and fried fish soon filled the air, and an exquisite living room, which Irene called The Parlor. There she and her husband placed their Cable Company piano, a fixture they viewed as necessary to any household as a bathtub. Set on a ridge about a mile east of Five Points, the house provided a view of the Candler Building peeking over a distant tree line. From his home, Dobbs could walk to the heart of Auburn Avenue in ten minutes. The house represented another tangible sign of his ascension in the black community. Colored men of standing now became his neighbors—a bishop, a school principal, another railway mail clerk. No one in John Wesley Dobbs's family had ever owned a home. This first home also was his last; Dobbs lived there the next fifty-two years.

In time, he became the sun and moon rising over his daughters' daily lives. "He was the king, the president, everything," Renie says. He placed restrictions and made demands upon them. He taught them about life, love and literature and mandated that each daughter take ten years of piano lessons, beginning at the age of seven. He sought to nullify any self-doubts that segregation in Atlanta might create. He fed them self-respect on a continuous basis as if it were one of the basic food groups. *You are equal to anyone*, he told them. *You will succeed.* That neither he nor his wife worked for a white family enhanced their credibility in the eyes of their daughters. He prohibited them from attending segregated events in Atlanta; never were his daughters to sit in the balcony seats reserved for blacks at the Fox Theatre or the Loew's Grand, the prized movie palaces in the city. They would go instead to the Royal Theater or the Ashby Street Theater, colored movie houses that showed films months after they had completed runs at white theaters. He took them on trips north to point out the greater freedoms that blacks had in public transportation and accommodations. History mattered to him. At Plymouth Rock his daughters were not merely to observe it, they were to touch it. At the Statue of Liberty, they climbed every step to the top. This, he believed, would make their experience permanent. He insisted that they outperform, outdress and outclass their peers in Atlanta. They were to get ahead and stay ahead. Quick to hug (often he returned from his train run with small gifts and trinkets), Dobbs was just as quick to criticize. He taught them about sexuality and the menstrual cycle. ("Oh, Wes, don't talk about that," Irene said. "Well, Babe," he replied, "the girls need to know these things.") He had a chivalrous code in the house, refusing to enter a room if his daughters were in a state of undress. Later, when boyfriends began to show up, he sized them up, methodically. He worried about an early pregnancy. His mother had given birth at sixteen, his sister at seventeen, and he determined to keep his daughters from the same path. His power over his family was absolute, undoubtedly a reflexive response to his own childhood when the absence of his father caused great hardship.

He ruled his daughters as he would attempt to rule all people and circumstances—with total fidelity to his sense of rightness. The personalities of his daughters varied, though each would develop an inner strength. At times they challenged, or defied, him, though it was a risky proposition. Challenges usually took the form of sneaking away to smoke a cigarette, or to apply lipstick, or to listen to blues music, things he considered beneath them. Millie so often challenged him that, naturally, she was said to be most like him.

In Dobbs's view, a woman was feminine and cultured, beyond

reproach yet somehow restrained. One of Dobbs's granddaughters explained the idealized image he wished for his daughters: "If you took a very refined, sophisticated European woman who had the best upbringing . . . and made her black." These were the qualities Dobbs's mother lacked but that he believed his wife possessed. Irene taught Sunday School and became a deaconess at First Congregational; she played whist and joined the Inquirers Club, a literary group, with some of the leading ladies of black Atlanta; she set out her finest linens and china for a Sunday family dinner, and she soothed her husband when he needed soothing. John Wesley Dobbs wanted his daughters to fit such a mold. Their future became his private crusade.

Alongside the blast furnace of her husband, Irene Dobbs seemed a cool summer breeze. The Thompsons were a prosperous family on the black side of Columbus, Mississippi. A co-owner of two barbershops in town (one for whites, one for blacks), her father, Kelly Thompson, was a mulatto born in 1856 to an Irish mother and black father. Upon graduating from a colored academy in Columbus in 1901, Irene intended to teach. When she met Dobbs, her plans changed. Dobbs did not want his wife to work. In time, part of her role as mother was to serve as a buffer between her daughters and her husband. She nurtured her children like the roses in her garden. Innately sweet yet devilishly coy, Irene knew how to hold her ground with John Wesley.

"You've got to fix the fish in lard, Babe!" he commanded once. She raised a kitchen fork at him. "It's time to leave, Wes," she said, biting off each word. He did.

"We're just like the big engine pulling the little engine," Dobbs once told her.

"Yeah, but who's the big engine?" she replied. "And who's the little engine?"

They had been married for a decade when Irene Dobbs, visiting her family in Mississippi in the summer of 1916, wrote to her husband. "My Darling Boy," she began. "I have been away from my Big Boy long enough. I do miss my sweet goodnight kisses and that strong arm that has carried me along through these ten years. Really, Darling if I should lose you for good, life would indeed be dreary for me, for I do not see any one else who interests me as you do, and I fear that without your sweet words of comfort, advice (and criticism, too, sometimes) I should be like a ship without a rudder. . . . If ever children devotedly loved their Daddy, ours do. Millie Doris [then four] is still worried lest you should be forced to go to the woods to eat worms."

Even on paper she tamed him. "Mama is quite well," she wrote, concluding her letter, "and tells me every day that I should lick you all over every day (as a cow does her calf) and thank the Lord every night for such a good sweet husband as you are.

"I told her I know you deserve it but I think the latter will be quite sufficient."

Barreling across the open spaces of Georgia and Tennessee, Dobbs feared a few of his more antagonistic white colleagues would push him from the moving train. He didn't know when it would happen. Maybe somewhere out in the countryside or perhaps on a bridge over a river during the humid summers. He worried that he might never make it home.

"They'll push me off when no one is looking, Babe," he told his wife, "and say it was an accident."

The number of postal jobs given to blacks in the south increased under Republican administrations in Washington, usually as a result of a patronage system guided by national committee members. But blacks encountered other problems once in the railway mail service. Few were allowed to rise to the rank of clerk-in-charge. Racially mixed crews were plagued with bickering over small matters, such as sharing closets and washbasins. Some rail lines were segregated intentionally, becoming "black lines." At one point the Atlanta & Birmingham, RPO had sixteen clerks, all black. Black postal clerks complained bitterly of "Bossism"— white superiors who gave preference to white clerks over blacks. L. D. Cunningham, a black Atlantan, spent a brief time in the mail service and surmised in 1906: "Colored men are put on daily duty and are not given any time for study, hence when they are called up for examinations, they fail and are dropped. . . . If a colored clerk has any trouble in the car with any of the white clerks, there are three white clerks to the one colored and they go into collusion and swear that he [the colored man] was to blame." At a convention in Chattanooga in October 1913, black railway mail clerks from across the South gathered to form the National Alliance of Postal Employees (NAPE). Within a few years, Dobbs became one of its more vocal members.

During these years Dobbs joined the Prince Hall Masons, a black organization that would become the centerpiece of his public life. Founded after the American Revolution for charitable and social purposes, the Prince Hall Masonic fraternity traditionally attracted a large portion of the black elite and became a bulwark of the black middle class. Its colorful rituals and long-winded language helped solidify socially conscious leadership within the black community. Between 1908 and 1924, the membership of the Georgia jurisdiction grew nearly fourfold to 24,000. Initiated in 1911, Dobbs became grand warden in Atlanta three years later. Masonry filled voids in his life. He thrived on its camaraderie and male fellowship, having been surrounded by females most of his life. If segregation denied his ambition to lead, Masonry provided an outlet to rise among those of his own race.

On his layover nights in Nashville, Dobbs usually could be found in his boardinghouse, reading. Much of what he read related to the race issue. He inscribed in a small black notebook some of his favorite phrases, those that spoke to the essence of the black plight. In later years he would draw from those notes in speeches to the Masons as well as in impromptu soliloquies on Auburn Avenue. On the cover of one notebook, he wrote: "J. W. Dobbs 400 Houston St. Atlanta, Ga. If found please notify." On the back: "My Armory Of Ideas."

Now thirty-five, a husband and father of three daughters, Dobbs was transforming himself into a "race man," a leader devoted to uplifting the black race. Some of the quotations in his notebook came from the Greeks, others from Lincoln, Du Bois, Grady and anonymous authors and soldiers.

> *"The problem of the 20th century is the problem of the color line."*
> Du Bois.

> *"The interest of Miss., not the African, dictates my conclusion."*
> Jeff Davis.

> *"If I forget these people may an infinite God forget me."*
> Henry Grady.

> *"In all things purely social we can be as separate as the five fingers and yet one as the hand in all things so essential to mutual progress."* Booker T. Washington.

> *"The fly sat upon the axle-tree of the chariot-wheel, and said, 'What a dust I do raise!'"* Aesop.

Interspersed with these quotations he tried a few self-truths.

> *"I cannot conquer age; all other fights I win."* J.W.D

> *"In the big cities you find both extremes—the most cultured and intellectual as well as the most perverted and depraved. It is a long drop from the top to the bottom of this abyss; yet, many are the souls that make the leap, and find too late, eternal woe."*
> J.W.D.

> *"Freedom is here but the spirit of slavery is also here."* J.W.D.

He made numerous visits during these years to the Kentucky birthplace of Abraham Lincoln in Hodgenville. These visits amounted to pilgrimages, for Dobbs admired Lincoln more than any other man, not only because he had emancipated his mother among the more than three million slaves but because he had risen from humble rural origins. Lincoln was the reason Dobbs was a Republican. Each time he left the Lincoln birthplace he felt a little freer and stronger and more optimistic about the white man.

John Wesley Dobbs visited the Lincoln birthplace so many times he claimed the tour guides knew him by name.

He tried to convince Jesse Dobbs, his young uncle and childhood playmate, to leave Kennesaw and move to Atlanta. "How can I support my family?" the sharecropper replied. Farming was all he knew. But Jesse Dobbs allowed his seven-year-old daughter, Isabel, to move to Atlanta to live with John Wesley's family so she could attend school for nine months instead of the three-month session in Kennesaw's one-room, one-teacher schoolhouse.

John Wesley Dobbs's devotion to family was pure. From Houston Street to Atlanta's Terminal Station, each week he carried a small woven basket containing Isabel's laundry and a letter to her parents. In these days before diesel fuel, all northbound trains from Atlanta stopped for water in Kennesaw. Jesse Dobbs usually was waiting when the train pulled in; he took the woven basket from his nephew. When the Nashville & Atlanta, RPO passed through Kennesaw on the return trip, he handed to John Wesley the same small woven basket—now filled with clean, folded laundry, freshly dug and cleaned peanuts, a pound of fresh butter, cut joints of syrup cane and a letter to his daughter. If Jesse Dobbs arrived a few moments late, he ran behind the train as it pulled away slowly. For five years this ritual continued. (Not until 1920, after the boll weevil left its signature across the South, did Jesse Dobbs move his family to Atlanta. His worldly goods atop his wagon, his sons atop the chicken coop, he made the twenty-five-mile trek several times; the last trip, he marched his cow straight up Lena Street in southwest Atlanta. John Wesley helped him obtain a job as a janitor at the lone black branch of the Carnegie Library and later at the Citizens Trust Bank.)

In late summer each year, Dobbs took his family to Kennesaw to help with "laying-by" time, a period of difficult chopping, plowing, banking and fertilizing. Elbert Dobbs, another of John Wesley's uncles who lived nearby, also brought his family. Jesse Dobbs had become the superintendent of the Sunday School of the Sardis Baptist Church and each summer coordinated the Sunday School picnic. Piling Renie, Willie and Millie and his own children atop the fresh hay, pillows and quilts, Jesse Dobbs drove his two-mule wagon on the five-mile trip to Marietta where he purchased hundreds of pounds of ice blocks to use for soft drinks and ice cream at the carnival. On the return trip, the Dobbs kids broke off small pieces of ice to quench their thirst.

Nearly ninety, Grandma Judie Dobbs seemed as fragile as crystal to her great-granddaughters, a serene old ex-slave in a taffeta dress. There was something mystical about her to Renie and something unsettling, too. Judie Dobbs's skin seemed as white as cotton, her hair straight and long enough to sit on. A precocious eight-year-old, Renie asked her mother, "Why is my grandma so white?" Irene Dobbs's answer came years later when her eldest daughter was valedictorian at Spelman College and capable of understanding what a slave woman's life had been like. Though only a child, Renie couldn't help but notice how the members of her extended family were of different shades, with hints of the African, the Cherokee and the white. "There was a whole lot of stuff and people would shut you up," Renie says. "They wouldn't let you talk—or listen, either." Grandma Judie Dobbs often asked Renie to sing hymns with her: "... *steal away to Jesus! Steal away, steal away home; I ain't got long to stay here! My Lord, he calls me by the Thunder! The trumpet sounds within my soul!*"

Once Judie Dobbs, an unlettered woman, handed Renie an old Bible. "Teach me," the freed slave said.

"Okay, Grandma," Renie said. Then she opened to the first page. " 'In the beginning God created the heavens and the earth . . .' "

Emancipation had come more than a half century before. No one knew an ex-slave in Kennesaw older than Judie Dobbs. Her teeth had decayed and fallen out and her lips seemed to collapse into her mouth when she spoke. She was an aged woman from another time. She shook her head. "How do you know it?"

"Because, Grandma, you have to go by every letter and certain combinations of letters make words. You have to learn the alphabet first."

Renie picked up two pencils and gave one to Judie Dobbs. "Try to follow," she said patiently, and began to write the letters of the alphabet.

Grandma Dobbs, she says, never did learn too much.

The Houston Street School was a conflagration waiting to happen. A dilapidated wooden structure without indoor plumbing or heating, fire drills were part of the daily regimen. On May 21, 1917, Renie and Willie heard the sirens from inside their classrooms, loud, piercing wails that seemed to draw closer by the minute. School let out early that day, and as their classes were escorted, single file, to the front of the building, the girls were surprised to see their mother out front, amidst a crowd of other parents, waving frantically to them. "Here I am! Come to me!" Irene Dobbs was a stickler about her appearance and, until now, her daughters never had seen her wearing her house dress outside. She had run the entire distance, about eight blocks, and now she raced back to the house with her daughters. As they ran, they saw police cordoning off streets behind them.

The Fourth Ward was engulfed in flames. The black section from Auburn Avenue to Old Wheat Street was wiped out. By one P.M. flames had swept north past Houston Street into the white residential areas near Ponce de Leon Avenue. At Five Points, John Wesley Dobbs heard the firebells sounding, saw the state militia marching to the northeast and felt soot falling from the sky. The fire had started near the Oakland Cemetery about noon. High winds carried sparks across the Georgia railroad toward Ponce de Leon Avenue. Hundreds of one- and two-story frame homes near Auburn Avenue were lost, as was the Wheat Street Baptist Church. Black refugees moved toward Peachtree. On Ponce de Leon twenty stately mansions were dynamited by firefighters in an attempt to contain the blaze. In a frenzy, Dobbs rushed for home but could not get past police barricades. As the flames approached Boulevard, Irene gathered important papers. She placed valuables in boxes and dragged them into the yard. Only six weeks earlier President Woodrow Wilson had declared war on Germany—and now rumors spread that the fire was part of a German conspiracy. ("Absolutely without foundation," the *Constitution* declared the next morning.) Dobbs had circled east, then backtracked through police lines to his home. When he arrived, he took out the hoses immediately and sprayed water on the roof. For eleven hours the fire raged. The Dobbses saw fine black families standing outside their gutted homes with nothing saved but a few portraits and papers. Nearly two thousand homes were destroyed; insurance companies estimated damage in excess of $5 million; more than ten thousand Atlantans, mostly blacks, were homeless. John Wesley Dobbs considered himself blessed because that night the inferno was halted at Boulevard, less than two blocks from the wife, three daughters and home he treasured.

# CHAPTER 6

→←

In the fall of 1907, only months before Henry Ford introduced his Model T automobile, Ivan E. Allen took a respite from the business grind to marry Irene Beaumont in the drawing room of her widowed mother's home at 282 Rawson Street in Atlanta. Several hundred guests sat before an altar decorated with tall palms and ferns. The Confederate widow Susie Allen of Dalton wore black silk and duchess lace, and her son Will served as his brother's best man. The new Mrs. Ivan Allen was an Atlanta native who carried herself in a stately manner, her appearance immaculate, never a hair out of place. At seventeen, Irene Allen seemed a child bride, particularly since her husband already was thirty-one, older than most men on their wedding day. She had married a man of her own social class who was on the rise and made no secret of his ambition to crack into the city's social elite. Her devotion to his ambition was total. "Mr. Allen is socially well-liked in Atlanta, and has a wide acquaintance in the east and west," *The Atlanta Constitution* wrote in its account of the wedding. "He is prominently known in business as a member of the firm of Fielder & Allen." Ivan and Irene Allen traveled to Cuba on their honeymoon and, in one striking photograph, he is wearing a black derby and holding a walking stick and she is wearing a flowing white dress and a dark hat with velvet flowers. Their smiles reflect a fresh, shared awakening.

They purchased their first home at 874 West Peachtree in 1910 in a booming residential section for young white families three miles north of Five Points. Here, in March 1911, their only child, a namesake son, Ivan Jr., was born. Because Dr. Nicholas Earnest did not arrive in time for the delivery, a black midwife named Bertha Lewis assumed his role. That the first hands to touch their son were black made little impression on the proud parents. The delivery was physically taxing on Irene, not a strong woman; she decided not to have any more children as a result.

Though the automobile age was dawning and he was among the city leaders lining Peachtree Street with New York–style skyscrapers—maybe not in brick and mortar, but certainly in grand vision—Ivan E. Allen remained rooted in his family's past. At times, his mother became his personal compass, reminding him of who he was, where he had been and where he aspired to go. He wrote to Susie Allen often. On Mother's Day, 1912, he sent a Western Union telegram: "Your Son, Grand-Son and Daughter in Law, Wish you every Joy and Happiness that you so richly deserve." He had compelling reasons to admire her: she had raised three children without a husband; she also had given him money to start in business in Atlanta. When infirmity made letter-writing impractical for Susie Allen, he sent a self-addressed, stamped envelope and asked her to fill it with petals from a flower in her garden—just to let him know all was well.

In November 1912, he was called back to Dalton for the dedication of a monument to Confederate general Joseph E. Johnston. Erected by the Brian M. Thomas chapter of the United Daughters of the Confederacy, of which Susie Allen was a charter member, the monument was unveiled by Allen's young niece, Suesylla Thomas. More than five thousand people filled the streets of tiny Dalton, including one hundred Confederate veterans. "General Johnston was the one who first took up arms in the defense of the South and the last to lay down arms after the great struggle was over," one speaker said. "And had General Johnston been left in command there would have been no 'March to the Sea.' " Twelve southern crosses of honor were handed out that day by General Johnston's grandniece. Allen rose from his seat next to his mother and accepted a cross for D. Earnest Allen, the father he had barely known, who a half century earlier had answered the call of southern honor.

As cities flourished across America, so did the Chamber of Commerce man with his signature calls of devotion to God, country and community. Sinclair Lewis's classic 1922 novel, *Babbitt,* created a vacuous real estate man/civic booster in a town he called Zenith. "It's the fellow with four to ten thousand a year, say, and an automobile and a nice little family in a bungalow on the edge of town, that makes the wheels of progress go round!" George F. Babbitt said in one civic speech. "Here's the new generation of Americans: fellows with hair on their chests and smiles in their eyes and adding machines in their offices. We're not doing any boasting, but we like ourselves first-rate, and if you don't like us, look out—better get under cover before the cyclone hits town!"

A cyclone in his own right, Ivan E. Allen spoke the Babbitt language and had similar civic impulses. He had arrived at a realization early in Atlanta: "The more I gave to altruistic work, the more my business seemed to grow." As a guiding principle, this amounted to civic paternalism—or what some Atlantans came to know as "enlightened self-interest"—and gave sharp definition to Allen's life. *What was good for*

*Atlanta was good for Ivan E. Allen, and vice versa.* Like the fictional George Babbitt (born in April 1874, two years before Allen), he chased money by day and civic improvement by night. Allen's entrée to the Atlanta business community was recorded in the minutes of the Chamber of Commerce on March 5, 1901, when, among the newly elected members, were: "Atlanta Daily News . . . Stewart and Ray, Excelsior Steam Laundry . . . Fielder & Allen."

In 1910, Atlanta was the second most populous city in the old Confederacy, trailing only New Orleans. As New South descendants of Henry Grady, the men of the Atlanta chamber created slogans and propaganda, made speeches and held committee meetings. In Atlanta, more than in most cities, the Chamber of Commerce was an aggressive body whose urban promotive schemes—and successes—gave rise to an exalted position in the community. Several Atlanta chamber presidents, including Robert F. Maddox and Asa Candler, later became mayor. The salesmanship of these Atlantans pushed their city toward the national mainstream and further from the rural traditions of Georgia. As a commercial hub, Atlanta became the South's first city of national import.

Ivan E. Allen looked the part of a man in a hurry. Taut and expressive, his face featured the deep-set dark eyes that had made his mother so alluring to a young ex-Confederate cavalryman. His brown hair turned prematurely silver. His chin had a determined upward tilt—the same as President Woodrow Wilson's, according to one *Atlanta Journal* story.

The Fielder & Allen office stood in front of the Henry Grady statue at 44 Marietta Street. Allen sat behind a large mahogany glass-top desk and dictated to his assistant the minutiae of the day—bids, checks, general correspondence—while he concentrated on the big picture, namely expansion. Allen's commands came with the sounds of an automatic weapon: "*Biff! Biff! Biff!* Steady, sure, no foolishness about it." Fielder & Allen sold pencils, pens, paper clips and carbon paper as well as ornate desks and steel safes. In a city on the make—with a Chamber of Commerce seeking to lure companies from the North and Midwest—office supplies seemed just the right sort of business. Whenever a business moved to, or sprang up, in Atlanta, Allen invariably was among the first to offer a hearty welcome and ask casually about office needs. Already in 1913, Allen was promoting Fielder & Allen as the largest office outfitter south of the Ohio River. He understood that his future was tied to Atlanta's commercial growth.

He sounded every bit the politician during the summer of 1912 when he wrote a story for *The Atlanta Journal*, beneath the headline "What Atlanta Really Needs." Among his suggestions were a central market, more parks, reduced water rates for families that used only one faucet, and curiously, a mausoleum. "Sentiment, everywhere," he wrote, "I believe, is turning toward the mausoleum." Over the next eight years he sold his city and himself with extraordinary single-mindedness. In December 1913, he led a two-week fund-raising campaign that netted more than $250,000 for Atlanta's Oglethorpe College. Earlier that year Allen joined the sons of Henry Grady and Joel Chandler Harris, author of the Uncle Remus tales, to found the Atlanta Rotary Club ("Service Over Self!"). In 1913, he became president of the newly created Atlanta Convention Bureau, inviting to town farmers and dentists, insurance men and automobile salesmen ("Tersely expressed, I might say that the Southeast is on wheels and Atlanta is the hub around which the wheels revolve," Allen wrote). The Convention Bureau pitched every imaginative advertising scheme to bring annual conventions to Atlanta, "The Convention City of Dixie Land." In his four years as president of the bureau, the city attracted nearly $4 million in convention business while spending just $30,000. "Beautiful, hustling, sunny Atlanta," Allen wrote in one brochure. (Though he did not promote it, he would learn of his city's darker side during this period when, in 1915, he sat on his front porch on West Peachtree and held a gun in case the mob rushing toward Gov. John Slaton's home turned on innocent bystanders. Slaton had commuted the death sentence of Leo Frank, a Jewish businessman convicted of murdering a factory girl named Mary Phagan; Frank vehemently denied guilt. Though Slaton was spirited away from Atlanta until emotions cooled, the vicious anti-Semitism around Atlanta did not quiet until months later when Frank was abducted from a jail in Milledgeville by vigilantes who drove him to Cobb County and hanged him from a tree. To Jews in Atlanta, the name Leo Frank carries the same haunting spirit today as the 1906 race riot for blacks.)

By 1916, the name Ivan E. Allen—he never wrote it without the middle initial—appeared in the newspapers with regularity. Always a civic do-gooder, Allen helped the Boy Scouts get a foothold in Atlanta, became a trustee of a local museum, president of the Southeastern Fair and director of an anti-tuberculosis society. "Here's the secret," he said. "To me, public business is private diversion. Now, every man must have some diversion, some slight let-up from the grind, or he goes stale. My let-up is in work that counts for public well-fare. That's my hobby. The hobby of some men is golf, some others bridge [or] whist, some others turkey-trotting. Well, it's no credit to me, but I just happen not to care for these diversions."

Before delivering a speech at the Ansley Hotel in the fall of 1913 on "The Value of Organized Effort in Convention Work," Allen heard friends suggest he might become Atlanta's next mayor. "You boys are kidding me?" Allen said. Soon, *The Dalton Citizen* boasted of its native son, "If Atlanta elects Ivan Allen as its chief executive, Atlanta will have one of the most wideawake, progressive mayors of any city in the South." *The Atlanta Journal* called him "the embodiment of 'The Atlanta Spirit,' that militant genius which has brought Atlanta from the ashes bequeathed by Sherman to her present status."

Allen opted not to run for mayor, though he waited a month before withdrawing. That was enough time to allow the compliments to pour in—good advertising for his business.

His immediate future was planned. On the list of chamber presidents, Allen in 1917 succeeded Victor Kriegshaber, owner of a building materials concern, and preceded William White, chief executive of a meatpacking company, and Sam Candler Dobbs, the Coca-Cola executive who not only was Asa Candler's nephew but a descendant of Josiah Dobbs's brother Elijah. "More smokestacks for Atlanta" was Allen's pledge as incoming president, though the First World War forestalled most of his plans. He devoted himself to the needs of the 43,000 military personnel in Atlanta's Camp Gordon and Fort McPherson. That number included foreign prisoners, whom he judiciously called "the guests at the German Barracks." He crafted his enthusiasm to meet the needs of the times. "Let us fly both the flag of our country and the flag of business optimism," Allen told the chamber membership.

Ivan E. Allen was an optimistic fellow, crisp and energetic, a southerner, and proudly so. He walked briskly and tipped his hat to the ladies on Peachtree. In the parlance of his day, he was a *business engine.* He liked good cigars and closing deals; he abhorred Bolsheviks and any criticism of Atlanta.

His friends called him the Atlanta Spirit, incarnated. The Atlanta Spirit was a phrase Allen used lovingly, and often, to describe what made his city great. He didn't argue the nickname because, if he had to say so himself, he thought it apt. The Atlanta Spirit, he once said, "is the love of home and civic loyalty that will, can and is building the greatest, cleanest, most prosperous city in all this glorious southland."

In a city that would become famous for excessive civic boasting, Ivan E. Allen's praise for Atlanta could have filled a fleet of balloons. He had verve, pep, self-love, civic pride, ambition, pluck, a namesake son, a colored cook, a devoted wife, Irene (whom he sometimes called Reno), a rambling frame house and a gasoline-powered Reo convertible automobile that he loved to drive through the leafy neighborhoods of his city as the summer sun beat warmly upon his face. Though a prohibitionist, he didn't mind a splash of bourbon in the privacy of his own home. His business was office supplies and, to make the right impression, he wore dark suits and clean white monogrammed shirts that proved not only that he had style but that he had all but cornered the market on vowels ("I.E.A.").

"How do you find business?" someone once inquired.

"By going after it!" Allen replied, with considerable voltage.

A man of commerce, Allen also was a Presbyterian, a Rotarian, a staunch Woodrow Wilson Democrat, an Ad Man ("Atlanta Always Ahead!"), a member of the Gridiron Club and, fraternally speaking, a Shriner, Mason, Knight Templar and Elk.

He defended Atlanta as though it were his family name, which in a sense it was. "An Atlanta man feels that he cannot say too much about Atlanta not only to an Atlanta audience, but any gathering in civilization," Allen said in 1914. Two years later a friend toasted him by saying, "If you should walk up to any Atlanta man and ask, 'Whoinell is this Ivan Allen I hear so much about?' you would be classified at once as a stranger from a very great distance."

He was typical of the chamber presidents leading Atlanta into the modern era. A Protestant born in Georgia who came of age during Henry Grady's years of sway, he arrived in Atlanta as a teenager and sculpted himself into the sort of highly specialized manager that American business was celebrating. His mentors were recent chamber presidents Mell Wilkinson, who owned a fertilizer and feed business, and Frederic J. Paxon, the local department store man. Allen shaped his public life in their image. His initiation into the Piedmont Driving Club in 1917 was another reflection of his rise. Already he had joined the Atlanta Athletic Club and the Capital City Club, where he lunched, smoked cigars and played gin rummy. At these clubs, Allen shared fellowship with peers from the chamber, except, of course, Victor Kriegshaber. The lone Jew to crack the chamber hierarchy, Kriegshaber was denied membership to Atlanta's elite social clubs and instead joined organizations created principally for Jews.

The recorded minutes of the Ivan Allen administration of the Chamber of Commerce in 1917 reflect a continuing passion for raising the stakes in the competition for commercial leadership in the south with Birmingham and New Orleans, but only one reference to elevating the living standards of local blacks. In February, two chamber officials solicited the support of the Fulton County commissioners to build a Bath House and Wading Pool for blacks. They appealed to the commissioners that little had been done for blacks, particularly in recreation and amusement. They said the chamber would contribute $2,000 to the new facility. But white citizens in the Sixth Ward, site of the proposed pool, were outraged. The notion of blacks splashing about in clear water in their midst had little appeal. The chamber backed away from its plan.

White supremacy was implicit in the chamber's continuing neglect of black Atlanta and this neglect would last for several more decades. The civic engines of Atlanta revealed only nominal interest in lifting the veil and offering solace to those behind it. Apparently, the Atlanta Spirit was not intended for blacks.

Ivan Allen believed in segregation. Separate but equal was the law of the land, established two decades before by the U.S. Supreme Court in *Plessy v. Ferguson.* He used the word "Nigger" freely in private conversation. "But Daddy didn't use the word with malice," Ivan Jr. recalls. His daily contact with blacks extended to his cook, Alvie Mobley, and a few other family servants, but that was all. His mother and father had been raised with blacks in their home and so had he. He liked the continuity of having blacks care for Ivan Jr. In Ivan Allen's eyes, black servitude was the way things had been, were and would be. Like his patrician peers, Allen believed black Atlantans had a living standard superior to that of blacks in other cities. Sometimes, the chamber even boasted of the black colleges on the west side. "Could it be true that these people, these earnest students are but one or two generations removed from the darkest jungles of Africa," *The City Builder,* official publication of the Atlanta chamber, wondered. "Where is the mother college which produced this negro culture? Is it Africa or Asia? No it has grown on Atlanta soil." The tone was typically self-congratulatory: "Here must be decided once and for all the vexed problem of race. . . . If the Christian spirit of Atlanta cannot settle the question then it is impossible of settlement."

As the sirens sounded for the Great Atlanta Fire on May 21, 1917, Allen rushed at once to the center of the crisis, as was his custom. With Mayor Asa G. Candler, he helped with the fire hoses, directed arriving soldiers to their places and, according to the morning paper, "in a hundred other ways lent aid to the fire fighters." He dispatched two men to Peachtree Street where they were instructed to redirect passing automobiles to nearby hospitals, in case patients required evacuation. The next morning, at an emergency relief meeting at the Chamber of Commerce, nearly $50,000 was raised, the sort of charitable response that Allen viewed as yet another example of the Atlanta Spirit. The donations were called out so rapidly, Allen repeated each one aloud so that the secretary had enough time to record them. Most of the city's leading men attended this meeting. Candler, the Coca-Cola Company magnate who had agreed only reluctantly to run for mayor, made a $1,000 personal contribution, as did banker Ernest Woodruff and businessman Edward Inman. Former mayors Robert F. Maddox and James English pledged sizeable donations as well. At one juncture, colored citizens were allowed to make contributions; Bishop Joseph Flipper and Rev. Henry H. Proctor pledged $100 and $50, respectively, amidst great applause. Ivan E. Allen announced plans to transform some of the burned-out areas in the Fourth Ward into a public park, ostensibly to allow for more breathing space and superior protection from future fires. He had an ulterior motive, though he allowed the *Constitution* to state it for him: such a park would settle "for all time the embarrassing problem of the 'fourth warders' of negroes living on the same streets as whites," the paper wrote.

"In a very few weeks," said Allen, who by now knew well his city's history, "I expect to see Atlanta rising from the flames, more progressive, more confident and more beautiful than ever."

In his patrician enthusiasm, he was not alone. Indeed, Ivan E. Allen was only one cog in a large well-oiled local machine.

The Atlanta chamber also was unresponsive during these years to the revived order of the Ku Klux Klan. Announcing Atlanta as its "Imperial City" in 1915, the Klan had set up its headquarters in a loft in the Georgia Savings Bank. Attracting a mostly lower-middle-class membership, the Klan held contempt not only for Jews, blacks, immigrants and the Catholic church but also for commercial clubs and "the autocratic Chamber of Commerce." In 1921, *The New York World* estimated that as many as forty-thousand Klansmen lived in Atlanta; undoubtedly an overestimate, this would have represented nearly 30 percent of the city's white population. As founder and imperial wizard, William Joseph Simmons of Atlanta preached a "one hundred percent Americanism," a theme popular across the country with a working class that felt an increasing dislocation in cities, often losing jobs to immigrants and blacks. At Klan meetings, Simmons placed two revolvers on the table before him and shouted, "Bring on your niggers!" His members rewarded him with a $30,000 house on Peachtree. The Klan's newspaper, *The Searchlight,* could be found at Atlanta newsstands and sometimes included advertisements placed by Coca-Cola and Studebaker. Klan initiations were held at nearby Stone Mountain and in Piedmont Park where Booker T. Washington had delivered his Atlanta Compromise. In 1922, Walter Sims, an avowed Klansman, was elected mayor of Atlanta and his victory capped a Klan sweep in Georgia: two Klansmen, Walter George and Clifford Walker, had been elected U.S. senator and governor during the preceding week. The Klan's baseball team played in an amateur league in

Atlanta, wearing crosses over the left breast of their uniform. The Klan team defeated the Baptist Tabernacle to win the 1924 Dixie League title in the city. The Chamber of Commerce did little to deter Klan activity in the city undoubtedly because the Klan pumped revenue into the city's economy. Not only did the Klan have several hundred employees, it also held "klonventions" and "klonvokations" in Atlanta.

In the summer of 1918, Allen was a politician without title, but that was about to change. The lure of public office proved irresistible. He entered the Democratic primary, which for the past decade had excluded blacks; in a one-party state such as Georgia, the Democratic primary was the only election that mattered, so Georgia's blacks effectively were without a political voice. Allen's campaign announcement read:

> As a native Georgian, always a democrat, in thorough accord with the administration's plans for full and complete victory over the Central Powers, thus forever putting an end to scientific savagery; with a sincere love for my state and a determination to further help in the upbuilding of our institutions, I announce myself a candidate for the office of State Senator from this, the 35th District, consisting of the counties of Cobb, Clayton and Fulton, subject to the vote of the White Primary. . . . I solicit your vote and influence for a plain business man.

He pledged better roads and better schools. He set up a campaign committee to contact every registered voter in the district. Already, Allen served as director of War Savings for Georgia and led the Liberty Loan campaigns across the Southeast. On September 18, 1918, when U.S. forces in Europe under Gen. John Pershing smashed through the concrete-reinforced first lines of the enemy in German Lorraine, Allen followed a long-standing tradition by appearing that night outside the offices of the *Constitution* to monitor election returns. At eleven o'clock, he telephoned Irene to give her the good news: he had won convincingly.

Once in the state legislature, he discovered a rural disdain for Atlanta and thought it wise to have his own bills introduced by legislators who were not from Atlanta. He chaired the Senate Appropriations Committee. His proudest moment—one he celebrated at cocktail hours for the next half century—occurred in 1919 when he helped stave off an attempt by Macon legislators to move the state capital from Atlanta to Macon. Allen researched the history of the capital carefully, and stated his case on the Senate floor. "If Macon is anxious to do something for Georgia, why doesn't she do something for the School of the Blind, which is located there?" Allen said. Some legislators broached the idea

of separating the state into North Georgia and South Georgia. By evacu-
ating Atlanta, Allen surmised, the state would give up a statehouse building worth $6 million. Ultimately, the bill was tabled, not to be revived.

Allen served in the legislature only two years. In 1919, his partner,
James Fielder, sold his interest to Allen and longtime employee Charles
Marshall. The two men changed the name of the firm to the Ivan Allen-
Marshall Company. Even to his eleven-year-old son this name change
sparked a realization. "That was the first time I realized that Daddy was
very proud of his own name, and that he wanted to build his reputation
around his name," Ivan Jr. says.

Certainly the name Ivan E. Allen was easy to remember. Yet the retiring state senator simplified matters further by dropping the middle initial.

*Ivan Allen*, he knew, was a name Atlantans would remember.

As much as he liked the sound of his name, though, he preferred
being called Senator.

The second Ivan Allen remembers the day in 1926 when his father
announced in the living room that he had purchased a mountain. A fru-
gal woman, Irene Allen blanched. She said, "You've got to be kidding,
Ivan." As a boy, the Senator had been told of the mysteries of Fort Mountain, which rises two thousand feet in the Cohutta range in north Georgia, about twenty miles from Dalton. In truth, the Senator did not buy
the whole mountain, just the 119 acres at its crest, which included the
stone ruins of a fort that some (including the Senator) believed had been
built by Spanish explorers. He thought his mountain might be converted
into a fine resort, with a golf course; Irene thought the whole matter
excessive. In 1934, he donated the mountain to the state and it has been
used as a park for more than sixty years.

From an early age, Ivan Jr. understood that his was a family of privilege. He grew accustomed to having a black servant in his home as a
cook, gardener or handyman. He was an only child of a prosperous businessman and a doting mother living in a growing southern city with big
dreams, a place that began to tout itself as the New York of the South.
"Life couldn't have been much more pleasant," Ivan Jr. says. "We had
what every American cherished. We had no calamities in the family.
Mother and Daddy were very compatible. Things were always improving." He showed his sense of industry as a boy by operating a drink stand
on the corner of Peachtree and 17th streets. Sometimes, the family cook,
Alvie Mobley, made potted ham sandwiches, which Ivan Jr. sold for a
nickel, profiting three cents on each. From the streetcars making the
turn at 17th, the conductor, motorman and passengers became his regu-

lar customers. At the Tenth Street Elementary School and later the Spring Street School, Ivan Jr. developed what would become lifelong friendships with classmates such as the future bankers Ed Smith and Jack Glenn. Watching their fathers, these boys one day would assume that civic mantle and serve Atlanta with a keen sense of history, gratitude and noblesse oblige.

By 1925, Ivan Jr. already had developed a sense of presence. With his parents he traveled to London where his father served as American representative to the annual meeting of England's stationery industry. The British asked the fourteen-year-old to say a few words. "I'd just like to say this," Ivan Jr. said. "You're all such a fine bunch of gentlemen that you make me right proud my father is a stationer." It was his first public statement and was received with applause.

A dynamic transition was afoot in Atlanta as the city broke from the past and leapt into the future: Monk, Prince, Dan and Rabbit, the police department's old and trusted horses, were retired, victims of a newly motorized force; businessman Samuel DuBose placed the city's first transcontinental telephone call to Paris; and upon the advice of a jug-eared city alderman named William B. Hartsfield, the city purchased the three-hundred-acre Candler racetrack in 1929 to transform into an airfield, the first step toward ensuring Atlanta's southern supremacy in aviation.

The Senator's own prosperity during the 1920s exceeded that of his city. Ernest Woodruff's Trust Company of Georgia, which in 1919 had transacted the $25 million sale of the Coca-Cola Company from Asa Candler to a syndicate headed by Woodruff, named the Senator as one of its directors in January 1923. Recalling his own inability to secure a loan from local banks decades before, the Senator urged the Trust Company to take more risks by making loans based on "character, energy and ability." The Ivan Allen-Marshall Company, meanwhile, celebrated its twenty-fifth anniversary in 1925 (dated to the founding of Fielder & Allen) and the Senator boasted how the original group of four employees had grown to forty-eight. In 1927, the Senator built a stylish brick English Tudor home in a shaded district beyond the trolley lines, six miles north of downtown. His new address was 2600 Peachtree Road. Among his esteemed neighbors were the former judge Shepard Bryan, publisher Clark Howell, Jr., businessman Clarence Haverty and Col. Robert Jones, father of the golfer Bob Jones, who in 1930 would win the celebrated Grand Slam of his sport.

Holding his cigar, squinting behind his wire-rim glasses and wearing his conservative suits, the Senator bubbled with robust self-satisfaction. At fifty his hair had turned fully gray, and he had become portly, the result of too much work and too little exercise. His rising affluence could be tracked by the history of his family automobiles—from a Willis-Knight to a Studebaker and then, by the time Ivan Jr. was at Boys High School in 1927, to a Cadillac. On Sundays, the Allens attended the First Presbyterian Church on Peachtree, a congregation that included some of the city's most influential families, such as the Inmans. In 1927 the Senator finally cracked into the Social Cities Register, the annual list of elites in Richmond, Atlanta, Charleston, Savannah and Augusta. At the Piedmont Driving Club, he and Irene danced on the terrace on warm summer nights. There, Ivan Jr. learned to swim and to play tennis in a quaint exclusivity.

When the city suffered a malaise of pessimism during the middle 1920s, brought on in part by the Millionaire-a-Minute boom in south Florida (even the Senator's brother, Will Allen, left his job as a buyer for Davison-Paxon to move to Fort Lauderdale), the Senator was among the businessmen to step into the breach. The competition with Birmingham, for sustained growth, intensified. Located about 150 miles to the west, Birmingham's population in 1920 was slightly less than Atlanta's 200,000. Unlike Atlanta, however, Birmingham did not have an indigenous business leadership. A steel town with absentee owners living in Pittsburgh, Birmingham lacked the necessary core group of civic visionaries with a vested interest in commercial development, arts and education in their city.

The Atlanta chamber in 1926, recognizing a critical need for the infusion of northern capital, began a nationwide "Forward Atlanta" campaign to sell the city. To the businessmen of the nation, the chamber touted Atlanta's advantages in distribution and manufacturing. The Senator was a natural choice to chair the campaign in 1926. The strategy was to inundate the nation's newspapers, trade journals and magazines, including *Forbes* and *The Saturday Evening Post*, with the same messages: namely, that the South had become the nation's fastest growing region; that central offices in the North no longer could serve the entire nation without the aid of regional branches; and that Atlanta, by virtue of its location and transportation facilities, was the most sensible and fiscally prudent city from which to serve the South.

The Forward Atlanta advertisements tolled the virtues of modern business Atlanta:

> Are you geared to modern conditions?
> Why did they all choose the same city?
> Freed from the Yoke of Cotton's Domination.

The Senator and his chamber colleagues bullishly promoted Atlanta's climate ("No extremes of heat or cold"), its schools, its cost of living ("7.5 percent below average for the country"), its capability to reach seventy million Americans with one day of travel and its laboring workforce—"Intelligent, adaptable, Anglo-Saxon," the latter serving notice that neither immigrants nor blacks would stand in the way of prosperity.

Lasting until 1929, the Forward Atlanta campaign lured 679 new factories, warehouses and sales offices during the four years, bringing seventeen thousand employees and payrolls that totaled more than $30 million. As part of this campaign, the Senator wrote a book in 1928, *Atlanta from the Ashes*, dedicating it to "the men in commerce and industry who have made America great." Sitting at his desk at 2600 Peachtree Road, he pulled out a typewriter, the instrument that first brought him to the city, and began: "In 1864 the city of Atlanta lay in smoking ruin." He filled his book with his trademark optimism as well as with evidence that justified Atlanta's "utmost importance to American business."

Just as Ivan Jr. knew of his father's energy and optimism, he knew of his explosive temper. Rarely did that temper reveal itself at home, but he had heard the stories about his father's fury being unleashed at the office by the smallest signs of incompetence or tardiness. His business success had not been forged by indifference. The Senator's wrath could be definitive, as in a 1928 dispute with a renter operating a small restaurant in an Allen-owned building at 240 Spring Street. When the renter complained that he needed more heat during evenings and weekends, the Senator told him he had enough heat already. After several months, with no additional heat forthcoming, the renter balked on his rent payment. The Senator promptly hauled the renter's furniture, fixtures and merchandise to a warehouse and locked the doors. In the ensuing lawsuit, the courts sided with the Senator.

Ivan Jr. enjoyed the spoils of his father's prosperity. Soon after entering Boys High School, he owned a Chevrolet two-door coupé, a gift from his father. Few students owned cars in 1928 and Ivan Jr. often drove his friends around Atlanta. "Ivan, the Bad Man," is what some of the girls playfully called him. "He always had a fancy car and he was a fancy operator. He was attractive. All of the girls were crazy about him," remembers Laura Maddox Smith, daughter of Robert F. Maddox. Less than serious as a student, Ivan Jr. once smugly signed his name to a blank sheet of paper during a final examination in a tenth-grade biology class. His teacher credited him with 15 points out of 100. When he asked the teacher for an explanation, she replied, "I thought it was worth at least that much because you not only signed it but you also spelled your name correctly." His father was his security: Ivan Jr. knew he could not be expelled from school due to his father's prominence. During his senior year at Boys High, though, he asserted himself and earned a spot on the honor roll.

One mile down the road from Boys High was the Georgia Institute of Technology. Founded in 1888 to allow Georgia a place to develop its own engineers, Georgia Tech became the school of choice for Ivan Jr. in 1929 for one compelling reason: it was in Atlanta and Atlanta was the center of everything he had ever known.

> *I gotta Eugene Dog, I gotta Eugene Cat,*
> *I'm a Talmadge man from my shoes to my hat.*

And then there was the rest of Georgia.

If Atlanta leaders aspired to Studebakers and Cadillacs, most Georgians, working the farms, aspired only to make it to tomorrow. Into the fiscal desperation of 1932 rode the motorcade of Eugene Talmadge, horns blaring, dust roiling. Rural Georgians had never seen anything quite like Talmadge, who would crow, "The poor dirt farmer ain't got but three friends on this earth: God Almighty, Sears Roebuck, and Gene Talmadge." As the state's agriculture commissioner in 1931, Talmadge had been charged with financial improprieties, but told a Senate investigating committee, "If I stole, it was for farmers like yourselves!" Urged to repay the state more than $16,000, Talmadge refused, state leaders buckled, and he emerged more popular than ever.

"Old Gene" was political moonshine, intoxicating and irresistible, an electrifying country orator with a brown forelock falling into his eyes, his sleeves rolled up to the elbows and pants hanging from his trademark red galluses. While Atlanta spoke the language of mainstream America, Talmadge spoke of the common man in the time-honored southern tradition. He cared little for Atlanta, even less for blacks. During his years of sway the expression "Two Georgias"—Atlanta, and the rest of the state—became a political, social and economic reality. The county unit system in Georgia, created in 1917, guaranteed rural domination of state politics and so perpetuated Talmadge's contempt and disregard for Atlanta. According to the county unit system, the eight most populous counties carried six unit votes apiece, the next thirty largest counties carried four unit votes each, and the remaining 121 counties were worth two votes each. Thus, three obscure rural counties could offset the vote of Fulton County in Atlanta. Conceivably, a candidate could lose the popular vote, but still win election based on the county unit votes. The inequities of the county unit system were even more acute during the 1930s when, for the first time, more Georgians lived off the farms than on them.

A cult figure, Talmadge was followed on the campaign trail by the Haggard brothers of Danielsville, who often listened to his speeches from nearby trees. On cue, the Haggards called out, "Tell us about it, Gene," and Talmadge would smile, lift his hand and say, "I'm a'comin' to that." Talmadge spoke on courthouse steps and in cotton fields and his cronies would boast later that Old Gene never won a voting district that had electric lights or trolley cars. His election as governor in 1932 began a family political dynasty in Georgia that would last a half century. "You farmers haven't had anybody fight for you since Tom Watson," Talmadge told a crowd at the Irwinton courthouse during the 1932 gubernatorial campaign. A spectator shouted, "We've got you NOW, Gene!"

The Senator knew Gene Talmadge, even served as an honorary lieutenant colonel on his staff, as he had for former governor L. G. Hardeman and as he would for future governors E. D. Rivers and Ellis Arnall. More than a Democrat, however, the Senator was a staunch Roosevelt man and he could neither understand, nor forgive, Talmadge's frequent attempts to undermine FDR's New Deal programs.

Besides, the Senator had enough to worry about at the Ivan Allen-Marshall Company. The Depression had cut revenues dramatically, though his rapport with the business community assured his company's survival. When Ivan Jr. graduated from the School of Commerce at Georgia Tech in June 1933, the Senator wrote his son a letter with typical directness. The two and a half typed pages read like a mandate. *"Dear Ivan: For many years I have been planning and educating you to join us here in the store and carry on the work in the years to come along the same lines and with the same people that have carried it along for the past thirty years."* Ivan Jr. had received offers from other companies, but he discounted them all. He had always planned to join his father. Smooth and handsome, impeccably groomed, with neat, wavy brown hair and blue eyes, Ivan Jr. had had a stellar career at Tech. His résumé read as you would expect from an aristocrat's son. He had been president of the student body, president of the Sigma Alpha Epsilon fraternity, a member of the honor roll and dean's list and a cadet colonel of the ROTC. He had passed his regiment in review once before Franklin Roosevelt, another time before Winston Churchill. His decision to enter the family business seemed to etch in stone his life's course. Nearly always, he would follow his father's path. *"You have expressed a desire to start at the bottom and learn the work thoroughly.*" The Senator would have his boy begin in the basement. He would learn from a black employee named Arthur Wright. "*Locate everything down there, go over the dark corners and find out why things are there, where they came from and whom they belong to—what use they are—rearrange them—change them, destroy them—clean them up, all tools, parts and hardware. Dark corners and backdoors are always danger points in a business.*" Ivan Jr. had been in the School of Commerce at Georgia Tech at a time when the nation offered a splendid economic case study: the stock market crashed and America went off the gold standard. "*You will appreciate the advantage of having our name on every piece of merchandise that gets out—in the past, much merchandise has creeped out of here not imprinted or improperly imprinted. Some of it has been imprinted almost to where it disfigures the merchandise and makes it objectionable to the customer.*" At Tech, Ivan Jr. studied social problems in the nation, which meant only the problems of its white citizens. The race issue never was discussed at Georgia Tech. It simply never came up. "*My greatest ambition for you now is to become a successful city salesman and to be able to go out and take orders at a profit to yourself and the Company.*" He began work that summer, in the basement with Arthur Wright, earning $100 per month. The Senator loved his son and was deeply proud of him. But business was business. He signed the letter to his namesake: "*Yours sincerely.*"

Of the Senator's many well-placed business friendships in Atlanta, one was about to pay an astonishing dividend. As a member of the board of directors of the Trust Company of Georgia, the Senator knew Ernest Woodruff. And Ernest Woodruff was an important man to know. The son of a prosperous flour miller from Columbus, Woodruff had become a business predator in Atlanta, buying small companies, or assuming control of financially troubled ones, and transforming them into the likes of the Atlantic Ice and Coal Company and Atlantic Steel. He served as president of the Trust Company of Georgia for nearly two decades, a position he had assumed from his brother-in-law, Joel Hurt. The purchase of the Coca-Cola Company in 1919 by a syndicate that did not reveal his involvement—he knew Asa Candler despised him and would not sell the company to him—had made Ernest Woodruff the biggest player on Atlanta's business scene. A short, bulbous man with a gray mustache and cold eyes, Woodruff was particularly harsh to his son, Bob, whom he believed his wife had spoiled. In 1908, after Bob Woodruff's poor grades prompted his dismissal from Emory College, a small Methodist school in Oxford, Georgia, his father warned, "Damn it, boy, it's only three generations from shirtsleeves to shirtsleeves. Learn something." Already a powerful personality in his own right, Bob had replied, "I'll take the shirtsleeves now." Though he never earned a college degree, Bob Woodruff later would flash an intuitive salesmanship and business acumen that even his father could not fail to miss. In 1923, at the age of thirty-three, Bob Woodruff was named president of the Coca-Cola Company. He would carry the company to unimaginable heights.

In November 1935, Ernest Woodruff sat in the Trust Company offices with the Senator and Tom Glenn, president of the bank and uncle of Jack Glenn, Ivan Jr.'s close friend.

"Ivan," Woodruff said, "I want you to buy some Co' Cola stock."

"But Mr. Woodruff," said the Senator, who was only thirteen years younger than Ernest Woodruff, but treated him, as most Atlanta men did, with supreme deference, "I don't have any money to buy with."

Ernest Woodruff was a notorious tightwad. Once he had traveled to New York with Glenn to buy bonds and, in order to avoid paying the required insurance premium on all bonds sent through the mail, he and Glenn had stuffed the papers under their shirts. "Every time we moved," Glenn recalled, "we rustled like a high school graduating class unfolding its diplomas." During the Depression, though, Woodruff offered to help some of his friends.

Now, he motioned to Glenn. "Tom," he said, "give him whatever he needs." And then Woodruff told the Senator, "Ivan, I want you to buy $25,000 of Co' Cola stock." The offer astonished. Depression conditions in Atlanta were severe. Only a year before Mayor James Key had announced that teachers and city employees would be paid in scrip for the final two months of 1934; Rich's department store showed its faith in the city by accepting the scrip at face value. The Coca-Cola Company, meanwhile, advanced Atlanta's city government $800,000.

When he returned to 2600 Peachtree Road that afternoon, the Senator found Irene and Ivan Jr. in the library. In a moment his son would recall with clarity decades later, the Senator told Irene what had transpired. "I thought I might just as well go bankrupt for another $25,000, if necessary," the Senator explained. "And so I bought $25,000 worth of Co' Cola stock today."

Once, she had listened to her husband explain why he had bought a mountain. Now, hearing him say he had bought $25,000 in Coca-Cola stock with money they didn't have rendered her speechless.

The Senator shrugged. "Tom Glenn let me have the money."

With its astonishing growth, Coca-Cola would prove a handsome investment for the Allens. Over the years, the Senator sold some of his

Coca-Cola stock, but gave most to Irene and to Ivan Jr., who, in turn, passed his shares to his children and grandchildren. Had the Allens continually reinvested their dividends through the years, their initial $25,000 investment in Coca-Cola would have been worth about $27 million in 1995, sixty years later; typically, investors did not reinvest dividends in those years, however. As it was, Ivan Jr. says "several million dollars" of Coca-Cola stock remained in his family in 1995.

In the summer of 1934, Ivan Jr. attended a swimming party at the Druid Hills estate of Asa G. Candler, Jr., son of the former Coca-Cola magnate. Candler's home included a lush wooded haven that had its own menagerie of elephants, lions and other animals; the guests of honor were the Candler twins, Helen and Martha. Ivan Jr.'s attention was captured that day by a girl wearing a blue dress and an oversized pink hat. Her name was Louise Richardson and she was an Atlanta blueblood. Her father, Hugh Richardson, was prominent in local real estate, and her mother, Josephine Inman, was the daughter of Hugh T. Inman, once said to be the wealthiest man in Georgia. Hugh Richardson had left his family hardware business in Vicksburg, Mississippi, to attend the 1895 Cotton States Exposition in Atlanta; while in Atlanta he met Josephine Inman. They were married the following year at the Inmans' summer home in Rome, Georgia. A train, chartered for the occasion, transported guests from Atlanta. For a honeymoon, Hugh and Josephine spent a year traveling the world, a remarkable exhibition of prestige and excess in 1896. Their daughter, Louise, in her pink summer hat, was only eighteen, nearly six years younger than Ivan Jr. She had attended a private school in Virginia, then the elite Rosemary Hall in Connecticut where the headmistress once took her class to the Metropolitan Museum in New York City so they could study Latin in the proper environment.

The courtship of Ivan and Louise lasted nearly two years. After her second year at Vassar College in Poughkeepsie, New York, Louise was offered a choice by her parents: would she prefer to make her debut in Atlanta or in a more formal presentation at the Court of St. James in London?

Louise soon set off for London.

Her friend Anne Alston, who was dating Ivan's close friend from boyhood, Jack Glenn, made the trip with her. The girls curtsied nervously before Queen Mary and Edward, Prince of Wales, then had supper at Buckingham Place with other members of the court in June 1935. Afterward, they traveled in Europe, seemingly oblivious to the Depression back in the States. Along the way they received letters from their two beaus in Atlanta. The girls returned to Atlanta on the train, but Ivan Jr. was not among those waiting at the station upon their arrival. He was in bed, at 2600 Peachtree Road, suffering from jaundice. "It was," Louise recalls with mock drama, "life's darkest moment." Ivan's face was a sickly yellow when he gave Louise an engagement ring. Soon after, on a visit to the Richardson family retreat near Lake Toxaway, North Carolina, Ivan Jr. told Louise's father of his wishes to marry. Richardson was a garrulous sort, about whom Ivan Jr. would say, "You could feed six people off the side of one chicken while he was telling a story." Sitting on the porch that day, Richardson asked Ivan Jr. about his financial stability. Ivan Jr. said he was earning $125 a month, an amount Richardson thought satisfactory. Richardson said Louise earned about $35 a month from her bank stock. "A pleasant chat," Ivan Jr. recalls.

Their marriage on New Year's Day, 1936, was the most celebrated of Atlanta's social season. The Richardson-Allen union was the most dynamic marriage of Atlanta Bourbons since businessman Joel Hurt wed Ann Woodruff nearly a half century earlier. On the wedding day, a snow and ice storm paralyzed Atlanta. "More people here than I thought would be," Robert F. Maddox announced to his daughter, as he surveyed the pews inside the First Presbyterian Church. The ushers comprised a veritable Who's Who of Atlanta's power elite: former governor John Slaton, the aged grand scion Hugh T. Inman, businessman John W. Grant (Louise's uncle, whose Pace's Ferry estate, Craigellachie, was the site of the rehearsal dinner and years later became the Cherokee Town & Country Club) and Philip Alston, the prominent attorney and former Atlanta Chamber of Commerce president. As his best man, Ivan Jr. chose Roy Collier, Jr., a descendant of Wash Collier, one of Atlanta's original settlers. Louise's sister served a matron of honor and Eleanor Spalding, daughter of King & Spalding senior partner Hughes Spalding, was maid of honor. *The Atlanta Journal* chronicled the wedding beneath an eight-column headline, describing it as "a marriage marked by impressive beauty and dignity and one of outstanding social importance."

In the spring of 1936, Susie Allen, the family's last link to the days of the Confederacy, died. She had lived most of her eighty-seven years in Dalton and the local newspaper was filled with tributes, including one that termed her a local landmark. "She was the widow of the gallant Confederate soldier, Daniel Ernest [sic] Allen," the United Daughters of the Confederacy wrote in *The Dalton Citizen;* the UDC members cited "her love and loyalty to the southern cause." *The Dalton Citizen* eulogized, "It was interesting to hear her talk of the old days when Dalton was not much more than a succession of cross roads, with no paved streets, and in rainy weather with plenty of mud-holes and in dry weather something akin to a desert." Ivan Jr. remembered "Mumpsie" as an elegant grandmother fastidious in her appearance, usually wearing a brooch at her throat. The Senator and Irene, Ivan Jr. and Louise made the ninety-mile trek to Dalton for the funeral. The Senator's two siblings, Will Allen and Mary Ruth Thomas of Athens, also attended. Susie Allen's open casket was placed for viewing in the front room in the house on Hawthorne Street. It was unseasonably hot for March. "It was hot as Hades that day," Louise remembers. "I thought I was going to faint." A family friend recited a poem in Susie Allen's memory: *From aristocrats descended, As portrayed in features delicate, Like a cameo. . . ."* Another friend read verse from Tennyson. Finally, Susie Allen's casket was interred next to the grave of her husband on the hillside that overlooked the Confederate graveyard.

In the fall, Franklin Roosevelt won Georgia en route to reelection. As treasurer of the state Democratic organization, the Senator reveled in FDR's landslide triumph that gave Republican Alf Landon only two states. Soon after, Ivan Jr. and Louise attended a dress ball at the Piedmont Driving Club attired as "The Landon Twins." He was Maine, she was Vermont. ("We thought it a clever idea," Ivan Jr. says, "but the average person there wasn't particularly impressed.") Signs of economic recovery appeared late in 1938 when the Senator waxed nostalgic about the insulated glory of the Piedmont Driving Club. In the olden days, he and Irene had danced on the Driving Club's terrace floor. Because it was made of unevenly laid octagonal paving stones, they had had to dance uphill. As for the stately oak beside the terrace, the Senator swore it had influenced Atlanta's social life; beneath it, marriages had begun, marriages had ended and Atlanta mayors had been elected.

Ivan Jr. and Louise were living in a home set amidst the woods on Northside Drive, on land owned by Louise's family, when their first son was born in October 1938. Though money was tight—they ate several meals each week with the Richardsons just to cut costs—they had enough to pay for a black maid, Viola Welch, who lived in the rear of their house. Welch was paid $6 per week. Almost from the moment he learned that Louise was pregnant, the Senator insisted that she would deliver a boy and that the boy's name would be Ivan Allen III.

He proved right on both counts.

With the birth of a new Allen generation—and a new Ivan Allen—times were changing. In order to keep up, Ivan Jr. and Louise rewarded Viola Welch with a raise. Now, she would earn $7 per week.

# CHAPTER 7

His white peers on the train held a growing contempt for John Wesley Dobbs. In October 1924, they revealed their hostility in a letter to the postmaster general's office in Washington.

> My Dear Sir, We the undersigned postal clerks of the Nashville and Atlanta, R.P.O. protest against clerk J. W. Dobbs holding two positions, one as a second clerk on Nash. & Atla trains 3 & 4 the other as Secretary and Treasury [sic] of the Masonic Order for the State of Georgia which carries a regular salary of twenty seven hundred dollars per year. . . . Refferring [sic] you to sections 160 and 1599 of the P.L.&R. if holding other positions is not prohibited, in order to be fair to all postal clerks we request that the P.L.&R. be amended so all clerks can hold other positions. In as much as the Atlanta Office have [sic] knowingly taken no action we are calling your attention to the fact.

Twelve signatures appeared at the bottom of the letter, scrawled in the bold manner of revolutionaries signing the Declaration of Independence. The protest was considered serious enough for a postal inspector, Frank Shumate, to begin an investigation.

With four daughters and a fifth on the way, Dobbs needed money to supplement his government salary. For years after World War I, he had sold insurance for the Standard Realty & Insurance Company. In an interview, he freely told Inspector Shumate he had been elected secretary of the Prince Hall Grand Lodge in June and that his primary responsibility was to receive and deposit monies. Dobbs said he was paid $225 per month, kept an office in the Odd Fellows Building on Auburn Avenue and, most important, used Masonic clerks to handle details so the job did not infringe on his government work. The railroad's chief clerk, Harry J. Graves, understood what had prompted the complaint. "A number of the clerks dislike Dobbs personally," he explained in a letter to Shumate. Graves noted that only twelve of the line's fifty-five clerks had signed the petition and that he had conducted an internal inquiry, determining that Dobbs conducted his Masonic work only during his layoff periods from the railway mail service. Dobbs, he wrote, "was ready at all times to respond to any call for emergency service or extra trips. . . . While clerk Dobbs is not what might be termed a very efficient clerk, his services in the R.M.S. are performed in the same manner in which he has always performed."

In his report, Shumate cited a central reason why the petition had been submitted: "Dobbs is a negro." As a matter of policy, the United States government did not attempt to legislate the religious or fraternal affiliations of its employees, not only to avoid sparking a legal controversy, but also, according to one interoffice postal memorandum, because such work tended "to uplift the employees and inspire them with the desire to attain the better things in life and to maintain good standing in the community." The complaint against Dobbs was dropped.

Two years later, John Wesley Dobbs, forty-four years old and in his twenty-third year of government service, was one of two blacks on the Nashville & Atlanta promoted to clerk-in-charge.

In a remarkable reversal, Dobbs would direct a crew of three white men.

Renie came first, in many ways. Among the six Dobbs daughters, she not only was firstborn but also the most intellectually gifted, the most facile on the piano and the quickest to develop fluency in foreign languages. More cerebral than combative, she proved the most compliant to her father's taxing demands. She had her father's eyes, her mother's diplomacy. On the color spectrum between John Wesley Dobbs's dark brown and Irene T. Dobbs's bright olive, Renie was the lightest, nearest her mother. She had what many blacks called "good hair," which meant it had a wavy, flowing quality typically associated with whites.

As she walked each day to the Houston Street School with her sister Willie, her mother's instructions remained fresh in Renie's mind: "Don't fight with the white children! Remember, *Sticks and stones may break my bones* . . .'" The troubles usually started near the Boulevard School for whites, on the corner of Boulevard and Houston Street. "Your mama tells me my papa is your papa!" the whites chided. Occasionally, harsh words prompted fistfights between the white and colored boys. Renie and Willie didn't stop to watch. They kept walking. "Children listen through closed doors and don't always know what they hear," Renie recalls, "and what the poor child didn't know was pretty often the truth—that they did have the same fathers [as white children] and some of them had the same mothers and grandmothers." As a young girl, miscegenation confused her. Once she heard a white man, holding a document of some kind, asking questions about his relative—a black who had graduated from

Atlanta University. The white man wanted to know if "my uncle George" wanted to come to the North to live with "our family"?

*What is all this stuff,* Renie wondered.

She excelled in the classroom, though in less than optimal conditions. Warmth inside the Houston Street School was provided during winter by janitors who carried big-bellied stoves from room to room, often interrupting class to do it. If she scored 98 points out of 100 on an examination, her father would say, "Humph! Who got the other two?" At home, Renie practiced the piano in the parlor for hours at a time, playing the sweet sounds of Bach and Chopin. Several times her mother took her across town to the Herndon family's white-columned mansion to play Jessie Herndon's piano during tea parties. Alonzo Herndon's second wife (Adrienne McNeil Herndon died of a blood disorder in 1910), Jessie Herndon, thought Renie's flourish on the piano added elegance to her parties. At the First Congregational Church, Dobbs family members sat in the main aisle in front of the Herndons, a sign of their rapidly improving social status. John Wesley Dobbs admired Alonzo Herndon, whom he soon joined on the church board of deacons, for much the same reason he admired Abraham Lincoln and Booker T. Washington: Herndon's rise from poverty was hard-earned, his greatness self-made. Jessie Herndon's expensive wardrobe was legendary in elite black circles and each Sunday Renie couldn't wait for her to arrive, to see the former beautician's clothes. Norris Herndon, Jessie's Harvard-schooled stepson, often came to church, too, though Dobbs cautioned Renie about him. "Norris had a reputation of being a sissy," Renie says. "Daddy would say, 'Leave him alone and don't invite him over here.' "

Renie loved and admired her father, even stood in awe of him. A man of mountainous pride, John Wesley Dobbs tried to set an example for his daughters that would prove a deeper human truth: like stars on a dark night they could shine despite segregation. He inundated Renie and her sisters with his beliefs and stories—"moralistic jewels that were often illuminating," June, the youngest daughter, recalls, "and sometimes boring." Education, Dobbs insisted, would unlock the door of segregation. His books were voluminous and often strewn all over the house; once he bemoaned a black doctor who "lives in that big mansion on Boulevard and hasn't got a book in the house." At night, Renie watched him study a simulation of the mail scheme on railcars, his face a mask of total concentration. Dobbs's intensity was apparent, his mission clear: he had to memorize the appropriate slots to sort mail so that he would pass the mandatory government examinations.

Cleopatra was black, Renie heard him say, and so were three popes.

He talked about Crispus Attucks, the black martyr of the American Revolution, and Frederick Douglass. On train trips to the North, he served as moral interpreter for his daughters. "Look at them," he barked once in New York City. He pointed at a group of European immigrants. "Just come in from Greece and Russia and they call this place their own." His voice rose: "They sit anywhere and they go anywhere if they've got the money. We've been living in this country for almost two centuries—WE WERE BORN HERE!—and we can't sit there, or go places in Atlanta—just because we are Negro."

Renie knew that her father could seem coarse. Though Dobbs's oratory had polish, his table manners did not, especially when compared to those of his wife. Irene Dobbs once cornered him in their bedroom to apply deodorant to his armpits ("I just bathed," Dobbs howled. His wife replied, "But you need this for later.") Yet to quantify how far her father's determination had carried him from the rural poverty of his youth, Renie only had to look a few blocks away. Minnie McAfee Hendricks Dobbs Banks, "Nannie" to her granddaughters, lived in a house on Irwin Street. Nannie's name now seemed longer than her patience, her last surname coming from her marriage to a freed slave named Charles Banks. He was a dark-skinned, soft-spoken older man, a retired janitor and drayman with a giant frame that made Renie wonder if he had ever been a prizefighter. Mister Banks is what Nannie called him, even after they had been married more than twenty years, another example of her exaggerated attempt to seem a woman of formality and high style. She did not attend his church and when he smoked his pipe she demanded he do it outside. Nannie was the family tornado, spoiled and high-strung and apparently less than fully appreciative that her son, "Buddy," was paying the rent on her house. After one argument with John Wesley Dobbs, she slammed every door in his house, then left. Nannie had few reservations about spending her son's money. When salesmen knocked at her door she told them, "Go 'round the corner to my son's house. Buddy'll buy something from you." Several times, John Wesley Dobbs learned of purchases made by his mother from the Brown-Hayes department store; they allowed her to buy on credit because they knew Dobbs. He bellowed in anger, then paid her bill. Nannie did not overextend herself. Once she told a young relative trying to crack a pecan, "Give it here," and she put it beneath her rocking chair, rocked back and split it open. Many times Renie tried to teach the illiterate Nannie to read and write, but, smart as she was, the old woman did not have the necessary focus. Instead, Nannie dictated letters to friends, ordering her granddaughters, "Write 'em just like I say it." The girls cleaned up her diction, anyway. She asked them to read the

Sunday comics aloud. "Read me Taz-zuhn," she would say and when her granddaughters laughed at her pronunciation, she told them, "I'll be dead and gone someday and you'll be sorry."

In her own way, Nannie worshipped her son, and he was devoted to her. "Mama came back to the farm to get me," John Wesley Dobbs reminded his daughters too many times to count. Still, his devotion had limits. He did not let her live in his house for fear she would destroy his marriage. Nannie cursed loudly and often enough to make Irene Dobbs blush. Once a truck passed her house and the driver whistled at her granddaughters. "Don't you whistle at them!" Nannie shouted. *These are some of the finest girls in Atlanta!*

Nannie seized every opportunity to flash her status. In the early years of the Depression, Dobbs took out a loan at the Citizens Trust Bank, against the advice of bank president L. D. Milton, to buy a Peerless automobile. ("Mr. Milton, I have six daughters and they see bootleggers and gangsters riding up and down Auburn Avenue," Dobbs said. "I want to give them a different symbol.") He paid a black chauffeur to teach Renie to drive. One of Renie's first driving chores was to carry Nannie on her Sunday afternoon social calls. Nannie's life centered around the Liberty Baptist Church where she served on the Board of Mothers. Her finest church attire included a hat with plumage. "She wore black taffeta, cream lace, bolero-type, and all those feathers on her hat were white," Renie recalls. "She was *Miss Nan!*" Nearly sixty years after her death, one church member recalls, "Mother Banks was a stately woman. You could tell just by the way she walked." Her granddaughters dreaded attending church with Nannie: more emotion was expended in one Sunday at Liberty Baptist than in one decade at the First Congregational Church. Once, Nannie stood from her pew to testify, shouting, "God's been good to me!" In her later years she never missed a funeral. Driving her on social calls, Renie heard Nannie recount the pastor's sermon from that morning with uncanny precision to friends who had been unable to attend. When Nannie's friends were not at home, she left her card outside the door. "Minnie Millie Minerva," her card read. Renie figured she had learned this practice from a rich white woman. On another occasion, Nannie visited Renie on the Spelman College campus, wearing black taffeta with a hand-crocheted collar and her finest aristocratic airs. Renie thought: "She looks like she stepped out of Rich's finest women's store!" Even her speech seemed affected. To Renie, odd as it seemed, Nannie sounded like an elegant white woman.

Morehouse and Spelman colleges stood in the red-clay hills of west Atlanta as symbols of hope and inspiration to southern blacks. Though John

Wesley Dobbs had attended the college only a few months (after four years at the school's academy), he was touched by what later would be called the spirit of the Morehouse Man. Growing up, Renie never doubted that she someday would attend Spelman. The product of missionary zeal and Rockefeller money, these colleges attracted the most ambitious blacks from across the south. Over time they would have a more profound historic effect on the quality of leadership in black Atlanta than any other single institution. Morehouse was founded as a seminary for freedmen in Augusta in 1867 by Richard C. Coulter, an ex-slave who had fled his master in Virginia and returned to Augusta after the war. The school was sponsored by the American Baptist Home Missionary Society; it was moved to Atlanta, a more central location, in 1879. Two years later, New England missionaries named Harriet Giles and Sophie Packard founded a seminary for black women in Atlanta. The women's seminary held its first classes in the basement of the Friendship Baptist Church. The old barracks and nine-acre field, used for drills by the federal army after the Civil War, was donated to the women's seminary. When philanthropist John D. Rockefeller visited in 1884, he was so impressed by Giles and Packard that he paid off the seminary's debt and donated additional monies. In appreciation, the women's seminary was given the family name of Rockefeller's wife: Spelman.

At the Spelman laboratory high school, Renie was the 1925 class valedictorian; her speech topic: "Harlem: The Center of Race Consciousness." Her years at Spelman College were the happiest of her young life. Some Spelman professors were white New Englanders who brought unique histories of their own: art teacher Rose Standish was descended from Miles Standish; the Dickinson sisters were great-nieces of Emily Dickinson. Renie heard that Harriet Giles, who died in 1909, once had worried that Spelman girls had lost touch with their heritage and had become too carefree and sophisticated, which made fund-raising in the North more difficult. Central to Giles's pitch for funds was the slave past. "We had gotten to the point where we didn't mention *that* anymore and we didn't want to be reminded," Renie says. "We were dressing beautifully in fur coats and giving parties and going to Europe in the summer. . . . *How did we get there so fast?*" Since childhood Renie's teachers had been advising her, and other elite black students, that when graduation day arrived, "You have got to leave Georgia and go somewhere else!" Renie accepted their advice as the gospel. She became the Spelman College Valedictorian, Class of 1929, having studied French at the University of Grenoble in southern France during one summer and at the University of Chicago during another. Upon graduation, she took a summer seminar at Middlebury College in Vermont.

France in the late 1920s was the greatest revelation of all. Josephine Baker, an American starring in the Folies-Bergère in Paris, had stirred the French fascination with blacks to a degree where "a funny little fat guy" once came backstage to ask Baker if he could draw a sketch of her. Baker consented, but made him pay her 25 francs first. His name, unknown to her, was Picasso. In France, Renie, for the first time in her life, forgot about prejudice—"the white business," as she calls it—and suddenly saw herself and Atlanta through a new lens. "The French loved black people! They wanted some of the things that we had. Like the color, the waves [of hair], the joviality, the optimistic way we looked at things no matter what," she says. "And they'd say, 'That's the way we have to live.'" To Renie, France was heaven.

When she answered the telephone at the Dobbs home at 540 Houston Street in the spring of 1932, Renie, now twenty-four and planning to leave in June for the University of Toulouse in France on a $1,200 one-year scholarship from the General Education Board (the board made only one grant each year to a black student for foreign study), listened to a man's voice that was rich and full, simply the most gorgeous voice she had ever heard. "Miss Dobbs, I was told to get in touch with you. They tell me you play the piano . . ." The caller's name was Maynard Jackson. As the new endowment secretary of Morehouse, he had invited several guests to his home that night and needed someone to play the piano. Hearing Jackson's voice, she agreed to play. In the calendar of her heart there would be a star by that night always. "Honey," she says, still aglow over the memory six decades later, "I got carried away at that wonderful piano."

With penetrating blue eyes and white features, Maynard Jackson hailed from the Negro-Creole society in New Orleans, bringing an alluring sense of mystery to the party. He could have passed for Italian or Greek, Renie thought. Disarmingly eloquent, the son (and grandson) of Baptist ministers, he was a Morehouse Man and trained at the Garrett School of Divinity at Northwestern University. He had modeled once for Hart Schaffner & Marx in Chicago; as national secretary of the Foreign Mission Board, he had spent time in Africa surveying missionary agencies. He later directed the African Import Company in Liberia, a group that aspired to make the African self-sufficient. He wore his pedigree well, Renie thought. His father, the Rev. Alexander Stephens Jackson, had pastored the New Hope Baptist Church in Dallas for thirty-four years. A member of Atlanta University's charter class, the Rev. A. S. Jackson had wavy brown hair and a thick walrus mustache that gave him the look of Theodore Roosevelt in his prime. A stern disciplinarian as a father, A. S. Jackson was progressive as a minister. His 1920 book, *The*

*Rebirth of Negro Ideals,* called segregation "legalized humiliation" and suggested that blacks should press for civil rights even if it meant leaving the United States for Brazil or Africa. Maynard Jackson was thirty-eight, fourteen years older than Renie. Later she learned that he had recently divorced. If some considered divorce a stigma, not Renie; to her it was just one more thread in the fabric of the mystery that was Maynard Jackson. She noticed how the women in the room were entranced by him. She sang with him and ate sandwiches that night and when she returned home she knew she would see him again.

Their courtship blossomed quickly. He sought new ways to raise funds for Morehouse. He performed with the school's quartet, traveled with its choir and made speeches in local churches. He struck up a friendship with John Wesley Dobbs, who arranged for him to meet his friends on Auburn Avenue. Dobbs invited him for dinner. Renie made her prized gumbo (with a shot of whiskey), then crossed her fingers: it was a hit. Maynard Jackson arrived often at the Dobbs home in the ensuing months. He put Mattiwilda and June in the rumble seat of his car and took them to the Krispy Kreme donut shop on Ponce de Leon Avenue. "What do people look like in Africa?" seven-year-old Mattiwilda asked. "What do they wear? Do they dance?" Maynard Jackson laughed. Renie had fallen in love.

Her departure for Toulouse was imminent. "I wish you could stay here with me all of the time," Maynard Jackson told her, as they sat in his cottage. Renie played it coy. She told him he would have to first buy the cottage and then let her redecorate it. "There are other homes. Atlanta is full of lovely homes," he said.

He needed several weeks to get the nerve to propose marriage. He took her to a small inn in the north Georgia mountains where they often went to fish, boat, hike and ride horses. The inn at Clayton was the only place for miles where blacks were permitted to lodge. Owned by the Bleckleys, a light-skinned black family, the inn had fourteen rooms, a screened-in sleeping porch and a wood-burning stove in the kitchen. It became a favorite summer retreat for professors and students at Atlanta's black colleges. There, Maynard Jackson said, "I want you to marry me— to let me marry you—and we'll live in a little home like the one I'm looking for." The nervous suitor's eyes lowered. "But I don't want to ask you because I think you'll be ashamed. Everybody knows about my divorce. I've talked about it a lot."

"Only men care about that," Renie blurted quickly, surprising even herself. "Maynard, you are one of the finest men I have ever met. Just because you've been disappointed once doesn't mean you have to mess your life up. Do you think you'll never get married again?"

"I thought that way," he said, "until I met you."

Renie was happier than she had ever been—but she still faced the responsibility of breaking the news to her father.

"Daddy," she began, "I'm not going to France."

John Wesley Dobbs's reply came without hesitation: "Yes, you are."

"But I'm going to get married. I don't need the degree, Daddy."

Dobbs's response would echo down through the years. He spoke warmly of Maynard Jackson, but also of the prestigious nature of Renie's scholarship and the rare opportunity it afforded. He spoke, too, of the uncertainty of the future and the need to be prepared for all things. "Someday," he said, shrugging, "your husband could die." Their love, if true, would withstand the test of time.

Though disappointed, Renie did not challenge him. Her fear of losing Jackson to another woman was allayed when he told her, "Go, and I'll meet you over there at the end of the year."

With Dobbs's help, Jackson rented a room next door at 546 Houston Street. Over the next year, Jackson took his meals with his future in-laws and read them Renie's letters, except the most personal sections. Over dinner he and Dobbs discussed politics and the black condition in Atlanta. They had philosophical jousts about whether the white man ever would see the moral wrong of segregation. "The white man is not gonna do what's right because it's right," Dobbs said. "He has the power. People don't give up power out of decency. They give up power because they don't have a choice."

"That may be," Jackson said, "but we have to insist on the moral side because it has more lasting value."

Jackson sailed to Europe the next summer and on June 20, 1933, he and Renie were married in Toulouse. They honeymooned in Spain. As their ship crossed the Atlantic on the return to New York late in July, Renie suffered what she thought was seasickness; it turned out to be morning sickness. She was pregnant with their first child, a daughter they would name Alexandra Irene, for his father and her mother, though she would be called Sandra. Upon the newlyweds' return to Atlanta, Dobbs had the marriage blessed by his neighbor, AME Bishop Joseph Flipper. Then he hosted a catered reception at 540. Dobbs, wearing his Masonic tuxedo, lifted his champagne glass for a toast.

Soon after, in answer to an urgent call, Maynard and Renie rushed to Dallas. From his hospital bed, the Rev. A. S. Jackson reached for his son. "Give me your hand, Maynard," he said to the former divinity student. "You are going to lose a father but New Hope will gain you as a pastor. I'll be happy and I'll go anywhere after I die—even if it's hell—if I know that you have taken over for me." The prospect frightened Renie, not for her husband (she had heard him as a stand-in preacher at New Hope several times and thought him wondrous), but for herself. She knew French and music, but she did not feel qualified to play the role of minister's wife. "You have to be another Mary," she says. "And I was not that good." But the pressure on her husband was overwhelming. His father was dying. How could he deny him?

In short order, Maynard and Renie packed their things and moved to Dallas.

On Irene and John Wesley Dobbs's silver anniversary, June 6, 1931, their family and friends crowded next to the piano inside the parlor at 540 to listen to the six Dobbs girls perform. In truth, only five performed that night—Renie and Josie on the piano; Willie in a brief recital of poetry; Millie, with her sultry voice, in a burst of song; and six-year-old Geekie, the future opera star, in a playful sing-along. Geekie and June were to perform together in a rendition of "When Your Hair Has Turned to Silver I Will Love You Just the Same," but the three-year-old June, left unsupervised, ate gobs of ice cream and cake and suffered from severe bellyache. So Geekie sang alone, with Josie playing accompaniment. June reappeared in time to vomit on her mother's dress.

In the darkness of the Depression, Franklin Roosevelt and Eugene Talmadge had been elected to lead the nation and Georgia into the light. The Prince Hall Masons gathered for their annual Grand Lodge in Americus in June 1932 to elect a new grand master to replace Dr. Henry Butler, the Atlanta physician who had died after thirty years as head of the Georgia jurisdiction. John Wesley Dobbs had labored for years, steeping himself in Masonic history and tradition, readying himself for the days of leadership that he hoped were ahead. At fifty years old, he wrote in a letter, "I feel that I am just at the right age to do some good work."

The black Masonic fraternity in which Dobbs would invest his future bore the name of Prince Hall, a mulatto born in the West Indies who later fought under George Washington in the American Revolution. Along with fourteen black colleagues, Hall was made a Mason by a white lodge in Massachusetts. When those whites later moved, however, the black members did not have a lodge affiliation. Hall petitioned the Grand Lodge in England and was issued a charter for African Lodge No. 459 in Boston. The Prince Hall fraternity flourished in the South after the Civil War when whites no longer could prevent blacks from meeting secretively. Nevertheless, white Masons have not recognized the Prince Hall Masons as part of their fraternity.

To become a Prince Hall Mason in Georgia in 1932 a black needed to have a good standing in the community, several recommendations from Masonic members, a firm belief in God and Christian values, and the $7.50 required for initiation fees. Already the Depression had caused membership in Georgia to drop from 24,000 to about 2,500. "Of this much I am certain," Dobbs said in Americus, as he presented his last financial report after eight years as secretary-treasurer of the Masonic Relief Association, "the year of 1932 finds us standing at the crossroads of our history."

Elected grand master that day, Dobbs considered it the crowning achievement of his life. In the intense heat and humidity, the Masons ended their two-day session by forming a large circle outdoors and singing in public, "What a Friend We Have in Jesus." Years later June Dobbs would recall an African rhythm in the men's voices that day and the way in which their harmonies "floated upward into the moist air like a soft cloud." Unaccustomed to such an emotional release when the song was performed at First Congregational, June sensed a touching, powerful mournfulness in these Masons.

To the Prince Hall Masons of Georgia, a politically moribund organization whose primary lure for many blacks had been the assurance of a proper burial, Dobbs delivered an astonishing jolt of confidence, political intuition and race pride. His plan to transform the Masons into a political force was not novel. (A grand master in Alabama had insisted in 1909 that, through the Prince Hall fraternity, black "farms could be owned, teachers trained to instruct us, soldiers trained to defend us.") But Dobbs's dynamic, single-minded leadership proved powerful. Furthermore, Masonic rules suited Dobbs's style: the grand master had dictatorial powers; his word was law. So the Georgia jurisdiction would be run exactly as 540 Houston Street had been run: as John Wesley Dobbs saw fit.

The Depression called for inspired leaders. Skillful oratory, in normal times an art form, suddenly became a necessity. With his chest heaving and his arms chopping the air for emphasis, Dobbs used colorful Masonic language and a cadence familiar to the black church to light a fire beneath his Masons. He believed he was put on earth to lead blacks, and if he had devoted his first twenty-five years to raising himself, the second twenty-five years to raising his family, now he would spend his final quarter century raising his race.

In the Masonic tradition, florid titles were heaped upon the grand master, known informally to members (and soon along Auburn Avenue) as "the Grand." Such reverence fed Dobbs's ego as few things had. In his first official proclamation, released from his office in the Herndon Building on Auburn Avenue, the Grand set a goal of increasing membership to thirty thousand. He cautioned the Masonic brethren, though, about choosing the proper men. "Go about it in a true Masonic way, ever keeping in mind the fact that this is a great Moral Institution, which has but one object in view, and that is to build character in men," Dobbs wrote. "Its purpose is to cement its members into one great brotherhood, whose deeds are all planned to charity." He also intended to build a Masonic temple on Auburn Avenue, and it would be a structure in the very image that the Grand held out for himself: stately.

In spare moments, the Grand and his brethren laughed, shared whiskey and played cards. Their initiation process sometimes included ritualistic hazing. "Lean forward and kiss the black casbah," blindfolded initiates were told once. As they leaned forward, their blindfolds were removed whereupon they discovered, with horror, that they were about to kiss the bare asses of Masons who had lowered their trousers. The gathered Masons howled with laughter. The Grand also was known to return from his train runs with some of Kentucky's finest blended whiskey. "Georgia was bone dry," J. Earl Acey, Dobbs's Masonic colleague, recalls, "But Dobbs always had a bottle or two."

The sinister realities of segregation in Atlanta during the early 1930s restricted virtually every aspect of black daily life. By law, blacks in Atlanta could not serve on juries. Their tax forms were a different color than those used by whites. City statutes prohibited interracial marriages. Mulatto children born out of wedlock were not permitted to inherit the estate of their white father. At the First National Bank, blacks used separate teller windows. Of the four elevators in the Rhodes-Haverty Building, three were marked "White" and the fourth "Colored." For some reason, blacks could not share an elevator with whites going up in the building but they could on the way down. (The peculiar logic behind this practice: whites thought blacks, upon dying, would go to a different heaven but to the same hell.) At the Davison-Paxon department store on Peachtree Street, the drinking fountain on the first floor was designated for whites, the fountain in the basement for blacks. At the Fox Theatre, blacks were made to enter through a stairwell on the side of the building, not the front. Though Booker T. Washington Park was created for blacks, all other city parks were off-limits. Some white philanthropists had donated parks to the city with the stipulation that they remain segregated. On the streetcars and buses of Atlanta, blacks sat in the back; only when buses became overcrowded did drivers permit them to sit in the emergency fold-up seat in the front. It's no wonder that the Fan-Tan Laboratories of Chicago advertised in *The Atlanta*

*Daily World* a facial bleach creme that would lighten a black's complexion. "A clear, whiter skin is the stepping stone to popularity, love, romance, and business success," the advertisement promised. "It unlocks golden doors of happiness and gladly beckons to you." In a 1934 editorial, the *Daily World* bemoaned the black as "a strange animal who will lick the hand that smites him."

Dobbs's first task with the Masons was to restore financial stability. Several Georgia fraternities had gone into receivership in 1932, including the Odd Fellows and the Knights of Pythias. Dobbs called for a special Grand Communication of Prince Hall Masons in Macon on January 28, 1933, to discuss the crisis. Wearing his black tuxedo, top hat, Masonic apron and symbolic cuffs before his brethren for the first time, the Grand appeared at the Pythian Temple in Macon before about five hundred members, the single largest gathering for a special communication in thirteen years. He spoke for several hours, quoting Tennyson, Napoleon, Georgia senator Ben Hill and author Robert Louis Stevenson. He cited the powerful effects of the nation's economic doldrums. "Just last week 14 banks went down in St. Louis, Mo.," Dobbs said, before listing other closings. "Is it any wonder then, that we too are face to face with grave problems?" The central problem, he said, was the Masonic Relief Association, which had been established in 1908 and now paid $300 in benefits to a Mason's family at the time of his death. Each Mason paid $6 annually to this fund, a rate that would require fifty years of membership to reach $300. When times were prosperous and new members plentiful, the system had worked. But now, when members were dropping out at an alarming rate, the fund could not keep pace with death benefits. Dobbs called for a controversial change to the so-called Texas Plan: two death-benefit payments would be paid out to families, the first for $100, enough for burial, and the second, for a larger amount, to be sent later, allowing Masons to earn interest in the interim. To explain the legality of this change, Dobbs brought two white lawyers from Atlanta: Shepard Bryan, a former superior court judge, and his son-in-law/partner, W. Colquitt Carter; both would help Dobbs and his Masons many times in the years ahead. With flourish, the Grand likened the fiscal woes to the violent hemorrhages suffered by the consumptive Robert Louis Stevenson. Once, as blood rushed from Stevenson's nose and mouth, his wife had panicked, the Grand said dramatically. Stevenson had motioned for pencil and paper, and wrote, "Don't be alarmed, I am not going to die!" With a soothing voice, the Grand said, "My brethren, the Masonic Relief Association, our boy is sick, and an operation is immediately necessary, but I am saying to you today, Don't be alarmed he is not going to die." Dobbs scored his first major victory when his proposed change passed unanimously in Macon.

The Grand almost did not live to see the fruits of his victory. Suddenly in great demand as a public speaker, he remained in Macon for several days and delivered a speech at a local church Sunday evening. He then began the ninety-mile trip home to Atlanta, accompanied by three Masonic officers. He pulled to the roadside in Griffin to rest for twenty minutes, then returned his high-powered Peerless to the road. Driving at sixty miles per hour, the Grand fell asleep at the wheel and the car slammed into a telephone pole, then came to rest against an embankment on the far side of the road. In the darkness, the windshields shattered, the car totaled, and the four Masons extricated themselves from the wreck. Bleeding profusely from the nose, Dobbs helped his companion, Dr. J. W. Madison, who bled from a deep wound to his head. They were fortunate to be alive. A passing white motorist stopped to lend aid, then drove the Grand and his three officers the remaining twenty-five miles to Atlanta's Grady Hospital. The Grand had suffered a severed artery at the bridge of his nose; Madison required nine stitches. All four were treated and released. "I have always believed that there was a good spirit that in some way looks after me," Dobbs wrote later. "I have had several experiences in my life to make me believe it. The result of this accident was but another. I believe it was a great warning, and I will take it in that spirit."

The Grand knew that some of his brethren had whispered criticism of the new payment plan of death benefits. As he approached the Grand Communication in Americus on June 13–14, 1933, he worried about his chances for reelection.

"Geekie, June, get down on your knees," Irene Dobbs told her two youngest daughters, "and pray to God that Daddy will be re-elected." (As they prayed, June also made a secret prayer that her father would not die, so that she would not be sent to live at the Masonic orphanage home in Americus.) Their prayers were answered when Dobbs was reelected to a position he would retain for twenty-nine years. Cheerfully, he reported that six thousand Masons had responded loyally by mailing in old relief fund certificates; he announced his expectation that other members would do likewise before year's end. Then, with a dictatorial air, he blasted those who questioned his authority to call for change in relief fund laws, terming the criticism "very unbecoming to the dignity and conduct of a good Mason." His first twelve months, he told the brethren with typical bravado, "would have proven too much for anyone with less experience."

Then, his voice rising to a crescendo, the Grand suggested that his Masonic ship had not yet escaped the economic storm: "We are just over Davy Jones' Locker and many brave hearts are asleep in the deep, so beware! . . . Only one thing is of vital importance at the present time, and that is that we outride the storm. The success of that will depend almost entirely upon the old Sea-Dog who goes to the Pilot House." He made the same point by quoting Kipling's "The Law of the Jungle": "For the strength of the Pack is the Wolf, And the strength of the Wolf is the Pack."

His word, the Grand was saying, never should be doubted.

Ten years had passed since the protest against Dobbs for holding two jobs. In June 1934, the protest was sounded anew by Cong. Malcolm C. Tarver of Dalton, a tough-minded member of the House Judiciary Committee. Tarver took his displeasure with the Grand directly to Harllee Branch, once city editor for *The Atlanta Journal* and now second assistant postmaster general in Washington. Tarver asserted that had he been informed that Dobbs had racked up too many demerits on his examinations; twice in 1933, Dobbs had received forty demerits for failing to pass an examination on time. Tarver blamed Dobbs's poor performance on his Masonic obligations. "He ought to be retired from the service," Tarver wrote.

James B. Hemperley, the chief clerk in Atlanta, did not like Dobbs. In his report, he recommended that the Grand be forced to give up one of his jobs. "Clerk Dobbs is not popular with the other clerks on the line," Hemperley wrote. "I think this is due largely to the fact that he talks too much and quite often breaks in on conversations among other clerks, which is resented."

Dobbs reacted quickly. First, he asked Shepard Bryan, the former judge, to write a letter on his behalf to Branch. "This man, I know, is a good upright man," Bryan wrote of Dobbs. "He has reared a large family and is a useful colored citizen. He is an influence for good amongst his people. . . . I am glad to say that I know this man Dobbs well and that I believe that the Government has no more faithful servant than he." In his own four-page response, sent to Hemperley, Dobbs again insisted that his Masonic duties had not infringed on his government service and stressed his thirty years of devotion, the last eight as clerk-in-charge. He cited his role as sole provider for a family of six daughters, in addition to his elderly mother and stepfather. "While these children were being raised and educated no one was able to work in my family except myself," Dobbs wrote. "I paid all the bills and expenses and counted it as my best investment." Dobbs stated that he was willing to retire—in fact, he included with his four-page letter an application to retire under the thirty-year plan—but not until he had worked an additional ten months. He had accumulated a $500 debt, which he attributed to "honest obligations," caused by the 15 percent pay cut suffered by all government employees. In July 1934, officials in Washington decided to allow Dobbs to retire as he wished, during the following spring, as long as his performance remained satisfactory.

Though he had been grand master for only two years, Dobbs already revealed a shrewdness and sophistication worthy of a veteran politician. With cunning and inventiveness, he had learned how to slip through the cracks of segregation. Twice during the next year he used personal contacts to reach the President of the United States.

On Randolph Street, around the corner from 540, lived his Masonic friend Irvin McDuffie and his wife, Lizzie. By trade, McDuffie was a barber at Herndon's shop and his wife a seamstress. But in the fall of 1934 both were in the employ of the White House. Lizzie McDuffie worked for the first lady, Eleanor Roosevelt, and Irvin McDuffie served as Franklin Roosevelt's valet. He gave scalp massages, using a special English tonic ordered through the Hotel Belmont in New York, and haircuts to the president, who often dictated letters from McDuffie's chair. (Roosevelt secretary Grace Tully, no admirer of McDuffie's, would later suggest that FDR could have received the same haircut by placing a bowl over his head and trimming around the sides.) By virtue of his position with Roosevelt, "Mac" was a hero among black Atlantans and his appearances in the city typically received front-page notice in the *Daily World*, such as in November 1934 when he attended the Clark-Morehouse football game with Dobbs.

During the fall of 1934, Dobbs became enraged when two black postal clerks on the Atlanta & Birmingham, RPO and the Atlanta & Jacksonville, RPO were passed over for clerk-in-charge positions in favor of lower-ranking whites. He wrote a letter to McDuffie, alleging discrimination in the two cases as well as in the hiring of the clerical and carrier force of the Atlanta post office. He asked that his complaint be taken directly to the President of the United States.

Later, Lizzie McDuffie personally handed his letter to Franklin Roosevelt.

On February 19, 1935, a White House memorandum was dashed off to presidential secretary Marvin McIntyre: "Will you speak to Harllee Branch about this the next time he comes in? F.D.R."

Dobbs's letter did not produce the hoped-for response. "I am sure that if Mr. Dobbs was familiar with the action taken in any of the cases mentioned by him," Branch wrote in his reply to Roosevelt, "he would agree that there was no discrimination." Nevertheless, Dobbs suddenly realized that he had a special access to Roosevelt and he was unafraid to use it.

Later that month, the government suddenly rejected Dobbs's application to retire, with annuity, citing the fact that he was fifty-three years old, nine years below the statutory age for retirement. The government's stated fear was that if such long-term annuity payments became common practice its retirement fund would be depleted. The Grand wrote immediately to Roosevelt's black valet. "If there is anything you can do to help me in this matter, I will greatly appreciate same. . . . I trust this will be the last request that I will have to make for myself in the Railway Mail Service."

Using official White House stationery, Irvin McDuffie related Dobbs's predicament in a May 10 letter to Postmaster General James Farley. "Will there be any way for this request to be granted?" McDuffie asked. He signed with a flourish: "I. H. McDuffie, Valet to President."

Five days later, Farley replied: "I will look into this matter and do whatever I can for Dobbs."

On May 31, 1935, just two weeks later, Dobbs worked his final day as a railway mail clerk. His annuity of $1,158 commenced the following day.

A Mason himself, Roosevelt is said to have mentioned to McDuffie, "I'd like to meet this grand master of yours." McDuffie was notorious for his inexplicable absences and for once having served a day in the navy brig on a presidential trip to Buenos Aires; his habits ultimately caused Eleanor Roosevelt to fire him. Before his removal, though, he arranged for Dobbs to meet Franklin Roosevelt at Warm Springs, Georgia. Roosevelt usually spent a few weeks during the Thanksgiving season luxuriating in the warm, therapeutic waters of the underground springs. Although no official records of Roosevelt's appointments were maintained at the Little White House, it is known that he kept an informal atmosphere and met with people from all walks of life. (In December 1934, after a radio speech in which he had declared "there are no more Napoleons," Roosevelt even met with Napoleon Hall, a nine-year-old black from Atlanta, to reassure him that he hadn't meant him.) Dobbs later told his family that Roosevelt became so engaged in their conversation about Masonry that the scheduled five-minute session in Warm Springs lasted forty-five minutes, delaying all other appointments.

Greatly impressed by Roosevelt, the Grand suddenly changed political affiliation. He went on the stump in 1936 to tell black voters in Mary-

land, Rhode Island, Delaware and New Jersey why they should vote for
the incumbent Democrat, Franklin Roosevelt.

Dobbs believed there was magic in Auburn Avenue, especially in that
two-block stretch between Piedmont Avenue and Butler Street. When
blacks spoke of Auburn, that's what they meant: the barbershops,
shoeshine stands, churches, clubs and small businesses between the
Rucker Building and the Yates & Milton drugstore. Once it had been
called Wheat Street, but in 1893 white residents successfully petitioned
the City Council to change it to Auburn Avenue, convinced it had a more
stylish sound. By the 1930s some called Auburn the "Black Peachtree,"
though, physically, that was a bit of a stretch since Peachtree wound
north of the city and continued for many miles. In its entirety, Auburn
Avenue ran little more than a mile and a half. Yet even as developer
Hemon Perry triggered a housing boom for blacks on the west side,
Auburn remained the spiritual center of black Atlanta. The three-legged
stool of black finance—the Citizens Trust Bank (of which Dobbs was
among the original directors), Mutual Federal Savings & Loan and
Alonzo Herndon's Atlanta Life Insurance Company—was located on
Auburn. To walk the Avenue on any summer evening was to experience
the vitality of black life in the city: the sounds of ragtime from the Top
Hat, the smell of fried chicken from Ma Sutton's and the constant hum of
animated street chatter. It became the place for black dreamers. You
knew you had arrived on the Avenue once you had your own pulpit or
your own cornerstone. Henry Rucker, Alonzo Herndon and Benjamin J.
Davis already had erected buildings on Auburn and soon Dobbs would
have his, as well. Mattiwilda and June had placed four-leaf clovers in the
cornerstone of Dobbs's Prince Hall Masonic Temple on the corner of
Auburn and Hilliard Street. But construction was halted for several
years during the Depression due to a lack of funds. Then, Dobbs had an
idea: he consolidated nineteen lodges in Atlanta into ten and rerouted
the savings to pay for construction. Finally, in 1937, the structure was
completed, the grand master's insignia was cut into the decorative molding across the upper rim, and John Wesley Dobbs had his temple.

    If Auburn Avenue had its own magic, in 1935 the black newspaper-
man I. P. Reynolds gave the street its own political machinery. Reynolds,
whose column in the *Daily World* was known as "What Sam of Auburn
Avenue Says," staged a mock election to raise funds for Big Bethel AME
Church; George Crumley of the Hanley funeral home emerged as unofficial mayor of Auburn Avenue, Reynolds as fire chief and J. W. Dobbs as
city attorney. Dobbs later would become its "mayor."

"Sweet Auburn Avenue" is what the Grand began to call it, in honor of the timeless Oliver Goldsmith poem from 1770, "The Deserted Village." *"Sweet Auburn! loveliest village of the plain, Where health and plenty cheer'd the laboring swain. . . ."* Money made the Avenue sweet, Dobbs said, and through voter registration he would make it even sweeter.

The Avenue provided a splendid spotlight for the race man to perform his oratorical tricks. Dobbs often stood in front of the Yates & Milton drugstore, handed to a bystander his Dobbs-brand hat with the punched-in crimp and then sprayed facts and figures and quotations from Bacon and Shakespeare, the Bible and Du Bois. His impassioned curbside speeches focused on the race issue and the importance of the ballot to blacks. "Our Buckle of Defense!" Dobbs termed the ballot. To many along Auburn, the Grand seemed larger than life, if not louder than life. The young minister William Holmes Borders (Morehouse Class of 1929) had listened to Dobbs as a collegian. "He'd come in from his [train] trip, clean his body up and then he'd go down to Auburn. He'd line them up and preach to 'em about race relations or anything that came up. Did it right on the sidewalk. You had to listen. He talked so loud. And then he had some information. He wasn't just blub-blub-blub-blub. He was cuttin' the cake. He'd stop traffic!" Accorded great respect, the Grand strode up and down Auburn as if he owned it. Usually his Masonic entourage walked with him, several paces behind. *"There's the Grand!"*

Like many blacks across the nation, Dobbs thrilled to the exploits of heavyweight champion Joe Louis during the 1930s. In his fists Louis packed the fury of his race. Dobbs frequently traveled to Louis's training camps and fights, returning to Sweet Auburn each time to tell his listeners "what Joe said," and to show how Louis had leveled another white opponent. "And Joe took that," Dobbs would say in the Silver Moon barbershop or Simmons Shoe Repair, as he crouched in a fistic pose, mimicking the Brown Bomber, "and then he came up with a left. *Pnnkth!*" Dobbs attended the September 1935 fight between Louis and Max Baer in Yankee Stadium. In his report in the *Daily World*, his enthusiasm for the moment was apparent:

> 90,000 mixed Americans from various nooks and corners of "The Melting Pot of the World" waited to see the 21-year-old boy wonder annihilate the highly-touted Hebrew boy, Max Baer. . . . Something was strangely tense in that autumnal atmosphere as Blackburn peeled off Joe's robe and crawled out of the ropes. Clang! . . . the bell! . . . and there were those two fine specimens of humanity representing two of the oldest races on earth, sparring for an opening with keen eyes and alert minds ready to take

advantage of every mistake. What a thrill as Louis' poetic left shot out repeatedly and Jack Dempsey's advice to Maxie (to rush Joe off his feet) backfired with the Bomber's rights and lefts working like pistons in a Lincoln Zephyr. In the fourth round a quick left hook and a terrible right cross sent Maxie to the canvas for the count—on the road to oblivion. They just don't survive a Joe Louis beating! That night in Harlem, sepia folk lifted the roof of the town and set it back again, signifying the dawn of a New Day.

Once, Dobbs entered Ma Sutton's restaurant on Auburn, an establishment noted for its fried chicken and barbecue ribs, and spotted musician Duke Ellington, already a star, his music an inventive blend of big band swing and mood-affected blues. Songs like "Soda Fountain Rag" and "What You Gonna Do When the Bed Breaks Down" were among his early hits. Meeting black celebrities on Auburn was a common experience for Dobbs. Since there were few hotels in Atlanta that accommodated blacks, black luminaries who visited the city often contacted the Grand in search of references for available accommodations; when New York congressman Adam Clayton Powell came to Atlanta, he and his entourage usually took meals at 540 with the Dobbses and spent nights at the Simmonses' next door. At Ellington's table, Dobbs pulled up a chair and boldly asked Ellington to visit 540 and play a few songs for his daughters.

Millie, Josie and Geekie were in the bedroom when they heard the familiar sounds. Millie said, "There's Duke Ellington on the radio."

"Let's turn it up," Josie suggested.

The three daughters bounded toward the living room. What they saw astounded them: the Grand standing next to the Duke. Thrilled by his daughters' incredulity, the Grand smiled broadly and playfully slapped Ellington on the back, one showman to another.

Dressed in a black coat and trousers with hickory stripes on February 12, 1936—Lincoln's birthday—Dobbs attempted to awaken the political consciousness of Atlanta's ninety thousand blacks. He spoke for two hours at Big Bethel on Auburn, beginning with a rousing assessment of Lincoln's political career. His purpose that night was to announce the formation of the Atlanta Civic and Political League, an organization devoted strictly to the ballot. Fewer than six hundred Atlanta blacks were registered to vote, Dobbs cried out. His dream was to register ten thousand.

"We have a city among ourselves right here in Atlanta," the Grand said, "and we are not doing anything to better our conditions." He cited Memphis where one-fourth of the city's 100,000 blacks were registered voters. "If 10,000 of you will register the white office holders of this state and city will come to you and ask, 'What is the meaning of this mass organization?' and consequently they will give us what we want. . . . We've got only one park and the city spends less than $5,000 per year for its upkeep. We want the right for our Negro doctors to intern at Grady Hospital. Our colored schools need suitable auditoriums and the colored teachers should receive the same pay as the white teachers. Atlanta should have colored policemen and firemen, as well as such southern cities as Knoxville, Louisville and Houston. . . . Here in Atlanta, Ga., we are asleep at the switch. If you will give me 10,000 registered Negroes on this ticket, I'll show you how to walk into Jerusalem just like John."

Dobbs promptly was elected chairman of the organization he proposed. The *Daily World* called him "fiery" and his speech "militant," though his militancy was a matter of tone and not strategy.

Leaders of the Atlanta NAACP branch believed the league was designed by Dobbs and C. A. Scott, twenty-eight-year-old *Daily World* editor, to undercut A. T. Walden, NAACP branch president since 1924. A reserved, though iron-willed black from the south Georgia peach belt, Walden used his University of Michigan law degree to help blacks facing prejudice in Georgia's courts. He was a precise, single-minded man, gifted in law, though not in organizing the masses. In the spring of 1934, Josephine Dibble Murphy, director of the women's auxiliary of the Atlanta branch, wrote NAACP secretary Walter White in New York to discourage awarding a prestigious NAACP medal sought by Walden for the creation of Citizenship Schools for blacks in Atlanta. The schools were created by Lugenia Burns Hope, wife of Morehouse president John Hope, not Walden, she wrote. Walter White's sister, Helen White Martin, had written to her brother in a similar vein earlier that spring: "So many people are disgusted with Walden as head and feel that he doesn't do anything with the branch." That July, Scott's *Daily World* concurred: "A rejuvenation is needed immediately. Either the organization should decide to behave as the N.A.A.C.P. should or else it ought to close up shop in Atlanta and quit reflecting discredit on the national association." In the decades ahead, Walden would become a personal rival of Dobbs's, a rivalry made unavoidable by their personalities and styles.

Walden was pushed aside in 1936 and replaced as NAACP branch president by Forrester B. Washington of the Atlanta School of Social Work. Washington noted the schisms in black Atlanta in a letter to Walter White, saying C. A. Scott "was responsible for establishing the

Atlanta Civic and Political League with J. Wesley Dobbs at the head with the deliberate purpose of killing the NAACP because Walden was the head of it. [Scott] was 'sore' at Walden because of 'what he considered' Walden's unfairness to him in the administration of the will of the late W. A. Scott [his brother, murdered by an unknown assailant in 1934]." Washington soothed relations between the organizations by placing Dobbs and Scott on the Atlanta NAACP's executive committee.

The next generation of black leaders had emerged on Auburn Avenue by 1936 with Dobbs, Scott and Walden among them. They would dominate black Atlanta for the next quarter century. At Wheat Street Church, the late Rev. Peter J. Bryant had been replaced by the demonstrative young preacher from Macon, the Rev. William Holmes Borders. At Ebenezer Baptist Church the death in 1931 of the powerhouse minister the Rev. A. D. Williams had passed the pulpit to his son-in-law, a short, squat man from the Georgia country, the Rev. Martin Luther King, Sr. As president of the local branch of the NAACP in 1919, Reverend Williams had spearheaded the first voter registration drive among blacks in modern Atlanta, producing more than two thousand black voters (some of whom laid out as much as $25 for back poll taxes). These black votes helped defeat a bond referendum that would have provided for construction of white schools only and, according to NAACP Atlanta branch secretary T. K. Gibson, served "notice upon the white people of this city that we had to be reckoned with in municipal affairs from this time forth." In 1921 a second bond issue passed, with strong black support, after another registration drive, including women as voters for the first time, increased the number of registered blacks to 5,905. As a result, black Atlanta gained five new schools, including the first public high school for blacks, Booker T. Washington High. But the voting registration passion among blacks subsided, not to be rekindled for fifteen years. Those years were squandered largely because of vying egos in the black community.

In the spring of 1937, Minnie McAfee Hendricks Dobbs Banks died. With her went the family's last blood connection to the days of slavery. Never had the Grand tried to explain, or deny, his mother's spoiled nature or tyrannical tendencies. He loved her as he loved his segregated country—unconditionally, despite her imperfections. Born in obscurity seventy-five years before on the McAfee plantation in Woodstock, Minnie Banks in death merited front-page mention in the *Daily World* because of her son's rising stature. The Liberty Baptist Church was filled for her funeral. The emotional response from the congregation, "startled the hell out of me," June Dobbs, then eleven, recalls. "They were whooping and hollering." Sitting with his family, the Grand wept uncontrollably, his shoulders heaving, his sobs long and profound. "If I can't see my mother in heaven I wouldn't be religious," he often told his daughters. His mother's death seemed to transport him to the days of his childhood in Kennesaw when he wailed, "Don't leave, mama!" His daughters had never seen him cry. Minnie Dobbs Banks was buried in a west side cemetery named for Abraham Lincoln.

The following spring, 1938, a headline appeared in *The Dallas Express*, a black weekly in Texas edited by the Rev. Maynard Jackson: "Unto Him a Son Is Born."

> Editor M. H. Jackson and Irene Dobbs Jackson became the proud parents of a healthy ten-pound son Wednesday morning at 3:00 o'clock at the Pinkston Clinic. The mother is reported to be resting well and the father is receiving the plaudits of his many friends.

Proud to have a male heir, Maynard Jackson presented his wife with a new Hudson seal fur coat, its fur so smooth his children would snuggle with it, as a security blanket, for years. (It was ruined during the middle 1950s when daughter Jeanne O. Jackson wore it to a Spelman College "Fright Night" on Halloween and it accidentally was doused with spaghetti sauce.) When the Rev. A. S. Jackson's second son had been born, he had named him Hubert, figuring he would have another son in the future to name for himself. But when that failed to occur, the minister took twelve-year-old Hubert to the Dallas courthouse to have his name changed, to Alexander Stephens Jackson II. Maynard Jackson did not make the same mistake as his father. He named his first son Maynard Holbrook Jackson, Jr.

Back at 540, the Grand couldn't believe the news. A boy? The first male born into the Dobbs family in about a half century! It is said that when the telegram announcing the birth reached 540, John Wesley Dobbs's exuberant yelp was so loud and pure the white folks heard him all the way over on Peachtree Street.

# CHAPTER 8

Irene Dobbs waited for Clark Gable. At the corner of Peachtree and Ellis streets, bundled against the December chill, with Geekie and June by her side, she waited for hours that seemed an eternity. If her overcoat weren't enough, she was warmed by proximity to the more than 300,000 people lining Peachtree. Only half as many people were in the combined armies that had fought in Atlanta seventy-five years earlier.

But that was only a war. This was the movie premiere of *Gone With the Wind.*

A former writer for *The Atlanta Journal Sunday Magazine,* Peggy Mitchell, as she was known to friends, had written a sprawling novel of more than one thousand pages that was a lullaby to the Old South and its agrarian traditions. Her tragic hero was Atlanta, which she painted as the indomitable hub of the southern sphere. "My novel is the story of a girl named Scarlett O'Hara who lived in Atlanta during the Civil War and the days of Reconstruction," Mitchell had said on WSB radio, in her first interview after the book was published in 1936. Her novel sold at an unprecedented pace, more than two million copies during the first three years. Her heroine, Scarlett O'Hara, demure and cunning, was Mitchell's personification of Atlanta: "pointed of chin, square of jaw . . . the seventeen-inch waist, the smallest in three counties . . . she could never long endure any conversation of which she was not the chief subject."

The daughter of an aristocratic Old Atlanta family, Mitchell had written a book that roared about Atlanta the Romantic, Atlanta the Resolute and Atlanta the Pillaged Symbol of an Old and Glorious Southern Empire.

On December 14, 1939, the arrival of stars such as Gable, Vivien Leigh, Olivia de Havilland and producer David O. Selznick stirred Atlanta's native pride and fulfilled the city's deep-seated longing for attention and validation. Beneath the surface sheen, the festivities also revealed a rigidly segregated city where, to white elites, blacks were largely invisible.

John Wesley Dobbs did not attend the parade. He had read Peggy Mitchell's book, but cared little for it. "That woman," he said, "has written it just to make sure she has a best-seller. It's not a great literary piece." Then the Grand made one of his less prescient predictions: "It won't last long." Geekie had read *Gone With the Wind* against her mother's wishes. Irene Dobbs thought the novel's love story unsuited for children. She had refused to let her daughters see *Camille*, with Greta Garbo and Robert Taylor, for much the same reason. Just twelve years old at the time, Geekie had enjoyed Mitchell's Civil War story.

As the nation watched Atlanta on newsreels, here was a moment made for Bill Hartsfield—and a moment made by Bill Hartsfield. The tin-smith's son had been elected mayor in 1936. His tenure (broken briefly during World War II) would last five times longer than the Civil War. The Hartsfield mayoralty represented a political epoch in Atlanta. His vaudevillian flair rivaled that of his contemporary, New York City mayor Fiorello La Guardia—though their backgrounds were not alike at all. La Guardia was the son of an Italian cornetist and a Sephardic Jew from Venice; he worked as a newspaper correspondent, an agent for the U.S. consul in Fiume, an interpreter at Ellis Island and as a lawyer represent-ing New York garment workers. In contrast, the dramatic persona of Hartsfield was shaped by his overpowering ambition to rise above his undistinguished lower-middle-class Atlanta roots. Unable to afford law school, Hartsfield, working as a secretary, had written to law school deans asking them to suggest which law books to read; he read them all at the library and later put himself through a law school in Atlanta. He liked to say his alma mater was the Atlanta Public Library. His pride as a working man made him appreciate the promotional glitz of *Gone With the Wind.* His sly management of the premiere rated among his finest municipal sales jobs. To Hartsfield, the premiere was the most important event in Atlanta's history since the burning of the city itself. If it wasn't, he would make it seem so. He wanted the premiere on November 15, the seventy-fifth anniversary of Sherman's flames. But Selznick's picture took more time to complete than anticipated since it stretched three hours and thirty-nine minutes. So Hartsfield settled for the seventy-five-years-plus-one-month anniversary. To show his gratitude that Selznick chose Atlanta, the mayor sent a box of home-grown magnolia blossoms to the producer in California. Later he wrote to *Life* magazine, instruct-ing its New York editors of the need to cover the event. As the premiere approached, he even encouraged Atlanta's ladies to rummage through their closets to find the hoop skirts and pantalets of their grandmothers. He asked men to wear tight trousers and grow whiskers reminiscent of the Civil War period.

From the moment his company had paid $50,000 for rights to Mitchell's Pulitzer Prize–winning story, Selznick was under siege. Various factions had wanted him to secure Lana Turner, Bette Davis or Katharine Hepburn for the role of Scarlett. His selection of Vivien Leigh, a native of England, prompted the United Daughters of the Confederacy to protest the choice of a foreigner to play a Georgia girl. As for Rhett Butler, the candidates included Gary Cooper, Ronald Colman and Errol Flynn, although the overwhelmingly popular choice was Clark Gable. In January 1937, Bing Crosby wrote Selznick to suggest a black actress to play the role of Mammy, the O'Hara family's feisty and protective house slave. "The little lady I have in mind played opposite Robeson in *Show Boat,*" Crosby wrote. He meant Hattie McDaniel, who got the part. ("Dear Bing: Thanks for the suggestion," Selznick replied. "Also for not wanting to play Scarlett.")

Selznick worried about Gable, who was not merely a star, but an empire—on loan from Metro-Goldwyn-Mayer. Gable had opposed the Atlanta premiere. Self-conscious and shy in crowds, he feared Atlantans would treat him as the Second Coming of Gen. Joseph Johnston and he did not want any part of it. Besides, Gable heartily disliked Selznick. The producer didn't want to stir the animus of his leading man. Though Selznick liked the idea of coming to Atlanta he fretted about the possibilities. "We are only motion-picture people, and the idea of a town receiving us as though we had just licked the Germans is something that I for one will not go through with," he wrote to a colleague. With a parting shot at Hartsfield, Selznick added, "I hope this doesn't upset His Honor and various others who want to make a Roman holiday out of this."

A band played "Dixie" as Gable and his wife, actress Carole Lombard, stepped onto the tarmac at Candler Field. Soon the motorcade moved up Whitehall Street toward Peachtree. Bands played as thirty convertibles drove into view. Dressed in costumes of the Civil War period, the ladies of the UDC occupied the second car. Gov. Eurith D. Rivers sat with Leigh and Selznick in car 16. When car 17 rolled down Peachtree, sitting next to Gable and Lombard was Bill Hartsfield. He mugged and waved to the crowd as if they had turned out to see only him. One observer noticed on Gable's face "an expression of mingled incredulity and amazement."

The motorcade of stars disappointed the Dobbses. When the automobiles passed Geekie and June, they were moving so fast as to make Gable and Lombard nothing more than a blur.

The Dobbses didn't notice the luminaries sitting in car 21, either—the governor's wife and the venerable official of the Atlanta Chamber of Commerce, Ivan Allen, Sr.

*            *            *

The arrival of the Atlanta Junior League costume ball that night came none too soon for Louise Allen. Only twenty-two, she chaired the league's patrons committee, having blended effortlessly into an organization traditionally associated with the city's aristocracy. For weeks, Louise had received calls from people in desperate need of tickets to the costume ball and premiere. In the City Auditorium, the ball began when forty-eight Junior Leaguers, in costume, nervously came onto the lighted dance floor to the warm applause of the more than five thousand in attendance; Louise and her close friends Eleanor Spalding and Anne Alston Glenn were among the lead group. As master of ceremonies, Maj. Clark Howell, publisher of the *Constitution*, introduced each of the stars and delighted the audience by calling Gable "Mr. Carole Lombard." A giant floodlight turned on him, Gable graciously stood and bowed to acknowledge the ovation.

The chieftains of Atlanta business, the men of the Capital City Club and the Piedmont Driving Club sat at the front tables: the Robert Woodruffs, the Robert F. Maddoxes, the Bob Joneses, the Shepard Bryans and the Ohioan, Gov. James M. Cox, who only that week had purchased the *Journal* and the *Georgian*. At other tables, luminaries from the north: William Paley of CBS, Harold Vanderbilt, Laurance Rockefeller and the famed pilot Eddie Rickenbacker. They saw on stage a reproduction of a Greek Revival plantation home, with its four eighteen-foot Ionic columns. Many of the Atlanta women in the audience wore tiny bonnets and wide hoop skirts with lace-trimmed pantalets showing beneath; their hoop skirts resembled multicolored balloons. Black butlers and chauffeurs scurried about, helping clear the dance floor of tables and chairs at the appointed hour. Ivan Jr. and Louise danced to the music of the Kay Kyser orchestra. The *Constitution* noted that Irene Allen wore a red velvet evening dress trimmed in sequins and that Louise Allen wore lavender taffeta.

"Social brilliance without compare," the *Journal* commented. Not since the 1895 Cotton States and International Exposition had Atlanta so unabashedly luxuriated in its own manufactured sense of self-importance. Whereas the Exposition tolled an Atlanta of the New South, the *Gone With the Wind* festivities celebrated Atlanta of the Old South— a portrayal not without its detractors. The NAACP had protested Mitchell's rendition of docile slaves and their seeming preference for servitude over freedom. Because black organizations pressed Selznick to remove the word "nigger" from his script, the producer replaced it with "darky." Walter White, the NAACP executive secretary, also had suggested that Selznick's screenwriters read Du Bois's *Black Reconstruction* to serve as a balance to Mitchell's perspective. Selznick, who was Jewish, was acutely sensitive about offending racial and ethnic groups, for reasons commercial as well as personal. He wrote financier John Hay (Jock) Whitney in February 1939, "I think these are no times in which to offend any race or people. . . . *I am most anxious to remove any impression (which I am sure is very wide-spread) that* Gone With the Wind, *this company, and I personally are enemies of the Negroes.*" Selznick's intention was to bring his black stars, Hattie McDaniel and Butterfly McQueen, to the Atlanta premiere. He hoped they would drum up publicity by conducting interviews with black newspapers and by circulating in the colored commercial community, which in Atlanta meant Auburn Avenue. But his advisors warned against it, fearing that McDaniel and McQueen would be forced to endure substandard lodging in Atlanta and that such mistreatment in a segregated southern city would provide fodder for groups antagonistic to the film. Ultimately it was decided that McDaniel and McQueen ought not go to Atlanta. The risk of alienating white southerners, it was decided, was too great. Hattie McDaniel's photograph was used in programs distributed in New York and Los Angeles but was removed from the program used in Atlanta.

Yet none of this seemed to matter to editor C. A. Scott and his *Atlanta Daily World*, thrilled by the festivities surrounding "that gripping story of the Old South."

In black Atlanta, the response to the segregated *Gone With the Wind* festivities was a bewildering mix of excitement and awe, envy and resentment. Among blacks, enthusiasm for everything touched by Hollywood was tempered by stark reminders of their own second-class status. The premiere arrived in Atlanta one year after Ralph McGill, on his first day as executive editor of the *Constitution*, had mandated that all future references to "Negro" would use a capital "N." An introspective Tennessean beginning to reconstruct himself into a moderate on the race issue, McGill already had become anathema to the powerful politician Gene Talmadge, who thought him the personification of all things wrong with Atlanta. (During the 1936 Senate race, a Talmadge henchman had punched McGill, banging his head against the columns of the Henry Grady Hotel, for having supported a Talmadge opponent, Richard B. Russell. "Next time I see you I'm gone have a pistol, and I'm gone kill the hell outta you!" the Talmadge man had promised.) During the month of the *Gone With the Wind* premiere, the *Daily World* columnist William A. Fowlkes called for blacks to "stop giving the opportunity for others hearkening [sic] back to the slave days by our acting the part"; his colleague, I. P. Reynolds, complained about Atlanta police raiding bars and locking up innocent blacks.

The *Daily World* celebrated the additional work the premiere meant for blacks and seemed pleased that Vivien Leigh brought two colored maids with her. Nearly three hundred blacks worked as ushers at the costume ball and were directed by Graham Jackson, Franklin Roosevelt's favorite musician, who was about to be initiated as a Prince Hall Mason by John Wesley Dobbs. Some black chauffeurs drove their white employers to the ball in horse-drawn carriages. "Dressed as did those carriage drivers and servants of the sixties," the *Daily World* reported, "they presented spectacular pictures on the downtown thoroughfares."

John Wesley Dobbs fretted over black Atlanta's capitulation to Jim Crow during the *Gone With the Wind* festivities. On New Year's Day, 1939, Dobbs had traveled to Cleveland to deliver an Emancipation Day address on *Wings Over Jordan*, a thirty-minute radio program of spirituals and anthems, backed by a thirty-five-voice choir and broadcast nationally. It was powerful recognition of his role as a race leader. He spoke with passion about blacks in America, tracing the history of the race from the cotton fields to the modern day. "Over the doorway of the Nation's Supreme Court building in Washington are engraved four words. 'Equal Justice Under Law,'" Dobbs said. "This beautiful American ideal is what the Negroes want to see operative and effective in Mississippi and Minnesota—in South Carolina and South Dakota—Nothing more or less." He spoke with such intensity and eloquence that he received a congratulatory note from the producers of the program: "The nation has gone simply ga-ga about your talk. We are being swamped with requests for copies."

Most astonishing and offensive to Dobbs was the performance at the Junior League ball by the sixty-voice Ebenezer Baptist Church choir, led by Rev. Martin Luther King, Sr. King was notoriously stubborn. Virtually unschooled when he first arrived in Atlanta in 1919 from Stockbridge, Georgia, he had suffered the indignity of entering a fifth-grade class at the age of twenty-one. Later he convinced John Hope to allow him to matriculate at Morehouse College where he earned a degree in theology in 1930. He joined Dobbs at the Atlanta Civic and Political League and together they became voter registration prophets. In November 1939, a month before the *Gone With the Wind* premiere, King had led more than one thousand blacks on a voter registration march to Atlanta's City Hall. "I ain't gonna plow no more mules," King said that day. "I'll never step off the road again to let white folks pass." But at the ball, his defiance and demand for equal status seemingly vanished. Dressed in slave costumes, his choir sang spirituals such as "I Want Jesus to Walk with Me," "Honor, Honor," "Get on Board Little Children" and "Plenty Good Room." The

*Daily World* wrote, "Each number swelled the hearts of the . . . lucky white persons attending the gay affair." Dobbs was outraged. He considered the Ebenezer performance an affront to race pride. "It is unconscionable that they cooperated," he told his daughters. The following week, the Atlanta Baptist Ministers Union concurred, censuring King for performing at a segregated event.

Martin Luther King, Jr., then ten years old, sang with the Ebenezer choir. The man who would lead the social revolution that transformed the South was on this night dressed as a pickaninny.

Irrepressible Bill Hartsfield sneaked Gable and Lombard out of the Georgian Terrace Hotel at ten o'clock the morning of the premiere for a two-hour tour of Atlanta. Hartsfield took the Gables past the fine homes in Ansley Park and the gleaming estates along West Pace's Ferry and Tuxedo Road, then down Northside Drive past the home of Ivan Allen, Jr., to the site of the Battle of Peachtree Creek. An amateur photographer who carried his 16-millimeter camera virtually wherever he went, the mayor brought his own film to the Gables' suite—a portrait of the city's historic sites.

That afternoon, at a reception in the governor's mansion, Ivan Jr. and Louise mingled with the stars. Now twenty-eight, working for Governor Rivers, Ivan Jr. served as treasurer of the State Hospital Authority in Milledgeville. When Louise sat down at the reception, she turned to her right and realized the man next to her was Clark Gable; Ivan Jr. sat at a table with Carole Lombard. Gable was every bit as graceful and charming as Louise had imagined, "so complimentary of Atlanta," Louise recalls. "I think they were all bowled over with the hospitality." In one way, though, Gable surprised her. "He was shorter than we expected. But Vivien Leigh was so small—she was tiny—that it didn't show up at all [on film]."

Margaret Mitchell did not make her first appearance until later that afternoon, at a reception at the Piedmont Driving Club, where she met Gable for the first time. Surrounded by admirers, Gable pulled her into a side room where they chatted privately for about fifteen minutes. "Our Peggy," as Atlantans proudly called her, had deep roots in Atlanta, having descended from a Methodist minister said to have performed the first wedding in Marthasville. Her father, Eugene, was president of the Atlanta Historical Society; years earlier, her uncle, Frank Rice, had helped start *The Atlanta Journal,* along with family friend Hoke Smith. Peggy Mitchell was diminutive, only four foot eleven, and beneath her floppy hats it sometimes was difficult to even see her. When her novel appeared in

1936 her old friend and former colleague O. B. Keeler of the *Journal* had admitted, "I'd never have guessed she could do one like this." Mitchell long had considered herself somewhat of a renegade. During her newspaper days, she smoked cigarettes, held her liquor admirably during those infrequent occasions in which she chose to imbibe and spewed four-letter words on a par with the notorious curmudgeons of her ink-stained trade. When her marriage to the bootlegger Berrien Upshaw foundered in 1923, after only ten months, she subsequently married Upshaw's best man, John Marsh, a reserved and frail publicity man for Georgia Power. (After Eugene Mitchell gave him approval to marry his daughter, Marsh's frayed nerves caused him to suffer a bout of hiccoughs that lasted for weeks.) The newly married Peggy Mitchell retained her maiden name as a writer, a bold statement for the times.

Her novel's celebration of the grandeur of the Old South fit with Mitchell's upbringing. As a child, she had spent many Sunday afternoons sitting on the laps of aged relatives who refought the Civil War. Cavalry knees, she said, were the worst. "Cavalry knees had the tendency to trot and bounce and jog in the midst of reminiscences," Mitchell said. Such bouncing had benefits, though—"kept me from going to sleep," she said. She was ten years old before she received the startling news that Robert E. Lee really had lost. Her racial views typified those of Atlanta's white patricians accustomed to having black servants and thinking blacks a subservient race. As a student at Smith College in Northampton, Massachusetts, in 1918, Mitchell was furious on learning that a black student was in her history class; she demanded, and received, a transfer to another class. She defended her paternalistic view of blacks by asking her teacher if she "had ever undressed and nursed a Negro woman or sat on a drunk Negro man's head to keep him from being shot by the police." Like most writers, she had difficulty accepting criticism of her work; she found criticism of her portrayal of docile blacks especially galling. She believed the radical press was using her novel to drive blacks to communism much as *Uncle Tom's Cabin* had been used to recruit abolitionists. "I do not need to tell you how I and all my folks feel about Negroes," Mitchell wrote in April 1939 to Susan Myrick, a Macon newspaperwoman serving as advisor in Hollywood during the filming of *Gone With the Wind.* "We've always fought for colored education and, even when John [Marsh] and I were at our worst financially, we were helping keep colored children in schools, furnishing clothes and carfare.

"Heaven knows," Peggy Mitchell added. "I had and have no intention of 'insulting the Race.' " In the decade that followed, she quietly made private contributions to Morehouse College to pay for the education of black medical students.

In front of the Loew's Grand theater on Peachtree that night, lights crisscrossed in the sky and cast a glow seen sixty-five miles away. About thirty thousand Atlantans, some leaning out the windows of buildings, waited for the stars to appear. Vivien Leigh arrived, wearing a gold lamé gown beneath a fox fur coat. Peggy Mitchell didn't want to watch the premiere sitting next to David O. Selznick, for fear that his nerves would rattle hers; she sat with her husband, John Marsh, and Jock Whitney. An organist played "Dixie" and the Senator and Irene, Ivan Jr. and Louise took their seats, paired separately. Louise's position with the Junior League enabled her to secure preferred seating, in the front right section, not far from the stars. They were among the 2,031 to obtain the $10 tickets. Mitchell's discomfort with the attention was plain to see, though she held up, admirably. "Really, Margaret Mitchell was amazing," Louise says. Some would recall how lumps had formed in their throat at the arrival of four Confederate veterans, all stooped old men, in their nineties, walking with canes, their eyes cloudy. The veterans received a standing ovation, J. R. Jones, born three years before Earnest Allen, had been with General Johnston at the time of his surrender to Gen. William T. Sherman at Durham, North Carolina. "The war looked just like that," Jones said, watching the film. "I feel like crying." Ed Smith and his wife, Laura, friends of Ivan Jr. and Louise, watched Gable and Lombard closely from their seats and noticed the unusual color of the Coca-Cola bottles in their hands. "They were blond," Ed Smith remembers, "from whiskey." Laura Smith: "They were drinking booze just as hard as they could."

The house lights darkened and on the oversized movie screen appeared:

*Here was the land of cavaliers and cotton fields called the Old South. Here in this proud world gallantry took its last bow. Here was the last ever to be seen of knights and ladies fair, of master and of slave. Look for it in books for it is no more than a dream remembered, a civilization "Gone With the Wind."*

The most emphatic response from the audience during the premiere occurred when a federal soldier advanced inside Tara, the family's home, and was shot dead by Scarlett O'Hara. The Loew's Grand erupted with applause and a few Rebel yells rent the air when the Yankee soldier hit the floor.

The Allens loved *Gone With the Wind.* "It's a great story. I enjoyed the hell out of it all of the way," Ivan Jr. recalls. "There's a lot of love in it. There's a great sadness in it. It tells the story of the poverty of the South. It tells the story of the problems of slavery, the devastation of war. Most of the characters don't come out of it very well. It's a sad book. I guess that was true."

June Dobbs, eleven at the time, did not see Clark Gable during the motorcade and did not see his film until much later. "Why was Scarlett any type of worthwhile role model for white girls?" she wonders decades later. "And for blacks, the woman Butterfly McQueen [who played the role of Prissy], her character makes you wonder if she was purposely stupid so she wouldn't have to get involved with [Melanie's] birth." Though Hattie McDaniel's performance as Mammy made her the first black actress to win an Academy Award, June says, "We didn't have any love in our hearts for her. The character she portrayed was obnoxious, servile. There was no pride or dignity. I mean, it was not Frederick Douglass. It had nothing for us."

In the days that followed the premiere, the *Journal* wrote, "The Old South's heart beats warm and friendly in the New South's stride." Hollywood publicity men promoted *Gone With the Wind* as "The Greatest Motion Picture Ever Made." At the Atlanta chamber, the Senator made a motion, seconded by Dick Rich of Rich's department store, to draft a certificate of distinguished achievement to his friend, Mayor Bill Hartsfield, for his management of the *Gone With the Wind* festival. And Hartsfield sent his homemade 16-millimeter film of the festivities to Clark Gable and Carole Lombard. Mrs. Gable replied with a note: "We ran it immediately and a very strange feeling came over us. It made us very homesick for you all, and again impressed on our memory what a great event it was in our lives." To Atlanta's budding municipal legend, she added: "You were one of the main highlights."

Upon the 1936 publication of *Gone With the Wind,* a *New York Times* book reviewer wrote of Mitchell, "She has set herself a hard mark to match with a second book." Peggy Mitchell was quoted four days later, saying, "I hope I never write another thing again." And she never did.

In August 1949, nearly a decade after the film's premiere, Mitchell and her husband, John Marsh, were crossing Peachtree Street en route to a theater to see *A Canterbury Tale* when Mitchell was struck by a 1949 Ford coach. The driver was an off-duty cabbie named Hugh Gravitt. Gravitt later told police he was bound for a pharmacy to pick up medicine for his ill stepson; Gravitt also said he had consumed one beer, maybe two. He left sixty-seven feet of skid marks along Peachtree. The forty-eight-year-old Mitchell held on for five days, but died in Grady Hospital. Convicted of involuntary manslaughter, Gravitt served ten months and twenty days at Bellwood Prison in Atlanta. He spent two of those months on a chain gang, pulling up weeds on roadsides. He lived his remaining forty-five years sadly, his sorrow produced largely by one moment he could neither change nor escape. Decades later people would pull into Gravitt's service station outside of Atlanta and ask, "Are you the one who ran over Margaret Mitchell?" Gravitt would reply, "No, I hit her, but I didn't run over her." To him, the distinction was important. As an old man, Gravitt said he wished he had killed himself after he had walked out of prison. *"I'll be haunted and hounded till the day I die."*

Some foreigners still visit the Oakland Cemetery and ask to be shown Scarlett O'Hara's gravesite. Instead, they see Margaret Mitchell's, next to her husband, who survived her by less than three years.

*Gone With the Wind,* a book Hugh Gravitt never read, has sold more than 25 million copies. Only the Bible has sold more.

# PART IV

# SEGREGATED CITY

TO: Mayor of Atlanta
July 18, 1941

Sir: There is a stretch of street on Beckwith Street Southwest between Chestnut Street Southwest and Raymond Street that is unpaved and that has long been a source of great inconvenience and danger to travelers. I have parked my car in a garage on this street for five years and sometimes it had been almost impossible to get in and out. Cars coming along Beckwith Street and striking this spot are seriously liable to accident. I am writing to ask if the city cannot arrange for the pavement of this block?

I am, Sir.
Very sincerely yours,
W. E. B. Du Bois.

# CHAPTER 9

➤✦

John Wesley Dobbs overheard the white man introduce himself to another passenger. *My name is Dobbs,* the white man said. Standing in the club car of the train as it passed through north Georgia, the Grand could not help but to eavesdrop on their conversation. The white man mentioned that he was from Cobb County, near Marietta, and the Grand began to make the connections in his mind. It was not uncommon for whites and blacks in a southern community to share the same last name. Frequently, the connection was more than coincidental. Though there was nothing particularly distinguished or even memorable about this man, Dobbs later said to his daughters, there was about this moment.

"That man's family," Dobbs told himself, "once owned my family."

Here, in this white man named Dobbs, was perhaps a piece of his family past, and therefore a piece of himself. But curiosity was one thing, self-respect and dignity another. In his retelling of this story, as with most of the autobiographical stories he told his daughters, Dobbs cast himself in a heroic role; undoubtedly, he sometimes stretched the truth, for certainly there were many times that had not ended in triumph for him. His purpose was to accentuate the positive and to develop in each of his daughters a powerful sense of self. In the presence of this white man named Dobbs, the Grand was as trapped in his way as any black man and had only two possible responses, submission or defiance. Certainly, he would not submit to this man, and he had no reason to be outwardly defiant.

If there was a historical connection here, he determined that he did not need to know it. He did not need to relive that part of the past. It was time to move past the shackles. Self-respect would serve as both his weapon and his shield.

And so John Wesley Dobbs stood in the club car and did precisely what his curiosity told him not to do.

Nothing.

And the train rumbled on.

During the early 1940s, the Grand streaked across the single-lane highways of Georgia in his green Lincoln Zephyr. He was bound for his

Masonic meetings where he intended to spread the gospel of voter registration. He drove his automobile hard and fast, just as he drove his Masons. His daughters feared riding in the car when the Grand was behind the wheel. He adored speed in an automobile. It was, after all, one of the few ways in which a southern black could make progress quickly. Among friends, Dobbs delighted in claiming for himself driving speed records, from Atlanta to Americus, Atlanta to Macon, Atlanta to any destination in the state. "He's one of the few drivers in the country who can hold a car in the road at 80 and 85 miles an hour while talking at a faster pace," his friend Lucius Jones of *The Atlanta Daily World* wrote.

Geekie and June often accompanied Dobbs to his Masonic district meetings during the summer months. Usually Joe Phinazee went, too. Dobbs had met the soft-spoken Phinazee at the Prince Hall Masonic orphanage in Americus several years earlier. When Phinazee turned seventeen, Dobbs took him as his foster son and arranged for him to live with his mother and her husband, Mr. Banks. Phinazee served as the Grand's personal assistant and part-time driver. While Phinazee drove, Dobbs, riding shotgun, often played old car games with his daughters, such as "Dogs" where the object was to count dogs along the way. When he played "Cats," scoring was based not only on the number of cats found, but also the color of the cat; invariably, the black cat was the most valuable.

When they drove outside of Atlanta, Dobbs explained to his daughters that they had entered a section of Georgia that was different from the one they knew. Rural Georgia was a harsher place than Atlanta not only for blacks but for whites. The economic upswing during the Second World War had had as little effect on black sharecroppers and tenant farmers in rural Georgia as on the whites. Electricity was not common in rural areas and even running water was not universal. Few blacks out in the Georgia countryside had received a quality education, Dobbs told them, even fewer had registered to vote. As Dobbs drove, usually with one hand fanning out to emphasize another important point, his daughters noticed how he seemed to know the location of every Confederate monument in Georgia. These monuments carried an irresistible lure to him. He drove to the center of dozens of small Georgia towns and pulled in front of yet another Confederate memorial. He turned off the ignition. Then he took a deep breath.

"This," he began, turning to his daughters, "is the white man's way of memorializing a diabolical system of human slavery." June and Geekie knew these as their prescribed moments of instruction, a time when Daddy's voice transformed into the voice of the Grand. The subject now was the old Confederacy. "What they fought for was to keep power and to earn a living off the sweat of slaves. And that was not right." His voice erupted with purpose. "IT WAS NEVER RIGHT!"

Rural Georgia was harsher to blacks in another sense as well. Dobbs felt his defenses rising as soon as the streetlights and the trolley lines of Atlanta were replaced by farmlands. In 1939, he had helped his daughter Josephine buy an automobile. Josie was doing postgraduate work in Savannah, about 250 miles away, and was tired of making the trek back home to Atlanta by train. "Send me off a telegram when you get to Savannah," Dobbs instructed his twenty-two-year-old daughter as she left 540 in her car. Dobbs told her that he wanted to know how long it took her to make the trip—"Remember, Daddy's got the record!"—but in reality he held deep-seated fears about one of his daughters driving alone across Georgia. Most of the service stations along the way did not allow blacks to use the rest rooms. "Stop and see Mr. Dudley in Dublin," Dobbs said, referring to a Masonic colleague, "and he'll look after you." Though Josie did not encounter troubles—she wired home from the Western Union office each time she arrived in Savannah—the concerns were well-warranted.

As a matter of principle Dobbs refused to purchase gasoline at a station that prohibited blacks from using the toilets. As their Lincoln Zephyr pulled into small towns across Georgia, June and Geekie felt almost as if they'd been shot in a capsule into a strange galaxy. They drew cold, angry stares from working-class whites as their father drove into small cities such as Griffin, Americus and Milledgeville. The Dobbses were well dressed. They drove a fine automobile. They had confidence and poise. These, local whites knew, were not typical blacks. These were Atlanta's blacks. "You never saw such evil stares in your life," Mattiwilda recalls.

The Grand had his own ritual at service stations. Having pulled next to a gas pump, he would say softly, "Geekie, go ahead in."

Mattiwilda would step out of the car and walk toward the bathroom in the back, her father watching her every step. A white would invariably emerge from the station, in a funk: "Hey, you can't go in there!" The attendant often stood in front of the rest room door, blocking Geekie. There was a toilet for blacks a few miles down the road, he said. Geekie returned to her father with her report, while another attendant stood beside the car, waiting. In these instances, Dobbs rolled down his window and said, "We're not buying," and drove off. It was a scene replayed, with small variations, all across south and central Georgia.

Once, Geekie went inside a service station rest room and immediately locked the door. The white attendant rushed out and knocked on the door furiously. "You can't stay in there!" he shouted. *"You can't stay in there!"* Geekie finished, then emerged. By the time she reached the car, the other white attendant already had pumped the gas.

This time, the Grand drove away victorious.

It became one of his favorite expressions on the voter registration circuit: "We need to stick with the blue-eyed boy—BUT WATCH HIM!" the Grand bellowed as he thrust an index finger toward his audience.

To Dobbs, Bill Hartsfield personified that blue-eyed boy. Hartsfield was a political animal, the lion of Atlanta's municipal jungle. Just as Alderman Hartsfield had understood the long-term importance of aviation, Mayor Hartsfield sensed, early on, the growing political sophistication of Atlanta's blacks. Dobbs believed Hartsfield was a good and decent man who would deal fairly with blacks. But he had to be watched.

Only several years before, the Swedish social economist Gunnar Myrdal had traveled though the South for his landmark study of blacks in America. Dobbs had driven with him through parts of Georgia and later spoke of how blacks had told Myrdal that southern whites never intended for them to vote once slavery had ended. In his groundbreaking two-volume *An American Dilemma: The Negro Problem and Modern Democracy*, published in 1944, Myrdal contended that "the Negro problem in America represents a moral lag in the development of the nation." He foresaw the coming changes in race relations in the South, changes he predicted would become the most significant since Reconstruction. Myrdal found that the two races in the South interacted largely through the medium of liaisons, or "plenipotentiaries." When a black was recognized as a race leader by whites it served to elevate his status within the black community, Myrdal wrote, though many whites still distrusted elite, educated blacks.

Dobbs was among a group of black plenipotentiaries in Atlanta who participated in periodic discussions with Hartsfield about the need for black police. The idea dated at least to 1932 in Atlanta when black voters helped then-mayor James Key stave off a recall vote that had been stirred by prohibitionists. Afterward, black leaders sought their political payback by asking Mayor Key to hire colored policemen. Aware of Key's black support, segregationists in the Georgia legislature responded to his victory in the recall election by halving the term of office for Atlanta's mayor from four years to two. Key told blacks that hiring black police in Atlanta would assure his defeat in the 1934 mayoral race, almost certainly to a segregationist.

Complaints of police brutality against blacks in the city multiplied during the 1930s. Not only were beatings all too common but Atlanta policemen frequently made disparaging, belittling remarks. White officers in Atlanta frequently referred to black women as "Annie Mae" or "Emma Lou" or "gal." The disrespect caused Atlanta University president Rufus Clement to bemoan, "I am just plain tired of going downtown and being told by the policeman on the corner, 'Okay, boy, you can cross the street now.'"

The group facing Hartsfield was an impressive one: besides Dobbs, there was editor C. A. Scott; Warren Cochrane, director of the Butler Street YMCA; Rev. Martin Luther King, Sr.; Rev. William Holmes Borders; and Col. A. T. Walden. Walden was known as Colonel not because of military rank (though he did serve as captain in Europe during World War I) but as an honorary title sometimes awarded to veteran lawyers. This title also gave whites in the courtroom an alternative to *"Mister* Walden."

These black leaders did not mince words with Hartsfield. The time was right for black policemen, they said. "We'll get colored policemen in Atlanta," Hartsfield replied, wryly, "just as soon as we get colored deacons in the white First Baptist Church." In this stinging rebuke, there was a lesson to be learned by the blacks in the room: the mayor was a politician who would be moved to action only by political leverage. Namely, votes. Dobbs and other black leaders redoubled their voter registration efforts.

Dobbs continued to try to galvanize black Atlanta through his Atlanta Civic and Political League. He decried the fact that fewer than two thousand blacks in the city were registered to vote in 1940 when he again went north to stump for FDR in colored communities. (Not until 1944 did Dobbs lose faith in FDR. Determining that the New Deal was a false promise to blacks, he returned to the Republican party and its presidential nominee, Thomas Dewey.)

Dobbs spoke about voter registration in Atlanta throughout the war years: in Masonic halls; in fiery speeches delivered at local black churches and black college campuses; in casual conversation while playing whist with other black leaders in the fourth-floor social club of the Odd Fellows Building on Auburn Avenue; and at the Butler Street YMCA—the "Black City Hall"—a half block from Sweet Auburn, where black civic leaders often congregated to talk political strategies. Dobbs created his own five-point program for black uplift: Religion, Education, Money, Political Security and Culture. Sometimes he abbreviated it to the Three Bs: "Books, Ballots and Bucks."

"Think about it for a minute," Dobbs wrote in *The Atlanta Daily World* in the spring of 1940, "right here in Atlanta, the Athens of the

South, where big brick schools and college domes adorn the hills about our town; where Negroes live on paved streets and in beautiful homes; where they strut every day in their tailor-made clothes; yes, where they angle along the boulevards in costly and expensive cars; and yet, it must be said, to their eternal shame and disgrace that less than 2,000 have earned the right to vote. . . . When 10,000 Negroes in Atlanta get registered, the Signal Light of Opportunity will automatically turn from red to green."

The poll tax often seemed an insurmountable obstacle to blacks, especially to those in rural areas; most did not own property and their poll tax usually went unpaid and grew to a prohibitive amount. In Atlanta, however, Dobbs discovered a tactical advantage, almost by accident, through the help of a white man. During the early 1940s, a white employee at the Fulton County courthouse pulled Dobbs aside, then pointed across the room. "Do you know those books over there, those books have 10,000 Negroes' names in there, who are already paying poll tax," he said. "Because when you pay your property tax, you have to pay your poll tax. So their poll tax is already paid. If you'll send somebody down here I'll let them copy all those names and addresses."

Dobbs conferred with other black leaders and all agreed that the Atlanta Civic and Political League should pay $300 to two young lawyers to copy the names of those ten thousand Atlanta blacks. The names were written on index cards, which then were organized by street address. Atlanta still was organized by the ward system and one black leader in each ward was designated, as they were for air raid purposes, to contact these potential voters. Since 1908, when Georgia became the seventh southern state to write black disfranchisement into law, black Georgians had been permitted to vote only in general elections and special elections, but not in the all-important Democratic primary. In 1942, however, black Atlantans put their voting strength to a test. In a special election, Bill Hartsfield was attempting to return to City Hall after Mayor Roy LeCraw left in midterm to enter the military. Because Hartsfield continued to hedge on certain issues, including the hiring of black police, blacks supported his opponent, a nondescript alderman named Dan Bridges. Hartsfield prevailed with 12,630 votes to Bridges's 4,867.

Nevertheless the political firmament was shifting. In the same year, Georgia elected Ellis Arnall governor. Though the thirty-five-year-old attorney from nearby Newnan, Georgia, believed segregation needed to be preserved, he proved a progressive thinker, abolishing the poll tax in 1945 and spurring a reform revolution that stripped away Eugene Talmadge's dictatorial system. Hartsfield continued to discuss the possibility of hiring black police. His latest response provided a window of opportunity: "If you have 10,000 registered voters in Atlanta I might talk to you." A gleam in his eye, John Wesley Dobbs liked what he heard.

The message was sent across black Atlanta. *Ten thousand votes.*

The Grand had learned to play partisan politics with a Machiavellian deftness. Once in 1944, after he had returned to the Republican party ("the Party of Lincoln"), he squared off in a scheduled debate with C. A. Scott at the Big Bethel AME Church on Auburn. At the time, Scott was a Roosevelt man and he remembered this debate always. The Grand spoke first and immediately denounced Scott as "A. T. Walden's right-hand man," a charge that didn't ruffle Scott. "Everyone knew I was a Democrat from reading the paper," Scott recalls. But Scott was ruffled by what occurred next. The church was filled with members of Dobbs's Prince Hall Masons. When the Grand finished his speech he gave the secret Masonic distress sign, signaling all devoted Masons to depart at once. The room emptied. Scott never made his speech. "Dobbs was a little tricky," he says.

After the state courts of Texas nullified the white primary in that state in *Smith v. Allright* in 1944, blacks in Georgia decided to test the decision in their own state. Among the challengers was a Columbus black named Primus King, who later would file a landmark lawsuit. The leaders of the Atlanta Negro Democrats announced their intention to attempt to vote in the 1944 all-white Democratic primary on July 4.

Three blacks climbed into the car with Clarence Bacote, an Atlanta University history professor, and drove to a polling place located in a barbershop, near Bankhead, a white working-class area in west Atlanta. In the car with Bacote were Walden, Eugene M. Martin, vice president of the Atlanta Life Insurance Company, and V. W. Hodges, assistant publisher of the *Daily World.* The men understood the gravity of what they were attempting to do. The tensions somehow seemed heightened in that the election occurred on the Fourth of July, a day traditionally set aside for celebrating American freedoms.

When the four blacks approached the barbershop, members of the local press waited. So did white residents, who stood on their front porches and stared down at the interlopers. Inside the precinct, Walden presented a receipt from the tax collector's office that qualified him to vote in the November 7 general election, though not Georgia's all-white Democratic primary. The clerks went through the motions of checking the voting lists.

"Your name's not on there," one of the polling officials said to Walden, finally. Then the official went down the list and told Bacote, Martin and

Hodges, one by one: "Your name's not on there." The crowd of whites surged forward and pressed against the windows of the barbershop. Quickly, the blacks departed. As they walked to Bacote's car, reporters followed along; then they drove away. "The Democratic primary passed in perfect order," *The Atlanta Journal* wrote the following day.

Yet the momentum was building. The signal moment that introduced the black vote as a force to be reckoned with in Atlanta occurred in February 1946. Nineteen candidates vied for the congressional seat vacated by the resignation of Cong. Robert Ramspeck. Tom Camp, Ramspeck's protégé, was considered the favorite. Because this was a special election, the 6,876 blacks registered in Atlanta were permitted to participate in the vote.

Only a few of the congressional candidates accepted an invitation to speak before a black gathering at the Wheat Street Baptist Church on Auburn Avenue. Addressing a black crowd was a risky proposition for an Atlanta candidate. Any black votes won could easily be offset by a backlash of white votes lost. Camp chose not to attend, but Mrs. Helen Douglas Mankin, a veteran state legislator, did, and seemed most at ease before the audience.

On February 11, 1946, the night before the election, Dobbs, Walden, Scott and businessman John Calhoun stood before another packed crowd at Wheat Street. Their purpose was to announce, in unified fashion, which candidate to support. They waited until 11:15 P.M.—after the evening radio programs had ended and too late to make the morning edition of the *Constitution*. If word leaked to the press, they feared their candidate would face the white backlash.

The 11:15 announcement was simple: "Vote for the woman." The news spread quickly throughout black Atlanta the next day. At eight P.M., one hour after the polls had closed, local newspaper reporters banged on the door of Precinct 3B on Ashby Street at the E. R. Carter Elementary School, the largest black precinct. "The election depends on the outcome of 3B," a reporter said. Reporters told Walden, the precinct manager, that Camp was 156 votes ahead of Mankin, pending the outcome of 3B.

Of the first fifty votes counted at the precinct on Ashby Street, Mrs. Mankin received forty-six. The word went out to the reporters: "Mrs. Mankin is in." In all, Mankin won 963 of the 1,038 votes cast at 3B. Camp took eight. Mankin's election to Congress in the Fifth District was more than a surprise; it was a revelation. Nationally syndicated columnist Thomas Stokes noted the import of the election. "Negroes contributed the margin of victory for Mrs. Helen Douglas Mankin," he wrote. "This is important as a matter of politics. . . . It explodes some myths, removes some old phobias, and points out the path for gradual extension of the franchise to Negroes in the South."

Fretting over increased black political participation, an angry Gene Talmadge, seeking a fourth term as governor with a platform that called for unrestrained white supremacy, began to refer to Mankin as "The Belle of Ashby Street."

The Grand had a decidedly different perspective. He saw John walking in Jerusalem. His was a crystalline image: the trumpets sounding and the dark clouds of racial injustice parting. Naturally, Dobbs saw himself in the role of John, a voter registration prophet who told of the inevitability of glorious days to come. In Dobbs's image, he saw himself blurring with the mission, becoming one. Yet the force of Dobbs's determination, and his hunger to lead, alienated him from many of his black peers, even though they shared his vision.

Dobbs felt betrayed in the spring of 1946 when the new All-Citizens Registration Committee was formed to oversee an intensified push to register blacks. His organization, the Atlanta Civic and Political League, had served in that role for a decade and he saw no need to create a new group. However, organizers of the new committee believed Dobbs's organization was too Republican in its orientation.

Dobbs appeared at an organizational meeting for the All-Citizens Registration Committee at the Savoy Hotel on Auburn Avenue. Bacote presided and had difficulty handling Dobbs's wrath.

"Bacote," John Calhoun whispered during the meeting, as Dobbs railed, "just let Dobbs talk. He can't stop you. You got all these people here with you. Just let him say everything he wants to say and then go on with your meeting."

When Dobbs finished, Bacote took charge. "Well, thank you, Mr. Dobbs," he said. "Now, ladies and gentlemen, we came here tonight to organize . . ." Dobbs stormed out of the Savoy.

On March 6, 1946, the All-Citizens Committee began its campaign. The goal was to register 25,000 blacks in Fulton County before the registration books closed in two months, in preparation for petitioning the courts to nullify the all-white primary. The campaign was directed primarily by Atlanta Urban League president Grace Towns Hamilton, who was, like Dobbs, a member of the First Congregational Church. Her Urban League colleague Robert Thompson was the lead strategist and organized workers by census tracts and blocks. Fifty thousand handbills, describing voting procedures, were distributed in the black community. Several hundred blacks lined up outside the Fulton County courthouse on many mornings, waiting their turn to register.

Within a matter of weeks, Dobbs, his ego apparently assuaged, was back in the fold. Thompson believes Dobbs returned because the registration movement was going on without him. "He could read the writing on the wall," Thompson says. At a special meeting, Dobbs's Atlanta Civic and Political League voted to donate $50 to the new All-Citizens Registration Committee. On March 28, Dobbs spoke at the Greater Mt. Cavalry Baptist Church in Atlanta and predicted the end of the all-white primary in Georgia. He spoke of the benefits to be reaped by voter registration. "We need better school facilities for our children and more schools," he said. "We need black men up and down Negro thoroughfares to police our areas, and if our white friends persist in maintaining separate books on which Negroes must make their tax returns then we need colored girls who will be called to take charge of these books. But none of these—not even police brutality, nor insults to us in the court rooms can be stopped until we can vote for these things. . . . We must not have one ballot but a flock of ballots before any perceptible change in our status can be assured." Dobbs spent the next two days touring the state and later reported an unprecedented pace of voter registration among black Georgians.

On April 1, 1946, the United States Supreme Court refused to hear an appeal on the Primus King case in which a Georgia federal district judge, following the Circuit Court of Appeals in New Orleans, had outlawed the all-white Democratic primary in Georgia. The courts held that its exclusive nature violated the constitutional rights of blacks.

The response was instant and dramatic. Talmadge suggested in his newspaper, *The Statesman,* that the death of the all-white primary meant "our southern traditions and heritage will be lost." About a mile down the road from Dobbs's Prince Hall Masonic Temple on Sweet Auburn, Speaker of the Georgia House of Representatives Roy V. Harris called for a special legislative session to devise ways to circumvent the court's decision. But Governor Arnall struck a different tone. "The courts," he said, "have spoken." Now the All-Citizens Registration Committee worked with an increased fervor. Over the next fifty-one days, nearly 18,000 blacks registered to vote as part of the local drive. Suddenly, the total number of black registered voters in Fulton County exceeded 24,000, and more than 21,000 of them lived in Atlanta.

John Wesley Dobbs had worked most of his life for this. After the Primus King decision he told the *Daily World* that "Negroes now will rapidly come into their full political rights and thereby firmly establish themselves as citizens."

But powerful forces were at work to keep this from happening, as

Mankin's cometlike fall later in the year showed. In July, Mankin—"that woman from the wicked city of Atlanta," according to Gene Talmadge—sought reelection to her seat. In the Democratic primary she was opposed by Judge James C. Davis, a Talmadge appointee to the state Superior Court bench in Stone Mountain. A former Klansman and state legislator, Davis once had sponsored a law in the General Assembly requiring a card index for all Georgians to specify whether they had an "ascertainable" trace of Negro blood. Since this was a Democratic primary, the county unit system, which had been removed from February's special election, was restored, much to Mankin's dismay. On election day, Mankin won more total votes (53,611 to Davis's 42,482), but Davis won a plurality in Rockdale and DeKalb counties to win eight unit votes; Mankin took only Fulton County's six unit votes. Despite a court battle, Mankin's name was not on the ballot in the November general election. Though she received more than 19,527 write-in votes, Davis's 31,444-vote total ended her congressional career.

Gene Talmadge, meanwhile, spoke in the name of southern tradition: "I believe in treating the Negro right but I want to deal with them with their hats in their hands, saying 'yessir' and 'nosir.' "

The Jacksons had returned to Atlanta in the spring of 1945 when Rev. Maynard Jackson accepted the pastorate of Friendship Baptist Church, a west side congregation with deep roots in the Atlanta University Center. The first memorable moment in Atlanta for seven-year-old Maynard Jr. was sharing in the joy of VE Day at 540 Houston Street. That day white Atlantans broke out in celebration on Peachtree Street and black Atlantans did the same on Sweet Auburn Avenue. The Grand was dressed in his trademark baggy suit with the wide lapels, and wearing white socks (the dye in colored socks inflamed a skin condition) when he announced the German surrender to his children and grandchildren in solemn and dramatic terms. It was, he said, simply a victory for democracy and the greatest nation in the world. His daughter Millicent Dobbs Jordan, whose husband, Bob, was in the army in Europe, wept tears of joy. There were hugs and kisses and Irene Dobbs brought out the fine china and the white linen tablecloth. The Grand leaned back in his chair to elucidate about what the end of the war would mean for blacks in America.

Dobbs was thrilled to have Renie and Maynard back in Atlanta. Soon, they joined in the Dobbses' weekly family fish supper, which was held every Saturday afternoon at 540. In truth, the Saturday supper began in earnest on Thursday when the Grand, usually with one of his grandchildren in tow, visited the Hooper Fish Market on Sweet Auburn. There, he took advantage of his friendship with the proprietor by walking behind the counter and scrutinizing every piece of fish. His daughters and their families usually arrived at 540 sometime before three o'clock on Saturday. The political discussions began and soon books were spread across the tables and floor. Though his other five daughters dreaded the Grand's wrath—whenever Josie heard his car pull in front of her home in Atlanta she immediately put out her cigarette and gargled with mouthwash for fear of detection—Millie was different. At these Saturday suppers, she challenged her father freely, their heated debates causing the Grand's emotions to boil over. After supper, the Grand often practiced an upcoming speech. Standing before his brood, he hitched up his pants, tugged on his suspenders and marched across the room as he orated, like a leopard on the prowl. "Then he'd point his finger right in your face," Bill Clement, Sr., recalls. As the second son-in-law to have entered the Dobbs family, following the Rev. Maynard Jackson, Clement understood the Grand's animation and passions. Back in the fall of 1941, when Clement, then a widower with a four-year-old daughter, had arrived at Dobbs's Masonic office on Auburn Avenue with the intention of asking for Josie's hand in marriage, the Grand had gotten right to the point: "Bill, I know exactly what you're up to. Josephine is a good girl, so don't mistreat her. And if you ever get to the point in your marriage where you cannot live with her and make it, bring her back to me, please." Part mandate and part plea, the speech had impressed Clement, who viewed Dobbs as a role model and later became a Masonic grand master himself, in Durham, North Carolina.

For his first son-in-law, the Grand had great admiration. A kindred spirit, though less bombastic, Rev. Maynard Jackson had been a progressive dynamo in Dallas's black community during the 1930s. He had inherited the church dynasty begun in 1899 by his father and lived in the Jackson family's elegant three-story white-colonnaded home on the corner of Caddo Street and Roseland Avenue. Jackson had edited a black weekly newspaper, *The Dallas Express*, and served as executive secretary of the Negro Chamber of Commerce of Dallas. With his close friend A. Maceo Smith, he had formed in 1934 the Dallas Progressive Voters League, a vehicle for voter registration among those of his race. A decade later, Jackson founded the National Progressive Voters League during the Ozark Conference in Hot Springs, Arkansas, and persuaded the Grand to assume the presidency of its Georgia branch. "We are conscious of the dangerous possibilities in a society ruled too largely by little men," Jackson once wrote. "We who are of the minority of the intellectual must concern ourselves more and more about the size of men, men to match our needs." Jackson often carried a medallion in his pocket that had been given to him years earlier by his former Morehouse instructor Dr. John Hope. On it was a phrase from Tennyson: "I am a product of all that I have met."

To John Wesley Dobbs, Jackson's personal mettle was beyond question. Nothing had proved that point better than Jackson's unprecedented run for an at-large seat on the Dallas school board in 1944, the first such attempt by a black. His platform had called for improved black schools and an equalization of salaries among teachers based on ability and tenure. A victory for the Rev. Maynard Jackson, the candidate contended, "would be a timely and democratic negation of the Nazi thesis and would be a simple act of Southern justice."

The day before the election, the Texas courts had abolished the white primary in the state. Though the decision had no direct effect on the school board race, it served to heighten racial tensions. That night, hours before Jackson was scheduled to appear on a local radio program, Renie had answered the telephone at home.

"Is this where that nigger preacher lives?"

The crudeness of the voice startled her. Her husband was in the bathtub at the time, preparing for his appearance. "No, this is *Reverend Jackson's* residence," Renie replied.

"That's what I mean," the voice said. "You tell him if he goes on the radio tonight we're gonna kill him. You got that? We're gonna kill him!"

Renie did not want to alarm her husband but she had no choice. He contacted the Dallas police department but was told that extra security was not available. Undeterred, he vowed not to miss his radio appointment. Renie insisted she was going with him, so they decided to take their four children, Sandra, Jeanne, Maynard Jr. and Carol Ann, to the home of friends who lived in a nearby government housing project. As they opened the front door of their home that night, clutching their children, Maynard and Renie Jackson saw a sight they were never to forget. Surrounding their property were deacons from the New Hope Baptist Church, each holding a hunting rifle to protect the pastor and his family. The headlights of their cars illuminated the front yard, producing a mystical light.

Jackson lost his race for the Dallas school board, trailing the winner by an eight-to-one margin. His presence in the race had scared white voters. More than 25,000 votes were cast, tripling the amount in the previous election. Jackson captured only 2,783 votes in spite of an estimated black voting strength of more than 6,000. He told *The Dallas Times Herald* that many blacks had voted against him because their employers had asked them to do so, while other blacks, unfamiliar with voting machines, had voted against him by mistake. Despite this defeat, his six-year-old namesake son would carry one moment with him forever: lying beneath the covers in the Dallas projects, listening to his father's voice on the radio as it rose above personal concerns, high above the mountain of racial hatred.

In Atlanta, Friendship was an elite church, much like the one he had left in Dallas. Both had been formed by freedmen after the Civil War and had developed highly educated, silk-stocking congregations. At Friendship, black members arrived for their Sunday sermon on time, dressed to the nines and demanding from their preacher a delivery founded on cool reason and smart biblical research without the hysteria common to the lower-rung Baptists. Jackson's move was made as much for the future of his four children as for his own ministerial career. Atlanta offered a greater cultural and educational outlet for blacks than Dallas. In addition, the Atlanta University laboratory school, known as Oglethorpe Elementary School, had a fine reputation as a place where the master teachers taught the student teachers. In the process, it was said, the students thrived.

The transition to Atlanta was not an easy one for the Reverend Jackson. The board of deacons at Friendship had promised him a comfortable home. Instead, what he got was 451 Ashby Street, a small, drafty place on a hill, poorly suited for a family that soon would grow to six children. To reach the front door you had to climb twenty-seven cement steps, stopping at least once to catch your breath. Furthermore, replacing the Rev. E. R. Carter at Friendship was fraught with peril. Within black Atlanta, Carter had achieved a near-mythic status. Born a slave in 1858 in Athens, Carter had set out for Atlanta in 1879 on foot, until a train engineer recognized him walking along the track and took him the rest of the way. During his first two months in Atlanta, Carter slept in a piano box and used his overcoat as a cover. He later graduated from the Atlanta Baptist Seminary and was befriended by Henry Grady, also from Athens. When he replaced the late Rev. Frank Quarles in 1882 as pastor of Friendship, the mother of black Baptist churches in the city, Carter began a tenure that would stretch sixty-two years. In April 1942, an interracial crowd of five thousand filled the city auditorium to commemorate Carter's sixtieth anniversary. "Can this be the little boy who used to pick up bones and rags and sell them to buy a little bit to eat?" Carter asked rhetorically that day, gazing across the crowd. At Friendship, three generations of churchgoers had come of age knowing no other pastor. Carter once had announced his retirement but later changed his mind;

during his final years he had preached, and even performed wedding ceremonies, while seated in a chair.

Jackson escaped the pressures of Friendship by driving to Clayton in Rabun County, precisely 114 miles from his front door. He had purchased an old farmhouse in the mountains in the northeast corner of the state, inside the triangle between North Carolina and South Carolina. There, the Dobbs family held reunions and educators from Atlanta University came for the weekend to ride horses and hike in the mountains. Jackson had hoped to transform the farmhouse into a resort for blacks— Jackmont he called it, an abbreviation for Jackson Mountain—but like many of his business dreams it never materialized. The Jacksons made the trip to Clayton often on weekends and holidays. They had memorized the country roads. They used a rest room at the Gulf service station off the main square in Gainesville, the only one available to blacks for many miles. Sometimes they stopped at a grist mill near Clarkesville where a white family gave them lemonade and let them use their toilets. (Twenty years later, when Maynard Jackson, Jr., campaigned for the U.S. Senate, he met a member of this family. "The only two [white] votes I got in north Georgia," Maynard Jr. says, "came from that family.")

In Clayton, the Jackson children did not have to share their father with his congregation and they luxuriated in his presence. They walked country roads and climbed mountains with him. Maynard Jr., still a young boy, hunted with him, using his father's long-range Wonder with the laminated barrel. The girls fished with him. The Jacksons were living the life of Atlanta's black elite, although money was not abundant—in fact, it would be tight throughout his remaining years.

While fishing alongside streams, or while gathered at dinner in the large country kitchen, Reverend Jackson and his children analyzed the problems of race in Atlanta and in the South. It was the defining issue in their lives, so pervasive that on occasion all they could do was laugh about it. Sandra once saw a letter addressed to her father with a "Col." next to his name, an identification used in Georgia for people of color. "Daddy," she said, "I didn't know you were a *Colonel.*"

Yet most of the time, the conversation about race was stark. "How do you ever get over seeing a picture of a black man hung and burned with screaming mobs standing around laughing and joking?" Maynard Jr. would say years later. His father, and the Grand, had shown such pictures to him during his childhood. Their moral lessons were complex. "They were designed to make sure that I did not grow up a fool but at the same time that I did not grow up a hater," he recalls. "The lessons always ended with why I should not grow up to hate white people. Most white people don't have any idea the lengths to which black families went to train their children in the facts of life and the necessity of avoiding hate. You'd come home and have some kind of incident and you sit and talk with your parents and they had to reassure you that you were as good as anybody."

Rev. Maynard Jackson spoke directly to his children about the color of their skin and the texture of their hair. His children were "trained down" on the issue and told never to accept praise from other blacks for having *good hair* or *good color.* Reverend Jackson was proud of his heritage, but he knew what it was like to have the color of his skin called into question. With his dark wavy hair and strong Roman nose and Caucasian appearance, Greeks sometimes mistook him for a Greek, Jews mistook him for a Jew and Frenchmen mistook him for French. On too many occasions whites had stared at Rev. Maynard Jackson for prolonged periods and some had even stepped forward to ask, "What are you?" Once, he sat with Renie on a park bench in Atlanta and a policeman asked them to move. "This is for older people," he said. As they left, the minister shook his head. "That wasn't the reason he asked us to move. I've been in this park on all these benches and nobody bothered me because they thought I was white," he told Renie. "But the minute you're with me and we sit here and we act like we're happy, they come and move us." He told his son of another occasion in which he had struck up a conversation with a Jewish man. Jackson spoke a little Yiddish and, it seemed, the man mistook him for a Jew. As they were leaving, the man asked his name. "Maynard Jackson," he said. "No, what was your name really, before you changed it?" "No, it really is Maynard Jackson." "That," the Jewish man said, "is one of our problems. Too many of us change our name." Then he asked, "Well, what do you do, Maynard?" "I'm a Baptist minister." The reaction was immediate. *"You mean you've changed your name and denied your religion?"* Once the Reverend Jackson tried to "pass"—as part of a movement by blacks in Dallas to integrate the federal building and post office. "They'd send me in to ride the elevators," the minister later told his namesake son, "and I would just listen and pick up all types of information." Nearly a half century later, Maynard Jr. positively beamed about his father's role: "He was being a spy almost, an undercover civil rights activist!"

*What are you?* It was a question ripe with insensitivity and condescension. It was a question Maynard Jr. heard often as a child, both in Dallas and Atlanta, more than thirty times by his own estimate. Whites became confused, even upset, when they couldn't determine his race, though he, for one, never could understand that. While an infant, Maynard Jr. contracted scarlet fever and the family physician, Dr. James Jordan, filed the case at City Hall in Dallas, as required. "But Dr. Jordan, how do you know when a colored kid has scarlet fever?" a white city health official asked. Jordan explained carefully that you had to look a certain way, sometimes examining their hands or the soles of their feet. The health official was so fascinated he asked if he could see the afflicted black child, and bring two white doctors with him. When they appeared at the Jackson house they found a plump Maynard Jr., his whole olive-toned body turned scarlet.

"See," Dr. Jordan said, "they turn red!"

*What are you?* It was insulting but Maynard Jr. had his responses down pat.

Answer: "What do you mean 'What am I?' "

Question: "No, I mean, what *are* you?"

Answer: "I'm a human."

Question: "No, I mean what *nationality?*"

Answer: "I'm American."

Those summer days in Clayton, playing in the mountains, had a warm, buttery quality for the preacher's kids. Yet the race issue collared the Jacksons there as well. In the summer of 1946, on a one-lane road in the mountains of north Georgia, Reverend Jackson's courage was tested. This time, on returning home from Clayton, he used the lightness of his skin as his armor.

When he first spotted a slow-moving line of cars in the twilight he thought it a funeral procession. Each car had its headlights turned on. As he drew closer, though, he looked into the cars and saw the white sheets and hoods. His instincts told him to reveal no emotion. His wife sat next to him; his four children were in the back. Jackson slowly pulled his car off the road, onto a turnaround. He kept the ignition running. "Get down," he said, firmly, though quietly. No one inside the car moved at first. From the back seat, Sandra saw the Ku Klux Klan members inside the cars. They reminded her of ghosts. "It was almost like seeing the bogeyman incarnate," she says. "It was terrifying." Her father became firmer. "Everybody hit the floor," he commanded. The kids fell to the floorboards of the car. Renie pulled a shawl snugly around her head and turned her face from the cars. From the driver's seat, Jackson watched the cars pass slowly. The Klansmen looked over and saw him. To them, he looked white—that much, at this moment, he was counting on. Occasionally there was a break in the line of cars and Jackson pulled his station wagon back onto the mountain road. When more cars appeared behind him, their headlights aglow, he pulled to the roadside again to let them pass, until finally he made his way for home. As members of a protective black elite in Atlanta that allowed for hope and ambition, the

Jackson children learned from this experience that blacks in Georgia still faced frightening dangers. Their comfort and security was restored by a father who, they believed, could handle every such danger.

This lesson, like their father's moral ones, was more complex than they realized.

Martin Luther King, Jr., and his younger brother, A.D., were sprawled across the linoleum floor in the kitchen at 540. They owned Broadway and Park Place, dozens of tiny green houses and a few red hotels. It was the summer of 1946, the game was Monopoly and their opponents were Geekie and June Dobbs. A couple of Morehouse Men versus two Spelman girls. Together the foursome laughed a lot, and the Dobbs girls wondered why the King brothers always won. Only later did they discover that the Kings had been stuffing their pockets with Monopoly money from their game at home, then sneaking it into 540. They had known each other for some time; June and M.L., as he was known, both had graduated from high school in 1944, she from the private Atlanta Laboratory High and he from David T. Howard High, a public school. For a time both M. L. and A. D. King seemed to have a romantic interest in June Dobbs. One day, John Wesley Dobbs, notorious for interrogating the beaus of his older daughters, even asked June, "Which one of them has a crush on you?" She had to laugh. Entering his third year at Morehouse, M. L. King, Jr., was still pondering a career as a lawyer or a physician, despite his father's heartfelt hope that one day he would assume his pulpit at Ebenezer. Both M.L. Jr. and June worked one summer on a student project, interviewing Baptist ministers in Philadelphia for a monograph their professor was writing. "M.L. and I got to know each other; we got into sociology," June says.

The Grand noticed M. L. King's affinity for young ladies.

"M.L. says he wants to be a preacher like his daddy," Dobbs once said to Renie. "If so, he better learn to *put his feet together.*"

The Kings and Dobbses lived only a few blocks apart and had known each other for many years. As far back as the 1920s, the Dobbs daughters had heard their grandmother rave about Rev. A. D. Williams, the powerful preacher at the Ebenezer Baptist Church. His daughter, Alberta, had married the Rev. Martin Luther King, Sr. In 1941, the Kings had moved from their home on Auburn Avenue to 193 Boulevard Street, a house situated on the Fourth Ward's most celebrated avenue of black mansions, only a short walk from 540. Martin Luther King, Sr., and John Wesley Dobbs had much in common, though Dobbs was seventeen years older and significantly more polished as a public speaker. Both had risen from meager beginnings to establish their base of power on Sweet Auburn. Dobbs's Prince Hall building was two blocks west of King's Ebenezer Baptist Church. "Daddy" King, as he was known, had joined Dobbs's Civic and Political League's executive committee in 1938 and was named vice president in 1945; the two men fought together on behalf of bond issues, black schools and black teachers. The obstinate Daddy King once had refused to remove his shoes as part of the initiation ritual of the Prince Hall Masons; as a result, he never became one of Dobbs's Masons. "Reverend King," the Grand muttered to his brethren, "is a stubborn old man."

By the fall of 1947, M.L. Jr. had decided to pursue the ministry. He preached his trial sermon at Ebenezer and immediately was licensed to preach at the church. June attended one of his early sermons. Raised in the sober First Congregational Church, she considered his effort, and the reaction, quite remarkable. "All of a sudden Mrs. Lewis jumped up. I thought she had had an epileptic fit," June says. "No one came to her rescue. She was whooping and flailing her arms. Then I realized this was directly involved with what M.L. was saying. She was bearing witness." After the Grand heard young M. L. King speak, he hugged him and said, "Young man, you're gonna deliver. You've got the stuff!"

June 7, 1948, was a red-letter day in the history of the Dobbs family. On that day June became the last of the six Dobbs daughters to graduate from Spelman. President Florence Read presented the proud parents, John Wesley and Irene T. Dobbs, with "The Order of Sixes" award in honor of the "six dauntless Dobbs daughters of Spelman." *The Spelman Messenger,* a college publication, later wrote, "We know of no other instance in the history of colleges in America where six daughters have been graduated from one college." The other five Dobbs daughters were present at the occasion and rose to acknowledge the achievement. *The Atlanta Journal* even published a story about the Dobbs family on graduation day on the front page, a remarkable achievement for any black family in 1948. The story began, "An elderly Negro couple sat through the Spelman college commencement exercises Monday with tears of pride in their eyes."

Bill Hartsfield had a political debt to pay. *Get your ten thousand colored voters,* he had said, *and I'll get your Negro police.* At the time Hartsfield said it, it was not so much a promise as a stalling tactic. Delivering sewers and streetlights to substandard black neighborhoods was palatable to white voters. Delivering black police was quite a different matter since black police would signify the erosion of white supremacy. The idea of a black licensed to hold a gun scared white Atlantans. And the idea of a black licensed to hold a gun and invested with the authority to arrest whites terrified them.

Hartsfield and Police Chief Herbert T. Jenkins had held long private discussions about the subject during the spring and summer of 1947. Over the next quarter of a century Jenkins would become a key player in shaping the racial tone in Atlanta. Dobbs would develop a rapport with the chief. He liked and even trusted him. Jenkins was a hard-nosed cop, tough though even-handed, and some black leaders were able to strike deals with him. He was, like Hartsfield, an up-by-the-bootstraps leader who once had served as driver to Mayor Key. Jenkins was a third-generation Georgia law enforcement officer whose grandfather, a county sheriff, was gunned down in a shootout with an escaped prisoner and whose father was killed when his police motorcycle slammed into a utility pole on a rain-soaked Atlanta street. In 1931, Jenkins had followed the ritual of all Atlanta police recruits by joining the Shriners and the Ku Klux Klan. The Klan was "your ID card, the badge of honor with the in group," Jenkins later wrote. As part of the Klan initiation, Jenkins stood before a burning cross at nearby Stone Mountain, where the modern Klan was founded. At the time he joined the Atlanta force, Jenkins had never befriended a black man. During the middle 1930s, he once drove Mayor Key to the Friendship Baptist Church, where he met the Rev. E. R. Carter. It was the first time Herbert Jenkins ever shook hands with a black.

Not long after he was named Atlanta's chief of police, in February 1947, Jenkins toured police departments across the nation. He learned that blacks had been hired by police forces in the Northeast and in border state cities, such as Louisville, but that they represented a negligible part of the department, usually less than one percent. In backroom meetings, Hartsfield and Jenkins structured their deal, then searched for supporters, in part to share the blame if the black officers failed. Public hearings were held. The *Journal* and the *Constitution* became advocates. On December 1, 1947, the Atlanta City Council approved the hiring of the city's first eight black policemen.

The agreement was one of the great political masterstrokes by Hartsfield, who already faced a constant barrage of accusations of being a "nigger lover." The new black police were to patrol only black districts, such as Sweet Auburn and Vine City, the Fair Street bottom, Summerhill, Pittsburg and Mechanicsville. Black officers could not arrest whites: they were to page a white supervisor to handle the arrest. Black officers also were forbidden to use the downtown police station. They were to keep lockers in the basement of the Butler Street YMCA. They were required to remove their uniform the moment they went off-duty. (Hartsfield feared the mere sight of uniformed off-duty black police might stir whites.) For the first month of service, black officers were to work only one day per week to allow the community sufficient time to adjust to their presence.

What Hartsfield accomplished with this deal was no small achievement. He had maintained the increasingly thin veil of white supremacy while simultaneously allowing blacks a tangible sign of progress.

And Hizzoner was not about to miss an opportunity to play the showman. Hartsfield wanted to demonstrate to the black citizenry that he had delivered on his promise. With increasing frequency, he began to say, "I am a mayor for all of the people." Before a packed crowd at the Big Bethel AME Church on Auburn Avenue in the spring of 1948, Hartsfield started his scheduled address by signaling to the doorman, who threw open the back door of the church. Eight black policemen, in uniform, marched in public for the first time. "Electrifying" was how Clarence Bacote described the moment.

For years Ernest Lyons, a young black with aspirations to become an Atlanta policeman, frequently had asked John Wesley Dobbs, "Are we going to have Negro police soon, Mr. Dobbs?" Dobbs had smiled. "Not yet, Lyons. Not yet."

Now it was time. Their names were Willie T. Elkins, Willard Strickland, Robert McKibbens, Claude Dixon, Johnnie P. Jones, John Sanders, Jr., Henry Hooks and Ernest Lyons. With great anticipation more than four hundred blacks stood outside the Butler Street YMCA on April 3, 1948, for the first official patrol by black police in Atlanta. There was a collective sense of accomplishment, pride, even emancipation. Hartsfield and Jenkins stood in the basement of the YMCA. The mayor played the role of inspirational leader. He gave a pep talk to the eight black officers, who nervously stared at their shoetops, only moments before they were to emerge in full public view. "You are more than just policemen. You are going out as the first representatives of your race in Atlanta," Hartsfield told them. "Your success is my success and the success of the City Council, the Chief, your race and the city at large." He cited Jackie Robinson, who had broken the color barrier in baseball the year before and had risen to stardom despite the insults and racial epithets. "Do the kind of job that Jackie did in Brooklyn!" Hartsfield said, thrusting his fist into the air.

John Wesley Dobbs stood on the avenue of his dreams, Sweet Auburn, his ten-year-old grandson, Maynard Jackson, Jr., at his side. A group of black ministers, including King, Borders and Maynard Jackson, Sr., congregated across the street. Finally, the eight officers emerged, walking in four separate pairs. The crowd reacted initially with a stunned silence. Then an elderly black woman stepped forward with a bouquet of flowers in her hand. "Lord," she said, "I want to give this to those boys." Others then rushed forward to shake hands with the new officers. About a hundred blacks followed Officers Lyons and Dixon as they walked down to Edgewood Street and then over to Courtland Street. "I felt almost like a god," Lyons would say decades later. Hartsfield and Jenkins trailed behind the officers. Some blacks cheered while others, disdainful of the officers' authority to arrest only their own race, jeered, "Nigger police! Nigger police!"

Suddenly, Maynard Jr. heard his grandfather's voice rising above the crowd. "Great God A'mighty! Look at those black boys in those uniforms!" When his grandson looked up he saw that Grandpa Dobbs's eyes were as big as saucers. Here, in the broad strides of eight young colored men, was a revelation, a Second Coming, and this time the Messiah came in the form of the ballot. Just as the Grand had promised. Awed, Dobbs repeated himself, only this time louder: "GREAT GOD A'MIGHTY! LOOK AT THOSE BLACK BOYS IN THOSE UNIFORMS!" Here he was on Sweet Auburn, a race man at his pulpit. "It was the vote!" Dobbs said, speaking to no one in particular and everyone within earshot. "The Negro vote! That's what gave us these police officers." He said it was a shame that the officers were not allowed to put on their proud uniforms with white colleagues. "But this is still progress," Dobbs added, "and the other will come."

In the spring of 1948, as the glory of the ballot rained down upon black Atlanta, John Wesley Dobbs, the power broker who soon would be known as the unofficial mayor of Sweet Auburn Avenue, said to the crowd, "I never thought I'd see this day, but now I know of my hope!"

# CHAPTER 10

>‹

Theirs was more than merely a relationship between a father and son. It was a transference of traits and ambitions from a self-made civic leader to his only heir. The Senator had given his name to Ivan Jr. and had shaped him in his own image. Acts of ego, yes; but done with unswerving devotion. A sober-minded Presbyterian, the Senator was not one for dramatic public displays of emotion or affection. He did not kiss or warmly embrace his son; a firm handshake, a pat on the back and words of encouragement sufficed. This most traditional of men adored dancing with Irene at the Driving Club, hosting dinner parties at 2600 Peachtree Road and bragging about his son to friends at the Rotary Club.

The father and son shared few recreational interests. As a boy, Ivan Jr. had adored hunting and fishing as well as the New York Yankees with Babe Ruth and Lou Gehrig (he scoured the box scores in *The Atlanta Constitution* each morning). In contrast, the Senator's favorite pastimes were lunch with the city's business engines and gin rummy at the Capital City Club. His dark broad-cut suits dramatized his shock of white hair and gave him the appearance of a bishop—though perhaps a light-hearted, martini-drinking bishop at that, for during most lunch hours, he could be found at local civic clubs with his cronies, businessmen such as Walter Hill, J. P. Allen, Carlyle Fraser and Chevrolet dealer John Smith. Together, they toasted themselves as the men who had rebuilt Atlanta. When he wasn't having his name etched onto the cornerstone of another new building, the Senator was posing for students at the Atlanta College of Art, having offered a $100 prize for the best portrait of him. He then took his fourteen portraits ("They were all perfectly awful," Louise Allen, his daughter-in-law, recalls) and gave them away, one at a time, to the civic organizations around town that had invited him to speak. "I think he had a very fine ego," Louise says. The Senator cherished his annual birthday lunch each March with Mayor Bill Hartsfield, Coca-Cola's Bob Woodruff and the Trust Company banker Bob Strickland— and he always brought Ivan Jr. with him. "I want you three fellows to know that I value your friendship and your affection and it is going to be worth our time to cultivate each other," he wrote in a letter to Hartsfield in February 1945. Of their birthday lunch, he added, "For the meeting next year, March 1, 1946, downtown at one of the clubs, or if the servant proposition improves, I would like to have . . . us at my home." Outside of his realm, the Senator seemed lost. Once, Ivan Jr. saw his father leaving for a rare hunting trip and thought to himself, *"Daddy looks like he's dressed to go golfing!"* Though the Senator's passion was history, especially his prized collection of valuable maps, his son thought it all painfully boring. When the Senator and Irene took fourteen-year-old Ivan Jr. to Europe in 1925 they had dragged him to business banquets and too many museums and cathedrals. Years later Louise would say the Senator had "actually ruined Ivan for traveling." If the Senator's affection for his son went largely unspoken, it yet was understood. "He was always very patient with me," Ivan Jr. says.

*"To the Greatest Dad In The World. Love, Ivan."* Only a boy when he signed the card on Father's Day, Ivan Jr. always felt love and respect for his father, admiring most his energy, optimism and strength. Ivan Jr. called him "Daddy" throughout his life, even as an adult, in the tradition of southern sons. In later years, Ivan Jr. would say he had not made the conscious decision to reenact his father's civic career, though reenact it he did. Nearly every move Ivan Jr. made in his first fifty years, his father had made before him.

The force of the Senator's personality was greater than Ivan Jr. was willing to admit. "Ivan was always very responsive to his father," Louise says. "I honestly don't think he ever bucked him." The Senator's influence was impossible to deny. The father became an enduring civic and political guidepost for the son.

Ivan Jr. had been taught by the Senator how to think (with optimism), how to vote (Democratic) and how to conduct himself in Atlanta (with civic devotion).

The Senator and Ivan Jr. took the train to Chicago for the 1940 Democratic National Convention. It became a Roosevelt lovefest, a celebration of a president who, despite the concerns of party conservatives, sought an unprecedented third term. A tried and true Roosevelt man, the Senator was an FDR delegate. When FDR was governor of New York, the Senator had written to inquire about the issue of home mortgage foreclosures. FDR later had appointed him to the board of the Federal Home Loan Bank in Winston-Salem, North Carolina. Over the years, the Senator had met with FDR several times at Warm Springs. Already he had signed on to chair the presidential campaign in Georgia in 1940.

As a young man, the Senator's ambition was to become governor of

Georgia. He had hoped that if his office supplies business prospered—it
now had branches in several Georgia cities—he might use that success as
a springboard into politics. But he never made the break from business,
fearing that his absence, even for a short time, might prove calamitous.
Business always came first. Even at age sixty-four, when most men consider
retirement, his business intensity remained unflagging and his tone often
turned severe. Upon discovering that Atlanta and Fulton County had purchased new steel voting machines from a firm in New York rather than from
the Ivan Allen-Marshall Company, the Senator telephoned Charlie Brown,
a county commissioner. "My company pays taxes to the city and county and
you should have bought the machines from me rather than sending off to
New York for them," he said. "Hold on, Mr. Allen," Brown said. "The decision wasn't mine. It was made by a committee named for that sole purpose.
I can't influence their decision." The Senator blurted: "Yes, you can." His
bullying often worked; this time, it did not.

His time to run for governor had passed. Now, to the Senator's friends
this much was clear: he was grooming his son to be governor.

In 1940, Ivan Jr. was twenty-nine years old, with a wife and namesake
son of his own, and a second son on the way, to be named Hugh Inman in
honor of Louise's family. Already Ivan Jr.'s marriage had moved him fully
inside the corridors of monied power in Atlanta. Each Christmas eve, he
and Louise attended a dinner for the extended family at the estate of
Louise's uncle John Grant. Grant rated among the standard-bearers of
Atlanta's old-guard elite. He had prospered not only in banking and real
estate but also by having married Annie Inman. In 1905, Grant's father-
in-law, Hugh T. Inman, had given him a memorable gift, the Kimball
House hotel. Inman owned nearly all the stock in the venerable downtown hotel; he required only that Grant manage the property, which
Grant was only too pleased to do. The Grants' breathtaking estate,
Craigellachie, stood on the rolling wooded acreage of West Pace's Ferry
Road. On Christmas eve, the Inmans, Allens, Richardsons and Grants
stepped inside the octagonal stone vestibule of Craigellachie and heard
the echoes as the great front doors closed behind them. There, on
Christmas Eve, 1938, Ivan III was christened. Arriving for a Christmas
feast, the family sang carols with the elder Grants—"Dearie" and "Big
Papa" to the younger generation—and stared with bright-eyed wonder
at the spectacular tree cut on the grounds of the estate. Lighted candles
illuminated the tree. Concealed behind the branches was a black butler
with a large bucket of water, just in case a flame caught.

His friends knew Ivan Jr. as a natural leader, sharp-witted, occasionally smug and uncommonly gifted at golf, a game he refined at the Capi-

tal City Club at Brookhaven. The spirit of noblesse oblige had been impressed upon him as upon most of his closest friends also born to privilege. They had been given much in life and understood that they, in turn, were expected to give much back. Politics provided a logical outlet. Ivan Jr. had worked in state government in the Gov. Eurith Rivers administration and, through his father, had tasted Democratic party national politics. As a member of Rivers's staff in 1937, Ivan Jr. had worn his honorary uniform with his leather boots and Sam Browne belt and had taken a special train to Washington for Roosevelt's inaugural.

Now, as he planned his future, in his ear he heard his father's voice.

The governor's mansion in Ansley Park had not been occupied by an Atlantan since Hugh Dorsey twenty years earlier. The rural antipathy for Atlanta had convinced most Atlantans that hell would freeze before a man from Atlanta would sit again in the governor's chair. Ivan Jr. knew this but liked the challenge that the governor's mansion presented.

Since Reconstruction, Democrats had held sway in Georgia, but now a new breed of Democrats emerged. Well educated, well heeled and, for the most part, from Atlanta, they recognized the decline of the cotton culture and the astonishing growth of the urban centers. These Democrats aspired to drive Georgia into the nation's mainstream. "The better element" is how they were known in the political vernacular of the times, and the Senator and Ivan Jr. counted themselves among them. If Roosevelt represented their champion on the national level, then Gene Talmadge, with his refusal to acknowledge the demographic shift to the cities, represented their nemesis in Georgia. For years Talmadge had waged a mean-spirited campaign against the New Deal. His contempt for FDR was legendary. Once, he reportedly said, "The next president we have should be able to walk a two-by-four." (Of this crude stab at the polio-stricken president, members of the Talmadge machine claimed either that Old Gene had been misquoted or that he wanted a president who would take more moderate positions.) A self-proclaimed champion of "the common man," Talmadge's true devotion was to big business. He had tried to subvert New Deal funds pegged for Georgia, and had termed the thousands of unemployed workers "bums and loafers," yet still won reelection in 1934. Talmadge and Louisiana governor Huey Long tried to prevent Roosevelt's reelection in 1936 by splitting the Democrats' Solid South. A grassroots convention was called in Macon to name a third presidential candidate. But Long was assassinated and Talmadge's bid failed. Though Talmadge lost races for the U.S. Senate against Richard B. Russell in 1936 and Walter F. George in 1938, he returned for a third term as Georgia's governor in 1940. There were indications, however, that his popularity among big business, including the Atlanta power companies and banks, was diminishing.

Old Gene cracked his despotic whip once too often in 1941. Stacking the state board of regents with men who answered his every command, Talmadge prompted the firing of two university educators. One, Dr. Walter R. Cocking, had been hired from out of state to study and improve the troubled School of Education at the University of Georgia (UGA). Cocking made recommendations that hinted broadly at integration. His study had been funded by the Rosenwald Fund, a liberal philanthropic foundation in the North. Sitting in Atlanta's WSB radio studio on July 25, 1941, Talmadge defended the firings. In the process, he invoked the names of the most illustrious orators of Georgia's political past. "I love the University of Georgia. I showed it. I sent my only son there. And I love the university enough to put up a fight for it when I think that any foreign element is trying to destroy the great traditions of that grand institution," Talmadge said. "We welcome people to come to our state. But we don't want them to come here to try and change our ideals of democracy, our ideals of humanity, our ideals of education. We don't want them to come here to try to make us believe that Alexander Stephens, Bob Toombs, Henry W. Grady, Thomas E. Watson, and a long list of others that I could name, were ignorant, prejudiced, Negro-haters." The firings triggered a controversy that overtook the governor. On October 14, the University of Georgia was stripped of its accreditation by the Southern University Conference, which represented all liberal arts colleges in the South. The conference conducted an investigation of the firings and determined that Cocking had been removed unjustly by a governor "with a chip on his shoulder." With typical vitriol, Talmadge, in a speech at the Ansley Hotel in Atlanta, told the Sons and Daughters of the Confederacy, "If foreign elements would just leave us alone down South, we'd get along all right." The next day hundreds of UGA students protested against the governor on the steps of the State Capitol. Their placards read, "To Hell With Talmadge" and "Why Can't You Be A Good Alumnus, Gene?" The national press feasted on Georgia's demagogue. "Here in the heart of Dixie," *The St. Louis Post-Dispatch* editorialized, "has developed a prize specimen of full-blown American fascism. . . ."

Once again, Talmadge seemed vulnerable. By autumn 1941, with war raging in Europe, the better element of the Democratic party in Georgia searched for a new, more progressive voice, a reformer whose vision and personal distaste for Gene Talmadge mirrored their own. Seizing the opportunity provided by the UGA fiasco, Ellis Arnall, the young state attorney general, announced his candidacy for governor. His promise to undo the damage wrought by the Talmadge machine made him a natural fit with the better element.

Roosevelt called out the reserves in December 1941, following the Japanese attack on Pearl Harbor. The following spring Ivan Jr. was in uniform in the headquarters of the Fourth Service Command in Atlanta. Far from battle, he spent nights at home. The Senator did not stand by idly. He served as Georgia's sugar administrator, a role related to FDR's federal rationing program, and through his work in the Atlanta chamber's industrial division helped lure the Bell bomber plant to Marietta.

When Arnall blitzed the Talmadge machine in the all-white Democratic primary of 1942, he became, at thirty-five, the nation's youngest governor. Ellis and Mildred Arnall, living in the governor's mansion in Ansley Park, soon became social friends of Ivan Jr. and Louise. Over dinner, the governor and Ivan Jr. shared stories of their earliest meetings. Arnall had been a student leader at the UGA Law School when Ivan Jr. was student body president at Georgia Tech. In April 1943, Arnall effected the transfer of Maj. Ivan Allen, Jr., to direct the field division of the Selective Service System. "They were having considerable trouble drafting farm boys," Ivan Jr. recalls. His new job was to change that. He crisscrossed Georgia, visiting every county, work that raised his gubernatorial aspirations by providing him with a broad understanding of the state. The cushiness of his role embarrassed him, though. While some of his closest friends served on naval aircraft carriers and destroyers, Ivan Jr. sat behind his desk in the Hurt Building at Five Points. "I did what I was told to do," he says. "I never felt very happy over it. I felt I wasn't making as great a contribution as I could have made."

The Japanese surrender was nearly formalized on August 20, 1945, when Arnall again intervened on behalf of Ivan Jr. This time, the governor maneuvered through the secretary of war in Washington to gain his military discharge, freeing Ivan Jr. to become his executive secretary at the statehouse. Ivan Jr. sounded like an aspiring politician when he told *The Atlanta Constitution,* "I've learned first-hand of the splendid character of our people and of the splendid way they have met all of the contingencies of the war effort. I've learned, too, of the land and of the resources of our state and of the wonderful opportunities, both in agriculture and in industry, that lie ahead of us. All we have to do is take advantage of them."

Working in the statehouse, he cultivated contacts in the legislature and studied the machinations of statewide power. He developed a friendship with the state revenue commissioner, M. E. Thompson, a future governor, and occasionally hunted with him. The only problem with the job was that it ended, abruptly, after six months with a phone call from the Senator.

Like all calls from his father, this one was blunt and to the point. His long-term business partner, Charles Marshall, in poor health, had decided to retire from the Ivan Allen-Marshall Company. The Senator needed his son to return to the company. Ivan Jr. knew the equation. *Politics was important, but the family business was all-important.* With apologies to the governor, Ivan Jr. resigned as executive secretary on March 1, 1946. By coincidence, that day was the Senator's seventieth birthday—though the proud, self-conscious man admitted to only sixty-nine. Hoping to keep his competitive edge, Ivan Allen, Sr., claimed to have been born in 1877, one year later than he truly was.

The Senator once boasted of his son, "I think one of the most outstanding things about him is the ease with which he makes friends and money. He seems to do both naturally." As the pace of business in America quickened in the postwar years, Ivan Jr. sought new opportunities for the company. He purchased surplus merchandise from army posts, including a trainload of steel shelving that had been used in Warner Robins, Georgia, and dumped in Macon. Since virtually all production of steel had been geared to the war effort, suddenly there developed an enormous demand for it. The purchase orders began to pour in from across the nation to the Ivan Allen-Marshall Company offices. "You could sell it at almost any price," Ivan Jr. says. The company's profits caused even the Senator to raise a brow in admiration for his son's acumen.

Atlanta's commercial landscape was dotted with family businesses, the foremost being Rich's department store, which had been founded by Hungarian Jews in 1867. As the Ivan Allen-Marshall Company approached its golden anniversary, it was among the city's most prominent family businesses. By 1949, it had more than two hundred employees, in excess of ten thousand charge customers and annual revenues of several million dollars. As bustling Atlanta grew, the office supplies company grew with it. "An office outfitter needs a medium-sized city," the Senator said. "In the little towns there's not enough business and in the big cities the factories have their own branch offices and do their selling direct." When Charles Marshall died without heirs in 1948, he bequeathed his half of the company to Ivan Jr., giving the Allen family ownership of the firm.

The Senator employed a handful of blacks, all of whom worked in the basement storage room. He particularly liked John Henry Hector, who had started at the company at thirteen and remained for decades. The Senator's paternal warmth for Hector was apparent years later when, while posing for a picture in the basement, he threw his arms around him and announced, "We've been here almost the same length of time. He runs this store. And this"—the Senator motioned broadly to the basement—"is where the Ivan Allen Company does its real business!" The Senator valued Hector's loyalty and in his will would leave him $1,000.

Were he not the Senator's son, the volume of civic and charitable services done by Ivan Jr. during these years might have seemed startling. He was a director of the Bank of Georgia, a trustee at the Georgia Tech Research Institute, an executive board member of the state's Family Welfare Society and of the Atlanta YMCA, president of the Young Democrats Club of Georgia and president of the local Boy Scouts Council. His name appeared in the newspapers with regularity, usually a notice about his civic endeavors.

In peacetime, the growing belief in America was that prosperity would be perpetual. Atlanta's city elites were too busy making money to detect the first rumblings of challenge to the city's existing social order.

Certainly Ivan Jr. did not attach any sociological significance when two blacks issued a golf challenge to him and Charles Dannals, Jr., his old friend from the Sigma Alpha Epsilon fraternity at Georgia Tech. Their names were Booker and John—Ivan Jr. and Dannals never could remember their last names. Booker served as caddie master at the Capital City Club golf course, in charge of the blacks who carried golf clubs and bags for white members. John cleaned the clubs in the back of the pro shop. Though blacks were not allowed to play on the segregated course, Booker and John called for a head-to-head competition. Ivan Jr. and Dannals were sufficiently intrigued and convinced the club professional to allow for the interracial match. The club professional made one stipulation: the challenge match had to be played at an obscure hour so club members would never know it had taken place.

The agreed-upon time all but assured secrecy. Not only would they play on Monday, when the course was closed, they would start at dawn.

When Ivan Jr. and Charles Dannals appeared on the appointed Monday, virtually every black caddie was there to support Booker and John. Some of the fifty caddies were high school students; others had gray hair and tired, leathery faces. Typically, these caddies earned 75 cents a round working for white members, with tips maybe a dollar. The only supporter on hand for Ivan Jr. and Dannals was Dannals's father, Charles Sr., a milling company executive who had known the Senator for nearly forty years, since the race riot days when they shared the same downtown boardinghouse.

Booker and John had fast, unorthodox golf swings and the distance of their tee shots exceeded that of their white opponents. "Booker could knock the tar out of a golf ball," says Dannals, who once had won the Atlanta Amateur Championship and would play with Bob Jones at the East Lake Country Club. A determined golfer, Ivan Jr. played a conservative game with an occasional burst of aggressiveness. In the challenge match against the two blacks, Dannals's putting provided the margin of victory. No money was gambled on the outcome. It was, after all, simply a challenge. "They were very humble darkies," Dannals recalls fondly.

The match was the first confrontation with blacks that Ivan Jr. had experienced in his lifetime. It did not leave a lasting impression. "It was just a way of life," he says.

For the time being, steel shelving had more relevance.

In December 1946, three weeks before returning to the statehouse, sixty-two-year-old Gene Talmadge, having been elected to a fourth term as governor, died before taking office.

His death set off a scramble to replace him and revealed to the nation the seamy, bawdy underside of Georgia politics. Talmadge had captured enough county unit votes to overcome the plurality won by James Carmichael, a two-term legislator from Marietta. The Talmadge machine had preached white supremacy in its campaign against Carmichael and former governor Eurith Rivers, calling for restoration of the all-white Democratic primary and the preservation of the county unit system. Before a speech in Moultrie, Carmichael discovered that thousands of leaflets spread throughout the black community invited his "colored friends" to a barbecue. Uncertain which rival campaign concocted the stunt, Carmichael could only reiterate his segregationist platform. Privately, he seethed.

No governor-elect of Georgia had ever died before taking office; succession was unclear. M. E. Thompson, who had won the primary for the newly created position of lieutenant governor, staked his claim. A former schoolteacher from Millen, Thompson contended that once he was sworn in as lieutenant governor the new state constitution made him the rightful successor. But Herman Talmadge, Gene's thirty-three-year-old son and manager of his father's campaign, also wanted the job. The young Talmadge bore a striking resemblance to his father—including the same unruly black forelock—and pledged to carry out his father's platform. He based his claim upon a provision in the state constitution that specified the legislature must elect a replacement for the deceased governor-elect from the two candidates who had received the highest number of write-in votes in the election. The initial write-in count gave

Carmichael 669 votes, Republican D. Talmadge Bowers (a salesman of tombstones) 637 and Herman Talmadge 617, an amount that would have eliminated the third-place Talmadge. But a recount of the write-in votes from Telfair County, home of the Talmadge machine, dramatically uncovered an additional fifty-eight write-in votes for Herman Talmadge. That moved him into first place, six votes ahead of Carmichael, who already had withdrawn his name from the gubernatorial derby to pursue private business interests. Years later, Herman Talmadge would say of that write-in campaign, "If I couldn't keep Papa from dying, at least I could keep him from dying in vain."

During the next fortnight, the M. E. Thompson and Herman Talmadge forces set up headquarters at the Henry Grady Hotel on Peachtree Street. Though the state attorney general ruled on January 5, 1947, that Thompson legally was entitled to become governor, Talmadge exerted enough pressure on rural legislators to win a late-night vote in the general assembly. With a swagger reminiscent of Old Gene, Hummon, as he was known fondly to his supporters, was sworn in as governor, only minutes after the vote was taken, at two o'clock in the morning on January 15 in the chambers of the Georgia House of Representatives. Then, with his entourage whooping up his victory, Talmadge marched to the second floor of the Capitol to take over the governor's office. There are different versions as to what happened next. His supporters either broke through the locked, heavy wooden doors, or somehow managed to find a spare key. Inside the inner offices, they came upon Gov. Ellis Arnall, who by state law had been unable to succeed himself as governor; one of Arnall's staffers stood by his side. Arnall refused to surrender his office. Arnall intended to remain as governor for four more days, at which point he would resign his position to M. E. Thompson. "Tell 'em, Herman!" Talmadge supporters shouted from the hallways. *"Throw 'em out!"* Arnall called Talmadge "a pretender." Still a political novice, Talmadge, with his mother, Mattie "Miss Mitt" Talmadge, at one side, turned to the man at his other side, Roy V. Harris, the deposed speaker of Georgia's House of Representatives and lead strategist in Old Gene's recent campaign. Harris whispered intermittently into Herman Talmadge's ear. In an adjacent office a fistfight broke out between supporters of the two governors. Already Talmadge had begun to make official appointments, and one of his appointees, Adj. Gen. Marvin Griffin, immediately cleared the room of the combatants. Roy Harris mounted a windowsill and calmed the Talmadge supporters. "I know you're happy over this great victory but we want you to leave quietly now. We do not want disorder or trouble." When the governor's office opened the next morning, the Talmadge staff moved in and physically removed Arnall's secretaries. One Talmadge man told a telephone caller for Arnall, "He is no longer governor . . . I don't know where he is . . . I think he is selling insurance." The Talmadge men later changed the locks on the doors. Arnall's only response was to set up a temporary office at the information booth inside the rotunda of the Capitol. It made for an outlandish sight.

Now there were two governors of Georgia with a third, M. E. Thompson, waiting for the state courts to approve him. On January 18, Arnall carried out his plan by resigning as governor even as Thompson was sworn in as both lieutenant governor and acting governor. Meanwhile, Talmadge continued to make appointments and formulate policy. On March 2, six weeks after Talmadge had assumed the role of governor, *The Atlanta Journal* loosened his precarious grip on state government by reporting that the fifty-eight write-in votes he had received in Telfair County were a sham. Some of the write-in voters were residents who had died or moved from the county; thirty-four voters were cited in alphabetical order. "It appeared impossible that 34 citizens anywhere could have appeared at the polls and been voted in alphabetical order, starting with the first letter and stopping abruptly at K," reporter George Goodwin of *The Atlanta Journal* wrote in his Pulitzer Prize–winning account. Soon after, the Georgia Supreme Court declared Thompson governor and Herman Talmadge's sixty-three-day reign ended.

The better element of the Democratic party was thrilled by Thompson's victory. Thompson's largest campaign contributor was Ivan Allen, Jr., his occasional hunting companion, who contributed $1,000. Ivan Jr. later cracked to Thompson that "it was the cheapest that anybody had ever bought a governor." Thompson made Ivan Jr. his chief of staff. During Thompson's abbreviated eighteen-month term (a special gubernatorial election was arranged in the fall of 1948 to coincide with the next scheduled statewide election), Ivan Jr. worked in statewide affairs, particularly in education. His own gubernatorial ambitions were apparent. Despite, or perhaps because of, the fiasco of 1947, Herman Talmadge had won many followers. He returned with a vengeance in the 1948 Democratic primary. Though he won only 53 percent of the ballots against Thompson, Talmadge won the county unit vote by more than a three-to-one margin.

For the next dozen years in Georgia, state government was dominated by Talmadge, Marvin Griffin and S. Ernest Vandiver. All fought a spirited and defiant battle for segregation in the face of a rising civil rights movement. Out of step with Georgia voters, the better element of the Democratic party quietly receded.

*     *     *

To the men who wanted power in Atlanta, leading the annual Community Chest charity drive was a rite of passage. A devoted son of the city, Ivan Jr. co-chaired the Community Chest drive in the fall of 1949 with Rock G. Taber, president of the Atlanta Gas Company. Their experience foreshadowed the racial dramas ahead.

Traditionally, the Community Chest paid the $500 National Urban League dues for the Atlanta branch and its director, Grace Hamilton. But now, as the white men on the Community Chest funding committee formulated the annual budget, several members charged that the Atlanta Urban League was a communist organization bent on funding the black rights movement. Only recently Ivan Jr. had met Grace Hamilton. He knew that her husband was a registrar at Atlanta University and that the Hamiltons were among the most respected black families in Atlanta. Beyond that, he liked her. After a brief discussion, though, the committee voted against Allen's advice and eliminated the $500 donation.

Whites and blacks raised funds separately for the Community Chest. The races had separate staffs, separate report meetings and separate expectations. Blacks were expected to contribute about $30,000 to a drive that, Ivan Jr. hoped, would reach $1,250,000. Ivan Jr. invited L. D. Milton, president of the Citizens Trust Bank, to serve as chief of the black division. Once Milton accepted, Ivan Jr. did not expect to see him again until the drive concluded. But several days after his appointment, Milton visited the Ivan Allen-Marshall Company offices. A self-impressed man of pedigree, Milton had been raised in Washington, D.C., and graduated from Brown University. Morehouse president John Hope had lured him to Atlanta in 1920 to direct the college's Department of Economics. After marriage to the daughter of David T. Howard, Atlanta's leading black mortician, Milton in 1926 began a forty-three-year tenure as president of the Citizens Trust Bank. He moved the bank's offices from Sweet Auburn to Piedmont Avenue to be nearer whites so they would "see Negroes advancing and growing and so they wouldn't get it in their minds that a Negro was somebody they could push around." As Ivan Jr. listened to Milton in his office, he realized this black man's education was superior to his own.

Then Milton said something shocking: "We'd like for you and Mr. Taber to come to our opening dinner." The request was unprecedented. White leaders of the Chest had never associated with blacks. And L. D. Milton knew it. "We think it would be a great help," Milton said. He told Ivan Jr. to discuss the matter with Taber, then departed.

Ivan Jr. did not want to make a mistake. He was thirty-eight years old, on the rise. One day he hoped to become governor. Maybe going to the dinner would be a mistake. *Maybe not going would be a mistake.* The worst mistake he could possibly commit was to transform a simple civic stepping-stone into a crisis that would bring into question his integrity. He sought outside counsel. He saw Clark Howell, Jr., publisher of the *Constitution*, and George Biggers, editor and publisher of the *Journal*. As newspaper-men, they shaped public opinion and had their fingers on the pulse of the city. But neither editor spoke decisively about the matter. "They quibbled over the decision and left me somewhat in a quandary," Ivan Jr. says.

Then he sought out his own trusted fountain of wisdom: the Senator. Ivan Jr. spelled out the problem. "Ivan," the Senator replied as he sat back in his chair, "let me have a very honest discussion with you." It was the first conversation between the Senator and his son about the way blacks in the South had been wronged. The Senator left no doubt this was a regional problem. He said mistreatment of blacks had restricted the South's business growth. He referred to "that banker Milton" and then spoke of "the Niggers," using the term in a casual, conventional way. The Senator said to his son, "My generation has failed in every way to enlighten or solve the major issue which our section of the country has—the racial issue. We haven't confronted ourselves with it. There is great prejudice, great trial and tribulation over the whole thing. We've kept the Nigger not in a second-class but a third- or fourth-class position and, as a result, we've impoverished him and we've impoverished this section of the country."

The Senator's tone was one of regret. He had given the subject deep thought and now expressed his views clearly and forcefully. "Here we are advocating human decency and freedom all over the world and we find ourselves with dirty skirts at home. It's time for some major changes."

Then the seventy-three-year-old patriarch made a prediction so unsettling that his son would cite it, verbatim, nearly a half century later: "Your generation is going to be confronted with it, and it will be the greatest agony that any generation ever went through."

Already, Ivan Jr. was experiencing agony over the dinner invitation. "Ivan," the Senator said, finally, "you should certainly go to this dinner."

Ivan Jr. noticed a thin smile on his father's face.

"Daddy, I'll do what you say, but what is it you're smiling about?"

"Well, I'm sending you," he said, "but I don't think that I would have the courage to go."

Ivan Jr. and Rock Taber appeared at the Savoy Hotel on Auburn Avenue promptly at seven o'clock on October 14, 1949, for the dinner of the black division. Like so many other structures along Auburn, the Savoy was in disrepair and in the upstairs ballroom the air felt stale and leaden. Sitting at the head table, they felt the eyes of the five hundred blacks in the ballroom scrutinizing their every move, searching for those telltale signs that would indicate their degree of sincerity. *Will these whites eat our food and drink our drink? Will they shake our black hands?* Small details, perhaps, but to southern blacks these were litmus tests of true goodwill. Ivan Jr. ate dinner with little sign of approval. ("Just acceptable," he later termed the food, "but that's all.")

Community Chest report meetings tended to be dull affairs that always ended on time. This meeting, however, was altogether different from any Ivan Jr. had experienced. It seemed more like a party. Announcements of every small pledge—pledges so small, in fact, they would not have merited an announcement at white report meetings—prompted raucous cheering and celebration. On this night, more than $5,000 was pledged. "A good beginning," the *Daily World* called it. Speeches by the team captains of the black drive were long-winded, prompting Ivan Jr. to wonder if this was their first public speaking opportunity, their last, or both. This Community Chest drive was known as "The Red Feather Drive" and in the front row of the Savoy Hotel sat a rotund black woman. She wore a tight blue knit dress covered with red paper feathers. She seemed like a spiritual siren, leaping from her chair at each pledge and shouting, "Hallelujah, A-men!" Ivan Jr. thought, *"So this must be what it is like in all of those African Methodist Episcopal churches . . ."* The woman made Rock Taber uncomfortable. "You're going to have to be careful about how you handle *that* situation," he whispered to Ivan Jr.

After a brief speech by Taber, Ivan Jr. followed with his trademark pep talk, the sort he would give often in the next dozen years. When the meeting ended, a line of blacks formed in front of the two white guests. It resembled a receiving line at a wedding. This, Ivan Jr. understood, was the blacks' way of expressing gratitude for coming to the Savoy.

During handshaking that seemed to last as long as the meeting itself, the rotund black woman in the blue dress with red feathers swept around the receiving line. Taber again whispered to Ivan Jr., "You'd better watch out, she's coming up front." Ivan Jr. lost sight of her until he half-turned and felt her meaty arms squeezing his neck in a loving embrace.

"Lawd, God, chillun," she bellowed, with Ivan Jr. lost inside her massive black arms, "this is *my baby*. I WAS HIS MAMMY'S NURSE THE NIGHT HE WAS BRUNG INTO THIS WORLD!"

Ivan Jr. did not know what to say. Bertha Lewis, for that was her name, some thirty-eight years earlier had served as midwife at his birth when

Dr. Nicholas Earnest, the family physician, failed to make it in time to the Allens' home on West Peachtree. He had not seen her since the day of his birth. What to say? *Nice to see you. Thank you for coming.* He stumbled over those few words.

"The greatest agony that any generation ever went through," the Senator had predicted. At this moment, Ivan Jr. felt not agony but rather something akin to regret. Like most of Atlanta's young elite, he had been raised with black servants in his home and still clung to notions of white superiority. But he also shared a historic closeness with blacks, a closeness that did not exist in northern cities or in less prosperous southern towns. That closeness, sometimes transformed into paternal affection, stemmed from guilt as much as from compassion. A few days later Ivan Jr. wrote a check for $500, from the Ivan Allen-Marshall Company account, to Grace Hamilton, for her National Urban League dues.

Bertha Lewis walked out of the Savoy Hotel that night with the rest of the crowd and Ivan Jr. never spoke with her, or saw her, again.

# Chapter 11

In 1950, Floyd Hunter, a graduate student in sociology at the University of North Carolina, conducted an intensive study of Atlanta's community "power structure." "I find that it will be necessary to run a separate study in the Negro community," Hunter wrote. "There is a power structure there that cannot be overlooked." While Coca-Cola Company president Bob Woodruff sat at the apex of power on the white side, aloof yet almighty, the black community had at its apex the socially reclusive Norris B. Herndon, president of Atlanta Life and son of the founder. Like Woodruff, Herndon operated through other men and did not actively participate in local civic groups. Through these civic operatives, Woodruff and Herndon pushed the necessary buttons to get deals done. The primary distinguishing factor between the city's separate leadership structures was that white leaders tended to be men of commerce and industry while black leaders largely were professionals or ministers who were politically oriented. In his role as a black plenipotentiary, Dobbs had no contact with the city's white business leaders, only its politicians, such as Hartsfield or Police Chief Herbert Jenkins, men who were subordinate to the top tier of white leadership.

Nearing seventy, the Grand looked the part of a political boss. He wore a three-piece suit decorated with a gold Masonic stickpin and a handsome watch with a chain that dangled from his vest pocket—the appearance of a man to be reckoned with. His name recognition in the black community, particularly among postal workers, was such that Hartsfield once bet him that he could mail a letter from Europe to "John Wesley Dobbs, U.S.A." and it would find its mark; when the letter arrived at Dobbs's office on Auburn Avenue, the Grand lost the bet. (Years later, Dobbs sent a letter from Europe to "William B. Hartsfield, U.S.A." and it arrived at Atlanta City Hall.) In his friskier moments, Dobbs played "Maple Leaf Rag" on the piano at 540 and his wife and daughters thrilled to his playful rhythm. During these years, he swept down Sweet Auburn with his Masonic entourage and patted small boys on their heads along the way. At the shoeshine stand, he broke into his favorite refrain: *"In Memphis it is Beale Street, in Nashville it is Cedar* and *Seventh, and in New Orleans it's Rampart, but in Atlanta, Ga., it is Sweet Auburn Avenue and it's gettin' Sweeter every day!"* When some-one along the Avenue asked to borrow a few dollars he reached into his pockets and pulled out a wad of bills. He gave his money freely, not because he had much to give but because the mere act reminded him, and bystanders, that he had the wherewithal to do it. Sometimes, he stopped at the *Daily World* to notify editors about a speech he was about to make or to recite the text of a speech he had just delivered, making certain they quoted him precisely. Occasionally, his young grandsons walked with him down Auburn. "THESE ARE MY GRANDSONS!" the Grand announced to his friends along the Avenue, all of whom knew that he had waited thirty years for a first male heir. As a child, Bobby Jordan was confused by his grandpa Dobbs's conversations on Auburn. As Mil-lie's eldest son, he even asked, "Grandpa, why do you argue so much?" The Grand broke into laughter. Not arguments, he explained, these were debates. "I'm just trying to make a point," he said.

To Dobbs, every moment could become a big moment, filled with purpose, drama and symbolism. At the college campuses on the west side, students knew him by his speeches that brought black history to life. Dobbs loved to tell the story of abolitionist John Brown and his raid at Harpers Ferry. "John Brown went to the gallows in 1859," Dobbs said, "but five years later General Sherman was marching through the South with a trail *sixty miles wide!* And behind him"—here his eyes grew wide—"there were four million slaves singing *'John Brown's body lies a-molderin' in his grave, His soul goes marchin' on!'* "

During these years, when black leaders in Atlanta sought political unity for their own race rather than confronting Jim Crow, Dobbs was at the top of his game. And he didn't mind flashing his good fortune. In Jan-uary 1948, he asked his newly hired Masonic secretary, Paul E. X. Brown, to pick up Geekie and Renie in Dobbs's Lincoln Zephyr and deliver them to the home of a friend where they were to perform at a wedding reception. Dobbs drove to the home in his new Mercury. When Brown pulled up in the Zephyr with Renie and Geekie, the Grand told him to wait until his daughters were ready to leave. The day was cold and rainy and the Zephyr did not have a heater. "I sat in that car, freez-ing, for two hours. I was numb," Brown recalls.

Brown believes the Grand had an ulterior motive for making him wait: "Dobbs just wanted to show everybody that he had two cars."

Though the Grand spent much of his public life challenging others, Brown learned the hard way that the Grand did not like to be challenged himself. Dobbs had hired Brown in 1947, having been impressed by his work as city editor of *The Chicago World* and as editor of *The Pyramid*, the black Shriners' national quarterly. Arriving in Atlanta, Brown took a weekend job, to earn extra money, on WEAS radio in Decatur, a white-owned station with a few black-interest programs. On Sunday mornings, Brown hosted *Hi, Neighbor,* and as part of this program he honored a different black woman in Atlanta each week for community service. At the very moment Brown saluted the woman on the air, a friend of his would arrive at her home, or at her church, to deliver a floral bouquet and a pass for a free Sunday afternoon dinner at Frazier's Cafe on Hunter Street. Dobbs listened each week and invariably on Monday morning called Brown into his Masonic office to criticize him for mispronouncing words. Though the radio station manager complimented Brown frequently, Dobbs never did. Brown believed the root cause of Dobbs's criticism was petty anger since he had never honored Irene Dobbs on the program. Finally, after another Monday morning round of criticism from Dobbs, Brown erupted. "Now, look, don't tell me how to speak. Remember, I grew up in the Midwest, I was educated in midwestern schools and my pronunciation is perhaps totally different than yours." The Grand backed off. Soon after, though, he fired Paul Brown from his job with the Prince Hall Masons. "When John Wesley Dobbs told you, that was it," Brown says. "You don't question the grand master.

"I did not realize that when I challenged him that day," Brown says, shaking his head years later, "I had cut my throat."

Two years after he had broken baseball's color barrier, the Brooklyn Dodgers' Jackie Robinson came to Ponce de Leon Park in April 1949 to break the color line in Atlanta. The stadium parking spaces reserved for local politicians included a space for John Wesley Dobbs.

The Grand admired Jackie Robinson, much as he had Joe Louis. To Dobbs, these two athletes proved their greatness by making the most of their God-given skills in the face of overwhelming racial challenges. During the next decade, he took his grandchildren to Ebbets Field in Brooklyn, where he pointed out the black players—catcher Roy Campanella, pitcher Don Newcombe and Robinson at second base. "It wasn't always this way," he reminded his grandchildren.

In the days before Robinson's arrival in Atlanta, rumors circulated that the Ku Klux Klan planned to appear at the ballpark. The KKK would demonstrate behind the magnolia tree in centerfield, or up on the railroad tracks behind the scoreboard where engineers sometimes slowed their trains to watch a few pitches. Robinson, who was born near Cairo, Georgia, though he was moved to California as an infant by his mother, had misgivings about the three exhibition games against the all-white Atlanta Crackers. During warm-ups before the first game, Brooklyn shortstop Pee Wee Reese, a white Kentuckian, and staunch supporter of Robinson, said to his black teammate, "Jack. Don't stand so close to me today. Move away, will ya?' " Robinson managed a small smile in response to Reese's joke.

As with many American cities across the Northeast, Atlanta had two professional baseball teams, the White Crackers and the Black Crackers. They played in separate segregated leagues. The Black Crackers played their games in several inferior locations, including Booker T. Washington High School. The White Crackers' home was Ponce de Leon Park, a colorful fifteen-thousand-seat stadium across the street from the enormous Sears & Roebuck Building. The magnolia tree stood 430 feet from home plate atop a four-foot embankment. Black spectators were restricted to the outfield grandstands. (Local whites called this section "Outer Senegambia," a derisive reference to a region in western Africa.) Typically, penny-ante gamblers sat down the third base line at "Poncey" and placed bets on obscure details of White Crackers games, such as whether the next out would be a strikeout. The Crackers, sometimes called "the New York Yankees of the minor leagues," won eighteen Southern Association pennants in sixty years. They even wore Yankee-like pinstriped uniforms.

Packing the outfield bleachers or standing in a semicircle on the hillside garden beneath the railroad tracks, black Atlantans cheered every move of Robinson and Campanella in the spring of 1949. Earl Mann, owner of the White Crackers, put a Coca-Cola stand among the blacks, beyond the centerfield ropes, and did a hearty business. The three games drew nearly 60,000 fans, including a record 25,000 for the third game. Nearly half the fans were black. Jackie Robinson did not disappoint. He had two hits in the first game and stole home in the third game. The sports editor of the *Journal*, Ed Danforth, noted after the opener that, for those who expected a race riot, "Atlanta double-crossed them. Not a cross was burned. If any of [KKK Grand Dragon] Doc Green's boys were there, they left their nightshirts at home and paid $1.10 for a grandstand seat. . . ."

The *Daily World*, meanwhile, celebrated Atlanta's black fans as "unsung heroes who have stood in centerfield quietly and patiently." An editorial in the *World* said the harmony during the city's first interracial games meant "Atlanta and all Georgia are the better for it in the eyes of the Nation."

*         *         *

For years, petty rivalries among black leaders caused fissures within the community. But in 1949, when blacks were allowed to vote in Atlanta's city primary for the first time since the 1946 court-ordered end to the all-white Democratic primary, black leaders understood they no longer could afford disunity.

In July, the Grand and A. T. Walden put aside their long-term rivalry to become co-chairmen of the new Atlanta Negro Voters League. The ANVL would hold political sway among blacks for nearly two decades. Now, blacks could stand behind their party in national elections, and unite to vote as a bloc in city elections. For the first time, white candidates would have to court the black voter, who represented roughly one-fourth of the city total. The ANVL would screen candidates and then announce its endorsement.

The union of Dobbs and Walden was no small achievement. The Grand was a Republican full of bombast and flourish; Walden, a Democrat and lawyer whose speeches were as direct as a legal brief. Dobbs sought black power through the ballot, Walden through the law. As a boy in Fort Valley, in south Georgia, Walden had shined shoes for whites to make money until "my Daddy saw me and he got me up and said, "Never get on your knees again in front of a white man.'" Because Walden had been a frail child, his parents sent him to school instead of putting him to work in the cotton fields with his brothers and sisters. Over time, he developed an immovable personal strength.

Seeking a fourth term as mayor, Hartsfield faced three challengers in 1949, though only Fulton County Commissioner Charlie Brown was a viable threat. The ANVL sponsored several debates in the black community with Dobbs as moderator, lecturing candidates about the need to speak candidly and directly to issues of importance to blacks. At the Allen Temple AME Church on August 31, a week before the primary, Dobbs told the candidates, "Negroes don't want any special privileges: all we want is equal opportunity. The vote is here to stay and we are going to use it from now on; we are not so much interested in what you were in the past as we are in what you stand for now! Tell us what you mean to do for the welfare of all citizens." Hartsfield reminded blacks that he had produced the city's first black policemen in addition to parks and libraries for blacks. He stated his support of rent control and superior public housing in the city. Brown attacked Hartsfield for saying different things to blacks than he was saying to whites. "Anything I tell you here," Hartsfield countered, "I will say over the radio, or to any white audience!"

Dobbs created the most dramatic moment of the campaign in the battle for black votes. Before a black crowd estimated at eight hundred in the white papers and more than three thousand in the black newspaper, Dobbs, by sheer force of personality, became a campaign issue, forcing himself onto the front page of the white newspapers for three consecutive days. He charged that blacks intended to have a black-operated fire station in the city "even if we have to construct the building and buy the fire engines ourselves." If Jackie Robinson could put more people in Ponce de Leon Park than anyone ever had, Dobbs contended, then "black boys can put out fires, too!" The city needed to hire its first black firemen, Dobbs demanded, and soon. He also said, pointing at the candidates: "We know that these men would not be here tonight if we did not have what they want—21,000 votes!"

Dobbs then chastised the local white newspapers for injecting the race issue into the campaign. In 1921, he recalled, the hostility of the white newspapers had prompted six thousand blacks to boycott them. Sitting behind him, Rev. Martin Luther King, Sr., added, "And we'll do it again." One of the peripheral mayoral candidates, a white supremacist named Bill Todd, stepped to the microphone that night at the Booker T. Washington High football field, and recited a poem: "Brown is too bleary, Salem is too light, Hartsfield is weary, Bill Todd is just right—and white!" The crowd jeered loudly. As Walden tried to grab the microphone, Todd added, "I challenge the right of John Wesley Dobbs [as a Republican] to participate in a Democratic primary."

The next day, Dobbs wrote a three-page letter to Hartsfield, praising him for verbally attacking Todd at the rally. "You have risen superbly the victor in every tilt with your opponents that I have witnessed," Dobbs wrote, adding, "Your record demonstrates that you have made a good mayor for all the people of Atlanta." Hartsfield replied, "Mr. Todd was merely trying to create publicity for himself. It is also a fact that Atlanta primaries have always been non-partisan."

For the first time, Atlanta's politicians were experiencing large doses of John Wesley Dobbs. The volume and tone of his voice caused them to recoil; but Dobbs knew no voice other than the roaring lion's. He always used force—the force of reason, the force of morality—as his form of diplomacy.

Todd later called Hartsfield "the fair haired boy of Dobbs and his associates." Meanwhile, Charlie Brown announced his intention to boycott debates sponsored by Dobbs because "the candidate for mayor backed by Dobbs and a few so-called leaders was picked months ago. . . . I solicit the votes of our colored community but they should be allowed to select their own candidates and vote their convictions free from dictation."

Dobbs and Walden tried to unify the black vote. Their success was recognized on September 7 when an estimated ten thousand blacks voted in the city primary, the overwhelming majority for Hartsfield. He needed nearly every vote. Hartsfield captured 20,092 votes to Brown's 17,258. Hartsfield's tally was 102 votes more than 51 percent of the total votes cast, barely enough to avoid a runoff.

This success enabled Dobbs to pry concessions from whites. It also established Dobbs as a political godfather in the black community, loved and feared, impossible to ignore. In any political decision of importance involving black Atlanta, he would have to be consulted.

Dobbs understood that Hartsfield now, more than ever, was obligated to the black community. He knew, too, that, in a segregated city, this was a precarious position for a white politician. Similarly, Hartsfield knew Dobbs required a political payback.

So, on a December night in 1949, when the mayor wanted to show blacks that he had delivered on another promise, he called upon the Grand. Hundreds of blacks gathered for the ceremony. They whistled and cheered. The David T. Howard High School band played. Hartsfield, and several city councilman, publicly acknowledged Dobbs and Walden. The mayor chose Dobbs to give the signal.

Wearing a gray suit and a felt hat, the Grand threw out his arm and suddenly there was light. More than three miles of newly installed lights, spanning the black areas of Sweet Auburn and Edgewood avenues and Decatur Street, were illuminated for the first time.

"The greatest policeman in the world," Hartsfield told the crowd, "is light."

For one splendid moment, John Wesley Dobbs seemed to have almost biblical powers. *Great God A'mighty! The Grand gave us light!*

The Grand pressed Bill Hartsfield to deliver on promises. In the summer of 1951, the mayor dedicated Pittman Park for blacks, which featured a gymnasium/field house, swimming pool, baseball diamond and tennis courts.

"I'm glad to see the city and county officials here. This park was one of the promises they made to us in the last election," Dobbs said in a speech that day. "We got this park because we could 'swap' votes, and we're not going to be satisfied with anything less than equal rights and opportunities for Atlanta Negroes."

Then he wagged a finger at Hartsfield. "We are still waiting for a Negro fire station in the West End area that was also promised us."

Dobbs's words were not soon forgotten. The governor of Georgia,

Herman Talmadge, would cite them, verbatim, in his 1955 treatise, *You and Segregation,* as an example of the dangers of the Negro bloc vote. "The 'captive' officials had to grin and bear it [that day in Pittman Park]," Talmadge wrote. "Bloc voting, as directed by the local branches of the N.A.A.C.P., can be and usually is one of the most dictatorial practices carried on in our nation today."

During the summer of 1952, the Grand lashed out against the Atlanta Terminal station ticket office for its poor treatment of black patrons. In a letter to the general passenger agent of the Southern Railroad, Dobbs, the old railroad man, wrote that blacks were made to stand in line at the Terminal station while ticket sellers hired to serve only white patrons sat idly nearby. He protested that iron bars were placed at the black ticket counter but not at the white counter. "This kind of treatment is not only separate but it is unequal," he wrote. He said blacks received more equitable treatment at train stations in Savannah, Meridian, Mississippi, Nashville and Memphis. "There is no reason to hurt people's feelings at the same time they are spending their money with you. They certainly deserve better treatment than this." The changes were slow to come.

When Hartsfield and Brown faced off again in the 1953 mayoral race, the mayor still had not produced the West End fire station for blacks. (Hartsfield's problem was that city firemen, unlike city policemen, slept in the same quarters; hiring black firemen therefore was an untenable proposition to most white Atlantans.)

Six days before the primary, the Grand shocked the ANVL by announcing his support for Charlie Brown. When Walden and ANVL leaders remained firmly behind Hartsfield, Dobbs went one step further and resigned from the league. To some blacks, it seemed a grandstand ploy, a simple case of Dobbs being Dobbs.

But the Grand simply could not support a mayor who had failed to deliver on a promise to blacks. His withdrawal from the league was front-page news in the *Daily World,* though no mention was made in the white papers. Rev. Martin Luther King, Sr., chastised Dobbs in a public meeting. "It was a fact that we got Negro police under the present administration," King said. It also was Hartsfield, King added, who had fought against the county unit system.

"It is a good idea," Dobbs answered, "for the Negro voters to be divided in some contests." The *Daily World* announced its neutrality in the race, agreeing, in principle, with Dobbs. "We have always maintained there is no justifiable reason for citizens to vote as a race when race is not a factor in the campaign."

Though the overwhelming majority of Atlanta's black voters had followed Roosevelt into the Democratic party, Hartsfield worried that Dobbs would take a large number of black Republican votes to Brown. Quickly, the mayor maneuvered behind the scenes. His chief political consultant, Helen Bullard, a cagy, straight-talking strategist who had many contacts in Atlanta's black community, sought advice from Grace Hamilton, Atlanta Urban League president. Hamilton responded with an unsigned, undated secret memo that outlined a plan of action for Hartsfield. She drew up a list of fifty-four black leaders and recommended Hartsfield meet them on their turf at the Butler Street YMCA. There, Hartsfield should point out that his opponents were calling him "the Negroes' representative," but that this was not true for he was "the mayor of all people." Hamilton also suggested Hartsfield admit that black Atlantans had legitimate complaints, among them the lack of black firemen.

After carrying out Hamilton's recommendations and with the endorsement of the ANVL, Hartsfield won a fifth term. Of the estimated thirteen thousand black votes cast, he won 88 percent.

When Brown complained that black Atlanta was controlled by a "powerful political machine." Hartsfield vigorously denied the charge. Why, some blacks, he said coyly, including John Wesley Dobbs, had supported Brown.

Hartsfield's margin of victory, about six thousand ballots, meant the black vote had again made the difference. "The Negro voters consider Mayor Hartsfield the most friendly mayor Atlanta has had," the *Daily World* wrote. The faith black Atlantans placed in the ANVL also was a factor.

As Hartsfield had outmaneuvered Dobbs, he would prove his political mastery many more times against many other political foes. In 1957, Hartsfield would run, and win, one more mayoral race, closing out twenty-three years in City Hall—and he would win in 1957 again without the support of John Wesley Dobbs.

Eighteen months after the Grand had quit the ANVL, a postcard arrived from Frankfurt, Germany, at the Prince Hall Masonic Temple on Sweet Auburn.

Addressed to Grand Master John Wesley Dobbs, the mayor of Atlanta, a politician always, wrote, "Having a wonderful time inspecting all German cities. Regards. W. B. Hartsfield."

*June 3, 1952.* "My name is John Wesley Dobbs," he began. Seven white men, who comprised the Metropolitan Atlanta Planning Commission, sat before him at a public hearing inside cavernous Municipal Auditorium. White city planners had proposed to clear black slum areas in the Fourth Ward and also to relocate the black business district from Auburn Avenue to the west side.

Already the commission had been barraged by black leaders decrying the assault on Auburn Avenue. Now, it was Dobbs's turn.

"I was born just 24 miles north of Atlanta at the foot of Kennesaw Mountain in Cobb County just 17 years after the close of the Civil War," he said. "It was part of my life to witness the eventful days of the Reconstruction.

"I have lived to see Atlanta and the State of Georgia rise above the ruin and devastation of war to places of power and importance in this nation of ours."

During his lifetime Dobbs would make perhaps more than a thousand speeches, in various forms and locations, but this, in many ways, was not so much the speech of his life as it was the speech about his life.

"I have made Atlanta my home since June 1897, which means that I have been a citizen here for the past 55 years. I have been a registered voter and taxpayer in Atlanta since 1904, a period of 48 years. Atlanta was chartered as a city in 1845, which makes it only 107 years old as a city at the present time. I have seen Atlanta develop and grow through the past 55 years, which is more than one-half of its entire existence as a city.

"I make no apology for being a Colored citizen in this community. God saw fit to send me into this world as a member of the Colored race and I have never for once in all my life seen fit to even attempt to question the wisdom of God's plans. My job is to do the best I can with the tools God gave me to work with. This I have always tried to do. My father, grandfather, and great grandfather have all lived and died among the red hills of North Georgia. I feel rather proud of that kind of heritage. Along with other good citizens we have helped to build America. The sweat from the brows of my ancestors has fallen in rice fields, cotton plantations, railroad cuts, in the forests, and along the mountainsides. In times of danger we have answered every call and spilled our blood for American ideals whenever it was necessary to do so. In this way I feel that we have purchased the right to equal citizenship and all opportunities that go along with it under the law."

Dobbs's presentation was reasonable, direct, unafraid. He spoke to the white city planners as an equal.

"I, too, love Atlanta. I think it is one of the greatest cities in all the world. I want to see it continue with the right kind of progress and prosperity."

He filed three protests against the plan known as "Up Ahead," which was drawing criticism from whites, as well, who feared that it hinted at integration. First, Dobbs protested that the Metropolitan Planning Commission did not have a black member even though blacks comprised one-third of Atlanta's total population; second, he protested the part of the plan that would relegate black residential areas to certain sections of the city, specifically beyond railroad tracks and highways; and third, he charged that among the "slum" sections scheduled for clearance was Auburn Avenue.

"I admit that the section north of Auburn Avenue to Forest Avenue and between Piedmont and Jackson Street could be so classed for your consideration. However, in the heart of this section mentioned in this recommendation is Auburn Avenue, known to us as 'Sweet Auburn.'

"In every city of America where Negroes live in large numbers they eventually develop a main business street for Negroes. In Atlanta, Georgia, Auburn Avenue happens to be that symbol of our business progress and achievement. On Auburn Avenue between Courtland Street and North Boulevard, Negroes have erected churches, built brick buildings and substantial business houses all along the street. Negroes own at least 90 percent of the property on Auburn Avenue. Big Bethel A.M.E. Church, corner Auburn and Butler, was built at the close of the Civil War when Atlanta was unpaved and open creeks were running through her streets. Big Bethel Church has done more to give a moral tone to this section of Atlanta than anything else in that section of the city. Big Bethel Church stands there today on the same corner as a moral Lighthouse for the welfare of the citizens in this part of Atlanta.

"It is true that we are poor people, liberated only 85 years ago, without education or money; and yet in the last 50 years we have acquired property along Auburn Avenue, built businesses like the Atlanta Life Insurance Company, which now has more than $25 million in assets; the Citizens Trust Company, a member of the Federal Reserve Banking System, with more than $5 million in assets; Atlanta Mutual Building and Loan Association, with more than $1.5 million in assets; *The Atlanta Daily World*, the only Negro daily newspaper in America; a broadcasting station, WERD, 860 on your dial, if you please. These are some of the businesses along Auburn Avenue that we feel justly proud of today. It takes sugar to sweeten things and, as you know, it takes money to buy sugar. The acquisition of this kind of wealth along Auburn Avenue has caused us to call it 'Sweet Auburn,' a name now known among Negroes throughout America as a symbol of the development of Negro Business in Atlanta, Georgia.

"Your proposed plan would destroy this development of ours, which represents two generations of sweat and toil. This attempt, ladies and gentlemen, is fundamentally wrong and unsound.

"Property rights have been held sacred in all ages and among all civilized people. Even among dogs, property rights have been held to be sacred. Throw a bone to the dogs and if a little dog gets there first, and places his foot upon it, the big dogs will back away in respect to ownership and possession of the bone. How much more sacred are property rights among human beings.

"One more illustration: Today on Manhattan Island in New York City Mr. Vincent Astor, one of the richest men in America, collects rent on land and brick buildings along Broadway on which 99-year leases have run out. This was made possible by the wisdom of John Jacob Astor, a great-grandfather of the present Astor, who first owned a farm on Manhattan Island and willed it to his heirs. The same thing is true in Pittsburgh, Pennsylvania, with the Mellon family. The same thing will be true along Peachtree Street in Atlanta, Georgia, in years to come, and the same principle ought to hold good for Negroes along 'Sweet Auburn' Avenue in Atlanta, Georgia.

" 'Sweet Auburn' Avenue, ladies and gentlemen, is not a slum street. Physically it looks just as good as Edgewood Avenue. 'Sweet' Auburn is not over behind the railroad tracks. It runs straight into Peachtree Street.

"When you go up 'Sweet Auburn,' you are going to town, that's all."

This speech, according to the *Constitution*, "climaxed an attack" against the removal of the business district from Sweet Auburn.

Later the same day, the chairman of the Metropolitan Planning Commission announced a clarification: in its final report, the commission would delete any reference to eliminating the business district on Auburn Avenue.

# CHAPTER 12

Two white policemen, working the black side of town in the summer of 1952, set their speed trap on Hunter Street. They placed two solenoid switches, inside rubber tubes, at the appropriate distance to measure the speed of passing automobiles. Officers Julius Smith and Hiram Durrett alternated roles: one held the electrical speed meter, the other chased the offender on motorcycle.

Suddenly, a blue 1949 Mercury two-door passed the second switch in a blur. The device in Durrett's hand registered fifty-five, thirty miles per hour over the posted limit. Two blocks east, at Ashby Street, the Mercury slowed as it neared a red light.

It was Officer Smith's turn—and his misfortune—to give chase.

At that moment, Rev. Maynard Jackson was en route to the Booker T. Washington High School where his second daughter, Jeanne, a gifted student, had finished her summer class. He drove a 1940 Cadillac, a car that appealed to his pragmatism and style. Its interior was wide and spacious, much like that of the station wagon the family had worn out. It had a fold-up seat that faced the rear, as in a London taxi. His young daughters Carol Ann and Connie were strapped in back.

At the lunch hour, 12:30, Jackson turned left onto White House Drive, named for the black musician, Graham Jackson, who lived on the street.

When Reverend Jackson recognized Smith's police-issue Harley-Davidson motorcycle coming toward him, he slammed on the brakes—but too late. The collision crushed Smith's leg against the Cadillac's front left fender. The policeman and his motorcycle landed about twenty feet away. Smith's mangled left foot hung from only strands of bloodied ligaments and tendons.

His young daughters heard Reverend Jackson say, *"Oh, my God!"*

He rushed from the car to help the white officer. He lifted Smith from a seated position by the curb. Aided by another black man, Jackson carried Smith across the street into the William A. Harris Memorial Hospital, a facility for blacks. Smith remained conscious and groaned in agony. After initial treatment, he was transferred several miles away to Grady

Hospital, a facility for whites. There, doctors amputated the lower portion of his left leg, six inches above the ankle. His agony was compounded when he suffered an allergic reaction to penicillin. His entire body swelled.

Terrified, Carol Ann and Connie had watched from inside the car as their father carried the policeman into the hospital. Everyone had seemed to move in slow motion. They had seen the policeman's blood soak into their father's starched white shirt. They had seen the exposed bone protruding through the ripped flesh at the officer's ankle. They had seen the pain on their father's face. Colored people had gathered and stared. Carol Ann was ten, Connie only five, and this scene would haunt them always. As adults they came to believe the accident caused their father irreparable harm. They believed it set free a flood of regret and self-doubt that washed away his mental stability. Their father never again was the mountain of strength they had known.

"That was going to take my daddy's mind right there because he was so into caring for human beings," Carol Ann recalls, opening an old wound four decades later.

"Last thing I remember was seeing my father's back, seeing him walk down the street with this man in his arms. He was really destroyed by that incident," Connie says. "It was all very confusing at the moment and bewildering. I couldn't see how anybody could challenge my father's integrity and his goodwill."

Within minutes, a group of white Atlanta policemen arrived. One spoke in a soft, polite voice to Jackson, who explained he had made a complete stop but that Officer Smith was unable to avoid a collision. Taking notes, the policeman asked, "May I see your driver's license?"

When this policeman noticed the "Col." next to Maynard Jackson's name, identifying him as a person of color, Connie noticed that his tone suddenly became "very nasty." Apparently, he had assumed that Rev. Maynard Jackson was white.

The afternoon of the accident several members of Friendship Baptist Church saw their pastor suffering his own despair as he pounded his fists against the church walls. "That policeman is only thirty-three years old," Jackson later told his children, "the same age as Christ at the time of his death."

"Patrolman Collides With Auto Driven By Minister," the front-page headline in the *Daily World* blared the following morning. George Coleman wrote the news story with remorse. Working the late shift, Coleman often had received newsroom visits from Jackson. The two men had discussed black affairs in Atlanta and Coleman had enjoyed the minister's warmth and intellect. He thought Rev. Maynard Jackson an impressive race man.

When a prominent black minister suffered an accident with a white policeman in Atlanta, it became big news in the black community. Not so in the white community. The accident merited four paragraphs on page six in the *Constitution*, "The South's Standard Newspaper Since 1869." The paper noted that the officer had lost his foot and then mentioned another traffic accident from the previous day.

Recording an event that would dramatically affect the course of the Dobbs family history, the *Constitution* cited the driver of the automobile as: "Maynard H. Johnson, 54, Negro."

Six weeks later, on September 2, 1952, a Fulton County deputy sheriff delivered the subpoena to 220 Sunset Avenue. Officer Julius Smith had filed suit against Rev. Maynard Jackson in Fulton County Superior Court, charging vehicular negligence stemming from an improper left turn. In his petition, Smith claimed that his life never again would be the same and sought from the black pastor $100,000 in damages, an enormous sum. "He will be a helpless cripple," Smith's lawsuit maintained, "so long as he lives."

The previous morning John Wesley Dobbs, in his trademark baggy suit, had shaken hands with Republican presidential nominee Dwight Eisenhower at the airport in Atlanta. "Glad to see you again," Eisenhower told him. Eisenhower had met Dobbs only two months before. The Grand had been one of several black members in Georgia's seventeen-member Eisenhower delegation at the Republican National Convention in Chicago. A battle had ensued with Georgia's pro–Robert Taft delegation. Dobbs and Elbert P. Tuttle, a white Atlanta attorney and later an Eisenhower appointee to the federal bench, made speeches to the Republican Credentials Committee on behalf of the pro-Ike forces. Ultimately, their delegation was seated and it represented a crushing loss of delegates for Taft. "I'm glad to be shaking hands with the next president of the United States," Dobbs told Eisenhower.

When Dobbs learned of the lawsuit against his son-in-law, he responded at once. He and Maynard Jackson hired a white attorney, W. Neal Baird. A senior partner of Marshall, Greene, Baird & Neely, Baird had been president of the prestigious Atlanta Lawyers Club only two years before. Dobbs understood the stakes of this lawsuit. He needed a white attorney whose name would evoke respect in the white man's courthouse. Renie's future, and the future of her six children, also were at issue. This was no time to take chances.

In the days that followed, black Atlantans began to notice something different about Rev. Maynard Jackson. He was not himself. He was adrift and wandering. He suffered mood swings and occasional outbursts.

Pressures were mounting on him from all sides. Money remained tight. As a younger man he had formed an export company in Liberia, in connection with the Baptist Foreign Mission Board; at the time, he had considered a career in business. Yet once he became a minister, he had made the conscious decision not to be swayed by money. "If I had gone into the ministry to become rich," he said, "all I would have to do is put on a turban, call myself 'Swami Maynard,' pitch a tent on the corner and have a revival three times a year." He had taken out an $8,000 loan to build a four-unit brick apartment house at 220 Sunset Avenue, in the Vine City section of west Atlanta. A leafy street in a middle-class black neighborhood, Sunset Avenue was known as "The Jewel of Vine City." The pastor used one unit for his family, rented two to other families and used the fourth as his church office.

The power struggles at Friendship Baptist Church, meanwhile, seemed never to end. They stemmed in part from a philosophical difference about the mission of the church. As a civic leader in Atlanta, Reverend Jackson served on a local interracial commission, organized the Atlanta Open Forum to spur political discussions and led the executive committee of the Morehouse College national alumni association. All these roles were consistent not only with his past work in Dallas but also with Friendship's position of eminence within black Atlanta.

He also reached out to underprivileged children who lived in the hovels surrounding the church. He set up a recreational center in the E. R. Carter Center on the church grounds. He played pool and checkers with the children and when he posed for pictures with them he was easy to spot—the light-skinned face in a sea of black. To the children, he spoke of faith and love; he hugged them often. He also organized a well-baby clinic, convincing doctors and nurses in his congregation to help the troubled and often unwed mothers in the area.

Some influential members believed the church ought to aspire to loftier chores. As Jackson saw it, these members were more concerned with enhancing the nearby black colleges than with saving the black underclass. The Rev. Murray Branch, a longtime member of Friendship who occasionally preached at the church during Reverend Jackson's absence, recalls overhearing one elderly church member say from her pew, "I don't see why our pastor insists on bringing those dirty little children into our building." For a time, Reverend Jackson remained undeterred. "Often you have to serve people in spite of themselves," he wrote in April 1952 to his old friend in Dallas, A. Maceo Smith.

The lawsuit magnified his emotional strains. His confidence and self-control were diminishing, particularly at the pulpit. Usually, his sermons were spare—eloquent and to the point—and he would set loose his congregation by 12:15. ("If you can't say what you've got to say in twenty minutes," he once said, "people have stopped listening to you, anyway.") Some church members remember him as a deep thinker, more like a college lecturer than a preacher; Branch says Jackson sometimes "put on a moan or a whoop and would move around vigorously to illustrate the absurdity or inappropriateness of the traditional black preacher." He moved his congregation with reason, not contrived emotion. But now his sermons became inexplicably longer and disjointed. "They didn't make any sense," one member recalls. "He'd start talking about one thing and end up talking about another. I would come home and say to my husband, 'I couldn't follow Maynard today.' " Once, during communion, his oldest daughter, Sandra, saw tears in Reverend Jackson's eyes; she had never seen him cry before. He became more irritable at home, more defensive in church. One day he was found wandering on the Spelman campus, where Renie was a professor of French. Searching for her, he said things to people that made no sense, sometimes muttering, sometimes loudly.

On another occasion, Renie answered the phone at home. "Come get Reverend Jackson," a church member said. "He's wandering around by the church and almost got hit by a car!" Renie went to get him. She pulled her children from school once, sat them down and explained what they already knew, that their father was not right. He is sick, she said, and together we will nurse him back to full strength.

W. Neal Baird filed a response to Officer Smith's petition on September 27, 1952. He maintained that not only had Maynard Jackson fully stopped his automobile before the collision but that Smith's motorcycle was moving at nearly sixty miles per hour along Hunter Street, not twenty-five miles per hour, as Smith stated in his petition. He contended that Smith's motorcycle left thirty-eight feet of skid marks in an attempt to avoid the collision. Baird also denied that Reverend Jackson "ran his car into plaintiff's motorcycle but on the contrary avers plaintiff ran his motorcycle into the left front fender of this defendant's automobile." If negligence was committed, Maynard Jackson's white attorney argued, it was committed by the officer.

In deposing the officer, Baird challenged his claim that Maynard Jackson's car was moving at the moment of impact.

Baird: "Was the Cadillac moving or stopped when you hit?"

Smith: "If he was moving he was moving very slowly, he was close to being stopped."

Baird: "Almost stopped, is that correct?"

Smith: "I wouldn't say he was moving, I wouldn't say he was stopped. As best I remember he was moving very slowly if at all."

Baird: "You don't remember; he might have been stopped, is that correct?"

Smith: "I wouldn't say yes and I wouldn't say no on that."

In some ways, Maynard Jr. was like any other fourteen-year-old. Asserting independence, he staged mild rebellions against his father's stern hand, usually in small daily matters, such as the time of the family's Sunday dinner. Grandpa Jackson, a man he never knew, and Grandpa Dobbs were legendary in the family for their strong guiding hands, and Maynard Jr. learned that his father had "a special hinged elbow." "He could reach around a corner and across the room if I was acting wrong, thirty-five feet away," he recalls, "and smack my face before I could blink."

Yet in other ways, the namesake son was unlike any other fourteen-year-old. He entered Morehouse College in the fall of 1952, three years early. A Ford Foundation fellowship propelled him from David T. Howard High's tenth grade straight into college. At Morehouse, he would be expected to "rise to the crown," in the words of President Benjamin Mays, an energetic educator creating the mystique of "The Morehouse Man." Aspiring to rise above the reach of Jim Crow, Morehouse strove to forge within each student "the mind of a scientist, the wisdom of the philosopher and the religious faith of the Negro slave." In his freshman year, Maynard Jr. saw *Gone With the Wind* for the first time. With his sisters at the Ashby Street Theater, he felt "sadness at seeing how black people were treated and disgust at the frivolity of the main characters," especially Scarlett O'Hara. "It didn't make sense to me that somebody as lamebrained as some of the whites in the movie should have the power to subjugate and oppress black folks."

The high expectations at Morehouse matched the expectations of his family. Born into the black aristocracy, Maynard Jr. was the family prodigy. Known as Buzzy because older sister Sandra thought he "buzzed like a bee" as an infant, he quickly developed a bravura that prompted aunts, uncles and cousins to tease him: *"Come here, Buzzy. You think you somebody!"* His cousin Bobby Jordan, five years younger, remembers the Dobbses, especially the Grand, praising Maynard's intellect. "As we got older," Jordan says, "everyone bragged on the fact that Maynard was so smart." Besides, he looked good. Uncommonly large—175 pounds by his twelfth birthday—Maynard Jr. was a light-skinned, green-eyed, wavy-haired kid with charisma and a gift for gab.

"The way that boy talks," the Grand often said, "he's boooorn to be a lawyer!" To be a lawyer, Dobbs thought, was to scale the heights. So Maynard Jr. aspired to become a lawyer, although the ministry also appealed to him; that was, after all, his father's calling.

During his freshman year at Morehouse, his father appeared on a program at Sales Hall. Reverend Jackson usually sang a hymn to set the tone for his sermon. This day he sang his favorite hymn, "His Eye Is on the Sparrow."

> I sing because I'm happy,
> I sing because I'm free,
> For His eye is on the sparrow,
> And I know He watches me.

Every time he heard his father speak, Maynard Jr. was thrilled to know this was the man for whom he had been named. "My father had a mellifluous baritone voice that literally caressed words," he says. To him, his father's Sunday service at Friendship was more than merely a sermon, it was an entire service with carefully selected music that spoke a deeper truth. Dobbs called Rev. Maynard Jackson "a dreamer" and it was that same dreamy quality that Maynard Jr. most admired and loved about his father.

On the day he sang of the sparrow, Reverend Jackson started his sermon only to lose his place and then his bearing. "It was like he was in a daze," Maynard Jr. says. "You could tell that he was just out of it." Trying to find himself, the minister told the Morehouse students, "Let's sing 'His Eye Is on the Sparrow.' I haven't heard that in a while." The students had just finished singing it. There came an uncomfortable pause. Benjamin Mays then led the disoriented minister back to his seat and moved the program along.

Sitting in the Morehouse audience, embarrassed, Maynard Jr. felt his safety net tearing. At fourteen, his values and ambitions still were tethered to his role models, primarily his father. For the first time, he thought about his father's mortality: "I mean here was this indestructible, indefatigable, righteous, loving father who all of a sudden was very human, very much subject to human frailty. . . ." The thought of losing his father terrified him.

The Jackson children—"P.K.s" as they called themselves, for Preacher's Kids—often saw their father writing his sermons on Saturday nights. Sometimes, Renie made revisions or suggested music. Sundays became magic for the family. Connie wrote in the back of the hymnals as she listened to her father. After communion, the P.K.s helped collect the sacrament glasses. On Sunday afternoons, Sandra, Jeanne and Maynard Jr. took part in the Young People's Round Table, a church group founded by their father for teenagers to discuss controversial issues, such as alcohol or premarital sex. Their father invited experts to speak. Sometimes, the Round Table met for picnics on the lawn at Atlanta University.

Rev. Maynard Jackson delivered his final sermon at Friendship during the fall of 1952. Once again, he railed against members who refused to help the despairing children and elderly. On this Sunday morning, as on all other Sundays, the P.K.s sat with Renie in the third row of pews. What they saw on this morning they would never forget. Their father chided and berated members for failing to meet the call of Christianity.

To the P.K.s, the man in the pulpit was not the pastor, or father, they knew. His voice and delivery belonged to an angry man. Carol Ann often had made the rounds with him on Saturdays to visit the elderly in the E. R. Carter Center. She even had scribbled notes during these trips. From the pulpit now her father spoke of those Saturday visits and looked to his daughter, about to turn eleven.

"Carol Ann, do you remember?" he asked repeatedly. "Stand up and tell them!" She twisted uncomfortably and said nothing.

On and on he railed. Twenty minutes became forty minutes. He had been at odds with several deacons at the church. Years later, Maynard Jr. would say that his father had "this tendency to be preoccupied with the minority opposition rather than with the majority support group. . . . But he was a minister more than he was a politician and I think he was driven by the notion that he had to save the souls of those who were most reluctant."

In retrospect, it would almost seem as if Rev. Maynard Jackson knew that this was to be his last sermon, the last chance for the shepherd to drive his flock toward safety. In the pews, members stirred. Their whispers grew louder. If this sermon left the congregation uncomfortable, it left the Jacksons in pain.

Forty minutes became an hour. Renie approached the pulpit. She tried to coax her husband to step down. "Maynard, come on, sweetheart," she said softly. Unyielding, he carried on for another long stretch. Renie approached him again. Now, looking into the eyes of the woman he had married nearly twenty years before, the woman to whom he had given a Hudson seal fur coat when she had given him a namesake son and the woman who would still light up at the mere mention of his name four decades after his death—Maynard Jackson wept and allowed her to lead him from his pulpit.

Carol Ann heard church members whispering. "What's wrong with Reverend Jackson? Why is he talking like that?" She could not contain herself. She turned and said, "He only said what you needed to hear."

As an adult, she reflects, "They didn't want him bringing those kids in there. They wanted to tear down the old Carter Center [to use] as a parking lot for their Cadillacs. His mind was just gone then, in a sense. Other people look at it that way. I don't. I think they deserved that talking to. He needed to get that out. . . . I realized that day that he'd had a nervous breakdown. But as far as I was concerned everything he said was dead on the money and sane. The insanity lay within the people of the church who wanted to call themselves Christians and would not go out and help these children."

Rev. Maynard Jackson, Sr., never fully recovered. "He was never as strong or as focused," Maynard Jr. says, "although he was able to function in a number of ways. But that began to deteriorate." On February 22, 1953, the pastor was unable to attend a celebration of his eighth anniversary at Friendship. His brother, the Rev. Alexander Stephens Jackson II, director of music at Bishop College in Marshall, Texas, and pastor of Jerusalem Baptist Church, came to Atlanta to preach the anniversary sermon in his place. His sermon: "This Thing Called Happiness."

Soon, the pastor was under a doctor's care. At times his vibrant personality resurfaced. Once, standing in the yard at Sunset Avenue by cherry, pine and Japanese tulip trees, he explained to his youngest daughter, Connie, what he saw as the enduring glory of the human spirit.

"Life goes on. It doesn't stop here," he told her. "It is sort of like a butterfly. It starts out as a caterpillar, and then it lives in that cocoon and has no activity, and when it emerges it emerges as a beautiful butterfly.

"Think of life like that," he said, "as you go from one transition to another."

In the spring, Reverend Jackson was sent to Marshall, where his brother could look after him. Renie faced the task of caring for their six children (the youngest, Paul, still a toddler) and explaining their father's condition. "I thought my father had gone away or that he was in prison or, you know, we were so poor, that he had robbed somebody or something," Carol Ann says, "because I always heard these things about money, and he needed more money, and he couldn't do this, and it was bothering him, and worrying him. Plus we had family financial meetings."

In April, Reverend Jackson was committed to the Rusk State Hospital in Marshall. To be near, Renie took a summer job teaching at Bishop College. She brought along four children: Sandra, nineteen (she soon left for Mexico on a scholastic program), Jeanne, seventeen, Maynard, fifteen, and the toddler Paul. Some of his friends remember the day Maynard Jr. left for Texas. "We were all very sad for him," one recalls. "We all knew what was going on." Carol Ann and Connie spent the summer with their Dobbs grandparents at 540.

The P.K.s never saw their father during his two months in the state hospital. They later heard that his hair, only flecked with gray when he left Atlanta, had turned fully gray and that he had lost weight and, apparently, his will to live. Though Renie visited him often, she decided the children should not see their father in this condition.

The telegram from Texas arrived at 540 on June 27, 1953. Irene Dobbs took her granddaughters Carol Ann and Connie into her bedroom and told them that their father had died. Remembering his story of the butterfly's transitions, Connie knew her father had moved on to another, happier place. She thought, "Anything that he may have encountered in his life as a challenge or anything that could have hurt him was removed from him." Because she thought sorrow was expected of her, she feigned sadness in front of arriving Dobbs relatives. What she really felt, she recalls, was "joy and peace [now] that he was in heaven."

When told of his father's death, Maynard Jr. was disbelieving. He had not seen him in several months. His father had been the central figure in his life—and, suddenly, gone. "I kind of went around expecting to see him walking around the corner one day," Maynard Jr. says.

Reverend Jackson was fifty-nine years old. On his death certificate, the cause of death was cited as "atypical pneumonia," stemming from "Schizophrenic reaction, paranoid type."

Back in Atlanta, the *Daily World* called him a "conscientious leader." *The Atlanta Journal* placed his death notice at the bottom of the obituary page, the traditional placement of death notices for blacks.

Her father's death, and his battles at Friendship, later would prompt Jeanne to renounce her Baptist faith. Years later, in a poem to her African husband, Francis Oladele, Jeanne would write: "*BAPTIST*—was my father/It killed him (and that killed *it*/for me!"). When Jeanne died a quarter century later in Oyo, Nigeria, her husband, in deference to her religious views, buried her not in the Baptist cemetery but across the road.

On September 4, 1953, W. Neal Baird notified the Fulton County Superior Court of his client's death. Nine weeks later, the sides reached an out-of-court settlement. Smith received an undisclosed sum, the Jackson family paid all court costs and the suit against the late Reverend Jackson was dismissed. The laws of Georgia gave protection, and twelve months' support, to Renie, now a forty-five-year-old widowed mother of six. Though permitted to keep the four-unit apartment house at 220 Sunset Avenue, she spent the ensuing years dealing with creditors. Officer Julius E. Smith, who maintained in his lawsuit that his earning capacity and projected lifespan were diminished by the accident, left the Atlanta police force and, according to city personnel records, died seventeen years later at the age of fifty. More than a generation later, Maynard Jr. would say, "In a school zone, at a time when there are school kids all over the place, to be going as fast as [Smith] was going, no siren, no light, and my father was already into his turn . . ." To him, fault was obvious.

Renie searched for her husband's spirit. Two or three times she attended services at Friendship, hoping to hear his voice. Foolish, she thought, just go on with your own life. Easier said than done, for he had romanced her always. On occasion, they had left the kids with family in Dallas, and gone away for a weekend. They had ridden horses together in Clayton. He had showered her with praise, particularly about her cooking, and understood her creative needs. After dinner, he often told their daughters, "You girls go in there and wash dishes and let your mother go practice her piano."

She never remarried. Renie told her children she would never find another man like their father. She dated a few times, several years after his death, though not with serious intentions. Once, she went out on a date and Jeanne, obviously concerned, asked her siblings, "What if he tries to kiss Mama?" Her older sister, Sandra, shrugged and said, "Well, if Mama wants to, she'll let him. If she doesn't, he won't." The thought of another man kissing her mother caused Jeanne's nerves to tighten and she threw up.

Sitting in a retirement home in Atlanta more than forty years later, Renie shook her head. "It never dawned on me that my husband was going to die. I mean he was a fine, healthy, you know, gentleman, and we had so many things in common: our music, and the way we liked things, and the way I helped him with his sermons, and the way we liked to read and travel." She shook her head. "He was such a sane person. I said to myself after he died, 'How in the heck could he be insane?' I never have accepted it."

Maynard Jr. would always hear the voice of his father in his ear, demanding, cajoling, loving, heroic, purposeful. The voice affected him, and guided him. He tried to fill the father role for his brother, Paul, a dozen years his junior. Paul Jackson never knew his father, so Maynard Jr. tried to compensate, talking of the man often. "I told Paul how much Daddy loved him," Maynard Jr. says. The brothers struggled with their relationship over the years, one of the many painful aftereffects of their father's death.

Renie never saw Maynard Jr. cry when his father died. "A young male has a problem," she says. "He feels like the devil and wants to boo-hoo and cry and carry on but he isn't supposed to do it." She believes her son's sorrow, held in, found release in a different way: he began to imitate his father. "His death was the biggest blow of my life," Maynard Jr. says. "He was my hero, you know."

Into this void stepped John Wesley Dobbs.

# Chapter 13

The model of the venerable Atlanta patrician was on display each morning at Woodhaven, the sprawling Buckhead estate of Robert F. Maddox, former president of the American Bankers Association and Atlanta's mayor in 1910. Maddox remained a formidable figure in town even past the age of eighty; Woodhaven, meanwhile, was noted for its terraced gardens, among the most magnificent in the South. Each morning a black chauffeur drove Maddox to his office at the First National Bank of Atlanta, always stopping first at his private gardens where Troy, the black yardman, emerged from the rosebushes to pin a rose on the lapel of Maddox's freshly pressed Palm Beach suit. The banker's car moved down the wooded avenues of Buckhead, which carried names that spoke of British gentry (Habersham Road, West Paces Ferry Drive). As a young man, Maddox had sat on the main platform at the Cotton States Exposition and heard Booker T. Washington's Atlanta Compromise address; he believed firmly in segregation and, in a book in his library, even had underlined Washington's phrase "In all things that are purely social, we can be as separate as the fingers, yet one as the hand in all things essential to mutual progress." Each noon Maddox lunched with his banker friends at the Capital City Club, then returned home in midday. Into this world of money and privilege in the summer of 1955 came a black student and future civil rights leader whose name was Vernon Jordan. He worked as a chauffeur/butler but was uninhibited by the circumstances. While Maddox took afternoon naps, Jordan spent time in the Maddox library. He did so despite protests of Lizzie, the black cook.

"You got no business in that room, readin', Vernon," she said.

One afternoon, as Jordan read, Maddox surprised him by appearing at the door. In his hand, the noted banker held a bottle of Southern Comfort.

"Vernon," he said, "what are you doing in the library?"

"I'm reading, Mr. Maddox."

"I never had a Nigger work for me who could read," Maddox said.

"Mr. Maddox, I can read well," Jordan replied. He had been given the summer job as a favor to his mother, Mary Jordan, often a caterer for the Maddox family. Now, Jordan brightened and said, "I'm colleged."

"You go to college? Where?"

"DePauw University in Indiana," Jordan said.

"White boys go to that school?"

"Yessir."

Maddox's voice lowered. "White girls go to that school?"

"Yessir."

"You know, Vernon, I have a place downstairs for the help to read or do whatever they want to do."

With the reasoning and appeal to a man's best nature that would serve him well in years to come, Jordan said, "But you don't want these wonderful books—Shakespeare, Longfellow, Wordsworth—downstairs," he said. "They belong in this library. I just like to read. I want to sit here and read." Maddox shook his head and walked away.

At dinner that night with Laura Maddox Smith and her husband, banker Ed Smith (friends of Ivan Jr. and Louise) and N. Baxter Maddox and his wife, the patriarch Bob Maddox brought the proceedings to a halt by saying, "I have an announcement to make."

Everyone looked up. "Yes, Papa?"

Vernon Jordan, with a white napkin folded over his arm, was serving vichyssoise when he heard the incredulous Maddox announce, "Vernon can read!"


Like his friend Bob Maddox, the Senator was not easily impressed by modern-age inventions. Toothpaste was a case in point. He didn't believe in it. He favored a good hard scrub with salt. His teeth had lasted seventy-five years, he figured, why change now? He did things his own way. He pronounced words as they suited him: the Atlanta mayor was "Mister Hartchfield" and the new contraption that was seizing control of America's living rooms was a "telly-vision." When he and his son purchased a large tract of land in Heard County, seventy miles west of Atlanta, Ivan Jr. fancied it as "The Farm," but the Senator corrected him.

"The Plantation, Ivan," said the son of the Confederate private. *"The Plantation."*

As the air-conditioning revolution transformed summer lifestyles in the South during the 1950s, Ivan Jr. casually mentioned to his father that he had purchased a new automobile. "And it has air-conditioning, Daddy," he said.

True to form, the Senator rolled his eyes. "That," he said, "is ridiculous. Y'all put so many gadgets in cars these days—cigarette lighters and windshield wipers—it's a wonder they can even drive."

Ivan Jr. had a Rotary Club speech scheduled in Macon and the Senator wanted to attend. Naturally, he was smoking a cigar when his son arrived at the Trust Company garage to collect him in his new car. It was a typical July day, hazy, humid with a piercing heat, and soon enough the Senator was commenting on the laborers he spotted working out in the open fields.

"We've got wonderful climate here in Georgia, son," he said, ever the booster.

They drove nearly ninety miles, the windows rolled up and the air conditioner circulating cool air, when Ivan Jr. finally pulled in front of the Dempsey Hotel in Macon. A black doorman opened the car door and said, solicitously, "Afternoon, Senator!"

The Senator stepped out of the car and was struck with a blast of warm, humid air. Only then did he comprehend the advantages of modernization.

"Is that that air conditioner you were telling me about, son?" he asked. Ivan Jr. nodded.

Holding his cigar, the Senator said, "Put one in my car tomorrow."

During the 1950s, both Atlanta and Ivan Jr. were uncertain of what they wanted, knowing only that they wanted more. Before the civil rights movement shattered the social system that had existed for nearly a century in the South, the ambition of Ivan Jr. was exceeded perhaps only by his naïveté about the dynamics and volatility of the race issue.

It seemed a simple time. A strictly segregated city, Atlanta slumbered in the southern sun. The red-brick Fulton National Bank at Five Points was said to be the only large structure built in the business district since the Depression. In 1951, the *Constitution* described the average Atlantan: "His social habits are discreet, and visitors from rowdier climes find him a sound, if dull fellow." The grandsons of the Confederacy inherited control of civic power in Atlanta, carrying their fathers' heritage and traditions with them. The city was guided by a powerful group of elite white men—the Coca-Cola-Trust Company crowd, the Georgia Power crowd, the Rich's crowd, the First National Bank crowd—and the overwhelming majority were paternalistic in their view toward blacks. Some of these leaders had been raised in the South by black mammies and had grown closer to their mammies than to their mothers. Paternalism, though based, like yahoo prejudice, on the notion of white supremacy, allowed for the expression of compassion. It was an acknowledgment of the black's human condition. In the years ahead, paternalism would separate Atlanta from many other southern cities, particularly Birmingham, where the expression of white supremacy took form in attack dogs, billy clubs and mean-spirited sheriffs.

A few colorful figures prevailed: Gov. Herman Talmadge ruled Georgia, while Bill Hartsfield and Ralph McGill ruled Atlanta, at least in the public's eye; the Coca-Cola magnate Bob Woodruff held sway in the city but from behind a discreet veil.

As a conservative tide swept the nation, Atlanta seemed a small and unsophisticated place. When the red traffic lights along Piedmont and Courtland streets slowed the governor on his daily trip from his mansion in Ansley Park to the State Capitol, Herman Talmadge simply telephoned the mayor's office and said, "Why, Bill, what in hell is wrong with your lights folks?" Just like that, the red lights were rejiggered and the governor made his trip at forty miles per hour, without interruption. The governor performed personal favors for the mayor as well. "[State Highway Chairman] Jim Gillis fired Hartsfield's mistress once," Talmadge recalls. "Bill came to see me and I overruled Gillis. Told him to put her back on the payroll." It was a period of divergence between rural and urban interests. By the latter 1950s, the state legislature, dominated by rural politicians, began to pass privileged resolutions, announcing antipathy for the civil rights movement. James Mackay, a state representative from Decatur, and a moderate on race, recalls how legislators "went to the coffee shop at the Capitol and read in the paper something about Thurgood Marshall, or someone like him. They'd write a resolution on a napkin or the back of an envelope and give it to the [legislative] clerk, Joe Boone. Joe would read anything you handed him. So before you had your second cup of coffee Joe would announce a resolution: 'Abolish UNESCO!' And the next day was 'Impeach Frankfurter!' Then you'd pick up the next day's *New York Times* and it said, 'The Georgia legislature unanimously passed a resolution to impeach the Supreme Court.' " Mackay would feel the repercussions of these legislative shenanigans years later when, upon election to Congress, several colleagues would shake their heads and chide, "*So you're the sonovabitch who voted to impeach Earl Warren!*"

The southern white man's relationship with blacks approached its third stage: first as master to slave, next as master of the house to servant and soon to be legislated as equals under law. At the Piedmont Driving Club, the esteemed old guard of the city drank martinis and threw verbal mudballs at Ralph McGill for the increasingly progressive tone of his newspaper columns. Years later, McGill reviewed his columns from the 1940s and 1950s, specifically those on race, and described them as "pale tea." McGill had made a slow conversion from his innate support of segregation. In the late 1940s, during an address at the Atlanta University Center, he pronounced the word "Nigras." June Dobbs, in attendance that day, said McGill's pronunciation fell upon black ears with an emphasis that "was like the roar of the ocean." Yet the native Tennessean moved toward a moderate position on race. Through the power and persuasiveness of his logic he dragged his city with him. To outsiders, McGill's voice became synonymous with Atlanta's. He made the city seem a less hostile place. During these years, the McGills entertained black dignitaries in their home, AUC presidents or African diplomats. The columnist's son, Ralph Jr., recalls that through uncommon politeness, his parents "would attempt to make it seem like it was just the most usual thing in the world to have black guests in the house."

In October 1953, when Hartsfield became president of the national mayors' association, McGill profiled him in *The Saturday Evening Post*. "You'd Think He Owns Atlanta" was the headline; it was also the truth. Driving through Atlanta, Hartsfield once drove past his intended exit at 14th Street. Realizing his blunder, he slammed on the brakes and then shocked his passengers by backing up along the shoulder of the road until he had returned to the 14th Street exit. Hartsfield sometimes invited McGill to meet him at the local wrestling matches during these years so they could discuss the latest racial quandary in the city without fear of being overheard. The mayor performed his own sleight-of-hand on race matters. Hartsfield had an uncanny ability to give blacks a sense of progress while, at the same time, reassuring whites that the line of segregation remained rigid. In 1944, Hartsfield had called for a federal investigation of subversive agents within the NAACP; seven years later, he delivered a cheery welcoming address to the NAACP national conference in Atlanta. Later, he implored city employees to write "Dear Mr. Jones" instead of "Dear Jim" in letters to blacks. "Hartsfield was somewhat like Lyndon Johnson," Herman Talmadge says. "Every waking moment was politics."

Hartsfield believed in segregation, but he believed more fervently in getting reelected; so he courted the growing black voting bloc, forming a coalition with north side whites, whom he termed "the Gold Toothpick crowd." "Hartsfield might not be the Great White Father," Grace Hamilton of the Atlanta Urban League would say, "but he can count."

On Saturday nights during the 1950s, Hartsfield often cruised his city past midnight, listening intently to the police radio he had installed in his car. Chief Herbert Jenkins and the mayor's old grammar school classmate Bob Woodruff came along for the ride. *The Atlanta Journal* police reporter, Aubrey Morris, sometimes joined them, privy to conversations between the mayor, his chief and Woodruff, the most powerful businessman in the city, who, because of his omnipresent Dunhill or Montecruz, was known privately as The Cigar. In the darkness, they drove through downtown streets, through black areas and along Peachtree Street.

Rising within this small universe, Ivan Allen, Jr., wanted to become governor of Georgia. He began his climb through the ranks of power in Atlanta. A merchant prince from the Gold Toothpick crowd, he had led a gilded existence. Though in his early forties, his smooth handsome features made him look younger. His breezy manner suggested that he had never known toil or inadequacy. Having inherited Charles Marshall's half of the Ivan Allen-Marshall Company. Ivan Jr., with the Senator, changed the name to the Ivan Allen Company in 1953. As its president, Ivan Jr. inherited his father's office decorum and strictness. One employee recalls how company salesmen, dreading the wrath of the arriving Ivan Jr., rushed out of the office (ostensibly, to make the business rounds) for fear he might think them lazy.

The wealth of Ivan Jr. was plain to see. In 1950, he and Louise built a summer cottage alongside the rolling green meadow of Broadlands, the Richardson family estate; their cottage was only a short walk down a winding path from the new home they were building for themselves on Northside Drive. Bordered by pines, the meadow would become an enduring Allen family symbol, a playground of privilege, a place to hit golf balls, ride horses, stage barbecues, a joyous ground where several generations of Allen children would laugh and romp. The local papers celebrated the Allen cottage as the first of its kind in Atlanta. It had an oval turquoise swimming pool, an outdoor fireplace and, in an attached Quonset hut, a gymnasium with large caged floodlights. During a year when Philco breathlessly announced an advanced-design refrigerator that featured a built-in home freezer ("With a Woman in mind!"), and Motorola introduced a new "Jewel Box" portable radio that, though small, "sounds like your living room radio console," the Allen cottage was a masterpiece of modernization and convenience. The gymnasium allowed Ivan Jr. and Louise to serve as hosts for a Tuesday night badminton and supper club, a weekly event that would endure for two decades and attract their closest friends, many of whom would guide the city in the days ahead.

"Now," the *Journal* wrote of the young Allens, "they have all of the advantages of going away for a vacation, with none of the disadvantages."

Ivan Jr. still took his cues from his father. The Senator and Irene liked to entertain at 2600 Peachtree Road. Their friends arrived for parties in chauffeur-driven automobiles. The Senator, in a conservative double-breasted suit, greeted guests at the door, along with a black doorman hired for the occasion. The chauffeurs parked behind the Allen house and were served dinner in the pantry area while their white employers enjoyed the cocktail hour. Irene Allen controlled the kitchen, where food was prepared by her cook and caterers.

History was the Senator's passion, particularly his own history and that of Atlanta. In 1954, he became president of the Atlanta Historical Society where he smoked his cigars, talked about the old days at Five Points and served with esteemed Atlantans such as the former governor John Slaton and attorney Stephens Mitchell, brother to the late Peggy Mitchell.

In his booklet *The Atlanta Spirit: Altitude + Attitude,* the Senator committed one of the most exaggerated examples of civic boosterism in a city noted for civic boosters. Of Atlanta, he wrote:

> It is a city of cool nights; an equable all-the-year-round climate; good working conditions. It is a city so healthful that it has never been found necessary to quarantine it against any disease epidemic. It is a city where the men walk fast and work fast and where the women have natural and beautiful complexions. . . . It is, in short, "The City of Pep". . . Ansley Park . . . Druid Hills . . . Peachtree Road . . . Morningside . . . these are but a few of the residential sections of Atlanta which more than counterbalance the "inner circle" of colored sections and the inevitable fringe of poor-white houses. Even Atlanta's mill villages are "different"—well-kept, painted, and in good repair.

That Atlanta was to be treated with devotion, much like a family heirloom, became clear to the Senator's son. As president of the Atlanta Improvement Association in 1951, Ivan Jr. oversaw a redesign of Marietta Street, an old, humpbacked boulevard that was home to most of the South's leading banks. Ivan Jr. intended to resurface the street and remove rail lines, placing the wiring underground. He also intended to move the statue of Henry Grady to Piedmont Park.

But the Senator wouldn't hear of it. "You don't move Henry Grady," he told his son.

And so, even as the redesign was executed, Henry Grady moved not an inch.

By law, Governor Herman Talmadge could not seek another term in 1954. Several groups in Atlanta believed that what Georgia most needed was a businessman as governor to energize the state's economy. They said Ivan Allen, Jr., might be that man.

He had waited for years to hear such talk; it thrilled him. Finally, his time had arrived. The first public notice of his potential candidacy appeared in July 1953 when the *Journal* reported that Ivan Jr. had expressed his availability: "he has sounded like a potential candidate in two or three speeches before out-of-town audiences."

At every opportunity for years, Ivan Jr. had delivered speeches to civic clubs, PTAs, 4-H Clubs, to anyone willing to listen anywhere in Georgia, and that curiously was one of his problems. Hard as he tried, he was not an able speaker. His written speeches were done with great care. When he spoke off the cuff, however, his mind sometimes outraced his tongue, leaving his syntax and message hopelessly tangled. His talks were filled with facts and figures. At times he seemed like a Chamber of Commerce press release brought to life. To rural Georgians who had grown accustomed to hearing fiery demagogues, Ivan Jr. seemed too impassive, too precise—too Atlanta. The timbre of his voice didn't help. It had a nasal quality and, at critical points of emphasis, its pitch rose even higher. In his conservative business suits and wire-rim glasses, Ivan Jr. came off as a young and optimistic man who meant well. Audiences trusted him and applauded politely but without the enthusiasm that fires a voter's soul.

On the speaking circuit in 1953, Ivan Jr. proposed an industrial development program for Georgia balanced with agriculture. He said eastern industrialists needed to learn more about Georgia's favorable climate, its reasonable tax structure and its finest attraction of all, an enormous white labor force. His position on race was stated without equivocation. Black Georgians needed to "learn to respect the traditional rights of segregation." With additional education and health facilities, he believed blacks in Georgia then could become good workers, too. Furthermore, he said, better-educated and better-employed blacks had left Georgia in droves, a trend that had to be reversed. (He neglected to mention one reason for this exodus: state universities refused to admit blacks as students.) Educated blacks must remain in Georgia, Ivan Jr. contended, to make tax contributions necessary to educate other members of their race.

As the gubernatorial field took shape, publisher Marvin Griffin, a zealous segregationist from Bainbridge in south Georgia, courted the Talmadge machine. Fred Hand, speaker of the House of Representatives, also entered the race. The better element of the Democratic party knew of the aspirations of Ivan Jr., but hoped for a bigger drawing card, someone not from Atlanta, perhaps Ellis Arnall or M. E. Thompson making one more run.

The field was crowded when the legal thunderbolt struck on May 17, 1954. The United States Supreme Court outlawed racial segregation in public schools. Its *Brown v. Board of Education* decision did not end segregation in schools immediately but provided an undetermined grace period for seventeen southern states where statutory segregation prevailed, including Georgia. The decision also affected Kansas and several states with permissive statutes. "In the field of public education, the doctrine of 'separate but equal' has no place," Chief Justice Earl Warren wrote. "Separate educational facilities are inherently unequal."

Nearly ninety years had passed since the end of the Civil War. In Georgia, as in all the South, white politicians prepared to battle what they perceived as federal intrusion. Gov. Herman Talmadge charged that the court "has reduced our Constitution to a mere scrap of paper."

Georgia Attorney General Eugene Cook insisted the federal court ruling did not apply to his state because Georgia was not named directly in any of the five lawsuits involved.

Georgia's U.S. senator Richard B. Russell asserted a state's right to self-govern and attacked the Supreme Court with sarcasm: "We should add trained psychologists to the court, or else provide for a court psychologist to attend and help the court in getting out its opinions." (Russell's stand against school desegregation elevated his already lofty position within Georgia but destroyed his hopes for the 1956 presidential nomination.)

Bill Hartsfield long had feared such a ruling. He urged calm while reminding voters that the city had a pending segregation suit in federal court; it had been filed in 1950 against the Atlanta board of education by a black woman on behalf of her children. Many black parents had joined her suit. "We expect to continue to defend that suit," Hartsfield said.

Newspapers across Georgia responded to *Brown v. Board of Education* with indignation. "Instead of benefitting the Southern Negro, it will hurt him," *The Savannah Morning News* wrote. *The Macon Telegraph:* "Georgia and the South today are not ready, nor able, to abolish segregation in schools, and until the time when we are, the principle pronounced by the court will remain in abstract." *The Atlanta Constitution:* "The decision—however much we may deplore it as individuals—becomes the law of the land. . . . [However] as our experience with prohibition proves, law without the force of public opinion behind it is not easily enforced."

The Democratic primary in Georgia was only months away. The gubernatorial candidates pledged to preserve segregation in public schools. Griffin, in the stinging voice of white supremacy that would dominate Georgia politics the next four years, said he was not surprised by the court's decision. "The meddlers, demagogues, race-baiters and Communists in the United States are determined to destroy every vestige of states' rights," he said.

Ivan Jr. wrote his own statement. Though ignored by the press at the time, his comments offer a revealing glimpse of Ivan Jr. as a forty-three-year-old southern man of tradition and pragmatism.

"The decision is even more far-reaching than most people realize at the present time," he wrote on May 18, one day after the court decision was announced. "Our entire anxiety and deliberation so far have been in regard to the public school system . . . [but] it also raises the issue of eliminating segregation entirely in public and semi-private places, such as railroads, streetcars, buses and taxicabs. It will also raise the question of segregation in barbershops, restaurants, hotels and many other service establishments."

The path to the governor's mansion, he knew, was the path of least resistance. In Georgia, a firm pledge to maintain segregation was that path. He said at the time, "Surely, with all of the white people and the great majority of Negroes in favor of the continuation of segregation of the races here, that end may be accomplished if we demonstrate the same wisdom and intelligence that our forefathers used before us."

Ivan Jr. soon faded from a gubernatorial race he never really entered. Marvin Griffin, the zealot segregationist, was elected governor in the fall of 1954. Already, Ivan Jr. had his eye on 1958.

By most measurements, Ivan Allen III seemed the perfect son. He followed in his father's footsteps, as his father had done before him. Ivan III was a high achiever, a driven and determined optimist who had a name that soon would become synonymous with Atlanta.

Being a child of Atlanta privilege meant that Ivan III learned to swim and play tennis at the elegant Piedmont Driving Club; it meant that, when he and his friends wanted to play baseball, they gathered, with their fathers, at the Allens' glorious meadow on weekend afternoons; it meant that, when he visited his grandparents at 2600 Peachtree Road he played at the pool table while listening to the Senator talk about Atlanta's old days, his collection of rare maps or the family business. "Granddaddy," Ivan III says, "was always talking about the business." The Senator lavished gifts upon his grandsons: first he bought Ivan III and Inman bicycles; later a 1956 two-door Ford Fairlane for Ivan and a 1959 Ford four-door for Inman. Privilege also meant that, when Westminster, a Christian prep school for boys and girls, was formed in Buckhead in 1951, Ivan III enrolled in the eighth-grade class. In those early days, Westminster even used the Allen meadow as their home field.

Ivan III circulated among the children of Atlanta's elite families. His lifelong friendships with F. Tradewell (Tread) Davis, Jr., and Mason

Lowance, Jr., began in grammar school. Though the boys' personalities were different—Davis was studious and serious; Lowance aggressive and often flip; Ivan III, mostly serious but occasionally a prankster—they were inseparable. Each was a namesake son of a family rooted deeply in the community. Davis's father was a high-ranking official at the First National Bank of Atlanta; Lowance's father was a noted physician who ran the Lowance Clinic and served as Bill Hartsfield's private doctor. Tread Davis recalls, "We had a sense that Atlanta was a place of destiny."

The headmaster at Westminster, Dr. Bill Pressly, became the boys' mentor. Pressly had left the elite McCallie School in Chattanooga to help found Westminster. He envisioned Westminster becoming the equal of McCallie or Woodberry Forest in Virginia. Beyond teaching geometry and the classics, Pressly taught his students civic duty and responsibility. He made clear they were Atlanta's future. "And we were constantly driving that home," Pressly says.

Allen, Lowance and Davis were class leaders with crew cuts and handsome cars. As a senior in 1956, Ivan III was the most decorated. He won the Hull Memorial Cup, the school's highest honor. He earned letters in football, basketball and tennis. He was president of the honor council and business manager of the annual.

The boys' interaction with blacks, apart from family servants, was rare. The boys spent many weekend nights together, co-hosting parties in the Allens' summer cottage. They played basketball and listened to Elvis Presley and Bill Haley records. Louise supplied hamburgers and Coca-Colas. The boys also had swimming parties in the summer and once threw a fully clothed Bill Pressly into the pool, with his gold watch on.

Ivan III dated Margaret Poer, a surgeon's daughter; they shared chili dogs at The Varsity and burgers at Rusty's. Sometimes they attended an Atlanta Crackers baseball game at Ponce de Leon Park.

When it came time to consider colleges, Pressly encouraged his students to look beyond the South. In so doing he was challenging a tradition of Old Atlanta families who had sent their sons to the University of Georgia in Athens or to Georgia Tech and Emory in Atlanta. "I thought they would get a better education outside of the South, to tell you the truth," Pressly says. The Class of 1956, the first to spend a full five years at Westminster, established the school among the nation's elite. Admission directors at several Ivy League schools sent letters to Pressly congratulating him on the quality of his students. Of the thirty-nine boys in the class, thirteen went to the North, mostly to elite schools, including Ivan Allen III, Tread Davis, Jr., and Mason Lowance, Jr. The trio chose to stick together, at Pressly's alma mater, Princeton University.

In September 1956, the Davis, Lowance and Allen families gathered at the Brookwood train station on Peachtree Street to see the boys off to Princeton. Ivan Jr. and Louise came, as did the Senator. Bill Pressly and his wife showed up as well. The boys' suitcases were full, their hopes high. They became roommates at Princeton, and joined a political organization known as the Whig-Cliosophic Club, which once counted as a member future President of the United States James Madison. Ivan III and Tread shared train rides from Princeton to Washington where they would rent a car to visit their girlfriends, who were at colleges in Virginia.

But as they boarded *The Southern* that day at the Brookwood station, bound for Princeton Junction, the three elite products of Atlanta privilege knew one thing for certain. One day they would come home.

The issue was not *whether* to resist the United States Supreme Court ruling on schools. The issue was *how*.

To Robert Troutman, Sr., the noted Atlanta attorney, the Civil War had proven that, in 1956, secession was no longer an option for southern states. "The fundamental question remains," Troutman said in a speech to the Atlanta Rotary Club, "how far are the states willing to go in interposing their sovereignty?"

Ninety percent of white Georgians favored segregation, recalls Ernest Vandiver, the state's lieutenant governor at the time. Gov. Marvin Griffin believed interposition by individual southern states was the only answer. In a February 1956 address before a joint session at the State Capitol, Griffin asked legislators to declare the Supreme Court ruling on schools "null and void," contending that the court had set out for the "destruction of the states." Resistance by whites was espoused in virtually every corner. Former governor Ellis Arnall suggested that delaying tactics in the courts could preserve segregation in Georgia's schools for another century. At Bill Hartsfield's First Baptist Church on Peachtree Street, the Rev. Roy McClain said integration "sounds like a good idea on the surface, but works in reverse. The idea of taking from those who have made gains, whether economically, socially or educationally and giving to those who haven't is no more than communism."

Ivan Jr. was listening closely, angling toward 1958. His name was gaining increased circulation, especially in Atlanta where those freshly scrubbed white delivery trucks fanned out across the city. Every truck bore the words "Ivan Allen" on the side, evidence of the Senator's romance with his own name as well as of the firm's continuing prosperity (eight stores in Georgia, Tennessee and South Carolina).

In the fall of 1955, Ivan Jr. and Herman Talmadge were named co-chairmen of a jointly sponsored fund-raising program for their alma maters, Georgia Tech and the University of Georgia. Together, they traveled Georgia, delivering speeches, at times joined by football coaches Bobby Dodd of Tech and Wally Butts of UGA. Their personal friendship strengthened and when Talmadge ran successfully for the U.S. Senate in 1956, beginning an unbroken quarter century in Washington, Ivan Jr. was among his supporters, for the first time. His support for Talmadge reflected not so much a political change as the fact that his friend M. E. Thompson had been a late entry into the race, too late to mount a serious campaign. Talmadge defeated Thompson by more than a four-to-one margin.

In Atlanta the rumblings of the civil rights movement were beginning to be felt. Law enforcement agencies in Georgia considered the NAACP a threat. The Georgia Bureau of Investigation (GBI), following a tip, discovered that the NAACP's southern region office had moved from Birmingham to Atlanta on September 28, 1956. The GBI found that Ruby Hurley, a black woman serving as NAACP regional director, had moved to the Waluhaje Apartments on West Lake Avenue in Atlanta and that thirty corrugated board cases filled with NAACP stationery had been transferred from Birmingham to the third floor of the Cannolene Building, a black hair-care business on Hunter Street. "Investigation is continuing," Lt. H. A. Poole of the GBI wrote in an internal memo in November.

In Montgomery, Alabama, a black boycott of city buses, led by Rev. Martin Luther King, Jr., finally ended after more than a year on December 21, 1956. The U.S. Supreme Court upheld a lower court ruling that Montgomery's segregated seating practice on buses was unconstitutional. Triggered by the arrest of a forty-two-year-old black seamstress named Rosa Parks for her refusal to give up a seat reserved for whites, the boycott spurred Atlanta's black religious leaders into action. Calling themselves "The Triple L Movement" (for love, liberty and loyalty), a group of black ministers led by the Rev. William Holmes Borders, boarded a trolley bus on Mitchell Street in downtown Atlanta on January 9, 1957. They sat in the front seats reserved for whites, in open violation of Atlanta's segregation laws. It made for a tense moment. A white transit company supervisor entered the bus and took the vehicle out of service. White passengers left immediately, but the black ministers remained. The supervisor called for mechanics to examine the bus—of course, there was nothing wrong with it—and soon it was taken to the bus barn, carrying the singing and praying ministers. The ministers rang the bell and told the driver they would leave through the front door. The driver consented. Reverend Borders had hoped for an arrest that would gain widespread publicity and force a legal test case of the state's segregation laws in federal courts. The challenge alarmed Griffin, who placed the National Guard on standby alert.

The last thing Bill Hartsfield wanted in an election year was a bus boycott by blacks similar to that just ended in Montgomery. If black Atlantans were going to protest segregated seating on city buses, the mayor, hoping to avoid unrest, wanted that challenge made in the courts. Through Chief Jenkins, Hartsfield secretly arranged for the black ministers to make another attempt to board a public bus the following afternoon. Six of the ministers, including Borders, were arrested in full view of the gathered press. Privately, Hartsfield had offered to send city limousines to take the ministers to City Hall for booking, but Borders refused, saying they preferred to take the police paddywagon. The mayor's choreography helped to produce the hoped-for legal test cases that ended segregated seating on Atlanta's buses.

That spring Hartsfield, seeking a sixth term, defeated Fulton County Commissioner Archie Lindsay in the Democratic primary. "Mr. Hartsfield has been in office so long," the *Journal* wrote in its endorsement of his candidacy, ". . . it is difficult to judge him objectively." Lester Maddox, an eccentric Atlanta restaurateur and ardent segregationist, emerged unexpectedly to oppose Hartsfield in the December general election. "I will never sell my birthright to Washington or the NAACP," Maddox announced. Of the more than 14,000 black votes cast in that election, Hartsfield took all but 353. What was equally significant, however, was that Hartsfield and Maddox ran nearly equal among white voters, Maddox taking most of the working-class votes in south and west Atlanta, a fact that injured Hartsfield's pride. Among many white voters it seemed that retaining segregation was more important than retaining Bill Hartsfield.

Into this racial maelstrom walked Ivan Jr. A businessman, he believed the race dilemma was an economic one requiring an economic solution. As a leading official of the Georgia Chamber of Commerce, Ivan Jr. wrote a concise letter to Gov. Marvin Griffin in 1957 that suggested an economic response while demonstrating that his racial views were not altogether different from those of such an arch-segregationist as U.S. senator Richard Russell.

Having called in 1953 for new incentives to keep educated blacks in Georgia, Ivan Jr. now urged Griffin to institute a one-cent sales tax to fund a program that would relocate Georgia's discontented blacks out of the state, perhaps even to Africa.

His secretary, Sylvia Porter, "must have rewritten that thing ten times after I dictated it," Ivan Jr. recalls. "Four beautifully spaced paragraphs, each one of them about the same number of sentences."

In the letter, Ivan Jr. used a quote he would not forget: "The race issue is chaos erected into a system without any loss to the chaotic and without any system." ("Where I got that from, I don't know. I think it was Robespierre in the French Revolution.")

The idea of relocating and colonizing blacks was not new in the South; the concept of African colonization dated to antebellum times. In 1949, Senator Russell had introduced a bill in Washington that called for the formation of a relocation commission and the appropriation of $500 million to establish credit for blacks who wanted to move from the South to other portions of the nation. According to the bill, each black family would be entitled to receive $1,500 to relocate. Russell sought a more equitable balance of the black population, explaining that the eleven states that once comprised the Confederacy contained fewer than one-fourth of the nation's total population but three-fourths of the nation's blacks. His bill never moved out of the Senate.

Ivan Jr. remembers that Griffin did not respond to his letter. He recalls his own thinking at the time: "If [Griffin] wanted to resolve the race issue—we couldn't go on forever with the strife we were living under, the confusion—[then] the best thing to do would be to provide the funds to move whatever people were dissatisfied back to Africa."

Nearly forty years later, an elderly Ivan Jr., at one turn, characterizes his letter as "a barb" at Griffin. "It was just . . . I couldn't define it."

At another turn, he shakes his head and says, "I thought that was smart as hell at the time."

In August 1957, Ivan Jr. resigned his position as president of the Georgia State Chamber of Commerce, hired a press agent and set out on a speaking blitz.

Over the next four months, he delivered sixty-five speeches across Georgia, hoping to catch the necessary spark for the 1958 governor's race. Already, battles were being waged behind the scenes between the Talmadge and Griffin factions. Lieutenant Governor Vandiver, who had married the niece of Senator Russell, had the backing of key members of the Talmadge faction, including Herman Talmadge himself; the Griffin group supported Roger Lawson, the former state highway chairman. The county unit system meant that power still rested in the rural areas. Of aspiring candidate Ivan Allen, Jr., Talmadge would recall, "Born rich, fingerbowl background. High society. He was not a good speaker. He was not a good mixer. He was a good man."

"Frankly," Ernest Vandiver would say decades later, "I knew Ivan was ambitious but I didn't know he was that ambitious."

For his speechwriter, Ivan Jr. hired a precocious twenty-two-year-old Harvard graduate named Gerald (Jerry) Horton. Horton was an Atlantan, schooled at Murphy High, and his father managed the F.W. Woolworth's store in downtown. He had been working at Rich's, writing the Monday advertisements that appeared each week in the *Journal* and the *Constitution* as well as writing an occasional speech for company president Richard Rich. During his interview, Horton recalls that Ivan Jr. played catch with himself, tossing into the air a football from the Georgia–Georgia Tech game. "Do you go to church?" Ivan Jr. asked. "How did you do at Harvard?" He told Horton that Ivan III was at Princeton, then stammered over a few more questions.

"He had no notion of what to ask," Horton says. "He asked me the silliest bunch of questions." Horton got the job that afternoon. The fact that Ivan Jr. hired a twenty-two-year-old Harvard graduate instead of a more experienced speechwriter proved he was a novice. Later, Horton met the Senator, who handed him a copy of *The Atlanta Spirit: Altitude and Attitude*. "As my son's speechwriter," the Senator told him, "you'll find this very helpful."

Together, Ivan Jr. and Horton crisscrossed the state, the speechwriter also serving as the candidate's driver. They spent the night at the finest place in each town, though often drove into the early morning hours so that Allen could return home to Atlanta and his family. They shared plenty of idle time along the open blacktopped roads. To Horton, Ivan Jr. seemed a decent, though naive fellow. On one occasion, after Horton had mentioned that he planned to buy a car, Ivan Jr. warned him never to buy unless he could pay for it in full. To Horton, it seemed as if Ivan Jr. didn't understand that most people couldn't afford to buy a car without a loan.

At each appearance, Ivan Jr. spoke of the need to improve education and agriculture and of the need to attract new industry and bolster tourism. He spoke about the race issue, too, in the ritualistic fashion of all southern politicians of the period. "Segregation is our way of life," he said that summer, "and not a political football. Healthy, prosperous and strong counties and a strong county unit system are one of our great advantages in maintaining segregation."

His tone had not changed appreciably, if at all, since 1953. He determined to focus on the economy during his speeches, not segregation. He knew more about business, after all, than he did about blacks. On the stump, he gave the appearance of a smooth, courtly man of business. He had few good stories to share. A raconteur, Ivan Jr. was not. "Deathly dull," Horton remembers of those speeches. "Ivan was not accustomed to speaking for an effect. He was accustomed to giving orders [in business]." Ivan Jr. tried to adapt, to appear as someone other than an upper-class Atlantan.

In early September, Allen and Vandiver were among a contingent of political friends invited to Herman and Betty Talmadge's plantation at Lovejoy, in Henry County, for the opening of dove-hunting season. It was an opportunity for the political boys to be boys and in one instance, when Ivan Jr. had stepped out of the room, Herman Talmadge cracked, "The only way Ivan can beat Ernie is if Ernie gets caught in a Nigger whorehouse two nights running."

Difficult as it was to win a gubernatorial race in Georgia without the support of Herman Talmadge, Little Rock made matters even more difficult for Ivan Jr. When nine black students arrived at the previously all-white Central High School in Little Rock, Arkansas, on September 4, 1957, beginning the court-ordered desegregation, members of the National Guard blocked their entrance. Gov. Orval Faubus had activated the state troops in open defiance of the federal government.

For the next three weeks, television cameras beamed to the nation images of racial discord in the South. Governor Faubus flew to Washington and met with President Eisenhower. He pushed Eisenhower's patience to the limit while his popularity among whites in Arkansas soared to new levels. When Faubus finally buckled to federal pressure and withdrew his National Guardsmen on September 23, local white mobs beat two black newsmen and broke windows at Central High. Local police saved several black students from mobs. Eisenhower sent in the 101st Airborne Division, a riot-trained unit. The desegregation of Central High proceeded amidst the glint of federal bayonets.

Ivan Jr. had planned to talk about tourism. But now, everywhere he turned in Georgia, white voters wanted to talk about the blacks.

On September 26, the second day of integration under federal protection at Central High, Ivan Jr. wrote another letter to Governor Griffin, this time asking him to call a special session of the Georgia legislature to leave "no stone unturned" in the battle to retain segregation in Georgia.

"Time and understanding, which have stood by us for so long are apparently running out," he wrote in a letter released to the press the same day. (Griffin announced the next day that a special session was not needed.) Ivan Jr. also called for new "extraordinary police powers at the state level" since "it is apparent that the National Guard can be immediately federalized at the whim of the President."

The announced candidates for governor reacted in a similar vein that day. Roger Lawson compared Eisenhower's moving the 101st Airborne

Division into Arkansas with the Japanese attack on Pearl Harbor. Vandiver announced that segregation in Georgia would be maintained "even if it means ultimately the abandonment of our public education system and the substitution of private education in its stead." (From the Capitol, Griffin blasted the president, charging that only two military chieftains ever dared occupy the South with federal forces: Ulysses S. Grant and Dwight D. Eisenhower.)

Typically, Bill Hartsfield had a different spin. "I'm proud of the fact that in the face of race trouble all over the South, you have seen none in Atlanta," he said on September 23. "Do you want boycotting, with the white people always losing?"

In the weeks that followed, Ivan Jr. spoke with firmness, yet moderation. Segregation, he told the Valdosta Exchange Club on October 7, "must be presented to the nation with thoughtfulness and dignity." He added, "Our position must be proved morally right to those who do not live in the thickly populated Negro areas as we do. This is necessary not only to protect our segregated way of life but also to promise the peace and tranquility necessary to continue our economic development program."

His campaign received only nominal coverage in the Georgia press. Of his speeches, the text of only one survives; written by Horton in November 1957, it was not delivered. Nevertheless, it offers insight into Allen's thought process. The speech read, in part:

> We are going to act with honor and dignity. This is a Southern custom too, just as segregation, and we believe in the Southern way of life. This is the first step in our fight against integration. . . . As I see it, the only way the South can win is to fight an aggressive battle. The future of segregated schools in Georgia depends on the picture we give to the rest of the nation. There will be only one way to set aside the Supreme Court decision, that is when people of the U.S. understand the problems of the South and realize that the Courts in the name of democracy are forcing a tyranny on the people which will destroy the life it has found since the days of Reconstruction. . . . We need to sit down and discuss the situation with the Negro leaders. The integration forces have told the Negro only one side of the story, they have distorted the facts. They've made him forget that we are his friend. They've told him the lie that he can't have equal opportunities under segregation. They've told him the white man in the South wants to keep him ignorant and always a servant. This is a lie, one of the worst lies ever to have been given a people. This lie has made the whites and Negroes of the South wary of each other. It has driven us

into opposing camps and we no longer speak. The old friendship of which the great Negro educator Booker T. Washington spoke, which was the white man and the Negro working together for a better south, is being destroyed.

Rural Georgians, in the fall of 1957, were not convinced that they had a problem with segregation. They believed that only Atlanta and other large, liberal cities with leaders like Ralph McGill and Bill Hartsfield had problems with their blacks. In November, eighty white ministers in Atlanta signed a six-point manifesto that supported blacks' rights to first-class citizenship, stressing the need to save public schools and to open the lines of interracial communication. "We approach our task in a spirit of humility, of penitence and prayer," the statement read. Among the signers was Rev. Harry A. Fifeld of the Allens' First Presbyterian church. Though Fifeld believed voluntary segregation "consistent with Christian truth," he thought "enforced segregation on the basis of color inconsistent with Biblical principles."

Ivan Jr. was discovering why no Atlantan in forty years had made it to the governor's mansion. "No matter how clear and unequivocal I made my support of segregation," he surmised, "I still was from Atlanta." Herman Talmadge tried to offer solace to his friend. "I'll try to get Ernie to appoint you to the Board of Regents," he told Ivan Jr. that fall.

The week before Christmas, 1957, Ivan Jr. announced he would not be a candidate for governor. "As a businessman I have analyzed the market and found I am not a saleable product."

The *Constitution* admired his statement. "This, we submit, is the most original political statement of our time and the only completely honest one in generations. . . . The people don't want a businessman. Most of them want one who says what they want to hear and one who endorses their prejudices. We think Mr. Allen would have made a fine governor. But he was right. He never had a chance."

He had learned a valuable lesson. "Making a decision promptly, as is generally done in business, just isn't the normal way in politics," he explained in a first-person article, about his brief campaign, written for *The Atlanta Journal Sunday Magazine* in February 1958. "You put it off just as long as possible, hoping the necessity for making it will go away. . . . You find yourself going through a sort of mathematical process to arrive at what you say and do. You add up 159 counties, multiply by two opponents—and then shoot.

"With all that calculating to do, you don't shoot from the hip very often."

*         *         *

Ernest Vandiver was elected governor of Georgia in a landslide in September 1958. He promised to maintain segregation and the county unit system. Vandiver also gave assurance that "No, Not One!" white child would be forced to attend a desegregated school. That same fall, a federal district court advised that *Calhoun v. Latimer,* a class-action suit filed in January 1958 by several black parents in Atlanta to end segregated schools in the city, would be decided by September 1959; this raised the specter of a desegregation order for the 1959–60 school year. In December, an organization known as Help Our Public Education (HOPE) was formed by a group of affluent white Atlantans; it became an effective lobby for desegregation in the ensuing years.

The inevitable racial conflict closed in on Atlanta. White families made an unprecedented rush toward private schools in 1958 to avoid placing their children in the same classroom with black children. At Westminster, where seventeen-year-old Inman Allen and his seven-year-old brother, Beaumont, were among the seven hundred students, more than eighteen hundred applicants were turned away that year.

Meanwhile, Governor-elect Vandiver walked into Herman Talmadge's living room in Lovejoy soon after his election and found, much to his surprise, a group of black leaders from Atlanta waiting for him. These blacks urged Vandiver not to defy the courts by closing public schools. "We supported you in the campaign," Warren Cochrane of the Butler Street YMCA told him, as businessman Clayton Yates sat by his side, "and we're hopeful that you'll be understanding of our situation now." Decades later, Vandiver says, "I was shocked, really, because I didn't quite understand Sen. Talmadge's relationship with the black community at that time." As governor, Talmadge says he once dispatched a state trooper to Miller County to protect attorney A. T. Walden, who was defending a young black charged with murdering a white. Of his relationships with black leaders in Georgia, Talmadge would say, "I don't guess anybody shouted it from the rooftop at that time."

During the 1950s, Atlanta's five-county metropolitan population grew by an astonishing 40 percent. As Hartsfield began to call his town "The City Too Busy To Hate," Atlanta became the twenty-second metropolitan area in the nation to arrive in "the one-million population class." City leaders were not about to let the moment pass unnoticed. A local committee named Donald C. Smith as "Mr. Million." Smith was a forty-year-old sales manager who had just moved his family to the city from Cincinnati. That he was a Yankee was symbolic to more than a few. "We roll out a red carpet for every damn Yankee who comes in here with two strong hands and some money," Hartsfield said. "We break our necks to sell him." Hartsfield called Atlanta "a city of destiny." To celebrate "M Day," $500 billion in Confederate money was printed by the city to promote the occasion; even Russian premier Nikita Khrushchev received a Rebel $1 million bill in the mail. *Newsweek* magazine knighted Atlanta as "the nerve center of the New South," though it noted, somewhat ominously, "The threat of closed schools hangs heavy over the city."

In 1958, Ivan Jr. received his own preview of the strife that lay ahead as a member of the Atlanta Citizens Advisory Committee on Urban Renewal. Gathered in an office on Auburn Avenue with a group of black leaders, the committee listened as the Rev. William Holmes Borders called for more black involvement in planning Atlanta's urban renewal program. Borders sharply criticized Hartsfield for his indifference.

Ivan Jr. listened quietly until he could take no more. He scolded the blacks in the room, saying they ought to appreciate all that the mayor had done for them over the years.

"Don't worry," he said, finally, in a phrase dripping with paternalism, "we'll take care of you people."

From his seat, architect Cecil Alexander, the white committee chairman, blanched.

Borders rose from his chair. A dark-skinned man with a resonant voice, he could be profoundly intimidating. His father and grandfather were ministers before him. "They were doing what was called 'Gettin' the slaves straightened out,'" Borders would say. He had left Macon for Morehouse College in the late 1920s and upon arriving in Atlanta had detected something different and exciting: "It had dash! It had a sympathetic drive in it."

Now, he stood before Ivan Allen, Jr. He let a few seconds pass, the tension rising. Then Borders reached out with the back of his hand. He stroked the cheek of Ivan Jr. in a symbolic gesture.

"Did anything rub off? Am I any different," Borders asked, "or am I a man just like you?"

On his cheek, Ivan Jr. felt a stinging sensation.

# Chapter 14

※

"I want to buy some perfume," the Grand said, and he said it the way he said all things, as a declaration. The white salesgirl at Rich's waited behind the counter.

Dobbs pointed inside the glass case. "What about this Evening in Paris?" The elegant blue bottle had gold embossed letters on the front and a colorful tassel falling lightly from its crown.

Dobbs planned to buy Christmas gifts for his wife, six daughters and a few secretaries at the Masonic lodge. Carol Ann Jackson, his twelve-year-old granddaughter, stood by his side.

Tilting her head slightly, the salesgirl eyed her black customer, doubtfully. Evening in Paris, she told him, was expensive.

Just then John Wesley Dobbs's right fist crashed down upon the glass top. The perfume bottles inside rattled and toppled. Heads turned from nearby aisles. Amazement, then fright, washed across the salesgirl's face.

"I DIDN'T ASK YOU HOW MUCH IT COST!" Dobbs roared. He reached into his right pocket, the side where he kept the big bills, and pulled out his money clip. He said he wanted to buy multiple sets.

He slapped the big bills on the glass counter, one at a time. *Thump.* He stared at the salesgirl, defiantly. *Thump.* So, you think a black man can't afford this? *Thump.* You, young lady, shall never forget this moment. *Thump.* Nor shall you forget me.

He was an old man now, yet he possessed a resolve that defied age. If he had self-doubt he would not show it, certainly not publicly. Self-doubt in a southern black expressed publicly was a victory for white supremacy. He fought all battles against prejudice armed with the certainty that his side was the right side. In June 1956, he rifled off a three-page letter to the Rev. Roy McClain, pastor of the white First Baptist Church on Peachtree Street, Bill Hartsfield's church, challenging him on his published sermon, "Is Racial Integration the Answer?" "I think that the decision for you, and your ministerial friends, to make is whether you will serve Jim Crow and Segregation on the one hand; or stand up for JESUS CHRIST and BROTHERHOOD on the other hand," Dobbs wrote. "Our moral short comings today are, largely, the result of these vile, inhuman living conditions to which we were subjected by your Master Race. . . . In God's name, just why are you, and your Christian friends, not willing to help us?" That fall, Dobbs gathered at the Steward Chapel AME Church in Macon with the Georgia Voters League, a statewide voter registration organization for blacks, and said, "Sometimes, the darkness of the night appears to get blacker and blacker. . . . We are, now, long past midnight; it certainly cannot be long until day."

One night during the summer of 1956, he heard a knock on the filigreed iron front door of 540. It was late, too late for someone to be knocking on the front door. Dobbs got out of bed. He called out, "Who is it?" and when the answer came it struck a nerve deep within him.

In a response drawn from the race riot days, he reached behind his bed and pulled out one of his guns.

Dobbs peered through a front window and saw his visitors. They were white men, looking for him.

"John Wesley Dobbs?" a voice called out, from the front steps.

"Who are you?" came the Grand's furtive reply.

"We have something for you."

"What is it?"

"Open the door."

"What is it?"

"Open the door and we'll show you."

"*What is it?*"

Finally, an answer: "A subpoena from Miller County. Open the door."

The Grand knew why they had come. He had cut too close to the truth about whites intimidating blacks trying to register to vote in Miller County. Now the whites had come after him. The Grand knew Miller County. It was a poor, mean place in the deep shadows of southwest Georgia. His Masonic lodge in Colquitt had sent him a letter, outlining voter registration difficulties. The Grand wrote his response at the bottom of the letter, then sent it back to his lodge. An Associated Press man soon phoned. He had researched the numbers in Miller County and learned that among nearly 10,000 residents, including 2,686 blacks, only 6 blacks were registered to vote.

His story disclosed these startling numbers and included several choice comments from the Grand.

And this was the result. An Atlanta standoff: the whites with a subpoena and the black, behind his locked filigreed front door in the darkness, with a gun. Their arrival under the cover of darkness only increased Dobbs's apprehension.

The Grand stalled. "Wait there," he called out. He phoned Herbert Jenkins, Atlanta's chief of police. In matters such as this, Dobbs believed, Jenkins could be trusted. Speaking quietly, so as not to be heard by the white men on his front step, he described the situation to Jenkins. The chief told Dobbs that he was not legally required to open his door. He also offered to send a City of Atlanta policeman to 540 to make certain these men were genuine in their announced purpose and that they were not hooligans bent on causing trouble. The Grand accepted the chief's offer. Once the Atlanta policeman arrived and the subpoena was served, Dobbs's problems were only beginning.

He did not expect to receive true justice in Miller County. The idea of appearing before a county grand jury in Colquitt convened in special session for the sole purpose of investigating his reported allegations that blacks in the county were being denied voting rights frightened Dobbs considerably. Grand juries were a prosecutor's tool; he knew this.

Dobbs had been down these legal roads before. When his Masons had stared down the barrel of multiple lawsuits during the 1930s and 1940s, he had hired high-powered white Atlanta attorneys, Shepard Bryan and his son-in-law, W. Colquitt Carter. When his own son-in-law, Rev. Maynard Jackson, had faced the police officer's lawsuit three years earlier, they had turned to W. Neal Baird, another prominent white attorney. This time, the Grand chose for his lawyer Hoke Smith, Jr., a Georgia state legislator from Atlanta. It was an ironic selection. Smith, after all, was the namesake grandson of the former Georgia governor and U.S. senator, Hoke Smith, the politician whose racially inflamed speeches had contributed to the race riot climate in 1906.

It was, the Grand later would write, "a terrible political experience." He ventured down to Miller County on September 19, 1956, and brought Hoke Smith, Jr., with him. "Good thing I did," he wrote the next day in a letter to Renie. "He was worth his weight in gold to me. We out-maneuvered them." Standing before the all-white grand jury, Dobbs was asked to produce the letter from his Masonic lodge, which he had signed at the bottom. Dobbs said he did not have the letter and signed an affidavit to that effect: "I do not have in my possession any letter or other written instrument that charges that Negro voters are being denied the right to vote in Miller County." Peter Zack Geer, Jr., attorney for the Miller County Board of Registrars and an avowed segregationist who later would win election as lieutenant governor of Georgia, reported that Dobbs told the grand jury that he had been misquoted by the Associated Press. The grand jury decided not to indict Dobbs and concluded that Miller County had an "honest, fair handling of our registration list."

Nearly four decades later, Geer recalls his friendship with Hoke Smith, Jr. (they served together in the Georgia General Assembly) and that Dobbs never was in danger. "Hoke didn't outmaneuver anybody. We had an agreement," Geer says. "Hoke called me and wanted to know if he would have any problems. I said, 'Hell, no, Hoke, we're civilized down here.' " Geer adds, "I guess Mr. Dobbs had been misled. . . . The Grand Jury invited him to put up or shut up and he shut up."

Privately, Dobbs vowed to continue to fight to register blacks in Miller County. He would do it carefully, though. "I don't want that experience again," he wrote to Renie. "It was almost like facing a 'Mob.' "

The Grand held several family reunions at 540 during the early 1950s, though the peripatetic nature of his brood made it difficult to gather everyone. Willie and her husband, Ben Blackburn, lived in Jackson, Mississippi; Millie and Bob Jordan, Sr., a dentist, in Nashville; Josie and Bill Clement, an insurance man, in Durham, North Carolina; unmarried, Geekie and June were overseas and in the North. Nothing thrilled John Wesley Dobbs quite like posing for a picture surrounded by his massive family. Invariably, he sat in the center, "Babe" to his right, and different variables of his six daughters, their husbands and his horde of more than a dozen grandchildren forming a forest of humanity all around him. In pictures taken during those reunions, Dobbs's chin always has an upward tilt and his old eyes are alight with pride. In the spring of 1952, he barely could contain his joy when Millie gave birth to twin sons, Jimmy and Dobbs. That gave the Grand nine grandsons and six granddaughters. At the time he wrote, "At my funeral I want 20 grands—well, now with two unmarried daughters [and fifteen grandchildren already] I . . . see that the quota was not set too high."

During these years when various personal crises struck his family, Dobbs remained the great stabilizer, the rock around which his family flowed in disparate directions. His responsibilities as husband, father and grandfather would take on a drama of their own. If voter registration became his public crusade, his family remained his private one.

When Irene suffered heart trouble, Dobbs secured a student from Morris Brown College to board at 540 (he paid for her tuition and books) so that someone would always be on call to look after his wife, particularly during those times when he was away on Masonic or Georgia Voters League business. His love for family remained unconditional but his tongue could be harsh. In January 1953, days before their planned trip to Washington for the Eisenhower inauguration, Irene returned from the beautician with her hair cut short and with a blue rinse that had turned her gray a purplish hue. Dobbs put his wife back in the car with orders to get the purple out.

For Renie, Dobbs would supply the necessary ballast to move ahead with her life, sometimes giving money, more often words of encouragement.

He also helped his two family stars to find their skies.

Geekie, his fifth daughter, who had that velvety operatic sound and the name, Mattiwilda, that caused people to scratch their heads, became his gift to the world.

And Maynard Jr., his rotund firstborn grandson with the driving ambition and impressive presence, became his gift to the future.

Sensing his mortality, Dobbs thought, too, of his own legacy. He pulled Geekie aside once, when her singing career in Europe started to blossom, and as they sat together on the porch at 540, he pointed to the house next door, 536 Houston, on the corner of Howell Street.

"Would you buy that house and tear it down," Dobbs asked his daughter, "so we could have a lawn around our house?"

"Daddy," Geekie replied, shaking her head in disbelief, "I can't afford to do anything like that."

It was a wild idea, Geekie thought, and certainly one that was financially beyond her means. But her father worried that one day 540 might not be around and that disturbed him. It was important to him that 540 never disappear. A lawn would increase its magnificence. In 1952, Dobbs had fulfilled a dream by adding a second story to 540. He did it over the objections of his daughters, who thought his money would be better spent moving to a new house on the west side. But Dobbs wouldn't hear of it. He was a Fourth Ward man, to the bone. He wasn't moving unless 540 was moving with him. He thought about posterity. On his top marble step out front he had engraved, "J.W. Dobbs, 540 Houston Street N.E." But a marble step was not enough. What if people forgot about John Wesley Dobbs? That's why 540 had to stay. "He wanted it there," Geekie recalls, "like some kind of museum."

For a time, Renie thought she wouldn't make it. Not in her worst nightmare did she ever imagine she would become a widow at the age of forty-five, let along a single mother of six. She felt abandoned and alone. Grieving still, her fears were real. *Where was the money going to come from? Who will discipline the children when they need disciplining? And what about me? Who's going to comfort me?* For her, every day seemed the same: she helped Carol Ann, Connie and Paul off to school, taught her French classes at Spelman and then returned home for a good afternoon cry. Sometimes she wept uncontrollably. Carol Ann consoled her and held her hand. Only fourteen, Carol Ann was growing up quickly. She had no choice. "Let me take a nap," Renie would say and Carol Ann would leave the room to cook dinner. To her children, Renie seemed like a robot during these lonely years, eyes glazed, perpetually in mourning, totally without joy and going through the motions in her life. "Kind of frozen over," Carol Ann recalls. Suicide entered Renie's thoughts, but then she remembered her husband's wish that she raise their children. Apart from the children Renie felt at times as if she had no reason to live.

The Grand played the role of surrogate father to her children. He had especially keen interest in Maynard Jr., his firstborn grandson. He openly questioned Renie for the free rein she gave him.

"Why did you let Buzzy do that?" he asked on more than one occasion. Dobbs wanted to take control of his grandson, as he wanted to control all things. Besides, he reminded Renie, he knew what it was like to grow up without a father.

But now, for the first time in her life, Renie lashed out at him for meddling.

"Daddy," she said, "you look after your son. I'll look after mine."

Accustomed to complete compliance from his oldest daughter, the Grand was shocked. "I didn't know you could |talk to your father like that," he said.

"Well, Daddy, remember, I'm grown now. I'm not fifteen years old and biting my tongue."

Twenty years before, Dobbs had insisted that Renie, as an investment for the future, wait one year before marrying Maynard Jackson and follow through with her prestigious one-year scholarship to study in Toulouse. "Someday," he said, "your husband could die." Now, he again encouraged her to broaden her career options and to enhance her earning potential; in 1956, Renie took the bold leap. That summer, she returned to the University of Toulouse to study for her doctorate. She brought Carol Ann, Connie and Paul with her. They lived for a few months in the same home where Renie had boarded as a student in 1933. None of her children spoke French so Renie hired a private tutor. Living alone in a foreign country—raised as southern black Baptists, her children now were attending French Catholic schools—increased their interdependence and brought her family closer together. In the fall, Renie sent Connie, who was nearly ten, and Paul, six, to a private boarding school, Val Fleuri, thirty miles away in an idyllic rural setting. The experience was not a good one, though, and soon she brought them back to Toulouse. She moved her family into a spacious third-floor apartment and hired a Basque woman, Madame Aillagon, to cook and clean; another family lived downstairs and they shared the bathroom, which was set between the floors.

Several times, Renie spoke to large audiences in Toulouse about the burgeoning American civil rights movement. In May 1957, she wrote a letter to an old family friend, the Rev. Martin Luther King, Jr., pastor of the Dexter Avenue Baptist Church in Montgomery, to congratulate him on his recent civil rights successes. "It is impossible to talk about the South today without presenting you and your philosophy," she wrote. Renie added:

> Daddy came by Toulouse . . . to see me and my three children who are going to public schools here. We talked of your tremendous courage and level-headedness and I decided to write you to let you know that I, for one, pray for your increased strength and know-how. If you never intended to become great—you are anyway and the world won't let you be anything less. . . . I will be home (Houston St.) after July 1st until Sept. 15th. There's so much spiritual depression here and there. Except for seeing dear ones, it won't be especially uplifting to come back to Atlanta. But then, the Algerian impasse is sapping the French in every way—especially spiritually. So it might be refreshing, at that, to live a few weeks among people who have right on their side.

During his visit in the spring of 1957, the Grand was horrified to learn that Renie, and his grandchildren, shared a bathroom between floors with another family. At once, he paid for the installation of a toilet inside a closet in Renie's apartment.

He was proud of Renie, especially her courage and intellect. His pride swelled even more in the summer of 1958 when he sent a note to all family members. "My dear ones," the patriarch began. "We received a Cablegram from Irene, at the University of Toulouse, this morning. It read—'Received Doctorate.' She had a hard struggle to complete a three-year course in two years. She deserves a lot of credit and commendation."

Nothing could stop him from bragging about Geekie. Sitting in a barber's chair on Sweet Auburn, the Grand rattled on about her latest smash success in an opera performed in some faraway land. Geekie was a coloratura soprano, an operatic style punctuated by florid ornamental trills and runs. Dobbs would pull from his breast pocket the most recent rave from Australia or Russia or Israel or Singapore or England and ask someone to read it aloud while he luxuriated in his own steam. "I know there's something of the divine in that child," Dobbs told one writer.

"It's a message of love you hear listening to her. . . . It's something you can't put into words, but it's there."

He considered Geekie the most fragile of his daughters and her timidity had been apparent in 1943 during one of her first solo performances as a student at Spelman College. Her teacher called her to the piano and advised her to lean against it for support. Watching from the audience that night Dobbs thought, "She's going to faint!" But over the years he had encouraged and soothed, praised and pushed Geekie. His wife, Irene, ever the family peacemaker and the sympathetic ambassador to the Grand, frequently added the cautionary, "Not too hard, Wes." A woman visiting from the North once heard Geekie perform at Spelman and asked to come to 540. "Take her to New York, Mr. Dobbs," the woman said, sitting next to the piano in the parlor. "Find her the best voice teacher in the city. I can tell you from my knowledge that she has the makings of another Marian Anderson." Anderson, a black contralto, had performed to great acclaim in Europe during the 1930s and was one of Geekie's idols. Years before, Dobbs had taken Geekie to hear Anderson perform at the Atlanta City Auditorium on a night when seating remained segregated but, according to Anderson's wishes, had been split directly down the middle, blacks on one side, whites on the other. (Typically, blacks were restricted to the balcony in the auditorium.) In 1946, Geekie, following Renie's lead, graduated as valedictorian of her Spelman class. Dobbs then took her to New York where she trained with the noted instructor Madame Lotte Leonard, once a lieder and oratorio singer in Germany. During this period, Geekie earned her master's degree in Spanish at Columbia University (where Millie and Josie also had earned master's degrees). Her young career was gaining momentum and focus when, in 1950, she traveled to Paris to study with Pierre Bernac on a John Hay Whitney Opportunity Fellowship, named for the same man who a dozen years before had financed Selznick's *Gone With the Wind*. She felt her father's firm, loving hand, always. "He pushed me into my career. I was very shy. I loved music. But I was afraid I wouldn't succeed. He was really behind me and paid for my studies in New York," she says. Geekie pursued opera even though blacks had scant opportunity. One of the leading operas of the period, *Aida* had a black heroine but the role was played by a white with blackened face.

On the brink of her breakthrough in Europe, Geekie's shyness faded. Her brown eyes flashed more confidence, less innocence. She learned the nuance of theater. She competed against many of Europe's most talented young singers in the International Music Competition in Geneva in October 1951. The night before the finals, twenty-six-year-old Geekie stepped off a curb and sprained her ankle; she suffered severe swelling. Doctors feared a sedative might temporarily damage her vocal cords and so on the morning of the finals they tightly wrapped her ankle with tape. She limped onto the stage and sang an aria from Mozart's *The Abduction from the Seraglio*. After finishing she took a sedative and went to bed. She learned of her victory the next morning when a hotel maid brought her a newspaper. The headline announced her arrival to stardom. Soon she was off to perform across Europe, in France and Sweden, Holland and Luxembourg. The Grand lived vicariously through her exploits. Proudly, he mailed copies of Geekie's letters to other members of the extended Dobbs family, a practice that later embarrassed Geekie for she had intended her personal thoughts for her parents only.

The Grand and Irene traveled to Europe in the spring of 1952 to witness, firsthand, how Geekie was spreading the glory of the Dobbs name across the globe. Their first trip overseas was a gift from the Masons. On March 7, 1952, they sailed from New York on the *Queen Elizabeth*. They visited England, Holland, France, Switzerland and Italy. Leaving his wife with Geekie in southern Italy, Dobbs flew on to Greece, Turkey, Beirut, Jerusalem and North Africa. Along the way he saw sites that amazed him. He felt the antiquity of man in the Middle East, and in Africa was overpowered by the dramatic human odyssey of the black race. In observing Geekie's successes, he saw the possibilities of a black, unfettered by artificial restraint, rising alone on merit and determination. Upon his return home, he told his Masons at the 1952 Grand Lodge in Savannah, "I am not the same man anymore because I have changed within." He wrote articles about his global travels in the *Daily World*. "I'm coming home to America more enlightened because of things I have seen on this trip and more determined to fight for human rights; yes, for Civil Rights, if you please; and for every bed-rock principle laid down in the American Declaration of Independence and the United States Constitution."

The Grand was introduced to Luis Rodríguez for the first time on this trip. Geekie had met the young Spaniard in Paris. He was studying law at the Sorbonne and lived near her in a campus community noted for its array of students of various races and nationalities. A romance blossomed and Geekie wrote often of Luis in her letters to 540. Rodríguez spoke, as Dobbs later would say, "very leetle Engleesh." He seemed nervous in the Grand's presence. The foursome spent one night at the Folies-Bergère where Dobbs noticed Geekie and Luis holding hands under the table. His first impression of Luis was that he seemed genuinely in love with Geekie. When Luis asked Dobbs for permission to marry her, Geekie, who spoke four languages, served as his interpreter.

Ever strict in such matters, Dobbs asked the young couple to wait one year. "I wanted Mattiwilda to be sure that this was really love and not a fleeting fascination," he explained. Irene chided him for it later, saying, "You really hurt the boy." Yet Dobbs gave his unconditional consent one year later. On April 4, 1953, Geekie and Luis were married in a small ceremony in Genoa, Italy, the historic home city of Christopher Columbus, where Geekie was performing in Mozart's *Magic Flute*.

Only one month earlier, Geekie had become the first black to appear in a principal role at the famed La Scala Opera House in Milan, playing Elvira in Rossini's *L'Italiana in Algeri*. Back at 540, the news was accepted along the same historic lines as Jackie Robinson's barrier-breaking effort in baseball. In Milan, though, Geekie says, "They didn't make any big hullabaloo over it. There was no color barrier there." Geekie's triumphs, however, were diminished by her growing concern for Luis, who was suffering from a severe liver ailment.

By the fall of 1953, Geekie had hired the noted impresario Sol Hurok of New York to handle her American performances. A Russian immigrant, Hurok was demanding yet effective. He had managed many of the world's leading opera performers, including Marian Anderson. Yet at times, it seemed as if the Grand remained Geekie's press agent and manager. When *Ebony*, a Chicago-based magazine of black culture, profiled Geekie's ascent in January 1954, its story centered on the Grand ("Boss Dobbs" according to the magazine) and not his daughter.

The provocative headline in *Ebony* read: " 'My Daughter Married a White Man'—J. Wesley Dobbs." When he first saw it, the Grand exploded in a double-fisted rage. The story read, in part:

> Many Negroes, particularly those born and bred in the deep South, would answer with an emphatic "No!" if asked "would you want your daughter to marry a white man?" Prejudice against interracial marriage is just as prevalent among colored people as it is among their white counterparts. . . . Some predicted that Dobbs would try to have Mattiwilda annul the marriage. Others went so far as to conjecture that he might even disown his most illustrious daughter. But in many ways peppy, garrulous John Wesley Dobbs is an unpredictable man. In this instance he did none of the expected things. "Why should I be up in arms because my daughter married a white man?" he asks. [The headline apparently was taken from a portion of that quote.] She didn't marry Luis because he is Spanish, but because he is the man she loves.

Dobbs told *Ebony* that Geekie and Luis could return to Atlanta without concern for stirring a racial tempest. "They can visit Atlanta any time they like," Dobbs said. "They can live in this house and be comfortable while they are here. Luis, you know, is Spanish, and doesn't look as white as some Negroes."

Later, Dobbs wrote an angry letter of protest to *Ebony*. "I positively did not attempt to stress the point that Luis Rodriguez was a white man," he wrote. "I stated to you that he was a Spaniard and explained that the Spanish people as a race are of mixed blood lineage. I have no apology to make about the man my daughter married—That was entirely her own business." He termed the headline "cheap and misleading." He added, "In the first place I did not say it; In the next, it suggests that I was either trying to brag about it; or, that I was ashamed of it. Neither suggestion is correct." He asked for a retraction and a public apology from *Ebony*. "You have also paid for advertisements in the *Atlanta Journal, Atlanta Constitution,* and *Atlanta Daily World* further exploiting my name and reputation. I am requesting that you will immediately stop that type of cheap publicity."

By now the European press had coined a new name for Geekie: "La Dobbs." Remarkably, she harnessed her skills at a time of enormous inner torment. Luis's health was deteriorating rapidly and in June 1954, only fourteen months after their wedding, he died in a London hospital.

His death occurred at a time of glory and optimism for black Americans. Several weeks earlier the U.S. Supreme Court, in *Brown v. Board of Education,* had outlawed "separate but equal" segregation, causing celebrations among blacks across the South. While Geekie was alone, in mourning in London, fully removed from her support system, the Grand was in Augusta, telling his Prince Hall Masons at the annual Grand Lodge, "Thank God for those nine Federal judges on our U.S. Supreme Court bench. . . . My brethren, these decisions have simply sounded the death knell to Jim Crow and Segregation in the United States of America."

Five days after Luis's death, Geekie was summoned to London's Covent Garden to perform before Queen Elizabeth II and the royal guests, Sweden's King Gustav Adolph and Queen Louise, in the French opera *Le Coq d'Or.* Aware of Luis's death, the audience rose to applaud the strength of Geekie's performance. Afterward, Geekie approached the royal box where the king presented her with Sweden's honorary Order of the North Star. Her fortitude never was more apparent.

At the dawn of 1955, Geekie was ready to make her American operatic debut. In January *Mademoiselle* named her one of the world's ten most outstanding women of 1954 (actress Eva Marie Saint and clothes designer Anne Klein were among those on the list); that same month Marian Anderson finally pierced the veil of discrimination to appear for the first time at the Metropolitan Opera in New York. These were wonderful omens for Geekie, signs that things were opening up. That autumn, she became the first black diva to perform with the San Francisco Opera. ("Miss Dobbs is easy to describe," a reviewer from *The Sacramento Bee* wrote in 1955. "She has everything.")

Yet if racial restrictions in opera were easing in Europe, New York and San Francisco, they were not in Atlanta. In November 1955, Geekie was scheduled to perform, in recital, before five hundred southern ministers and educators of both races at the Atlanta City Auditorium as part of a southwide conference on compliance with the Supreme Court ruling on segregation. It was to be her coming-out party in her hometown. But politics intruded. In September, U.S. senator James O. Eastland of Mississippi, chairman of the Senate Internal Security Subcommittee, called for an investigation by the Justice Department to determine whether the Southern Conference Educational Fund, sponsor of the southwide conference, was a communist front organization. The fund had been created to improve race relations through conferences and publications; among its directors were Morehouse College president Benjamin Mays, Clark College president James P. Brawley and John Wesley Dobbs. Dobbs refused to allow Geekie to become embroiled in the controversy. "We feel that she should, under no circumstances, be subjected to a political or controversial issue that might damage her future career in any way," he wrote in a letter to SCEF secretary James A. Dombrowski. Geekie withdrew from her commitment to perform in recital. Earlier, Dobbs had written a letter to the chairman of the Republican National Committee, blasting attempts by the committee to link the fund, and the NAACP, with communism. Dobbs stressed his allegiance to both organizations, while noting his position on the Republican State Central Committee of Georgia. He wrote, "I do not need to tell you that Negroes, all over America, will resent this kind of tactics and hold the Republican Party responsible for it."

And so Atlanta would have to wait for Geekie.

But the Metropolitan Opera of New York would not.

The Grand was euphoric when he learned that Geekie was to perform the following year at the Met, playing Gilda in *Rigoletto* on November 9, 1956. In that role, she would become the third black to appear in New York's most prestigious opera house, following Anderson and Robert McFerrin, and the first to sing a principal role.

Naturally, the Grand bragged about the news up and down Sweet Auburn; when Irene, still plagued by heart trouble, was cleared by her doctor to make the trip to New York, the Grand sent her straight to Rich's where she bought a new $165 gown. "Believe me," Dobbs wrote in a letter to Renie, in Toulouse, "she will look lovely." For his wife, he took every precaution to assure her comfort: she would eat her meals in the compartment of the train, and at the stations in New York and Atlanta she would have a wheelchair. Dobbs wanted his entire family to attend. History, he knew, tolled. If Renie could not attend, then he decided Maynard Jr., now in Boston University Law School, must come in her place. The round-trip bus fare from Boston to New York City was $9.52. The Grand would pay for it. "I wore out my tux pants this summer having to work in them every day," Maynard Jr. explained in a letter to his grandfather, preparing to attend Geekie's big night. "Would my charcoal gray suit be sufficient?" The Grand would take care of this, too. On the train he brought a spare tuxedo jacket and a pair of dress pants, which he had a tailor loosen at the waist in order to fit his grandson's enormous frame. "I want him to be there," he wrote to Renie, "to represent you and your family. He will live to tell it to the coming generations."

Geekie was a bundle of nerves when she made her first appearance during Act II. "Her body was tense and her breathing was deep," reviewer Douglas Watt of *The New York Daily News* wrote the following day. "But her lovely voice delivered for her." He added, "Miss Dobbs is alone among her contemporaries in being able to combine florid vocalism with warmth of expression. I, for one, attribute this happy circumstance partly to the characteristic veiled tones that distinguish the Negro voice from any other." Melvin Tapley of *The Amsterdam News*, the leading black newspaper in the city, viewed the effort largely through the racial prism. "The NAACP might consider Verdi for a posthumous Spingarn medal. Both of the precedent-shattering appearances of Mattiwilda Dobbs and Marian Anderson were in roles from operas by Verdi."

When Geekie came home to Atlanta in January 1957, the cheers of the Met still resounded in her ears. Treated as a conquering hero by hometown blacks, she was hounded by autograph seekers when she sang at the Wheat Street Baptist Church on Auburn Avenue. But her opportunities in Atlanta remained limited. The city did not yet have an opera of its own. Furthermore, because Geekie stipulated in her contract that she would not perform before a segregated audience, whites in Atlanta effectively were prohibited from her appearances, though a few attended her recitals at black churches.

Several weeks later the Grand gathered the family around the television set at 540 to watch Geekie appear on Ed Sullivan's *Toast of the Town*. The program was ill-suited for opera but was one of America's most popular television shows. Geekie's appearance represented another stroke of pride for the Grand.

She wrote to 540 after the show, "It was nice to know that I was singing to you right at home on TV while you were sitting in your own living room. I'm sorry I couldn't sing 'Russian Nightingale' but 'Summertime' wasn't bad. They paid me $1,500, which isn't bad, either."

Traveling the globe, Geekie's loneliness intensified. Only thirty-two, her world was a small and insulated place. Sometimes, a family member, usually one of her sisters, visited her in Madrid, or met her on tour. Geekie sent money to family members often, including $200 per month to Renie, in Toulouse. "I have no one to spend my money on but myself," she wrote to Renie in July 1956, "and am only too glad I can do something for my loved ones when they need it."

She met a Swedish newspaperman, Bengt Janzon, in February 1957. Later in the year, they were making wedding plans. In one sense, Geekie was following a family tradition. In choosing their husbands, the Dobbs daughters showed an unusual strength and willingness to challenge the conservative social standards of their times: Renie had married a divorced minister, Josie a widower with a young daughter and Geekie a Spaniard and now a Swede. She knew that marrying Bengt in Atlanta was out of the question. The Grand told her Atlanta was not ready for it, that an interracial marriage was certain to cause a stir. Besides, he feared his wife's heart might not stand the stress.

Geekie and Bengt decided to marry in New York, at Grace Congregational Church, two days before Christmas, 1957. A black minister presided and a Swedish minister delivered a prayer, in Swedish. The Grand and Irene attended, as did Willie, Millie, Josie and the youngest sister, June, who served as matron of honor. A family dinner followed at the St. Moritz Hotel.

Though the *Constitution* had failed to take notice of most of Geekie's European successes, and even her appearance on Ed Sullivan's *Toast of the Town*, the newspaper did not miss her second marriage.

Its brief notice about the wedding made one point eminently clear: "Janzon is the second white newpaperman husband for Miss Dobbs."

From the beginning, Maynard Jr. seemed a man-child, broad as a bear, with a sharp mind, meaty hands and a huge laugh. "He was a personality," Renie says, "from time go." With two older sisters and two younger sisters, he became their playful knight. In ballroom dancing, he was Connie's first partner. ("Do you mind," he told her, after a few steps, "if I lead?") He was a heavy sleeper, and his younger sisters often sneaked into his bedroom in the morning to tickle him, just so they could hear his remarkable laugh. He had a knack for making his presence felt, intentionally and unwittingly. Once, as a boy at his uncle Alex Jackson's drug-store in Texas, a woman entered and asked for "douche powder," though to young Maynard it sounded like she had asked for "dish powder." He called out to his uncle, "Do we have any dish powder?" His uncle seemed perplexed. "Dish powder?" Maynard Jr. repeated, a little louder. "Do we have any?" Seeing the embarrassed woman, an equally embar-rassed Uncle Alex told his nephew to run along. His sisters playfully called Maynard Jr. "The Garbage Disposal" because on most nights he ate whatever they had left on their plates; he found ice cream particu-larly irresistible. At David T. Howard High School, he stood more than six feet tall and weighed about 250 pounds. No one in the family knew of any ancestor who had ever been so large. He would grow taller and heavier yet and his heft gave him an intimidating presence. His size did not translate into athletic prowess, however. As an eleven-year-old, he was among the elementary school students invited to play in the annual Milk Bowl Classic at Herndon Stadium at Atlanta University. When the coach called him into the game, as an offensive guard, "I was in the stands showing off my uniform to my mother," so he never played.

Growing up, his family challenged him. "If you didn't bring home straight As in our house, there was something wrong with you," May-nard Jr. recalls. An intellectual atmosphere prevailed. Renie often spoke French inside the house and Maynard Jr. considered himself nearly flu-ent in that language when he was fourteen. To be criticized at home, he understood, was to be a member of the Dobbs-Jackson family. "I grew up in a family where if you criticize that's one manifestation of love. It shows you care." Criticism usually related to deportment or expression, from manners to diction to appearance. Criticism came at the breakfast table, the dinner table, virtually anywhere at any time. Family criticism, it was reasoned, bred self-criticism, which, after all, had bred an opera star, a minister, college professors and, of course, the Grand. If Maynard Jr. and his siblings used poor grammar, or even the wrong word alto-gether, they were corrected, then sent to a dictionary to look it up. That way they wouldn't make the same mistake twice.

His father and grandfather had made him feel the urgency of his spe-cial place in family history. Maynard Jr. knew that he was descended from a line of black men and women who, because of segregation, had been unable to shape their own destiny. He also knew that, as a matter of fate, his own coming of age was coinciding with the slow rupture of legal segregation in the South and that this presented him with opportunities that previous generations had never known.

In May 1954, Maynard Jr. sat in the student assembly at Morehouse when the announcement was made of the *Brown v. Board of Education* ruling. The students erupted with glee, shouting and hugging over the promise of a new day. "It was like the second Emancipation. We didn't know the first one, but we imagined what it was like for a slave to hear that you are free," Maynard Jr. says. "This was unbelievable. *Unbelievable!* And unanimous? It was too good to be true."

His most defining quality, aside from his physical heft, was his voice. It made people stop. It was not so much its depth—Maynard Jr. entered Morehouse a first tenor and graduated a second tenor—as its precision and formality. He had an entirely different sound from, the Grand, smoother, less emotional. His delivery was precise, his sentences perfectly punctuated. His voice impressed people, particularly his new college classmates. "Some of us came straight from the country to Morehouse. Maynard had the advantages of a particular kind of parentage that equipped him early in life, in terms of leadership and eloquence," said Otis Moss, Jr., a Morehouse peer.

Even in his letters to the family, Maynard Jr. was beginning to sound like a lawyer. In the summer of 1954, when he was just sixteen, he wrote to Renie and tried to describe his affections for a girl. "I have concluded that I am, for the first time in my life, in love!" he wrote. "To be frank, the whole situation is somewhat of an enigma to me."

Following his graduation from Morehouse in 1956, he determined to attend law school in the North, at Boston University. It was an adventure, his first chance to live outside the South. Only eighteen, an age when most students are college freshmen or sophomores, he competed against law students three and four years older. He worked that summer as a waiter at a country club in Cleveland to earn money for school. Apparently he did not earn enough. In September he wrote to the Grand, asking to borrow money, a request for which he later would apologize. "I had no intention of implying that I was in some type of trouble, for I wasn't, am not, and will not be," he assured the Grand. "As long as this combination of Jackson and Dobbs is in me, I have sense enough to keep trouble off my doorstep. Grandpa, I'm a big boy now, even though I sometimes do childish things (like asking you for money)."

The young law student notified his grandfather that he would not return home to Atlanta for Christmas. He planned to get a job in Boston during the holiday season, as the Grand had mandated. "I may be out of line, but I am going to be frank with you," he wrote in November 1956, "I am in love with a girl who is at Spelman, and we had planned on this trip [to Atlanta]. I say 'we' but actually it was all my idea. . . . I suppose [remaining in Boston] is the price one must pay for growing up."

The Grand laid it on the line to his grandson in a letter sent four days later. He reminded him that years earlier, when Millie and Josie were in the master's program at Columbia University in New York City, they could not afford to come home to Atlanta for Christmas, either. "You knew from the start it would be a struggle for you to remain at Boston University Law school with little money," Dobbs wrote. "You took that chance and I thought it was a wise thing for you to do. I still want you to realize that your father is gone and left a widow with six children, of which you are the only big boy in the group. In fact it now devolves upon you to assume the responsibility of a Man. I want to help you realize and face that responsibility. I know what it is because I had to face it myself. I worked hard and made the 'grade.' You can do it, too. I am willing to help you, but I am not willing to help spoil you."

More than money was troubling Maynard Jackson. He had fallen behind in his law classes. He failed to make passing marks in several courses. His lack of maturity was showing. The Boy Wonder's freight train was derailing. Suddenly in November 1957, at the age of nineteen, he found himself out of law school and working in Cleveland as a claims examiner for the state of Ohio's Bureau of Unemployment Compensation. Discouraged, yet still hoping for another chance at law, he wrote to his mother in Toulouse in December, updating her on all aspects of his life. He remained upbeat. "Tell [Carol, his sister] there are a couple of new dances called The Calypso & The Slop (a good 'un). Carol, always stay your sweet self. There are so many girls with beauty & nothing else. Also, I've observed (other factors being equal) that Southern girls have 'it' all over Northern girls. This is true in terms of general attractiveness, personality, warmth, deportment, and sincerity."

Just as he protected and promoted Renie and Geekie, Dobbs tried to open closed doors for his first grandson. In May 1958, Dobbs visited Cleveland where he introduced Maynard Jr. to Thurgood Marshall of the NAACP. The following week, he reminded Marshall of the meeting in a letter in which he asked for help in getting Maynard Jr. into the Howard University Law School, which counted Marshall among its most illustrious alums. Of his grandson's travails at Boston University Law School, the Grand wrote to Marshall, "Seemingly he did not know how to properly grasp the study situation. For that reason he did not make the passing mark in two or three subjects. . . . He seems quite determined to succeed, if given another chance." (The Grand also tried to pull strings with a letter to the Howard Law School dean, James M. Nabrit, of an esteemed Atlanta family. "When I think of your dear old father, I am constrained to say that you are truly a 'chip off the old block,'" he wrote. "Your daddy, too, was somebody!") The Grand's influence did not get his grandson into Howard, though.

In June, he sent a letter to his grandson, giving him the bad news. "I'm rather glad you had told me first," Maynard Jr. wrote, "in that the blow was definitely softened."

As Maynard Jr.'s personal struggles deepened, he became nostalgic for his father and those summer days spent together fishing and hiking. "Mother," Maynard Jr. wrote in November 1958, "I think of Clayton quite often and long to stretch my legs on its dusty, memory-laden roads and hills and drink of its colorful vistas." He kept the Grand apprised of his jobs, his plans and his political views. In February 1959, he inquired about the school desegregation movement in Atlanta. "I saw 'The Second Agony of Atlanta' on T.V.," he wrote, "and was a bit disappointed that there was such an apparent lack of responsible Negro leadership on the program. Further, Chet Huntley's supposed 'editoral' in the closing minutes was, I felt, unfair in that it allowed no immediate rebuttal. I missed the following Sunday's program when Roy Wilkins was on, but I hear that he did a tremendously effective (considering that he suffers under the handicap of having no Dobbs or Jackson blood in his veins) job of public speaking."

Energetic and eternally optimistic, Maynard Jr. soon found a job perfectly suited for his verbal skills: selling encyclopedias for P.F. Collier & Son. He worked in Boston, Cleveland and Buffalo and soon was promoted to assistant district sales manager. He made more than $20,000 during one year, a heady amount. But his heart remained in law and when given a second chance at Boston University Law School in the fall of 1959 he was eager to prove himself. "My desires are simple," he wrote to Renie, a month before his return to law school, "to be successful familially, professionally, ethically, financially, etc." He added, "I miss my family very much and eagerly await our reunion and its consequent gratification."

His optimism soon faded in the face of those old law school difficulties. His five classes—Bills and Notes, Equity, Evidence, Taxation and Wills—quickly overwhelmed him. As a result, he quit his job with Collier's. "I am behind in three of my five courses," he wrote to Renie in October 1959, noting that he was "working like a Trojan to catch up." By now he was attempting to play the role of the man in the Jackson family as well. He advised Carol Ann to stop dating a classmate ("The argument that she would be out of the social picture but for her present status is fraught with invalidity."). On another occasion, he threatened that older sister Sandra's now former husband "had best keep this continent between himself and me." He told his mother, "[Sandra] needs our love and support now. She has mine."

His second try at Boston University law ended much like the first: Maynard Jr., in search of himself and his future, did not make the grades. In 1961, he left Boston, and the North, to enter the law school of North Carolina Central University in Durham.

His law school difficulties in Boston remained a deep source of embarrassment to Maynard Jr. Through the years, he did not speak of it publicly; graduating from law school at the customary age of twenty-five would make it easy to conceal his lost time in Boston. "I always told Maynard that he should talk more about that [failure in Boston University]," one family member says. "It would make him seem more human to people."

Yet at times it seemed that Maynard Jackson was trying to be something more than human. One experience in Boston during the fall of 1959 sent him spiraling into disillusionment about racial prejudice. A law school friend, a light-skinned black often mistaken for white, shared a few beers with a group of white classmates. Among the group was Jackson's white roommate. Conversation became heated when it shifted to the subject of Jewish fraternities at the University of Connecticut, where some of these whites had been schooled as undergraduates. Maynard Jackson's roommate chimed, "They even let Niggers in!" At the time, the roommate was unaware that a light-skinned black was seated at the table; the black promptly got up to leave and, despite the urging of several of the whites to overlook the slip, did not return. A week later this black friend told Maynard Jr. what his roommate had said. Maynard Jr. responded by sending a sprawling six-page handwritten letter to Renie, making plain his discontent with some whites:

> I've had it! Up to here! I'm so disgusted and disillusioned that I don't really know what to think. . . . Too often I have found that my trust in "them" was ill reposed. I have never believed in racial behavior, but now I don't know. Is the presumption to be one of distrust and skepticism until the contrary is proved? Or, shall we even go further and make that presumption irrebuttable? I don't know what to do or what to think.

As the man-child of the Dobbs family, and its standard-bearer for the future, Maynard Jr. began to see in a new light the moral lessons delivered to him long ago by his father and the Grand. He was twenty-one and learning, firsthand, the full dimensions of racial division. It was too all-encompassing for him to grasp. In his letter to Renie, he admitted that he and his white roommate were "not the closest of friends, but we have had our mutual confidences and shared experiences." He wrote:

It's not that this one thing is so vastly important, but a combination of incidents have led me to know that an answer which is equitable and just and realistic, is vital to me for my understanding of Mankind and its ways.

His future was taking shape. With resignation, he wrote, "Please give me what help you can. My love to you and all. Your son, Maynard."

"There is no doubt that M. L. King is the outstanding Negro in America today," John Wesley Dobbs wrote in a letter to Renie in Toulouse in January 1957, the same month in which King founded the Southern Christian Leadership Conference. "He is well prepared and represents everything we are standing for. . . . Believe it or not he is the greatest orator for his Race in America today. It is almost unbelievable! He outranks Borders and all the rest!" The following month, Dobbs spoke to students in the chapel of Morris Brown College and held high above his head the current issue of *Time* magazine. On its cover was a picture of M. L. King, Jr. The Grand challenged students to equal the accomplishments of King by attempting to rewrite history at a young age. He also sent a congratulatory note to King the same day: "I was certainly happy to find your likeness on the cover page of *Time* magazine this week. You could not have accomplished so much, in so short a time, unless you had decided to let God use you. Keep up the good work." Only seven months earlier, however, Dobbs had questioned whether King's good work in Montgomery's bus boycott ought to be applied in Atlanta. "We don't want that," he said in a meeting of the NAACP's Atlanta branch. "It's not the right way." But Borders and Daddy King protested against Atlanta's segregated buses anyway. In Martin Luther King, Jr., Dobbs saw much of himself. He saw King as the young man he could have been, had their eras been reversed. King believed in many of the same principles as Dobbs. The very themes Dobbs had been stressing to blacks for decades—namely, the moral wrongness of Jim Crow—King now delivered directly to whites in the form of protest.

In March 1957, the Grand, funded by his Masons, traveled to Africa, where he crossed paths with King during the independence celebration of Ghana, formerly a British colony. A large American delegation attended, including Vice President Richard Nixon and prominent blacks such as Cong. Adam Clayton Powell and Charles C. Diggs, A. Philip Randolph, president of the Brotherhood of Sleeping Car Porters, and Dr. Ralph Bunche of the United Nations. Kwame Nkrumah was installed as the first prime minister of Ghana and the Grand was among a group to meet him in his office. Nkrumah even autographed a copy of his autobiography for Dobbs. After stopping in Toulouse to visit Renie, Dobbs passed through Paris and visited the Louvre. There, he spotted M. L. King and his wife, Coretta. "I moved over with them and we really enjoyed talking Africa, Europe and America," he later wrote. "It is so wonderful that they can travel around so young."

Age was taking a toll on the Grand. By spring 1958, he could barely get out of bed on some mornings. His bones throbbed unmercifully, his muscles ached and his joints stiffened as if they were made of cement. He was seventy-six years old and tired. Stairs became increasingly troublesome. Doctors had difficulty diagnosing his ailment. Meanwhile, the Grand prepared for death. He divided fifty-five of his seventy-five shares of Citizens Trust Bank stock among his children and grandchildren. To each daughter, he gave five shares, each grandson two shares, and each granddaughter one. He retained the remaining twenty shares for Irene. "I'm also grateful to God," he wrote to Renie, "that I have been spared to help, and that Mama, too, has been left with us to stimulate and cement family affections." Later that year he drew up elaborate plans for his funeral and submitted copies to his six daughters and to his wife, for safekeeping. When the time came, he wanted his funeral done right.

In October, the Grand expressed outrage when a hate-monger's bomb ripped through the Hebrew Benevolent Congregation, a Jewish synagogue on Peachtree Street known to Atlantans only as the Temple; the bomb caused considerable damage, though no injuries. The Grand sent a $100 donation from his Masons to Rabbi Jacob Rothschild to help pay for the reconstruction. "It is the crop of things sown," Ralph McGill wrote after the bombing, in a column that would bring him a Pulitzer Prize. "It is the harvest of defiance of courts and the encouragement of citizens to defy law on the part of Southern politicians. It will be the acme of irony if any one of four or five Southern governors deplore this bombing." Hartsfield quickly denounced the unknown bombers and promised that every effort would be made to assure their apprehension, a performance that led President Eisenhower to praise the mayor. (Several years later, Hartsfield would gloat in telling the Public Relations Society of America that his prompt PR effort had transformed the Temple bombing from a story about hatred in Atlanta to one about law and order and heartfelt compassion in the city.)

That summer Dobbs had told a Masonic gathering in New Haven, Connecticut, "The real disease is deeper seated in the very bloodstream of the body politic of the South." The Irish, he reminded, had fought for seven centuries before securing their liberation from Britain. "When seventeen million American Negro citizens become obsessed with a determination to put up a fight like that," Dobbs said, "then the stars in their courses will fight for them, the breezes on Earth will blow for them and the angels, in Glory, will shout for them."

Dobbs faced personal challenges in other areas. The Internal Revenue Service sought payment from him on back taxes for the years 1951, 1952 and 1953. Though it is unclear what prompted this IRS challenge, it might have stemmed from cash gifts he received from his Masons. Dobbs had been rewarded with many such gifts over the years, a traditional way to show affection for Masonic leadership. A 1952 Grand Lodge resolution offered by his friend, W. S. Holloman, an Atlanta insurance man, had rewarded Dobbs on his twentieth anniversary as grand master with an array of financial gifts, including paying off his debt to the Masonic Relief Association (an unspecified amount), assuming his $5,000 bank loan (to pay for new construction at 540) and $2,650 in cash donations from lodges across the state. In January 1959, Dobbs paid more than $15,000 to the federal government and more than $1,800 to the state of Georgia. These payments nearly depleted his life's savings but removed a worry that had weighed heavily upon him. "Already I feel like a new man," he wrote to John Lewis, Jr., his close friend and the grand master of Louisiana's Prince Hall Masons. "Maybe I can make it now for a few more years."

When Renie and her family returned from Toulouse in 1958, they rejoined the Saturday afternoon family dinners at 540. Once, as Renie helped in the kitchen, the Grand whispered to her children in the parlor, "Psst! Come with me!" They followed him to the kitchen, whereupon he threw open the door and announced, "Look it there! I want you to see this and never forget it. There's your Mama, she doesn't have any shoes on, and she's right there frying fish for me! She may have her Ph.D., but she's got her feet on the ground!" The room filled with laughter and Dobbs squeezed a smiling Renie in a bearish hug.

More than five years without her husband had toughened Renie, awakening a formidable inner strength. In Atlanta, Renie would fight her own battle for justice in May 1959. She would do it over a library card.

Among large southern cities, Atlanta was among the last to end enforced segregation in its main library. Already, Miami, Charlotte, Louisville, Chattanooga, Knoxville and New Orleans had desegregated library systems.

Since the Supreme Court decision in 1954, several black groups had sought permission to use the downtown library in Atlanta on the same basis at whites, to no avail. The Atlanta public library system had several small branches reserved for blacks. In the main branch, blacks were still permitted to read books, but only in the basement. In the spring of 1959 a few blacks had attempted to obtain library cards at the main branch. None had succeeded.

When Dr. Irene Dobbs Jackson walked into the main library in downtown Atlanta that May, she was a well-dressed fifty-one-year-old Spelman College professor of French.

"I want to become a member here," she told the white man at the front desk.

Renie was frightened by her own words. She did not view herself as a heroine. She simply wanted a library card. In France she had been free to visit any public library and to check out any book she wanted.

Waiting patiently for a reply, she watched as the man at the front desk walked to the back of the room and engaged in a heated debate with his superiors. Finally, the man returned and handed her a form. He told Renie to sign it, and she did.

"We'll call you later," he said. Renie did not believe him. Later, the Grand told her to hire a lawyer, and let the courts handle it. Yet already the Atlanta library board, along with Hartsfield and Chief Herbert Jenkins, was holding secret discussions about desegregating the city's main library.

Finally, on May 19, 1959, the library board agreed to give black Atlantans the same privileges as whites at the main branch. Hoping to minimize the possibility of an antagonistic response, the board opted not to announce the change.

Not until four days later did the local newspapers discover it. Only when pressed did library director John C. Settlemayer admit that a new policy was in place. But Settlemayer said the change likely would have little effect since records indicated that few blacks had used their own branches over the years. Gov. Ernest Vandiver denounced the new policy, contending it "does not represent the thinking or the wishes of the vast rank and file of colored citizens who would prefer to use their own library facility." But Vandiver predicted that segregation would continue on a voluntary basis at Atlanta's main library despite the change. Hartsfield chose his words more carefully. "A public library is a symbol of literacy, education and cultural progress. It does not attract troublemakers," he said. He stressed Atlanta's good reputation in race relations and said he expected those relations to continue.

For Renie, the trouble started when the *Constitution* wrote that "the first card issued to a Negro by the downtown library went to Mrs. Maynard H. Jackson, 220 Sunset Ave., N.W." Her phone started ringing at home that morning. "Doncha know niggers cain't read?" one caller said. That night a few unfamiliar cars drove along Sunset Avenue, moving slowly and surreptitiously, searching for 220. Once they spotted the apartment house, they stopped out front. From the street, a few shouted obscenities and honked horns. Dobbs family members congregated that night to offer support and protection to Renie. Millie Dobbs Jordan wouldn't stand for any harassment of her older sister. When the phone next rang, she waved away Renie, picked up the receiver and heard the racial epithets. Millie erupted. "Y'all must be nigger lovers! You keep on calling here to talk to us!"

As the controversy subsided during the following days, Renie, alone with her thoughts, wondered about Atlanta. Civil rights for blacks were inevitable, she knew. Whites in Atlanta had to see the judgment day coming, didn't they? She decided that her father was right about white southerners giving up their old prejudices. The Grand had said that such changes would come slowly, grudgingly, like the sun fading at dusk, until finally, one day, the old prejudices would be gone. Renie couldn't wait for that day. She thought, "It is just like somebody giving up a religion."

# PART V

# CIVIL RIGHTS

"Atlanta has given the South a Southern example to follow. Southerners have complained about Yankees telling them what to do. Now the South has a Southern example to follow.

> —NBC News, after Atlanta peacefully desegregated four public high schools, August 1961.

"Atlanta was no different than any other place—Baton Rouge, New Orleans, Nashville or Jackson, Miss. Segregation was just as rigid in Atlanta."

> —JAMIL ABDULLAH AL AMIN (né H. RAP BROWN, black militant)

# Chapter 15

→←

The full-page advertisement in the *Constitution* struck Ivan Allen, Jr., as it struck all leaders in white Atlanta, with a jolt.

"AN APPEAL FOR HUMAN RIGHTS," it read. "We, the students of the six affiliated institutions forming the Atlanta University Center . . . have joined our hearts, minds and bodies in the cause of gaining those rights which are inherently ours as members of the human race and as citizens of these United States." The March 9, 1960, advertisement sounded the beginning of the black student movement in Atlanta. Signed by student leaders from each of the six schools, the manifesto, filled with idealism and surging anger, called for an end to racial injustice across the spectrum of life in Atlanta.

Only six weeks earlier, four black freshmen from North Carolina A&T had sat at the whites-only lunch counter at Woolworth's in Greensboro, North Carolina. Store operators closed the counter. The "sit-in" movement took flight and moved across the South. The same night the sit-ins began in Greensboro, Rev. Martin Luther King, Jr., was celebrated in a going-away party in Montgomery. King had decided to return to Atlanta, his native city and the home base of his Southern Christian Leadership Conference (SCLC), an organization he aimed to strengthen. The governor of Georgia, Ernest Vandiver, had made plain his views about King. "Wherever M. L. King, Jr., has been there has followed in his wake a wave of crimes including stabbing, bombings, and inciting of riots, barratry, destruction of property and many others," Vandiver said. "For these reasons, he is not welcome to Georgia." Vandiver's views were echoed, privately, by many at the Atlanta Chamber of Commerce who feared that Atlanta might become another Greensboro. Even some of the established black leaders in Atlanta worried about King's return. When news broke of King's intentions, Paul Delaney, a young black reporter for the *Daily World*, was brought by editor C. A. Scott to cover a private meeting of the city's black leadership, and "those guys hit the ceiling. They didn't want Martin Luther King, Jr., to come to Atlanta. They felt Atlanta already had black leadership," Delaney recalls. "I was supposed to be a reporter at the meeting, but C.A. told me not to write what they were saying about

King." To Delaney, these meetings were about control. "They didn't want Atlanta to have the same image as Birmingham and Montgomery. Their idea was to make sure there were no racial incidents and if there were to help the mayor and the white leadership. And it worked."

King's return to Atlanta would transform the city into the headquarters of the civil rights movement; he set up his office on Auburn Avenue, on the first floor of the Prince Hall Masonic Temple that John Wesley Dobbs had built during the Depression. The superior accessibility of flights from the Atlanta airport was one reason for King's return. King traveled widely across the South and most planes in the region were routed through Atlanta, where a $20 million terminal was being constructed. The men of the Atlanta chamber had celebrated the airport as a jewel of the city, an instrument of growth. They boasted that the airport would lure people to the city. Now it had lured the spiritual leader of a black movement they hoped to suppress.

The AUC students had watched the Greensboro events closely. Lonnie C. King, a student at Morehouse College (unrelated to the Rev. M. L. King, Jr.), began to organize a similar demonstration in Atlanta. One day at the Yates & Milton drugstore, a favorite student hangout near the campus, the AUC president's secretary located him. "Mr. Mays wants to see you in the president's conference room in the administration building," she told him. When Lonnie King arrived, he found not only the presidents of the six AUC schools but most of the student leaders he had contacted about arranging a sit-in in Atlanta. Dark-skinned and powerfully built, King commanded great respect from his fellow students. At twenty-three, he was older and more mature, having served on a naval aircraft carrier in the Far East. Already he was married and a father. His mother was a domestic and his stepfather served as a foreman of the Southern Bakery. The presence of the presidents "scared us to death, man," King recalls. "Some of these folks we'd never seen. We'd only heard about them." Atlanta University president Rufus Clement had a warning for the students. He said the presidents were not philosophically opposed to student protests but the students still had to make passing grades. This was difficult to do, Clement said, from a jail cell. Lonnie King admitted that he had been planning a protest in Atlanta for the following week. Benjamin Mays, forceful and outspoken, tried to dissuade King by suggesting that the NAACP was better equipped to handle a protest, since segregation remained primarily a legal issue. But the students were impatient.

Clement told the students, "We are not going to tell you what you can or can't do but let us give you some advice. Before you take action, pick-

eting or demonstrating, you should draw up a bill of particulars as to
what your grievances are. If you do a good job, we will see that it gets
printed in the local newspapers."

A committee of students, including Roslyn Pope of Spelman College
and Julian Bond of Morehouse, then drew up the "Appeal for Human
Rights." Clement raised the $1,500 necessary to publish the appeal in
the local papers. On March 8 he strode into the advertising office of the
*Constitution.* Moments later the phone was ringing in editor Gene Patterson's office. "Gene, you better come in here," an advertising executive
at the newspaper said. "I'm in something way over my head." The revolutionary tone of the advertisement shocked Patterson. Years afterward
he would recite one sentence from it, by memory, nearly verbatim: "We
do not intend to wait placidly for those rights which are legally and
morally ours to be meted out to us one at a time." "I thought this was
communism," he recalls. "Are you going to print it?" Clement asked. Patterson believed he had no choice but to print it. The *Constitution,* after
all, had been printing the segregationist diatribes each week in ads
placed by the eccentric Lester Maddox, owner of the Pickrick, a restaurant noted for its fried chicken.

The response to the students' published advertisement was immediate. "A left-wing statement," Governor Vandiver called it, "calculated to
breed dissatisfaction, discontent, discord and evil." Within hours of
Clement's arrival at the *Constitution,* Hartsfield seemed to be transforming a previously scheduled appearance on local television into a rebuttal
to the students. He patronized them, suggesting that in Atlanta, unlike
most southern cities, there was no reason for a black to demonstrate.
"He can walk, instead of march, right into City Hall and talk over his
problems with city officials," the mayor said. "Here, he can get a hearing." The next day, when the "Appeal for Human Rights" appeared in his
city's newspapers, Hartsfield reacted as if it were nothing more worri-
some than a box score from a Crackers game. "Constructive," he called
it. "It must be admitted that some of the things expressed . . . are, after
all, the legitimate aspirations of young people throughout the nation and
the entire world."

To Hartsfield, who had passed his seventieth birthday, it was clear
that a generational divide had developed in black Atlanta. The old-guard
aristocracy—Walden, Dobbs, Milton, Clayton Yates, Daddy King and
the college presidents—had served for decades as instruments of nego-
tiation and compromise. Virtually all of the elder black leaders had
passed through the AUC, either as students or professors. Now they
were being challenged by a younger, restless generation.

The tempo was too fast now for Hartsfield. The rush of daily events didn't allow a wily old mayor time to apply his practiced and calm response. A fast tempo in business in Atlanta was considered a godsend. But in race relations, it was not. For all the pronouncements by civic boosters of racial fairness and moderation, Atlanta in March 1960 remained a stiffly segregated city where water fountains at City Hall still carried signs that read "Colored" and "White."

Even Rev. M. L. King, Jr., recognized that he had to be mindful of moving too fast, or too radically, in Atlanta. He was concerned about the city's black leadership. "I grew up with these people," King told a colleague in the SCLC. "They'll eat me alive if I make a mistake." Now a figure of national renown, King had thrilled his father by agreeing to join him as co-pastor at Ebenezer. In explaining his desire to leave Montgomery, the young King had told his closest friend, Rev. Ralph D. Abernathy, that his father needed him and that the membership at Ebenezer was in decline. "Now I've got to help him." Daddy King, a short, bullish man who had little regard for those who dared challenge him, was a central player among Auburn Avenue's old guard. Now, upon his son's return to Atlanta, Daddy King made clear that he, and other black leaders, had worked diligently for decades to make Atlanta what it was. His son got the message. He would not lead mass marches in Atlanta. "They didn't have to say it to him," recalls Andrew Young, who joined King's SCLC staff in 1961. "He knew it."

The AUC students felt no such inhibitions. On March 15, nearly two hundred black students staged sit-ins at nine cafeterias and restaurants at City Hall, the State Capitol, the Fulton County courthouse and at the train stations. The students were largely middle class; for demonstrations they dressed handsomely, the women in dresses and the men in crisp shirts and sometimes even suits. Atlanta police made seventy-seven arrests that day, among them the Rev. A. D. King, the younger brother of Martin Luther King, Jr. A recently passed state law made it a misdemeanor to refuse to leave a business establishment when asked by management to do so. After the protest, the Atlanta newspapers each remarked that black students had made their point, but urged them not to belabor it by staging more protests. Ever conservative, the *Daily World* wrote, "Since the students had so intelligently and, we believe, impressively presented their position through the press [in the "Appeal for Human Rights"], we wonder if there is a necessity here in Atlanta to continue the demonstrations." Scott refused to print student demands in news stories. The AUC students denounced Scott and the *Daily World* as too cautious and too unwilling to pursue needed change, a rift that led to the creation of *The Atlanta Inquirer,* a black newspaper more sympathetic to the student movement.

The day after the first widespread Atlanta sit-ins, President Eisenhower, while admitting peaceful protests were protected by the U.S. Constitution, called on southerners to convene "bi-racial conferences in every city and every community" in hopes of resolving the segregation issue.

In April, black students from across the South gathered at Shaw University in Raleigh, North Carolina, to found the Student Non-Violent Coordinating Committing (SNCC). Rev. Martin Luther King, Jr., attended, and lent his spiritual support. Julian Bond of Morehouse, a handsome and eloquent young black, whose father was an admired educator at the AUC, also attended. Though greatly impressed by Reverend King, Bond, like so many others in Atlanta's black community, did not yet perceive the Atlanta minister as the prophet of the broadening movement. "He was a hometown boy . . . so it was hard for us to look at him as *Martin Luther King, Jr.,*" Bond said, adding, "It was hard for us to revere him, I think, the way other people did."

The Atlanta students mounted one more major demonstration before the summer. On May 17, 1960, the sixth anniversary of *Brown v. Board of Education,* the largest gathering of black students in Atlanta's history marched through downtown. The *Constitution* estimated three thousand marchers, though student leaders claimed four thousand. ("The white papers always underestimated the numbers," Lonnie King says. "And they changed our verbs in quotes to make us sound uneducated, too.") Their destination was the State Capitol, where, only four years before, defiant Georgia legislators had redesigned the Georgia state flag to place upon it the markings of the Confederate battle flag. Vandiver had been warned about the student march and had surrounded the Capitol with state troopers. They were armed with pistols and billy clubs.

Several blocks west of the Capitol, Chief Herbert Jenkins joined the line of black marchers.

"I'm turning you," Jenkins told Lonnie King. Jenkins motioned King to turn north, onto Broad Street, away from the Capitol and a potential conflict with state troopers. A few students announced their intention to defy Jenkins and to march to the Capitol. But Lonnie King, who hours before had listened to Benjamin Mays ask him to cancel the march for fear of inciting a riot, did not resist. Fearing violence at the Capitol, King turned the marchers to the Wheat Street Baptist Church on Auburn Avenue, one block from SCLC headquarters. From the church's altar, Martin Luther King, Jr., told the students. "You have been an inspiration to people all over the world who are struggling for freedom and dignity.

Old man segregation is on his deathbed. The only thing we are uncertain of is when he will be buried."

Among Atlanta's white leaders, the black protests were of secondary importance in the battle against desegregation. The public schools represented the main battlefront. Vandiver and the Georgia legislature created a School Study Commission during the spring of 1960 to examine the state's options for desegregation. The committee was composed of nineteen members, all white. John Sibley, a seventy-one-year-old Atlanta aristocrat, was appointed chairman. Sibley was chairman of the board of the Trust Company Bank and a confidant of Coca-Cola's Bob Woodruff. To Vandiver, Sibley was "just as much a segregationist as Herman Talmadge was. But he was a fair, impartial man who had tremendous respect." The so-called Sibley Commission had held ten hearings during March to determine what Georgians wanted: Did they want to circumvent desegregation by setting up a private school system, in which students would receive tuition grants from the state? Or did they prefer the existing public school system, even if districts in Atlanta, and elsewhere, were integrated? Existing state law mandated that if one school was integrated its entire district would shut down.

None of the Sibley Commission hearings carried the emotional voltage, or a wider range of views, than the one held in Atlanta on March 23 in the gymnasium of Henry Grady High School.

The Atlanta Chamber of Commerce had met briefly the night before. Ivan Allen, Jr., read the chamber's official position, in favor of the local option, which would allow desegregation to proceed in Atlanta. He did not attend the hearing the following day when John Sibley pounded his gavel for five hours, trying to quiet the raucous ovations that followed any support of segregated schools in Atlanta.

"This is no popularity contest, no rivalry," Sibley warned. Jack Dorsey, an Atlanta plumber and arch-segregationist, testified, "I'd rather die fighting this godless, communistic integration than to live under it." A dozen blacks, including A. T. Walden, called for a strict adherence to the court-ordered desegration. One avowed local leader of the United States Knights of the Ku Klux Klan told the commission that thousands of Klansmen in Atlanta favored closing public schools rather than desegregating them. The position of the Atlanta chamber was introduced for the record. The chairman of the Atlanta school board decried the private school plan, maintaining that it would require more than a decade to place each of Atlanta's 115,000 students. Former gubernatorial candidate Tom Linder called for the three-school plan: white, black and mixed. This represented a change of heart for Linder, who years earlier had said that anyone favoring mixed schools ought to be sent to the state hospital in Milledgeville.

The grand master of Georgia's Prince Hall Masons, John Wesley Dobbs, also testified. In an extended self-introduction, the Grand cited the size of his family. "I mention this because one of my daughters is Mattiwilda Dobbs . . . of the Metropolitan Opera."

"I know," Sibley replied, ". . . one of the greatest singers in the country."

Dobbs thrust out his chest: "Of the world!"

Not to be outdone, Sibley deadpanned, "All right, let's make it the universe."

Speaking with flair and conviction ("A hatred for discrimination . . . was stamped in every act, word, look and thought," the *Daily World* wrote of Dobbs's testimony), the Grand said, "I believe I reflect the thinking of my wife, who I have been married to for 53 years, when I say public schools should never be closed and facilities should be made available on a non-segregated basis, for equal justice under law."

On April 28, the Sibley Commission released a majority report, which recommended that the state legislature enact a constitutional amendment that would keep public schools open while allowing parents in newly integrated districts to accept state tuition grants and send the children to private schools. In Atlanta, the process of desegregation would proceed, under court order.

Already, the Atlanta Chamber of Commerce had learned an important lesson: black protests were bad for business. Now, in late spring 1960, rumors circulated that AUC students planned a widescale purchasing boycott of segregated downtown department stores. When students asked the chamber for a meeting, the chamber's board refused.

Only Ivan Allen, Jr., and Mills B. Lane of the Citizens & Southern Bank were willing to hear the students' grievances. The enigmatic Lane was a banker from Savannah, full of quirks and full of himself, a self-professed liberal noted for his collection of antique cars and colorful neckties, including one that featured a bursting sun beneath the C&S bank logo and Lane's favorite credo: "It's a wonderful world!"

In the meeting, Ivan Jr. and Lane heard sharp criticism of the segregated policies of downtown stores, specifically Rich's, the largest department store in the Southeast. Not only were blacks forbidden to sit at the Rich's lunch counter, they also could not try on clothes before buying them. The Atlanta department store's rule of thumb was that white customers would not buy clothes if they knew blacks once had sampled them.

As chairman of the student movement, Lonnie King was the black spokesman in the meeting. "It fell my task to articulate to these two white millionaires that we were human beings—educated—and that we were entitled to certain rights that they shared as a matter of birth," King recalls. To Lonnie King, Lane appeared unnerved by the tone of the discussion. "Mills Lane's position was that he went to Yale, he was a liberal, and he didn't quite understand why we were doing what we were doing. He was an arrogant man."

Though he spoke infrequently, Ivan Jr. had made a small statement by his presence: he was willing to listen. He was a creature of his own discoveries and now, for the first time, he was beginning to discover blacks. "The minute I got into it, it was showing, this great antagonism of race," Ivan Jr. recalls. *"You'd begin to learn as you went along."*

Days later, at a meeting of the board of directors at Rich's, Ivan Jr. reported the black grievances. The board's response was predictable if reactionary. It calculated the exact volume of black business at Rich's. Then board members discussed the possibility of transforming Rich's into an all-white store. The idea never took shape. They decided to risk a black boycott.

By the fall of 1960, Ivan Allen, Jr., was on the brink of change, about to be recast, by changing laws and political realities, into a southern liberal. He was a lifelong Democrat fascinated by Sen. John Kennedy's style and panache. On October 10, he stood at the Little White House in Warm Springs with Vandiver, attorney Griffin Bell and other members of the state Democratic party. There, amidst a crowd of nearly twenty thousand, he was mesmerized by Kennedy's charm, magnetism and his call to "a new generation of Americans" to rendezvous with destiny.

For nearly a decade, Ivan Jr. had lurked in the backstage of Georgia politics. In his brief moments as a candidate, wearing wire-rim glasses and freshly pressed suits, he had issued public statements that were carefully balanced and purposely inoffensive. He seemed tenuous and unnatural: an Atlanta businessman masquerading as a politician. He held on to segregation as if it were a breakable heirloom, refusing to wave the bloody shirt in the manner of the Talmadges and Marvin Griffin. He seemed a rabid moderate.

Over time, his private transformation on the race issue would seem much like John Kennedy's: as the dark clouds of civil protest gathered, his response would be shaped by pragmatism and expedience. For Ivan Jr. to reinvent himself as a champion of the black cause would require uncharacteristic boldness. It would require him to oppose what had been a basic tenet of life nurtured in the cocoon of his elite Atlanta upbringing. It would require him to ignore his Boy Scout's code of honor, which called for submission to the wisdom of elders. It would require him, for the first time in his forty-nine years, not to mirror the ruling class of white Atlanta, but to outpace it. Even to oppose it. He would retain his deep respect for traditions and appearances. He would remain ambitious, fair-minded, optimistic and acutely driven by business forces. His political rise in Atlanta would coincide with the rise of the civil rights movement. He could not move away from the black social revolution any more than it could move from him. Moderation would prove his great strength.

In October, the student boycott of downtown stores gained support among blacks in the city. Students intensified plans to storm the gates of Rich's, the symbolic castle of the white merchants. "We were exponents of the John Foster Dulles 'Domino Theory,' " Lonnie King says. "When Rich's falls, the rest of them will fall."

At the Atlanta chamber, the matter of presidential succession was in question. Because of the volatility of race relations in the city—desegregation of Atlanta's schools would be the paramount issue for the chamber's next president—no one was rushing for the job. Traditionally, the chamber's board elected a vice president to ascend to the one-year presidency. In the fall of 1960, Ed Smith, president of the First National Bank of Atlanta, Ben S. Gilmer of the Southern Bell telephone company and Ivan Allen, Jr., served as vice presidents. "They had difficulty getting anybody to be president," Ivan Jr. remembers, "because nobody wanted to face this [school] issue."

For nearly a year, Ivan Jr. had been developing his own comprehensive proposal for the chamber. The Six-Point Program, as he called it, reflected a businessman's prudence and a dreamer's ambitions. Sweeping in scope, the program seemed more the platform of an aspiring mayor than a blueprint for a Chamber of Commerce leader. It called for completion of all projected expressways by 1970, the construction of a coliseum-auditorium and a stadium, the development of a rapid transit system, support of urban renewal and low-income black housing opportunities and a nationwide advertising program called "Forward Atlanta," a concept and name borrowed from a chamber program his father had championed more than three decades before. The final point of his program called for open schools, in support of the Sibley Commission.

The Atlanta chamber was especially leery of his motives. Was he angling for something larger? Why was he so willing to compromise with blacks? Neither Ed Smith nor Ben Gilmer had a plan to offer. When leaders of the Atlanta chamber approached Ivan Jr. about assuming the presidency, they did so with reluctance.

"I will serve," Ivan Jr. told them, "only if you accept my program." That, he said, meant an acceptance of all six points, including open schools; though the chamber publicly had supported open schools, it remained a divisive issue among members. "Everybody was walking on eggshells," Ivan Jr. says. "There had been very bitter resentment on the chamber board against my position."

On October 19, 1960, black students mounted more protests, and Atlanta discovered its own vulnerability. On that day, Richard Rich, a chamber stalwart, sat down and wept after Martin Luther King, Jr., was arrested at Rich's and led away in handcuffs. His crime: violating an anti-trespass law by refusing to leave Rich's when he was denied service at a restaurant inside the store. Fifty-one students were arrested after simultaneous protests at other downtown stores, including Davison's, S. H. Kress, Woolworth's, Newberry's and Grant's. Most students had agreed to remain in jail rather than post the $500 bail, a tactic they hoped would increase pressure on white merchants.

Martin Luther King, Jr., also refused bail, telling a judge, "I don't feel that I did anything wrong in going to Rich's and seeking to be served. We went peacefully, non-violently and in a deep spirit of love." He then spent the first night of his life behind bars.

Some students had planned for jail by packing a toothbrush and a bar of soap. In the segregated city jail, women were placed on one side, men on the other. It was a new experience for the Spelman students. From her cell, Herschelle Sullivan, the Spelman student body president, who had recently returned from studying at the Sorbonne in Paris, heard the men across the way singing "We Shall Overcome." Their treatment was acceptable, Sullivan would say, though the food was not. The pregnant inmates were given fresh milk, the other women buttermilk. Reverend King and Lonnie King, arrested with him, received noticeably better treatment at the county jail where black guards provided them with phone messages, books, a checkerboard and news on the protest. On Thursday, reports suggested that nearly two thousand picketers were on Atlanta's streets, including many whites in counterdemonstrations.

As black protests mounted, Bill Hartsfield attempted to manage the final crisis of his twenty-three years as mayor. On Saturday, Hartsfield called a meeting with sixty black leaders, a bloated number that reflected the continuing fracture of black leadership in Atlanta. Virtually every segment of Atlanta's black leadership was represented, including the students, college educators (Clement, Mays, Albert Manley and

Frank Cunningham of Morris Brown), the old guard of the ANVL (Walden, Dobbs and John Calhoun), the leading ministers (Daddy King, Borders, Sam Williams) and business leaders (Warren Cochrane of the Butler Street YMCA and E. M. Martin and Jesse Hill of Atlanta Life, the latter of whom would become a major political force in black Atlanta in the decades ahead).

Black leaders demanded the release of the jailed protesters, but Hartsfield was empowered to release only those students held in the city jail and not those (including Reverend King) who were detained on state charges in the county jail. Only the state prosecutor or the criminal complainant, Richard Rich, had that power and neither was inclined to use it. Rich feared that yielding to black pressure would cost him the trust of his white customers.

After hours of intensive negotiations, Hartsfield agreed to drop the charges and to secure the release of the students from the city jail, and pledged to continue to negotiate with merchants for the desegregation of all downtown lunch counters. He also promised to lobby for the release of those held in the county jail. In return, the students gave assurances that their demonstrations would cease for thirty days, which, Hartsfield believed, was ample time for him to broker an agreement between the two sides.

Reverend Borders called it "the best meeting we've ever held in the City of Atlanta," then recited for the gathered press one of his favorite quips, that "the shortest route to Heaven is from Atlanta, Ga."

In Washington, Harris Wofford, an aide in the Kennedy campaign's civil rights section and a friend of Reverend King's, wondered if he could engineer the minister's release. Acting impulsively, Wofford phoned Atlanta attorney Morris Abram, who subsequently spoke with Hartsfield during a break in negotiations with black leaders. A series of telephone conversations ensued between Hartsfield, Abram and Wofford whereupon Hartsfield came up with an idea: he would announce, unilaterally, that Sen. John Kennedy had requested him to gain King's release. The idea was vintage Hartsfield: brash and cunning, an imaginative scheme concocted solely for effect. Hartsfield believed such an announcement not only would lend greater credence to an Atlanta settlement, but, with Kennedy's name recognition, would mute some of the criticism that was certain to arise with the release of King.

Wofford pleaded with the mayor not to make that announcement, certainly not until the candidate could be reached in Kansas for approval. Hartsfield could not be dissuaded. He reentered the aldermanic conference room and announced that Kennedy had called to ask him to spring

King. "Now, I know that I ran with the ball farther than you expected, Harris, my boy," Hartsfield later told an enraged Wofford, "but I needed a peg to swing on and you gave it to me, and I've swung on it."

When the news of Kennedy's involvement became public, the candidate's aides were furious. They issued a brief, unspecific statement from Kennedy, asking for an inquiry. "The Senator is hopeful," the release indicated, "that a satisfactory outcome can be worked out."

The black students were released from the city and county jails on Monday, October 24, though authorities detained Martin Luther King, Jr. Judge Oscar J. Mitchell of neighboring DeKalb County had issued a warrant denying King's release. In May, King had been stopped by a DeKalb policeman, as was the custom, while driving a white woman, author Lillian Smith, back to Emory University's hospital after having dinner. (Smith was undergoing cancer treatment at the facility.) King was charged with driving without a proper license, paid a small fine and was given probation.

When Lonnie King had called to ask him to participate with the students in the Rich's protest, Reverend King had initially resisted. He was still on probation. He knew the legal risks.

"But M.L., *we need you!*" Lonnie King had pleaded.

"L.C.," Reverend King replied, "what time do you want me to be there?"

Reverend King's concerns proved valid. On Tuesday, October 25, he was transferred from the Fulton County jail to DeKalb County. Handcuffed, he sat in the back seat of a DeKalb sheriff's car, a German shepherd sitting beside him. Suddenly, he was at the legal mercy of Judge Mitchell, a noted segregationist. Several years later, when the DeKalb County courthouse water fountains were to be desegregated, Mitchell would call for a fountain to be installed inside his office so he would not have to share one with blacks; upon learning that all water lines in the buildings were connected, he ordered bottled water.

Whites sat on one side of the courtroom, blacks on the other. More than two hundred supporters of Reverend King showed up. Donald Hollowell, King's attorney, needed persuasive voices as character witnesses. To him, John Wesley Dobbs was one obvious choice. "Dobbs was not only a solid, hard-hitting sort of person, he dealt in a few histrionics," Hollowell says. "He knew what to do to arouse people. That was part of his nature." In the courtroom, Dobbs spoke of his long relationship with the King family and of his admiration for young M.L. Though no records of his testimony survive, whatever the Grand and several other character witnesses said made no difference. Mitchell's mind was made up.

He revoked the minister's probation and sentenced him to four months in the state's public work camps. In the darkness that night, King was shackled and taken to the state prison at Reidsville.

Her husband was already in solitary confinement when Coretta King called Harris Wofford to ask for Senator Kennedy's help. Kennedy, in response, made a sympathetic call to Mrs. King. "He wanted me to know he was thinking about us and he would do all he could to help," Coretta King told *The New York Times.*

Once news of the Kennedy call reached the press, John Calhoun, director of Richard Nixon's campaign in black Atlanta, wanted his candidate to declare his support for King. Calhoun spoke with Val Washington, vice chairman of the Republican National Committee. "Val, this is gon' have some terrific repercussions," Calhoun said. Nixon declined to make a public statement.

During this same frenetic period, Kennedy's brother and campaign manager, Robert, phoned Judge Mitchell. On Thursday, October 27, eight days after he first had been jailed in Atlanta, King was released from Reidsville on a $2,000 appeal bond. Daddy King immediately switched his support from Nixon to Kennedy, whom he had previously opposed because of his Roman Catholic faith. Wofford and other campaign staffers produced a pamphlet, " 'No Comment' Nixon Versus a Candidate with a Heart, Senator Kennedy." Pamphlets were sent to black churches across the nation on the Sunday preceding the election; many of them went to Chicago, which was being hotly contested. On election day, in one of the closest presidential elections in history, black voters provided the margin of victory for Kennedy in several states, including Michigan, Illinois and South Carolina; Kennedy also won Georgia, handily.

In the days that followed the election, Atlanta was full of individuals who claimed to have played the instrumental role in the Kennedy victory, from Hartsfield to Abram to Daddy King to the AUC students. Thurgood Marshall of the NAACP later joked to attorney Hollowell, "They tell me that everybody got King out of jail but the lawyers." Ironically, Nixon won the black precincts in Atlanta, due largely to the organizational work of John Calhoun.

Several weeks after his release from prison, Reverend King sent John Wesley Dobbs a note, thanking him for serving as a character witness. He wrote, "I don't know any way to pay you back for your kindness and genuine concern, but by promising that I will always strive to prove worthy of your confidence and delve deeper into the struggle for freedom and human dignity for our people."

The Grand's response to the young M. L. King was deferential: "My life has been made better, more useful and more ennobling by having known you."

Atlanta, and the South, were on the cusp of historic social change. Bill Hartsfield, his negotiating magic at an end, failed to secure a lasting agreement between the white merchants and black students in his allotted thirty days. By Thanksgiving, downtown Atlanta again filled with black pickets. The 1961 mayor's race in Atlanta was less than a year away. Hartsfield was hinting that he might not seek a seventh term. The prospect of Atlanta without Hartsfield produced uncertainty in the city. To Atlanta moderates, black and white, the one man who could keep Atlanta from falling over the edge of racial moderation into the clutches of the yahoos was Bill Hartsfield.

Now, who would be there for them?

In February 1961, only one month after Atlanta's Hamilton Holmes and Charlayne Hunter became the first blacks to enter the University of Georgia, Robert B. Troutman, Sr., and A. T. Walden, venerable attorneys from opposite sides of town, arrived in the Ivan Allen Company offices. Troutman was legal counsel for Rich's, having once served in the same capacity for Bob Woodruff at Coca-Cola. At seventy, he was closing out a distinguished career as a senior partner in the firm of Sibley, Spalding, Troutman, Meadow & Smith. Walden, a rotund black Buddha now seventy-five, had retired the previous month from his legal practice after nearly a half century of devotion to civil rights cases. When black students asked him to serve as their negotiator, Walden accepted at once. To students who considered him too old and conservative, Walden admitted readily that he had grown up in a different era, while saying, "If I had been militant when I was the age of the young people today I would not be here now."

These two counselors came to discuss the impasse between the white merchants and black students with Ivan Jr., president of the Atlanta chamber. They agreed the boycotts hurt both sides. For three months, seventy downtown stores resisted student pressures. The closing of lunch counters had cost many blacks their jobs.

Even in this amicable meeting there was drama. It was prompted by a simple question.

"May I use the rest room?" A. T. Walden asked.

His question, simple only on its face, signaled a personal dilemma for Ivan Jr. The toilets for black employees at the Ivan Allen Company were in the basement; they were poorly maintained. Ivan Jr. knew he could not send Walden there. The bathroom for white employees was down the hall. But that was not an option, either. *"My sales organization will blow their stacks if I take him in there,"* Ivan Jr. thought. Some prejudiced whites believed sitting on the same toilet as blacks was the surest way to infection or disease. Undoubtedly, Troutman knew Allen's predicament. In the years ahead, Ivan Jr. would come to admire Walden; on Walden's death in 1965 his daughter, Jenelsie Holloway, looked onto the front porch of the family home and saw Ivan Allen, Jr., with a single red rose in his hand. But now, in February 1961, his relationship with Walden, much like his grasp of interracial negotiations, was in its infancy.

His ability to locate a moderate position, however, already was evident.

"Come over here," Ivan Jr. said, rising from his chair and leading Walden into the adjacent office. "Use Daddy's rest room."

Days later, Ivan Jr., and Troutman convened a meeting of twenty-five downtown merchants to gauge their views on the impasse. Their businesses were suffering a slow bloodletting. The boycotts had deflated the traditional buoyancy of Christmas shoppers. In February, a new wave of sit-ins resulted in eighty arrests. The exasperated merchants resigned themselves to desegregation. These businessmen, Ivan Jr. believed, were more liberal than merchants in other southern cities, though he sensed their readiness to negotiate with blacks was more a product of pragmatism than evidence of any moral imperative. He also knew some merchants, particularly Rich's chairman Frank Neely and the new executive director of the Atlanta chamber, Opie Shelton, from Baton Rouge, preferred firm resistance. When the meeting with white downtown businessmen ended, Troutman told Ivan Jr. and Shelton, "You boys have got to handle this. I've taken it this far." Ivan Jr. told Shelton he intended to meet with black leaders immediately. Shelton was shocked.

Ivan Jr. worked to set the parameters for the negotiations. Sessions would be held in the fourteenth-floor boardroom of the Commerce Club, the new building Mills Lane had built across the street from his C&S Bank. ("You want a downtown club?" Lane had asked Ivan Jr. a year earlier. "All right, I'll build one if you get out of my way. And you're going to be the president of it!") Ivan Jr. liked the idea of inviting black negotiators into the Commerce Club, where the Atlanta chamber had moved its headquarters the previous fall. The boardroom had three chandeliers suspended above a long, smooth cherrywood table with thirteen leather high-backed chairs on each side. An ornate Chinese rug covered the parquet floor. "It was rather lavish quarters, a very impressive place to the black people," Ivan Jr. says, "and this raised their estimation of our position, I guess." The setting spoke to class distinctions, a modern rendition of slaves called into the master's Big House. White businessmen felt more comfortable on their own turf.

Ivan Jr. also met editors of the Atlanta newspapers to explain the negotiations. He implored them to minimize publicity, for fear it would undermine chances for settlement. The *Journal* and the *Constitution* long had been members of the downtown establishment and often seemed more inclined to excessive civic promotion than even the Atlanta chamber. Ralph McGill had been a member of the chamber; Gene Patterson was about to join the chamber's board. The newspapers privately agreed to a virtual news blackout on the negotiations. Patterson would recall years later how Atlanta newspapers often were reminded of their shameful role in setting off the 1906 race riot. "It takes a few decades for a newspaper to get over something like that," Patterson says. In this case, apparently it took more than half a century.

AUC students feared the Auburn Avenue old guard might try to reach a settlement to desegregate lunch counters without their input. The old guard, meanwhile, worried that desegregation of downtown would fall to the students, many not even Atlantans. A few members of the old guard were in failing health. John Wesley Dobbs was bedridden with rheumatoid arthritis. Walden was beginning to have small lapses in concentration; several times in court hearings, students turned to Walden and discovered him asleep. A core of about a dozen black leaders was formed for the negotiations, though as many as two dozen participated. Besides Walden, this group included Daddy King, Clement, Borders, three student leaders (Lonnie King, Herschelle Sullivan and Otis Moss, Jr.), businessmen Jesse Hill and Q. V. Williamson, attorney Leroy Johnson of the ANVL and Mrs. P. Q. Yancey of the Student-Adult Liaison Committee (a group devised to bridge the generations in black Atlanta).

Negotiations were long and tedious. Black leaders wanted answers. To them, these negotiations were not only about segregated lunch counters; they also were about the right to try on clothes, and shoes, before making a purchase, the right to use the same bathrooms as whites and to drink from the same water fountains; they were about the beauty salons and the elevators. Inside the fourteenth-floor boardroom, hours dragged into days and days into weeks. "Every one of them," Ivan Jr. recalls of black negotiators, "had to make speeches and out-talk the others. What in the name of dear God they were talking about!"

The negotiations became a test of patience and endurance. Lonnie King sat next to his chief adversary, Frank Neely of Rich's. Neely was not inclined to bend his racial views. In later years, when Rich's hired blacks to greet entering customers, Neely ordered a subordinate, "You get that goddamned Nigger out of there! Bad enough to have them in the store, but we don't have to parade them around." During one meeting at the Commerce Club, King felt Neely's walking cane, beneath the table, tapping against his thigh. ("It was a nervous tic, okay, but the man was still hitting me," Lonnie King says.)

For the first time, black Atlantans began to know Ivan Jr. On the one hand, Herschelle Sullivan thought him "very much a white southerner," traditional in racial views. On the other hand, Moss was impressed by Allen's firmness when challenged by white merchants. When several merchants asked for removal of a clause referring to "and other facilities" from a tentative agreement, Ivan Jr. removed his glasses, rubbed his tired eyes and said, "We have come a long distance. 'And other facilities' is written in the agreement. We should not tear it up. We should move forward." A merchant asked, "What do you mean by 'and other facilities'?" Ivan Jr. replied, "I would assume it means what it says."

On March 6, nearly a month later, a settlement was near. Ivan Jr. approached various downtown merchants with the proposed terms. Richard Rich—"He had more guts than any of them," Ivan Jr. says—had reached the breaking point. A year before, Rich had sat in the Capital City Club and told Gene Patterson, "I'll never yield to the N-Double-A-C-Pressure!" But now his tone was different. He told Ivan Jr., "Open the goddamned stores and give it to them, if you need to. But for God's sake do something! I'm so damned tired of this thing. Get me off the hook."

Downtown merchants were willing to desegregate lunch counters *and other facilities* but not before the city's public schools were desegregated in the fall. Lonnie King knew AUC students wanted the lunch counters desegregated immediately. "It was clear that if there was trouble with the school desegregation," he recalls, "this would fall apart, too." But Ivan Jr. remained firm, insisting upon the six-month delay to allow for gradual acceptance among whites. King asked for permission to bring the proposed terms to the students to make certain of their approval.

Suddenly a voice thundered across the fourteenth floor of the Commerce Club.

"BOY, I'M TIRED OF YOU!"

An enraged Daddy King wagged a finger at Lonnie King. "This is the best agreement that we can get out of this," he said. The students long had doubted the wisdom of an alliance with Daddy King. "He was obviously a traditional man with conservative views," Sullivan recalls, adding, "I don't think we had a lot of respect for his political courage." Astonished by the excoriation, Lonnie King was equally astonished when the man to his left came to his defense. "I think he's right," Frank

Neely said. "[Lonnie] King ought to be able to go back to the students and see if they want to go along with this."

During a recess, black leaders cornered Lonnie King in a hallway. Clement, Borders and Hill urged him to sign the agreement. John Calhoun also came by and said, "I've been segregated all of my life. I don't see where another six months is going to make a difference." Daddy King walked by, his jaw jutted in defiance, without acknowledging Lonnie King. There, in the hallway, the student leader buckled to the pressure. He signed the pact. (Later that day he and Sullivan offered their resignation as leaders of the AUC movement, insisting they had signed against their better judgment. AUC students, still confident of their abilities, refused their offer.)

The following day, March 7, 1961, the agreement between white merchants and black leaders of Atlanta was announced. Walden presented the settlement to the newspapers. Ivan Jr. made the announcement for the chamber. Lunch counters would reopen immediately on a segregated basis, but would be desegregated in the fall in concert with desegregation of city schools. In the meantime, the black student protests would end.

Lonnie King heard Ivan Allen's voice over his car radio, praising the "Nigras." King hated the pronunciation.

The agreement's language was vague and clearly protective of white merchants. Nowhere did the word "desegregate" appear. The accord cited only the merchants' willingness to act in the "same pattern" as established in the Atlanta public schools. The obligations of black leadership, however, were stated explicitly: "Every effort will be made to eliminate all boycotts, reprisals, picketing and sit-ins." The optimistic tone of the statement was a vintage ray of Chamber of Commerce sunshine: "We feel that the fine relationship which has existed between the races for a long number of years should be reinstated in Atlanta in every way as soon as possible."

Lonnie King believed that Ivan Jr. intentionally had made the agreement seem more vague than it was. He recalls that he telephoned him immediately. "Mr. Allen, you are creating an inordinate amount of problems for the students in this matter," he said. He remembers Ivan Jr. responding, "That's your problem, Lonnie. I take care of my problems and you take care of yours." Then, he says, Ivan Jr. hung up. For his part, Ivan Jr. has no recollection of such a call.

Ivan Jr. already was under fire from conservative elements in white Atlanta. At Rich's, many white customers canceled accounts. Lester Maddox, head of an anti-integration group called Georgians Unwilling to Surrender (GUTS), resigned as a member of the Atlanta chamber.

To Ivan Jr., the refrain among resisting whites was always the same. *"You're giving it away to the Niggers. You don't understand: the majority rules!"*

His response was evenhanded: "There's certain things the majority can't take away," he said. "Or else there would have been one race long ago." Without knowing it, or perhaps simply unwilling to admit it, Ivan Jr. was becoming something his father never would have been: a southern liberal.

Gene Patterson celebrated Ivan Jr. just as Henry Grady once celebrated the spirit and verve of the New South. "To call this businessman ambitious, in the uncomplimentary sense, is inaccurate," Patterson wrote in the *Constitution* two days after the agreement was announced.

"[Ivan Jr.] seems more intent on living up to his name than living on it. If he desired approbation he would shrink into his set and settle for tea, tennis and tired blood. He has repeatedly chosen to go into combat. . . . [He] laid aside his lesson in state politics without rancor, and plowed his intense blend of idealism and pragmatism back into the earth of Atlanta."

Patterson would praise Ivan Jr. often in the years ahead. The columnist would become his advisor and confidant, stirring his conscience and, at times, prompting him into action. Though twelve years younger, Patterson understood Allen's struggle to find middle ground on race. He was undergoing the process himself, though his liberal leanings in 1960 were more pronounced than Allen's. Raised on a two-mule farm near Adel in south Georgia, Patterson had come of age abiding by the rules of segregation. His perspective broadened with his experiences. He served as a platoon leader during World War II in a light tank division that followed Gen. George Patton to the Rhine. He became London bureau chief for United Press International before returning to Georgia in 1956 as editor of the *Constitution*. Already Patterson had begun to peel away his racial insensitivities and to assume the liberal ideologies of his boss and idol, Ralph McGill. "Before you had the guts to declare yourself, there was a long period where you did things, said things, that you wished you hadn't," Patterson says. "I've written some things I'm deeply ashamed of. If you were in politics, like Ivan Allen, or if you were in journalism, like McGill and me, through this period each day was a new page in your life and you learned something."

Among AUC students, the agreement with merchants caused the confusion and hostility that Lonnie King had feared. Too much, they argued, had been compromised and not enough had been won. The six-month wait was a stalling tactic, many students believed; and if it was true, as black negotiators were contending, that the agreement specified that the desegregation of Atlanta's lunch counters would occur no later than October 15, why was that date not spelled out in the contract?

A group of Black Muslims circulated handbills criticizing black negotiators for "selling out to the Chamber of Commerce." Finally, students called for a mass meeting.

More than a thousand blacks filled the Warren Memorial United Methodist Church on Friday night, March 10. They represented the broad spectrum of black Atlanta, young and old, students and workers, educators and ministers. Some couldn't find seats, and stood outside the church, listening to the proceedings over a loudspeaker system. A few white leaders attended, as well. Ivan Jr., as chief negotiator of the accord, stood at the back of the sanctuary.

The gathered blacks sang songs of the movement. They cheered as heroes the student protesters released from Atlanta jails.

Ivan Jr. was apprehensive. In this church, he felt the ingredients of a riot. He realized there was more at stake than simply the agreement. He felt a racial unrest like nothing he had felt before. He watched with horror as the audience jeered A. T. Walden. When the old man said desegregation of the counters was certain, and punctuated his belief by saying, "You'll have to take my word for it," laughter rippled through the crowd. At the announcement of "the Rev. Martin Luther King," blacks cheered—only to fall silent when they realized the speaker was Daddy King. "By your saying I've sold out bothers me very little," Daddy King said. "I keep my record up and my business is to keep any of that from being true." He added, "For the first time in years, as far back as I can remember, the Chamber of Commerce agreed to take it upon itself the responsibility of working with the merchants to agree and settle this thing." When Daddy King reminded them that he had been working for civil rights in Atlanta for three decades, a woman in the audience stood and shouted, "And that's what's wrong!" The audience erupted in cheers. Borders and Rev. Sam Williams, president of the local branch of the NAACP, also were treated with little respect on this night. But the crowd stood to applaud another minister, Rev. J. A. Wilburn of Union Baptist Church, who said, "I don't see how in the name of heaven after going through all of this toil, all this suffering and sacrifice, humiliation, downgrading and degrading . . . any self-respecting Negro can go downtown."

Ivan Jr. thought: *The whole thing is going to blow up in our faces.* After three hours of heated discussion, Rev. Martin Luther King, Jr., did in fact speak. The young minister had seen his father's humiliation; it affected him deeply. As he approached the lectern, "his eyes were a little glassy," Lonnie King recalls, so deeply was he affected by the crowd's rejection of his father. Then, in a voice familiar to everyone in the church, Reverend King, Jr., began, "I'm surprised at you." He delivered a twenty-minute oration in which he said, "We must see in this struggle that Aunt Jane, who knows not the difference between 'you duz' and 'you don't,' is just as significant as the Ph.D. in English." Misunderstandings are not solved "trying to live in monologue; you solve it in the realm of dialogue." He spoke of the "cancer of disunity" and the "palpitation of purpose."

"If this contract is broken it will be a disgrace," Reverend King said, his voice exploding through the public address system into the streets of black Atlanta. "If anyone breaks this contract let it be the white man."

By the time he finished, remarkably enough, Reverend King had achieved a unity of spirit among the crowd's disparate groups.

With Atlanta's first written agreement between whites and blacks in danger of unraveling, Ivan Jr. had heard blacks refer to Martin Luther King, Jr., as "Little Jesus." Never again would he wonder why. Martin King would be more celebrated in other places at other times, but the Warren Memorial United Methodist speech was his greatest moment in Atlanta, his hometown.

The following Monday, Mills B. Lane dropped a postcard on Ivan Allen's office desk. "What do you think?" he said. It was a perforated two-sided card, known in the industry as a "12-cent mailer." The recipient would tear it in half and return the signed portion. On the back it read, "Count me among those who would like Ivan Allen, Jr., to become mayor of Atlanta."

An eccentric noted for stubbornness as much as originality, Lane said he had mailed 88,000 cards. Ivan Jr. figured this mailing cost about $11,000. Lane paid for it himself. That afternoon, March 13, a news story on the mailing appeared in the *Journal*. In short order more than 9,000 responses arrived in Lane's office; nearly all favored Ivan Jr.

His ambitions for the governor's mansion had come to naught, but in Atlanta, he saw a political landscape more favorable. Walden, Borders and Daddy King told him he would make a good mayor. He could count on his friends at the newspapers, particularly Gene Patterson. Most of the leading bankers in town were regulars at the Tuesday night badminton/supper club on the Allens' meadow. Beyond that, the Ivan Allen name had held a position of prominence in the city for nearly sixty years. The Senator had made sure of that.

Still, one question remained: what was Bill Hartsfield going to do? Hartsfield was more crotchety and argumentative than ever. During the spring of 1961, with rumors of Hartsfield's retirement circulating, Dan

Sweat, the City Hall correspondent for the *Journal,* prodded the mayor for his plans.

"Give me the scoop," Sweat said. "Everybody knows you're not gonna run again."

"Who says I'm not gonna run?" Hartsfield snapped. The mere implication that people—voters—were saying such things provoked his ire. Sweat's relationship with the mayor was alternately playful and adversarial.

"Well," Sweat said, backpedaling slightly, "you are getting sort of old."

Sweat had gone too far. The mayor rose from his chair and grabbed the reporter by his shirt collar, yanking him into the City Hall anteroom.

"OLD!" Hartsfield howled. "I'LL SHOW YOU WHO'S OLD!" He spat out the words in a rage, venting not only at Dan Sweat but at the passage of time. "I CAN OUTRUN, OUTFIGHT AND I CAN OUTFUCK ANY MAN IN THIS CITY!" Thrusting an index finger into the air, Hartsfield said, "I challenge you to a race around the City Hall block." Sweat was twenty-seven years old, the mayor seventy-one; Sweat recently had returned from a three-year hitch in the navy, young and fit.

"Mr. Mayor, I ain't about to go out and do that," Sweat said, "because you'll embarrass me. *You'll outrun me.*" That concession brought peace, for the moment, anyway.

Awaiting Hartsfield's political plans, Ivan Jr. remained active as chamber president. He met black leaders throughout the spring to plan a format for desegregation of lunch counters. White merchants on the Plans and Procedures Committee presented "control programs" to black leaders in which they outlined the optimal time of day to begin the desegregation process (off-peak hours) as well as a recommended number of blacks to appear at each location. At Rich's, it was agreed that eight blacks would lunch in the Magnolia Room for six consecutive days, but not during the peak hours of eleven A.M. to two P.M. At Davison's Tea Room, four to six blacks would lunch for a six-day period during off-hours. During one session, a white merchant asked if light-skinned blacks could be designated to begin the desegregation; the merchant believed this would make the transition more palatable for white customers. (His request was denied.) Walden and Borders agreed to allow store managers to meet blacks in the control groups. Ivan Jr., meanwhile, again offered to seek the newspapers' cooperation to keep coverage of desegregation to a minimum.

Allen's primary focus now was the 1961 mayor's race. In May, he went to see Helen Bullard. This much Ivan Jr. knew: if he was going to run for mayor, Helen Bullard was going to direct his campaign. Bullard was Hartsfield's longtime political advisor and a vice president at the

Charles Rawson & Associates advertising agency in Atlanta. A stout spinster from Dalton, Bullard was a legendary figure in Atlanta politics, married only to liberal causes. She was said to be the only Atlantan, man or woman, who could tell Bill Hartsfield to shut his mouth and get away with it. She was a fifty-two-year-old curiosity piece, a woman who had broken into the male-dominated political world of smoke-filled rooms. She wore her hair in the roughly chopped manner of a small boy. Years later, a local newspaper described her as "nondescript" and her friend, Cong. James Mackay, wrote her a note suggesting she was "one of the most descript people" he knew. Bullard never received a driver's license, instead moving about town in taxis. To gather anecdotal wisdom she often spent a few hours riding through downtown, changing from one taxi to another, asking each driver for his opinion. Her access to black Atlanta was hard-won; she was said to have known almost every black minister in the city. She spoke slowly and with authority and, almost invariably, with a cigarette dangling from her lips. She once wrote that she had entered politics because of the realization that Adolf Hitler's rise to power in Germany "could not have happened if the government itself had not become a part of the nightmare. And in my own little way I decided that this must never happen in this country." By the time her career finished in the mid-1970s, Bullard estimated that she had managed 165 state and local campaigns with a winning rate of 96 percent. Her devotion to Atlanta was total. "If anything good spills over into the South," she once said, "it comes from Atlanta." What had made her most invaluable to Hartsfield was her contacts in the black community.

"Helen," Ivan Jr. began, "I want to run for mayor." Bullard was famous for giving the silent treatment to prospective clients. It allowed her time to size up body language and intent. Now, as cigarette smoke clouded her visage, she paused for a long moment. "Ah-vin," she said, finally, "where do you stand on the issue of race? You can't be serious about running for mayor without appealing to the Negro vote."

Ivan Jr. walked across the room. When he turned to face her, his conviction was apparent. "I've decided the Supreme Court has told us what the law is," he said. "I want us to obey the law of the land. I want to get this devil behind us." A small smile creased Bullard's lips. "I believe I can work with you," she said. First, though, she told him she had to be certain Hartsfield would not run again.

Privately, Ivan Jr. canvassed every source in the city during the following weeks. The consensus was that Hartsfield was not going to run. In fact, the word was out that Bob Woodruff, whose power in Atlanta seemed limitless, had indicated to Hartsfield it was time for a new mayor. *"The Boss thinks it's time for you to move out."* Hartsfield told Patterson about Woodruff's message. The editor recalls the mayor was "extremely disappointed and angry."

Ivan Jr. could not wait for Hartsfield to put an official end to the guessing game. On May 30, he announced his resignation as president of the Atlanta chamber, saying he would make "a political announcement" in mid-June. Then he arranged a meeting with Hartsfield.

On June 6, 1961, Ivan Jr. arrived at City Hall, moments before his scheduled two o'clock meeting with the mayor. Hartsfield was nowhere to be found. By the time the mayor ambled into his office, Ivan Jr. had waited seventy-five minutes. Allen smoldered with anger. Hartsfield offered no apology. Instead, he launched into a diatribe about a mayor's hardships, the endless papers to be signed, the small-minded aldermen to be lobbied, the business leaders to be tracked down on golf courses or at the Driving Club. He rambled on for more than forty minutes.

"Mr. Hartsfield, I wonder if you'd let me make a simple statement," Ivan Jr. said. The mayor listened. "I think you can be re-elected. I'll put $10,000 in your campaign fund and take a leave of absence from my company so I can be your campaign manager. I can help you with the younger people, and you can be re-elected."

Hartsfield knew political shrewdness when he heard it. He replied, "You wouldn't make an offer like that unless you wanted something, would you?"

Ivan Jr. was direct. "No, sir. If you're *not* going to run again, I'd like for you to make an announcement so that the rest of us can get in the race."

He performed admirably, stroking Hartsfield rather than provoking him. The mayor then walked to his office window, staring out at his city. Ivan Jr. sensed an overwhelming sadness. More than his job, City Hall had been Hartsfield's life. His marriage had been irretrievably broken for years and his relationship with Tollie Tolan, a former campaign volunteer about half his age, was well known. ("Helen, do you think people will be surprised when they hear I'm going to get divorced?" Hartsfield had asked Bullard. To which the irrepressible Bullard had replied, "Bill, I think most people will be surprised to hear that you were married.") A generation of Atlantans had grown up without knowing another mayor. "I've had this job for 23 years," Hartsfield told Ivan Allen. "I'm 71 years old, and I've been married for 48 of 'em, and now I'm in love with a very wonderful young lady and I want to marry her. I can't get a divorce and be re-elected mayor. If you'll send Helen Bullard over here tomorrow, I'll make an announcement and get out of the race so you boys can go on about your business. I've been around long enough."

The headlines in the *Journal* and the *Constitution* were of the boldface magnitude reserved for spectacular moments. "MAYOR BOWS OUT" . . . "Hartsfield Calls It Quits After 23 Fateful Years." In an emotional press conference, Hartsfield declared himself mayor emeritus. For the first time, the newspapers began to examine the five likely mayoral contenders: Ivan Allen, Jr.; the segregationist Lester Maddox, defeated by Hartsfield in 1957; the state senator Charlie Brown, defeated by Hartsfield in 1949 and 1953; the state representative M. M. "Muggsy" Smith, Hartsfield's floor leader in the statehouse; the Fulton commissioner, James Aldredge. Hartsfield declined to support any candidate. Privately, he told friends that if a segregationist, such as Maddox, won the primary he might enter the general election.

On June 19, Ivan Jr. announced for mayor. As a band played lively music, he was surrounded by nearly five hundred supporters, including his father, the ever-buoyant Senator. The announcement was made at his new campaign headquarters at 60 Peachtree Street, several doors down from where Fielder & Allen had been located in 1900, only a few steps from where the Confederate Armory had been located ninety-seven years earlier. Within days, Hartsfield announced that, with the impending desegregation of the public schools, "peaceful racial calm" would be the central issue in the mayor's race. "We have learned that racial disorder soon shows up at the cash register," the mayor said.

The media at the announcement included two black correspondents, news director Paul E. X. Brown of radio station WAOK and reporter George Coleman of the *Daily World*. Helen Bullard had invited them. The Senator, now eighty-five years old and vigorous, approached the two black journalists, introduced himself, and said, "My son is going to make a good mayor." He told Brown and Coleman they needed to consider his son's candidacy with an open mind. Brown was struck by the Senator's friendliness and directness. "He had no qualms," Brown says, "about taking us into his friendship."

With a reassuring voice, the Senator spoke proudly of his son. He said to the reporters, "You will not have anything to worry about."

Soon, Ivan Jr. learned the art of Atlanta politics from Helen Bullard. For the first time in his life, he was an announced candidate. He rolled up his sleeves and prepared to go to work.

Bullard began with some of the basics. "Say Negro, Ah-vin," she said. He said it as he had said it always: "Nig-ra." Bullard shook her head. "Say it like this: Knee-grow." Aspiring to become mayor of his hometown, Ivan Jr. looked squarely at Bullard.

"Knee-grow," he said.

# CHAPTER 16

In the summer of 1960, the Grand took the train to Boston where he was scheduled to deliver a speech about Crispus Attucks, the freed slave who was the first to fall in the American Revolution.

Maynard Jackson, Jr., his twenty-two-year-old grandson, visited his hotel room on the eve of the speech to ask him to co-sign a loan for a two-door Chevrolet Bel-Air. He told his grandfather he needed the car for his work as an encyclopedia salesman for P. F. Collier in the company's district office in Boston. He said he expected to earn more than $20,000 a year.

"Look," the Grand said, finally, "I'm going to sign this for you but not because I believe you can earn that much money—because I don't believe you'll earn that much—but because I believe *you can sell somebody on the idea* that you can earn that much money."

The grandson inquired about his speech: "Are you going to use 'Will'?" a reference to the Ella Wheeler Wilcox poem.

Sitting on the edge of the bed in his hotel room, the old man seemed surprised. "And what do you know about that?" he asked.

"You told me it was your favorite poem and told me to learn it."

"Well," Dobbs said, "did you?"

"Yes, sir. I did."

"Say it for me."

"You mean right here? In this hotel room?"

"Right here. This is as good a place as any."

Maynard Jr. felt his body tighten.

In a moment, his hands moved in sweeping motions and his words carried force. *"Gifts count for nothing; will alone is great/All things give way before it, soon or late."* This was a rite of passage for a Dobbs, any Dobbs, but particularly this one. Maynard Jr. was the closest thing John Wesley Dobbs had to a son. He wanted the boy to know how to transform words into an arsenal, to learn words which needed to be caressed and which crushed. *"What obstacle can stay the mighty force/Of the sea-seeking river in its course."*

The next day, August 16, 1960, the Grand delivered his address about Attucks and heroism. It was the final impassioned public speech of his life.

"[Attucks] made the down payment on Liberty and Freedom for all members of his racial group who were to live after him in the United States of America," the Grand said. "Crispus Attucks made the down-payment for you and me, when he died in Boston, March 5, 1770, with a stick in his hand."

Dobbs spoke of blacks' devotion to America and to democracy. The current struggle for civil rights represented the continuation of a historic battle. "Our Negro college students, often assisted by white fellow students, are walking picket lines, and staging 'sit-in' demonstrations for the recognition of these rights, today," he said. "Again, a moral issue is at stake! Our college students will not be willing to wait another hundred years, like their fathers did. They are protesting to High Heaven, and in God's name, for Justice—right now—if not sooner! They know that the world rises on protest."

Passing businessman, black and white, hearing the emotion in Dobbs's voice, gathered in Boston Common. Soon, the crowd numbered in the hundreds. The Grand's speech was so powerful, Maynard Jackson recalls, applause at the close was sustained.

But one moment during this address, so small as to be undetected by anyone but a Dobbs, signaled a larger, more frightening prospect to the grandson.

John Wesley Dobbs had referred to his notes. It was the first time Maynard Jackson had ever seen him do it. The realization settled in: "Grandpa was beginning to lose some of his powers."

The voice on the telephone was old and heavy. It was the voice of a weary old general still longing to fight. "When you get ready to march at Rich's tomorrow," John Wesley Dobbs told the Rev. Otis Moss, Jr., "let me know."

As the civil rights movement in Atlanta gained momentum, the Grand lost his own. His mind retained its clarity and sharpness but pain crippled his shoulders, hands and knees. He spent days on the couch at 540, too stiff to move. Sometimes, his grandsons Bill Clement, Jr., and Bobby Jordan, both students at Morehouse, lifted him from the sofa for a conversation. The Grand had good days when the cortisone injections restored the old fires and bad days when he seemed nearly inanimate except for the groaning. "It was depressing for us," Bill Clement, Jr., recalls, "and traumatic for him."

The Grand's views had changed since 1956 when he believed that Atlanta need not duplicate the bus boycott in Montgomery. He believed Atlanta a superior and more reasonable place than any other in the

South. But now, four years later, the younger generation, and especially M. L. King, Jr., had convinced him that direct action was needed to break through the intransigence of white Atlanta.

The South had become a lead actor on the American stage. It stood alone in a spotlight, forced to justify its social customs. In Atlanta, white leaders struggled to maintain the appearance of racial moderation, but black college students made that increasingly difficult.

John Wesley Dobbs made his final public stand in Atlanta by marching in support of the students in front of Rich's on October 19, 1960, as part of the same protest for which the Rev. Martin Luther King, Jr., was jailed, then sent to Reidsville. One month earlier, Dobbs had returned his charge card and closed out his account, paying $159.88. In a letter to Rich's officials, he said his family had spent more than $3,700 at the store in 1959 and 1960 and that "my Conscience and Self-Respect will no longer allow me to support a business that shows so much unfairness to its Colored Patrons." He noted that dialogue between Rich's and black leaders, including one conference in which he and Daddy King met Richard Rich, had produced no results. The store's discriminatory policy, Dobbs wrote, would subject esteemed blacks such as Dr. Ralph Bunche of the United Nations and his own daughter, opera star Mattiwilda Dobbs, to Jim Crow humiliation if they so much as ordered a sandwich at Rich's lunch counter. "You are caught on the wrong side of a MORAL ISSUE," he wrote. "Already cities like St. Louis, Mo., Louisville, Ky., Nashville, Tenn., Durham, N.C. and Tampa, Fla., have done something about this condition. You continue to do NOTHING about it."

Frank Neely, chairman of Rich's, responded in a letter five days later: "So far as we are aware, we have tolerated no so-called 'Jim Crow' or unfair practices to race or color, and while it has not been the custom . . . for white and colored to dine together, accepting such social differences, we long ago provided a restaurant and rest rooms for our colored patrons equipped as those of the white customers, and food cooked in the same kitchens." Neely added, "In my memory"—here he was deferential to the Grand—"no citizen has been more respected or honored than John Wesley Dobbs, and our pride in your status and the talents and character of your offspring is equal to yours. We are sincerely sorry for your attitude, and regret the turn of events which has promoted it."

As Dobbs stood outside Rich's in the autumn chill, Reverend Moss watched with awe. The young pastor of the Providence Baptist Church in south Atlanta had heard the Grand speak years earlier in the Morehouse Chapel. That discourse ranged from the glory of the ballot to the fiery destruction caused by John Brown at Harpers Ferry. Once, in a visit to 540, Moss heard the old man speak in admiration about New York congressman Adam Clayton Powell, Jr., an occasional visitor in the Dobbs house. "He preached the gospel on Sunday and walked the picket lines on Monday," the Grand said. Moss accepted that description as a blueprint for his own career.

In his final hour of protest in Atlanta, the Grand wore a fine three-piece suit and a gray trench coat. His wing-tipped shoes shone and his Dobbs-brand hat set low on his head. An oversized sign was draped from his shoulders. "Wear Old Clothes With New Dignity," it read. "Don't Buy Here." He stood straight-backed and his countenance held supreme resolve. To those who knew him well, he looked unmistakably old. The flesh on his face sagged from his high cheekbones and somehow made his Indian features stand out. He walked with a group of elder black leaders, including realtor John Calhoun and ministers such as Sam Williams, Daddy King and William Holmes Borders. As chairman of the Adult-Student Liaison, Borders had called for the old guard to demonstrate at Rich's after learning that dozens of black students and M. L. King, Jr., had been arrested. Like the students, the adults protested at Rich's in shifts, some arriving as others departed.

Dobbs's first steps were slow and small. A few of his fellow protesters expressed concern about his stamina. But as he turned from the south end of Rich's and marched around the block his strength surged. He walked faster and longer than anyone had expected. "He walked that day just like he did the first time I had ever seen him," Moss recalls. Across the street, members of the Ku Klux Klan in their white robes shouted threats and obscenities. The Grand seemed not to hear them.

"How do you feel?" Calhoun asked him, after he had marched for some time.

"I feel good," the Grand said, "on the inside. This is one of the best experiences of my life."

The Grand demonstrated in front of Rich's for nearly two hours. Organizers of the demonstration finally told him to stop. He smiled. "If you think so, I will," he said. His old brown eyes sparkled. "But I could go on."

Thirty years later Maynard Jackson, Jr., saw, for the first time, a photograph of his grandfather as he marched in front of Rich's. "Look at that jaw set. He would've walked through hell—*bare feet, if he had to!*" Tears streamed down Maynard Jackson's cheek. "What a man!" he said.

During the spring of 1961, a poll revealed division among black leadership. Now that Hartsfield was out of the picture, a pair of veteran legislators, Charlie Brown and legislator Muggsy Smith, reached for the black vote in the mayor's race. Smith had labored in the General Assembly for many years and believed his fights to remove the county unit system and to unmask the Ku Klux Klan had proven his virtues to black Atlantans. Brown, meanwhile, had received a large percentage of black votes in his victory over Everett Millican in their race for the state Senate.

John Wesley Dobbs was for Brown, as he had been in 1953 and 1957. Along with a handful of other black leaders, he questioned the sincerity of Ivan Allen, Jr. These leaders believed Allen's courtship of black votes was motivated solely by politics.

"There have been some questions about Allen," the Reverend King, Jr., said. But his father, Daddy King, put it this way: "Ivan is strong and can grow; we can support him." Both Kings said their first choice would have been Hartsfield.

As he passed his seventy-ninth birthday, Dobbs's physical condition weakened considerably. Doctors had been unable to diagnose his ailment. The Grand did not like uncertainty. He attacked it the way he attacked injustice: with all his might. The previous spring, he had flown with his foster son, Joe Phinazee, to the Mayo Clinic in Rochester, Minnesota. Their plane had landed in a rainstorm; the clinic was closed. The Grand and Phinazee had spent the night at a hotel. At seven o'clock the following morning, he announced himself as an emergency patient at the clinic and immediately checked in.

To remove the swelling from his wrists and joints he was given various treatments, massage therapy and massive doses of aspirin.

"My Dear Babe," he wrote to 540, after his first day of treatment. "Well, at long last I'm here at the famous Mayo Clinic. I should have been here long ago. . . . I haven't seen another colored patient on my floor. The white people are all very nice indeed." He praised the clinic for its thoroughness. "These Doctors feel and examine every bone, muscle, tendon, grizzle, and every thing else. They miss nothing. . . . You can put this down for sure—At the end of the line, they will be able to give you all of the FACTS. They seem to think this is Arthritis—and of course that is one of the diseases that still have them 'guessing.' "

Finally, doctors diagnosed rheumatoid arthritis. The Grand then studied arthritis. "They know about 70 different kinds, but boil them down to a 7-point category," he wrote to his daughter Willie.

Back in Atlanta, the Grand wrote a letter to friends and family. He described his experience at the Mayo Clinic and urged them to keep the letter for future reference. At all times, he meant his life to be transformed into a learning experience for his family.

The irony was, his daughters had worried for the past decade about their mother's heart condition. John Wesley Dobbs was the rock. But his physical decline was made clear to his daughter Willie when she visited from Mississippi over Mother's Day, 1961. She had heard him, in his bedroom down the hall, moan in pain through the night. Until that time she had no idea his condition was so severe. The next morning she sat in the front parlor, next to the piano, and her father trudged in.

"I heard you last night. How are you feeling this morning, Daddy?" she asked.

"Well, I'm not well. I don't feel good," he replied.

A serious look flashed across the Grand's face. "I want to talk to you about something," he said, gravely. His daughter knew instantly that he was going to talk about family life after he was gone. She didn't want to hear such talk. The Grand pressed on: "I know I've got six children and I love them all and you all love your Mama. But you are more disposed than any of the others to looking after Mama. Josephine is, too. Between the two of you I want you to look after her."

"You don't have to worry, Daddy," Willie told him. "Mama has always got a home with us in Cook County." Then she changed the subject.

Events in Atlanta, and across the South, moved beyond the Grand. In the spring of 1961, Atlanta's sit-in movement, at full throttle, drew in several of Dobbs's grandchildren. Bill Clement, Jr., went with Morehouse College friends to sit-ins at Rich's lunch counter. "Everybody participated. You either went down there and did the outside thing, that is, walking around, or you actually went in and sat at the counters," Clement recalls. "It was not as hostile as in other cities. . . . It was almost like they would just ignore you." As the Atlanta movement unfolded, Carol Ann Jackson of Spelman joined a group of AUC students determined to desegregate the Roxy movie theater on Peachtree Street. She was appointed to buy the tickets. "I guess they looked at me and I was the whitest thing in the room," she says. After she handed the tickets to an usher, her black classmates appeared and swept into the theater. When the manager came inside the darkened theater to ask the students to leave, they refused; the manager relented rather than create a scene, easing the nervous knot in Carol Ann Jackson's stomach.

Mayor Hartsfield worried about the desegregation of public schools scheduled for August 30. Hartsfield walked into Gene Patterson's office at the *Constitution,* put his feet up on the desk, as was his custom, and said, "You know we've got five hundred national media coming into Atlanta." Hartsfield worried that violence might break out on the campuses and damage the city's hard-won image of racial moderation.

Patterson suggested: "Why don't you give them all of the news? Why don't you have one central place [for reporters], if you don't want them on the campuses, a place where everything is available to them. Why don't you clear out the City Council chamber and put in press tables with typewriters and coffee and free Coca-Cola."

Hartsfield perked up. "I've got it," he said. The mayor was about to claim Patterson's idea as his own. "We'll bring the police chief in there and the school superintendent. We'll have loudspeakers and every time the chief gets his reports from the various campuses he'll give them over those loudspeakers."

"You've got it, Mayor," Patterson said. Hartsfield set the plans in motion.

Moving more rigidly with each passing week, the Grand spent a few hours at his Masonic office each morning during the early part of summer 1961. He made calls, answered mail. The dutiful Joe Phinazee dropped him off each morning and then picked him up. The Grand had hired a woman to help with the housecleaning chores. B. B. Beamon, the Auburn Avenue promoter/restaurateur and Prince Hall Mason, frequently sent a cook to 540 to prepare meals for the grand master and his wife.

At the Grand Lodge Communication in June, the Grand was reelected for the twenty-ninth time—and the last as he immediately announced his intention to step aside as grand master in June 1962. His plan was to write the history of Sweet Auburn Avenue. In his office, he made copious notes for the book.

At times, Dobbs sat on the porch at 540, staring into the distance with a vacant expression, as if lost in pain. He wrote a letter to Maynard Jr., on July 31, 1961. It amounted to a call to family duty. Renie had accepted a position as chair of the Foreign Languages Department at N.C. Central and Dobbs had smoothed the transition by purchasing for her a small house in Durham. Her mortgage payment was $72 per month. Further, he explained in his letter, the house needed repairs.

"Now, Maynard," he wrote, "I am calling this to your attention to see if you will be able to help your mother, and the children, in this financial dilemma. I don't know how you are financially situated, but if you are able to help her out, I believe you will be willing to do so." He asked his grandson to contribute $100 per month.

The Grand suffered a stroke on August 21 and was checked into Grady Hospital. He was placed in the Hughes Spalding Pavilion, a separate facility for blacks. During the next nine days his six daughters rushed in to visit. When Willie arrived, she located him in the general ward. She had him transferred at once to a private room and secured round-the-clock care.

On August 30, 1961, the summer air in Atlanta was redolent with the overtures of history. At 8:45 that morning, nine black students began integration of the city's schools. They entered Northside, Murphy, Brown and Grady high schools to mark Atlanta's first step toward compliance with the Supreme Court order, now seven years old. As Dobbs lay near death in a segregated public hospital, Bill Hartsfield watched his meticulously planned desegregation of public schools executed almost without a hitch. The mayor aimed to prove Atlanta was not Little Rock. Much to his delight there was barely a hint of violence. At two schools, four youths and an avowed member of the American Nazi Party were arrested. Police monitored developments at the schools from cars, motorcycles and helicopters. Most members of the national media remained in the City Council chambers where Hartsfield's media flaks spoon-fed them news reports. The mayor had arranged a parade of "news" including press conferences with the superintendent of schools, Police Chief Jenkins and, naturally, with a mayor who kept saying how proud he was of his city. When three white men picketed City Hall that afternoon, Hartsfield rushed to the media center and called out, " 'Stop the presses!' We said we'd tell you everything. I have news for you. We are being picketed. Out in front of City Hall!" The mayor also delivered a more serious news flash from the White House. President Kennedy, in a news conference, had congratulated Atlanta for its heroic effort. The president said, "I strongly urge the officials and citizens of all communities which face this difficult transition in the coming weeks and months to look closely at what Atlanta has done."

By day's end, one reporter stood inside the media center and said to Gene Patterson, "There's something wrong here. We've been had, haven't we?" Patterson simply smiled. "I think you have," he said.

The headline in *The New York Times* the next day was a Hartsfield dream come true: "Atlanta Integration Is Peaceful."

Shortly before six o'clock that evening, with the *Atlanta Journal* already on the streets, its headline declaring, "Negro Students Make Historic Move," John Wesley Dobbs died at Grady Hospital.

The deputy grand master of the Prince Hall Masons, X. L. Neal, sent a Western Union telegram to the brethren later that evening: "Grand Master Dobbs passed this afternoon at five fifty five Funeral 12 o'clock Saturday at Big Bethel AME Church."

The first person from outside the family to pay condolences at 540 was Ivan Allen, Jr., candidate for mayor.

The mayoral primary was two weeks away. Black votes would be of paramount importance. The visit by Ivan Jr. likely was suggested by a campaign aide familiar with the black community. Ivan Jr. had never met John Wesley Dobbs.

He didn't stay long.

Years later, he did not even recall making the visit.

Irene Dobbs wanted her husband's funeral at the First Congregational Church. They had been members nearly six decades, were married there in the race riot days of 1906 and there had christened their daughters. Her husband, however, wanted the funeral at the Big Bethel AME Church, on Sweet Auburn. Irene Dobbs considered overruling his wishes, but her daughters convinced her otherwise. The idea of moving the funeral to Big Bethel irritated leaders at First Congregational, some of whom considered it a personal slight from a man of insatiable ego. *Typical John Wesley Dobbs,* they said.

But in his funeral request, read at Big Bethel by the Rev. Homer McEwen of First Congregational, John Wesley Dobbs wrote, "I hold not the slightest ill feeling toward that church. . . . My reason for this request is my undying love for 'Sweet Auburn Avenue'; and, also, the fact that Big Bethel Church has always been an 'Open Forum' for the Civil and Political rights of my people. It is, therefore, my wish and desire that my remains be taken directly from Big Bethel Church, and 'Sweet Auburn Avenue,' to their final resting place."

The smallest details were carried out as the Grand had wished: the spirituals performed, the midnight Masonic kadosh service, specific hours that his body would lie in state (ten A.M. to noon), the length of the funeral service (not to exceed one hour) and the handling of his bier by a mortician from Sandersville who was a Prince Hall Mason.

The old guard of Auburn Avenue attended in full. The array of funeral guests ranged from Shorty, who, selling pencils from his wheelchair, seemed a fixture on Auburn, to Thurgood Marshall of the NAACP, who, having been named an honorary pallbearer, came wearing his Masonic attire.

The Grand chose with great care the men who would speak for him. They celebrated him not for his public wars on behalf of the ballot and his race, but for his private crusade in elevating his family. "A people recently escaping from subjugation," Reverend McEwen said, "will find their domestic life in chaos. And this is part of the strategy of the oppressor. And only when wholesome family life can be revived again is there chance to throw off the inner and outer shackles of slavery and become free. And this he did well for us."

Rev. Martin Luther King, Jr., had not forgotten that he and the Grand had playfully agreed that whoever died first, the other would speak at the funeral. "Martin talked about him a lot," Coretta Scott King says. Once, the Reverend King had told his wife, in admiration of Dobbs, "He educated those six girls. They have a large family and they've all done so well." King wanted a large family of his own and to his wife cited the Dobbses as his model.

At the funeral, King offered the Lord's Prayer. "We thank thee for his love for people and his unswerving devotion to the cause of freedom and human dignity," King said. "Especially do we thank thee for the beauty of his family life, for his greatness as a husband and his magnanimity as a father. We thank thee for his matchless love and affection for his wife and children. . . . We do not come here to question Thee, but to praise Thee, for giving to Atlanta, for giving to Georgia, for giving to the Masons, for giving to America, such a noble life that has stood for seventy-nine years as a refreshing oasis in the midst of a desert world sweltering with the heat of oppression and cynicism."

The Grand wanted Reverend Borders to deliver his eulogy. In black Atlanta, there was no greater honor in death then to have the Reverend Borders offer your eulogy. As a teenager M. L. King, Jr., was known to slip from his father's Sunday sermon at Ebenezer and walk a few doors away to Wheat Street Baptist to hear Borders's electrifying sermons. Decades earlier, Borders had sent love letters to his future wife, Julia Pate, and when she had received them she noted that a railway mail clerk who processed the letter had signed his name on the back of the envelope—"J. W. Dobbs." Borders and Dobbs shared a mutual respect—in fact, Borders was the Prince Hall Masonic grand chaplain in Georgia—and now, in his eulogy, the minister spoke of the Dobbs family as "compassionate in love, brilliant in mind, magnificent in beauty, sweet in spirit, unified in fellowship and Christian in attitude."

As the Dobbs family—now six daughters, nineteen grandchildren and two great-grandchildren—comforted Irene Dobbs, Reverend Borders's voice rose. "Twenty-five, thirty, forty years ago, when the Klan was really riding and when prejudice held a death grip from Sugar Creek to the Chattahoochee, and from the bright lights of Tybee to the lines of Alabama, John Wesley Dobbs was saying loud and long, 'Friends, let's get the ballot! The ballot is your weapon! You can put them in and put them out with the ballot!' "

"No person in Atlanta praised Negro businesses more than Dobbs. The Atlanta Life. The Citizens Trust. The Atlanta Federal Mutual Building. The *Atlanta Daily World*. WERD. And his refrain from Sweet

Auburn Avenue: '*In Memphis it's Beale Street, in Nashville it is Cedar and Seventh and in New Orleans it's Rampart. But in Atlanta, Ga., it is Sweet Auburn Avenue and it's gettin' sweeter every day!*'"

At the end of the service, Maynard Jr. helped his grandmother down the front steps of Big Bethel. A hearse took the body of John Wesley Dobbs to the Southview Cemetery where much of Atlanta's black gentry is interred. Row after row of black educators and ministers and professionals line the rolling hillside cemetery in south Atlanta. Dobbs was buried in a prominent location, along a gravel path. In another year, the Masonic broken column, signifying the demise of a leader on whom the brethren once had leaned, would be placed above his grave.

Over the next five weeks, June and Josie stayed at 540 to pack up their father's personal effects collected over the past fifty-five years. What they found brought them to tears. The Grand had kept memorabilia from all six daughters—"The dauntless Dobbs girls" of Spelman College. Report cards. Letters. Programs from their performances. A paper trail of his private crusade. "I didn't know my father was so sentimental," Josie recalls. Like a wispy cloud that had lost its sky, Irene Dobbs moved to Durham where she lived with Bill and Josie Clement for her remaining eleven years.

"When Roosevelt died," Borders said, in closing his eulogy, "newsboys ran up and down the streets hollering, 'Extra! Extra! Extra! The president is dead! Extra! Extra! Extra! Franklin Delano Roosevelt is dead!'" Borders paused, then said, "I'm glad to be God's newsboy today. They sold their extras for a nickel. This is my extra. It's free." He spoke of the Resurrection and, at fever pitch, said, "You can't kill goodness! You can't murder death! The cemetery can't hold love! The grave can't grip goodness!

"DEATH CAN'T DESTROY A FAMILY LIKE THIS!

"EXTRA! EXTRA! EXTRA!"

# CHAPTER 17

>‹

"Mister Maddox, let you hear this!" Ivan Allen, Jr., said. The first shot in the 1961 mayor's race would be fired low and hard. Ivan Jr. had planned a safe-as-your-next-mayor speech for the first debate among the five candidates. But he could not forget what he had seen. He had seen Lester Maddox in the flesh, his jug ears aflame, his spindly body twitching with anger as he sounded a zealot's shrill call for resistance to desegregation. That image alone caused him to reconsider.

How Atlanta would react to court-ordered school desegregation remained the crucible. Ivan Jr. believed resistance, especially a zealot's resistance, would cause the city irreparable damage. Hartsfield put it pragmatically: "When have you heard of Little Rock or Montgomery getting a booming industrial plant?" Ivan Jr. believed the old mayor was exactly right. If plain economics wasn't enough to place him squarely in the center on the race issue, Lester Maddox surely was. Ivan Jr. considered Maddox an urban Gene Talmadge who would play the old rural trump card. As the harsh euphemism went, Maddox would "out-Nigger the field."

Instead of conciliation or caution, Ivan Jr. decided to attack Maddox. Standing before three hundred observers at an elementary school, Ivan Jr. was tense, even jittery. He was about to tangle with a political alley cat.

"You represent a group which would bring another Little Rock to Atlanta," he said, jabbing a finger toward Lester Maddox. "You spread hatred and lawlessness, but we will settle it this summer with God's help."

On the stump, Lester Maddox possessed a vaudevillian genius and a populist's appeal. He had a biting wit, worked crowds well, and sometimes even used props. Once during the campaign he pulled a pair of his wife's stockings from his pocket and called out to Ivan Jr., "You're the silk-stocking candidate so you ought to have some silk stockings to go along with it." Now, hearing Allen's assault, Maddox struck back. "We are teaching love," he said, *"and racial pride."* He insisted he would fight forever against mass integration of public schools. Then, to the audience: "Special interest groups are fighting me and spending a lot of money. The pinks, radicals and Communists are trying to eradicate freedom. I am trying to keep Atlanta in your hands, trying to protect your homes, your jobs and your churches." Later, Maddox put his own spin on his opponent's "violent" attack: "Had he not stopped when he did, I was planning to ask that he apply for booster rabies shot."

Since the election in 1848 of Moses Formwalt, a tin and copper salesman, virtually every Atlanta mayor had been elected largely on the strength of his personality; few elections had turned on a local issue, the last in 1940 when insurance man Roy LeCraw defeated young incumbent Bill Hartsfield by promising to end the practice of policemen hiding behind billboards to ambush speeding drivers. In 1961 personality was defined through the prism of race.

The patricians had tapped one of their own in Ivan Jr., the Senator's son. He had promise, bloodline and respect for the elite. He would look after business. Enough said.

Maddox was the polar opposite to Ivan Jr. In his defiance of desegregation, the crude populist struck a chord old and deep. If his campaign lacked finances, it had raw emotion. Beneath the surface sheen of Hartsfield's "City Too Busy To Hate" simmered a racial unease. Not since the first decade of the century, when blacks were disfranchised, had racial invective been so freely and callously expressed in Atlanta.

Ivan Allen, Jr., and Lester Maddox shared little, save Atlanta. Ivan Jr. was a scion of the business elites; his pedigree was so apparent that Bullard advised him to chew gum on the campaign trail to make him seem more like a common man. Maddox was the son of an Atlanta laborer who had lost his job at the Atlantic Steel Company during the Depression. While Ivan Jr. drove his two-door coupé to Boys High, Maddox, who later dropped out of school after the tenth grade, sold newspapers on street corners and raised hogs, cows and chickens behind his family's home near 14th Street. While Allen moved in social clubs and the upper echelons of state politics, Maddox followed his father's path and became a steelworker. "I couldn't get into the Capital City Club unless I was a delivery boy," he would say. Maddox worked his way into the restaurant business and in 1947 opened the Pickrick near Georgia Tech ("You PICK it out, we RICK it up!"). He poured iced tea refills and knew most of his customers by name. He made politics part of his business and his business a platform for his politics. He published advertisements that not only announced his famous fried chicken but also his segregationist views. In 1957, after a friend, Fulton commissioner Archie Lindsay, lost in the mayoral primary to Hartsfield by a small margin, Maddox entered the general election. First, though, he took a Dale Carnegie course to learn how to influence people. Calling for a strict separation of the races, Maddox won 36 percent of the vote, including the majority of white ballots, but lost virtually the entire black vote to Hartsfield. His segregationist's message clearly held great appeal to many Atlantans.

Helen Bullard wanted to reduce the five-man mayor's race into a battle between only Allen and Maddox. Then she could portray the race simply: Good versus Evil. Bullard aimed to re-create the coalition of liberal north side whites and the black bloc that had carried Hartsfield in city elections since the late 1940s. Bullard knew the Hartsfield name carried weight in black Atlanta; she made certain that Ivan Jr. invoked it often.

The presence of five candidates made a runoff virtually unavoidable. The Allen camp believed the sentiment for segregation remained strong enough to land Maddox in a two-man runoff. The key battleground for Ivan Jr. was the black vote, roughly 29 percent of the total. Bullard worried; she knew that candidates Muggsy Smith and Charlie Brown, career local politicians, had friends in black Atlanta. Bullard also knew the old guard on Auburn Avenue held a lingering skepticism about Ivan Jr., not having forgotten his past days as a segregationist. In addition, many AUC students believed the settlement negotiated by Ivan Jr. to desegregate lunch counters would not be put into force as scheduled in the fall.

Bullard decided Smith and Brown had to be frozen out of the campaign. Throughout the summer, Ivan Jr. effectively did that with relentless attacks against Maddox. It pleased him when Maddox willingly returned the criticism, always ignoring the other candidates.

Ivan Jr. mounted one of the most expensive campaigns in the city's history. While funds remained a constant concern for each of his opponents, Ivan Jr. had more than enough. For the primary alone, he spent $175,000, more than twice the amount spent by all other candidates combined. "We decided that as long as people were saying that we were spending a lot of money," Ivan Jr. says, "we might as well do it."

He was the first mayoral candidate to appear on television. On June 30, he delivered a full-scale address, in which he invoked Bill Hartsfield's name five times. He also said 90 percent of voters responding to his postcard survey had indicated that peaceful race relations was Atlanta's top priority. Television became a useful tool for Allen. Not only could he afford to buy time, he looked good on TV: neat, smooth, courtly. As for Lester Maddox, television magnified his intensity, not a good thing. It made him appear wild and excessive, as if he were about to leap through the screen into Atlanta's living rooms.

Ivan Jr. enjoyed other advantages. The four hundred employees of his company were a campaign force. At a moment's notice, they mobilized for rallies with placards in hand. In Helen Bullard, Ivan Jr. had a proven political strategist with a pipeline to black Atlanta. In the business community, the Ivan Allen name was golden. His social standing, and network of friendships, provided access to all of the important sources of finance and influence.

On July 13, two months before the primary, a day on which he was quoted in the *Atlanta Journal* saying, "Shoot, I'm no silk-stockinged boy," Ivan Jr. began to solidify his contacts with Atlanta's leading white power brokers. He sent out the first in a series of weekly confidential memoranda to seventeen men: leaders of five local banks, businessmen (such as Richard Rich, developer John O. Chiles and newspaper executive Jack Tarver), Bill Hartsfield, Ivan Allen, Sr., and, of course, Bob Woodruff. These notes provided updates on the campaign and solicited suggestions. "We are making twice as many public appearances than anyone else, and . . . the stress is being laid on the south side," Ivan Jr. wrote in the first memorandum. "The colored problem is in a good position at the present time."

At a campaign forum in late July, Muggsy Smith and Charlie Brown attempted to strengthen their positions in the black community. Standing before a packed audience at Wheat Street Baptist Church, Brown, a state senator in his third mayoral race, charged that Ivan Jr. was a "political opportunist" and that City Hall was "too important to entrust to a man without prior political experience."

Muggsy Smith alleged that Ivan Jr. was "a novice" and Brown "a loser." He called himself "an old friend seeking a new job." Smith, who had earned his nickname a half century earlier with tenacious play on the baseball field that reminded friends of the professional John "Muggsy" McGraw, then held his fists in the air, striking a fighter's pose. The black audience applauded warmly.

Afraid the forum was about to be lost, Ivan Jr., in his turn, admitted he had once been a segregationist but said "our views on segregation were changed by the Supreme Court decision." He ripped into Charlie Brown for "his distinguished record of doing nothing" and resurrected a quote attributed to Brown after his defeat in the 1953 mayor's race. "[He] said, 'I was defeated by the colored vote,' " Ivan Jr. said, adding, "Except he didn't use the word 'colored.'

"You remember that."

Gene Patterson of the *Constitution* sat in the pews that night. The next two months he would write favorably of the Allen candidacy. In fact, one column was used as a paid advertisement in the *Daily World*. In the pews of Wheat Street, Patterson was struck by the rage of Ivan Jr. "[Allen] laced into his enemies, real or imagined, with an indignation that marooned him in mid-sentence without breath," Patterson wrote. "But suddenly he was stirring something in the crowd. He wound up saying, with passion . . . that he would be guided by what is 'decent' and what is 'right.'" When Ivan Jr. finished he received the evening's most sustained applause.

Four nights later, on July 31, Muggsy Smith took the offensive before another black gathering, at Tabernacle Baptist Church. Smith's campaign was strapped for funds and rumors swirled that his withdrawal from the race was imminent. Days before, Hartsfield had told Smith he could not support him, that Ivan Jr. had been knighted by Atlanta's powers. Hartsfield had urged Smith to do the sensible thing and drop out. The mayor said he would make certain all of Smith's campaign debts were paid and that he would get a little extra money, besides. Smith was aghast. For fifteen years, he had been Hartsfield's point man in the legislature. He had been a devoted lieutenant, paying his dues. Now he felt betrayed by Hartsfield, their friendship irretrievably broken. Smith's son, Scott, remembers how his father viewed the mayor as Judas. So bitter, he would refuse even to attend Hartsfield's funeral years later.

Smith would not withdraw from the race. He began a month of intensive criticism of Ivan Jr. designed to strip his black support. Smith pointed out that he was the only legislator voting for open schools in 1958 and that he had supported a bill to unmask the Ku Klux Klan. (Smith's memory was selective in this regard; he once favored interposition to thwart school desegregation and once supported a bill designed to facilitate impeachment of U.S. Supreme Court justices.)

Allen responded, "I'm perfectly willing to acknowledge anything I said in 1957, 1956 or 1955. What I have learned is what a lot of Americans have had to learn, and that is a social conscience. If you elect me mayor, I want you to send me over there on my record of the last few years, since I got a social conscience."

Smith, a robust, square-jawed man noted for a short temper, took to the microphone and rolled his eyes. "*Since I achieved a social conscience*," he said, mocking Ivan Jr. "It takes a man, some men, about 50 years to achieve a social conscience."

Weeks later, Smith continued the assault with an advertisement in the *Constitution* that ridiculed Ivan Jr. as an "On-Again-Off-Again-Finnegan." "No one ever knew his real convictions. Neither did he," the ad said. "Just a few years ago he was dancing cheek to cheek with Lester

Maddox. . . . Yesterday he was saying the things he felt Georgia wanted to hear—today they're the things he feels Atlanta wants to hear. What will it be tomorrow?"

Despite his verve and hustle, Smith's campaign foundered. Lost in the Allen-Maddox crossfire, he couldn't establish a presence. During the week of the September 13 primary, Ivan Jr. received a tip that Smith would attend a rally with a band of black supporters. Smith, he was told, intended to make a dramatic statement about the renewed vitality of his campaign. But the Allen staff undercut Smith by announcing a free supper followed by a free bus ride to the rally. Originally, Allen campaign aides planned for enough buses to carry eight hundred. But when the Coca-Cola and fried chicken buffet was served, sixteen hundred blacks showed up. Another twenty buses were ordered. When Ivan Jr. arrived at the black church for the rally that night, he saw a beaming Muggsy Smith with fifty supporters. Allen's forty buses rolled in moments later. On their sides were signs that read, "Allen for Mayor." Ivan Jr. saw the color drain from Muggsy Smith's face.

The criticism of Ivan Jr., and his segregationist past, had various effects. Ivan Jr. learned that his opponents had obtained a copy of his 1957 letter to Gov. Marvin Griffin, in which he had called for a special legislative session to "leave no stone unturned" in the battle to retain segregation in Georgia. Though this letter was less problematic than his letter to Griffin that had suggested an African colonization program, Ivan Jr. met with Rev. William Holmes Borders in hopes of limiting the damage. He gave him a copy of the letter. Borders read it carefully, then smiled. "Mister Allen, don't worry," he said. "We Negroes don't like anybody better than a reconstructed Southern white man."

Not everyone was as easily convinced. Paul E. X. Brown, now working as news director of the black radio station WAOK, decided to observe the candidate closely. "We were not sold on somebody from that part of society—rich and powerful—being able to bring about changes," Brown says. During one appearance in the black community, Brown noticed that Ivan Jr. did not take a soft drink or coffee. "He did not even take a sandwich," he recalls. Brown wondered about the sincerity of a candidate who asked for the black's vote but would not accept his hospitality.

Even Helen Bullard had doubts about the conversion of Ivan Jr. In early August, over lunch at the Dinkler Plaza Hotel with Cecil Alexander, the white architect helping to manage the Allen campaign, Bullard said, "Cecil, I'm concerned we're creating someone who doesn't exist." Alexander trusted Bullard's instincts but expressed confidence in Ivan

Jr. Bullard admitted she felt pangs of guilt for having abandoned Muggsy Smith, whom she had always supported.

In previous Atlanta campaigns there had been a gentlemen's agreement among candidates that appearances in the black community would not be publicized. Maddox ignored that agreement and charged daily that his opponents courted the black vote, once saying Charlie Brown "has dinner nearly every night on Auburn Avenue." Ivan Jr. responded by publishing weekly notices of his appearances, black and white, effectively silencing the thunder of Maddox's accusations. He also opened a campaign office on Auburn Avenue. Within days both Brown and Smith followed suit, even on the same block of Auburn.

Ivan Jr. gained entrée to black Atlanta from various sources, including Reverend Borders, A. T. Walden, Daddy King and the local Urban League president, Grace Hamilton. In courting their vote, Ivan Jr. mingled with blacks daily. Once, at the home of Mrs. P. Q. Yancey, a member of a prominent family in black Atlanta, he was surprised to be served from a sterling silver set. Never before had he known a black family to exhibit such wealth. On another occasion, he spoke to black leaders at the home of L. D. Milton of the Citizens Trust Bank. There, Ivan Jr. described himself as a fiscal conservative; Milton, whose wit was based on sarcasm, replied, "Yeah. We known that you've always been close with your money." Milton then announced his support for Allen: "Of the five candidates, you are the least harmful." The room filled with laughter. Ivan Jr. smiled.

Later that night, Ivan Jr. stopped by Gene Patterson's office.

"Mr. Patterson," he said, sitting back in his chair, "I have just had the damndest experience in my life."

"What happened?" Patterson asked.

"I have just been to dinner where I was the only white person in the room. And that is a strange experience."

"You better get used to it," Patterson said, "if you're running for mayor. Did you not like it?"

Patterson saw the sparkle in the candidate's blue eyes. "They were wonderful people," Ivan Jr. said. The candidate's pure joy reminded Patterson of a Boy Scout who had just done a good deed.

By August 3, Ivan Jr. was confident of his support from black voters. For an endorsement meeting at the Waluhaje Apartments several days earlier, 170 black religious, civic and political leaders attended. "Mr. Milton introduced and endorsed me," Ivan Jr. wrote in his weekly memo to the power brokers. "Mr. Walden followed my talk with an overall endorsement, and Mr. C. A. Scott [editor of the *Daily World*] voluntarily arose and said he would support me editorially and news-wise."

That night, in a rally of candidates at the Capitol View Elementary School, a pro-Maddox contingent heckled and booed Ivan Jr. "I've got the courage to go from one end of town to the other and say the same thing," Ivan Jr. said, as boos cascaded upon him. "I will represent all the people, white or colored . . . who make up this city of Atlanta." His oratorical skills had improved as the campaign unfolded. He toyed with the booing Maddox crowd: "If you think this town has been built and developed, and has thrived and provided jobs because you can ignore 30 to 35 percent of the population just because they have one color and you another, then go vote against me."

The crowd chanted, "We want Maddox!" In a moment, their man stood at the lectern and said, "I can't understand how Mr. Allen is going to do all those things *with me mayor of Atlanta*." The audience cheered. Maddox then criticized Ivan Jr. for buying a 1961 Lincoln automobile in Cobb County. "He has gone to the high exalted job of president of the Atlanta Chamber of Commerce, but he doesn't represent the Atlanta businessmen. He went to Marietta to buy a $9,000 automobile and thus deprived an Atlanta businessman of a commission," Maddox said with mock incredulity. To thunderous applause, he went on, "Mr. Allen, you don't have any more business in this race than Martin Luther King." As mayor of Atlanta, Maddox said, he would not permit a court-ordered integration of municipal swimming pools; instead, he would set up community corporations empowered to retain segregation. Though he said he would not close public schools in defiance of the courts, Maddox said, "I will put my efforts into teaching racial pride, into teaching the Negro people they do not have to lean on the white people, or eat with them, or go to school with them."

The divisive tenor of the campaign spread beyond the rallies. At the Allen home, telephone death threats became a frequent occurrence. Because most were racially motivated, Ivan Jr. assumed they came from Maddox supporters. "They were the meanest people in the world," he recalls, "and they hated me." Some threats were directed at his family. He did not worry about his sons Ivan III and Inman, both adults. (Ivan III was in the naval reserves in Philadelphia, though he returned home occasionally to make campaign speeches. Inman, who had finished his sophomore year at the University of North Carolina, also participated in the campaign, stuffing envelopes and answering telephones.) His most immediate concern was his nine-year-old son, Beaumont, so the Allens hired two police detectives to stay with their young son through the night. George Royal, who worked in the police homicide division, slept across from Beaumont and even accompanied him around town. Raised in a lower-middle-class area in southwest Atlanta, Royal was amazed by the Allen lifestyle. "We were sitting at the dinner table," he recalls, "and they had servants that served the food. I had never seen anything like it." Royal arranged for Atlanta police to place a recording device on the Allens' telephone to monitor the threats. The family installed a second line with an unlisted number they gave only to friends.

The Kennedys had made good use of polls during the 1960 presidential campaign. Ivan Jr., who considered Kennedy a political hero, also used polls. The first poll commissioned by Helen Bullard suggested Ivan Jr. would receive between 50 and 60 percent of votes cast. Because Ivan Jr. believed Bullard's poll unsound, he asked Joe Heyman, a vice president and economist with the Trust Company, to refine her system. By the end of August, Heyman's poll indicated Ivan Jr. would win about 40 percent of the vote in the primary, more than any other candidate but not enough to avoid a runoff with Lester Maddox.

In the campaign's final weeks, Ivan Jr. received the expected endorsements from the *Constitution* and the *Journal.* ("Mr. Allen will keep us in the main stream of progress," the *Journal* wrote. "Mr. Maddox's policies mean stagnation in the brackish backwaters.") In the Allen camp, though, all attention was focused on black Atlanta, where Muggsy Smith continued to batter away. Attorney Donald Hollowell was Smith's most high-profile black supporter; together, they were pictured in the *Daily World.* Years later, Hollowell would say, "We knew what Ivan's record was and we weren't enamored by him. . . . Muggsy Smith, who was no angel, did have some credits." But on September 7, the week after Atlanta schools desegregated peacefully, Ivan Jr. paid for a full-page advertisement in the *Daily World* that named eighty-one black supporters, including religious and civic leaders.

Ivan Jr. knew of the generational split in the black community. He had campaigned hard for the old guard's support. On September 5, C. A. Scott delivered on his promise when the *Daily World* endorsed Ivan Jr. On the same day, Reverend Borders called for a united black voting bloc for Ivan Jr.

Smith knew an Atlanta Negro Voters League (ANVL) endorsement of Allen likely would mean the end of his own campaign. On September 8, the day before the ANVL would announce its endorsement, Smith was angry. He charged that Ivan Jr. was buying black votes. "Some of these votes and influence can be bought," Smith said. "But the young Negro people will not be sold down the river. They are fighting the old men of Auburn Avenue."

Later that day, A. T. Walden categorized Smith's accusation as that of a "raving candidate who recognizes that he has already lost." Walden also said, "It is true that the younger group, which has wanted changes overnight, has made some attack on this leadership and we can well understand their impatience. This is an attribute of youth and not of mature leadership."

The following evening, Ivan Jr. received the endorsement he coveted—from the Atlanta Negro Voters League. Traditionally, the ANVL waited until election eve to announce but now, hoping to unify black voters, the league endorsed Ivan Jr. five days before the primary. Walden praised Ivan Jr. "for his comprehensive grasp upon and penetrating insight into the problems now facing our city as well as the even more difficult and complex problems with which it shall inevitably be confronted in the immediate future; his mental alertness and extraordinary initiative; his broad human sympathies; his prodigious mental and physical energy; his deep sincerity; his quick perception and sound judgment; his forceful directness and his cool courage."

On the eve of the September 13 primary, the traditional ANVL rally was held at Wheat Street Baptist Church. For three months, Ivan Jr. had been on the campaign trail. He had worked white rallies by day, black rallies by night. Rare were the nights when he ate dinner at home. Louise had been drawn into the spirit of the campaign, though she made few public appearances. During the spring she had visited her friend Laura Maddox Smith, sat on her couch and said, "They want Ivan to run for mayor. I don't know what to do about it. I think if I said I didn't want him to, he wouldn't, and yet I don't want that [burden]." On this morning she surprised her husband: "I'll be glad to go with you to the rally tonight if you want." Ivan Jr. shook his head. "I don't think you should try to move into an area that you don't know anything about." But when he came home from the office that day, Louise was dressed for the rally. "I'll be glad to have you," Ivan Jr. said, "but I can't protect you from the press."

The Allens arrived late at the church on Auburn Avenue, a common ploy among candidates eager to make a grand entrance. When the doors opened at the back of the dark sanctuary, they saw Reverend Borders standing at the altar, speaking from behind a white marble lectern. Seeing the candidate and his wife, Borders stopped in mid-sentence. All heads turned from the wooden pews, to look back at the Allens as they walked down the aisle on bright red carpet and turned toward the altar.

More than fifteen hundred blacks had crowded into the historic church. As Ivan and Louise Allen glanced into the balcony they saw the image of Christ in an enormous stained-glass window. Every wooden pew was filled. Among the few whites in the church were Charlie Brown and Muggsy Smith. Several blacks in the front row offered their seats to the Allens.

From across the dimly lit room, an elderly dark-skinned black man stood and walked slowly toward the Allens. Large and broad-shouldered, the man wore a seersucker suit that made his snow-white hair sparkle. An extraordinary preacher who knew drama when he saw it, Borders watched the byplay in silence. As the old black man walked out of shadows into shafts of light, the Allens recognized Grant Carter. He had served as the liveryman for the Edward Inmans, Louise's uncle and aunt. As a child, Ivan Jr. often had played at the Inman estate with Edward Inman, Jr.—and they did so under the watch of Grant Carter. In later years, Carter chauffeured Robert Woodruff and philanthropist Lettie Pate Evans. As he neared the Allens, Louise blurted out, "Grant!" She rose and greeted him warmly, placing her left hand on his shoulder and her right hand in his. She acted spontaneously, instinctively, without artifice, and more than fifteen hundred blacks in the church on Auburn Avenue saw it. When Louise sat back into her pew, Grant Carter, smiling, stood in front of her and, as a knight to his patron lady, bowed from the waist.

Watching the scene from the balcony, Raleigh Bryans of the *Atlanta Journal* thought Louise Allen had guaranteed her husband's election. "If Ivan didn't already have every Negro vote in Atlanta," Bryans thought, "he does now."

The Allen polls proved remarkably accurate. Of the more than 100,000 votes cast, an unprecedented total in Atlanta history, Ivan Jr. won 38,000 and Maddox 20,000 to finish second. (Charlie Brown and Muggsy Smith had followed with 17,000 and 15,000.) In the twelve predominantly black precincts, Ivan Jr. took 60 percent, outpolling Smith two to one. At Allen campaign headquarters at 60 Peachtree Street, reporters gathered around the Senator, eighty-five years old and aglow at the prospects of his son becoming Atlanta's forty-fourth mayor. With his typical zest, Ivan Allen, Sr., told the family story, dating to the early death of his father, the Confederate veteran, and their life in Dalton. "I could have stayed there," the Senator said, clutching his cigar, "but I chose to come to Atlanta and sell typewriters." Louise had placed a notice in the newspaper that morning, inviting campaign volunteers to drop by for coffee and an election night party. Many showed up, including blacks, to mingle beneath red, white and blue bunting and a placard that read: "I'M FOR IVAN."

The Senator walked into his son's campaign office the next morning. "Got any money left over?"

Ivan Jr. said he did not.

"What's this other two weeks going to cost?"

"I don't know, Daddy," he said. "Whatever's necessary."

"When you get through," the Senator said, "send me a bill for half of it." Ivan Jr. would spend in excess of $200,000 on the campaign, the most ever spent in a municipal race in the South. He appreciated his father's support, particularly since the Senator had wavered initially over his decision to leave the family business and run for mayor. The Senator became so enthralled, in fact, that he made small bets with friends about the accuracy of his son's campaign polls.

Signs pointed to an Allen victory. Just the possibility of the segregationist Maddox as Atlanta's mayor healed the generational split in black Atlanta. Up and down Auburn Avenue, across the halls of the Atlanta University Center and in black churches on Sundays, the call was the same: "Vote Ivan Allen." Even Bill Hartsfield, who seemed to believe no mere mortal could follow him as mayor, was quoted saying that Ivan Jr. would win the runoff. The *Journal* felt the historic imperative of the moment: "It is customary, if not trite, to declare at election time that we stand at the crossroads. But the statement was never more appropriate than now."

On September 20, two days before the runoff, the ANVL sponsored a meeting at Warren Memorial United Methodist Church in hopes of reuniting the black bloc. Smith and Brown had announced their support for Ivan Jr., though grudgingly.

Maddox recognized he would not win the liberal or moderate white vote or the black vote. So he sought conservative white voters with the fervor of a segregationist grasping for survival at any cost. During a September 19 television appearance he pounded his fists on a table and said "we will provide for the Negro, but we will not surrender everything else." The Maddox newspaper advertisements took on a more aggressive tone. "I am absolutely opposed to integration of the races being voluntarily extended beyond the law," one advertisement said. "I AM UNWILLING TO SURRENDER ON THIS ISSUE." Maddox supporters spread rumors that Hartsfield had decided to enter the general election; they hoped to convince Allen backers not to vote in the runoff. *Why vote for Allen now, when you can vote for Hartsfield later?* Finally, Hartsfield denied the rumor, saying, "This talk is dangerous and simply is not true."

During the campaign's final days, Maddox called Ivan Jr. "a turncoat segregationist" who had become a member of the NAACP. Ivan Jr., who had come to enjoy trading barbs, countered by saying Maddox was a member of the Ku Klux Klan. At a rally in his stronghold of southwest Atlanta on September 20, Maddox said, "I don't say that Ivan Allen would intentionally do anything communistic, but surely he must know his platform is identical with the Communist platform for America." One supporter shouted, "The white people of Atlanta have their last chance in this election. If we don't win, we might as well leave town."

On the eve of the runoff election, Maddox published the campaign's most racially inflammatory advertisement. It featured a photograph of blacks and whites socializing at Allen campaign headquarters on the night of the primary, the work of an unknown photographer. Below the photograph, the advertisement prophesied, "This is what Atlanta can expect if Ivan Allen, Jr. is elected! . . . If you love your FAMILY, CHURCH, HOME, SCHOOL AND YOUR CITY, VOTE FOR LESTER MADDOX! His stand is the same as yours."

One night earlier, Gene Patterson had telephoned Cecil Alexander. "I shouldn't be telling you this," Patterson said. Then he described the Maddox ad. "We have to run it," Patterson said. His tip was helpful. Hours after the ad reached newsstands the following afternoon, Ivan Jr. appeared on television with pictures in hand. He said the pictures showed what really happened at his campaign offices on the night of the primary. It was, he declared, simply a celebration among Atlantans united for a better city. Nothing more, nothing less.

At the West End Kiwanis Club that day, Ivan Jr. accused Maddox of race-baiting. "You have done more harm to Atlanta in the last 10 days than the good people of this town have hardly been able to overcome," he said. Maddox, in turn, stressed Allen's elitism. "He's not worried about the [public] swimming pools. He's got a great big nice swimming pool in his backyard, but everyone doesn't have one like that," Maddox said, his left hand fanning wildly. "Unless you don't go along with his crowd—and he says his crowd is goin' to run City Hall—then you are the scums of the earth." A Maddox administration, he said, would be an administration for all people. "When Ralph [McGill] comes down, I'll say, 'Ralph, go back to Forsyth Street. City Hall belongs to the people!'"

The inevitability of an Allen victory prompted *The Augusta Herald*, on the eve of the runoff, to caution observers outside the South not to overstate the significance of Atlanta's mayor race. "It is to be remembered that Atlanta, because of its heavy infiltration by people from other sections in recent years, no longer can be rightly termed a typical Southern city—or even one that speaks for Georgia as a whole. Hence, whatever happens there is not to be construed as representative of a change in Southern sentiment on racial matters or any other issues."

Ivan Jr. won the runoff election with an impressive mandate, capturing 64 percent of the 100,000 votes cast. His victory was a duplicate of Hartsfield's 1957 victory, just as Helen Bullard had hoped. Answering the call of the ANVL, voters in black Atlanta turned out in greater numbers than they had in the primary.

Of the nearly 22,000 votes cast in the twelve predominantly black precincts, Lester Maddox won only 237. The likelihood was that the blacks who voted for Maddox mistakenly pulled the wrong lever in the voting booth.

In the newsroom of the *Constitution* that night, the Rev. Martin Luther King, Jr., stopped by to congratulate Ivan Jr. As the men shook hands, Maddox was heard to squeal, "Lookee! Lookee! He's goin' ta *kiss* him!"

"This victory," Ivan Jr. said to the media, "shows Atlanta is the finest city in the South in many respects." He extended an olive branch to Maddox. "Let's heal our wounds right now," he said.

"Depends on you, Mr. Allen," Maddox said. "I cannot go along with forced integration."

Ivan Jr. walked down Marietta Street, toward his campaign office, with his right arm wrapped around the shoulder of the invaluable Helen Bullard. As he entered his campaign office, a group of supporters, which included two Georgia Tech freshman and A. T. Walden, struck a rendition of "For He's a Jolly Good Fellow." The mayor-elect stood on a small platform, squinting into the lights. "Daddy," he said, "where are you?" The Senator, elected to the legislature with significantly less fanfare forty-two years before, moved next to his son; Inman and Beaumont stood with them. Ivan Jr. wrapped his arm around his father and squeezed tight. Using his father as a symbol, the mayor-elect said, "These are the men who built Atlanta and made it what it is. Now, we must carry on their work."

No longer was Ivan Jr. only a businessman selling office supplies. No longer was he the chosen leader of local businessmen. With his election, he represented more than 400,000 citizens, one-third of them black, in a city that claimed to be the South's most enlightened. Atlanta's racial division was pronounced; the runoff with Maddox had emphasized it. Ivan Jr. had won 98 percent of the black vote, but he took office knowing that Maddox won more than half of the white votes.

The precipice of the most critical juncture in Atlanta's history since the Civil War, the 1961 mayor's race became the foundation on which the modern city was built.

Like Bill Hartsfield before him, Ivan Allen, Jr., was elected mayor of Atlanta on the hopes of its blacks.

Several weeks after the election, Ivan Jr. received an invitation from Bob Woodruff to a dove hunt at Ichauway Plantation, Woodruff's thirty-thousand-acre preserve in south Georgia. He knew that if winning the black vote had been essential for election in Atlanta, remaining in Bob Woodruff's good graces was essential to governing. Ivan Jr. was thrilled by the invitation. Since childhood, he had heard his father speak of the Woodruffs with reverence. If New York had the Rockefellers and Pittsburgh the Mellons, Atlanta had the Woodruffs. Bob Woodruff was the genuine wizard of Atlanta's Oz, working his wonders quietly, discreetly. Woodruff was admired for his philanthropy and his business acumen. Like most cities, Atlanta had a surfeit of parochial thinkers, but Bob Woodruff thought in global terms. He had assumed command of Coca-Cola in 1923 and, during the ensuing decades, engineered its rise to international eminence. Among Atlanta's Bourbons a favored maxim passed through generations: "Buy property on Peachtree Street and hold it; buy Coca-Cola stock and hold it." At times, Atlanta seemed to be a part of Coca-Cola, not vice versa.

In his mansion on Buckhead's Tuxedo Road, the seventy-year-old Woodruff was a benevolent civic dictator and a museum piece of the free-market system. As he sold his soft drink to Third World countries, he decided that Atlanta, the city whose name was stamped on the back of every Coke can, would rise above all other southern cities to become a bastion of civility. Woodruff did not merely encourage this. He demanded it.

Ivan Jr. stood in the corner of a field at Ichauway in the autumn of 1961 as Woodruff whistled the beginning of the hunt. The mayor-elect heard the plantation's black workers, riding on horseback through the woods and yelling to scare doves into flight across the open fields. Ichauway (pronounced Itch-uh-way), the Creek Indian phrase for "where the deer sleep," was a hunter's paradise, a spread of old farms and woods in Baker County. Woodruff ruled the place in the manner of an Old South master. Black sharecroppers and servants sometimes gathered inside the white-board Big House to sing spirituals to Woodruff and his guests on Saturday nights. Each morning, a black servant knocked softly on bedroom doors to awaken guests. "Mornin', suh. Care for a fire?" Some guests rode out for the morning hunt on horseback, others in a mule-drawn wagon. Afterward, lunch was served, dove pie with nutmeg and corn pancakes dripping with Georgia cane syrup. Sometimes, a second hunt followed in the afternoon. Woodruff adored his hunting dogs; his favorites had their own marble tombstones in a much celebrated canine cemetery. "You had to be pretty good to rate being buried in that cemetery," Woodruff once said. On this afternoon, a black "pickup boy" accompanied Ivan Jr. into the field to collect the doves he shot. Typically, there were a half-dozen or more shooters at Ichauway, including a few Atlanta men.

Ivan Jr. shot with an accuracy that astonished the black workers. "I killed the limit [twelve doves] before you could say 'jack rabbit,' " he recalls. He told W.H., a black worker at Ichauway, "I better stop."

"No, suh," W.H. said, as if acting on prior order. "I put those way in the back in a paper bag."

"Is that all right with Mr. Woodruff?"

"Yes, suh," W.H. said.

Ivan Jr. shot a second limit, and then a third. By the time Woodruff blew the come-on-in whistle, he had bagged thirty-seven doves in about ninety minutes.

The shooters and "pickup boys" gathered around Woodruff. In his presence, Atlanta's mayor-elect behaved like a schoolboy cowed by his principal. Blacks at Ichauway called Woodruff "Boss."

Woodruff walked over to the black laborer and whispered, "W.H., how many birds did he get?"

"Thirty-seven," W.H. said.

Ivan Jr. was worried now. Had he misjudged W.H.'s advice in the field? The last thing he wanted to learn was the extent of Woodruff's wrath. He was relieved to see the Boss smile.

"That's fine," Woodruff said, holding his trademark cigar. Then he said to W.H., "We've got a couple of hours before dark. Take him quail shooting."

Before returning to the Big House, Woodruff turned back toward the mayor-elect and said, "Anytime you want, you have a bed here."

As his adrenaline surged, Ivan Allen, Jr., thought, "I've hit the jackpot!"

# CHAPTER 18

When Mattiwilda Dobbs came home to perform before a desegregated audience at the Atlanta City Auditorium on a winter night in 1962, Ivan Allen, Jr., was in his twenty-ninth day as Atlanta's mayor. He would serve more than 2,900 days.

To his City Hall office, Ivan Jr. had brought high-backed rocking chairs, the type John Kennedy was using in the Oval Office. Kennedy had spoken to the nation as the dreamer in his inaugural address a year before about "a new generation of Americans" bold enough to "explore the stars, conquer the deserts, eradicate disease, tap the ocean depths." He had exuded optimism and a New England grace when he reminded the nation "that civility is not a sign of weakness, and sincerity is always subject to proof."

Ivan Jr. had spoken with a similar dreaminess in his inaugural on January 2, 1962. He suggested the bell of history tolled for Atlanta. "We are a legend that has become real in our own lifetime," Ivan Jr. had said. He cited Atlanta's leading role in the field of human relations. "It is in this area that we must face up to the cold, sober fact that in the national and the international scene, we are an extremely necessary factor in the sum of things. Whatever doubtful comfort we may have had when we were small is gone. What we do and how we do it affects the United States and its place in the world."

John Kennedy had become Ivan Allen's liberal compass and, as the campaign against Maddox had revealed Allen's toughness, the responsibilities of City Hall would reveal his Kennedy-like idealism.

On his first full day as mayor, Ivan Jr. had ordered the removal of all signs in City Hall that designated "Colored" and "White." He had done it without fanfare, though little else of this nature would go unnoticed. Race would dominate his administration. "If there wasn't a race issue," Ivan Jr. told friends, "I could play golf every afternoon." Bill Hartsfield had left him a government lean and efficient; he also left a city that, apart from its buses, golf courses and a few parks, was segregated strictly. Already, Ivan Jr. was on record in support of empowering Atlanta's black police to arrest whites. Through Helen Bullard, he had forged an open-door policy with black radio and newspaper reporters, giving them more access to City Hall than Hartsfield ever had. Foremost, Ivan Jr. had an economic agenda and he did not want racial problems in the way.

"By the time I got into the mayor's office," Ivan Jr. recalls, "I became convinced that there wasn't a single decision ever made in the South that wasn't warped or misused some way or the other on account of the race issue."

The Allens and Dobbses had flourished on opposite sides of a segregated city for sixty-five years, their paths never crossing. They had walked different streets, eaten at different restaurants and prayed at different churches. Jim Crow guaranteed as much. The nation had waged the Spanish-American War, two world wars and the Korean War. Yet the Allens and the Dobbses lived parallel lives in parallel worlds, sometimes no more than a few city blocks separating them.

As an aged man, the Senator often strolled Peachtree Street, tipping his hat to the ladies, while the Grand had held court on Sweet Auburn. The streets intersected but the patriarchs never did. A chance meeting between Ivan Allen, Sr., and John Wesley Dobbs could have occurred, perhaps even in 1924 when the First Congregational Church, according to church records, purchased $8.55 cents worth of paper at the Allen & Marshall office supplies store. It is also possible the men met, in passing, in 1940 when both were avid Roosevelt supporters.

Yet when the Allens and Dobbses had their first public meeting on January 31, 1962, it was no coincidence of commerce or politics. It was evidence of the changes wrought in Atlanta by the civil rights movement.

It also was evidence of Helen Bullard's manipulative genius.

Ivan Allen, Jr., and Helen Bullard, his most valued political aide, were an odd couple: "The crispest gentleman and the most unmade bed of a woman I have ever known," attorney Morris Abram observes.

Not once during her decades as a political consultant had Bullard sought a client. Each year she had written the names of preferred candidates in local and statewide races in her private black book; if those candidates asked for help she gave it. Ivan Jr. named her executive assistant to the mayor, a title that told nothing of her wide-ranging duties. She was the sounding board for Ivan Jr., his strategist, his fount of ideas and, most vitally, his liaison to the black community. At aldermanic meetings, Bullard sat in the back of the room, knitting, her fingers working even as she absorbed every word spoken. Ivan Jr. said, "Helen Bullard is the only person I know who loves Atlanta more than I do," and this was a compliment that Bullard cherished more than any other.

Even before he took office, Bullard had begun to feed Ivan Jr. a steady diet of memoranda. She always wanted to be one step ahead. When she received a tip that Gene Patterson had asked questions about the city's Urban Renewal Department in November 1961, Bullard wrote, in a memo to the mayor-elect, "It might be a good idea to mention this department to [Patterson] casually and see what it is that is bothering him. Every so often the newspapers see the Pulitzer Prize dangling in front of them, and this could be an area that they might think about." Blunt if need be, Bullard also could be subtle. During his first week as mayor in 1962, she reminded Ivan Jr. that the City Hall press room would be moved but that she could make the transition palatable to even the most cantankerous reporter. "I think we might gently start putting some excess equipment in there," Bullard wrote, "so that when it comes time to move they won't be too sorry to move!"

And then Helen Bullard heard that Mattiwilda Dobbs was coming home from Stockholm. The opera singer would perform at the recently desegregated Atlanta City Auditorium. Bullard passed a message to the mayor: "You need to go."

What better way for Atlanta's new mayor to show his political gratitude to black Atlantans than by appearing with Mattiwilda Dobbs, the coloratura soprano and a member of one of black Atlanta's most distinguished families?

Geekie was thirty-six years old and had performed in front of kings and queens, in communist nations, at the Met and in the Holy Land. She had received rave reviews on every continent. Yet the idea of singing to a desegregated audience in her hometown left her uneasy. The Atlanta City Auditorium was the only segregated theater her father had allowed her to attend. John Wesley Dobbs had compromised on segregation in opera because it was high culture. He had wanted his daughters to know and to understand high culture, even to become a part of it. If that meant sitting in a segregated section reserved for blacks to hear Marian Anderson, he did it. Returning to Atlanta, Geekie felt a sadness because her father had died five months before. He had traveled abroad to see her, to the Caribbean and Great Britain. For her homecoming performance, Geekie knew that the Grand's breast pockets of his finest suit would have been filled with the most recent rave reviews of La Dobbs. *Why, Daddy might have stood by the front door and passed out mimeographed copies!*

The moment she arrived at the Atlanta airport, Geekie was startled. There to greet her was Sam Massell, vice mayor of Atlanta, who awarded her a key to the city. A familiar group of elite black women, including

Julia Pate Borders, Evelyn Frazier and Geneva Haugabrooks, stepped forward to exchange hugs. Geekie came home, without her husband, Bengt Janzon. Four years before, when her father had told her Atlanta was not ready for an interracial marriage, Geekie had married the Swede in New York. Not until 1967, when she would return to sing with the Atlanta Opera, would Bengt Janzon make a visit to Atlanta.

On this night, Geekie performed Brahms, Mozart and Rossini as well as Creole songs and black spirituals. A reviewer in the *Constitution* wrote, "She won the hearts and the ears of most of her audience before the concert was half completed." She did it, despite a cough and horrid acoustics in the old pavilion. Her back straight in a formal pose, Geekie's voice was mellifluous and full. She bowed after each song, left the stage and returned to acknowledge warm applause. One thought dominated her attention that night. *"Daddy would have been so proud to have been here!"* Until this night, all of Geekie's performances in Atlanta had occurred either in black churches or at the black colleges. When she had come home in 1952, John Wesley Dobbs had arranged recitals for her, each time before a black audience, with Renie playing accompaniment. Typically, when a performance in Atlanta was under black auspices, seating was not segregated and a few whites attended. But all concerts in the city sponsored by whites, even those with black performers, were rigidly segregated.

As her eyes surveyed an audience where blacks mixed with whites, Geekie recalls, "It was a very moving experience for me." Yet she could not fill the emotional void of her father's absence. John Wesley Dobbs had died just as the civil rights movement was making substantive gains. To Geekie, fate seemed cruelly unjust.

Mayor Ivan Allen, Jr., rose from his seat in the audience and moved to center stage to stand with Mattiwilda Dobbs. He dressed impeccably, in a dark suit and gray silk tie; she wore a flowing dress and a shy smile. They were symbols of white Atlanta and black Atlanta, indisputably linked, yet indisputably apart. On stage, Peachtree met Sweet Auburn.

Ivan Jr. presented Geekie a bouquet of roses and struck a pose with her for photographers. He said into the microphone, "You have brought great honor to Atlanta by your appearances all over the world." Softly, Geekie replied, "My heart is so full."

"This is a great moment," the mayor said, "a moment we are proud of. Thank you for letting me be on the program with you."

The following morning the *Daily World* featured a front-page photo of the mayor and the opera star.

Once again, Helen Bullard had done the job.

# CHAPTER 19

➤✦

In his City Hall office, Ivan Allen, Jr., mounted dozens of shiny steel shovels, each from a ground-breaking for a multimillion-dollar building. Atlanta was in a period of unparalleled growth and development, the leader among the nation's Sunbelt cities. The metropolitan Atlanta population was increasing by thirty thousand a year. In 1962, the city issued a record $120 million in building permits. A new downtown skyline included the thirty-one-story Life of Georgia Building, the Southeast's tallest. "The gracious belle of the old South," *Time* magazine wrote of Atlanta in 1962, "has become the nation's newest boom town and managed to turn the trick without losing her poise or showing an ankle."

Set amidst rolling fields and pines in Franklin, Georgia, seventy miles west of Atlanta, the Allen farm was a two-thousand-acre refuge from business and political pressures. Not that it was much of a farm. The soil was marginal and several attempts to raise cattle had yielded limited success. What made the farm special to the Allens was its peacefulness. They could walk alone or fish the ponds or sit in a rocker on the back porch. It became the mayor's weekend retreat.

But on June 3, 1962, a Sunday, the world intruded on the farm's morning stillness. Louise called from Atlanta to tell her husband that an Air France jet had crashed outside Paris. A large contingent of Atlantans was on board. The mayor rushed back to Atlanta and soon was en route to Paris. More than a hundred Atlantans died in the crash, many of them cultural leaders of the city; they had been visiting Europe's arts centers in hopes of raising Atlanta's image to national distinction. Notable names such as Candler, Ragsdale and Bleckley were among the casualties; so were a few of the mayor's childhood friends. Landing at Orly only twenty-four hours after the crash, Ivan Jr. felt unprepared. He did not speak French and his grasp of French protocol and international relations was limited. In addition, he never had experienced tragedy in his life. He could only let his instincts guide him. He knew most of the victims and promised himself to represent them, and their families, with dignity. An odd thought came to him: *"What if Lester Maddox had become mayor instead of you?"*

He did not criticize Air France even as European newsmen prodded him. He spoke instead of loss. "I knew them all," he said. "We were boys and girls together." Aborting takeoff, the jet had run off the eleven-thousand-foot runway, through a fence, across a public road and into a small stucco cottage. The collision broke loose the tail section, which saved the lives of two stewardesses. The mayor walked through the wreckage and debris. He saw a pastel dress that, he felt certain, had belonged to Nancy Frederick, his first date. "I rode my Indian bicycle over to her house to have a date with her when I was twelve years old," he recalled. That night, he visited five morgues. He insisted upon seeing each corpse, all burned beyond recognition. It was a gruesome task but he wanted the victims' families to know he had done what he could. Aubrey Morris of WSB radio, traveling with the mayor, admired his stoicism. "He had absolute and complete control of himself," Morris says. An ecumenical service for the victims was held in the American Cathedral in Paris. "Life is eternal and love is immortal," one minister eulogized, "and the horizon is only the limit of our sight."

Returning to City Hall in Atlanta, Ivan Jr. received a telegram from Eleanor Roosevelt, expressing sympathy. Secretary of State Dean Rusk wrote, too; like Ivan Jr., Rusk had attended Boys High in Atlanta and also had lost friends on the flight. The actress Vivien Leigh, who had a special fondness for Atlanta, cabled the mayor from London: "Have just read with grief and horror of the fearful air disaster. May I, through you, convey my deepest sympathy to all."

At Orly, Ivan Jr. had exhibited resilience and diplomacy under duress. Roby Robinson III, whose parents died at Orly, wrote the mayor: "It is indeed a rarity to have such a warm and profoundly human man as yourself as the symbol of all that is good and honorable in our city."

Gene Patterson's office phone rang early on the morning of December 19, 1962. Bill Hartsfield shouted into the phone, "I'm so happy! I want to come see you." Later that morning it seemed almost like old times to Patterson when Hartsfield's hat came sailing into his office followed moments later by the mayor emeritus himself.

"Have you seen the goddamned thing that my successor has done?" Hartsfield said. "He's made a mistake that you can make a picture of. *You never make a mistake that you can make a picture of!* He's done it! He's done it!"

Little in life pleased Bill Hartsfield in 1962 more than a blunder by the new mayor, especially a blunder so overt that Atlantans would say, "This never would have happened if Bill Hartsfield was still mayor."

Even though he had given most of his assets to his wife in their divorce settlement, the retired Hartsfield was well provided for: Bob Woodruff had made certain of that. Hartsfield was placed on retainer by Coca-Cola, the Trust Company of Georgia and Georgia Power, and was hired as an editorial commentator on WSB television. Woodruff also occasionally put him into a stock syndicate; soon Hartsfield was earning $60,000 annually, more than he had made as mayor. Now, he gleefully traveled the town telling every familiar face that he had warned Ivan Allen, Jr., about not making mistakes that could be photographed. Never mind that he never had said such a thing directly to Ivan Allen, Jr. It made for a good story and Bill Hartsfield liked to tell good stories.

The picture in question was of two barricades that the mayor, supported by a 13–1 vote of the Board of Alderman, had ordered raised near Peyton and Harlan roads in southwest Atlanta. Racial tensions had escalated after white residents accused black realtors of attempting to buy homes in their neighborhood. "Block busting," as it was called, referred to violation of racial purity. A block was "busted" when one home in an all-white area was sold to a black.

On the morning of December 19, the mayor's mistake was there for all Atlantans to see, a mistake more harmful to him politically than even the defeat of an $80 million bond issue from his first summer in office. The *Constitution* printed a front-page photograph of a two-foot-ten-inch barrier of steel and wood. An affixed sign read, "ROAD CLOSED."

The barricades created a shocking image: physical barriers separating the races.

Black leaders likened the barriers to the Berlin Wall, remembering what Ivan Jr. had said in his inaugural address. "It was in Berlin," he had said, referring to a recent visit to Germany with other U.S. mayors, "that the tragic and dramatic lesson of what happens to a divided city came home to me, and if I could make you see it as I saw it, you would share with me my feeling that Atlanta must not be a city divided."

Had the mayor forgotten his own words?

"We must let Mayor Allen know we're not going to forget it," said the Rev. Ralph D. Abernathy. Q. V. Williamson, a black realtor, added, "These are the darkest days I've seen in Atlanta as far as race relations are concerned. We have pointed to New Orleans and Little Rock, but Atlanta is the first town in the South to build barricades across public streets."

For Ivan Jr. the central problem was that blacks were not sharing proportionally in Atlanta's civic boom. The median income of a black family in Atlanta was less than half of the median white family's $6,350. Atlanta's 200,000 blacks represented 40 percent of the population but lived on 24 percent of the residential land. Blacks lived mostly in a belt that ran from the west side through the city's center. Most black housing was woefully deficient.

During the summer of 1962, black realtors habitually had driven through the Utoy–Peyton Forest subdivision of Cascade Heights, a white, upper-middle-class section in west Atlanta where houses sold for $50,000. These realtors made their excursions on Sunday afternoons when white residents were most likely to be at home. Driving through the subdivision, realtors pointed at homes and wrote notes, which stirred the apprehension of white residents watching every move. Realtors later telephoned white residents to ask if they were interested in selling their homes. When one white, who owned a home and fifteen lots in Utoy-Peyton, threatened to sell to a black broker, panic set in. White residents turned to Ivan Jr. for help. They asked him to close the two roads that separated Cascade Heights from an adjacent black neighborhood in hopes that the closings would discourage black encroachment.

As he considered his alternatives, Ivan Jr. knew the city had commercial buffer zones separating white and black housing areas. A decade earlier, Hartsfield had faced a similar dilemma with the transition of Mozley Park from white to black, but with one significant difference: then, blacks had accepted Westview Drive as the unofficial boundary for their expansion southwest.

In his inimitable way, Hartsfield always had made black leaders grateful by consulting them, even though these consultations often failed to yield substantive gain.

In December 1962, however, with black expectations rising, black leaders made no such concessions. Mayor for only eleven months, Ivan Jr. had not yet understood the rapidly changing tenor of the times. His blind spot, a lack of sensitivity to black needs, lay exposed by Peyton Road. Once again, black Atlantans examined his racial views.

Ivan Jr. made a compromise offer: to rezone several hundred acres in a nearby commercial district for black residential use. He hoped that would please both sides; it would increase black housing opportunities while easing concerns of whites who feared black encroachment. "I saw it as a happy compromise between two very serious problems," Ivan Jr. recalls, "and thought maybe I could be Solomon before it was all over."

But the visual power and symbolism of the barricades made compromise impossible. Ralph Moore, a leader of the Atlanta student movement, sent a wire to Ivan Jr. on December 22. He threatened several mass protests at City Hall as well as 175 picketers in the West End business district each day unless the barriers were removed at once.

"This action will focus the eyes of the world on the Atlanta City Wall," Moore wrote. "We do not want Atlanta to have this type of publicity. Therefore we encourage you to remove the wall and save the good image of Atlanta while there is still time."

In politics, as in business, Ivan Jr. did not respond favorably to pressure. He sent a letter to Moore citing fifty-one instances where black expansion, or encroachment, had occurred in Atlanta in 1962, all of which had been handled without incident. Peyton Road, Ivan Jr. wrote to Moore, was "an artificial, unnatural condition created by unscrupulous parties, both white and Negro, who have attempted through unethical, disloyal and false misrepresentations to panic the residents of an established community. . . . [The barrier] has merely served as a warning to unscrupulous real estate dealers that Atlanta will not tolerate under the guise of 'race discrimination' the destruction of fundamental values among any of its citizens."

Each day the Peyton Wall stood, pressure on the mayor grew. Black leaders filed lawsuits against the city and refused the mayor's offers to join in biracial negotiations until the barricades were removed. The Atlanta Wall, as it was known to blacks, drew coverage in the national press. In Atlanta, both white and black newspapers opposed the barriers. Gene Patterson called them "silly" but wrote in a forgiving tone of the mayor's miscalculation. "A charitable view toward an occasional insobriety is owed to a city government that has done so much so well," Patterson wrote in the *Constitution* on December 22. A week later, he added, "The mayor, who is quite properly getting the blame for the fence, is not an anti-Negro demagogue, but a fair man who fumbled the 52nd fly ball after he had fielded the first 51 neighborhood transition problems of his administration without a bobble."

On a Friday night in late February a segment of the barricade on Harlan Road was sawed through by persons unknown and thrown into a nearby creek. The next day, white residents filled the breach with bushes and tree limbs.

Throughout the early portion of 1963, the Atlanta Wall stood, as the civil rights movement intensified across the South. In the spring, Rev. Martin Luther King, Jr., arrested in a protest in Alabama, wrote his "Letter from a Birmingham Jail." Birmingham police commissioner Eugene "Bull" Connor turned police dogs and fire hoses on black demonstrators several weeks later and made mass arrests that crowded the city's jails. Meanwhile, the U.S. Supreme Court upheld *Sanders v. Gray,* which ended the county unit system in Georgia, washing away rural power with it. Justice William O. Douglas wrote, "The concept of political equality from the Declaration of Independence to Lincoln's Gettysburg Address to the Fifteenth, Seventeenth, and Nineteenth Amendments can only mean one thing—one person, one vote."

On March 1, seventy-two days after the Peyton Wall barricades had been erected, Fulton County Superior Court Judge George Whitman ruled them unconstitutional. Whitman gave the city until March 4 to remove them. Ivan Jr. had them taken down within twenty minutes.

He announced that the city would not appeal the decision and asked the aldermanic board to form a biracial panel of realtors to create a code of ethics. His moves were applauded by the *Daily World*. But, the *World* suggested, "The real problem is that of an inadequacy of housing. The barriers are down but the basic problem continues to exist." During the three weeks that followed, thirty white residents of Utoy–Peyton Forest—half the total in the subdivision—decided to move from the area.

Reflecting the tenor of the times, all thirty put their homes on the market through a black broker. The white-middle-class exodus from Atlanta was beginning to pick up speed.

Fourteen months into his administration, the mayor seemed at a political crossroads. A telegram arrived at City Hall:

> *We are in the deepest depths of a financial emergency—Woodruff has taken all our money at Gin rummy Repeat All our money including the stake you gave us. We would like to come home and Be "Wit Choo"—Please send bus fare in care starving cactus saloon—plastered view california—we hope to make it by fall—keep a light in the window! Adair and Talley.*

The telegram was from two of the mayor's old friends: Lee Talley, the recently retired president of the Coca-Cola Company, and real estate investor Jack Adair. They were vacationing in Palm Desert, California, with Bob Woodruff. Their note reminded Ivan Jr. of the privileged life he had given up for, among other things, Peyton Road.

John Kennedy, in an address to Congress on February 28, 1963, noted that one hundred years had passed since Abraham Lincoln's Emancipation Proclamation. Blacks in America, Kennedy said, now lived in despair: they earned half as much as whites, lived seven years less and were twice as likely to become unemployed. It was time "for a sober assessment of our failures."

Certainly the Kennedy administration, slow to act on civil rights, shared in the failure. But now a push was on to pass civil rights legislation before the 1964 presidential campaign. Kennedy cited many reasons for this push, but stressed that "the basic reason is because it is right."

In Atlanta, Ivan Jr. dealt with race nearly every day. He found the tests changing him. His heart and heritage told him one thing but his intellect began to tell him another—that racial separation and distinctions were wrong, that changes needed to be made.

As mayor, Ivan Jr. acted intellectually, not emotionally. He gained a reputation as a cool-headed moderate. He removed the separate registers at City Hall. He lobbied successfully for Atlanta's first black firemen. He empowered black policemen to arrest whites. Seating was desegregated in Atlanta's baseball park, downtown theaters and Municipal Auditorium. In June 1963, Ivan Jr. made the city's swimming pools available to both races. That same month, the Atlanta Chamber of Commerce asked downtown businesses to desegregate to "maintain the city's healthy climate." The chamber's request, along with the mayor's backroom negotiations, prompted thirty restaurants and eighteen hotels to desegregate voluntarily.

Though the tide of equality rose, Ivan Jr. had no illusions that a moral transformation was sweeping his city. "The principal motivation," he says, "had been one of business pragmatism."

His confidence grew. His connections in the black community were improving. He delivered speeches filled with anecdotes and folksy tales rather than statistics. His pronunciation of the word "Negro" never deviated from "Knee-grow." He ruled, as Hartsfield had, by force of personality—and necessarily so, because Atlanta's mayor operated under a so-called weak-mayor system. Technically, this system meant the Board of Alderman ran city government since department heads reported to the board, not to the mayor; the mayor's strength derived from power to appoint chairmen of aldermanic committees. Regardless, Ivan Jr. felt that, as mayor, he had the authority to do what needed to be done.

Above all, Ivan Jr. acted in accordance with a basic tenet of the Hartsfield years: Atlanta's reputation as a place of racial moderation was to be treated as the city's most precious asset. That reputation had drawn business to Atlanta. The battle for southern eminence between Atlanta and Birmingham was long since decided. Birmingham was being diminished further as it confronted black protests with attack dogs and fire hoses. Atlanta, with its more mild lunch counter protests, grew in stature as it confronted race behind closed doors. In 1950, Atlanta was the nation's twenty-third largest city, Birmingham twenty-seventh. By 1970, Atlanta was nineteenth, Birmingham forty-eighth.

Seldom were the differences in the cities more painfully clear than in May 1963. On May 10, after weeks of demonstrations in Birmingham in which more than two thousand blacks were arrested, the Rev. Martin

Luther King, Jr., announced that white leaders in that city finally had agreed to a desegregation plan. The next night, bombs detonated directly under and outside of King's vacant motel room, prompting blacks to riot until the morning light. The next week in Atlanta, a group of Atlanta University Center students, commemorating the ninth anniversary of the *Brown v. Board of Education* decision, followed Mrs. R. Pruden Herndon, a black attorney and associate of A. T. Walden's, into the basement cafeteria of City Hall where they were refused service. Ivan Jr. intervened on their behalf.

"Mrs. Herndon, do you have a problem?" the mayor asked.

"They won't let us eat," she said.

"You understand what the ordinances say that only city employees and their guests can go into the cafeteria?"

"Yes," she said, "but I think there was another reason."

The mayor agreed. "What can we do?" he asked. Herndon asked for his help.

"Okay," Ivan Jr. said. "I'm inviting you to be my guests."

The mayor of Atlanta, in a scene most remarkable, led the group into the City Hall cafeteria. The students had been protesting segregation in downtown restaurants. Now, they arrived in the city cafeteria during an afternoon coffee break with their mayor. Nearly a hundred white city employees watched the mayor's every move.

Ivan Jr. approached the white woman at the cash register and said, "I want you to serve my guests."

"I'm not going to do it," she said.

"I said these are *'my guests.'* I want you to serve them."

She refused again, at which point Ivan Jr. snapped, "Then come out from behind there, and I'll serve them."

The cashier yielded. "If you put it that way," she said, sneering, "I'll do it."

Ivan Jr. bought soft drinks and led his guests to a table as if they were aldermen or department heads. But it wouldn't be that easy to lighten history's burden on Atlanta. In an instant, a few white employees left the cafeteria. Soon, the entire room emptied. George Royal, the mayor's devoted police aide, stood in the corridor. As employees walked past, Royal said, "You're a bunch of damned fools, giving up your cafeteria just because some young students want to cool off with a Coke."

Because Ivan Jr. had acted on impulse, he wondered if he had made a tactical error. But in a few moments, the white city employees returned: first a few, then all.

The mayor had believed always in the decency of his city. Now, he had more reason for such belief. The City Hall cafeteria was desegregated.

\*            \*            \*

The summer of 1963 is represented in civil rights history by startling images. The governor of Alabama, George Wallace, rigid with defiance, stood in the schoolhouse door on June 11 vowing to halt integration of the University of Alabama. That night John Kennedy told the nation, "We are confronted primarily with a moral issue. It is as old as the Scriptures and as clear as the Constitution." Hours later a shot rang out in Jackson, Mississippi, and Medgar Evers, statewide leader for the NAACP, fell dead in his carport. By late August, Rev. Martin Luther King, Jr., stood at the Lincoln Memorial and told more than 200,000 listeners, "I Have a Dream." Each man's moment became an unforgettable piece of history. Wallace was southern resistance; Evers was the human cost of racial hatred; Kennedy was the eloquent if slow-moving national leader; and King the spiritual lightning rod of the black race.

A piece of this mosaic was missing that summer: the southern patrician with a moral conscience. That image, less well known, was provided by Ivan Allen, Jr.

Although reluctant to leave behind the society that had shaped him, Ivan Jr. moved ahead irrevocably. He assured Atlanta's reputation as a city of hope and justice.

In the spring of 1963, Kennedy mobilized forces to forge a civil rights act. His proposed legislation included a public accommodations bill designed to eliminate discrimination in restaurants and hotels. During hearings before the Senate Commerce Committee, the lines of battle were drawn predictably. Southern conservatives expressed outrage over federal invasion of private enterprise. Gov. Ross Barnett of Mississippi accused John and Robert Kennedy of encouraging black demonstrations. Governors of the old Confederate states, including Georgia's Carl Sanders, united against the bill.

In early July, the lawyer Morris Abram paid a visit to Ivan Allen, Jr. Formerly from Atlanta, Abram recently had joined the prestigious New York firm of Paul, Weiss, Rifkind, Wharton and Garrison. In 1954, Abram had run for Congress in Georgia; if being Jewish hadn't subverted his hopes for victory, his candor and directness had. As a student at UGA, Abram had debated classmate Herman Talmadge on the question "Should Eugene Talmadge be reelected governor of Georgia?" Herman Talmadge had called out, "Who reduced your utility rates?" and his friends in the audience shouted, "Gene Talmadge!" Given his chance to respond, Abram attacked Herman Talmadge's methods. "He copied his father's techniques without improving on them," he told the assembly, and then he laid out his own case. A panel of judges ruled Abram the winner. An advisor to the Kennedy administration, Abram had been dispatched to meet with Ivan Jr. about the public accommodations bill.

"I don't know a single important official in the South," Ivan Jr. said, "who's come out for it."

Sitting in one of the mayor's Kennedy rocking chairs, Abram had an answer for that. "Ivan, the President wants you to support the bill. He wants you to go to Washington to testify."

Surely Abram was kidding, Ivan Jr. thought. But Abram's severe expression indicated otherwise. The mayor didn't understand: why him? He was a mayor, not a governor, not a senator. He'd been an elected official for only two years of his life! Besides, the idea of testifying in Washington frightened him. He held a schoolboy's reverence for the place. Entering City Hall, he held no illusions of becoming a politician of national import or renown. In fact, he had sent Vice Mayor Sam Massell as his stand-in at conferences of the nation's mayors. Ivan Jr. wanted only to be a good mayor, nothing more. Now the President of the United States was asking him to do what no other politician in the South would do: stand up and declare himself a Kennedy liberal.

Abram said Kennedy needed such support and that Atlanta, with its moves toward desegregation, fit the president's needs. And who, if not Ivan Allen, Jr., spoke for Atlanta?

Abram's argument continued. He said reputations mattered in moments of crisis because reputations assured credibility and gave weight to testimony. With passage of this bill, Abram said, the black vote would go to Kennedy in the 1964 presidential campaign. So the president needed Ivan Allen's help.

"You know the dilemma I'm in on this thing," Ivan Jr. said, finally. "I've got a large Negro population down here, and they support me because I've done more for them than anybody else on the political scene in the South. But if I go up there I'm not going to pass the bill or even have a strong influence on it, and if I go I won't stand a chance of getting reelected in '65.

"It would be suicide for me to go," he told Abram, "and you know it."

Ivan Jr. understood that the career of a southern mayor mattered little to a president. His thoughts were a jumble of conflicting emotions—fear and dread, mostly, but also pride that Kennedy had chosen him and Atlanta. Complicating things even more, Ivan Jr. had not yet decided his position on the bill.

"I'll leave it this way," the mayor told Abram. "Please tell the president what I said and ask him to weigh it. Discuss it with him personally, Morris, and be sure he fully understands all of the angles. And then if he calls on me and still wants me to do it, if he recognizes that I can't be reelected and that my testimony isn't going to pass the bill, then I'll go."

Soon after the meeting with Abram, Ivan Jr. was notified by his secretary, Ann Moses, that John Kennedy was on the line. He had met Kennedy, but only in passing. But now, in that New England voice so familiar, Kennedy said, "You're right, your testimony alone is not going to pass the bill. But I don't think you are correct in thinking your testimony will defeat you. I think there will be sufficient change in the country by 1965." Ivan Jr. did not agree with Kennedy on this last point, but then he heard the president say, "It not only will not defeat you, it will help you get reelected."

Hoping Kennedy had superior insight, a reluctant and uneasy Ivan Allen, Jr., agreed to testify. He had two weeks to prepare, to formulate his testimony, to discuss it with select quarters of Atlanta—two weeks to prepare for what he believed would be his political suicide. "I was reluctant to go even after Kennedy called me," Ivan Jr. recalls. "I was suffering some qualms about it." Some of his uneasiness was born of the possibility he would be made to look foolish by U.S. senators cross-examining him. "I thought I had gotten in over my head," he says. "I didn't have the give-and-take in conversation and that's what worried me."

Yet the more he studied the public accommodations bill, the more he saw elements he liked. Voluntary desegregation in the South had run its course, he believed, and guidance from the federal government was needed. For the next week, Ivan Jr. worked on his testimony with Bill Howland, formerly Time-Life's bureau chief in Atlanta for eighteen years, and an occasional hunting companion of the mayor's. A native New Yorker, born to wealth, Howland had majored in Latin at Princeton and later married a woman from Decatur, Georgia. As an Atlanta newspaperman, he counted Ralph McGill a close friend, and had named Margaret Mitchell godmother to his son. Only recently he had been hired by the mayor as a part-time advisor/speechwriter. A facile writer with a liberal bent to his thinking, Howland shaped the mayor's thoughts into testimony.

With a draft of his testimony in hand, Ivan Jr. visited Bob Woodruff at Coca-Cola. In the patriarchal southern society, Ivan Jr. seemed an obedient son. Years earlier, in times of restlessness, he had turned to his father. But now the Senator was eighty-seven years old and in fading health. Woodruff had become more than the mayor's advisor. He had become his civic superior, truly the Boss. Ivan Jr. understood that Woodruff's racial views were typical among southern patricians of his generation. In 1960, Woodruff had written a private letter with sarcasm about civil rights legislation designed to assure "the right of a chimpanzee to vote."

Woodruff listened to Ivan Jr. describe his dilemma with JFK's bill. "I know it's going to be an unpopular thing to do," Woodruff said, "but you've made up your mind and you're probably right about it, and I think you should go." Woodruff suggested the mayor propose a delay for smaller locales to allow for more gradual implementation of the law, a concept Ivan Jr. agreed to include in his testimony. Typically, conversations with Woodruff put the mayor at ease. He knew Woodruff, who once paid a public relations agency to keep his name *out* of newspapers, would never violate his confidence. Typically, they talked about the city, Coca-Cola and hunting. They laughed while playing gin rummy. The Boss always enjoyed a good dirty joke. The mayor viewed Woodruff as a man's man. Above all, Woodruff was a pragmatist who knew what was best for Atlanta. Woodruff, meanwhile, viewed Ivan Jr. as an extension of the lengthy relationship he had had with Bill Hartsfield. "Mr. Woodruff always stood with me," Ivan Jr. says. "I think he never admonished me." A reclusive man always in great demand, Woodruff chose his friendships with great care. "He avoids dreary characters like the plague," Lucille Huffman, his former secretary, once said. "He never gets caught with tedious ones twice." At times, Woodruff seemed a father figure to the mayor. Joe Jones, Woodruff's personal secretary for decades, says, "[Woodruff] liked the kind of fellow that Ivan was—he liked to play golf, he liked to shoot, to ride."

To defy Woodruff on an important issue, Ivan Jr. believed, would have been to incur his wrath, an unsavory prospect for any mayor of Atlanta. "As far as I was concerned," Ivan Jr. says, "what he said was what you'd do, that's all."

Even with Woodruff's approval, the mayor fretted about his testimony as the July 26 Senate hearing approached. If he decided not to testify, no one, other than John Kennedy, Morris Abram and Bob Woodruff, would question him, and, of the three, at least Woodruff would understand his decision. It was Louise, who usually stayed clear of politics, who crystallized her husband's decision. "You'll have a hard time living with yourself the rest of your life if you don't do it, Ivan," she said. "I don't think you can be re-elected if you do go, but if you feel it's right, then go and accept the consequences."

On July 24, Ivan Jr. gathered with two dozen black leaders at the Butler Street YMCA. There, he told Daddy King, Rufus Clement, Benjamin Mays, the Rev. William Holmes Borders, A. T. Walden, Leroy Johnson, Jesse Hill and others of his intention to leave for Washington the following night to testify for Kennedy's bill. In a stifling second-story room where a fan generated the only movement of air, the mayor read a portion of his 3,500-word testimony. When he finished, his listeners exchanged glances and raised eyebrows. They knew Bill Hartsfield never would have dreamed of giving such testimony. They told Ivan Jr. they admired his stance and, even more, his courage. State Senator Johnson said, "This is the kind of leadership we need in the South." But Daddy King told the mayor he should not testify, that he was too valuable to sacrifice for testimony that would go unheeded in Washington and was unlikely to help the bill pass. When these black leaders took a straw vote, all but a handful agreed with Daddy King.

With the majority of local black leaders on one side and John Kennedy, Morris Abram, Bob Woodruff and Louise on the other, Ivan Allen, Jr., boarded an Eastern Air Lines plane the following night and flew to Washington.

"Are you sure you're going to say this part?" Margaret Shannon asked the mayor. Then she read a few lines from his prepared text. It was Friday morning, July 26, 1963, and Shannon, the Washington correspondent for *The Atlanta Journal*, sat in Ivan Allen's room at the Madison Hotel. Ivan Jr. thought Shannon incredulous at the text. But Shannon was making certain that the mayor did not intend to deviate from the text she planned to quote in the early editions.

The mayor was tense. Dressed in a dark suit, he knew he was about to make the most significant political statement of his lifetime, one certain to make him very unpopular among many of his closest friends in Atlanta. And how ironic that he would deliver it not in Piedmont Park or at a Peachtree storefront, but to United States senators. Later that morning, he walked into Room 318 of the Senate Office Building with Georgia congressman Charles Weltner. He noticed television cameras and reporters filling the room.

It was customary for senators to introduce witnesses from their home state. But Georgia's senators, Herman Talmadge and Richard Russell, were not in attendance. Both opposed the president's bill and felt no obligation to the mayor of Atlanta. "I figured he was playing domestic politics," Talmadge says of the mayor, "cementing his relationship with the black voters in Atlanta." Ivan Jr. was thankful for Weltner's presence.

He took his place alone at a table facing the Senate Commerce Committee members. His testimony would be one of the most important addresses by a southern politician on the race issue since the Civil War. And this from a scion of Atlanta society who once had suggested returning disenchanted blacks to Africa, and who seven months earlier had supported the construction of a wall in his city to separate whites from blacks. Now, he told U.S. senators, the race problem should be confronted by the power of the federal government.

Many histories of the South celebrate politicians who refused federal intervention at every turn. Ivan Allen's testimony then represented not only a dramatic breakthrough for John Kennedy, but for Ivan Allen, for Atlanta and for the South.

Speaking in a manner that British writer Alistair Cooke described as "a soft, almost apologetic Southern tone . . . without bombast and without much self-esteem, either," Ivan Jr. presented an assessment of race relations in Atlanta with an arresting candor. It was the most honest portrayal of race division, and race achievement, in Atlanta ever delivered in public by a white native son.

"It is true that Atlanta has achieved some success in eliminating discrimination in areas where some cities have failed, but we do not boast of our success," he testified. "Instead of boasting, we say with the humility of those who believe in reality that we have achieved our measure of success only because we looked facts in the face and accepted the Supreme Court's decisions as inevitable and as the law of our land. Having embraced realism in general, we then set out to solve specific problems by local cooperation between people of good will and good sense representing both races."

Seventy-seven years had passed since Henry Grady spoke to the elite New England Society of New York in December 1886. On that night, in an elaborate chandelier-lit banquet hall in Manhattan, before an audience that included Gen. William Tecumseh Sherman, Grady spoke with a disarming eloquence about a New South, reconstructed from war, rapidly industrializing and intent on solving its racial troubles without federal intervention.

"To liberty and enfranchisement is as far as the law can carry the Negro," Grady had said. "The rest must be left to the conscience and to common sense."

Ivan Jr., the mayor of Grady's city, was challenging Grady's assertion, suggesting that conscience and common sense were not enough to liberate blacks. Federal law was needed as well. Ivan Jr. cited the steps Atlanta had taken toward eliminating racial discrimination during the previous two and half years. Some were triggered by court order, he said, and others were carried out voluntarily. He praised Atlanta's black colleges and black press. He praised Ralph McGill of the *Constitution* as a "world famous editorial spokesman for reason and moderation." But his caution exceeded his optimism. "It has been a long, exhausting and often discouraging process," he testified, "and the end is far from being in sight."

Ivan Allen, Sr., poses with sister Mary
Ruth and older brother Will in
Dalton, Georgia, circa 1882.
Ivan Allen, Jr., files

Daniel "Earnest" Allen,
ex-Confederate cavalryman,
died at the age of thirty-one in 1879.
Ivan Allen, Jr., files

Cobb County farmer Josiah Dobbs died in 1851 and his estate inventory lists his thirteen slaves. The most valuable— the field hand Wesley, worth $800—was John Wesley Dobbs's grandfather.

Because his personal estate was valued in excess of $20,000 after the Civil War, Dr. John Miller McAfee had to apply for a pardon under President Andrew Johnson's amnesty program. Here, on September 3, 1865, in Canton, Georgia, he signs an oath indicating he has freed his slaves, including his mulatto daughter Minnie.

John Wesley Dobbs (about ten) poses with older sister Willie, circa 1892.
Amistad Research Center, New Orleans, La. (J. W. Dobbs Papers)

The freed slave Judie Dobbs is said to have lived 101 years. She poses here, circa 1885.
Muriel Gassett James files, Sacramento, Calif.

Ivan Allen, Sr. ("The Senator"),
circa 1920, poses as the stylish Atlanta
Chamber of Commerce man. "Daddy
was always ready for the cameras,"
Ivan Jr. says.
Atlanta History Center

Ivan Sr. and Irene Allen
on their honeymoon trip
to Cuba, November 190
Ivan Allen, Jr., files

Ivan Allen, Jr., listens to his
father's watch, Atlanta 1912.
Ivan Allen, Jr., files

Irene Thompson arrived in Atlanta
in 1905 from Columbus, Mississippi.
The following year she married
John Wesley Dobbs.
Josephine Dobbs Clement files

Irene Beaumont Allen poses with
six-year-old son Ivan Jr. in Atlanta in 1917.
Ivan Allen, Jr., files

The Senator in 1920, during
his tenure in the Georgia
legislature, in a pencil sketch
with black porters.
Atlanta History Center
(Ivan Allen, Sr., Papers)

Louise Richardson dressed elegantly when she bowed before the royal court in England in June 1935. On New Year's Day, 1936, she married Ivan Allen, Jr.
Atlanta History Center (Ivan Allen, Sr., Papers)

Minnie McAfee Hendricks Dobbs Banks, mother of John Wesley Dobbs, usually dressed to the nines on Sunday when she went to the Liberty Baptist Church.
Amistad Research Center, New Orleans, La. (J. W. Dobbs Papers)

Ivan Allen, Jr., about sixteen,
at summer camp, 1927.
Atlanta History Center
(Ivan Allen, Sr., Papers)

John Wesley Dobbs, 1934.
*The Atlanta Journal-Constitution*

The three Ivans—
the Senator, Ivan Jr. and
Ivan III—in the library
at 2600 Peachtree Road
in 1942.
Ivan Allen, Jr., files

The Grand in his Masonic regalia.
*The Atlanta Journal-Constitution*

Mattiwilda ("Geekie") and
Bengt Janzon in a wedding toast
in New York in December 1957.
*The Atlanta Journal-Constitution*

The Senator at poolside with Ivan Jr., Inman and Ivan III at his home
on Northside Drive, 1951.   *The Atlanta Journal-Constitution*

The six Dobbs sisters at Mattiwilda's Spelman graduation, 1946 (*from left to right*): June, Mattiwilda, Josephine, Millicent, Willie and Irene (Renie). Spelman College archives

Geekie, the opera star, circa 1955.
*The Atlanta Journal-Constitution*

The Rev. Maynard Jackson (*with hand on son Maynard, Jr.*) and Renie pose with their children (*left to right*) Maynard, Jr., Sandra, Carol Ann and Jeanne, circa 194

Sandra Irene Jackson Baraniuk files

The Rev. Maynard Jackson, pastor of New Hope Baptist Church, Dallas, Texas, 1942.
Sandra Irene Jackson Baraniuk files

The 1959 Dobbs family reunion at 540 Houston Street, Atlanta.
Amistad Research Center, New Orleans, La. (J. W. Dobbs Papers)

On tour in Europe, Geekie with visiting parents, Irene and John Wesley Dobbs.
Amistad Research Center, New Orleans, La. (J. W. Dobbs Papers)

When Mayor Bill Hartsfield (*in glasses, second from right*) added streetlights to the Auburn Avenue area in 1949, he called upon the two black leaders who had helped to reelect him months earlier to symbolically "throw the switch"— John Wesley Dobbs (*arm outstretched*) and A. T. Walden.

*The Atlanta Journal-Constitution*

Ivan Allen, Jr., 1958.
*The Atlanta Journal-Constitution*

The Senator, circa 1952.
*The Atlanta Journal-Constitution*

Primary night 1961: Ivan Allen, Jr., and segregationist Lester Maddox prepare for a runc
*The Atlanta Journal-Constitution*

In this 1961 ad placed in *The Atlanta Constitution*,
mayoral candidate Lester Maddox made clear his
segregationist views.
*The Atlanta Journal-Constitution*

Election night, 1961: Atlanta's new mayor, Ivan Allen, Jr., throws his arm around ten-year-old son, Beaumont, as the Senator and Inman (*looking down*) join the celebration.
Marie Dodd files

In 1962, when Mattiwilda Dobbs came home to sing before a desegregated audience at the Atlanta Auditorium, Mayor Ivan Allen, Jr., presented her a bouquet of roses.
Mattiwilda Dobbs files

On April 4, 1968, the night of her husband's murder, Coretta King is escorted back to her home, from the Atlanta airport, by Mayor Ivan Allen, Jr.
Associated Press/Wide World Photo

Two views of the Atlanta skyline, taken a decade apart from the same spot
(near 540 Houston Street), reflect the growth of Atlanta's downtown skyline
during the 1960s when Ivan Allen, Jr., served as mayor.

Atlanta Chamber of Commerce

Vice Mayor Maynard Jackson, Jr., 1970
*The Atlanta Journal-Constitution*

Sworn in as Atlanta's first black vice mayor in January 1970, Maynard Jr. poses with (*from left to right*) mother Renie, brother Paul, daughter Beth and wife Bunnie.
Bunnie Jackson-Ransom files

Atlanta's Powers That Be: Ivan Allen, Jr. (*right*), with retiring mayor Bill Hartsfield (*center*) and the Boss, Bob Woodruff, holding his trademark cigar.
*The Atlanta Journal-Constitution*

In the summer of 1963, Mayor Ivan Allen, Jr., was the only elected southern official to testify in Washington in support of President John F. Kennedy' public accommodations bill.
*The Atlanta Journal-Constitution*

In 1960, Ivan III married Margaret
Poer in the First Presbyterian
Church on Peachtree.
*The Atlanta Journal-Constitution*

Mayor Ivan Allen, Jr,. poses with Louise and sons Inman and Beaumont
*The Atlanta Journal-Constitution*

On his eighty-sixth birthday in the spring of 1962, the Senator receives a kiss from Irene Allen.
*The Atlanta Journal-Constitution*

In October 1960, only ten months before his death, an ailing John Wesley Dobbs demonstrated against segregated practices at Rich's in downtown Atlanta. The Rev. William Holmes Borders walks behind him.
*The Morehouse College Torch, 1961 annual*

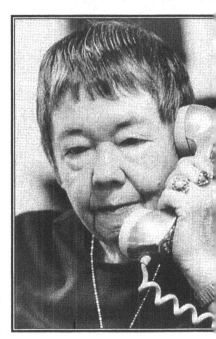

Helen Bullard, the savvy political
consultant, works the phone.
*The Atlanta Journal-Constitution*

Trailing by 27 percentage points in the 1973 primary, incumbent Mayor Sam Massell
came up with a hard-driving slogan in the runoff: ATLANTA'S TOO YOUNG TO DIE.
Harry Jacobs files (Jacobs formerly was with the advertising agency Cargill, Wilson & Acree)

Maynard Holbrook Jackson, Jr.—the South's first big-city black mayor—
gives an election night hug to Renie (*left*) and Bunnie in October 1973.
*The Atlanta Journal-Constitution*

Coca-Cola's Bob Woodruff wasn't
often photographed. Yet here,
in 1978, he poses with Mayor
Maynard Jackson.
*The Atlanta Journal-Constitution*

In one of the most enduring images of modern Atlanta, Mayor Maynard Jackson sits before the $100,000 reward money offered during the Missing & Murdered crisis of 1979–82.
*The Atlanta Journal-Constitution*

A slimmed-down Mayor Maynard Jackson feels his mother's warm touch on reelection night 1977, as Valerie Richardson watches. Three days later, he married Valerie in her hometown of Richmond, Virginia. *The Atlanta Journal-Constitution*

In 1979, Mayor Maynard Jackson whispers to the Rev. Martin Luther King, Sr. (aka Daddy King).
*The Atlanta Journal-Constitution*

Mayor Maynard Jackson, in a playful moment, with daughter Brooke and son Buzzy.
*The Atlanta Journal-Constitution*

Mayor Maynard Jackson,
serving his third term,
with former Mayor Ivan
Allen, Jr., in front of
Atlanta City Hall, 1991.
Photograph by Billy Howard

The Jacksons pose in their Buckhead home (*from left*): Brooke, Maynard Jr., Valerie,
Alexandra and Valerie Amanda.   *The Atlanta Journal-Constitution*

In 1982, Maynard Jackson turns over
Atlanta's City Hall to Andy Young.
*The Atlanta Journal-Constitution*

In an Allen family hunt in Georgia in 1992 (*from left to right*): Ivan III, Inman
and Ivan Jr.    Ivan Allen, Jr., files

Former Mayor Ivan Allen, Jr., turning eighty, surrounded by his family—
Ivan III, Inman and Beaumont and their families—at the Commerce Club in 1991.
Photograph by Ross Henderson

Ivan Jr. and Louise in their
backyard on Northside Drive.
*The Atlanta Journal-Constitution*

Atlanta Mayor Bill Campbell (*left*) joins Renie and Maynard Jr.
at the dedication of John Wesley Dobbs Avenue.
*The Atlanta Journal-Constitution*

At the 1992 Summer Olympics in
Barcelona, Mayor Maynard Jackson
waves the Olympic flag.
Photograph by Joey Ivansco

At the Marietta City Cemetery, the monument of Dr. John Mill... McAfee stands prominently inside the front gate.
Photograph by Steve Sternberg

The tombstones of the freed slaves Wesley and Judie Dobbs lie in an overgrown, century-old graveyard near Kennesaw Mountain, Georgia.    Photograph by Joey Ivansco

His humility was effective. "I am not a lawyer, Senators," but "I beg of you not to let this issue of discrimination drown in legalistic waters.

"Surely the Congress realizes that after having failed to take any definite action on the subject in the last ten years, to fail to pass this bill would amount to an endorsement of private business setting up an entirely new status of discrimination throughout the Nation. Cities like Atlanta might slip backward.

"Are we going to say that it is all right for the Negro citizen to go into the bank on Main Street and to deposit his earnings or borrow money, then to go to department stores to buy what he needs, to go to the supermarket to purchase food for his family, and so on along Main Street . . . but when he comes to the restaurant or the hotel, are we going to say that it is right and legal for the operators of these businesses, merely as a matter of convenience, to insist that the Negro's citizenship be changed and that, as a second-class citizen he is to be refused service?"

Ivan Jr. invoked his "Woodruff clause," allowing smaller communities time to adjust. Then he harkened to the Civil War.

"We cannot dodge the issue. We cannot look back over our shoulders or turn the clock back to the 1860s. We must take action now to assure a greater future for our citizens. A hundred years ago the abolishment of slavery won the United States the acclaim of the whole world when it made every American free in theory.

"Now the elimination of segregation, which is slavery's stepchild, is a challenge to all of us to make every American free in fact as well as in theory—and again to establish our Nation as the true champion of the free world."

Sen. John Pastore of Rhode Island, acting committee chairman, responded first. "Let me say that I am humbled in your presence," he told Ivan Allen. "I think that President Kennedy, when he wrote *Profiles in Courage,* must have been thinking of men such as you."

A committee member raised his hand. "Senator Thurmond," Pastore called out.

This was the moment Ivan Allen, Jr., had been dreading. Strom Thurmond of South Carolina, the old Dixiecrat and a rabid segregationist, had his line of questioning prepared. ("I couldn't cope with him legally in the interpretation of the Constitution," Ivan Jr. recalls. "He had a very sharp tongue.")

"I observe from what you say," Thurmond said, "that the progress that has been made in your city, though, in almost all cases, has been by voluntary action."

"Yes, sir," Allen replied.

Thurmond went down his list. "In the lunch counters and department and variety stores, this was voluntary action?"

"That is correct, sir."

"And downtown, in the arts and theaters, I believe this was voluntary action."

"That is correct, sir."

"On separate employment listings, I believe this was voluntary action."

"That is correct."

"The handling of real estate, I believe, was voluntary action."

"That is correct."

Finally, Thurmond arrived at his point of attack: "Don't you feel that less tension results when there was voluntary action?"

Ivan Jr. replied: "I repeatedly heard businesspeople say that if there had been definition by the Congress, or if there had been a court order, that it made it so much easier to do what they felt that they were being forced to do under the Supreme Court's decision. . . . Sometimes we can't clearly define where we should go and what we should do, and yet these pressures are always there."

Thurmond's tone became accusatory. The mayor did not waver. ("One thing about it was I knew more about it then he did," Ivan Jr. says. "That's what saved me.") Thurmond continued laying traps for the mayor, the mayor slipping away. Thurmond questioned him about the application of the proposed law to interstate commerce. Ivan Jr. stressed that his position was based on practical experience, not legal understanding.

Finally, Pastore intervened on the mayor's behalf. "I hope we won't begin to fling at these witnesses the type of 'when do you stop beating your wife' sort of questions because that, I think, is most unfair. It is only done for the purpose of embarrassment to the witness."

Thurmond was provoked by Pastore. Suddenly, the southern conservative and northern liberal began a harsh exchange of their own. "It seems to be that you are casting an insinuation that my questions were improper, and I resent that, and I tell you I resent it," Thurmond said.

"Let the Senator from South Carolina resent it," Pastore said.

"If you want to hear only one side of this hearing, now is the time for the people of America to know it," Thurmond said. "It is a matter of bringing out the truth and I expect to bring out the truth."

"Your truth is not my truth," Pastore said.

Using the chairman's gavel effectively, Pastore cut off the South Carolina senator—to cheers from the public gallery. ("We got under his skin

pretty bad and he lost his temper," Ivan Jr. remembers. "I had the audience 100 percent.")

"I am surprised," Thurmond told Pastore, "that you permit applaud-
ing in this room. . . . You did nothing to stop it."

"I can't stop it after it happens," Pastore said.

Strom Thurmond then turned his blade on the gallery. "I can tell you
who is in here. It is a bunch of leftwingers who favor this bill, and who
are taking your position, and you know it."

That night, Ivan Jr. flew to Lake Toxaway, North Carolina, for a weekend with Louise and a few friends. He telephoned Gene Patterson in
Atlanta. "Mr. Patterson," he said, "I want you to know that I went up to
Washington today and I came out for the public accommodations bill
right out in pubic in front of the Congress of the You-nited States, ahead
of *The Atlanta Constitution.*" With unrestrained joy, the mayor poked at
his friend, *"What are you waiting for?"*

When Henry Grady returned to Atlanta in December 1886 after his
New South address, a brass band and a thousand people greeted him at
the train station. The people took Grady to the Kimball House hotel to
celebrate.

Ivan Allen's return to Georgia prompted no such festivities. When a
friend called to congratulate the mayor, Ann Moses, his secretary, said,
"I think you better come down here and tell him. He doesn't have many
friends right now."

The *Rome* (Georgia) *News-Tribune* editorialized about Allen, "We are
grateful, indeed, his peculiar philosophy is at least far removed from
Rome." Months later, the Atlanta Board of Aldermen voted 9–3 to forbid
the mayor to speak to them about a public accommodations resolution.

Postcards and letters poured into City Hall, some venomous. "I have
often wondered how Benedict Arnold felt when he had time to reflect,"
one began. "If I ever see you personally, you can tell me." Another:
"Dear Mr. Allen, I believe the City Hall's executive office is high enough
to do the job. Why don't you do the city of Atlanta a favor and jump."

A third: "How much Nigger blood have you got in you?"

Two days after his testimony, *The New York Times* wrote, "On rare occasions the oratorical fog on Capitol Hill is pierced by a voice resonant
with courage and dignity. Such a voice was heard when Mayor Ivan
Allen, Jr., of Atlanta testified before the Senate Commerce Committee in
support of President Kennedy's bill to prohibit racial discrimination in
stores, restaurants and other public accommodations."

A letter from John Kennedy arrived several days later: "You made a number of very effective points and I believe your excellent presentation will prove to be extremely helpful. Under strong leadership the people of Atlanta have been able to recognize and understand a difficult, complex problem and resolve it—at least partially—in a direct and mature fashion."

Within five days positive letters to City Hall outnumbered negative nearly two to one. On July 20, Gov. Carl Sanders offered his own testimony in Washington. Sanders opposed the president's bill, maintaining it would "put the cork in the bottle of mutual cooperation and will make this great moral issue one which is dependent upon federal force alone for its correction." Sanders was introduced to the committee by Sen. Herman Talmadge; Sen. Richard Russell attended the hearing as well. Under questioning that day from Sen. Strom Thurmond, Sanders said the testimony of Mayor Ivan Allen, Jr., did not represent "the feeling of the majority of the people of Atlanta or Georgia."

*The Atlanta Constitution,* meanwhile, opposed the bill, calling instead for further voluntary action. Nevertheless, the newspaper allowed, "We praise the mayor's presentation and agree with the principles he stated. We differ only with his hitch-up of the cart before the horse." The *Daily World* wrote, "Mayor Allen has ignored the myths, stereotypes and regionalism to project Atlanta as the city of the future."

The moral weight of the mayor's testimony was cheered by liberals. McGill wrote the mayor a letter: "Two years from now things will have progressed to show your statement as a moderate one." Benjamin Mays, the president of Morehouse College, told Ivan Jr. that many whites in Atlanta agreed with his position but lacked the courage to say so. Morris Abram predicted that the mayor's testimony would lure new business to the city. Helen Bullard, who once wondered about the sincerity of Ivan Allen's promise to help blacks, wrote: "In the scheme of time, this is no small thing."

The following summer, nearly eight months after JFK's assassination, the 1964 Civil Rights Act, with its public accommodations section, became law. Because of his testimony, Ivan Jr. forever would be considered a liberal, even though Ann Moses insisted her boss was only a "progressive moderate."

Some of the mayor's friends at the Piedmont Driving Club dropped him following the testimony. "That was the end of the rope for most of them," Ivan Jr. says. Thirty years later, the old mayor discovered that many of his contemporaries still thought the Civil Rights Act "was all my fault."

# Chapter 20

Herbert Jenkins sat in the mayor's office, smoking his cigarettes so rapidly he seemed to be eating them. The chief's usual practice was to amble into City Hall unannounced, sit in one of the mayor's rockers and start talking. But in a rare show of formality, he had requested this meeting. In his sixteen years as Atlanta's chief, the size of the force had tripled and his own impressive reputation had grown at a commensurate rate. But now, in 1963, Jenkins sat across from the mayor, smoking as he rocked, obviously ill at ease.

"What are you so nervous about?" Ivan Allen, Jr., asked.

"I want to talk to you," Jenkins replied. Then he added, more cautiously, *"About your father."*

The mayor feigned indignation. "Well, what's wrong with my father?" He suspected Jenkins would tell him the same thing members of the First Presbyterian Church had told him: his father's driving had become a real problem. Already, an edict had been issued quietly at the Ivan Allen Company that employees were not to ride with the Senator. The Senator continued to barrel down Peachtree Street as if he owned it, running through red lights and taking his corners too wide. Though his vision had diminished, his pride had not. He was a terror on the road.

"No policeman in Atlanta is going to arrest your father," Jenkins said. "They're sure not gonna arrest him while you're mayor. But if he keeps running through red lights sooner or later he's gonna have a wreck. That's what I'm worried about."

The mayor agreed to speak with the Senator. It was not coincidental that he arrived at 2600 Peachtree that afternoon after the cocktail hour had already started and the Senator had poured his first old-fashioned. At eighty-seven, the Senator still drove to the office each morning, though by midafternoon on most days he was home scrutinizing his collection of rare maps with the aid of a magnifying glass. A portrait of robust self-satisfaction, portly with a shock of snow-white hair, he dressed each morning in coat and tie. He had outlived most of his contemporaries and privately longed to become the oldest living member of the Atlanta Chamber of Commerce. Robert F. Maddox, who was ninety-three, currently held that distinction. Once, the Senator had said to his friend, "Bob, you look so good. You're gonna be around forever. *Come on, Bob, how much longer are you gonna be around?*" For her husband's eighty-seventh birthday in March, Irene had pulled out the fine china, the silver and linens for a catered dinner (Virginia ham, broccoli with lemon sauce, colored ice cream balls) for fifty of the Senator's closest friends. He remained vigorous. Sometimes, he phoned Marie Dodd, a young woman not yet thirty who worked in the company's advertising department. "Mare-ee," the Senator would say, "are you busy?" She came to his office, he pulled out the dictation slide on his desk, then reached into a drawer and pulled out a deck of cards. They played gin rummy for one-tenth of a cent per point, and he waxed poetic about the old days in Atlanta, the days of wagons and carriages, the majesty of the Hurt and Candler buildings. He told her he believed the best way to market his company was through his name. The fact that his first name began with an "I" was, he thought, unique, and when the company's advertising department decided to change the company's logo, spelling Ivan Allen in lowercase letters, the Senator complained. "He said we took away his total identity," Dodd recalls. To Dodd, he was a lovable grandfather figure. Once, she asked if he would accompany her to an industry-wide dinner and he showed up wearing a white ruffled tuxedo shirt. "He looked like one of those pouter pigeons that can throw their chest out," Dodd says. "He was just so full of himself and I thought how interesting that at age eighty-seven he was willing to escort this young woman to a dinner. He was so full of energy." At Christmas, the Senator still was quick to hand Capt. George Royal a few dollars ("This is for your boys, George!") before he and Irene left for a stay at The Cloister, a swanky place at Sea Island on the Georgia coast.

Yet, despite his vigor, the Senator prepared for death. He had placed a smooth white marble tombstone in a prestigious location at Westview Cemetery, near his friends, the Woodruffs, and not far from the family vault of Henry Grady, the New South dreamer. The Senator's was the only family marker on the hillside with more than a surname. "IVAN ALLEN," it read, conspicuously. He loved his name and planned to carry it with him into eternity.

On this day in 1963, the mayor took a deep breath, "Daddy," he said, "are you having trouble with your driving?"

"Not a bit," he replied, without hesitation. "I just get in my car and drive straight to town."

After another old-fashioned, the mayor tried from a different angle. "Daddy," he said, "are you having trouble with the red lights?"

"I certainly am," the Senator admitted. He shook his head. "But if those damned things weren't there on Peachtree when I first started driving, I don't pay a bit of attention to them."

That the Senator held seniority over the red lights on Peachtree was impossible to dispute.

The mayor gave up. Later, he instructed his police aide, George Royal, to keep a close watch on his father's driving.

The Allens had become the First Family of Atlanta. As Democrats and aristocrats, they were Atlanta's version of the Kennedys. As a civic dynasty, they moved through Atlanta with ease and grace, socializing in high society at the Driving Club, lunching with the business engines, golfing with the elites at the Peachtree Country Club and spearheading charitable efforts with frequency. Already the family had produced two generations of civic leadership in Atlanta and now Ivan Allen III (president of the Jaycees, vice president of the Atlanta Boy Scouts and vice president of the family business by the age of twenty-eight) was beginning to walk that same line. At times, the Ivan Allens seemed like a continuum, one civic soldier in Atlanta indistinguishable from the next. The tradition, and the name, continued on June 5, 1964, with the birth of Ivan Allen IV.

Like the Kennedys, the Allens became a synonym for a place. "Sometimes I think people get mighty tired of us," Louise Allen would say.

The Allens, in every other respect, were as different from the Kennedys as Atlanta was different from Boston. The Kennedys were Catholics and career politicians who, with their daring and their rakish charm, sought the limelight. The Allens were Presbyterians and city boosters who, though aggressive and ambitious in business, were careful about appearances. The Kennedys had their family vacation compound at Hyannis Port; they played touch football on the beach as the paparazzi tried to sneak photos. The Allens had their retreat at the family farm in Franklin where they hunted and fished in solitude. The mayor and Louise migrated to a compound in exclusive Buckhead in northwest Atlanta—the old Richardson estate, Broadlands—where their home was joined over the years by homes built by their three sons. A dense stand of trees shielded the houses and some of the most premium land in the city from passing cars on Northside Drive. While the Kennedys courted danger, controversy and tragedy, the Allens lived in a manner as secure and enduring as Coca-Cola stock. Ivan Jr. once had boasted, "I was born with money, I married money and I made money." Years later his comment surfaced and was quoted often, "much to my chagrin," he says. But the fact was his comment was absolutely accurate. As Ivan Jr. ascended toward City Hall, he also made an extraordinary investment, using Ivan Allen Company funds to buy newly issued Xerox Corporation stock. By June 1965, the company owned more than eleven thousand shares of Xerox common stock, which had a fair-market value in excess of $1.5 million.

The Allens' Presbyterian modesty was kept in check by Ruby Hutchinson, their stout black cook. Hutchinson had worked for years for the Robert Alstons, one of Atlanta's leading families. After the death of the widow Alston, Louise had asked her to become the Allens' cook but Hutchinson declined; Ivan Jr. later decided, with good humor, that Hutchinson did not believe the Allens were of the Alstons' class. Instead, Hutchinson accepted a position with another family. But months later a taxi pulled in front of the Allen home. Out stepped Ruby Hutchinson, with her life's belongings. With few questions asked, she began to work in the Allen kitchen, where she became a mainstay for nearly two decades. Conservative and opinionated ("Like Mammy in *Gone With the Wind*," Beaumont Allen says), Hutchinson lived in the Allen home and expounded upon her worldly views whenever the occasion suited her. She insisted that Beaumont call her "My Brown Mamma." When Vice President Hubert Humphrey once visited Atlanta, he stopped at the Allen home. "Look," Ivan Jr. told him, "I've got this cook who doesn't quite believe that Louise and I are, you know, high-class enough for her. Could you go in and say hello to her?" Humphrey, who had strong support among black Americans, played the role splendidly. He strode into the kitchen and put on a show. "Miss Hutchinson, Mayor Allen sure is a fine man, one of the finest we've got in this country. I want you to take good care of Mayor Allen and Mrs. Allen," he said. Then he threw his arms around the cook in a warm embrace. Ruby Hutchinson stood amidst the pots and pans, wide-eyed and speechless.

At that point, the mayor believed, "Ruby decided we were satisfactory to work with."

The warnings about the Senator's driving proved well founded. While attending the funeral for another friend at Patterson's funeral home, the Senator suddenly became lethargic. After the service, he remained in his chair, the last to leave.

"Are you all right, Senator Allen?" someone asked.

"Yes, I'm all right," he said.

He drove along Peachtree Road toward home and as he turned into 2600, he lost control. He failed to steer his Chevrolet through the two pillars at the front of the driveway; instead, the car bounced over the curb and passed over the front lawn. The car hit the edge of the front terrace with a thud and came to a stop. Drawing from his remarkable reservoir of determination, he made it to the front door, rang the bell, and then fell heavily against the door. When Irene Allen opened the door she found her husband at her feet. She called out for Jesse, their black handyman, who carried the Senator inside and placed him on the sofa. Irene Allen immediately called for a doctor.

The Senator was coherent when the doctor arrived. He explained his dizziness.

"Mr. Allen, when did you first have this feeling?"

"At Patterson's," he said.

"Who brought you home?"

"I drove home."

"You couldn't possibly have driven home," the doctor said. "You've had a major stroke."

The Senator shrugged. "Well," he said, "I'm here."

The stroke cost him partial use of his right side and his right eyelid drooped noticeably. He would survive the stroke but never again was quite the same. In addition, his wife had grown aged and infirm. Both required attendants. Irene grew distrustful of her servants and attendants and carried her purse around the house, from room to room, fearful that it would be stolen. Marie Dodd occasionally visited the house, updating the Senator on the company's advertising department and bringing him treats. Once she brought an old photograph found at the office. It pictured the Senator and several elegant gentlemen posing with a beautiful young woman, a picture undoubtedly from one of his many civic groups. When Irene saw the photograph she blanched. "Mrs. Allen did not approve of it and was highly indignant," Dodd recalls.

As he waited for death, the Senator reworked portions of his will, adding several codicils. Virtually his entire estate (which included the silver cups, urns and pitchers given to him for civic duty) were to be left to his wife and their only son, the mayor. In February 1964 the Senator added a codicil that awarded $1,000 to four longtime employees of the Ivan Allen Company. In an apparent fit of anger the following year he revoked a clause that would have awarded $15,000 to his niece, Suesylla Thomas of Dalton.

Once, during a stay at St. Joseph's Hospital, the Senator was visited by Marie Dodd and Bill Glenn, the tall, gentlemanly president of the Ivan Allen Company. *"Mare-ee, pssst! Come here."* the Senator said. She stood next to his bed. "I want you to step outside. Billy and I are going to change clothes. He's going to put on my pajamas and I'm going to put on his suit. But you be there to walk me out of here 'cause I'm going home." The Senator had not lost his spirit just yet.

When Robert F. Maddox died, at ninety-five, during the spring of 1965, Ivan Allen, Sr., became the oldest living member of the Atlanta Chamber of Commerce.

But the Senator, who had waited so long for this moment, was not well enough to celebrate with his old friends at his favorite clubs. Besides, most of his old friends already were gone.

The Rev. Martin Luther King, Jr., in 1960, had said, "People cannot devote themselves to a great cause without finding someone who becomes the personification of that cause. People cannot become devoted to Christianity until they find Christ, to democracy until they find Lincoln and Jefferson and Roosevelt, to Communism until they find Marx and Lenin and Stalin."

By 1964, his third year as mayor, Ivan Jr. personified Atlanta. He was ambitious and prosperous, optimistic and constantly in motion. "Our Mayor a-go-go," is how some locals knew him. Anne Rivers, then a newly hired young writer for *Atlanta* magazine, sometimes lunched at the Commerce Club, where the mayor and his old friends slapped backs and discussed policy over London broil. These were the men redoing Atlanta, Rivers knew, and some were using their own money to do it. "The aura of power was just palpable," she recalls. "It was like watching perfectly adapted creatures move through their world, absolutely not one false move because they were so sure of themselves and their environment. Such a perfect entity. Like you were watching a Fabergé Egg." Together, the mayor and his city were on the rise. Atlanta's 2 percent unemployment rate represented less than half the national average. Its housing starts during 1963 increased by more than 40 percent over the previous year. The city's new airport terminal, opened in 1961 and expected to last a generation, already was inadequate.

Ivan Allen's victory over Maddox in 1961 not only set a mood but seemed part of a larger political trend in Atlanta: racial moderates began to unseat the segregationists. With the death of the county unit system in 1962, Charles Weltner unseated Cong. James Davis and Augusta's Carl Sanders was elected governor, defeating the rabid segregationist Marvin Griffin. The creation of a congressional district near Atlanta in 1964 made an opening for James Mackay, a former legislator and racial moderate. A movement was afoot in the city. "We were going to absolutely solve all of the problems overnight," businessman Larry Gellerstedt, Jr., recalls. "Nothing was impossible."

On most mornings, Ivan Jr. dropped his son Beaumont at Westminster, a private school, then drove directly to City Hall. (His black yardman and handyman, Watson Plummer, picked up Beaumont in the afternoon carpool.) Ivan Jr. ran the mayor's office as he ran his business. He kept his City Hall desk spotless, in contrast to the debris of Bill Hartsfield's office. He signed papers quickly, then transferred them from the in basket to the out. His neatness was compulsive. "I hate dirt," he says. He kept a few golf balls and a putter in his office and at times during conversations he struck a few putts. Gripping a golf club put him at ease.

He delegated freely and expected results immediately. He relied heavily on the experience of administrative aide Earl Landers, who had worked in city government for thirty-four years, most recently as comptroller. Landers taught Ivan Jr. the inner workings of city government: he knew where all the city's skeletons were buried. Landers made two demands upon being named to Allen's staff: "One, I won't make speeches. Two, I won't get involved in any racial issues. I'm not suited for either."

Meanwhile, Ivan and Louise continued to serve as hosts for the Tuesday night badminton supper club in the field house on the Allen meadow. There, they were joined by their closest friends, including some of the leading bankers and attorneys in the city.

While Ivan Jr. looked after Atlanta, Atlanta—through Bob Woodruff and the badminton group—looked after him.

The strict order of his life, however, was about to be disrupted by the rumblings of racial discord in his city.

Black demonstrators marched into Leb's restaurant on Forsyth and Luckie streets late on a Saturday afternoon; many stayed into the evening. They filled the booths and the counters. Demanding service, they received silence. Some downtown restaurants had desegregated voluntarily, but, as of January 25, 1964, Leb's was not among them.

Outside, protesters sang freedom songs. Up the street, a group of robed Klansmen held a counterprotest in front of several newly integrated restaurants. "Please stay out. Negroes and whites mix here," the Klan placards read. From inside Leb's, Dick Gregory, a black comedian and social activist, led a chant: *"The old K-K, she ain't what she used to be . . ."*

When owner Charles Lebedin arrived, he closed his restaurant at once. A group of blacks refused to leave. Because Lebedin locked the bathroom doors, several protesters urinated on his floor. Enraged, Lebedin told reporters he employed two hundred blacks and always had been a friend to the race. "I was never a segregationist," Lebedin said. "But I am today. They [the demonstrators] made me one." The next day, protests at Leb's resumed. When Lester Maddox saw the paddywagon loaded with protesters pull away from the restaurant, he said, "Man, that sure does look good. I ain't seen nothing look better than this in a long time."

For Atlanta, the protests could not have come at a worse time. A United Nations panel on human rights had arrived in the city the previous day. Group members hailed from thirteen nations, including American representative Morris Abram; the purpose of their two-day trip was to study the interracial calm and cooperation of Atlanta. Ivan Jr. was embarrassed by what the U.N. commission witnessed. Earlier in the week, A. T. Walden, the aged chairman of the Atlanta Summit Leadership Conference of nine civil rights groups, had broken off negotiations with white restaurant and hotel owners. In the days that followed three hundred arrests were made; a dozen people were injured.

The mayor pledged firmness. "Atlanta will accept no ultimatums and bow to no threats," he said. "At the same time it will not lag in its efforts to ensure all of its citizens their full rights of citizenship." The national press weighed the significance of the Atlanta protests. *U.S. News & World Report:* "There is widespread fear that January's troubles will bring a halt to years of quiet progress in interracial cooperation in Atlanta."

By mid-February Ivan Jr. was back in the fields of Ichauway in south Georgia with Bob Woodruff, the third consecutive winter the mayor had made the trip. Allen would term his day-long hunt "a capital letter day in my life," in a note of appreciation to Woodruff. Later in the year, the mayor, Louise and Beaumont traveled on the Coca-Cola Company jet for a two-week vacation at Woodruff's sixty-thousand-acre ranch and hunting preserve in Cody, Wyoming, once owned by Buffalo Bill Cody himself. There, the mayor resumed his competitive gin rummy match with Woodruff while Beaumont and the children of Coca-Cola president Paul Austin were chaperoned each day by Woodruff's butler, Charles, who dressed in a traditional black suit, tie and cap. "[Charles] would even go down to the creek with us dressed like that," Beaumont says. Ivan Jr. believes Woodruff took a personal interest in him as well as other emerging civic and political leaders such as realtor Jack Adair, banker Charles Thwaite and Gov. Carl Sanders. He understood Woodruff's magnanimity toward Atlanta and he continued to take advantage of it. "I would like to talk with you when you get back to Atlanta," Ivan Jr. wrote to Woodruff in February 1964, several weeks after the Leb's demonstration. "I will give you a ring on Sunday or Monday and when it is convenient, hope you can hear me out for a few minutes."

When the time came to vote on President Lyndon Johnson's 1964 Civil Rights Act, U.S. Cong. Charles Weltner, now a political soulmate of Ivan Allen's, was the only one of Georgia's ten congressmen to support it.

Nonetheless, the bill became law on July 2, 1964. That day, Georgia senator Herman Talmadge admitted that "there is no alternative but compliance."

Lester Maddox disagreed.

Everything that Ivan Allen and Atlanta would achieve during the 1960s would occur despite Lester Maddox. The day after the Civil Rights Act was enacted, three black students from the Interdenominational Theological Center (ITC) of the AUC drove to Maddox's Pickrick restaurant. Their intention was to integrate it, putting the new federal law into local action. When they pulled into the parking lot, Maddox appeared, brandishing a pistol.

"Get out of here and don't ever come back," Maddox yelled. He kicked their car while customers, including women and children, held pick handles Maddox had stored in crates inside the front door for moments such as this. As the black theological students drove away slowly, Maddox slammed a pick handle across the top of the car.

In Fulton County Criminal Court on July 7, Maddox was charged with pointing a pistol at one of the young black ministers. Judge Osgood Williams said, "Such conduct would create in our land only anarchy and tyranny." Maddox told the judge he would not comply with the Civil Rights Act. When the Rev. George Willis, the black student who brought the charge against Maddox, was asked to explain why he had attempted to enter the Pickrick, he said, "I'm a preacher and we like chicken, you know." Maddox denied he had pointed his pistol in Willis's face, insisting he merely intended "to protect my life, liberty and property." He also said that he had entered Leb's during a protest in January and had heard blacks chant, "Lester Maddox gotta go! Lester Maddox gotta go . . . Pickrick is next!"

The stakes in the Maddox case, and in another lawsuit brought by the U.S. Department of Justice against the Heart of Atlanta motel, brought a coterie of government attorneys to Atlanta, including Assistant Attorney General Burke Marshall. Jack Greenberg, chief counsel for the NAACP, and associate counsel Constance Baker Motley joined William Alexander, a local black attorney, in representing the black plaintiff against Maddox.

Maddox's attorneys contended that the Pickrick did not fit within the terms of interstate commerce as defined by the public accommodations section of the Civil Rights Act. In response, the black plaintiff introduced witnesses who testified to the out-of-state license plates they saw in the parking lot of the Pickrick; attorneys for the plaintiff also maintained that bottled catsup served inside the Pickrick was made out of state. As the drama unfolded inside the courtroom, Maddox, in his weekly advertisement for the Pickrick published in the *Constitution* on July 18, thanked his supporters "in our fight for our 'Civil Rights.' " He broadly defined those rights as the freedom to operate his business within the American system of free enterprise. "Much of the blame belongs to White citizens who have used [black] people to make their own gains in the political world possible," Maddox wrote.

In a landmark ruling four days later, the federal court upheld the constitutionality of the Civil Rights Act and enjoined the Heart of Atlanta motel and the Pickrick restaurant from discriminating against blacks. The three judges, Chief Judge Elbert P. Tuttle of the Fifth Circuit Court of Appeals, and District Judges Frank A. Hooper and Lewis R. Morgan, determined that both enterprises were accountable to the interstate commerce regulations of the Civil Rights Act.

"I'm not going to integrate," Maddox told reporters that day. "If I lose everything, I'm not worried. Lyndon Johnson said he's going to eradicate poverty, didn't he?"

Once his appeals had expired, Maddox allowed the Pickrick to expire with it. In August he picketed against LBJ at the 1964 Democratic National Convention in Atlantic City and announced his support for Republican Barry Goldwater. Maddox then placed a mock coffin in front of the shuttered Pickrick along with copies of the U.S. Constitution and the Declaration of Independence. Free enterprise, he declared, was dead. Maddox also sold souvenir pick handles in front of the restaurant. He called them "Pickrick Drumsticks."

On April 21, 1965, an all-white jury found Maddox not guilty on two charges that he had pointed a pistol at the black minister. The jury deliberated for only forty-four minutes.

Maddox's victory was a small one. But his reputation as a symbol of resistance was strengthening. Soon to come was an even more remarkable victory.

The news from Norway broke on October 14. The Rev. Martin Luther King, Jr., had been awarded the 1964 Nobel Peace Prize. Within days Atlanta's white leaders fell into an apoplectic fit over what to do about it.

The thirty-five-year-old Baptist minister became the twelfth American to win the honor, joining the likes of Theodore Roosevelt, Woodrow Wilson and Cordell Hull, and the second black American, following former United Nations under secretary Ralph Bunche. King learned of the honor at St. Joseph's Infirmary in Atlanta where he was suffering from a severe virus and exhaustion. When the former police commissioner of Birmingham, Eugene "Bull" Connor, heard the news, he reacted with disbelief: "They're scraping the bottom of the barrel." In St. Augustine, Florida, Police Chief Virgil Stuart wondered aloud, "How can you win the Peace Prize when you stir up all the trouble he did down here?"

As mayor of King's home city, Ivan Jr. sent a congratulatory telegram to the Southern Christian Leadership Conference offices on Auburn Avenue. He also complimented the black minister in a press conference with local reporters. "He has displayed remarkable leadership at both a national and international level to the 20 million American Negro citizens," he said, "and has been instrumental in bringing full American citizenship to them."

The Nobel announcement started a flurry of activity, most of it hidden, among leaders in black Atlanta and a select group of whites who believed the city needed a public display to honor King.

But in the halls of the Commerce Club even the mention of King's name reminded members of how he had reduced Dick Rich to tears with his demonstration at Rich's in October 1960. Their anger would rise again in November when King supported striking black workers at Atlanta's Scripto Inc. by calling for a national boycott of the company's products and joining the picket line. Few white civic leaders wanted to honor King because it was the right thing to do or even out of courtesy.

But they recognized one compelling reason to honor the Nobel laureate: anything less would embarrass the city, exposing a racism they couldn't admit to anyone, least of all themselves. Soon a committee formed to organize a testimonial dinner for King. The co-chairmen were four liberals: Ralph McGill, Rabbi Jacob Rothschild, Morehouse College president Benjamin Mays and Roman Catholic Archbishop Paul Hallinan. In mid-December, they sent letters to more than a hundred civic leaders urging them to sponsor the affair scheduled for January 27 at the Dinkler Plaza Hotel on Peachtree. The letter went unanswered by most whites.

McGill had made his views plain long before the letter was sent. In his front-page column in the *Constitution* on October 16, McGill had written, "The South one day will be grateful when it realizes what the alternative would have been had Dr. King, with his capacity to stir and inspire, come preaching violence, hate and aggression. These Europeans have a view of Dr. King that is clearer than ours, which has become befogged by emotions and prejudices."

At what should have been his crowning moment, King was suffering a crisis of self-confidence. For months, the Federal Bureau of Investigation had waged an intensive operation to discredit him, wiretapping his phones and bugging his hotel rooms. There were rumors of extramarital affairs. As a moral leader, King understood that any moral failure on his part could cripple the entire movement. In late November, he met FBI director J. Edgar Hoover in Washington for what he later told reporters was a productive discussion. That was an overstatement. Hoover only intensified his subversive operations against the minister.

In Oslo on December 10, King accepted the Nobel Peace Prize and told of his "abiding faith in America." He accepted the Nobel as "profound recognition that non-violence is the answer to the crucial political and moral question of our time—the need for man to overcome oppression and violence without resorting to violence and oppression." He announced later that he planned to donate to the civil rights movement the $54,000 that accompanied the prize. His family and close associates knew of King's depression over the FBI invasion into his private life. In early January, Coretta Scott King, at home in Atlanta, received an audiotape that she assumed was a recording of one of her husband's speeches. As she listened, though, she was shocked. She heard her husband tell dirty jokes. At another moment, she heard the muffled sounds of people engaged in sex. A horrifying letter, addressed to her husband, was included with the tape: "King, like all frauds your end is approaching." The tape was a product of FBI wiretaps.

The FBI also tried to subvert the King dinner in Atlanta. An agent told Gene Patterson that King engaged in illicit sex, and that, during an upcoming weekend, was scheduled to leave from a Florida airport for an island tryst. The agent urged Patterson to write about it. "Look, we're not a peephole journal," Patterson said.

Twice, Herbert Jenkins told Ivan Jr. that the FBI had called with tips that King was engaged in a sexual liaison at the Waluhaje apartments in west Atlanta. The bureau wanted the Atlanta police department to stage a raid. "Jenkins told me there wasn't anything to it," Ivan Jr. recalls. "He didn't put any credence in it."

The mayor, unaware of the extent of the FBI's surveillance of King, so firmly believed the city should honor its only Nobel Prize winner that he lobbied business leaders. In December, he visited Ichauway to discuss the crisis with Woodruff, now seventy-five. It pleased the mayor when Coca-Cola's Paul Austin approached him in the field, during a hunt and, speaking for the Boss, said, "We feel that the city must move ahead as you suggested."

So the mayor and Austin gathered at the Piedmont Driving Club with twenty business leaders. Harvard-trained, still in his forties and exuding confidence, Austin spoke powerfully. The fact that he spoke for Woodruff added to his persuasive power. Soon enough, the group agreed to sponsor a biracial dinner for King. The mayor understood that his friends had been moved to action not by morality but by pragmatism.

Austin asked Ivan Jr. to close the meeting. He looked at the men in the room, some of them lifelong colleagues. "I have listened to your reasons for support," the mayor said, "and I am sure I'll find that you will support it financially and that you will glory in the very fine national publicity that you will receive.

"But on the night of the banquet it's my guess that very few of you will be present. Most of you will be out of town or sick, and you'll send someone else to represent you.

"Don't let it worry you, though," he said. "The mayor will be there."

Though McGill played a central role in organizing the King dinner, the local papers did not write about the rift among white leaders. "I do not understand the local papers' silence," Archbishop Hallinan later wrote to Rabbi Rothschild.

On December 29, four weeks before the dinner, *The New York Times* reported on Atlanta's civic disharmony. Only then did the Atlanta newspapers present the issue to their readers. The *Times* said one "high-level bank executive" had mounted a private campaign against the dinner. Mills Lane of the C&S Bank, fearful that some might think the *Times* meant him, telephoned friends to say, "I was not the one they were talking about."

The mayor insisted there was no controversy, though Bill Hartsfield admitted some tensions had developed. Hartsfield, on record in support of the dinner, said he would "hate to see my town held up as a city which refused to honor a Nobel Peace Prize winner."

The magnitude of the crisis should have been clear to readers when Ralph McGill, in a staff-written story about the King dinner in his own newspaper on December 29, declined comment.

Privately, though, McGill defended the need to have the testimonial dinner. "I don't agree with everything about Dr. King," McGill wrote in a letter to local attorney Granger Hansell, whose firm represented the *Constitution*. But, McGill added, "I don't see any need for the business community to brush off the Negro community. Whether we like it or not, Dr. King is their leading symbol, both in this country and abroad. Atlanta has too good an image, in my opinion, to act in a petty manner." When McGill received a hostile letter from an Atlantan who suggested that the editor was closely linked with King, he responded with anger. "I have seen [King] only three times and then casually," McGill wrote. "It is odd how people who don't know what they are talking about imagine things that do not exist."

*The New York Times* story—proof that the nation was watching Atlanta closely—and the knowledge that Woodruff supported the King dinner combined to produce a sudden burst in ticket sales. White leaders responded in a rush. Banks and department stores telephoned requests to purchase tickets in blocks of twenty. Already a group that included Helen Bullard and Janice Rothschild, wife of the rabbi, had purchased a $430 Steuben bowl, inscribed with a dogwood blossom, symbol of Atlanta, as a gift for King.

King, meanwhile, participated in voter registration rallies in Selma, Alabama, where on January 25 he watched a hefty, middle-aged black woman named Annie Lee Cooper punch Dallas County Sheriff Jim Clark in the head. Clark, who with Bull Connor would become the symbolic gargoyles at the gate of the civil rights movement, responded by slamming his billy club across Cooper's head, an act captured in a photograph that appeared in the nation's newspapers.

Reports of the difficulties with the King dinner disturbed King. "At one point Martin was so agitated he almost pulled out," Coretta King says. "It was almost like they were doing him a favor."

On the eve of the dinner, King left Alabama for Atlanta, where his father gave him more discouraging news. Chief Jenkins had told Daddy King that, in a recent personal conversation with J. Edgar Hoover, the FBI director spoke of the young King with an alarming distaste.

A biracial crowd of fifteen hundred attended the dinner. An announced protest by the Ku Klux Klan never materialized, and restaurateur Charles Lebedin of Leb's sounded a lonely call of protest from the street, yelling at the arriving King, "Peace with violence! Peace! A lot of baloney!"

Many of those who attended the event would recall its tense nature. As Vice Mayor Sam Massell left the ballroom that night, he walked with his wife toward their car, feeling fearful. "Everybody, I think, was nervous," Massell says. "We could get shot, bombed, whatever.

"I watched over my shoulder."

The Morehouse glee club performed and plainclothes detectives walked through the ballroom. As the mayor predicted, many of the leading white businessmen in the city did not attend. Among the missing: Paul Austin and Robert Woodruff.

Ivan Jr. that night sensed uneasiness among both whites and blacks, many socializing with the other race for the first time. "It was one of those occasions when I would say that things were kind of sticky," Ivan Jr. says. The mayor tried to generate conversation but had little success, until an organizer of the event approached to say that the dinner would start forty-five minutes late.

"Don't worry about that," Ivan Jr. said, motioning to the Rev. Sam Williams, president of the local NAACP. "My friend Sam Williams has been waiting for 100 years to get in that ballroom, and 45 minutes one way or the other isn't going to bother him much." As laughter filled the room, Ivan Jr. felt the tension release.

Later, the mayor told the audience, "Through the years, as history is wrought, some men are destined to be leaders of humanity and to shape the future course of the world. Dr. Martin Luther King, Jr., is such a man. I take great pride in honoring this citizen of Atlanta who is willing to turn the other cheek in his quest for full citizenship for all Americans." Rabbi Rothschild and Archbishop Hallinan saluted the Reverend King in brief addresses, as did state senator Leroy Johnson and Morehouse president Benjamin Mays.

The mayor sat at the head table with Martin and Coretta King; the King children, Yoki, Marty and Dexter, played beneath the table. That night Ivan Jr. presented King with an official proclamation from the city.

King delivered an address the mayor long would remember, at one point declaring there were "in the white South millions of people of good will, whose voices are yet unheard, whose course is yet unclear, and whose courageous acts are yet unseen." King called on those unseen people to rise into view. The evening closed with a rendition of "We Shall Overcome," the anthem of the civil rights movement. For an hour afterward, King shook the hands of whites and blacks, who stood in line for the honor.

Bullard called the dinner "the first thing Atlanta had done that they didn't have to do," though, in truth, a city conscious of its image could not have refused to honor King.

The coverage in the *Constitution* and the *Journal* the next day was relegated to pages nine and twelve. King later wrote a note of appreciation to the dinner organizers: "It was a testimonial not only to me but to the greatness of the City of Atlanta, the South, the nation and its ability to rise above the conflict of former generations."

*Time* magazine praised Atlanta's racial moderation and, with amazement, suggested that the interracial King dinner "was remarkable even for Atlanta." The fact that the magazine credited Ivan Jr. and Hartsfield with organizing the dinner, and not the city's religious leaders, irked Archbishop Hallinan, who, in a handwritten note to Rabbi Rothschild, contended the oversight was done in "true Time style—totally secularistic." But Hallinan added, "Enough griping! The goal was achieved—our community reflects progress and good will—the segregationists are dwindling—and we heard a fine address from a real leader."

King left Atlanta the next day for rest at a hotel in New York. The FBI preceded him to plant its recording devices.

Ivan Jr. sent a note to Bob Woodruff along with a copy of an editorial from *The Philadelphia Inquirer*, which called the King dinner "right and proper." The editorial expressed hope that Philadelphians understood that "this could only come about with basic good will and endless hard work by all concerned."

"Dear Boss," Ivan Jr. wrote. "This is a right sound editorial and is a reflection of the type of comment that I think we received over most of the country.

"Looking forward to being with you on the week of the 15th. Sincerely, Ivan."

Muggsy Smith never had a chance in the 1965 mayor's race. When no one else challenged Ivan Jr., Smith filed his entry fee in the final hours of the registration period in July. He said the people of Atlanta deserved a choice.

But Allen's popularity was high, bolstered by the city's unparalleled growth. Not since Reconstruction, when Atlanta rose from the ashes of the Civil War, had the city undergone such a transformation. Every economic index showed Atlanta's promise. Department store sales rose by 11 percent in a year. A $21 million expansion of the runway at the Atlanta airport, now the nation's fourth busiest, had not cost the taxpayers a cent. Construction began on a $9 million convention hall in the Buttermilk Bottom slum area. The mayor rewarded municipal employees with raises, costing more than $1.5 million. In April 1965, the $18 million Atlanta–Fulton County Stadium opened; the mayor, with some magnificent behind-the-headlines work, had received assurances that baseball's Milwaukee Braves would move to Atlanta for the 1966 season. Unbridled optimism moved Ivan Jr. to perpetual boasts about his "major-league city."

"We continue toward our destiny of greatness," he had said in his State of the City address in January 1965. The fact that thousands of poor blacks in Atlanta's blighted areas had been displaced by the mayor's building boom seemed to Allen only a small complication in the overall scheme of progress; many of the dislocated blacks moved from the city into DeKalb County. With the creation of Economic Opportunity

Atlanta in 1964, Atlanta became one of the first cities to create an anti-poverty program, but its success in creating housing opportunities for dislocated blacks was limited.

Muggsy Smith would learn that Ivan Jr. had solidified his strength. He lunched with Boss Woodruff at Coca-Cola and played badminton, dressed in whites, with city bankers and businessmen. Unlike Bill Hartsfield, an agent of the power structure, Ivan Jr. was *of the power structure.* When his friend Mills Lane of the C&S Bank financed the stadium deal, Ivan Jr. crowed, "We built a stadium on ground we didn't own with money we didn't have for a team we hadn't signed." In November 1964, Bullard had privately worried that, because the city had spent an additional $900,000 to have the stadium ready within one year, the "stadium standing vacant will probably determine the next mayor's race."

But Ivan Jr. made certain the stadium would be filled with life. Within a year, he also would lure the National Football League to Atlanta.

Just like that, Ivan Jr. was the father of professional sports in Atlanta. Even segregationists could applaud that. Muggsy Smith struggled to find a point of attack during the 1965 campaign. When the Watts riots burned in Los Angeles that summer, leaving thirty-four dead, Smith suggested a similar riot could break out among blacks in Atlanta. Ivan Jr. disagreed. "We do not have large areas of poverty and discontent in Atlanta like they do in Los Angeles," he said. In the meantime, the mayor called for an assault against the city's worst slums.

Two years earlier, John Kennedy and Ralph McGill had told Ivan Jr. that his testimony in support of the president's public accommodations bill would enhance his 1965 reelection bid. They were right.

Into every black rally during that race, Ivan Jr. carried a green leather-bound book with the gold-embossed letters: "Testimony by Ivan Allen, Jr. Civil Rights, Public Accommodations, 88th Congress." He had learned from observing Borders and Daddy King that, in church, blacks responded to drama.

"It was as though I was carrying a Bible under my arm," Ivan Jr. would say. At times, blacks reached out to touch his book. Some asked to read it. "There aren't many people in political life who can walk in and completely dominate an audience as I was able to do with Negro audiences during that campaign," he recalls.

On September 8, the morning of the mayoral primary, Ivan Jr. visited the Senator at 2600 Peachtree Road. He also visited his mother at Piedmont Hospital. Both were in poor health but had made certain to vote by absentee ballot. Ivan Jr. won the election with 70 percent of the vote, leaving Muggsy Smith to contemplate a real politician's real power.

Yet the vote did carry a troubling message: the mayor won only 51 percent of the white vote. His racial policies had alienated virtually half of Atlanta's white voters.

That night, at a victory party, a telegram, purportedly sent by the Beatles, was read: "Dear Ivan Baby. It couldn't have happened to a sweeter boy." The ballroom erupted with laughter. The jubilant mayor threw his arms around his son Ivan III, an image carried on the front page of the *Constitution* the next morning.

At a time when Lyndon Johnson forged his Great Society, Ivan Jr. became a favorite of the administration. He received feelers for federal positions, first to head a civil rights commission and later to serve as director of the Community Relations Service. His interest, however, was Atlanta. As he studied other mayors, he came to admire Richard Lee of New Haven, Connecticut, Henry Maier of Milwaukee and John Lindsay of New York.

The big-city mayor he watched most closely during these steamy summers of urban discontent was Sam Yorty of Los Angeles. In Yorty, Ivan Jr. saw a stunning example of how not to govern. Yorty was a maverick, feisty and prepossessing, a mayor who turned politics into a streetfight. The first Democrat elected mayor of Los Angeles in half a century, he had supported Republican Richard Nixon for president in 1960; he also wrote a pamphlet entitled "I Cannot Take Kennedy." During the Watts riots, Yorty had remained aloof. Subsequent studies suggested blacks in Watts were among the most isolated in the nation.

"Yorty was the sorriest white man's mayor that ever stepped on two feet," Ivan Jr. says.

In July 1966, Yorty and Ivan Jr. were among eight mayors to appear before the Senate Subcommittee on Executive Reorganization during its hearings on the plight of American cities. Ivan Jr. was treated with enormous respect, Yorty was not. Chairman Abraham Ribicoff of Connecticut chastised Yorty for his neglect of the Los Angeles ghettos, saying, "You are shortchanging a few generations by doing absolutely nothing for the disadvantaged groups." Sen. Robert Kennedy of New York, who had not forgotten Yorty's support of Nixon, said, "The mayor of Los Angeles I would like to have stay here through all of these hearings, and I think he could safely do so, because as I understand from your testimony, you have nothing to get back to." A disgusted Yorty replied, "That is sort of a ridiculous statement."

As mayor, Ivan Jr. drove through Atlanta's ghettos frequently, scribbling notes. At times he left his car and approached black bystanders to inquire about the quality of city services.

Early in the summer of 1966, Ivan Jr. hired Dan Sweat, a former *Atlanta Journal* reporter who more recently had helped set up the War on Poverty program in the city, to serve as federal aid coordinator for Atlanta. Most federal funds were to be used to clean up Atlanta's ghettos.

Ivan Jr. gave Sweat three months to coordinate a new federal aid package for the city.

But on Sweat's second day he was called into the mayor's office. Ivan Jr. was red-faced with anger. "I thought he was gonna blow a gasket," Sweat says. One by one, the city department heads arrived.

The mayor paced, waiting. "Everybody follow me," he said, finally. The department heads crowded into several cars and followed the mayor to Vine City, a black ghetto on the west side. There, they found a group on the sidewalk. What they saw was worse than crude. It was nauseating. Decayed houses on the brink of collapse. Black children playing in the gutter with a dead dog. Ivan Allen's voice was high-pitched.

"I WANT YOU TO CLEAN IT UP!" he told the department heads.

The mayor barked out orders to the city building inspector, the public works director and the water works director. Then he turned to Dan Sweat.

"Sweat," he said, seething, "I'm holding you responsible that we don't have any riots in the city this summer."

"Wait a minute, Mr. Mayor," Sweat said. "You told me I have three months—"

"YOUR TIME'S UP!"

Ivan Jr. believed federal funds could save the ghettos of his city. "Most southern cities wouldn't dare take any federal funds because they were dogging you about segregation all of the time," he says.

Like its mayor, Atlanta was a favorite of the Johnson administration. There were several reasons for the city's preferred status: Ivan Allen's 1963 testimony in Washington; the city's two congressmen, Charles Weltner and James Mackay, were liberal Democrats; and Gov. Carl Sanders was a friend of LBJ's. (In March 1967, Atlanta became the first city in the nation to apply for Johnson's Model Cities Program; approval came eight months later.)

Ivan Jr. had no patience for bureaucratic delay. If a task wasn't performed well, and quickly, there would be hell to pay. As a leader, he was a quick study. En route to deliver a civic speech, he read Ann Moses' notes in the back of the car and memorized the essentials. Then he delivered the speech off the cuff. Once, he invited radio newsman Aubrey Morris to hear him address the Rotary Club in Rome, and along the way he told his driver, police captain George Royal, to stop at the Ivan Allen

Company branch office in Rome. As Morris walked inside the store, he watched the mayor, on his surprise visit, rub his finger along a shelf in the front of the store. The shelf was covered with dust. Ivan Jr. invited his store manager into a back office where he berated him for his lackadaisical effort, a bullying style of management that surprised Morris.

Ivan Jr. used his friendships to get things accomplished. In 1966, Sweat borrowed an idea from John Lindsay's Tot Lot program in the ghettos of New York City and initiated a Play Lot program in Atlanta. To brighten the gloom of the ghetto, sand boxes and swing sets were to be placed in vacant lots. In the second phase of the program, portable swimming pools would be added.

"How much is this thing gonna cost?" Ivan Jr. asked.

Sweat was afraid to tell him. "Six thousand dollars each," he said.

The mayor pulled out his personal checkbook. Sweat raised an eyebrow, though he had seen the mayor do this before. Once, Ivan Jr. had promised blacks in Summerhill that the city would pave a road in the area. When the city didn't respond, residents complained. The mayor then asked Sweat how much the paving would cost, and then wrote a personal check. "You've got to stop doing that," Sweat warned him, respectfully, "because the poor son-of-a-gun who follows you [as mayor] probably ain't gonna have a checkbook and you'll put him at a disadvantage."

Now, in the matter of sandboxes and swing sets, the mayor said, "We can't wait for them," meaning the Board of Aldermen. Ivan Jr. handed Sweat a check for $6,000.

"Here," he said. "I'm buying my Play Lot." Then the mayor said, "You call Billy Sterne [at the Trust Company]. You call Dick Rich." The mayor cited several more names. "Tell each one of them to send you a check for $6,000. Then call Mr. Woodruff's office and tell him we want him to match the total."

To Sweat's amazement, everyone ponied up the money. "Nobody blinked an eye." Sweat says. "We put those Play Lots in there and got the program rolling."

On the afternoon of September 6, 1966, when the late summer furnace cast a hazy glow across Atlanta, the WSB news bulletin sounded from Beaumont Allen's transistor radio. *"Duh-duh-duh-DUH-DUH!"* Louise and her youngest son were at work in the garden at the Allen family estate. *"Duh-duh-duh-DUH-DUH!"* Suddenly, they heard breaking bottles and raised voices. An excited reporter said a few cars had been turned over, blacks were angry, and that something in Summerhill, maybe a house, was burning. But the words Beaumont heard best, the words that froze this moment in time as the news of the Kennedy assassination had, were "mayor" and "riot." The reports came every two minutes, and each time the reporter said Ivan Allen, Jr., was walking in the midst of the storm, somewhere between the bricks and the bottles and the angry blacks. Louise listened in silence. She remembered something the mayor had told her: "If trouble breaks out in Atlanta, it's going to break out over me." Just fifteen, Beaumont was frightened. He thought: *"Dad might get killed!"*

The summer of 1966 was one of Lyndon Johnson's worst on the homefront. Riots broke out in black ghettos in twenty cities. In San Francisco, Chicago and Cleveland, blacks fed up with overcrowding, poverty and unemployment lashed out. Watts in 1965 had been not an aberration but a portent.

Atlanta's problems on September 6 were complex. The city firemen were on strike. Anti–Vietnam War pickets and firefighter's pickets marched in front of the mayor's office. Construction had been preempted by striking carpenters.

Late that morning, an aide told Ivan Jr. that Stokely Carmichael, the black power apostle, was waiting outside his office. "Well, tell him to c'mon in," the mayor said. Carmichael was followed by several young blacks, including several women. When the mayor introduced himself, Carmichael refused to shake his hand. "Would you like to sit down?" the mayor asked the women. They remained standing. Carmichael had assumed leadership of the Student Non-Violent Coordinating Committee (SNCC) earlier in the year and, according to reports in the mayor's possession, had led the organization toward militancy. In the mayor's office, Carmichael railed against police brutality against black Atlantans. He demanded the release of a dozen anti-war protesters in Atlanta's jails.

"Mr. Carmichael, that's a federal matter," Ivan Jr. said. But Carmichael was unconvinced, saying, "The city ought to do something about it." Ivan Jr. asked Carmichael if he was a registered voter in the city; Carmichael said he was not, and Ivan Jr. offered to escort him, and his group, to the Fulton County courthouse to help them sign up. Carmichael and his group soon left, but moments later George Royal rushed into the mayor's office to say they were blocking the front door to City Hall from the inside. Several aldermen were unable to enter, Royal said.

"Hell," Ivan Jr. said, "let's just go walk through them." The mayor and Royal walked through Carmichael's group, pushed them aside lightly, and opened the door. Carmichael departed moments later.

The mayor's day had only begun. That afternoon, a white policeman shot a black car-theft suspect who, in resisting arrest, had fled. Wounded in the leg and the hip, the suspect was brought to Grady Hospital. Within hours, a SNCC soundtruck circulated through Summerhill, with the cry, "Black power! Black power!" Rumors spread that the black suspect had been handcuffed and murdered. Black children returning home from school listened as the rumors grew more frenzied.

*"What's up?"*

*"They shot a kid in the back who stole some grapes, man!"*

Stokely Carmichael urged blacks in Summerhill to "tear this place up." Blacks, he charged, were "tired of these racist police killing our people."

Summerhill was a tinderbox, a riot waiting to happen. Only one year earlier, the mayor's interracial Commission on Crime and Juvenile Delinquency had pinpointed Summerhill as the neighborhood most vulnerable to unrest. Once it had been a favored tree-lined neighborhood for whites, its two-story frame houses only a brisk walk, or trolley ride, from the Capitol. But now ten thousand blacks, many recently arrived from rural areas, crowded into 354 acres. The decrepit houses and trash-filled vacant lots represented the troubled side of Ivan Allen's shining Atlanta. Summerhill stood in the shadow of the new stadium, tucked inside the developing network of interstate highways. Hopelessness and despair haunted Summerhill.

At 4:30 P.M., George Royal, responding to a police radio call, again rushed into the mayor's office. "My God, Mr. Mayor, a riot!" he said. Ivan Jr. had made the decision long ago: he would not be Sam Yorty. He wanted to send a message to black Atlantans and to America's mayors. If a riot broke out in Atlanta, he would not run, or hide.

"I'm going down there," he said. Within ten minutes, the mayor and Royal reached Summerhill. Fewer than twenty policemen had arrived; a command post had been set up on Capitol Avenue. The mayor approached Capt. Oscar Jordan and asked if Chief Jenkins had arrived; he had not. Ivan Jr. then determined to take charge. He motioned to Capt. Morris Redding. "Come on, Morris," he said, "you and George. Let's walk through this damn thing."

Before him, the mayor saw several overturned cars and a crowd of nearly a thousand blacks. On the periphery, he saw Stokely Carmichael hustle into a Buick convertible with the top down and leave the scene. The mayor's hopes for a calm resolution soared with Carmichael's departure.

As Ivan Jr. walked into the crowd of blacks, with a uniformed Redding to his right and Royal, wearing a "Police" armband, to his left, both carrying police-issue thirty-eights, it was the longest walk of his life. "I get shaky very easily," Ivan Jr. says. At times of stress his hands trembled. Doctors termed it a familial tremor, and said it was genetic. The Senator had the same tremor in his hands. Walking toward the crowd of blacks, the mayor's hands trembled noticeably. The black faces were a blur to him, some old, some young.

"Everybody go to your homes," he said. "Let's go home. Come on, let's go home."

He moved quickly, waving his arms, beseeching and cajoling the crowd, buying time for more policemen to arrive. He had been instructed never to confront a mob until he had police power sufficient for containment. Some blacks shouted obscenities at the mayor; others spat at him. A pregnant woman ran in front of him. She yanked her dress, half off, and shouted at Ivan Jr., "A white man put this in my belly. What the hell you gonna do 'bout it?" The mayor was startled by her action. "That thing was hanging out like she was ready to deliver," he recalls. He said nothing, and walked on.

Strategically, he had prepared for this moment. He had created an emergency list of twenty-five leading black ministers who were to be called, then brought by Atlanta police directly into the crisis area. He also had arranged with the governor to have two hundred state troopers ready.

But how do you prepare for such a moment, emotionally? If most of his close friends could not understand his friendships with blacks, certainly none could understand his willingness to enter a riot where he would be a prize target for a shotgun or a knife.

For nearly an hour, Ivan Jr. walked with Royal and Redding through Summerhill. He tried to keep the lid on Atlanta's first major race riot since September 22, 1906, nearly sixty years earlier, almost to the day. That riot happened after a mob of whites had been inflamed by rumors of black men violating white women. Now, it was a mob of blacks who had been inflamed by exaggerated rumors of white policemen violating black youths. When Atlanta mayor James Woodward tried to calm the white mob in 1906, the mob had shouted down their blustery leader.

But now Ivan Jr., elected on the hopes of blacks and carrying a reputation that far exceeded Woodward's, had to prove himself. In the crowd on Capitol Avenue, he spotted a black with a pack of Winston cigarettes. "Give me a cigarette," he said. The request so surprised the black man he handed over the entire pack. "Give me a match," the mayor said. Then the man grabbed back the cigarettes. "I ain't giving you no match, too," he said.

Flashing blue lights told Ivan Jr. that additional police units had arrived. An armored truck, owned by the city police for years but never used, pulled to the command post. Policemen took shotguns and riot helmets. Royal asked the mayor if he wanted a helmet. "Cover up all this gray hair?" the mayor said. Royal, whose devotion to the mayor would be lifelong, saw in the joke evidence the mayor had no fear.

Ivan Jr. pleaded with the shouting blacks, "How about listening to me for a minute now? How about letting me speak? I'm going to walk up Capitol Avenue to the stadium and if you want to come, let's go."

"Why are there only white people with shotguns?" a black asked.

"I'm not here with anything," the mayor replied. "Ain't nobody gonna get killed and you know that."

Several SNCC leaders foiled the mayor's attempt at negotiations. "We ain't going to no goddamned white man's stadium," one shouted. "They'll get you in there and the po-*leeces* will shoot you down."

Suddenly, bricks flew at the policemen. A bottle, launched from the top of a nearby house, exploded on the pavement. In this chaos, some-one had a bad idea. Someone suggested the mayor stand atop a nearby police car and reason with the crowd through a bullhorn.

The mayor climbed atop the car roof, his weight causing it to buckle slightly. Immediately, Ivan Jr. knew he had made a strategic error. The image was devastating: a white patrician mayor, in his gray suit, looming high over worn and weary blacks. His words, heard by only a few, were drowned out by jeers. "You could hear his voice cracking," one black in the crowd remembers. "There was fear in his voice." Ivan Jr. handed the bullhorn to a young black minister and asked him to lead a prayer. Instead of praying, the minister saluted the mob spirit. "This is the best way for you to be heard," he called out. Then another young black, in a faded blue sweatshirt, shouted through the bullhorn, "Atlanta is a Cracker town. It's no different from Watts. The Mayor walks around on plush carpet and wears $500 suits and eats big steaks, while we eat pig foots and chitlins."

Blacks pressed closer to the police car and then lifted it slightly. As the car rocked, side to side, Ivan Jr. lost his balance. The mayor fell from the car to the ground, where Morris Redding, holding the mayor's belt, and George Royal half caught him. Hosea Williams, one of the SCLC lieu-tenants to Rev. Martin Luther King, Jr., arrived at Summerhill in time to see Allen climb atop the police car. "I couldn't believe some white man had that nerve," Williams says. "He was crazy! He had the guts of a lion. [But] Stokely was a master at starting riots . . . and would have paid Ivan Allen to jump up on that car." One SNCC leader present in Summerhill, H. Rap Brown, recalls, "Ivan Allen was a chump, man. Like all the rest of the chumps at that time. A dude who took advantage of the situation. He was a champion of segregation. He saw things changing, some of the momentum of the movement. But he used everything he could to maintain the system as it existed."

Now, as the mayor bounced up uninjured, bedlam set in on Capitol Avenue. A press photographer was struck in the face with a brick. A policeman was met with force when he tried to keep blacks from looting a candy machine at a nearby service station. Ivan Jr. dispatched Royal to telephone Ann Moses to page the black ministers and have them brought to Summerhill at once. Another call was placed to the governor to request the activation of state troopers. Ivan Jr. called for police to clear the streets. They responded by firing their pistols into the air and letting loose with tear gas. The crowd of blacks began to scatter. On the run, one punched Royal in the stomach, knocking him to the ground.

The mayor had never experienced tear gas. It burned his eyes, nose and throat. He used his white handkerchief to cover his mouth. He continued to exhort, "Go to your homes!" Soon, the black ministers began to appear. Daddy King was one of the first. "If I only had my strength, I would tell these people we have got to have law, else we have no protection," he told the mayor. Ivan Jr. held King's hand and said, "You've got your strength, old friend."

The tear gas, and the appearance of the armored truck, restored order. In a moment, the mayor, drenched with sweat and enervated by the experience, spotted Chief Jenkins. Now, Herbert Jenkins said, "For God sake's, mayor, you've hit a home run. Now get out of here and get straightened out while you've got the chance."

By eight o'clock, nearly 750 policemen and 300 state troopers in riot gear kept guard over the calm in Summerhill. "If it had broken out, with the impetus it had," Ivan Jr. says, "the whole population was just across the expressway, with another 100,000 black people."

When the mayor arrived at City Hall, his wife and Dan Sweat were there. Sweat watched him remove his clothes and, to his surprise, saw the mayor wore shin guards, similar to a baseball catcher's. For an instant, he wondered if the mayor had foreseen the violence of the day. But as Ivan Jr. removed the shin guards, Sweat saw gruesome blisters on his legs, a result of a trash-burning that had flared out of control in the mayor's backyard several days before.

The mayor who once had risked his political life before the Senate Commerce Committee—and enhanced his reputation, and that of his city, in the process—now had risked his physical safety on Capitol Avenue with much the same result. Ivan Allen, Jr., was not Sam Yorty. He had entered the fray and stopped the Summerhill riot from spreading. Sixteen people were hospitalized and seventy-five arrested. A dozen cars were damaged, a one-story frame building burned. Yorty's riots ended with thirty-four deaths; Allen's had none.

In a press conference the next day, Ivan Jr. praised his police force. "I saw plenty of brutality," he said, "but it was all directed toward the Atlanta police and the mayor." Jenkins renamed SNCC "the Non-Student Violent Coordinating Committee," and Ivan Jr. announced, "If Stokely Carmichael is looking for a battleground, he has created one, and he will be met in whatever situation he chooses."

The praise that followed Summerhill was reminiscent of that which had followed his 1963 testimony. Vice President Hubert Humphrey said, "If there is a hero on the domestic scene today, it's Ivan Allen of Atlanta." McGill praised the mayor's performance: "No other mayor of any city experiencing the trauma of riots has so behaved. Even the more angry and bitter could not fail to respect him."

He received congratulatory letters from Robert Troutman and Mills Lane, from a city official who compared his heroic acts to those of comic book heroes Batman and the Green Hornet, and also from the aged counselor, John Sibley, one of the Senator's old friends, who wrote, "The late Mr. Jack Spalding often made the remark that 'blood counts.' He applied this to race horses as well as to men. Your courageous leadership and action during the recent riot again evidences the truth of that statement."

There was also criticism. "You've given dinners for such scoundrels as Martin Luther King and have brought Atlanta to the point of nothing much better than Harlem itself," one Atlantan wrote in a letter to the mayor following Summerhill. Another wrote, "Dear Ivan: The next time you get on top of a car down in Nigger Town we suggest you wear a parachute. You really took off like a jet."

Ivan Jr. responded to the crisis by announcing a plan to build sixteen thousand low- and moderate-income housing units by 1971, an ambitious goal he would fail to reach.

That Ivan Allen's style of liberalism and racial moderation did not have broad appeal in Georgia became clear three weeks later. On September 28, Lester Maddox defeated former governor Ellis Arnall in the Democratic gubernatorial primary. Maddox was helped, in part, by Republican voters who crossed party lines to support him, believing he would be easy to defeat in the general election.

After Maddox won the primary, Rev. Martin Luther King, Jr., announced that he was "ashamed to be a Georgian." Cong. Charles Weltner went one step further, announcing he would not seek reelection because, as a matter of principle, he could not support Maddox, as the state Democratic party oath required.

In an angry funk, Ivan Jr. said, "It is deplorable that the combined forces of ignorance, prejudice, reactionism and duplicity of many Republican voters have thrust upon the State of Georgia Lester Maddox, a totally unqualified individual as the Democratic Nominee for Governor. We cannot permit our state's progress to be stopped and reversed by yesterday's mistake."

The mayor's vicious statement carried little weight across the state.

Republican Howard "Bo" Callaway outpolled Maddox by only three thousand votes in the November election while virtually all fifty thousand write-in votes were for Arnall. Since no candidate captured a majority, the Democratic-dominated legislature was empowered by state law to choose from the two leading finishers—Callaway or Maddox. Callaway's attorneys challenged on constitutional grounds. It took two months before the U.S. Supreme Court, in a 5–4 decision, upheld the law. As a Republican, Callaway had little hope for victory in the legislature.

On January 10, 1967, by a 182–62 vote in the legislature, Lester G. Maddox, who two and a half years before had used a pistol to chase blacks from his Atlanta restaurant, was elected governor of Georgia.

# CHAPTER 21

Near dusk on April 4, 1968, as rain fell on the Allen meadow, swelling the banks of Nancy Creek, Ivan and Louise Allen saw the news bulletin flash on their bedroom television: "Martin Luther King, Jr. Shot in Memphis."

The mayor rose from his chair in disbelief. "First Kennedy," he said, "now King."

A sketchy first report said King was in Memphis to lend aid to striking sanitation workers. He had been standing on a balcony at the Lorraine Motel when a single shot rang out. A bullet struck him in the shoulder or neck. The severity of his injury was unknown.

As the mayor paced in his bedroom, decrying the senselessness of violence, he said to his wife, "I must go to Mrs. King."

First he made a phone call to her. Only minutes before Coretta King had received a panicked call from Jesse Jackson, one of her husband's aides. From Memphis, Jackson had said, "Coretta, Doc just got shot. I would advise you to take the next thing smoking."

The mayor asked if she had heard the news. Coretta King said she had and wanted to get on the 8:25 P.M. Eastern Air Lines flight to Memphis. The plane would leave in an hour.

"I'm coming over myself," he said, "and I'll try to get there before you leave. I'll send an officer to go with you." He phoned ahead to the Atlanta police department and asked that a patrol car be dispatched to the King home in Vine City.

"What are you going to do?" Louise asked.

"I'm going to Mrs. King," he said.

"I'll get a coat. I'm going with you," she said. For years, Louise had been her family's strong emotional foundation. She had raised three sons while her husband pursued his business and political objectives. A newspaper story years later would liken her to a "tall ship on a fine day" and the image was appropriate; with her wealth and lifestyle, she had a ladylike grandeur. She revealed her inner thoughts to few people. She was a hard person to get to know; even her daughter-in-law called her "Mrs. Allen." Some of her friends described her as a "steel magnolia," southern grace masking a harder edge; one friend suggested, "You may think the mayor is strong but Louise is even stronger." Accompanying her husband to Coretta King's seemed only proper to Louise: "A lot of times a woman can do better with another woman. It was perfectly natural on my part." Initially, Ivan Jr. was reluctant to bring her with him, fearing an outbreak of violence. Louise had made up her mind. She was going.

In the rain, the Allens sped down Northside Drive, toward the King home. As he drove into the darkness of the Vine City slum, the mayor thought about the thirty-nine-year-old preacher. He had seen King mostly in times of stress, but he had begun to grasp the depth of the man, his humor and his sincerity. In 1965, he had attended a dinner for King in New York City, an affair sponsored by the American Jewish Committee. Before nearly two thousand guests, King had expressed his gratitude for the testimonial, then said, "But adding to the honor is the fact that I have been accompanied here by the mayor of Atlanta, Georgia: my good and close friend, Ivan Allen, Jr." His kind words had surprised the mayor. The applause that night for Ivan Jr. was loud and sustained. Finally, someone tapped him on the shoulder and told him to stand. That night Ivan Allen, Jr., learned what King undoubtedly already had known—that there was a world, and a viewpoint, beyond that of Atlanta.

On another occasion, the tenth-anniversary dinner of the SCLC at the new Hyatt Regency Hotel on Peachtree Street in August 1967, King had arrived late. He explained that he was caught between different time zones: "Central Time, Eastern Standard Time and CPT." The mayor, sitting with Ralph and Mary Lynn McGill, fell into King's trap. "CPT?" he asked. "Colored People's Time. We're always late," King said, before breaking into a disarming laughter.

Ivan Jr. also recalled his discussions with King in his office on the first floor of the Prince Hall Masonic Lodge on Auburn Avenue, Dobbs's building. The mayor and King had spoken freely about race, as it affected the nation and Atlanta. After one such talk, King had driven the mayor back to City Hall and handed him an autographed copy of his book *Where Do We Go from Here: Chaos or Community*. He had signed it: "To my good friend, Ivan Allen, Jr., for whom I have great respect and admiration. Martin."

Ivan and Louise arrived at the red-brick King home at 234 Sunset Avenue, next door to the four-unit apartment house built nearly two decades earlier by the Rev. Maynard Jackson. Coretta King was being escorted to a police car. The mayor joined her, though she sat in the back seat. When Capt. George Royal suddenly appeared in another police car, the mayor moved in with him so he could radio ahead to hold Mrs.

King's plane. The convoy began for the airport, with Louise Allen and Billye Williams, wife of the Rev. Sam Williams, trailing behind in the Allen family Chevrolet.

Ivan Jr. knew he needed to show the black community that he understood and was responding with all due speed and sympathy. He knew the media monitored police radio and hoped they would spread the word of his response to the black districts where the despair over the shooting was beginning to deepen. As far as Ivan Jr. knew, Martin Luther King, Jr., was still alive, but the mayor feared that the deep-seated fury in Atlanta's black ghettos was about to be unleashed. Crime in Atlanta was rising, and a record 142 murders had been committed the previous year. During the summer of 1967 riots in America's black ghettos had seemed to mirror the Vietnam War. Cleveland, Washington, Louisville, Omaha and Montgomery erupted. Twenty-six were left dead on the streets of Newark, forty-three in Detroit. Stokely Carmichael had fomented a rock-and-bottle-throwing disturbance in Atlanta's Dixie Hills section in June after a black policeman had shot and wounded a black youth. Ivan Jr. testified later that summer before a Senate committee that Congress no longer could delay funding to cities trying to cope with the black migration from rural areas. In a speech at Harvard on July 10, 1967, Ivan Jr. also had made the point that Carmichael was jeopardizing the civil rights movement. Lyndon Johnson had responded by forming a commission, led by Illinois governor Otto Kerner, to study the root causes of black unrest in America. Known as the Kerner Commission, its report in March 1968 suggested that America fast was becoming two nations, one black and the other white, separate and unequal. "What white Americans have never fully understood—but what the Negro can never forget—is that white society is deeply implicated in the ghetto," the commission reported. "White institutions created it, white institutions maintain it, and white society condones it."

The convoy arrived at the Atlanta airport and the mayor handed $200 to Capt. Morris Redding. "Morris, for God's sake, get two tickets for Memphis," he said. With Coretta King, he rushed through the Eastern Air Lines terminal toward the gate, where the 8:25 for Memphis was being held. A few newsmen accompanied them.

"It is such a senseless thing," the mayor told her. "When will people ever learn?" Suddenly a page for Coretta King sounded over the public address system. Dora McDonald, secretary to King, rushed over to the group, her expression grave. "Come on!" she said, grabbing Mrs. King's arm. "We need a room where we can sit down." They went into the outer area of the ladies' rest room.

An Eastern Air Lines official told Ivan Jr. that someone was trying to reach him by telephone. At a nearby phone, he listened to a voice, identified as an Eastern Air Lines official in Memphis, say, "I've been asked to inform you that Dr. King is dead." The mayor's response was deliberate. "I want you to go back and reaffirm your statement and be positive that this is right."

The voice had not a particle of doubt. "Mayor Allen, I have been instructed to affirm and *reaffirm* to you that Dr. King is dead. We're trying to furnish you the information as quickly as possible."

The mayor put down the phone and, when he turned, Louise knew at once what had happened.

Together, the Allens walked to the ladies' rest room. When the door opened, they saw Coretta King and Dora McDonald embracing, and quietly weeping. Mrs. King had not been told officially. That duty fell to the mayor. He performed it formally, with the words he had just heard: "Mrs. King, I have to inform you that Dr. King is dead." Coretta King could not restrain her tears. Seeking to be helpful, Louise instinctively reached for a paper towel and handed it to her. The mayor snatched the paper towel, then gave her the silk handkerchief from his breast pocket.

"Mrs. King," the mayor said, "is it your wish to go to Memphis?"

"I should go back home and see about the children," she said. "And then decide about going to Memphis."

The mayor escorted her through the terminal, back to the car. Television cameras captured their grim expressions. Rain was falling across Atlanta. The mayor held an umbrella over Coretta King. Together, they drove back to the King home, along with her sister-in-law, Christine King Farris, and Christine's husband, Isaac. They drove in silence.

At the King home, policemen and family friends were waiting. In the confusion, seven-year-old Dexter King asked, "Mommy, when is Daddy coming home?" Coretta King spoke with her children privately, then retired to her bedroom.

By the time President Johnson called the King home that night, riots had erupted in dozens of American cities. According to the police reports received by the mayor, Atlanta remained mostly quiet, with only a few flare-ups.

Later, Lyndon Johnson appeared on television to urge Americans to search their hearts. "I ask every citizen to reject the blind violence that has struck Dr. King, who lived by nonviolence," the president said. Ivan Jr. watched the address from the living room of the Rev. Martin Luther King, Jr.

\*       \*       \*

By ten o'clock that night the media had crowded into the mayor's office at City Hall. They asked him what would happen next. He released a brief statement, expressing outrage over the murder and calling for calm. He placed all City of Atlanta policemen on emergency twelve-hour shifts. He telephoned the local newspapers and the presidents of the AUC, outlining his plans and asking for suggestions. His hope was to make it through the night without bloodshed. Herbert Jenkins, who operated best in crisis, was with the mayor. The television set at City Hall showed blacks throwing bricks and lighting fires across the nation. A grocery store was on fire near the AUC. Near midnight, twelve hundred Atlanta University students met in the Morehouse gymnasium.

For the first time as mayor, Ivan Jr. was compelled to telephone the White House. He wanted to assure the president that, in King's hometown, all necessary precautions were being taken. Within minutes, LBJ returned the mayor's call.

"What does it look like down there?" LBJ asked.

So far, Ivan Jr. told him, Atlanta's streets remained mostly peaceful. Rain was keeping the streets clear, he said. "I'm worried, but I'm hopeful."

"We've had to commit a lot of troops already," Johnson said. "I hope we don't have to send anybody down there. I hope if it gets bad in Atlanta the National Guard can take care of it."

A short time later a long-distance call came through to the mayor's office from Bob Woodruff at the Mayflower Hotel in Washington. He had been trying to get through for hours. Woodruff and former governor Carl Sanders were on a social call to LBJ at the White House when King's shooting was announced. The president was handed a piece of paper. He then showed it to Woodruff and Sanders. "I'm sorry that I have to be the bearer of this news," Johnson told them.

Ivan Jr. apprised Woodruff of the situation in Atlanta but Woodruff had called for a different reason. "I want to give you a little advice," he said. Nine times out of ten, when Bob Woodruff gave the mayor advice, he did so only after it had been solicited. Woodruff did not bother with the daily affairs and political minutiae of the city, only the big picture.

"You've got to start looking ahead, Ivan," he said. "I mean really look ahead." Ivan Jr. listened intently. "The minute they bring King's body back tomorrow—between then and the time of the funeral—Atlanta, Georgia, is going to be the center of the universe.

"I want you to do whatever is right and necessary, and whatever the city can't pay for will be taken care of. Just do it right."

In his haste over the past six hours, Ivan Jr. had not had time to address the full implications of the next five days. Now, he knew that

Woodruff was right. In the days ahead, many whites in Atlanta would remain indifferent to the King funeral. The Boss had provided an open checkbook to the city to make certain that such feelings would not show.

By the time Ivan Jr. slid into his bed at 3700 Northside Drive, it was past four o'clock in the morning. He stared into the darkness as the Boss's words penetrated his soul. *Just do it right.*

By seven A.M. the mayor was awake, jittery before his first cup of coffee. On his kitchen table, Ralph McGill's column burned in the *Constitution:* "At the moment the trigger man fired, Martin Luther King was the free man. The white killer (or killers), was a slave to fear, a slave to his own sense of inferiority, a slave to hatred, a slave to all the bloody instincts that surge in a brain when a human being decides to become a beast." McGill praised Ivan Jr. for having escorted Coretta King to the airport, calling him "another symbol of the South." "He, too," McGill wrote of the mayor, "was a free man." If a major black protest was going to happen in Atlanta on April 5, the mayor knew it most likely would occur at the Atlanta University Center (AUC). He canceled his appointments and phoned Gene Patterson. "They are going to march," the mayor told him. "I'm going to go out there and see what I can do. You want to come with me?" Patterson, hoping for a good story, agreed.

At 9:30 that morning, the mayor met with the six presidents of the AUC on the second floor of the Clark College administration building. Outside, nearly a thousand marchers formed a line in a driving rainstorm. Ivan Jr. stood by the window, watching. The presidents urged him not to confront the students. They said the students would reject him.

Finally, the mayor swung around and said, "I'm going down there." Wearing a tailored brown silk suit, he walked into the rain, with Patterson trailing behind. His hair falling across his forehead in soaked gray strands, Ivan Jr. approached the marchers, stuck out his hand and with a Boy Scout's sincerity, said, "I'm Ivan Allen." ("Ivan was just a gutsy little guy," Patterson recalls. "His heart was in it. This wasn't politics; it was a different kind of visceral thing.") Arthur Burghardt, an organizer of the march, cautioned the mayor, "This is a black people's march. We don't want white people mixing in."

"I'm just as sorry as you about what's happened to Dr. King," the mayor said. He asked to join the march, even to lead it, but was refused. Ivan Jr. then said, "I want you to know that you are welcome to march in this town."

The mayor and Patterson entered a car driven by Redding. "Get well out in front of them, Morris," Ivan Jr. said. "Don't let it look like we're leading them." He was surprised, and pleased, when the six AUC presidents joined the march. He believed their presence would have a calming effect. The students marched across the west side, occasionally chanting, "Black power! Black power!"

The mayor told Patterson, "I was afraid they'd be breaking every window along the street right now." Not a single pane of glass was broken.

Mattiwilda Dobbs was preparing to leave for an Australian tour when a reporter from the Swedish television news agency phoned her Stockholm apartment to say that Martin Luther King, Jr., was dead. It took a moment for her to know what to say. "How?" she asked. Later that day she was interviewed about King at the Stockholm airport. "We were so proud of M.L.," she said in the glare of the television lights, "to see him become that great a figure."

On the way to Australia, Geekie stopped in Bombay, where she was joined by her older sister Millie. The Peace Corps in Bombay asked her to sing at a memorial service for M. L. King; in his memory she sang several black spirituals.

When her younger sister, June Dobbs Butts, first learned of the murder of Martin Luther King, Jr., while at her home in New York, she booked a flight to return to Atlanta. The day before the funeral, June, and her friend Juanita Sellers Stone, arrived at Daddy King's home to pay their respects to the family.

Hoping to be of some assistance to the family, June was assigned a task. She would sew veils on the black hats to be worn at the funeral by the King family women.

The mayor and his staff first estimated that the King funeral would bring to Atlanta a crowd of ten thousand.

They underestimated by about 140,000.

On Friday afternoon, Ivan Jr. and Vice Mayor Sam Massell waited at the Atlanta airport for the flight from Memphis that brought home King's body. The next night, he and Chief Jenkins drove through the black areas of Atlanta. In Summerhill, Mechanicsville and Pittsburg, the mayor and his chief parked and walked the streets, talking, listening, wondering if violence was about to break out. In the darkness of Sunday morning, U.S. Attorney General Ramsey Clark phoned the mayor at home, waking him. Clark said the Third Army at Fort McPherson in Atlanta would be placed at his disposal for the funeral, just in case. After four nights of rioting in the country, twenty-five were dead, more than a thousand injured and six thousand arrested.

Chartered planes of mourners arrived in Atlanta from the Midwest and the West Coast, Greyhound buses from New York and from small outposts across the South. Hundreds of federal agents poured into the city.

Ivan Jr. couldn't sleep. The inherited tremor returned to his right hand. He ordered liquor stores in the city closed from Monday night until Wednesday morning. He ordered City Hall closed Tuesday morning; city employees would be permitted time off to attend the funeral.

He worried, too, about the governor. Lester Maddox began each day at the Capitol in prayer at his desk, afterward leaving open his Bible to a new passage. Maddox had enforced a dress code among state employees (skirts down to the knees for women, hair up to the ears for men), pushed through penal reforms, secured raises for Georgia's teachers (even as the General Assembly made shambles of his 1968 state budget) and surprised his critics by hiring blacks to state boards and commissions. Yet he remained a vocal opponent of race mixing and of Martin Luther King, Jr. He rejected a request from the Georgia Teachers and Education Association to close schools on the day of King's funeral. State government, Maddox said, would operate as usual.

On Tuesday morning, April 9, rain continued to fall. One hundred and sixty state troopers surrounded Maddox at the State Capitol. "We were told," Maddox recalls, "that there were approximately 150,000 people in town that were coming by the Capitol and that their intention . . . was to storm the capitol." Maddox decided to keep the Capitol open, but well protected. He told intelligence sources, "If they do storm the Capitol they had better be prepared to meet their maker!" Early that morning, Ivan Jr. looked out his window at City Hall and saw Maddox across the street, walking to the flagpole at the Capitol. Maddox began to raise the flag, which had been lowered in respect to half-mast. "There were three television crews, CBS, NBC and ABC, and they had every camera trained on him," Ivan Jr. recalled in 1971. "I will never forget how utterly perplexed he was as he realized the eyes of television were watching him." The governor left the flag at half-mast and returned to his office. Maddox recalls, "I didn't think we oughta use our flag to honor an enemy of our country." The mayor and his wife went to the airport that morning to greet Vice President Humphrey, his wife, Muriel, and New York mayor John Lindsay.

Earlier that morning, across town, June drove with Juanita Sellers Stone and her husband to Coretta King's home, where well-wishers gathered outside. Inside, June saw two widows of political violence, Jacqueline Kennedy and Betty Shabazz, share their grief with Coretta King. The sight of the wives of John Kennedy, Malcolm X and Martin

Luther King, Jr., carried undoubted power. "It struck us," June recalls, "as an affair of state." She saw the widows pose for a picture. "It was so poignant."

June shared only a moment with Coretta King, a hug and a kiss. Her own sense of loss was profound. She had known the Rev. Martin Luther King, Jr., years earlier, before his fame, a time when he was simply "M.L." She had known him as a youngster, when he would not play cards or dance or drink or smoke. She had shared a conversation with M.L. and Coretta in New York once about the crazed black woman from Georgia who had stabbed him in the chest with a letter-opener in 1958 as he autographed his new book *Stride Toward Freedom* at Blumstein's Department Store in Harlem. The blade grazed his heart and nearly killed him. "Have you ever been afraid since then?" June asked. No, he said, he did not fear dying, though he knew death was approaching. When he was stabbed he said he was more curious to know who his attacker was than if he was going to live. Listening to him, June cried. She recalls, "I loved him. I didn't understand him. I'm not blessed to be in communication with God. At that point, I didn't believe in God."

In the procession bound for the funeral at the Ebenezer Baptist Church on Sweet Auburn, June rode behind the King family. The people crowding the streets left her in awe. "They were like rows of poppies," she says. Ebenezer was the Reconstruction-era church where Daddy King and M.L. had served as co-pastors. The sanctuary seated about thirteen hundred. By the time June reach the church, fifty thousand people stood outside, surging. With each appearance of a famous face— Robert and Ethel Kennedy, Wilt Chamberlain, Harry Belafonte, Richard Nixon, Nelson Rockefeller, Marlon Brando—the murmurs became roars. Sweet Auburn had never seen anything like this.

The King family had difficulty entering the church. "It was like trying to stuff everybody into a size one shoe," June recalls. The Rev. A. D. King, brother of the slain leader, stood atop a hearse outside and pleaded for the crowd to part so the Kings could enter. Ebenezer's heavy oak front door had been bolted; Stokely Carmichael, with six bodyguards, demanded to know why white dignitaries could enter and he could not. "You better let him in!" his group shouted. "He's a black man!" June watched incredulously as Carmichael and his group struck the front door of the church with a battering ram. She was horrified but transfixed by the scene. The crush of humanity, the pushing and shoving, scared her. Suddenly, a policeman pulled her group through a side door into the church.

There were no seats available. As she stood behind a partition, football star Jim Brown and his girlfriend shoved past. The fragrance of what seemed to be ten thousand floral arrangements overpowered her. She watched Carmichael, escorted inside, rush to Coretta King. Her five-year-old daughter, Bunny, lay across her lap. Carmichael hugged the widow, then knelt beside her.

Secret Servicemen quietly brought the Humphreys and the Allens into the church through a fire escape in the rear of the building and into the back of the sanctuary. The Allens sat in the second row, behind the vice president and his wife. As he waited for the service to begin, the mayor worried because in death, as in life, Martin Luther King, Jr., had defined the racial divide in Atlanta. Among white Atlantans there was little anguish. Few whites participated in the memorial services. Lenox Square Mall in Buckhead was filled with Easter shoppers. Most downtown stores had closed, including Rich's and Davison's, but the mayor knew the closings were due to fear of rioting blacks. Because the service at Ebenezer started late, it gave the mayor a chance to visit with John Lindsay, Michigan governor George Romney and Carl Stokes of Cleveland, the nation's first black mayor. Louise, meanwhile, admired Mrs. King's stoicism. "Coretta, she's a cool lady," Louise says. "I never really did see much emotion [from her]." The service began when the Rev. Ralph D. Abernathy took the altar, calling the murder of his closest friend, "one of the darkest hours of mankind." Two months before, on February 4, King had delivered a sermon at Ebenezer in which he had discussed his own funeral. On tape, mourners heard that familiar voice one more time, saying, "If any of you are around when I have to meet my day, I don't want a long funeral. . . . I'd like for somebody to mention that day that Martin Luther King, Jr., tried to love somebody." June remembered her father telling M.L. one of his favorite stories. Once, John Wesley Dobbs said, a general's army was surrounded by the enemy and he commanded his drummer to beat the sound of retreat, but the drummer boy told the general he knew only how to sound the advance. "Play what you know," the general said and so his drummer beat the advance. "I want to be the drummer boy in God's Army," the Grand had said on that day. Now, inside Ebenezer, June heard M.L.'s voice on tape saying, ". . . if you want to say that I was a drum major, say that I was a drum major for justice; say that I was a drum major for peace; I was a drum major for righteousness. And all of the other shallow things will not matter."

When the lengthy service ended, King's coffin, made of African mahogany, was placed atop a crude farm wagon pulled by two Alabama mules, a scene rich in symbolism. The sun broke free over Atlanta and the temperature climbed to 80 degrees.

The marchers, bound for another memorial service at Morehouse, made an astonishing sight. Behind the wagon were some of King's staff members. Fred Shuttlesworth, Hosea Williams, Andrew Young and Jesse Jackson. Behind them marched congressmen and African envoys, members of the black underclass and famous actors and athletes. About 10 percent of the marchers were white. Women carried umbrellas against the boiling sun as they walked past rows of helmeted policemen and National Guardsmen. "It was," *The New York Times* wrote, "one of the strangest corteges ever seen in the land."

June removed her heels and changed into soft-soled shoes to make the long walk. The mayor's sixteen-year-old son, Beaumont, marched with ten members of his history class from the private Westminster School. At six foot two, Beaumont was able to look across the mass of humanity, an unforgettable sight.

Ivan Jr. marched with other mayors, Lindsay and Stokes and San Francisco's Joseph Alioto. As they passed the State Capitol, Ivan Jr. thought of the segregationist Lester Maddox and gave thanks to God, "that I was on the side I was on, instead of on the side of the racists who have plagued Georgia and the rest of the South for more than 100 years." From inside the Capitol, Lester Maddox saw a sight he would not forget. "I saw George Romney and Bobby Kennedy," he says. "They was [*sic*] supposed to be in mourning and they was all waving, shaking hands, and laughing, having a good time."

Maynard Jackson, Jr., also marched. An attorney now, having resumed law school at North Carolina Central, graduated cum laude and then married soon after, he marched with his uncle, Rev. A. S. Jackson, pastor of a small church in Berkeley, California. On the previous day, Maynard Jr. had watched the birth of his first child, a daughter he named Brooke in honor of his father, whose middle name was Holbrook. The birth occurred at St. Joseph's Hospital, only a few blocks from the marchers' route. "I was just reflecting on birth to death and the meaning of this new life in my life," he says. He broke off from the cortege and went to the second story of the Morehouse chemistry building, a perfect vantage point.

Mourners crowded on the Morehouse Quadrangle, some standing atop parked cars or perching on tree limbs. Mahalia Jackson sang "Precious Lord Take My Hand"; the Morehouse glee club sang "O God Our Help in Ages Past" and Benjamin Mays, who had served as King's mentor, said in his eulogy, "Jesus died at 33, Joan of Arc at 19, Byron and Burns at 36, Keats and Marlowe at 29 and Shelley at 30, Dunbar before 35, John Fitzgerald Kennedy at 46, William Rainey Harper at 49 and Martin Luther King, Jr., at 39. It isn't how long but how well."

Praise for Atlanta's performance came from across the nation. Even Maddox admitted that the peaceful day had been "really miraculous." Bill Hartsfield, not inclined to applaud his successor publicly, said Ivan Jr. had done an admirable job. "There was nothing," Hartsfield said, "to tarnish the good name which Atlanta has abroad."

Yet, as ever, what appeared on the face of Atlanta belied the emotions within. A study conducted by the Center for Research in Social Change at Emory University during the two months after the funeral indicated that 41 percent of whites in the city had either disapproved or had no reaction to the way the mayor had rushed to Coretta King's side and orchestrated the city's memorial services. Polls aside, the mayor always remembered Daddy King's words, "I want you to know I will die being your friend."

June followed the hearse and the King family's limousines to Southview Cemetery at day's end. The celebrities were gone now and the number of mourners had shrunken considerably. The dinner hour had arrived, which meant the memorial services of Martin Luther King, Jr., had extended nearly seven hours, much longer than he had wanted. Clouds gathered and a cool wind blew across the open field at Southview, where generations of Atlanta's black leaders are buried.

Abernathy said, "This cemetery is too small for his spirit but we submit his body to the ground." Across the cemetery path, June saw her father's grave, where a broken column, symbolic of the Masonic grand master, rose from the center.

The world had watched, but June believed the moment belonged truly to the Atlantans, black Atlantans, the people who had known M.L. and loved him, to the people who knew, as June would say, that "M.L. was a person of transcendence." His epitaph was etched into stone: "FREE AT LAST. FREE AT LAST. THANK GOD ALMIGHTY I'M FREE AT LAST."

# Chapter 22

➤⬅

Maynard Jackson was home alone and stayed up late, watching the returns from the Democratic primary in California. He'd left his wife, Bunnie, and their new baby in Durham, with Bunnie's parents, and returned to Atlanta alone to inform a group of supporters that he had decided not make a run for the Georgia state legislature. He felt good about his decision not to run. He was thirty years old, had a family and decided that he would do the sensible thing and build a law firm—black-controlled but integrated. Someday, he believed, his firm would rival the prestigious King & Spalding in Atlanta.

It was past three o'clock in the morning in Atlanta on June 5, 1968. In the dim glow of his television Maynard Jr. watched Robert Kennedy, who had just won the California primary, say to a few supporters gathered in the Ambassador Hotel in Los Angeles, "So my thanks to all of you and it's on to Chicago and let's win there." Moments later, Kennedy was struck by a bullet fired from close range.

At that late hour, the news coverage in Atlanta was fragmentary and when it ended Maynard Jr. still wasn't certain if Bobby Kennedy had survived. Before he turned out the lights, the local news recapped the day's events. With a hint of boredom, the commentator said, "It looks like Sen. Herman Talmadge is going back for another term unchallenged. Today is the last day for qualifying."

Lying in bed, in an east Atlanta neighborhood that was in the process of transition, from white to black, Maynard Jr. thought about Bobby Kennedy and the more he thought about Bobby Kennedy the more he thought about Herman Talmadge. To him, Talmadge seemed a distillation of the best and the worst the South had to offer; he had power and intellect and hailed from a politically gifted family, yet he was using it, as Maynard Jr. saw it, "to keep a people in virtual bondage, economic bondage and in political segregation." Only eight weeks had passed since Maynard Jr. had walked in the cortege at the King funeral. In King and Kennedy he saw visionaries who had tried to bridge the racial and class divisions in America.

Herman Talmadge and his political machine represented the kind of bigotry and narrow-mindedness that was killing the dream. In the summer of 1968, Maynard Jackson was young enough, bold enough, dreamy enough and perhaps foolish enough to believe that, in the political kingdoms of Kennedys and Talmadges, he could find his own place and somehow make a difference. From the Grand's lectures to his father's Sunday sermons, Maynard Jr. had been raised to believe in the ballot and in the ultimate triumph of God's goodness.

Only one day before he and Bunnie had agreed that she would take a maternity leave from her job at the anti-poverty agency Equal Opportunity Atlanta. He would become the sole wage earner of the family, helping to pay the mortgage on their $17,000 home. But with the liberal Kennedy felled and Talmadge breezing to another six years, Maynard Jr. felt "it was almost like a sign. That's when I decided not to do the intelligent thing. . . . My intellect told me no but my heart told me I could [win]. I never admitted to anyone, including my wife, that I could not win. I had serious doubts. But I wouldn't let myself say we could not win. I did tell myself a number of times that it would be a miracle if I did win."

The next morning he walked into his offices at the Emory Community Legal Services Center, where, for the past nine months, he had represented low-income Atlantans. He told his boss, Frederick LeClercq, that he had decided to challenge Herman Talmadge for his U.S. Senate seat. LeClercq, a young white attorney from the South Carolina low country, knew about such dreams. Only two years before, he had run for office in South Carolina against "as vicious a racist as there is," though he had lost.

Maynard Jr. needed $3,000 to pay the required entry fee, and he had to get it before five o'clock that afternoon. He and LeClercq worked the phones throughout the morning. Most of the aspiring candidate's friends responded the same way—"Herman Talmadge? ARE YOU CRAZY?"— but by early afternoon he had raised about $1,000, most of it from his friends in the black community. He decided to call Leila Ogden, a white jewelry designer he had met when he and Bunnie had been looking for a wedding ring. Though the young couple had been described to her by a Rich's saleswoman as "two Indians," Ogden didn't mind what race they were. She was a free spirit, well read and, by the standards of the time, a liberal on the race issue.

Maynard Jackson told her he needed to borrow $2,000 to run against Herman Talmadge and promised to sign a guarantee of repayment. He said he needed the money in cash, fearing that the State of Georgia might not accept a check at this late hour. Ogden agreed at once, told him not to bother signing a note, and immediately instructed her butler to retrieve the money from the bank. An hour later she learned that the bank manager was uneasy about giving her money to a black.

Fifteen minutes before the filing deadline, the butler stood on the steps on the west side of the Georgia Capitol near the statue of the legendary race-baiter Sen. Tom Watson. When Maynard Jr. extended his hand to greet butler Albert Sullivan he saw tears streaking his cheek.

"If only he had seen this now," the sixty-two-year-old Sullivan told Maynard Jr., as he handed him $2,000 in cash. "He dreamed about this kind of thing."

"What do you mean?" Jackson said. "Who?"

"John Wesley Dobbs," he said. Sullivan explained that he had been a Prince Hall Mason years earlier, "raised" by the Grand. He said the Grand had bragged often about his oldest grandson. "He dreamed about the day when someone in his family would run for office. If he could see you now, all of his work would be justified."

Maynard Jr. embraced the butler. Then, feeling a surge of strength, and the guiding spirit of John Wesley Dobbs, he walked inside the State Capitol.

After his withdrawal from Boston University Law School in 1960, Maynard Jr., at a loss about his future, had answered a blind advertisement in *The Plain Dealer* of Cleveland. Six foot two and nearly 275 pounds, he became one of the most physically imposing encyclopedia salesmen in the history of P. F. Collier. Working in Boston, Cleveland and Buffalo, his success had been immediate. He had a presence about him, an amiability that charmed and a voice that was firm, credible and impressive.

*"Hello, I'm Maynard Jackson, interviewing a few of the families in the neighborhood. Have you got a minute?"*

"What's this about?" a prospective customer would ask from behind a half-opened front door.

"It's about two minutes," Maynard Jr. would reply, his smile bursting like sunshine. "May I step in?"

Each sale had renewed his self-confidence. When a respondent declined to allow him inside, he had asked, without hesitation, "Do your neighbors next door have children?" He recalls, "About three minutes into the house you went for a commitment. It was called a qualifier to determine interest, and to determine if it was worth your while to spend another twenty or twenty-five minutes on the presentation. If they didn't qualify, you very politely thanked them and packed up and went to the next house." He had risen quickly in the company, recruiting and hiring applicants and training salesmen.

But his heart had not been in it fully. Hearing the Grand's voice in his ear—*"That boy's boooorn to be a lawyer!"*—Maynard Jr., in the autumn of 1961, had entered the North Carolina Central University Law School in Durham, where his mother served as head of the Foreign Languages Department.

While in law school, he had met Burnella "Bunnie" Hayes Burke. Twenty-two years old, divorced with a young daughter, she was pursuing her master's degree in business while working as a secretary and researcher for an anti-poverty program. She first met Maynard Jr. when he had knocked on the front door and asked, in that booming second tenor, for Ralph Frazier, one of several housemates: "IS RALPH FRAY-ZUH HE-UH?"

Bunnie Hayes Burke had raised a brow but let the young man in.

She asked if he would like something to drink.

"Cognac," he had said, "Hennessy cognac."

Bunnie had never seen anyone like him, such a smart aleck. "Maynard has this tendency to do these little things to test people to find out their sophistication," she says. By coincidence, she had some Hennessy that day. That had impressed him.

"And his voice, of course, impressed me."

He had excelled in moot court competitions during college and Bunnie suggested he take advantage of his unique skill and run for political office, either for the school board or perhaps the state legislature. But he had other ideas. "He wanted to be an F. Lee Bailey," she says. "He wanted to be a trial lawyer. He wanted to stand up before a judge and argue cases."

Bunnie had been raised in tiny Louisburg, thirty miles from Raleigh. Her family had used an outdoor toilet and she had bathed in a tin tub. Her father was a schoolteacher and Bunnie was the valedictorian of her high school class. The family lived better than most blacks in town. At least they had electricity.

By the time Maynard Jr. graduated from law school in June 1964, he had been away from Atlanta for eight years. His involvement in the civil rights movement during those years was, by his own admission, "not as active as I wanted." In Boston he had picketed Woolworth's once with a group of students, most of whom were white, protesting the dime-store chain's segregated lunch counters in the South. At N.C. Central, he had demonstrated at a Howard Johnson's restaurant. "They arrested most of the folks around me, but not me," Maynard Jr. says. Later, he would turn defensive about his participation in the movement, maintaining that he had been involved with the NAACP, voter education and voter registration activities. "Maynard was selling encyclopedias while we were down here facing the mob," Lonnie King, a contemporary at David T. Howard High School, says pointedly. Bunnie had been involved in the student movement in Durham in 1960–61, demonstrating at bus stations and downtown department stores.

Soon after Maynard Jr. returned to Atlanta, Bunnie and her daughter also moved to the city, to be near him. He was admitted to the Georgia bar in January 1965, then served as the first black attorney in the Atlanta office of the National Labor Relations Board. Later that year, Bunnie bumped her knee on the bedpost. "I was hobbling around and I guess he felt sorry for me and he said, 'Let's get married.'" They were married on December 30, 1965 ("Before the last day of the year so we could have it on our income taxes," Bunnie recalls), in a chapel on the Morehouse College campus. Paul Jackson, still a teenager, served as his older brother's best man. The reception was held at Millie Dobbs Jordan's home.

Bunnie entered an unfamiliar society in Atlanta. "Maynard was a part of that group, he was born into that group," she says. "It was, I don't want to say racist, it was color conscious. If you were fair-skinned with straight hair, which he was, you were accepted." Bunnie's complexion was darker than her husband's, though she said she could pass the Brown Paper Bag Test used in some elite black quarters: if a black's skin was no darker than a brown grocery bag, he or she was accepted as a cultural peer. "I just passed," Bunnie says. "Plus, I had straight hair, which made me more acceptable." During her first years in Atlanta, she saw the frustration of dark-skinned blacks who arrived in the city with great hopes but failed to penetrate society.

She admired her husband's dreams, his tenacity and his sensitivities; at times, she thought, Maynard Jr. allowed himself to be moved to tears in a way most men wouldn't. He had adopted Bunnie's daughter, Beth, and later insisted on being present in the delivery room when their daughter Brooke was born in April 1968, long before it became a popular practice among expectant fathers. He and Bunnie had to conduct a small search before they found a physician who was willing to allow it.

Before long, she noticed the reverential tones her husband used whenever he spoke about his father and grandfather. Indeed, any member of the Dobbs family might recall John Wesley Dobbs, and his thoughts about the ballot or his moral lessons. Bunnie felt the Grand's "power from the grave. He was awesome." She saw that her husband idealized both John Wesley Dobbs and the Rev. Maynard Jackson, Sr. "I almost think Maynard read things into their memories that were a figment of his imagination at some point because Maynard is such a dreamer," she says.

"It's like he had made them into deities. I used to say to myself, *'They were real men at some point, so there had to be something wrong with them. Nobody's perfect. They could not have been infallible.'*

"[But] they were supergods in his life and he had to please them. He had to live up to the standards that they set."

His decision to challenge Talmadge shocked Bunnie. She saw their best-laid plans for his legal career and her maternity leave vanish into thin air. She recalls, "I could have had a duck."

"You've got to be out of your mind," she told him. "What are we going to live on?"

Though she thought his dream "pie in the sky," Bunnie returned to work at Equal Opportunity Atlanta and her mother came to Atlanta to care for the baby. To Bunnie, "Talmadge was the guy you'd see the statue of at the Capitol." In truth, the statue was of Herman's father, Gene. Bunnie thought all Talmadges alike.

She felt the daily strain. "I was the bitch," she recalls, "because I had a baby, a [mortgage] note and a job and nobody to help me. I have to admit I was not the easiest woman to get along with during that particular period. Plus, I was afraid for my husband."

She knew he would campaign in rural outposts in Georgia, places unlikely to view a black candidate favorably. She feared for his life.

She found herself asking a simple question: *"How is Maynard going to fight this statue?"*

Maynard Jackson's appearance was unusual. A black neighbor recalls, "I saw him on the street for the first time in 1967, his hair slicked back. He was fat and his clothes were ill-fitting. His features appeared white. He looked like the old Watkins salesman who came to the house selling bedspreads and liniments."

Yet Maynard Jr. was a smooth talker, articulate beyond his years and this became his most precious and effective political weapon.

One Jackson campaign slogan took off on the old cigarette advertisement "Lucky Strike Means Fine Tobacco." Maynard Jr. remembered seeing "L.S.M.F.T." on a billboard across Mitchell Street from his father's pulpit at Friendship Baptist Church. "We all knew what that meant," he now told the press, " 'Lord, Save Me From Talmadge.' "

Taking on a Talmadge was Georgia's political equivalent of throwing yourself in front of a cement truck. In the four decades since Gene Talmadge first had become Georgia's agricultural commissioner, the Talmadges had become a political dynasty as durable as the Longs in Louisiana or the La Follettes in Wisconsin. Herman Talmadge had not had serious competition since the 1950 gubernatorial race. In 1962 an Atlanta attorney named Henry Henderson had opposed Talmadge but did not mount a campaign. He won 110,000 votes and Talmadge supporters believed that figure represented the height of the anti-Talmadge vote. ("Hank Henderson, I was in college with that boy and we were good friends," Talmadge recalls. "I never did know why he went off on that fruitless venture.")

Few took the Jackson candidacy seriously. The black vote in Georgia had swelled to nearly 350,000 in 1968, yet still represented only about 20 percent of the total. The lone black serving in the U.S. Senate at the time was Edward Brooke of Massachusetts.

The local press attempted to figure out exactly who this light-skinned, articulate and portly black attorney was, without much success. On the campaign trail Maynard Jr. termed himself a "fifth-generation Georgian," referring to his Jackson side, though he was also fifth-generation on his Dobbs side, dating to the slaves Wesley and Judie.

Like any underdog, Maynard Jr. called immediately for Talmadge to meet him in a debate and, like most incumbents, Talmadge refused. "I knew that no black at that time could be elected senator of Georgia," Talmadge says, "particularly a black without any reputation. I knew that the best course of action was to ignore him completely. . . . I knew that it was a foolhardy venture on his part."

Maynard Jr. had thrown his hat into the ring so impulsively that he had not first consulted with black leaders in Atlanta. He had believed that he could count upon an automatic loyalty from all blacks to the shared causes of civil rights and political advancement. He was naive. He found that several members of the Auburn Avenue old guard, including businessman Clayton Yates, were supporting Talmadge.

State senator Leroy Johnson, who had his own political ambitions, told Maynard Jr., "You've messed everything up!" then chided him for having broken the accepted chain of command in black Atlanta. Maynard Jr. left Johnson's office in a state of shock. "I knew he was jealous, frankly, of my move and felt threatened," he says. Johnson recalls their discussion very differently. "[There was] nothing he could mess up with reference to Talmadge. I do know the [Atlanta Negro] Voters League felt Maynard betrayed them when he did not come before them and say, 'This is what I plan to do.' "

As he traveled the state, Maynard Jr. discovered a subterranean network of blacks with strong ties to Herman Talmadge. He became convinced the veteran senator was working behind the scenes to undermine his campaign. Only one hundred people attended a Jackson rally at the Macon Civic Auditorium—including a high school band. The echoes resounded.

"I got betrayed down in Macon," Maynard Jr. says, suspecting black leaders with debts to Talmadge. "That's what I learned: Talmadge would do anything. I mean he'd help a [black] kid get a scholarship. He would get a [black] kid out of jail. But he would go right back to the Senate and vote every single time to keep us second-class and subjugated." At the very least, Maynard Jr. knew none of the black leaders favoring Talmadge would dare to announce their support publicly.

Maynard Jr. also made courtesy calls on the white leaders of Atlanta. "What in the world are you running for the Senate for?" Gene Patterson asked him. "Well, I think I'm fully qualified," Maynard Jr. replied. Patterson recalls the young black candidate as "a very merry guy," attractive and smart, but with no hope of winning. "Just for the hell of it," Patterson says, retrospectively, "I would've enjoyed endorsing him but it wouldn't have been a very credible thing for the *Constitution* to do. If you go out and head up what you know is a lost cause then you've taken the paper so far out of the mainstream. But in the case of Maynard, he was such a charming guy, I was tempted to do it. Herman was no friend."

One night, Maynard Jr. stopped at City Hall to speak with "Night Mayor" Wyche Fowler, the Emory law student and former administrative aide to U.S. congressman Charles Weltner. Fowler had been appointed to the position in June by Ivan Allen, Jr.; he worked after hours until midnight and on weekends answering telephones at the mayor's office. Fowler thought Maynard Jr. striking and compelling. He also believed Jackson was the consummate salesman, cocksure, though remarkably naive. Fowler got the impression that Maynard Jr. really thought he could defeat Herman Talmadge.

"Do you think they'll let me speak at the Kiwanis Club in Wilkes County?" Maynard Jr. asked Fowler, as they discussed the willingness of whites in south Georgia to receive a black candidate.

"They are not going to *want* you to speak, and they are not going to vote for you, but they want to see you as a curiosity piece: as a fool running against Herman Talmadge. And a black fool, at that."

Maynard Jr. said, "But if I have a chance to speak they might find my message very compelling . . ." Fowler couldn't decide which was greater, the young man's sincerity or his naïveté.

On the afternoon of July 10, 1968, Maynard Jr. walked into the mayor's office at City Hall for his appointment with Ivan Allen, Jr. Along one wall,

Maynard Jr. saw the Kennedy high-backed rockers and the stainless-steel shovels emblematic of new construction in Atlanta. As ever, the mayor's desk was in perfect order, not a paperclip out of place. It was this typical efficiency that made afternoon visitors wonder if the mayor had enough to do. With a courtly southern air, the mayor made his trademark offer to his guest.

"Co' Cola?"

Bob Woodruff had been providing free Cokes to City Hall since the Hartsfield years. Ivan Jr. had enjoyed other perquisites from the Boss. He and Paul Austin had used Woodruff's seats at the Kentucky Derby in May. In June, he and former governor Carl Sanders had taken the Coca-Cola jet to Robert Kennedy's funeral. In New York, the Boss even had a car waiting for them.

Ivan Jr. noted Maynard Jackson's boyish good looks, his sheer size and his eyes, which were an iridescent green. When he first heard the candidate's name the mayor had not made the connection to the Dobbs family. Recent newspaper accounts had reminded him of Mattiwilda Dobbs, the opera singer, whom he had once met on stage, and of John Wesley Dobbs, the old black political leader who had died seven years earlier.

The mayor introduced Raleigh Bryans of the *Atlanta Journal,* who sat in on the conversation. This was not a private visit, but simply a matter of political protocol: Maynard Jackson, Jr., thirty-year-old attorney, paying his respects to the mayor of Atlanta by telling him, in person, what the mayor already knew, that he had become the first black to seek statewide office in the modern history of Georgia.

"How does it feel to be taking on the king?" Ivan Jr. asked.

Maynard Jr. leaned back in the rocker and smiled. "I could say it's a ball," he said, "but I don't have any feeling other than an absolute and total commitment to do what I think needs to be done for the cities in this state, for the farmers—for all of the people in Georgia."

He told the mayor that funding for his campaign would resemble Lester Maddox's gubernatorial race of 1966 when Maddox, driving a station wagon and posting "Maddox Country" signs across the state, won the Democratic nomination by spending just $36,000. "The byword of the campaign is 'Send Money,' " he said. "I'm already preparing 'This is Jackson Country' signs. Of course, we're going to have to post them very high up on the poles."

"How are you going to get about the state—by car?" Ivan Jr. asked.

"By bicycle if I have to," he said. Already, Maynard Jr. said, he had visited Albany, Marietta, Norcross and Roswell. Soon he would make stops in Cedartown, Rome, Waycross, Brunswick and Augusta. His campaign, he said, was for real.

He complimented the mayor on his control of civil disorders in the city and his management of the King funeral. "You have demonstrated a feeling of concern for all people, which I think is extremely important," he said. "It's made a difference in Atlanta's hot summer."

During the thirty-minute conversation, Herman Talmadge's name was not spoken. The candidate's disdain for his opponent was clear.

Ivan Allen, Jr., had a more complicated view. He had known Herman Talmadge for thirty years. Ivan Jr. and Ivan III had hunted in south Georgia with Talmadge and his son. The Talmadge position on race offended the mayor's sense of decorum, though he admired the Talmadge family's political staying power. Over the years Ivan Jr. had worked against the Talmadge machine, in the camps of Rivers, Arnall and Thompson. Nevertheless, Herman and Betty Talmadge had been guests in Ivan and Louise Allen's home on several occasions.

Maynard Jr. did not ask for the mayor's support during this meeting and the mayor didn't offer it. "He had to protect Atlanta," Maynard Jr. recalls, "which meant he expected Talmadge to win. He didn't want the U.S. senator mad at Atlanta and at the mayor of Atlanta. That was the reaction everywhere, I mean 99.9 percent of the people, black and white, in the power structure."

The men shook hands and promised to talk again. "You are courageous," Ivan Jr. told him.

The next morning's *Constitution* quoted Ivan Allen, Jr., on Maynard Jackson: "He's a nice young man but he's climbing Heartbreak Hill."

Maynard Jr. traveled the state by car and airplane and set up Georgians for Jackson organizations in more than three dozen cities and counties. Each had one black and one white chairman. His populist campaign was intended to appeal to the black and the farmer. When he greeted Georgians on the street, in churches and in grocery stores, his meaty hand seemed to swallow theirs in a broad handshake and his smile engaged them. "He had reached his calling," Bunnie says. "Maynard was born to campaign." Outside of Atlanta, he was not well known, but in many rural outposts blacks knew him as John Wesley Dobbs's grandson. That gave him instant credibility.

He hammered Talmadge on urban issues, anti-poverty programs and federal aid to education. He promised, if elected, an investigation of the U.S. Agricultural Department. "It's a scandalous situation," he said. "The small farmer is suffering." When Talmadge commented that $1 million was required to make a serious bid for a U.S. Senate seat, Maynard Jr. called a press conference. He said, "I don't have a million dollars and I don't have a political machine. But I'm in this race all the way." His press conference was televised by WSB in Atlanta and he used the forum to support gun control and a cease-fire in Vietnam. He also said that, if drafted into the army, he would serve at once. At a time when the Kerner Commission suggested that a substantial number of blacks had lost faith in America and were turning toward more militant leadership, Maynard Jr. suggested his own definition of Black Power. In his definition were echoes of the Grand's words. "To me it means the ability and capacity of black people to determine the course their lives will take through the exercise of ballot power. I do not nor will not endorse any power—black, white or green—if it endorses violence."

Later, he stood at the Tift County courthouse and proposed the creation of a Small Farmers Administration to provide interest-free loans and help with farm surplus programs. The proposed agency would give small farmers in Georgia a fighting chance, he said.

Talmadge treated Maynard Jr. as if he did not exist. When Maynard Jr. appeared in Carrollton, forty miles west of Atlanta, an organizer of the event read the usual letter from Talmadge, blaming his absence on a previous commitment. A few laughs were heard in the audience. "They know what's going on, those people," Maynard Jr. said.

An apprentice politician, each of his speeches had three parts: "The Opening, the Diatribe and the Close." The purpose of the diatribe was to assault Talmadge "for his record, for his bigotry, for trying to impede the progress of the South," Maynard Jr. recalls. "This man was a throwback to the old days. I'd eat him alive on boll weevil exploitation and all that kind of stuff. And about keeping black and white poor separate from each other. He was an instrumentality for keeping people apart based on an irrational distinction."

The young candidate received support from unlikely places. In early August an anonymous farmer called from south Georgia to say a group of farmers had decided to support him since Talmadge had given up on the agricultural industry. "Understand, I ain't never lost no love for Colored folks," the farmer said, "but I have to admire one who can rise above that background." Later, Maynard Jr. would say, "I was insulted at first, but then I realized what it took for him to say even that." The next day a cashier's check for $39 arrived in the mail. Several weeks later, in Valdosta, deep in south Georgia, he addressed the Ten Oaks Country Club, a private institution for blacks. He spoke of a fast-approaching time when Lowndes County would be ruled by a metro-wide government. He spoke, too, of developing a computerized health care center where a patient would be billed on a sliding scale relative to his ability to pay. He also spoke of the troubled statewide educational system. Forty percent of Georgia's young men were rejected at military induction centers. Eleven whites attended his speech at the black club. *The Valdosta Times* wrote in an editorial, "We like some of Mr. Jackson's ideas . . . Mr. Jackson is worth hearing."

It wasn't so much what he said—though his campaign proposals had wide appeal—as how he said it. His voice was resonant and expansive, filling rooms and exploding across radio airwaves. He spoke with a lawyer's diction. His campaign targeted white Georgians. "I am not running as a Negro," he told the *Constitution.* "I am running as a Georgian and as a citizen of the United States." One of his advertisements in the Atlanta newspapers began, "Forget for a Moment that Maynard Jackson is a Negro." Then it cited his plans to represent all Georgians with fresh ideas. "Maynard Jackson also happens to be Negro," it suggested, in closing. "Doesn't make much difference does it?"

The Jackson campaign placed a quarter-page ad in *The New York Times* on Sunday, July 28, seeking to touch the purse strings of the nation's liberals. It read:

> Maynard Jackson is fighting the battle for America. The odds are against Jackson. The Talmadge forces are well-entrenched; their resources are almost limitless. Jackson's supporters have little money. And Maynard Jackson's a Negro. A Negro who's running against the forces which invented "white supremacy." Maynard Jackson doesn't intend to be a "Negro Senator." He is dedicated to representing all the people of Georgia.

The tone was reminiscent of another campaign advertisement, from a bygone era. It had been nearly a quarter of a century since Rev. Maynard Jackson, Sr., seeking a Dallas school board seat in 1944, published in his campaign platform, "I am running as a citizen, not a Negro." During that war-torn time, Reverend Jackson suggested that, although he did not view the school board as a political office, his election "would be a timely and democratic negation of the Nazi thesis and would be a simple act of Southern justice." He won only about 12 percent of the vote.

On September 9, two days before the Democratic primary, *The Atlanta Journal* termed the Jackson Senate bid "a good thing." "Mr. Talmadge is a survivor of the old state Democratic party and Mr. Jackson foretells of things to come," the *Journal* wrote. The following day, two dozen black leaders in Atlanta held a press conference to announce their support for Maynard Jackson. Standing alongside legislators Ben Brown and Julian Bond and Jesse Hill, the Atlanta Life Insurance Company executive and rising political force in black Atlanta, Sen. Leroy Johnson watched the political star of Maynard Jr. rise above his own in the black community. Even Gov. Lester Maddox, on the eve of the primary, predicted that Maynard Jr. would win as much as 16 percent of the white vote. "He's not a deadhead," Maddox said. "He's a live wire and he's working hard. No one can play down his candidacy and ignore it."

Herman Talmadge defeated Maynard Jackson by more than a three-to-one margin, winning nearly 700,000 votes. But when Maynard Jr. stood before an interracial group of supporters at his campaign headquarters at a Forsyth Street storefront in downtown Atlanta, he said, "An historic victory has been achieved tonight. Georgia told the world that any American—black or white, rich or poor, liberal or conservative—can run for office in this state. This is a victory." He captured more than 207,000 votes, though of Georgia's 159 counties, he won only one: Hancock County, which had a large percentage of black voters. He won about 13 percent of the white vote in the state, which disappointed him.

But Ralph McGill wrote, "All things considered, the Jackson campaign remains something of a moral achievement. It illustrates how much a Deep-South state has changed when the first black candidate, against a long-entrenched incumbent, can make a statewide race and attract, under extremely difficult conditions . . . 200,000 votes."

The most immediate repercussion of the Senate race was that Maynard Jackson no longer was an unknown. Suddenly, he was a viable political force. Black voting strength in Atlanta, and across the South, was rising with each passing day. Of all the numbers generated by his Senate race one glistened with a revolutionary promise: in the city of Atlanta, where black voters represented about 40 percent of the total, Maynard Jr. had defeated Talmadge by six thousand votes. That small victory was an omen.

# CHAPTER 23

→←

When Mayor Ivan Allen, Jr., walked out onto the floor of the Alexander Memorial Coliseum at Georgia Tech on October 16, 1968, the crowd of more than five thousand cheered him warmly. As he "bounced out" the first ball before the Atlanta Hawks' National Basketball Association game, Ivan Jr. had completed a sports trifecta: in three years, he had lured major league baseball, football and basketball to Atlanta. Sitting with former governor Carl Sanders and developer Tom Cousins that night, the mayor luxuriated in the fact that Atlanta had made one more stride toward becoming one of the nation's major league towns.

He had watched the game for only a short time before a city policeman rushed in to tell him that at 8:10 P.M., almost precisely the time of the opening ceremony, Ivan Allen, Sr., had died at Piedmont Hospital.

Because the ninety-two-year-old Senator had been in poor health, his death was not unexpected. Only four days earlier he had undergone surgery for an intestinal blockage. Four years had passed since his first stroke and a series of smaller strokes had stolen his mobility and effervescence.

The mayor ran the city but had been largely unable to counsel with his father. And he missed him. He missed his father's self-assurance, and his incomparable understanding of Atlanta's civic history. He missed their occasional talks, over old-fashioneds, about the first Forward Atlanta campaign of 1926, or about the time he sold typewriters to Asa Candler and Tom Watson. In the Senator's telling, Atlanta's history came to life in ways that were constructive and relevant.

The Senator would have reveled in the local newspapers' front-page coverage of his passing. In the *Constitution* he was "one of Atlanta's most valuable citizens"; in the *Journal,* the "dean of the city's businessmen." "The name Ivan Allen had meant movement in Atlanta for more than 70 years," the *Constitution* wrote. And the *Journal* added, "He outlived his generation and his deeds will outlive him."

The Ivan Allen Company closed on the day of the funeral. The First Presbyterian Church's pews were filled, the altar crowded with floral arrangements. The mayor looked after his mother, Irene, now seventy-eight. Married to the Senator for sixty-one years, she would live only three years past his death.

On a warm, overcast autumn day, the funeral procession entered Westview Cemetery and passed the family vault of Henry Grady, and the curious graveside marker, which resembled an oversized moonrock, of the author Joel Chandler Harris. With the sons of Grady and Harris, Ivan Allen, Sr., had founded the Atlanta Rotary Club sixty-five years before. Across the nearby path was the modest family monument of Ernest Woodruff, who had helped the Senator buy $25,000 worth of Coca-Cola stock in 1935. Ivan Allen, Sr., would lie among the Atlantans he had known and most admired, those who had rebuilt Atlanta.

The Senator's casket was lowered into the ground in front of a smooth granite marker he had placed there years earlier. Into the stone were etched the two words that meant everything to him: IVAN ALLEN.

Having served in City Hall for nearly seven years, Ivan Jr. had decided, with Louise, that he would not seek a third term. The pressures of city administration and of volatile racial politics during the 1960s had been severe, and the tremor in his hands had worsened as a result. Unlike Bill Hartsfield, Ivan Jr. had a full life outside City Hall, and he aimed to enjoy it. He had entered City Hall with his Six-Point Plan and four of the six points had been accomplished. The public schools had met the issue of desegregation without closing. The Forward Atlanta advertising campaign had scored a terrific marketing success. The planned ribbons of expressways were nearly completed. A new stadium and Civic Center had been built.

He fell short only on rapid transit and urban renewal. These failures suggested problems far beyond the control of any mayor. On November 6, 1968, the day Richard Nixon defeated Hubert Humphrey to become the nation's thirty-seventh president, voters in Atlanta, Fulton County and DeKalb County rejected the referendum for the Metro Atlanta Rapid Transit Authority (MARTA). It was a stunning defeat for Ivan Jr. and for Helen Bullard, who managed the referendum, especially in light of the state's enabling legislation and the federal funds that would have covered most of the construction costs; the local portion would have been paid by property taxes. Black leaders, however, opposed the referendum, because the planning of the transit system had not included enough input from the black community and because it would not, as proposed, sufficiently serve poor black neighborhoods. Allen's first response was to name Atlanta Life executive Jesse Hill, a loud critic of the referendum, to the MARTA Board.

The MARTA failure was a signal of things to come: the black community, sensing its growing strength at the ballot box, had broken from its decades-old coalition with Atlanta's white business elites. The political firmament was shifting and the change carried deep racial implications. During the 1960s, sixty thousand whites had moved from the city, many fleeing so that their children would not have to attend school with black children. During the same period, seventy thousand blacks had moved into the city. Blacks had become the majority in Atlanta city schools during the 1964–65 school year. Now, in 1968, the black population in Atlanta was 46 percent and rising. Many whites began to believe that black control over Atlanta politics was only a matter of time.

For all his accomplishments in the area of human rights, Ivan Jr. was losing his battle for low-cost housing. Twenty-one thousand blighted housing units had been removed during the decade as part of Atlanta's urban renewal program, but only five thousand units had been built to house the displaced residents. It was clear that Ivan Jr. would not reach his stated goals for low-cost housing. Statistics indicated that housing segregation in Atlanta was two and a half times more prevalent in 1966 then it had been in 1940. Meanwhile, crime also was spiraling beyond control. Atlanta set murder records throughout the 1960s and ranked second only to New Orleans in 1965 for the nation's highest per capita murder rate. By 1968, Atlanta's 183 murders (a 30 percent increase in one year) represented the nation's highest figure.

As Ivan Allen entered his final year as mayor, it also became clear that, without an heir apparent, a form of leadership in Atlanta—driven by a tightly knit oligarchy of business elites and dominated by Bob Woodruff—was about to end after more than three decades.

With the death of his wife, Nell, Woodruff seemed lonely, sad and solitary. Nearing his eightieth birthday, and his fiftieth anniversary of running the Coca-Cola Company, Woodruff was prone to dramatic mood swings. To Louise, the Boss gave some of his late wife's jewelry, as a show of his friendship and affection. Deeply moved, Louise thanked him by delivering beautiful freshly picked lilies that "reminded me of Miss Nell." In a personal note, she also thanked him for his friendship and "for your confidence in Ivan these past several years." Yet despite his fading health and spirits, Woodruff's every word still was heeded in Atlanta. At a Commerce Club meeting, Dick Rich initiated a motion that newly popular turtleneck sweaters be allowed as proper attire among Commerce Club members; the motion was seconded promptly. Presiding, Ivan Jr. called for a vote. Woodruff, whose hearing was failing, nearly shouted to the mayor, "WHAT'RE Y'ALL TALKING ABOUT?" "Turtleneck sweaters," the mayor said. Chewing on a cigar, Woodruff said, "I DON'T LIKE 'EM." Instantly, Dick Rich withdrew his motion and the mayor asked, "Any other new business?"

When Lt. Jim Mulliford of the Atlanta police department was assigned to the Buckhead beat in 1969, Chief Herbert Jenkins called him into his office and gave him specific instructions: Mulliford was to check in at the Woodruff estate on a regular basis.

"Which one," Mulliford asked, "Mister Bob's or Mister George's?" George Woodruff, brother to the Boss, lived a short distance from Woodruff's Tuxedo Road estate. "Mister Bob's," Jenkins said. "And I want you to check in with him at least once a day—maybe more." Then Herbert Jenkins leaned forward in his chair and said, with an expression that was nearly bloodless, "Is that understood, lieutenant?"

Jenkins instructed Mulliford to park his car against the brick wall alongside Woodruff's home, and, when necessary, to use the telephone in the office next to Woodruff's kitchen. Mulliford soon realized that Woodruff was fearful of being kidnapped and held for ransom. He kept a handgun on either side of his bed, hired a Pinkerton detective who was to remain at his home twenty-four hours a day and kept two attack-trained German shepherds at his estate.

Woodruff took a special liking to Mulliford, particularly after he learned that the lieutenant hailed from Baker County and had grown up on land adjoining Ichauway. "I always thought Ichauway *was* Baker County," Mulliford told Woodruff, prompting a chuckle from the Coca-Cola magnate. Mulliford worked the three-to-eleven shift in Buckhead, so before he retired each night he made a final check at Woodruff's estate. A police radio was turned on inside the Woodruff home at all hours. Sitting in the kitchen and listening to it, Mulliford sometimes heard the elevator door opening and saw Woodruff step from it in his pajamas. Mulliford got the impression that Woodruff had come to see him simply to talk. "Anything happening?" Woodruff would ask. Mulliford would tell him of the crimes committed in Atlanta that day. Woodruff wanted to know every detail of robberies and murders. Mulliford often saw the mayor's car, or the police chief's car or the car of Coca-Cola president Paul Austin pulling into Woodruff's magnificent winding tree-lined driveway. He began to understand that he was at the control center of Atlanta.

Once, Woodruff asked Mulliford if he wanted a Coca-Cola.

"Do you have a Pepsi?" Mulliford responded, playfully.

Woodruff's valet, Luther Cain, Jr., grabbed Mulliford's elbow and pulled him aside. "Don't do that," Cain cautioned. "Out here we don't joke about *that*."

\*　　\*　　\*

On January 6, 1969, a headline in the *Constitution* read: "Retiring, Allen Tells City Today." Privately, Ivan Jr. had shared his decision with friends. He told Gene Patterson, Jack Tarver and Jack Spalding at the newspapers. He told Mills B. Lane, the banker who had supported his entrance into the 1961 mayor's race with a postcard campaign. He took a memorandum to Woodruff's estate to explain his plans to the Boss. Only hours before his seventh State of the City address in the aldermanic chambers, Ivan Jr. made his retirement announcement at the Atlanta Rotary Club, an organization that held special meaning to him and his father. In the back seat of his Chevrolet en route to the Rotary Club, Ivan Jr., dressed in a fine suit, was interviewed by WSB-TV. "I'm anxious to have the privilege to speak to the white community of Atlanta," the mayor said, "with the complete freedom where no one says it is being said because you are seeking the Negro vote."

At the Rotary Club, he pounded on his favorite theme. "Our only hope is to continue to develop, redevelop a better status for the poor Negro," Allen told an audience of nearly four hundred. "We can't go to a polarization of the races and survive as a dynamic city. We have got to achieve a feeling of unity."

In his State of the City address later that afternoon, Ivan Jr. praised Atlantans for their response to the murder of Rev. Martin Luther King, Jr. "Even in the face of despair and grief, never has a city exercised its responsibility more," he said. He boasted of Atlanta's continued economic surge and blamed the failure of the MARTA referendum on bickering government officials and an apathetic public. Ivan III, with his wire-rim glasses and taut expression, spoke for the family when he told WSB television, "In some respects we're sorry to see him make this decision but in other respects glad to know he's going to have some time on his hands to develop other interests."

A lame duck in his home city, Ivan Jr. remained a national figure, a progressive southerner who had broken the solid sectional antagonism to the public accommodations bill. In April 1969, he joined other big-city mayors at a White House meeting with President Nixon. The group included Carl Stokes of Cleveland, John Lindsay of New York, Richard Daley of Chicago, San Francisco's Joseph Alioto, Baltimore's Thomas D'Alessandro and Richard Lugar of Indianapolis.

The mayors spoke of urban problems such as crime, racial and class divisions, urban renewal and rural-dominated state legislatures that were antagonistic to the needs of the cities. The cordial session lasted about an hour. But when Nixon departed and left Vice President Spiro T. Agnew in charge, the tone of the meeting changed.

Agnew railed in an extended attack against cities. Spend less time trying to understand the demonstrators in their cities and more time putting them in jail, Agnew said. He pointed to his own toughness as a former governor of Maryland as a model for how mayors might act, particularly in the areas of housing and welfare.

Thus did the mayors come to realize they were no longer dealing with a Democratic administration inclined to aid urban centers. Agnew's diatribe moved Ivan Jr. to rage. He had spent seven years trying to rebuild his city's ghettos. Much of his success, he knew, was a result of federal funding. "You're sitting there with the vice president of the United States, who was carrying out the president's orders, telling you that you're a bunch of skunks," he says, "and then this guy just tears you to pieces and lets it be known that you're not going to get a damned cent out of Washington; indirectly he was saying that."

Ivan Jr. knew the political risks of offending the vice president of the United States; not to himself—he was a lame duck—but to his city. A verbal brawl with the new vice president could harm Atlanta in the long run. But with every word Agnew spoke, Allen's rage grew. Finally, he could not remain silent. He stood and said, "Mr. Vice President, I came to this meeting concerned about my city. But after listening to you here, I am now worried about my country. Everything we have said here has gone in one of your ears and out the other. You have no more understanding of what we are talking about than the man on the moon." The mayor of Atlanta then suggested to the vice president of the United States that this meeting ought to be adjourned "right now."

Agnew fired back. "Don't tell me I don't understand; you're not listening," he told Ivan Jr. "The whole trouble is you people think you have the only approach and it is the right way and that is what has gotten this country into trouble."

Attempting to reestablish a sliver of diplomacy, Cleveland mayor Carl Stokes thanked Agnew for his views and said the mayors would draw up a statement for the press. Agnew shook the hand of each mayor in the room, including Ivan Allen's. Ivan Jr. achieved a remarkable feat of detachment in which he shook Agnew's hand while seeming to be outside his reach.

A presidential aide soon entered and told Stokes and Ivan Jr. that Nixon wanted to speak with them in the Oval Office. At his desk, Nixon sipped from a cup of tea. He said he had been informed about the harsh words with Agnew: "I want you to know I am very distressed about it. I think that probably it was the result of misunderstandings of positions on everybody's side, because I know of the vice president's concern for local government."

Nixon then asked what the mayors would say to the press.

"Mr. President," Ivan Jr. said, "are you asking me not to say anything about the discussion I had with the vice president when I go out to the press conference?"

"I just don't see how that would help the cause of any of us," Nixon said.

Ivan Jr. was firm. "I am not going to promise you what I will say or not say. I am not really sure myself. The only thing I can say to you is that Vice President Agnew seriously concerns me."

At the press conference, neither Agnew nor the mayors mentioned the abrupt end to their meeting. "There are some feelings the mayors have that I don't share and there are some that I have that they don't share," Agnew said. News of the Allen's disagreement with the vice president leaked to the press. Reporters waited for the Atlanta mayor after the conference, some even followed him to his car. When he arrived at the airport in Washington, Ivan Jr. saw more reporters waiting for him. He steadfastly declined comment. Privately, he worried for the future of American cities.

In Atlanta, mayoral candidates already were angling for position for the fall primary. Vice Mayor Sam Massell and Alderman Rodney Cook, a Republican insurance man, were considered the front-runners. Two blacks, state senator Leroy Johnson and Vernon Jordan of the Southern Regional Council, were rumored to be interested in the vice mayor's seat. According to one newspaper report, attorney Maynard Jackson was expected to offer himself for the aldermanic board.

Maynard Jr. had other ideas. Quietly, during February, he had begun to lay the groundwork for his own emergence in Atlanta city politics by forming a skeletal campaign organization. His showing in Atlanta against Talmadge four months before had stirred his ambition.

The political kingmakers of the black community gathered in a Hyatt Regency suite on March 7, 1969, to hear M. Carl Holman of the National Urban Coalition speak about setting up a local branch in Atlanta. But about an hour earlier, across town at Paschal's restaurant, Maynard Jackson had announced his candidacy for vice mayor of Atlanta. Maynard Jr. told reporters his showing in Atlanta in the U.S. Senate race had proven that the city's voters believed in him. "They recorded in black and white their confidence in me," he said. For an aspiring black candidate, the vice mayor's seat, traditionally a ceremonial position, was a political plum. It would provide the inside track for the mayor's race in 1973 when the black vote was expected to rise to nearly 50 percent in Atlanta. Meeting with Holman, the former deputy director of the U.S. Civil Rights Commission and former *Atlanta Inquirer* editor, some of the black leaders privately fumed at Jackson's nerve, running for office for the second time in a year without consulting with them. A few vowed not to support him.

Jackson's decision to enter the vice mayor's race had a brash, single-minded quality about it. Once upon a time, the Atlanta Negro Voters League had been run by John Wesley Dobbs and A. T. Walden, to determine which white candidates the city's black voters should support. But the death of Walden in 1965, coupled with the growing number and independence of black candidates, had diminished the ANVL's clout. Besides, Maynard Jr. believed his future was his own and that the only decision for the black establishment to make was whether to join him or fight him. He had decided they were not going to dictate to him. He had spoken of his planned candidacy with a group of black ministers, some of whom had known his father. Members of the ANVL had expected him to make his pitch to their organization, too. He did not do it. "Maynard had not been in town long and many people felt he had jumped the gun," Jesse Hill recalls. "I think he jumped the gun. He probably should have given deference to the Voters League. . . . There's no telling how much of this came from sitting on the floor in front of his granddad and his granddad talking about the ballot."

The ANVL seemed in a constant state of flux with the aging Warren Cochrane of the Butler Street YMCA and Rev. William Holmes Borders receding as Jesse Hill and Leroy Johnson were emerging. Sitting in the hotel suite now were the likes of Hill, Johnson, builder Herman Russell, activist Johnnie Yancey, Alderman Q. V. Williamson and Lonnie King, former student leader at the AUC who recently had returned to Atlanta to become president of the local NAACP branch.

Quickly, Holman and David Franklin, a twenty-six-year-old colleague at the National Urban Coalition who hailed from Atlanta, sensed that Atlanta's black leadership was not receptive to forming a local branch of the NUC, an urban advocacy organization formed two years earlier to help bridge cultural and racial divides in American cities. "[They believed] Atlanta was different," Franklin says. "They didn't want us to come down and organize at that time because they had an election coming up." Holman inquired about the most pressing needs for blacks in Atlanta. Leroy Johnson answered, "We are going to start the process of black political power." The consensus among the leadership was that the time was not right for a black candidate to run for mayor or vice mayor. Vernon Jordan had decided not to run for mayor or the congressional seat in Atlanta's Fifth District held by Republican Fletcher Thompson.

Johnson also had decided not to run. But the strong showing of Tom Bradley, a black Los Angeles city councilman and former policeman, complicated their decision. If the time was right for Tom Bradley to win the primary in the mayor's race in L.A., where the black vote was less than half of Atlanta's 41 percent, then why was the time not ripe for a black to make a similar ascendancy in Atlanta?

But the black leadership of Atlanta decided that the sixteen-member aldermanic board should become the primary focus of 1969, not the mayor's or vice mayor's seat. The agreed-upon goal was to gain five more aldermanic seats in addition to Williamson's. It was a modest quest.

The anger expressed toward Maynard Jr. at the meeting was pronounced. "There was a feeling among blacks that Maynard was a maverick," Johnson says, "that he was concerned about his own political interest, that he made no consultation with anybody and that part of his strategy was to move in and then to paint blacks into a position of having to support him vis-à-vis the white element. . . . 'Either you vote for me or you're voting for whites. And if you don't vote for me you're not living up to the Cause. You're an 'Uncle Tom' or you're an 'Oreo.' " To the black kingmakers, Maynard Jr. was an opportunist, almost a carpetbagger despite his lengthy Dobbs family history in Atlanta. If Maynard Jr. had attempted to make a presentation to black leaders regarding his candidacy, almost certainly they would have attempted to dissuade him from it.

If Atlanta's black leadership had decided to run a black for mayor or vice mayor in 1969 the preferred choice would have been either Johnson or Jordan. The first black legislator elected in Georgia since Reconstruction, Johnson would be termed "the single most powerful black politician in Dixie" by *The New York Times* in 1970. The son of an Atlanta mortician, Johnson would be a protégé of A. T. Walden who, with Walden's help, became the first black hired in the Fulton County prosecutor's office. He had earned his law degree from North Carolina College in Durham in 1954, graduating seven years before Maynard Jackson arrived at the same school. (Ironically, Johnson later offered Jackson a position at his Atlanta law office, though Jackson chose instead to work for the NLRB.) A political deal-maker, Johnson could deliver large blocs of black votes in city, county and statewide elections. When Walden died, Johnson had assumed the chairmanship of the Georgia Association of Democratic Clubs, a black organization. He wore expensive suits and a two-carat diamond ring, smoked eight-inch-long Tabacalera cigars imported from the Philippines and believed that, when the time came for a black to run for mayor of Atlanta, he had earned the right to be that man or, at the very least, to determine who that man would be.

Vernon Jordan was perceived as more conservative than Jackson and more willing to play by the rules established by black leadership. Jordan had curried favor with the members of the ANVL while serving as director of the Voter Education Project for the Southern Regional Council in Atlanta from 1964 to 1968. Charming, with a terrific sense of humor, Jordan had been raised in the University Homes housing project on the west side, later serving as summer chauffeur for Robert F. Maddox. Like Jackson, he was an articulate and refined attorney, a massive man with a commanding presence. Unlike Jackson, Jordan had traveled north, to DePauw University in Indiana, where he became the only black in his class. His complexion was a smooth deep black and, during the student sit-ins, it was said that you could be certain a restaurant in Atlanta had desegregated if you saw Vernon Jordan inside since he was too dark to "pass." Jordan knew that some light-skinned black elites believed his ebony complexion undermined his potential. Windsor Jordan recalls that older brother Vernon, as a teenager, once had attempted to court a light-skinned black classmate but was told by the classmate's mother that he was too dark for her daughter. When she learned of this exchange from her son, Mary Jordan drove her 1941 green Pontiac to the classmate's home where she read the riot act to the girl's mother, who immediately apologized. White liberals in Atlanta in 1969 liked Jordan and called him "The Black Prince." Though some of these white liberals believed it was time to share political power with blacks, a few thought Jordan too dark to win that role in a city election. White voters, they reasoned, would be threatened by his darkness. Sensing broader financial opportunities in the north, Jordan moved to New York in 1970 to become executive director of the United Negro College Fund. Within two years, he was a director on the boards of Banker's Trust and J. C. Penney; later, he told an old Atlanta friend, "Now you know why I had to leave."

As the discussion continued inside the hotel suite, the door opened and Vice Mayor Sam Massell entered the room. Massell announced his intention to run for mayor and shook every hand in the room. Privately, Massell already had received the support of Johnson and was received warmly by the group. Franklin was convinced that Johnson had cut a deal. "I knew that Leroy was carrying Sam's water," Franklin recalls. "And I knew right then that Massell would get 80 percent of the black vote [in the fall election]."

Later that afternoon, after the meeting with black leadership had ended, Franklin told Maynard Jr., "Those people are pissed off with you. They said they won't support you."

"They can't tell me what to do," Maynard Jr. said.

In the years ahead, the friendship between Maynard Jr. and David Franklin would blossom. Recently graduated from American University Law School in Washington, Franklin had met Maynard Jr. at a wedding several years earlier, though their families both hailed from the Fourth Ward and had known each other for generations. Franklin's maternal grandfather was a Presbyterian minister who arrived in Atlanta in 1900 and later lived near the Grand and Irene Dobbs. While Franklin had attended Morehouse College during the early 1960s, one of his closest friends had been Bill Clement, Jackson's cousin. Franklin was so light-skinned that he was frequently mistaken for white. Though he had a severe stutter, his intellect and his street savvy were evident in conversation. Like Maynard Jr., David Franklin had big plans for the future. Already he was agent for two young black recording artists, Donny Hathaway and Roberta Flack.

Despite the lack of support from black leadership, Maynard Jr. remained undeterred. "When I ran against Talmadge," he told Franklin, "they didn't give me a thousand dollars."

"But this is not Talmadge," Franklin replied. "We're talking about *real power* here."

Maynard Jr. vowed to move ahead without them. That summer he learned his opposition in the vice mayor's race would be Milton Farris, the most powerful of Atlanta's white aldermen. At sixty-two, Farris was twice as old as Jackson. He was an executive with the Gulf Oil Company and had served as an alderman for eighteen years, most recently as chairman of the powerful Aldermanic Finance and Budget Committee.

Soon, Farris would tell voters, "To allow a young boy to handle the intricacies of a city as large as ours could be disastrous."

Maynard Jr. would counter by saying, "Nobody running for the office of vice mayor has experience in the office of vice mayor, and being an alderman doesn't necessarily prepare one for the office of vice mayor."

On May 27, Sam Yorty shocked many political observers by rallying to defeat Tom Bradley in the mayoral runoff in Los Angeles. Yorty had suggested that Bradley was under the control of black militants and that the election of a black mayor would prompt hordes of white city policemen to resign in protest. Bradley's defeat slowed the momentum of black political advancement.

Maynard Jr. campaigned aggressively in the autumn of 1969. Seeing his picture on the sides of public buses, some blacks believed he was white, or of another ethnic background. "People thought he was Greek," Franklin recalls. He ran hard in the black community, appointing block and street leaders and visiting as many as four or five black churches on

Sunday mornings. Neither Maynard Jr. nor Farris used race as a campaign issue, but race was impossible to ignore.

On October 1, six days before the primary, the candidates for mayor and vice mayor appeared at the Hungry Club luncheon at the Butler Street YMCA. Here, where the Grand had orated and occasionally played whist, was a setting perfectly designed for Maynard Jackson. He spoke of transforming the vice mayor's seat into "the voice of the people" and promised to create a "Kitchen Cabinet" that would be filled with people from all walks of life who would serve as critics of city government. His eloquence far exceeded that of the other candidates. When he spoke, his hands swept in broad arcs and his nearly three-hundred-pound frame made him seem bolder and more convincing. Never before had a candidate for vice mayor of Atlanta quoted Aristotle and the black poet Langston Hughes in a speech about crime. The *Constitution* noted that Jackson "received the longest applause by far" of any candidate at the forum.

"If Atlanta is to grow and prosper," the *Constitution* editorialized, "if it is to remain a viable and integrated city, if it is to become a shining symbol of cooperation for the world to see, we believe the leadership must be shared. Atlanta needs a recognized Negro leader who can speak with vision and humanity the dreams of his people. And she needs a Negro leader who can bridge that chasm between the races. Jackson is the best hope we see for realizing that goal."

The following day, six black leaders, including Leroy Johnson, Jesse Hill, Daddy King and the Rev. Sam Williams of the Friendship Baptist Church announced their support for Massell and Maynard Jr. Their endorsement came late, but Maynard Jr., who knew that he had forced their hand, accepted it willingly.

On election day, Jackson campaign staffers predicted he would win between 56 and 59 percent of the vote against Farris. They chartered buses to carry black voters to the polls. Late on election night, Maynard Jr. and his supporters awaited the returns in a dimly lit restaurant on Peachtree Street. By 2:15 A.M., when the black precincts began to report, he swept past Farris by more than eight thousand votes. As Farris watched from his headquarters, he gave up hope. The election, Farris said, "shows that whites are willing to vote for a black man but blacks are not willing to vote for others." When tabulations were finished the next morning, Maynard Jr. had won 58 percent of the vote to become Atlanta's first black vice mayor.

His victory was made possible by having won more than 96 percent of the black vote and nearly one-third of the white vote. The *Constitution* termed Jackson "a giant-killer in Atlanta elections" and noted the strong biracial support he had developed. The mayor's race was headed for a runoff in two weeks hence, between Sam Massell and runner-up Rodney Cook; Horace Tate, a black educator who ran for mayor without support from black leadership, had finished third, several thousand votes behind Cook.

The day was fast approaching when Atlanta would elect its first black mayor. In the fall of 1969 many believed Maynard Jackson, Jr., would be that man.

In early September, Vice Mayor Sam Massell requested police protection for the final month of the 1969 mayor's race. He asked for Capt. Buddy Whalen, a former vice squad lieutenant. Asking for security was one thing but asking for a captain (and a particular captain) was something different. "Good Lord, we've got more candidates than you've got captains," Mayor Ivan Allen, Jr., told Chief Jenkins; the mayor relented.

On September 20, Whalen reported to his superiors at the police department that for the past eleven days he had been assigned by Sam Massell to Howard Massell, the candidate's brother. According to Whalen, Howard Massell had been soliciting campaign funds from nightclub and strip club owners with Whalen by his side. Whalen felt his rank, and reputation, were being abused. He asked for a transfer, Chief Jenkins agreed, and assigned a different detective to Massell. Jenkins did not mention his lieutenant's complaint to the mayor.

So when the story of Howard Massell's campaign solicitations splashed across the newspapers less than a week before the runoff, Ivan Jr. was caught by surprise. Publicly, he called for a complete investigation. Massell, meanwhile, lashed out against Rodney Cook for leaking the story, terming it "the dirtiest, lowest, meanest method of campaigning"; Massell also admitted his brother had acted in "bad judgement."

Privately, and financially, Ivan Jr. had been supporting the Republican Cook, though his personal favorite would have been the former congressman, Charles Weltner, a principled liberal but a man the white business elites of Atlanta simply would not support. With broad black support, Massell was almost certain to win.

Ivan Jr. and Massell were not, in the truest sense, compatible. Their relationship during the previous eight years was not poor as much as it was distant. They communicated infrequently. The city charter under Atlanta's weak-mayor system did not demand interaction between them: the vice mayor ran the bimonthly aldermanic board meetings, the mayor made all appointments to the aldermanic committees and the department heads in city government reported to the aldermanic board. (Already, however, there were rumblings in Atlanta to change to a strong-mayor system.) As vice mayor, Massell did not even have an office at City Hall. Once, when Ivan Jr. left the city, Massell assumed the position of acting mayor and issued a statement of no real import from Allen's desk. When Ivan Jr. returned, he made clear that he did not agree with Massell's statement and then told the vice mayor, plainly, "And don't use my desk when I'm out of town."

Massell had emerged from Atlanta's Jewish community. His uncle, Ben Massell, had been a leading force in commercial real estate in Atlanta for many years and once ranked among the largest taxpayers in Georgia. The three Massell brothers—Ben, Levi and Sam Sr. (the vice mayor's father)—had joined to form Massell Realty in the early part of the century. The brothers split up during the Depression. Sam Sr. became a lawyer, as did his son, though Sam Massell, Jr., now the aspiring mayor of Atlanta, held a full-time job selling real estate.

On Sunday, October 20, two days before the runoff election, the *Constitution* published copies of checks written by nightclub owners on behalf of the Massell campaign. In sworn affidavits, two of these owners said they had made the contributions with the understanding that Sam Massell, as mayor, would allow their clubs to remain open two hours later.

Ivan Jr. felt compelled to make a statement. He knew that a public condemnation of Massell would not sway the election; there was even the possibility that it might help Massell. He called a press conference on Sunday afternoon. With several television and radio microphones positioned at his desk at City Hall, the grim-faced mayor said, "It is my personal feeling that it is the vice mayor rather than his brother or Captain Whalen whose judgment is in question in this sorry situation.

"Moreover, it is my considered conviction that the vice mayor has badly misused his position and that, if he is a man of conscience, he should immediately withdraw from consideration for an office which requires intuitive integrity and instinctive withdrawal from even the suspicion and appearance of evil."

At that moment, Massell and Cook were engaged in a campaign forum on WQXI-TV. Massell reacted calmly when told of Allen's statement but, off-camera, his wife, Doris, erupted.

"Anti-Semitic WASPs," she snapped.

The next day, election eve, Massell called a press conference at his home. Surrounded by his wife and children, he charged that "five angry adversaries" were opposing him because he was a Jew: Mayor Ivan Allen, Jr.; Alderman Rodney Cook; banker Mills B. Lane; newspaper executive Jack Tarver and Atlanta Chamber of Commerce president Frank Carter, who happened to be the mayor's next-door neighbor. "The same men," Massell said, "who don't want me to sit in their clubs." Acting now as an underdog, Massell went on the attack. "Never before has the 'power pack' pushed the panic button so madly," he said. "The attempted assassination has started, but they will discover that it's easier to kill a man than it is to kill his reputation." With Shakespearean splendor, Massell then said, "In the eyes of my Maker, I ask the people to decide . . . and I do so with faith."

In short order, public opinion turned, decisively, against Ivan Jr. Some believed he was attempting to choose his own successor. Some of his strongest black supporters, including the Rev. Sam Williams, the Rev. Andrew Young, Jesse Hill and Coretta Scott King, accused him of "a base power play on behalf of the downtown power structure." A few blacks even began to call for Ivan Jr. to resign. Massell spent the final day of the campaign accusing his opponents of anti-Semitism, a charge that would leave Atlanta's Jewish community with lingering questions about Ivan Jr. and his attitude toward Jews. In part, this charge stemmed from guilt by association. Ivan Jr. was a member of social and athletic clubs that excluded Jews and blacks, an exclusion that was inbred and systemic more than overtly egregious. Once he had been a segregationist and many Jews believe that a person who makes distinctions based on color likely makes distinctions based on religion: southern history was full of segregationists who also were anti-Semites. His tight-knit circle of close friends held no Jews. Cecil Alexander, the Jewish architect who had helped to manage the Allen campaign in 1961, says, "Ivan doesn't go out of his way to associate with the Jewish community and some of his friends are what I would call 'Locker Room Anti-Semites' who might sit around and tell jokes [about Jews]. But I never saw any covert or overt anti-Semitism from Ivan. Never." The charge was difficult for Ivan Jr. to rebut. He let the accumulated weight of his human rights record speak for him.

Both the *Constitution* and the *Journal* endorsed Rodney Cook, but Massell, winning nine of every ten black votes cast, won the Atlanta mayoral runoff with 55 percent of the vote. His victory represented the end of a thirty-year political coalition in Atlanta between blacks and white downtown elites. Massell became the first mayor in the history of Atlanta to receive more votes from blacks than whites. In fact, he had received less support from whites (27 percent against Cook) than Maynard Jackson (33 percent against Farris in the primary). That Massell's strength was black Atlanta would prove problematic four years later. "Sam was standing on a banana peel," Maynard Jr. recalls. "His base was my base." Meanwhile, five blacks were elected to the sixteen-member aldermanic board, one fewer than the modest goal established by the ANVL.

To the world, Atlanta now began to crow that it had a Jewish mayor and a black vice mayor, not only fodder for jokes about "kosher chitlins" but proof that the City Too Busy To Hate, one of America's fastest-growing cities, remained one of its most enlightened. Yet, as ever, the racial truth in Atlanta remained more complicated. On the night Sam Massell was elected as his successor, Ivan Jr. was "eating crow." As he walked down a corridor at City Hall, one of Massell's zealous supporters yanked the mayor's elbow and shouted into his face, "You just couldn't pull it off, could you, Mr. Mayor?"

Enervated by two terms at City Hall, Ivan Jr., now a fifty-nine-year-old former mayor, sought a personal rejuvenation the following spring when he traveled to Africa to hunt in the lush expanse of the Okovanggo Swamps in northern Botswana. He killed two prime trophies, an oryx ("It had a perfectly gorgeous long horn, fifty-five or sixty inches long") and a kudu ("two beautiful fifty-to-fifty-two-inch spiral horns"). After two weeks hunting, he met Louise and their friend Marisa Adair at a dirt landing strip outside the delta, then returned to camp.

His sporting vacation nearly proved fatal. Several days later, Ivan Jr. felt feverish. Soon his body temperature reached 105 degrees. The Africans knew that he had been bitten, probably while poised in the brush of the Okovanggo, by infected tsetse flies. The tiny village of Maun, about 150 miles away, was said to have a Portuguese intern who operated a small commissary and dispensary. In Maun they could get an airplane to Johannesburg.

Ivan Jr. was placed in the back of an open Land Rover, on a mattress. "They hauled me seventy-five miles with an African sitting on either side of me, fanning me to keep the flies off," he recalls. "They didn't want the flies to bite me and then bite them because then they might have [the disease]." At a camp along the river, Louise was told that a mineral prospector had just arrived and that his plane was nearby. Wasting not a second, she found the prospector, woke him, and explained her husband's plight. He agreed to fly them to Maun, but said his plane was a two-seater. Louise stretched her now-inert husband across the floor of the Piper Cub. He was wearing his pajamas and slippers and was wrapped in a bathrobe. The former mayor of Atlanta slipped in and out of consciousness en route to Maun. There, he was diagnosed with try-panosomiasis, a disease commonly transmitted by the infected tsetse, and which often causes sleeping sickness. The next morning a small plane arrived. The pilot had been flying emergency flights all night. But late that morning he flew Ivan Jr. and Louise to Johannesburg. Rushed to a fever hospital where he would spend the next two weeks, Ivan Jr. slowly regained his health.

He returned to Atlanta in mid-May, more exhausted than when he had first left. He learned later that of the other five Americans to have suffered similar bites in Africa only one had survived.

In January 1970, Maynard Jr. became a founding partner in Jackson, Patterson & Parks, an all-black law firm. Their offices were located at 40 Marietta Street, once home of the Ivan Allen-Marshall Company.

Early that month, Jackson, with his wavy hair combed straight, was sworn in as vice mayor of Atlanta. His mother, Renie Dobbs Jackson, wearing white gloves, and his younger brother, Paul, with his thin Errol Flynn mustache, attended the ceremony. With Ivan Jr., Sam Massell and eighty-year-old Bill Hartsfield (now only thirteen months from death) sitting behind him inside the aldermanic chamber, Maynard Jr. promised, "Our city will not be measured by the quality of our structures, but the quality of our souls." The *Daily World* wrote, "For the first time since Reconstruction days, all of the people of this city are well represented in the city government."

That Sam Massell and Maynard Jackson were destined to become adversaries became clear within the first hundred days of the administration. Not one for ribbon-cutting, Maynard Jr. tried to force himself into negotiations with striking city garbage workers. He called his own press conference. "I can no longer hold my peace," he said. He had recommended binding arbitration, then advisory arbitration, then mediation, he said, then simply an independent fact-finder to help settle the strike, but the city had rejected each. "I am firmly convinced that this dispute can be settled, and could and should have been settled, several weeks ago." He reminded reporters that he had been an attorney for the NLRB, and cautioned them not to confuse him with someone speaking out of turn. The vice mayor believed the garbage workers' request for a pay raise was fair.

Question: "Has the mayor taken any initiative in drawing you into the consultations on how to settle the strike?"

Maynard Jr.: "No, he has not."

Question: "Why do you suppose he hasn't?"

Maynard Jr.: "Well, I am not able to delve into the inner workings of a man's mind."

Massell thought his vice mayor a publicity hound, "playing to the gallery." Clearly, Maynard Jr. adored the attention.

Already their relationship was fractured. In his dealings with the aldermanic board, Massell made certain to sidestep the vice mayor. Maynard Jr. had a knack for making headlines. In May, he called for city department heads charged with racism to prove their innocence or face firing. Furthermore, in city hiring practices, he charged, "things ain't what they ought to be." Massell became convinced that every political decision Maynard Jackson made was made for the sole purpose of bene-fitting blacks at the expense of whites.

And Massell was not alone in this view. In August 1970, a group of white aldermen criticized Maynard Jr. for his "high-handed" manner of presiding over meetings. Several aldermen tried, unsuccessfully, to strip him of his ex-officio voting powers on committees. Alderman Wade Mitchell, a white executive with the Trust Company and a racial moder-ate, recalls that some of his white aldermanic colleagues "didn't like black folks" and that their dislike for Maynard Jackson was especially intense. "They were smart enough not to make a public display of it," Mitchell says, "but in the corridors they'd grouse about Maynard's appointments." Massell perceived the vice mayor as a threat and cer-tainly the vice mayor did little to make him think otherwise. Maynard Jr. criticized Massell often.

Massell proved a capable marketer of the city. In July 1971, Eastern Air Lines opened a route to Mexico City, Atlanta's first nonstop interna-tional flight. "Now we can truly call ourselves an international city—a city of the world," Massell said. Trying to keep pace with civic ambition, the city's recently named William B. Hartsfield Atlanta Airport was renamed, four months later, William B. Hartsfield Atlanta *International* Airport.

The specter of race politics loomed over City Hall. In October 1971, Massell delivered the most dramatic speech of his mayoralty at the But-ler Street YMCA. He warned Atlanta's blacks that their preoccupation with gaining political control of Atlanta could ruin the city. "The word around town is that you and I . . . the black and white liberal leadership of Atlanta, are committed to Atlanta becoming an all black city. . . . What a terribly confined and costly ambition that would represent." Massell cited Newark, New Jersey, as an example of what Atlanta might become if white-middle-class families continued to leave the city and poverty-stricken blacks continued to take their place. With a declining tax base, Atlanta needed to annex outlying areas. Massell urged blacks to "think white," to make the city more attractive to induce white families to remain in the city. "We must not let the vast majority of blacks be sold out for the little prestige of a few demagogues," Massell said.

Maynard Jackson—a black demagogue to Sam Massell—blasted the mayor for encouraging blacks to "think white" and for his indifference toward poor blacks.

The MARTA referendum passed in Fulton and DeKalb counties in 1971, but only after black leaders had received a number of assurances, including better service in black areas and a promise that affirmative action programs, consistent with federal guidelines, would be applied to MARTA hires and contracts. During the 1972–73 school year, Atlanta NAACP branch president Lonnie King struck a deal with white leaders in which he agreed to give up his demand for broad-scale forced busing in the city in return for a dramatic desegregation of the city school system's administrative staff, including the appointment of its first black superintendent. Viewing this compromise as a sell-out, the national office of the NAACP removed King as branch president. Yet whites comprised only 23 percent of the city's student population and forced busing likely would have diminished that number even further.

Through these grinding negotiations, racial anxieties were rising, though white business leaders, aware of black Atlanta's increased electoral strength, carefully cultivated support from the city's black middle class.

Publicly, the mutual dislike of the mayor and the vice mayor was well known. Privately, both awaited their inevitable showdown in 1973.

# PART VI

# BLACK CITY GOVERNMENT

"After a decade of virtually unrelieved boosterism, Atlanta is moving into a period of introspection. Everyone recognizes that the city is in transition, and many are apprehensive about how it will emerge."

—*The New Republic*, 1975

# CHAPTER 24

The vice mayor's son was born in January 1971, the midpoint of his four-year term, and when it came time to put a name on the birth certificate there was not a moment of hesitation. It would be Maynard Holbrook Jackson III, as the vice mayor always had wanted. Like daughter Brooke, his son's name would honor his late father. Bunnie liked the sound, especially its fullness. "But 'Maynard,' " she decided, "is such a big name for a little baby."

So the vice mayor and his wife searched for an appropriate nickname. The one she determined not to use was Buzzy. But that's what the family started calling the baby, anyway, including the vice mayor. It stuck and the child had not only the same name as his father, but the same nickname as well. Bunnie sensed her husband had big plans for the boy: "He definitely wanted him to be a superachiever."

Buzzy Jackson made headlines for the first time at the age of two.

On March 5, 1973, Bunnie, running errands with Buzzy in tow, stopped at a barbershop in the Campbellton Plaza Shopping Center in west Atlanta. It was not the usual place, but Buzzy needed a haircut.

"We don't cut blacks' hair here," a barber told her. His words left her speechless. He repeated: *"We don't cut blacks' hair here."*

Bunnie proceeded straight to a telephone. "I want their license!" she thought. Calling her husband from an aldermanic board meeting, she told him what had occurred. When he returned to the meeting, Maynard Jr. requested a "special privilege" to address his colleagues. He related his wife's tale and said that she was "very, very upset." He told his colleagues that a city ordinance prohibited racial discrimination in public facilities, including barbershops; he said he planned to seek advice from the city attorney.

"This is to reinforce to you," Maynard Jr. said, wagging his finger with purpose, "that in this day and time we still have problems."

Television cameras descended upon the vice mayor and the barbershop. "I didn't mean to start such a riot," Bunnie would say years later. But she was beginning to recognize that when a ruckus needed to be raised in the name of racial justice in Atlanta, then, by God, her husband, Maynard Jackson, Jr., was going to raise it.

*　　　　*　　　　*

When Maynard Jr. first spoke about running for mayor of Atlanta in 1973, Bill Clement, Jr., one of his Dobbs cousins, figured it was another case of the dreamer dreaming. But Jackson had studied Atlanta's changing demographics carefully, and he liked the numbers. Atlanta's reputation as a mecca of opportunity was attracting droves of young, ambitious blacks from across the nation. Meanwhile, the pace of white flight was accelerating, part of a nationwide urban trend. At the dawn of 1973, Atlanta's black population, only 38 percent in 1960, had risen to 54 percent. "Atlanta is the best city in America for black people to live," Maynard Jr. said. Not entirely, said Julian Bond, a state representative: "This is the best place [for blacks] in the United States if you're middle class and have a college degree, but if you're poor, it's just like Birmingham, Jackson or any other place." Most critically to Jackson, black voting strength in the city was 48 percent—and still rising.

Most of the black leadership privately conceded that Sam Massell would serve a second term as mayor, then step aside for a black mayor in 1977. Maynard Jr. was unwilling to wait. In the summer of 1972, he met on Saturdays with his cousin Clement, a Wharton graduate and stockbroker for Robinson-Humphrey in Atlanta; David Franklin, his new law partner; and Chuck Williams, a friend who had helped in his vice mayoral campaign and was building a black public relations firm in Atlanta. Clement had arrived from North Carolina, Williams from New York and Franklin was in the process of moving back home from Washington, D.C. Together, they held informal discussions about campaign strategies. Once, in Adams Park, near Jackson's west Atlanta home, they sat on picnic benches and stared up at the promising blue skies: young black men, each in his thirties, talking about making political history.

Maynard Jr. was an idealist, and moralist, who believed there was a right and wrong, a good and an evil, in all things and all people, and he tended to discount the range in between. You were either with him, or against him. To Jackson, victory was meant to be absolute and surrender unconditional. He had been raised to think in broad terms, of principles and morals, of things ephemeral and timeless. He was a race man, as his father and grandfathers before him. Their world—the world in which he had been raised—was crystallized in black and white. His world was an intensifying gray, a merging of two different worlds, as the 1973 mayor's race would reflect. A race man by birthright, he wanted to be more than that. To be mayor of Atlanta, he would need to be all-inclusive, to represent whites as well as blacks, allaying white fears and fulfilling black expectations. If most whites thought this inherently impossible to achieve, Maynard Jackson, the idealist, did not, because victory—his victory—would be absolute and timeless, a victory for all people.

He thought the time was right for a black mayor. But knowing how to execute such a political conquest was another thing. "Maynard is a great talker, but somebody had to reduce that stuff and organize," Clement says.

Franklin became the key strategist. He thrived on his proximity to power. An entertainment lawyer who soon would add comedian Richard Pryor to his list of clients, Franklin's political experience had amounted to yeoman fieldwork. In the 1961 mayor's race in Atlanta, he and Julian Bond, a fellow Morehouse classmate, had organized a Muggsy Smith student group in the race against Ivan Allen, Jr. In 1965, he had helped Bond win a seat in the Georgia legislature. As part of his work for the National Urban Coalition, Franklin participated in Carl Stokes's 1967 mayoral victory in Cleveland, and subsequently worked in a steelworkers' election in Baltimore.

The Jackson campaign began in the fall of 1972 on the strength of $40,000 put up by Franklin and Clement. Next, Maynard Jr. solicited support of Atlanta's black leadership for the first time in three campaigns. It was a sign of maturity, but also of necessity. In the process, he encountered a familiar resistance, particularly from Jesse Hill.

To run for mayor, Maynard Jr. knew he needed Hill on his side. Hill had been a central figure in 1972 when Andrew Young, campaigning in a redrawn district, became the first black congressman from the Deep South since Reconstruction. Young's victory solidified Hill's political power in black Atlanta. Hill's name lent credibility, money and more than a few votes. He was chief executive of Atlanta Life, which, with $85 million in assets, was the largest privately held black business in the nation. Over the years, Hill had proven his willingness to help those laboring in the civil rights movement. He had supported the AUC students during the sit-ins in the 1960s, at times paying their bail. In 1960, he had co-founded *The Atlanta Inquirer,* a progressive black newspaper, to serve as an alternative to the more conservative *Daily World.* During the early 1970s, Hill became the first black named to the Georgia Board of Regents and to the board of Rich's. Raised in St. Louis, and educated as an actuary at the University of Michigan, Hill was a complex figure. "Carl Holman once told me, 'As long as I've known Jesse, there are two Jesses,' " Franklin would say. "One is the benevolent one we see and the other is a raging ego who wants to be recognized as on center stage." Franklin viewed Hill as the black rendition of banker Mills B. Lane, a behind-the-scenes force who wielded his civic power like a hammer.

Hill was not enchanted with Jackson's plans to run for mayor. He thought 1977 the right time for a black mayor in Atlanta, not 1973. Hill was forty-seven, a dozen years older than Maynard Jr., sixteen years older than Franklin. He was entrenched in black Atlanta; they were not. And so a generation gap emerged. "[Hill] said Atlanta was not ready for a black mayor," Maynard Jr. recalls, "and that it was going to disrupt the plan for black political progress." Maynard Jr. had heard it all before. Privately, he seethed. "It was the old mentality that we had to kind of keep on getting handouts from the white power structure rather than assert ourselves and be responsible ourselves and work for coalition with whites," he says. He sensed that Hill felt threatened by his candidacy.

Early in 1973, Jackson, Clement and Franklin met with Hill, John Cox of the Butler Street YMCA, Lyndon Wade of the local Urban League branch and other black leaders in the offices of the Atlanta Urban League. Their conversation was animated, the sides were clearly drawn: they wanted Maynard Jr. to wait. Moreover, some black leaders were convinced that whites thought Maynard Jr. too radical, too quick to take the black side in every issue. As Maynard Jr. discussed his intended mayoral platform, he was interrupted by an exasperated black leader, who said, "We want you to say what we want you to say."

"You don't want a candidate," Maynard Jr. replied, his voice rising, "you want a parrot!"

Hill recalls that "there were some efforts to want to coach Maynard." Clement remembers, "People were saying that Maynard was an upstart. And so our response was, 'Well, you know, Mr. Dobbs paid his [grandson's] dues.'"

As Franklin walked about town with Maynard Jr., he saw working class blacks react to the vice mayor with unrestrained admiration and respect. Blacks leaning from the windows on city buses shouted, *"Hey, Maynard!"* Others, uncertain how to address a vice mayor, stammered, *"Hi, uh, Mister, er, Honorable, Sir."* But Franklin needed something that accurately reflected this popularity. He was tired of listening to Hill say what black Atlantans were thinking, particularly when he knew Hill was wrong.

Franklin spent more than $8,000 to commission a survey of 400 whites and 218 blacks in Atlanta. The results of the survey by Pat Caddell, whose Cambridge Survey Research had gained credibility in 1972 for the McGovern presidential campaign, exceeded Franklin's wildest hopes. In a field of six possible candidates, Maynard Jr. received 45 percent of the vote, more than double the runner-up, Sam Massell. The poll indicated that, in a head-to-head election, Maynard Jr. would receive 54 percent of the total vote, Massell 28, with 18 percent undecided. Among blacks, Maynard Jr. received 95 percent of the vote. Mystified at the perception that Maynard Jr. was too extreme, Franklin included a question about that issue in the poll. An overwhelming majority of whites disagreed when asked if Maynard Jackson was "too radical." Franklin had hoped only that Maynard Jr. would be within striking distance of Massell. Seven months before the primary, he nearly had to restrain his joy. Years later, he says he didn't know which was more shocking—the numbers that were tilted so heavily in Jackson's favor, or that "Maynard wanted to know why he was doing so poorly." His sizeable ego led Maynard Jr. to expect voters to commit to him on faith alone.

Franklin and Maynard Jr. immediately called for another meeting with Jesse Hill at the Atlanta Urban League offices. Franklin explained the survey, and its significance, meticulously and powerfully. The shock in the room was palpable. Hill asked several questions, then said, "It's very clear that you should run."

Days later, Hill carried the poll to the Action Forum, an interracial group of business leaders, founded in 1971 by Mills B. Lane and black realtor Bill Calloway, to bridge the city's racial divide. The forum met monthly, on a Saturday morning in a shirtsleeves, get-to-the-heart-of-the-problem format. Forum members, like everyone else, were stunned by the Caddell findings.

On March 9, word of the Caddell survey leaked to the press, though its results had not yet been revealed. "Who Hired Mayor Survey?" *The Atlanta Journal* headline read. Handing the newspaper to his wife, Shirley, that afternoon, David Franklin slapped his finger against the headline, smiled broadly and exclaimed, "I did!"

Sen. Leroy Johnson had promised to support Maynard Jackson's mayoral bid. But in March he said he had had a change of heart. He would run for mayor himself.

"But you said you were going to support me," Maynard Jr. said.

"That's true, and I would support you against the whole world," Johnson said, "except myself."

It was perhaps fitting that, nearly twenty-five years after John Wesley Dobbs and A. T. Walden had co-founded the Atlanta Negro Voters League, Dobbs's grandson and Walden's protégé vied to make the breakthrough at City Hall. Jackson's strategists worried about Johnson's ability to gauge political winds and to deliver blocs of black votes. In October 1970, Johnson had brought the Muhammad Ali–Jerry Quarry heavyweight fight to Atlanta, an accomplishment of backroom genius. It was Ali's first fight since he had refused military induction in 1967. In the intervening three years, local politicians across the country had feared the conservative backlash. But Johnson brought Gov. Lester Maddox to his side, no small trick, then secured the necessary legal rights. Not only had Johnson received a standing ovation at the auditorium moments before the fight, he had earned a reported $175,000 in the process.

It was indisputable: Leroy Johnson was a gifted politician and his candidacy threatened to split the black vote in the 1973 mayor's race. Some of the younger blacks, aligned with Maynard Jr., had not forgotten Johnson standing at the State Capitol in January 1966, a cigar dangling from his lips, as AUC students led by Rev. Martin Luther King, Jr., protested the Georgia legislature's refusal to seat Rep. Julian Bond. The students believed Johnson should have participated in the protest, not observed it.

A pair of Morehouse Men, Jackson and Johnson made a joint campaign appearance April 11, 1973, before 250 students at the AUC. Maynard Jr. told the students he would "never . . . never . . . never . . . never . . . never . . . NEVER sell you out." He maintained that he had transformed the vice mayoralty into a position of significance. "I haven't been Sam Massell's boy," he said. "I'm not going to be anybody's boy." At one point during his rebuttal, Johnson removed his sports coat, hoping to add a more personal touch and to distance himself from the formality of Maynard Jr. Johnson told the students, "I'm one of you. He [Jackson] is not." Over the next two days a mock election was held at the six schools of the AUC. Of the nearly 2,400 votes cast by students, faculty and clerical workers, Maynard Jr. won 2,113, nearly 84 percent. Johnson won only 286 votes.

Jesse Hill asked David Franklin to commission another poll to gauge the effect Johnson's candidacy would have on the black vote. The survey, conducted during the third week in April, was devastating to Johnson's hopes: Maynard Jr. received 80 percent and Johnson only 7. Sam Massell received just 2 percent among the surveyed black voters. Undeterred, Johnson vowed to press on.

But Jesse Hill was convinced. On May 15, he told the *Constitution*, "If the election were held [today], Maynard Jackson would be mayor. . . . I would hope that Sen. Johnson would not qualify for the mayor's race." Then, Hill added, "I think the wheeling-dealing type of politician has no place in the office of mayor of this municipality."

During this period, Hill, Cox and Calloway met with members of the white business elite, including bankers Mills Lane and A. H. "Billy" Sterne. "We told them that in the past they had picked, then brought us a candidate," Hill says. "We told them that we had our candidate for mayor." The black leaders asked for support of the Jackson candidacy. "They would have preferred not to, but it was clear to them that we were not there to ask for their permission or ask for their endorsement of the candidacy," Hill says. "It was a done deal in our minds."

Soon after, Hill invited Massell to a lunch meeting at the Kimball House restaurant on Decatur Street. Hill had been a strong supporter of Massell's over the past four years, but now his tone was serious and distant. He told the mayor that he had been sent by the black leadership to convey a message.

"Sam, we don't want you to run this time," Hill said. "We want to go for a black."

Massell felt as if he had been sucker-punched. Without the black vote, his hopes for reelection were nil. As mayor, Massell had been a devoted friend of Atlanta's blacks. Sitting across from Hill, he remembered something his friends had been telling him: *You're doing all this stuff for the blacks. But they're going to forget you as soon as they get the numbers!*

Sam Massell didn't believe it then. He did now.

In the corridors of power in white Atlanta, there were other ideas about the next mayor.

Ivan Jr. began his letter to Bob Woodruff on May 24 in a familiar, deferential fashion: "Dear Boss." Over lunch at the Commerce Club, and in the clubhouse at the Peachtree Golf Club, Allen had heard the whispers about how polls in the black community made Maynard Jackson the favorite. After a couple of false starts, "I subsequently advised Charles Weltner that I was going to support him in every way possible," Ivan Jr. wrote in his letter to Woodruff, "and forwarded a check for $5,000, payable to Charles Weltner Campaign Fund. I hope you will consider giving Charlie your blessing and support and that we can assist in building him into a major candidate." His appeal apparently had the desired effect. David Franklin would say, "We only got the 'B' money from Coke. Weltner got the 'A' money." Bob Woodruff had taken a liking to Maynard Jr. after asking his valet, Luther Cain, Jr., who had correctly predicted Massell's 1969 victory, for his thoughts about the upcoming mayor's race. "Black people," Cain advised Woodruff, "love Maynard Jackson."

Maynard Jr. had not risen through the political ranks in Atlanta and therefore had not been raised on the city's style of interracial give-and-take. He was a maverick, beholden to no single group or special interest, in the black or white communities.

Already troubled by crime in the 1960s, Atlanta became one of the nation's most crime-infested cities during the Massell years. The reduction of crime became the central plank in the platforms of Jackson, Weltner and Leroy Johnson. Jackson played down the race issue at all times, seeking an interracial coalition. He tried to allay the concerns of whites who feared that a black mayor would shape policy to reverse the oppression of blacks that had marked southern history.

"I fully intend to do everything within the power of the office to see that the racial injustices to which black citizens have been subjected in the past are not repeated," he said in a campaign speech in August.

"I am not, however, on a crusade to prove black people superior to anybody—either racially or legally. . . . I am and always have been committed to equality for all of the people of Atlanta." His rhetoric was strong, but carefully worded. "Bigots and fear-mongers . . . tell us that blacks are 'taking over,' " Maynard Jr. said. "They talk about the city 'going black.' The fact is that black people are simply availing themselves of the joys and the woes of citizenship. These bigots neglect to mention that the black majority has come about not because of some nefarious plot, but because of the high attrition rate among whites who are moving away from what they have been taught to fear and hate. We urge our fellow citizens, do not abdicate your citizenship."

On June 2, he officially opened his campaign headquarters in a storefront at 41 Pryor Street, near Five Points. When the buses arrived each morning at 5:30 and 6:00, Maynard Jr. was there to greet the workers who stepped off. As a campaigner, Maynard Jr. had an extraordinary capacity to give each bystander a singular moment of eye contact and total attention and then to move on to the next. He drew strength from an admiring crowd. "Maynard could go on for eighteen hours a day," Franklin says. Not even Bill Hartsfield, the consummate municipal politician, had possessed such total command of hand-to-hand campaigning. Franklin had seen Bobby Kennedy campaigning once in Washington. To him, Kennedy had seemed a small man with a big head, but, working the crowds, he had had a style and a magnetism that made him seem much larger: Bobby Kennedy "vibrated strength." Maynard Jr. projected larger, too, and he was already six foot two and more than three hundred pounds. Such outsized projection was a trait a candidate either had or didn't. Maynard Jackson had it.

To many blacks in Atlanta in 1973, Maynard Jackson became more than a mere candidate. He was a cause, a symbol, a spiritual manifestation of black hopes and dreams a century old. Whites could not comprehend it. He was fourth-generation Atlanta, third-generation Auburn Avenue. He was the Morehouse Man who, with verve, intellect and oratory, would attempt to assume ultimate political power in the city that once had served as the arsenal of the Confederacy. Only thirty-five years old, he exhibited a remarkable grasp of history, black history, family history and Fourth Ward history. He seemed older and wiser than his years, as if he had been groomed for this moment. He spoke often of family and of Grandpa Dobbs. He was fastidious in appearance, formal in his carriage, gracious in conversation. His strict morals and manners suggested another, earlier time. Some of the city's older blacks considered his style self-serving and arrogant, not unlike that of his grandpa Dobbs. But he spoke to—and for—the young and aspiring blacks of Atlanta.

An urbane young Morehouse professor named Michael Lomax, on leave from the faculty to write his dissertation, volunteered for Jackson's 1973 campaign. With the help of his wife, Pearl, a local television producer, Lomax wrote a speech for Maynard Jr. to deliver to a group of veterans. The next day a car appeared in Lomax's driveway and out stepped Maynard Jackson. "This," Maynard Jr. said, waving the speech in his hand, "is the best speech that's ever been written for me." Soon, Lomax was on the inside, helping to write the position papers for the campaign: Maynard on Neighborhoods, Maynard on Transportation, Maynard on Crime, Maynard on Maynard. Raised in Los Angeles, and graduated from Morehouse in 1968, Lomax felt an almost biblical quality to Jackson's quest. "Maynard was the Second Coming," Lomax recalls. "I think for all of us who were in there, he was your father, he was your older brother, he was your role model. I just can't tell you the kind of goose pimples, the sense of exhilaration, I would get from hearing Maynard speak. It was like you just needed to be near him."

Alderman Wyche Fowler, a candidate for city council president, learned that a small group of white businessmen, having accepted the inevitability of Maynard Jackson's political ascendancy, were attempting to undercut him with a power play. Fowler told Hosea Williams, the renegade civil rights activist, that white power brokers were trying to elect banker Wade Mitchell as council president to counteract the likelihood of a black mayor. "They wanted one of their own—a conservative white businessman from the Trust Company to basically 'run the city,'" Fowler says, "and they were willing to acknowledge this black mayor—'not fiscally responsible'—as only a figurehead. They didn't even know that with the [city] charter changed that wasn't even possible."

Fowler described the scenario simply to Williams: "They are trying to pull an inside straight."

Hosea Williams already knew about the deal. He had been told that a few black power brokers, including Jesse Hill, were centrally involved as well. Once one of the most ardent and volatile lieutenants to the Rev. Martin Luther King, Jr., Williams was a gadfly who would march for a cause on a minute's notice. During the 1960s, King had deployed him as his rabble-rouser; Williams's role was to stir the passions of the entrenched white establishment in a southern city targeted for protest.

Williams responded to this news in typical fashion.

He announced his intention to run for the city council presidency, "to break up the deal."

Soon, Williams met with Jesse Hill and other black leaders at the Butler Street YMCA. "They told me I couldn't run," Williams recalls. His reply was defiant: "It takes $600 to qualify. I've got $400 on me. I'm goin' out to beg for the other $200.

"I'll meet you at the courthouse in two hours."

The slogan—"Win It Again, Sam!"—was simple, upbeat and positive. Sam Massell believed it accentuated his record as mayor. So he liked it.

Massell had been elected in 1969 by black voters. As mayor, he had responded to their needs. He had called for blacks to comprise 50 percent of all city government employees and, in four years, he had raised the total by nearly 20 percent, to 42 percent. Three of the five new city department heads were black, as were two of three local judges appointed by him. He had created an Office of Affirmative Action. He had successfully lobbied for the passage in 1971 of the MARTA referendum, which had been defeated during Ivan Allen's tenure. He had struck a financing deal with developer Tom Cousins so taxpayers would not have to pay for the Omni, the $17 million, seventeen-thousand-seat downtown arena. Massell also could accept credit for the creation of Central City Park, near Five Points, which had been made possible by a $9 million gift from an "anonymous donor"—the decades-old code words for Bob Woodruff.

Sam Massell and Maynard Jackson had been running against each other for more than three years. As for their relationship as mayor and vice mayor, Massell says, "There wasn't one." In early July, Massell had charged an "unholy alliance" between the white power brokers and Jackson, reiterating Fowler's allegation that a deal had been cut to support Jackson and Wade Mitchell; Massell likened the deal to the Watergate scandal. Struggling to generate his own campaign, Leroy Johnson blamed the woes of the city on the "Massell-Jackson administration." Maynard Jr. responded carefully: "We all know that Mayor Massell seldom made a move without consulting Mr. Johnson. . . . What we really had was a Massell-Johnson Administration."

Massell and Jackson were mutually petty. Maynard Jr. presented a ceremonial key to the city to comedian Pat Paulsen, then complained, "The mayor has refused to give me any more keys." Massell's response: "I give keys to people who represent me." Their bickering had become so common and excessive that candidate Weltner said, "While the mayor and the vice mayor argue over such petty things as who will pass out keys to the city, Atlanta has deteriorated into the third most crime-ridden city in America."

There was some dissension in the Jackson campaign. One campaign staffer, John Barber, believed Jesse Hill and developer Herman Russell, as heavy campaign contributors, controlled Maynard Jr. Brilliant, though eccentric, Barber, a former Morehouse valedictorian, feared their control would cause Maynard Jr. to become more compromising with whites and turn his back on the black community, a notion that surely would have astounded white business leaders. Meanwhile, questions were raised about how efficiently campaign funds were spent. The Jackson campaign reportedly was $60,000 in debt by mid-September and would spend more than $200,000 before the October 2 primary. As a result, Hill was handed the title of campaign chairman and Russell, an emerging force in the black business community, assumed control of campaign financing. Two of Cong. Andrew Young's staff members, Stoney Cooks and Tom Offenburger, also joined the Jackson campaign in the final weeks before the primary; Cooks took control of the field operations, including election day get-out-the-vote fieldwork. Franklin, meanwhile, arranged for a fund-raising concert at the Omni, featuring two of his clients, Donny Hathaway and Roberta Flack, as well as Gladys Knight, a graduate of Atlanta's Archer High School. The concert raised at least $40,000, sorely needed by the campaign.

The local press was divided. The *Journal* endorsed Weltner, the *Constitution* Johnson. The *Daily World*, whose influence was in rapid decline in the black community due to the emergence of two rival and more widely read black-interest newspapers, chose Massell. "We have in this contest two officials of our racial group," the arch-conservative *Daily World* editor C. A. Scott wrote, "but the persons who have made up the political coalition should have exerted the leadership to discourage their contending for mayor at this time. . . . Mayor Massell has done a good job and will do a better job with the new officials elected next Tuesday." *The Atlanta Inquirer*, controlled by Jesse Hill, endorsed Jackson. So did the newest black-owned newspaper, *The Atlanta Voice*. Founded in 1968 by businessman Lowell Ware, the *Voice* was considered the most liberal of the black newspapers.

In the primary, Maynard Jr. won nearly 47 percent of the vote, including better than 80 percent of the black ballots. He was headed for a runoff with Massell, who had edged Weltner by fewer than one thousand votes to finish second, 19.8 percent to 19.1. Leroy Johnson finished with a microscopic 4 percent. The "single most powerful black politician in Dixie" was in a precipitous decline, soon to lose his state senate seat to black educator Horace Tate (who never forgot Johnson's refusal to support his 1969 mayoral bid) and then to serve a brief prison term for a tax law conviction.

Maynard Jr. had finished only 3,500 votes short of a majority. Standing at the Atlanta American Hotel primary night, he said, "It is important for us to remember what we are about. We are fighting for the rock of ages, that lady at the bus stop with the shopping bags around her feet who made it possible for many of us to go on to school, for many of us to have a decent house to live in, for many of us to have nice clothes."

Across town, Hosea Williams was feeling something akin to shock. With nearly 30 percent of the council president's vote, Williams had edged Wade Mitchell for second place and the right to meet Alderman Wyche Fowler in the runoff. Williams credits John Barber, who, after his departure from Jackson's staff, assumed control of his campaign. Fowler posed with Williams on the night of the primary, holding hands for the cameras as they prepared for a runoff. Fowler was ecstatic that the power structure favorite, Mitchell, was out of the race.

"All I had to do to get elected [against Williams]," Fowler knew, "was not die."

It was past two o'clock in the morning when Helen Bullard, participating in her final Atlanta mayor's race, gathered with Sam Massell and his staff at the Peachtree Towers. The mood was nearly funereal.

Jackson's lead was a commanding 27 points. Massell's only window of opportunity was that Maynard Jr. had fared poorly among white voters, netting less than 5 percent.

Bullard's health was fading. She was sixty-four but looked much older. She walked with a cane. She lived in an apartment near Piedmont Park where she fed every stray cat and aimless waif that wandered past. She was managing Fowler's campaign and working as a volunteer for Massell. One member of the Massell campaign's advertising agency, Ralph McGill, Jr., son of the late newspaper editor, recalls how "the top people in the agency talked in whispers about [Bullard]. They kept using the word 'guru.' She was considered the 'guru' in Atlanta and Georgia politics and whoever had her would win." To Massell, Bullard was campaign manager, with or without the title. To the young McGill, Bullard seemed only "very old and sort of bent over a little bit."

"Sam," Bullard said finally, speaking softly as the room fell into a hushed silence, "if you keep doing this"—she motioned to the campaign poster, "Win It Again, Sam!"—"you won't win. *You need something stronger.*"

Everyone in the room understood. "Fear not only hit the campaign," Ralph McGill, Jr., says, "it also hit the agency."

If Maynard Jackson was elected mayor of Atlanta, Sam Massell believed the already accelerated white flight to the suburbs would increase even more and the tax base would wither, causing the inner city to decay at a faster rate than ever. Massell believed every decision Maynard Jackson had made as vice mayor was along racial lines and that if his pattern continued as mayor, whites simply would leave the city. It should not be a question of color, as Massell saw it, but rather a question of experience and managerial capability. It was a question of what was best for Atlanta.

The task for the advertising agency of Cargill, Wilson & Acree was to put Massell's views into a powerful, driving theme. Before the primary, the agency had focused on Massell's accomplishments, producing full-page advertisements and leaflets beneath the heading: "What Has Sam Massell Done For You Lately?" But the guru had spoken: Massell needed something stronger.

The Massell campaign was not merely trying to overcome 27 percentage points. It was trying to turn back the tide of racial history. Already, blacks had won mayoral positions in six other major U.S. cities, although none in the South: Los Angeles; Cincinnati; Cleveland; Dayton; Gary, Indiana; and Newark. In several weeks, Coleman Young would win the Detroit mayor's race over a white opponent. By the end of 1973, there would be 105 black elected officials in Georgia, ranging from Congressman Young to 27 members of local school boards. Though this represented only a fraction of the more than 7,000 elected officials in Georgia, the movement was afoot and gaining momentum daily.

For the Massell account, Cargill, Wilson & Acree put together a group of writers and artists, each young, energetic, politically inexperienced and white. A graduate of Westminster and Vanderbilt University, McGill, at twenty-eight, was the youngest in the group. He had shied away from his father's famed journalistic footsteps. Instead, he entered advertising. He had started in 1967 at McCann-Erickson and his father had sent him "little doodles" to use for the agency's Coca-Cola account. "They were real teeth jarrers," the son recalls. "They usually had the word 'nifty' or 'swell.'"

The agency's art director, Bob Shira, located a photograph of urban decay in a book of thematic photos. The photograph showed trash and debris scattered in front of vacant storefronts, precisely the image Massell evoked when he spoke of his fears of an Atlanta governed by Maynard Jr.

Late one afternoon, McGill, Shira and copywriter Mark Doyle sat together in a back booth at the Brothers II bar in midtown, a hangout for advertising copywriters. They were searching for the right headline to use with Shira's photograph. Suddenly, after a couple of drinks, Doyle perked up.

"I've got it," he said. In the mid-1960s, Doyle had been a member of the advertising team at the Leo Burnett agency in Chicago that had created Pop 'N Fresh, the Pillsbury Doughboy. Now, he scribbled a few words on the back of a bar napkin, then held it up for his colleagues to see.

"ATLANTA'S TOO YOUNG TO DIE," it read.

McGill remembered the collective response: "That's it!" followed by hand slaps of celebration.

To Mark Doyle, "it was not really created as a slogan. It was just a headline for a picture."

But "Atlanta's Too Young To Die" would become the most infamous campaign slogan in Atlanta's political history, outstripping even the racial imagery of Lester Maddox's campaign ads of 1961.

Before "Atlanta's Too Young To Die" was shown to Massell, Shira says, "Mark and I were having reservations about it. I thought it was too mean."

Doyle remembers, "[The slogan] was created to say that Sam Massell was a better manager, that the infrastructure would deteriorate if Maynard Jackson was elected. I'm a naive guy. I thought people would take it at face value."

McGill, however, worried about the racial implications of the slogan. "The race thing scared me," he says. "It went against everything that my family had to do with. At the same time, everybody around me [in the agency] was, well, 'This is what we have to do.' Then came the dissembling part: how to call it race without calling it race. You can't very well get on television and say, 'This guy's white and this guy's black and vote for the guy who is white.' Hardly. TV stations wouldn't let you do that. But you could say that 'if this guy gets in, the confidence of the community will be lost, business will be lost, families will leave town, schools will be closed, business will leave and downtown Atlanta will become a wasteland where, at five o'clock, it turns dark and nobody will be there.' "

As the agency's account supervisor, Ron Scharbo took the layout of the new slogan, blown up to full poster size, to Massell's office where Massell and Bullard waited. "You wanted something really powerful to get your message across," Scharbo told Massell. "Here it is."

The mayor's expression was serious as he examined it.

To Massell, the slogan implied "that I can run the city better than he can. Economically, physically, by any category. . . . [Helen Bullard] never would have let me do it if it was racial. She would have gotten up and walked out of that room." Massell agreed to use it. He adds, "I absolutely, positively did not see any racial overtones in this. It was just the furthest thing from my mind."

Once approved, the "Atlanta's Too Young To Die" campaign became a clinical exercise in advertising. "It was very much, I would think, the same sort of mental process that you would go through," McGill says, "once you decided to drop an atomic bomb."

McGill helped to produce the television commercials for the "Atlanta's Too Young To Die" campaign. In one commercial, the agency set up cameras on Peachtree Street, shooting south toward Five Points, at five o'clock in the morning. The agency placed a wind-blowing machine on one side of Peachtree, beyond the camera's eye, and filmed tumbleweed as it blew across the vacant downtown thoroughfare, as the streetlights changed from green to red. In another commercial, they filmed through the padlocked chain-link fence at the McEachern School in Atlanta: the implication was that Jackson's election would cause schools to close. The agency ran into trouble on location at the school, though. "We were run off by the police," McGill recalls. "We didn't have permission to shoot there."

Part of the Massell campaign strategy now was to associate Maynard Jr. and Hosea Williams as a team, so that Williams's image as a black radical would rub off on Jackson in the minds of conservative and moderate voters.

The first print advertisement in the "Atlanta's Too Young To Die" campaign appeared in *The Atlanta Journal* on October 10, six days before the runoff. The photograph, spread across two pages, showed debris scattered before a vacant storefront. The text began, "The thought of a Maynard Jackson–Hosea Williams administration is scaring some Atlantans to death."

When Shira's wife saw the *Journal* that afternoon, she asked him, "Did you do this ad?" The art director said he had. "You ought to be ashamed of yourself," she said.

Worse yet, Shira knew the photograph used wasn't even taken in Atlanta. "It was," he says, "from Philadelphia."

When he first saw the "Atlanta's Too Young To Die" slogan, Maynard Jackson thought: "The man has made my campaign for me. *We are going to ram that phrase right down his throat, and make him choke on it!*"

\*          \*          \*

The morning after the primary, Maynard Jr. had phoned the home of Beaumont Allen, the twenty-two-year-old youngest son of the former mayor, who had served as media director for the now-expired Weltner campaign. "I want to thank you for running a clean campaign," Maynard Jr. told him, "and welcome you into our fold." The phone call was standard political protocol, though it impressed the naive Allen; he considered it kindhearted and thoughtful. The Jackson campaign contacted Ivan Jr. as well. They asked the former mayor for a public endorsement now that Weltner was gone from the race. Ivan Jr. declined, citing his botched involvement in the 1969 mayor's race. "I made such a mess of the last one," he said. Privately, he pledged his vote to Maynard Jr.

On the day after the primary, Maynard Jr. issued a public challenge to Massell. "We are going into a two-week runoff that can either build up Atlanta or tear Atlanta down. I believe in building," he said. It was the classic position for a front-runner to take.

With only thirteen days until the runoff, Jackson's lead seemed invincible. The combined number of votes won by the second-, third- and fourth-place finishers in the primary totaled 48 percent, only one percentage point more than his own total. Maynard Jr. sought to ride out the remaining days of the campaign by avoiding controversy.

Incumbent underdog Massell took the opposite path. On October 7, he appeared on *The Candidate and I,* a program on WQXI radio, and characterized Maynard Jr. and Hosea Williams as "racists." He said most whites in Atlanta perceived Jackson and Williams as "a racial team."

"Right or wrong that's the feeling in the white community," Massell maintained. "For me to pretend [fear] is not there would be to mislead you." If Maynard Jr. and Williams were elected, Massell predicted the city's real estate would "really drop to the bottom."

His campaign rhetoric was loaded with racial innuendo. "One can almost see them dancing in the streets," Massell said, "in anticipation of a black takeover."

"He's running whites out of the city with these scare tactics," Maynard Jr. said later that day in an appearance at Friendship Baptist Church. "He's in the gutter with this type of attack."

In a joint appearance held the next day before the Atlanta Press Club, Maynard Jr. again called for unity among the races in the city, to "unite our city under the banner of brotherhood, peace, prosperity and love." Courting the white conservative vote, Massell suggested that, over the years, many Atlanta whites had voted for able black candidates, including Cong. Andrew Young, school board president Benjamin Mays and Alderman Q. V. Williamson. "But I don't think that means they have to support every black who runs for office," Massell said. "Maybe Atlanta has gotten to the point of sophistication where it can realize that you aren't great just because you're black."

By linking Jackson with Hosea Williams, Massell was engaging in raw racial politics. The implication was that all black politicians were alike or, at least, in cahoots. He knew that if the prospect of *Mayor* Maynard Jackson worried Atlanta's whites, the prospect of electing Hosea Williams to any political office terrified them. Before black crowds, Williams spoke often of his years with King, evoking memories of the slain civil rights leader.

But his campaign needed money more than nostalgia. Several days after the primary, Williams spotted Fowler leaving a church and, as Fowler prepared to enter a car driven by a young campaign staffer, Williams said, "Wyche, seeing as how we're gonna spend the next two weeks together, and if we're gonna be debating the great issues, don't you see, at the clubs and the radio stations, and seeing as—"

"Hosea," Fowler interrupted, "what do you want?"

"Well, yo' man there who sort of whisks by and carries you."

Fowler was incredulous. "*You want me to pick you up?*"

"Well, we are goin' to the same places," Williams reasoned.

And so Fowler, who was fond of Williams, drove his opponent to joint appearances. Williams's campaign antics both astonished and delighted Fowler. When the candidates for city council president appeared together before white audiences, Fowler says, Williams was "perfectly coiffured, hair combed back. Got him a $400 suit on, pocket puff flowin', shootin' his cuffs. We'd walk in and he'd say, 'I am a research chemist. I am a graduate of Savannah State University. Like you, I am a businessman. I have to meet a payroll. I know the problems you face in our society with too much government influence and regulation.' " Fowler remembers how whites in the audience, expecting to hear Williams's renegade diatribes, dropped their jaws in disbelief when he delivered an eloquent address. "Then we'd get into my car, head to Ebenezer for an afternoon debate with the [black] ministers," Fowler says. Before his eyes, Fowler watched Williams transform himself into a *black candidate.* "All of a sudden, Hosea gets out of the car, rips open his [shirt] and puts on his chain," Fowler says. Then, and only then, did the trademark renegade appear.

No such humor permeated the mayor's race. Hearing "Atlanta's Too Young To Die," some campaign aides wanted Maynard Jr. to strike back. Not A. Reginald Eaves, once a Morehouse classmate, now Boston's penal commissioner for Mayor Kevin White and commuting to Atlanta on weekends to serve as advisor to Jackson's campaign. Eaves told Maynard

Jr., "That stuff only works [for Massell] if you jump into the same sewer bag." Maynard Jr. understood the dynamics. Tempted though he was, comfortable with a twenty-seven-point lead, he refrained from a counterattack.

David Franklin understood the political logic of the Massell slogan ("We knew the race already was over," he says), but wondered about the advertising men who had created it. "It was almost like those people didn't understand the city. No one from Atlanta would ever think that someone from Atlanta created a slogan like that. Atlanta can't die. Maynard Jackson can die. Sam Massell can, but the city can't die . . . Birmingham can die. Not Atlanta."

On October 11, the day after Vice President Spiro Agnew abruptly resigned from office and pleaded no contest to a charge of federal tax evasion, the *Constitution* editorialized, "Atlanta is indeed too young to die. She is also too wise to be fooled . . . [Massell's campaign] is sowing the seeds of bitterness which will come to harvest for years to come."

The Cargill, Wilson & Acree slogan was backfiring. It was driving blocs of moderate whites and blacks, formerly sympathetic to Massell, into the Jackson camp.

Soon, both the *Constitution* and the *Journal* endorsed Maynard Jr., citing as one reason the divisive tone of Massell's campaign. A group of leading white attorneys, who previously had supported Weltner, also endorsed Maynard Jr.

Massell insisted his campaign slogan was motivated not by racism but by truth. He began to run a print ad, which included a provocative headline: "Atlanta's Greatest Black Leader Doesn't Happen To Be Black."

The black leaders, and you know who they are in this election, talk a smooth game. But, let's face it. They haven't done diddley squat for you. The black community. Mayor Massell has clearly demonstrated his ability to lead all Atlantans. The Jackson-Williams Team has not. . . . And if such a team attempts to lead this city, many blacks and whites (we're in this together) fear a new trend of flight from Atlanta. They fear an end to progress. An end to opportunity. An end to faith. If that faith dies, Atlanta dies with it.

Four days later, on October 15, the Massell campaign published an advertisement in the *Journal:* "He Loves Atlanta So Much He's Got The Guts To Tell The Truth."

"He gave Atlanta the straight story about Maynard Jackson and Hosea Williams," the ad began. "And he got labeled a racist in return. Seems like you're labeled that if you have the guts to tell the truth on this subject these days."

Years later, Maynard Jr. would say, "Isn't it interesting that all these bright [advertising] minds had no appreciation, no understanding of the revolution that was taking place in thought and voting patterns? They were still dealing with manipulative politics and this was about movement. People were voting from the heart on this thing and they're kind of playing with these cutesy little phrases. . . . The people around Sam gave him bad advice. They really didn't give a hoot about Sam in my opinion. They could not if they gave him that kind of advice. That was not a moral stand."

Yet editor C. A. Scott remained one of Massell's most devoted supporters. Many blacks in the Jackson camp had come of age during the sit-in days of the early 1960s. They believed Scott's refusal to endorse Maynard Jr. smacked of the same old-guard conservatism Scott had exhibited during the halcyon days of the movement when he had insisted upon urging caution and a continued respect for the existing social system. On October 9, the *Daily World* had suggested that Williams's presence in the runoff, coupled with the assurance that five blacks had won seats on the nine-member school board and at least nine blacks on the eighteen-member city council, has "raised the question of just how much control we should seek at this time." The *World* printed a picture on its front page on October 11 of Maynard Jr. surrounded by a group of smiling black children, two of whom had their right arm upraised and their fingers balled into a fist. Scott believed this picture—which had been printed on postcards circulated by the Jackson campaign—was an emotional appeal to black power. "Most white southern politicians made this appeal to emotions and race 100 years ago and the Supreme Court finally outlawed the objectives they achieved," the *World* maintained. "The Germans adopted an emotional salute and it almost brought them to destruction."

The prevailing view among white voters was that all blacks stood united behind Maynard Jackson. Not only was this assumption wrong, it was one more example of how little whites in Atlanta knew about the people who lived on the other side of town.

Maynard Jr. voted during the early morning hours of the October 16 runoff, then posed for waiting photographers. He held two-year-old Buzzy and flashed a victory sign. His campaign staff then dispatched into the black precincts two flatbed trucks, one carrying Maynard Jr., the other Jesse Jackson, former aide to Rev. Martin Luther King, Jr., and a firebrand capable of drumming up excitement in the streets. Music blared and the resonant voices of the two men backed it up, calling for strong voter support.

The candidate's every moment had been scripted during the campaign's final days. He had traveled the Sunday morning circuit of black churches; to those congregations he was unable to reach, the staff had sent a surrogate to spread the word: "Vote Maynard!" Vans and cars were rented to transport thousands of black voters to the polls. These were the election day rituals in black Atlanta, and, as history tolled, they weren't going to be overlooked by Jackson's aides. A poll in the paper on the morning of the runoff indicated that Wyche Fowler led Hosea Williams by a three-to-one margin and that Maynard Jackson would win election with between 59 and 65 percent of the vote, depending on the size of the black turnout. Meanwhile, Lomax recalls Jackson staffers contacting black radio stations to spread the lie that black turnout was expected to be light; the idea was to frighten blacks into voting. *If you don't vote for Maynard, Sam will win!*

That night, members of the national press crowded into Jackson's Pryor Street headquarters. Maynard and Bunnie, Renie, assorted Dobbs aunts, uncles and cousins, and top aides gathered in a suite at the Sheraton-Biltmore Hotel on West Peachtree Street. Early returns from the white precincts, though giving Massell a slight lead, were promising: Maynard Jr. was scoring more than 20 percent.

Then the black precincts began to report. At Precinct 2-G at David T. Howard High, the candidate's alma mater, Maynard Jr. outpolled Sam Massell, 650 to 80.

At Precinct 3-L at Alonzo Herndon High, named for the millionaire black businessman and freed slave who once sat in the pew behind the Dobbses at First Congregational Church, Maynard Jr. won 736 votes to Massell's 32.

In the Sheraton-Biltmore ballroom, anticipation became exhilaration. Black musicians played to a crowd that was predominantly black. Men with afros and beads, women wearing plaid and wide-brimmed hats waited for Maynard Jr. As the hour of victory approached, an intense vibration energized the room.

Upstairs, staffer Michael Lomax had the nearly impossible task of keeping well-wishers out of the already overcrowded Jackson suite. Arthur Langford, a young black, shouted his credentials: "I just got elected to the city council." But Lomax replied, "I don't care what you just got elected to. You ain't coming into this room!" Reginald Eaves drew back the curtains and saw people dancing in the streets. Bob Jordan, Jr., made it inside the suite largely because he, like the mayor-elect, was a grandson of John Wesley Dobbs. Jordan happened to be a general assignment reporter for WGN television in Chicago. Years later he remembered the night "as one of the few times in my reporting career that I was very moved and overwhelmed by a story, feeling pride in having my cousin elected mayor of the city where I was born." He conducted an interview that night with Maynard Jr. for WGN radio, during which the mayor-elect of Atlanta "referred to me as 'Bobby.' I'm known either as Robert or Bob Jordan. The fact that Maynard referred to me as Bobby was a dead giveaway. Then he mentioned that we were cousins." Their interview took on a more relaxed, familiar tone, two of John Wesley Dobbs's grandsons expounding upon the meaning of the moment.

Maynard Jr. already had prepared his acceptance speech, yet as a phalanx of security escorted his entourage toward the ballroom, he began to think of personal history—his father and grandfather.

Walking into the spotlights, Bunnie says, "the crowd was so hot. I moved from the front of the ballroom all the way to the stage and my feet never touched the ground." Lomax says, "We walked out onto that stage and it was a great high. You never will have that kind of rush again. . . . We knew that what we had done was historic beyond Atlanta." And David Franklin recalls, "They lifted me off my feet, carried me by my arms. That was the first time, and the only time, I thought that if someone slipped, we all would be crushed." Reginald Eaves was moved by the scene. "Very unlike Boston politics," he says, "where people were happy but they were plotting the whole time. This was genuine. *Things are going to change.*"

As she moved to the stage, next to her husband, Bunnie was struck by a realization. She had not been an active part of the campaign. Most of her time had been spent at home, raising three children and caring for her mother. Her husband had been away, campaigning. Now she felt the crowd surging and she understood what it all had been about. "Maynard was it. He was the most important thing that had ever happened to black people in the City of Atlanta." The significance of her realization was powerful: "At that point, Maynard becomes not my husband. He's not mine anymore. He belongs to everybody else."

It was past eleven o'clock when Maynard Jackson leaned toward the ballroom microphone and said, "Did we send Sam a message?" The crowd erupted with cheers. Renie stood to her son's right, in a floral dress, the fingers of her right hand forming a victory sign. At times, it was difficult to see her because the ubiquitous Jesse Jackson, with his afro and broad shoulders, moved in front of her, next to the mayor-elect, where the cameras couldn't miss him. Benjamin Mays and Lonnie King stood on the crowded platform as well. So did a handful of Dobbs family members and staff aides.

Maynard Jr. won 59 percent of the more than 125,000 votes cast. He took 95 percent of the black vote and 21 percent of the white vote. Fowler won the presidency of the city council over Williams by nearly two to one.

Atlanta, with a black mayor and white council president, nine black and nine white council members, now claimed a victory not only for racial moderation but for racial balance.

From his headquarters, Massell said, softly, "My only motive was to tell the truth. That's all I wanted to do, and all I felt I did." His political career was over.

His arms draped around the shoulders of his mother and wife, Maynard Jr. became nearly solemn. "I come with my father in mind," he told the crowd. "My father died when I was fifteen. . . . He was the first black person ever to seek office in Dallas, Texas." Obviously, his father's tragic demise remained a deep wound, so deep he never even discussed it with Bunnie. Then he spoke of John Wesley Dobbs and his years of toil in the voter registration movement, the vineyards where the fruits of 1973 truly had been sown.

But now, on a historic night for black Atlanta, Maynard Jr. connected the significance of his victory to his father and the Grand and the whole history of racial uplift, saying, "It is not solely the culmination of a campaign waged against another candidate. It is not the petty conquest of a choice political plum. This election means more than that. Not just me, or not just to me. But to all of us."

The Dobbs family reveled in the victory. Two of the mayor-elect's aunts, Josie Clement of Durham, North Carolina, and Millie Jordan of Atlanta, took part in the jubilation at the Sheraton-Biltmore. "I had a hard time digesting it," Josie recalls. "For those of us who had been reared under a different time it was hard to believe things had come to this point and that the city had elected a black mayor."

"Wouldn't it have been something if Daddy could have been here?" Millie said to family members in the hotel suite.

Josie replied, "Somehow, I think Daddy is here. He wouldn't have missed this for the whole world!"

"We are the city whose people refuse to become bogged down in the mire of demagoguery and inflammatory rhetoric," Maynard Jr. said that night. "And like the Phoenix, which is the symbol of our city, today we have arisen from the ashes of a bitter campaign to build a better life for all Atlantans."

His cadence changing, the preacher's son suddenly made like the preacher, saying to the charged crowd: *"No matter how many suns may set, no matter how many moons may glow . . ."*

"Well?" an old man in the crowd said, in singsong style.

*"No matter how many pebbles may rest on the beach, no matter how many times the tide may come . . ."*

"Well?"

*"Never, never . . ."*

"Never!" a few members of the audience shouted.

*"Never . . ."* Maynard Jackson said, a smile breaking across his face.

"Never!" the crowd, his crowd, replied.

*"Never . . ."* the mayor-elect said, tears forming.

"Never!" the audience roared.

*"Never, never, shall I let you down."*

Later that night, he met the media. "I don't hate Sam. I don't dislike Sam at all. I just regret what he did. I think that it was avoidable. But I was never without confidence that Atlanta was going to rise to the occasion. We're kind of like one big family where brothers and sisters might fight among themselves, but don't let somebody else mess with us, okay? Sam is one of the family except that he was holding Atlanta up to national scorn and obloquy and ridicule and that is something which Atlanta does not tolerate.

"So Atlanta came through, as I see it. It came through to say to the nation and to the world, 'We are not divided. We are above racial appeals and we can cut across racial lines to support the best people.'

"I never doubted that would happen."

A decade had passed since Bill Hartsfield, a mayor's mayor, bemoaned the continuing white flight from Atlanta. "What good will it do the Negro citizen [for whites] to go off and leave the town to him," Hartsfield said at the time. "The worst element of his own race will rise up and take over."

Bill Hartsfield was not wrong about many things, but this was one of them. Maynard Jackson was a member of the black aristocracy, who hailed from an elite family Hartsfield had known and respected. Given their respective upbringing, the argument could be made that Jackson's political emergence was more logical than that of Hartsfield, the tinsmith's son.

Sixty-one relatives made the pilgrimage to Atlanta for the January 7, 1974, inaugural. John Wesley Dobbs's brood had been in Atlanta for more than seventy-five years but on the day Maynard Jr. was inaugurated, whites reacted as if the Dobbses had pulled into the train station on the *Crescent* only that morning. The mayor-elect's aunt Mattiwilda came from Stockholm, his sister Jeanne from Nigeria with her husband, Francis Oladele. Cousins, uncles and siblings arrived from points across the globe; their complexions varied from light to dark, some had earned master's degrees, some doctorates. They were educators, doctors, businessmen.

Never had Atlanta witnessed an inaugural like it. Hartsfield, Allen and Massell had had decidedly unremarkable inaugurals, each held in the aldermanic chamber where the mayor-elect placed his hand on a family Bible and made a brief speech before friends, family and reporters. ("The shorter they are, the more the newspapers will publish," Hartsfield advised Ivan Jr.)

The Jackson inaugural had to be different for it carried implications that stirred the conscience of the city. The swearing-in of the city's first black mayor was to be liberation night to black Atlantans, a confirmation of a victory for the race that one black city official said felt every bit as meaningful as "the Supreme Court saying, 'You don't have to sit in the back of the bus anymore.' " If the 1906 race riot and the Martin Luther King, Jr., funeral in 1968 represented the two moments of deepest despair to Atlanta's blacks, now there was a matching pair representing monumental joy: the spring day in 1948 when eight black men wearing the crisp blue uniform of the Atlanta police force for the first time walked along Sweet Auburn Avenue, and the night in 1974 when Maynard Jackson, Jr., was sworn in as the first black mayor. Jackson's ascendancy also stirred many young blacks across the nation, whose résumés already were stacking up at Atlanta City Hall.

Maynard Jr. did not lack for broad vision. (Says one Jackson advisor, "Maynard could turn a parking ticket into a world event.") His inaugural would mimic the grand style of the mayor-elect himself. As mayor, Maynard Jr. intended to take Atlanta to new levels of culture and interracial understanding. He wanted his inaugural to begin the process.

With vivid imagery and racial symbolism, the inaugural not only gave expression to black hopes but was a logical extension of 540 Houston Street, dating to the hard days of segregation: Renie playing accompaniment on the family piano in the parlor as Geekie sang a spiritual and the lacy fairies, made of terra-cotta, danced from the ornate molding by the fireplace. Geekie would perform at the inaugural as well, and to her it seemed appropriate that her nephew had emerged as Atlanta's first black mayor for, in the context of his times, that is what the Grand had been on Sweet Auburn, and because "I don't know of anybody else in the family who is more like Daddy than Maynard. . . . He has that same drive, that same personality. His speeches are like his. Daddy was always saying, 'I want to be in touch with the common man.' Like a king with his subjects."

Of the nearly five thousand in attendance at the inaugural gala inside the Atlanta Civic Center, about 90 percent were black. Most were middle aged and middle class. They understood better than most that the coronation of Maynard Jr. was also a coronation of Atlanta's black middle class, now in its fourth generation. Coretta Scott King appeared in a flowing red cape. Vernon Jordan, successor to Whitney Young as head of the National Urban League and a man who might have been Atlanta's first black mayor if his complexion had been lighter, said, "There's no better time to come home than today." To Hank Ezell, a white reporter for the *Atlanta Journal,* the significance of the moment carried through the years: "Few occasions in my life have I felt the spirit moving, but I did that night. As a reporter you couldn't respond to it, but as a human you couldn't miss it."

The Atlanta Symphony and a choral group performed the "Ode to Joy" from Beethoven's Ninth Symphony and on stage Wyche Fowler, new city council president, felt the explosive power of their voices passing through his body. The Morehouse glee club, which once counted Maynard Jr. as a member, sang "Lift Every Voice and Sing," often called the black national anthem. Finally, Geekie, resplendent in a sequined gown, sang a French aria, "Je Suis Titania," the spiritual "A City Called Heaven," then closed with "He's Got the Whole World in His Hands." Despite its high style, the Jackson inaugural did not approach the scope of the celebration held the previous week in Detroit to honor its first black mayor, Coleman Young. Jackson's ceremony lasted ninety minutes; Young's went on for three days.

At thirty-five, Maynard Jackson was not only Atlanta's first black mayor, but also its youngest. In the television lights, he dabbed a handkerchief to his sweaty brow. "I was so involved and so caught up in it and so wanting to do the right thing and to be understood, but more than that, wanting to give good direction," he recalls. "I almost couldn't enjoy the occasion. . . . I was working that night."

Among the whites in attendance were Ivan Allen III, now second in command at the Atlanta Chamber of Commerce, and his wife, Margaret. They came to show support for the new mayor. Margaret would describe the Jackson inaugural with polite discretion: "It was, well, grandiose." Showing up was more difficult for Sam and Doris Massell. His defeat was a bitter one, and his slogan "Atlanta's Too Young To Die" would become his albatross. More than two decades later, Massell insists, "To this day, I test people in other cities, or strangers to politics, or strangers to [the 1973 campaign] and say, 'Suppose somebody used this slogan, do you think that's offensive or do you think it has a bad connotation?' Never, ever once have I had somebody say, 'Well now, that would be racial.' "

Maynard Jr. labored over his inaugural address. He was a perfection-ist in all things, but especially his oratory. He fashioned himself in the same cloud-of-dust oratorical style of the Grand: *"Start low, Go slow; Strike fire, Move higher, and then Sit Down in a Storm."* He also consid-ered himself an idealist who could weave disparate themes with the mastery his father once had used in his Sunday sermons. His inaugural address was a collaborative process. Pearl and Michael Lomax, rising stars in the black community who joined the new Jackson administra-tion, helped to craft it.

"Let's talk about what you want to say," Pearl Lomax said to Maynard Jr., whose responses always related to effect rather than the substance of the speech.

"I want to rock 'em," the mayor-elect said, enthusiastically, "and move 'em."

His central theme was a politics of inclusion. That meant everyone: rich and poor, white and black, haves and have-nots. The number of drafts was countless ("Shitloads," by Michael Lomax's estimate). Work-ing scrupulously with the words, Maynard Jr. didn't finish his inaugural address until he had no choice. "[It] was not ready until thirty minutes before he gave it," Lomax recalls.

He used the word "we" fifty-four times in a fifteen-minute address. His speech focused on ideals more than programs. Of the Atlanta police department, Maynard Jr. said, "We will respect it and require its respect of us," a notion that brought warm applause from an audience long famil-iar with charges of police brutality against blacks.

"We stand, not so much as a gateway to the South, but as a gateway to a new time, a new era, a new beginning for the cities of our land," he said. "It is a great moment for us. Many eyes are watching us; many cities are examining us.

"It is awesome to consider, but true: we stand at a decisive point in history. Everyone knows that the Old South is dead forever."

"Right on! Right on!" a black man in the audience shouted.

"But in spite of much propaganda to the contrary, we have not yet seen the birth of a really New South. Now we stand with a choice: we can live as if this were simply the worst of times, as if there were no path for Atlanta save the terrible mistakes of the Urban North. Or we can strike out in still uncharted directions."

He quoted Aristotle and the black poet Langston Hughes. He cited a former mayor, saying, "We use the Hartsfield slogan, 'A City Too Busy To Hate,' but equally as important, we must ask during the difficult days ahead, are we a city too busy to love?"

The most personal quotation came from his grandfather—not the Grand, but the Rev. Alexander Stephens Jackson, his father's father, who died before Maynard Jr. was born. He found the quote in a monograph his mother, "Mama Renie," had kept over the years. In his inaugural, Maynard Jr. said, "If the 'haves' do not help the 'have nots' we will see the truth in the words of Alexander Stephens Jackson when he said, 'The blight will fall on master and man equally, different only in phase.' There can be no glittering International City as long as grim poverty and dangerous despair tarnish our glow."

This quotation captured one of his driving themes: that white power brokers in Atlanta need not fear a city governed by a black mayor. *Those who have power are not going to lose power because more share power.* His idealism unmasked, few whites were in the audience that night to hear him. "That," Maynard Jr. recalls, "was like a signal."

According to the *Constitution,* his inaugural address was interrupted by applause sixteen times. The *Daily World,* suddenly enamored of a politician it had refused to support during the campaign, now calling him "Black Atlanta's favorite son," counted twenty-five interruptions for applause.

To Massell, the Jackson inaugural was excessive. "A bore. Terrible and pompous," he says.

"And taxing to the fanny."

In the hours following his inauguration, Maynard Jr. gathered with his sixty-one relatives. "This is the happiest moment of my life," he said. "This inauguration is a step that goes way back in our family. There's something unusual about this family—it has a history of strong people and moral leaders. It has a spirit of never giving up."

This adrenal high failed to resonate beyond the next morning. J. Paul Austin of Coca-Cola had extended an olive branch a week earlier when he, along with thirty white businessmen, agreed to offset the Jackson campaign's $30,000 debt. But most of white Atlanta was seized with dread. For several years, new glass and steel skyscrapers and town centers had been sprouting in Buckhead and neighboring Cobb County. The city's black population—roughly 54 percent in 1974—would rise to 66 percent in six years; blacks represented about 80 percent of Atlanta's public school system in 1973 and that number would soon surpass 90 percent.

Racial battle lines already were forming when someone in Maynard Jackson's hotel suite on the night of his inauguration shouted, "Long live the king!" As their laughter rippled across the arc of time, the Dobbses sang in unison, "Aaaa-A-men, Aaaa-A-men, Aaaa-A-men, A-men, A-men!"

# CHAPTER 25

→←

As the Braves' Hank Aaron sought to claim baseball's most treasured record on April 8, 1974, at the stadium Ivan Allen built, Allen sat in a private suite with Bob Woodruff and Mayor Maynard Jackson sat in a field-level box with entertainer Sammy Davis, Jr. On television, the nation watched, and waited.

To baseball fans, Babe Ruth's record 714 home runs had seemed as inviolate as Jim Crow laws once had seemed to white southerners. Ruth was an American icon with the New York Yankees during the Golden Age of Sports. Boisterously excessive in his social habits, Ruth had redefined the game with his garrulous personality and home-run-hitting prowess. Aaron was a black outfielder for the Atlanta Braves, a quiet man raised in segregated Mobile, Alabama, who guarded his privacy closely. Aaron's personality did not demand attention, though his astonishing number of home runs year after year certainly did. As he closed in on Ruth's record in 1973, Aaron had received numerous death threats from whites and required personal security. Though Aaron did not have deep roots in black Atlanta—he had arrived in the city just eight years before, having hit most of his home runs as a member of the Milwaukee Braves—his wife, Billye, widow of Atlanta NAACP president Rev. Sam Williams, was well connected. The mayor knew Hank and Billye Aaron personally.

Sammy Davis was a fan of baseball and of Hank Aaron. Once a member of Hollywood's "Rat Pack" with Frank Sinatra, Dean Martin and Peter Lawford, Davis was the son of vaudeville dancers, a tiny and dynamic entertainer who playfully called himself "the little one-eyed colored guy." Having finished a performance in Atlanta, he had accepted an invitation for dinner at the mayor's house. Davis had made one request—he wanted soul food. Bunnie didn't know how to prepare it; so she found a caterer. That night Davis and his entourage had arrived at the Jacksons' home at 1272 Oakcrest Drive for a soul food feast of fried chicken, chitlins and "mountain oysters," the latter a delicacy Davis had requested. "What are mountain oysters?" Bunnie inquired. "Pigs' nuts," someone said. She wished she hadn't asked.

When Davis mentioned during dinner that he planned to fly to Houston in a few hours, Maynard Jr. told him, "Sammy, you can't leave now. Hank Aaron's going to hit his record-breaking home run tonight."

Davis had offered to pay $25,000 for the ball Aaron hit for his record-breaking 715th home run, an offer that went unheeded. "If I go to the game," Davis told Maynard Jr., "that would probably curse him." But the mayor replied, "If he hits that ball tonight and you're not there you will never forgive yourself." Davis agreed and delayed his flight.

In the season opener in Cincinnati, Aaron had struck the home run that tied Ruth's mark. Before that game, he had requested an official moment of silence to honor the sixth anniversary of the murder of the Rev. Martin Luther King, Jr. Cincinnati club officials refused, however. "It is inconceivable to me," Maynard Jr. said, in a statement at Atlanta City Hall on April 5, "that Cincinnati would turn down this request for such a modest tribute to a fine American who gave his life for his belief in justice and freedom."

Now, as Aaron prepared to face Los Angeles Dodgers veteran pitcher Al Downing in the fourth inning, Allen, who as a boy had followed Ruth's exploits in the daily box scores in the *Constitution*, turned to Woodruff.

"It's not gonna happen tonight, Boss," he said. "The wind's blowing in."

Just then Aaron connected for his historic home run.

Ivan Jr. and Woodruff stood and applauded. Two Emory University students bolted from their seats in the grandstands and ran onto the field to congratulate Aaron as he rounded the bases.

From his seat, Sammy Davis, Jr., leaped in celebration. "He literally seemed to jump seven feet in the air," Maynard Jr. says. "That was one of the highlights, just watching him celebrate.

"I've never seen anybody that excited in my life."

The mayor wrote a letter to the stadium authority four days later proposing that the name of the Atlanta ballpark be changed to Henry Aaron Stadium. A local ordinance, however, prohibited the naming of city facilities in honor of any living person.

Maynard Jackson didn't fight the ordinance.

Atlanta's first black mayor already had enough fights in progress.

Twenty years later, Maynard Jr. would describe the two most difficult obstacles he faced in 1974 as Atlanta's first black mayor: "Exaggerated expectations in the black community and exaggerated fears in the white community. A lot of things flowed from that."

At the dawn of his mayoralty, he became an articulate symbol for black political progress in the nation and for New South potential. He spoke frequently on college campuses during his first year as mayor, commanding as much as $2,000 per speech, a sizeable amount. He varied his cadences and themes to suit his purposes, and was a masterful storyteller. Campaigning to get out the black vote for Chattanooga developer Franklin Haney's unsuccessful 1974 gubernatorial bid in Tennessee, Maynard Jr. walked on stage during a Stevie Wonder concert in Memphis. Wonder was in the middle of a set and mayoral staffer Michael Lomax recalls, "Maynard interrupted him and got away with it. He obviously had tremendous command of an audience." In virtually every address, the mayor sold himself and Atlanta. Once, a group of African students from Duke University arrived at Atlanta's City Hall unannounced. Maynard Jr. had spoken at Duke several days earlier; at City Hall the students asked to see him.

One of the Africans explained to a bewildered mayoral staffer: *"He invited us to come to Atlanta!"*

As mayor, Maynard Jr. was in a hurry to make lasting social change. He says, "I felt that things [in Atlanta] that were wrong ought to be changed right away. And there was no mandate for gradually *unwronging* things. They'd been wrong for too long already. I didn't help it along by being a gradualist because I was not a gradualist."

There were black mayors in other American cities, but Atlanta, where educational and entrepreneurial opportunities for blacks had been a historical constant, seemed an essentially fertile testing ground for black political power. To ambitious young blacks, the city seemed to open up as a gleaming palace of opportunity—and all of those opportunities flowed from the second story of City Hall. A whole cadre of young blacks angled for position, currying favor with the new black mayor. To be iced by City Hall meant that you were left out and might as well move to another city. Morehouse Men, such as David Franklin, Michael Lomax and A. Reginald Eaves, became his chief political lieutenants. They felt almost like revolutionaries, certain there was no other place in America quite like Atlanta, at least not for blacks. In Washington, D.C., blacks could aspire to federal jobs, but in Atlanta in 1974 they believed they could aspire to real power.

The mayor's commitment was total. He spent nearly every waking hour thinking or talking about politics, arriving at the office early and leaving late. He demanded the same dedication from aides, though often they disappointed him. "Maynard surrounded himself with people who were inexperienced," says Lomax, who was among the novice political staffers, "because there were no black people who had experience in government then." Maynard Jr. became notorious for calling staff members during the wee hours of morning to discuss City Hall issues. Many of his staffers, lured to their jobs by the mayor's magnetism and his call for a historic change in Atlanta, were suffocated by his inability to delegate authority.

In Atlanta, elite white businessmen bemoaned their loss of civic clout, and the need for new power alignments. Chamber of Commerce leaders wanted a white go-between at City Hall (they had one already in city finance director Charles Davis, hired during the Allen administration, though Davis tended to be scrupulously independent), and helped the mayor land as his chief administrative officer Jule Sugarman, a career civil servant, working in Mayor John Lindsay's Department of Human Services in New York City. Many complaints against Maynard Jr. were irrational and unfounded. One charge—that he hired only blacks—was amended after he hired Sugarman: "He only hires blacks and *outsiders.*"

The most deep-seated fear among white business leaders was that a black mayor would hold them accountable for hundreds of years of racial injustice. Chamber leaders became convinced Maynard Jr. would filter all decisions through the racial prism, a notion the mayor thought racist in its own right. He became anathema to white business elites not only because he was black but because of his impeccable style and lofty speeches filled with words that sent Georgia Tech and University of Georgia boys scurrying to their dictionaries.

The black mayor's determination proved indomitable. He was the embodiment of the Ella Wheeler Wilcox poem, "Will," which the Grand had treasured and made him memorize: *What obstacle can stay the mighty force/Of the sea-seeking river in its course.* In 1974, the black mayor was the sea-seeking river.

He wore fine suits and black alligator boots, was chauffeured around town by police detectives in a black Lincoln, and was quoted as rejecting "the vapid, jejune trappings of American middle-classness."

If Bill Hartsfield had lived to the age of seven hundred, never would he have used words like "vapid" and "jejune." The black mayor said he would be the mayor of all people—and it was his honest ambition—but deep within he also was a race man who felt the need to champion the cause of his people, as his father and his grandfathers had before him. More than his mission, this was his birthright. Every speech reflected it. Oratory was his passion, the Grand had made certain of that. The mayor memorized poems, biblical passages and historical facts. He often sounded like a lawyer arguing his case. He had conviction about what he was saying. To him, the orator who lacked conviction was a charlatan, no matter how convincing his words. He traveled to Chicago in June 1974 to address a banquet sponsored by the Rev. Jesse Jackson's Operation Breadbasket. There, he railed against the anti-poor and anti-black policies of the Nixon administration. "Throughout our history," Maynard Jr. said, "we, the poor people of this nation, have been exploited and then cast aside. The policy of the power brokers has always been, if they couldn't abuse us, then they didn't want to use us."

In Atlanta, a press release was issued that day quoting portions of his speech. The whites in Atlanta could not help but notice the pronouns—*Us* and *They*. Over time, *Coloreds* had become *Negroes* had become *Blacks*. But it seemed two terms in race relations had remained unchanged in Atlanta—*Us* and *They*.

Marriage, professional ambition and the passage of time had scattered in different directions John Wesley Dobbs's daughters and their families. Of the six daughters, only Millie, a Spelman professor, still lived in Atlanta in 1974. Thirteen of the Grand's twenty grandchildren had attended, or were about to attend, Morehouse or Spelman; all but a few graduated and a number already were building prestigious careers, including the mayor, Ben Blackburn II (a dentist), Bob Jordan, Jr., (a television news anchor) and Wesley Dobbs Clement (an eye surgeon).

Forged by the Grand, the Dobbs family bond took different shapes during these years. Family reunions were held in Atlanta in December 1975 and in the summer of 1977, continuing a tradition that dated at least to 1931 when the twenty-fifth wedding anniversary party for the Grand and Irene was held at 540. In 1976, Bill Clement, Jr., created Dobbs Associates, Inc., an investment club for members of the extended family. In September 1977, Willie Blackburn, the Grand's second eldest daughter, founded *The Dobbs Family Newsletter*, a quarterly that provided family updates, family history and a few of the Grand's favored poems.

To his children, Maynard Jr. spoke often of family history, usually about his father or the Grand. Just as the Grand had burnished his family tales, neglecting to mention, or smoothing over, his stories of slavery and personal defeats, Maynard Jr. stressed only the positive and inspirational aspects of his family's past to his children. His daughters, Beth and Brooke, would reach adulthood without knowing that their grandfather, the Rev. Maynard Jackson, had died in a state institution in Texas, knowing only that, as Brooke says, "he was supposedly a really romantic husband." Neither would the mayor's daughters learn that their father had been unable to make passing grades at Boston University Law School, only that, as Beth says, "Daddy is so intelligent, super-smart." Maynard Jr., meanwhile, continued a family tradition as a stickler for table manners and grammar. ("I couldn't get through a sentence at the table without being corrected," Brooke says.) Also in the family tradition, Maynard Jr., at nearly every turn, hugged and kissed his daughters and son, Buzzy, often giving what Beth calls "Daddy's Coach Speeches." Typically, those speeches were a variation of the same theme: "I love you, I'm proud of you, and there's no limit to what you can do with your life!"

Adopted by Maynard Jr. at the age of seven, Beth, Bunnie's child from her first marriage, habitually forewarned her dates to read *The Atlanta Constitution*, cover to cover, before coming by to pick her up.

"Daddy always asks something about current events," she warned. "Don't sound stupid."

It is easier to govern during prosperous times, more challenging during times of economic hardship.

If Ivan Allen, Jr., had ascended to Atlanta's City Hall in 1962 at an opportune moment that provided his political launching pad—a time of Kennedy liberalism, urban prosperity and minuscule unemployment in his city—Maynard Jackson entered office a dozen years later under conditions so inopportune as to be insurmountable. In 1974, the nation was in the throes of a recession with spiraling inflation, the most severe economic downtown since the Depression. Atlanta's unemployment rate exceeded 7.5 percent, more than triple the rate during most of the Allen years. The Watergate scandal caused widespread distrust of politicians. Furthermore, Maynard Jr. assumed a new city charter that transformed government from a weak-mayor system to a strong-mayor system, a change long wanted by Hartsfield and Allen that hurriedly was pushed through the state legislature during the Massell administration by young, farsighted Atlanta leaders who understood that legislators would be unlikely to make the change under a black mayor; the change made department heads answerable to the mayor and required a reorganization of city government, a process that assured turmoil. Beyond that, Ivan Jr. had entered office at the age of fifty. Maynard Jr. was just thirty-five.

Maynard Jr. also was victimized by sweeping demographic changes that left the central city with a declining tax base and unable to compete with the booming white suburbs; the suburbanization process of middle-class blacks already was in motion, producing black enclaves in DeKalb County and south Fulton County. What some myopic white Atlantans would define as a failure of black government was, in fact, a product of broader societal shifts.

Among the various first-black mayors in large American cities two frequent sources of crisis were the local press and the police department.

Two years earlier, Chamber of Commerce president Larry Gellerstedt, Jr., a construction company executive, had lobbied for the annexation of Sandy Springs, an affluent white north side suburb. Gellerstedt claimed the city needed annexation in order to increase its tax base. But years later, he admitted, "What I wanted to do was get those [white] voters in Sandy Springs so that in 1973 we wouldn't elect Maynard as mayor. . . . The fear was that he would bring in a black police chief and that we would have the tearing down of the image we had built in Atlanta."

Placing the city's weapons in the hands of a black police chief frightened white business leaders. Statistics proved that the overwhelming majority of violent crime in Atlanta was committed by blacks. Many whites believed a black police chief would show preferential treatment to members of his own race, placing the city at risk. To blacks, on the other hand, the white police chief long had represented the modern rendition of the plantation overseer.

From the beginning, Maynard Jr. intended to remove Atlanta's police chief, John Inman. For generations, the Atlanta force had been laced with an institutionalized racism and, as the mayor was quick to say, more people were killed by Atlanta police in 1973 than by any other police department of equal size in the nation. Inman was a tough career cop (unrelated to the elite Atlanta family of the same name) hired to the force in 1949 by Chief Herbert Jenkins. As a longtime police detective, Inman had a network of informers and stooges across the city. He had been appointed chief by Massell in March 1972, after receiving a recommendation from Massell's controversial brother, Howard.

Inman made it well known that he would not leave his job without a fight. Besides, Inman said, his contract was signed under the old charter, stipulating an eight-year tenure. By that agreement, Inman contended he had six years still to serve.

On February 4, 1974, Maynard Jr. proposed a reorganization of city government, reducing twenty-six departments to nine super-agencies. His proposal called for a new level of top managers, called "commissioners," to whom department heads (now termed "bureau chiefs") would report. His announced intention was to create more efficiency in government, but it was clear that his plan also would neutralize John Inman. Inman would be made subservient to a new commissioner of public safety, or "superchief," who would oversee the police, fire and civil defense departments. When the mayor's reorganization plan passed the City Council on March 4, he announced that his search for a superchief would begin at once.

Inman filed suit in Fulton County Superior Court and a judge issued a restraining order barring the mayor from naming a superchief. Not until May 2, nearly two months later, did City Hall receive word that the restraining order was about to be lifted; Maynard Jr. told Sugarman, "I want [Inman] out the moment we can do it."

The next afternoon, the restraining order lifted, Sugarman and former Morehouse classmate A. Reginald Eaves, Jackson's chief of staff, met with Inman in the police chief's office. Expecting trouble, Eaves brought Eldrin Bell, a black policeman, and told him to stand outside the door with orders to enter at the first sound of discord. "I'll leave the door cracked," Eaves told Bell. Eaves and Sugarman sat before Inman. "[Inman] was playing games with us," Sugarman recalls. "He took out his revolver and started twirling it around. Reggie and I sort of moved apart so [if he fired] he wouldn't hit us both at the same time. It was pretty scary because Inman was so unpredictable." Sugarman told Inman he had been relieved of his duties. Inman showed little emotion. He was told that Capt. Clinton Chafin, a personal rival, had been named acting chief of police. Inman asked to come back Monday to clean out his desk.

When Inman returned on Monday, May 6, he found Chafin's car parked in the space allotted for the chief. He entered his office and brought twenty-five armed members of the city's Special Weapons and Tactics (SWAT) unit with him. Then he announced that he would not leave. A brief confrontation with Chafin ensued, a tense and confused moment: two chiefs, surrounded by twenty-five armed officers uncertain whose orders to take. Inman announced that Chafin had broken the law by serving as acting chief; though he was suspended himself, Inman told the press that he had suspended Chafin.

The scene was preposterous and reminded many of the three governors debacle of 1947 when Herman Talmadge's band of men had stormed the State Capitol. Maynard Jr. was out of town at the time. At City Hall, Sugarman heard reports from the police radio network that large numbers of black officers, enraged by Inman's coup, were en route to the police station to lend support to Chafin. Only after several intense moments did Inman leave the building, his battle still to be fought in court.

The story made national news that night, embarrassing Maynard Jackson. For the next ten weeks, a war was waged between Atlanta's black mayor and his white police chief, in the courts and in the press. It worked as a corrosive acid on Jackson's credibility, even in the black community, because it was taking so long to make good on his promise to remove Inman. This crisis threatened to drive a wedge more deeply between the races and to tear down the Jackson administration before it had had a chance to gain momentum. Quietly, the city offered Inman a new job, with a raise. He refused. The chamber leaders tried to meet with Inman, but he rebuffed their efforts, too.

The mayor's typical response to resistance was to try to overpower it. Maynard Jr. was at his political best as an advocate, fighting for a cause. He had helped to kill the proposed Interstate 485, which jeopardized in-town neighborhoods, and that advocacy had helped him garner support from whites during the 1973 mayor's race. Like Interstate 485, John Inman became a cause. "The best police chief Maynard ever had, in one sense, was Inman," Michael Lomax says, "because Inman was a foil. . . . Maynard had somebody he could say was the evil devil incarnate."

White business leaders had little affection for Inman, in part because they associated him with Sam Massell, never their favorite. Nevertheless, few white leaders were willing to publicly support Maynard Jr. in his struggle to remove Inman, a fact that registered clearly with the mayor.

Among blacks, the contempt for Inman deepened daily. The mayor determined to await the court's ruling. But when Inman commented publicly that City Hall had attacked him in every way except with "a hit man," Maynard Jr. could not contain his anger. He charged that, in an impassioned speech the *Constitution* called "the most extraordinary of his career," Inman and a group of conservative white businessmen were attempting to destroy his administration.

"I have tried to keep my peace as demagogues have pounced upon this situation and used it as a platform for racial polarizing, fear-mongering and the spewing of hatred," Maynard Jr. said on June 6, 1974. But silence, he said, no longer was possible. Recalling Inman's actions from the previous month, he added, "The spectacle of a man who is sworn to uphold the law, surrounding himself with understandably confused police officers armed with automatic weapons, and shouting his defiance from behind those men is one spectacle I hope I will never, never see repeated in our city." He also decried the call by members of "Inman's group" for state government to assume control of the Atlanta police force, a plan he viewed as racially motivated.

"I have come to believe," the mayor said, "that they are carefully calculated efforts to undermine confidence in government and public officials and to create an atmosphere of fear in which Mr. Inman and his colleagues may act at will unrestrained by any of the normal rules of government. It is you, the citizens of Atlanta, your husbands, children and families who would be the ultimate victims of such a plot."

The theme of this speech at Covenant Presbyterian Church was reminiscent of the Grand's Masonic oratory. Maynard Jr. had portrayed himself as the champion of the masses who had become the tragic-heroic victim of a "plot" constructed by evil-spirited men bent on deceiving and dividing his constituency. That much of what the mayor said that night was true, if somewhat overdramatized, failed to register among white business leaders, who became more certain that Maynard Jr. was a paranoid black mayor who cared more about his race than his city.

During these difficult times, Maynard Jackson, unlike Ivan Allen, Jr., in 1962, did not have friends at the white newspapers sympathetic to his administration. Even at the time of Allen's most egregious blunder as mayor—the erection of the Peyton Road barriers—Gene Patterson urged readers to focus on the mayor's many favorable achievements. By 1974, though, the more progressive editors, such as the late Ralph McGill and Patterson, who left for *The Washington Post* in 1968, had been succeeded by less forgiving writers.

In fighting the white newspapers, Maynard Jr. was fighting a battle he had little chance of winning. Throughout the century, the *Constitution* and the *Journal* had served as tireless boosters of Atlanta, and in the process assumed the perspectives, and biases, of the city's white business structure. This did not bode well for Maynard Jackson. One enduring journalistic trademark of Atlanta was a reluctance to write critically of the city's corporate heavyweights, such as the Georgia Power Company and the Coca-Cola Company.

The festering Inman problem was magnified when the Federal Bureau of Investigation, during the first quarter of 1974, rated Atlanta as the worst city in the country for per capita violent crime. Major crime in Atlanta, according to the Atlanta Crime Commission, had increased by nearly 300 percent since 1965, the middle of the Allen years. Neither Jenkins nor Inman had been able to stabilize the problem.

The pressures on Maynard Jr. mounted; the courts moved too slowly. He would not—could not—back down from Inman. To do so would be to lose public confidence in his administration. Blacks, meanwhile, could not afford for Atlanta's first black mayor to fail.

At City Hall, staff members saw signs of the mayor's personal strain. Tension in his marriage was growing. Occasionally, staffers heard him, in his office on the telephone, engaged in a shouting match with Bunnie. "You could tell Maynard was troubled," Sugarman says.

Soon after his election, Ivan Jr. had passed along a piece of advice to Maynard Jr. "When Peachtree Creek floods there may not be anything you can do about it, but be sure to go and wade out there to the middle, where the television cameras can see you, showing concern." In times of crisis, the people of Atlanta needed to know that their mayor was on the job.

Maynard Jr. knew he needed to respond to crime in a demonstrative way.

But how could he? "I wasn't talking to Inman that much," Sugarman says. "And anything that got done between them got done through me."

On June 29, a Sunday morning, Marcus Wayne Chenault, a deranged young black student from Ohio State University, carrying two pistols and claiming to be the "Servant Jacob," entered the Ebenezer Baptist Church on Sweet Auburn. He fired at random, killing a church deacon and seventy-year-old Alberta Williams King, the mother of the Rev. Martin Luther King, Jr., as she sat at the church organ playing "The Lord's Prayer."

Police learned later that Daddy King, who witnessed the shooting, had been Chenault's intended target. Now, with his wife and namesake son murdered, and a second son, the Rev. A. D. King, having drowned in a swimming pool accident, all within the span of six years, Daddy King had just one remaining member of his immediate family, daughter Christine King Ferris. "How much more can a man take?" the seventy-four-year-old minister asked an old friend.

Maynard Jr. arrived at Ebenezer just as word was announced inside the sanctuary that Alberta King was dead. His arrival was not merely a matter of *wading through the creek*. The Dobbses and the Kings had been friends for generations. Renie Dobbs had seen the romance of Daddy King and Alberta Williams blossom. Geekie and June had been friends with M.L. Jr.

"We need something from you now," Maynard Jr. told the members of the Ebenezer congregation. "The city needs you to be strong. Let's cry our tears in silence."

Finally, on July 3, the Georgia Supreme Court ruled that Atlanta's new city charter was constitutional. Though the court ruled that the mayor did not have unilateral power to fire Inman (because he had been hired under the old charter), the City Council could conduct a trial for his ouster. The court also allowed the mayor's reorganization plans, which meant Maynard Jr. could hire a superchief. Inman was forced to accept a diminished role as director of the Bureau of Police, where he completed his career in relative obscurity, far removed from City Hall. For the mayor, this victory was monumental.

The candidates for superchief included blacks and whites in law enforcement across the nation. Lee Brown, the black police chief in Portland, Oregon, seemed to be the top candidate until the mayor's interviews led him to believe that Brown did not possess a forceful personality. Finally, the mayor told Eaves, "I've got my candidate."

"Great," Eaves said, assuming the mayor had selected Brown.

"You're my candidate," the mayor said.

Eaves swallowed hard. He did not want the job. He still held the frightening image of John Inman and the gleam of the automatic weapons held by his twenty-five white commandos. "I'm not going over there," Eaves told the mayor. When Jule Sugarman learned of Jackson's intention to name Eaves, he understood the logic. "Maynard went from picking the person with the strongest qualifications," Sugarman says, "to picking a person he thought was politically supportive, a person he knew the best."

For nearly a month, Eaves resisted. Then, the mayor tried a new tactic. "He called back on my fraternity stuff, Morehouse stuff and friendship," Eaves says. Finally, Eaves relented.

When the mayor announced Reginald Eaves as his candidate for commissioner of public safety, the opposition was loud and immediate. Some charged his selection was a product of cronyism. ("I did not appoint him because of our friendship," Maynard Jr. responded, "but in spite of it.") City Council president Wyche Fowler, the *Journal* and the *Constitution*, and leaders of the Atlanta Crime Commission believed Eaves's arena was politics, not law enforcement.

Maynard Jr. was furious. He blamed the opposition on racism. The white newspapers recoiled, the *Journal* suggesting that the mayor's emotional blast "emphasizes the shaky ground on which this particular appointment rests." But in mid-August, with all nine black council members voting in support, Reginald Eaves was confirmed as the city's first public safety commissioner.

When he learned of the vote, Eaves sat in his office and held his head in his hands. "I did not want that job," he would say.

In time, Reggie Eaves would prove even more divisive than John Inman.

Across the nation, white-owned businesses in big cities were abandoning the urban core. In Atlanta, the problem was severe. Friends rushed to Sam Massell, who had predicted such a decline during the 1973 mayor's race, and told him, "Sam, you were right!" When photographs of Atlanta's decaying downtown business district appeared in local papers, Massell felt a small vindication. "It brought a smile to my face and a tear to my wife's," he says. The problem, however, had been building for some time.

On September 16, 1974, Central Atlanta Progress (CAP), an association of downtown businessmen and property owners, sent the mayor a letter with ominous overtones. Signed by Rich's chairman Harold

Brockey, the letter warned that crime and racial problems were among the primary reasons that businesses were leaving downtown Atlanta. The letter was accompanied by a fourteen-page addendum that included a sampling of comments made by some of the fifty business-men who had participated in a CAP discussion two weeks earlier. One comment noted the "perceived attitude of the mayor as anti-white."

The consensus among CAP members, Brockey wrote, was that the alliance between business and City Hall needed to be reforged in order to restore vitality to downtown. "The dilution of this partnership over the past five years has resulted in a major communications/action vac-uum," wrote Brockey, who also served as president of CAP.

At the time Maynard Jr. entered office, armed with his arsenal of ideas and moral lessons, he had established virtually no personal relationships with the white business community. Years later, he would say, "I knew but did not fully appreciate the extent to which relationships made the difference. I really still, naively, thought that issues would carry the day, that if you were right, and that I, the lawyer, could bring forth the case or the point, that that would carry it. I now understand, in my more mature years, that the reverse is the case: the first thing that must be established is the relationship. People cannot hear the facts if they do not trust you. Trust is something that develops because they get to know you and to see that you don't have horns."

He made attempts to establish the relationship. He held several "Pound Cake Summits" in his City Hall office with the city's economic leaders. Informal discussions conceived as constructive give-and-take sessions, they didn't work. The hostility and distrust were visible through the transparent courtesies. "The two times I went," says Bob Holder, president of the Holder Construction Company, " 'give-and-take' consisted of somebody asking a question and fifty-nine minutes later Maynard's monologue ended. His monologue would become, in about the tenth or fifteenth minute, a lecture and, by the end, was a total harangue about his discomfort, his insecurity and his paranoia about things. It was just a complete turnoff. He by us, and us by him. So I quit going to these breakfasts because I thought they were depressing and they reinforced my theory that the mayor was a bad guy."

The white businessmen of Atlanta now longed for the days of Ivan Allen, Jr. Then, they had not only a friend but one of their own in City Hall. They missed their easy access to power. During a period of eco-nomic tension and constant strife with a black mayor, their fondness for Ivan Jr. bordered on hero worship. They romanticized about the former mayor to a degree that made one local columnist wonder if on "some

Tuesday soon [Allen] may be declared a saint, stuffed, and placed in living color in Central City Park."

Since leaving City Hall nearly five years earlier, Ivan Jr. had kept a low public profile. At sixty-three, he was a vintage Atlanta patrician, working at the Ivan Allen Company and spending leisure time at exclusive golf and social clubs.

When the Atlanta Board of Realtors sponsored a public forum on September 25, 1974, entitled "Atlanta—Where Do We Go From Here?" both Allen and Jackson participated. A panel of white business leaders suggested that blacks in Atlanta needed to worry less about maintaining political control of the city and more about the welfare of the city. The business group, which included former governor Carl Sanders, called for a study of a new metropolitan-wide form of government linking counties. The group also called for a second airport north of the city, near the predominantly white suburbs from which the airlines contended they would draw most of their clientele. Sanders said Maynard Jr. ought to stop "pussyfooting" with the idea of a second airport south of the city, nearer the black community.

Ivan Jr. agreed with most of Sanders's forcefully expressed views but spoke with a broader understanding than his business peers, casting blame on whites as well as blacks.

"Too many of us have been too concerned to see the failure of a black government here," he said. "Unless we can rise above racial prejudices, on both sides, as much on the Black Side as on the White Side; unless we can get ourselves together, we're going to kill ourselves by crying in our own soup."

Ivan Jr. recognized that annexation of white districts to the north of the city, such as Sandy Springs, was a double-edged sword: whites in those districts did not want to pay for services used by the black underclass, while blacks in the city did not want to yield to whites a political majority that had required more than a century to build.

"White people in the suburbs will have to give up their prejudices," Ivan Jr. said, "and the blacks in the city will have to give up their selfishness about not wanting to dilute their power."

Privately, Ivan Jr. worried about his city and its first black mayor. He thought Maynard Jackson too combative. He also believed Jackson's staff was ridiculously bloated and as a result unnecessarily expensive to taxpayers. (With reorganization, Maynard Jr. had a staff of more than thirty, compared with Allen's staff of ten.)

But as a matter of principle, Ivan Jr. never criticized Maynard Jr. in public, as Massell often did. In fact, Allen rooted for Jackson to succeed.

The success of a black mayor, he believed, would be a success that belonged to Atlanta.

Some of the former mayor's social peers viewed Maynard Jr. with contempt. A few even blamed the city's ills on Allen, recalling his testimony for integrating public accommodations more than a decade earlier. One acquaintance approached Ivan Jr. at the Piedmont Driving Club and got right to the point.

"Now that you have given these Niggers all these rights," he asked, "what're you gonna do about the way they conduct government?"

Among white civic elites, a star was rising. His name was Ivan Allen III. He was gentlemanly, though to those who did not know him intimately he could seem aloof and cold. Not handsome in the classic sense, as was his younger brother Inman, everything about his appearance seemed solid and effective. Ivan III was a young man with a big heart and often wrote thoughtful personal notes to employees at the Ivan Allen Company. With his wife, Margaret, he had two children, a boy and a girl. By the time he came of age as a civic player in Atlanta, his father's long shadows cast across the city and those shadows covered him as well.

Over time it became clear that Ivan III was driven, absolutely, by a sense of duty to his family, his city and, above all, his name.

Like his grandfather and father, he was gung ho and optimistic, though he preferred to work in the background, Woodruff-like. He lacked his father's native courtliness and charisma. The more he was asked about his father's accomplishments, and about whether he would continue the legacy, the more Ivan III settled into the background, working for good causes, working not to be noticed.

Close friends knew him as an occasional prankster and as a man who loved the outdoors. But his no-nonsense quality predominated. Ivan III set goals and achieved them. When a decision had to be made, he made it. That was his *modus operandi* as president of the Ivan Allen Company, a role he assumed in 1971, and as fund-raiser for a wide array of groups, such as the Boy Scouts, the United Way and Westminster. He had little patience with bureaucratic red tape. He worked hard—harder than hard—and he worked often. He was not a social climber, or even a social clubber, though, from a sense of family duty, he was a member of all the proper Atlanta clubs.

"Every now and then, when the Atlanta Chamber of Commerce runs out of other names," the *Constitution* wrote in December 1974, "Ivan Allen turns up president again."

A dozen years had passed since Ivan III had returned to Atlanta from the navy, and his ascent to the presidency of the Atlanta chamber reassured Old Atlanta's elite white families; to them, the idea of having an Ivan Allen involved in local leadership was a comforting sign of continuity in their city.

At thirty-six, Ivan III was the youngest president in the modern history of the Atlanta chamber. His rise made the Ivan Allens the only family to produce three generations of presidents at the Atlanta chamber. His career took root in the accepted ways of Old Atlanta. Not only had he risen to the presidency of the family business, he was deeply involved in community service. His mentor, Bill Pressly, headmaster of Westminster, had shared long conversations with Ivan Jr. about Ivan III during the 1960s on their return trips from the Allen vacation home at Lake Toxaway, North Carolina. Pressly recalls, "I was conscious then that Ivan Jr. was stimulating Ivan III for civic service. . . . We were all stimulating him to keep up with his grandfather and his father."

During 1975, the year of his chamber presidency, with young children at home, Ivan III was drawn into the vortex of civic leadership in Atlanta. In her daily calendar book, Margaret wrote, night after night after night: "Ivan Out." "Ivan Out." "Ivan Out."

As chamber presidents, the Senator in 1917 had called for more smokestacks in Atlanta; Ivan Jr. in 1961 had called for widespread downtown construction and for open schools in the face of court-ordered desegregation in Atlanta; and Ivan III, assuming the presidency of the Atlanta chamber on December 4, 1974, called for a mutual understanding between the races, a coming together of the black mayor and the cadre of white business leaders in the name of economic development in the city. He also called for opening international air routes.

"The Chamber and city government cannot and will not agree on every issue," Ivan III said at the Fairmont Colony Square Hotel. "But we can work harder on cooperating, and we can work to resolve our differences quietly and effectively.

"Today, as our black community exercises its role in the leadership of Atlanta, the entire community will benefit," he said. "The opportunity must not be lost in ill-founded fears, but captured through commitment to full participation in economic growth."

If Ivan Jr. had "developed a social conscience late in life," his son became a progressive in his racial views at a much younger age. His schoolboy friend Mason Lowance, Jr., recalls that Ivan III refused to listen to racial jokes; he would interrupt and put an end to the joke or simply walk away. During the 1960s, Ivan III was a leader of the Atlanta Jaycees and sought to build bridges with the black community. "We had a big luncheon at the Dinkler Hotel once," Ivan III recalls with relish. "We had a big crowd to hear Lester Maddox. When the [Jaycee official] announced, 'Next week's speaker will be Dr. Martin Luther King, Jr.,' there was big applause and Lester turned red." As Ivan III recounted this story, his eyes were alight with joy. He was involved with the 1969 founding of Leadership Atlanta, an organization that brought together young leaders of both races. In the background, he also labored in the early 1970s to help blacks break down barriers in Atlanta's social and business clubs. In May 1972, he co-sponsored the first black members of the Commerce Club—developer Herman Russell, realtors Bill Calloway and T. M. Alexander, and Vice Mayor Maynard Jackson. In 1972, his sponsorship allowed Morehouse College president Hugh Gloster to became the first black member of the Atlanta Rotary Club. Impressed by the sincerity of Ivan III, Gloster landed the former mayor's son as a Morehouse trustee in 1973. Along with elites such as Morris Abram, banker George Craft and attorney Hughes Spalding, Jr., Ivan III joined a board that also included Mayor Maynard Jackson. The majority of the Morehouse trustees were white, and many were from the North, including Chairman Charles Merrill, of the Merrill-Lynch family. "I tried to get people who were wealthy and who were deeply interested in elevating the status of blacks in the United States," Gloster says. "Ivan III was a great leader with a great desire to improve race relations."

In the fall of 1974, when most white families on the north side had removed their children from public schools rather than face court-ordered integration, the Allens sent their son, Ivan IV, to the Warren T. Jackson Elementary School, a public school that attracted children from some of the city's noted black families. Eleven-year-old Ivan IV was joined at the school the following year by seven-year-old Brooke Jackson, the mayor's daughter, though they were in different classes.

Suddenly, two decades after *Brown v. Board of Education*, the great-grandchildren of John Wesley Dobbs and Ivan Allen, Sr., shared the same school.

But when the city discussed adding a new dimension to its desegregation scheme, pairing schools in white districts with those in black districts, it opened the possibility that six-year-old Amanda Allen, younger sister of Ivan IV, would be bused across town to the predominantly black West Manor Elementary School.

"We were all for public education but we were for public education in our own neighborhood," Margaret recalls. "We weren't ready to send a six-year-old on a bus." And so Ivan IV and Amanda were sent to private school at Westminster, their parents' alma mater.

The Allen and Dobbs children shared the same school for only one year.

Muhammad Ali's eyes grew wide just thinking about Maynard Jackson. "He's so big," Ali cooed. "He's like a balloon. If you hit him, he'll bust."

In a playful moment in January 1975 the mayor took on the heavyweight champion in a one-round exhibition for charity. Ten thousand people showed up at the Southeastern Fairgrounds to witness a scene that bordered on the absurd: the sleek Ali matched against a bulbous mayor dressed in black boxing shoes, red-striped socks, an Atlanta Falcons T-shirt and baggy paisley shorts pulled high on his mountainous girth. As referee, state senator Julian Bond, between the two fighters, appeared so thin as to look like a child's stick figure drawing. Before the fight, the mayor turned poetic and, mimicking Ali's fanciful style, said, "They tell me the champ is Muhammad Ali, But that's just because he never fought me. . . . Liston is strong and Foreman was tough, But when you mess with the 'Big M' the going is rough!" Ali made a pantomimed fall to the canvas and the Big M claimed victory.

In his State of the City address earlier that month, Maynard Jr. said, "Not since the 1930s have as many people in our city suffered from such a poor economy as now." But the mayor also said the city now had 50 percent more police officers patrolling its streets than before he had named Reggie Eaves as his superchief. Yes, the mayor admitted, crime had increased by 7 percent in Atlanta, but that rate was less than the 16 percent increase across the nation, and the 20 percent increase in the Atlanta suburbs.

"We will succeed," Maynard Jr. said with flourish, "because our foundation does not rest on the sands of despair; it is rooted in the bedrock of our hopes, our dreams, our hard work and our willingness to stand together to make this truly the world's next great city."

The Atlanta police force remained the mayor's Achilles' heel. Every day, it seemed, there emerged a new controversy concerning Reggie Eaves. In February 1975, his twenty-year-old nephew, Larry Eaves, obtained one of 225 Comprehensive Employment Training Act (CETA) jobs for which nearly 4,000 had applied. The younger Eaves said, "My uncle told me the people to see at City Hall." A public outcry prompted Larry Eaves to quit his job several days later because "it was too much of a hassle." Years later, Reggie Eaves would say that his nephew had been given a job raking leaves, though, as superchief, he had never been told about it. Later in February, city officials discovered that Eaves had sidestepped official procedures by hiring as his personal secretary Daniel

Odum of Brooklyn, New York. Odum had a criminal record that included convictions for possession of drugs and illegal draft cards. His hiring prompted the Georgia State Intelligence Network in late March to suspend the Atlanta Bureau of Police from membership, thereby denying the bureau access to the intelligence files of other law enforcement agencies. Eaves insisted that Odum had never been exposed to sensitive information.

Reggie Eaves was a fighter. He was a dark-complexioned man from Jacksonville, Florida, with almond-shaped eyes. His father was a native of the West Indies, a railroad man who married a black Jew, converted and later became a rabbi. The ninth of thirteen children, Reggie Eaves was raised Jewish. During his days at Morehouse in the middle 1950s, Eaves was known to classmates as "Mister Civil Rights." While at Morehouse, he once participated in a boycott of Atlanta's Jim Crow buses. Taking his seat in the front of the bus, he refused to move to the back when asked. A white girl he had known years before was sitting in an adjacent seat. Spotting him, she called out to him. He did not react. She asked, "Reginald, don't you know me?" Eaves had been forewarned by NAACP leaders that fraternizing with a white woman could jeopardize a protest. He steadfastly refused to acknowledge her acquaintance. "Guess I have the wrong guy," she said, finally.

Eaves would become a double-edged sword of the Jackson administration, proof of racial advancement and tenacity. On his first day as Atlanta's superchief in August 1974, Eaves said, "Things will remain the same at least until tomorrow." And he meant it. In short order, four assistant police chiefs, six majors and fifty-seven sergeants were demoted. The Fraternal Order of Police responded by charging Eaves with reverse discrimination.

Like Maynard Jr., Eaves attempted to play hardball with white leaders, but lacked the mayor's command and personal skills. His popularity among blacks grew steadily as charges of police brutality against blacks declined precipitously. He aimed to change attitudes, white and black, and flexed his political muscle to do it. When a group of white businessmen asked for additional policemen in downtown, fearing crime would detract from tourism, Eaves not only refused but said he intended to remove officers from downtown and place them in black areas where the crime rate was higher. Statistics aside, the white leaders were aghast. Years later, one Chamber of Commerce leader recalled Eaves as "slippery as a snake in lard."

Reggie Eaves became every worst nightmare to the white business elites. As his political missteps increased, white leaders pressured the mayor to fire him. On April 14, Maynard Jr. publicly reiterated his confidence in Eaves but announced that his role as superchief was designed as interim. Though this was true (Eaves had agreed to take the job for two years but asked that the interim nature remain confidential so as not to undermine his effectiveness), Eaves understood that the mayor was caught between politics and friendship.

Two days later, on April 16, 1975, Maynard Jr. and several of his aides met with Eaves at his home. During his eight months as superchief, Eaves had accepted criticism from whites as inevitable, but believed Atlanta's blacks had appreciated his work. In Eaves's living room, however, one of the mayor's aides said, "Not one black person in this town is willing to stand up for you." The comment hurt. Eaves already had offered to resign. He had told the mayor that he was considering a move back to Boston. Now, hearing the criticism from a black aide, Eaves told the mayor and his aides, "You can take this position and stick it up your ass."

Later that morning City Council president Wyche Fowler, in a press conference, demanded Eaves's resignation. "He has abused [the mayor's] confidence," Fowler said.

Eaves returned to his office in late morning, intending to resign. Press secretary Pearl Lomax arrived to help him write his resignation letter, but before doing so, she wanted Eaves to clear his thoughts, to consider all of the variables. They went for a drive. Passing through the west side, Pearl Lomax reminded Eaves of his historic role as the city's first black head of police and of the fact that Atlantans—black Atlantans—knew he was making a difference in their lives. No longer were they being called "Boy" or "Girl" by city policemen. Police brutality was disappearing, in part because the mayor had sent down the word—any policeman, black or white, found guilty of brutality would be fired and vulnerable to prosecution by the district attorney. Eaves appreciated Pearl Lomax's kind words but had made up his mind. A press conference was called for that afternoon. As word of Eaves's plan to resign leaked out, a group of black policemen and local black politicians, including City Councilman Arthur Langford and Fulton Commissioner Henry Dodson, converged on Eaves's office. They told him not to give in to white threats. Maj. Claude Dixon, one of Atlanta's first black policemen, walked in and put his fists on Eaves's desk. As the blood drained from his knuckles, Dixon said, "For the first time in twenty-seven years I feel like a man. I feel like a police officer with authority. Do you know what kind of support you have?"

Tears formed in Eaves's eyes. It was past four o'clock, the announced hour of the press conference. Eaves apologized to everyone in his office. He said he had no choice but to resign. He opened a back door leading to the conference room where the press waited. What he saw in the back hallway stunned him: a group of black policemen blocking his path. Stepping forward, one said, "You can fire me, but when you quit it doesn't mean anything. And if you don't quit, I'll take the consequences."

Eaves returned to his desk and telephoned Maynard Jackson. Together, Atlanta's first black mayor and first black police chief determined to hold firm—Reggie Eaves would remain. The press conference canceled, reporters and Eaves's supporters waited beside his car in the parking lot. But Eaves snuck out a back door, through the city jail, where a friend drove him away. "You're a helluva man," a black officer told Eaves as he left. The superchief smiled and said, "Yes, I am."

Though often charged by whites with being anti-business, Maynard Jr. supported virtually every major development initiative during his mayoralty, including projects inherited by his administration such as MARTA rail line construction and the slum clearance and revitalization of the Bedford-Pine district. What prompted much of the grumbling by white business elites was having to conduct business with a mayor they perceived as self-absorbed, demanding of their respect and bent on helping blacks at the expense of whites. Yet Maynard Jr. formed his social programs not to obstruct development but in a way that conformed to it; he aimed to give blacks a larger piece of the economic pie while, at the same time, increasing the size of the pie.

Other cities were putting affirmative action programs into place, but few local governments pursued their goals as vigorously as Atlanta. Jackson established a goal of 25 percent minority involvement in all municipal contracts, either directly or through limited "joint-venture" partnerships with white-owned companies. Stricter contract language allowed the city to unilaterally declare a breach of contract and to seek damages. Maynard Jr. met periodically with aggrieved white contractors "to let them know this was not a blindly unfeeling government but that our policies were going be put in place. No matter what." When he enforced his joint-venture program in the construction of the $400 million airport terminal, all hell broke loose. It had taken years to even make the final decision to expand the Atlanta airport rather than to build a second facility. To make the expansion, an interstate had to be moved, no small obstacle. Astutely, Maynard Jr. had sought the help of his former opponent, U.S. Sen. Herman Talmadge. Talmadge arranged a meeting with several dozen local, state and federal bureaucrats in his crowded Washington office. There, he spoke of how an expanded airport would benefit all of Georgia, and the entire southeast. When an official from the federal highway department balked, saying, "If we do it this time, we'll be moving expressways all over the nation," Talmadge used a power play. "I understand how difficult it is to make decisions. When I review your budget, I find myself unable to make a decision and *that may be the case even more so in the future.*" After a short break, the highway official returned, suddenly a supporter.

But over the ensuing months white contractors argued with Maynard Jr. over his minority programs, insisting there were only a handful of eligible black firms, most of them unqualified. The airlines, already locked in to pay for the construction, announced their refusal to fund the mayor's social agenda. Jackson was unshakable, immovable. In 1974, he said minority contractors earned little more than one percent of the $73 million in city contracts. "Now, if anxiety attaches when the black community gets one percent . . . just imagine what happens when we double it to two percent," he said. The airport impasse would last about a year, raising tensions in the city. Gov. George Busbee fretted over the impact of delays, and the legislature once again pondered turning over airport management to a new state authority.

Technically, affirmative action programs had started in September 1965, eight years before Maynard Jackson was elected, when President Lyndon Johnson signed Executive Order 11246. At the time, affirmative action required only that employers search for qualified minority applicants and then make a hiring decision without reference to color. But over the ensuing years, as the federal government stepped up its minority preference programs, so did many cities. Soon after his election as San Diego's mayor, Pete Wilson in 1971 persuaded the city council to adopt a five-year plan to increase the number of minorities hired to city government as well as the number of minority-owned companies doing business with the city.

In Atlanta, Maynard Jr. felt the weight of morality on his side. Such changes, he knew, had to be made. As a matter of principle, he also refused to set foot inside the Piedmont Driving Club as long as blacks were unable to join as members. When invited to a function at the Driving Club, he sent a letter, asking that the site be changed; sometimes it was. He governed with total fidelity to such principles, and the results were beginning to show. In 1975, the percentage of city contracts in Atlanta awarded to minorities reached 5 percent.

As Atlanta Chamber of Chamber president, Ivan Allen III tried to mediate in the airport struggle between the white businessmen and the black mayor.

"You know, Maynard," Ivan III said, "you need to understand that these [white] people are trying to adjust, and they don't understand why you are pushing so hard."

For the first time in his life, Ivan III stepped into the spotlight. He sought to become, like his father before him, a bridge of compassion and pragmatism between the races in the city. "It is time to stop talking about 'we' in the white community and 'they' in the black community," Ivan III had told a black audience at the Butler Street YMCA early in 1975. "If I may be forgiven a cliché, we are all in this together, and it is time we ended the kind of politics of confrontation which has characterized many of our efforts in the past." He also asserted a commitment to restoring vitality to downtown. "Atlanta is here to stay and we in the business community are going to stay and grow with her."

The chamber attempted to counteract the adverse publicity with a national advertising campaign that praised the can-do qualities of Atlanta. In one advertisement, published on *The New York Times* opinion page on March 12, U.S. congressman Andrew Young, dressed in a sweater and standing in the woods, was quoted saying that no problem "is too big for this city to solve." A former aide to the Rev. Martin Luther King, Jr., Young also was quoted saying, "Atlanta doesn't live by its fears and anxieties. It lives by its hopes and aspirations. And it doesn't matter what color the leadership is. The most important thing is that we have people who are willing to work together."

By late March, Maynard Jr. seemed all but buried by criticism. In a seven-part series entitled "A City in Crisis," the *Constitution* laid waste to his administration. Based on interviews with thirty city leaders, the series concluded that the city's first black mayor had caused the rift between the races to widen. "Camelot has faded," the newspaper contended. Some city leaders were even more harsh. "I'm ready to give up," John Portman, Atlanta's leading downtown developer, said. And banker Mills B. Lane, now retired and moved to Savannah, added, "Maynard Jackson's no good. He's lazy on top of everything else. Damn, when Ivan was mayor he ran around in a little Ford. This guy's got a big black Lincoln as big as anything Mr. Woodruff had." The newspaper reported alarming demographic shifts, namely the exodus of whites from the city. "Can I deliver what I think is important?" Maynard Jr. told the newspaper. "The answer is yes, but it will take longer." The *Economist* of London had published a biting profile of Atlanta earlier that month, reprinted in the *Constitution* on April 3. The story contended that many charges against Atlanta's black mayor were unreasonable. But the *Economist* also wrote of the black mayor, "For a nice guy with good intentions, he seems to have lost a lot of friends in just one year." The American

South's city of glory from the 1960s now had a murder rate that exceeded Ulster's in Northern Ireland, the *Economist* reported, though its downtown commercial building boom continued. "The only way this could all go sour is if the city loses its precarious self-confidence and succumbs to internecine warfare. . . . Atlanta could join the urban cadavers of the north." It was as if Sam Massell's campaign ad was coming to life.

In responding to the negativism, Maynard Jr. borrowed a phrase from Franklin Roosevelt's 1933 inaugural address. Atlanta, the mayor said, had "nothing to fear but fear itself."

In both the *Constitution* and the *Economist*, a rumor spreading throughout Atlanta's boardrooms for months was put into print. The British newspaper referred to Ivan Allen III not only as chamber president and son of the former mayor but as "a possible successor to Mr. Jackson." Ivan III told the *Constitution* that he often was asked if he intended to follow his father into City Hall. "I think it's a natural reaction for somebody to have," he said. "But I have not got any inclinations in that direction."

Nevertheless, the rumor of his impending mayoral candidacy fast was becoming an expectation. Maynard Jackson had heard it himself.

On the same day the *Economist* story was printed in Atlanta, Maynard Jr. and Ivan III were together, with their wives, in Paris.

They were attempting to attract new international commerce to the city, including an air route between Paris and Atlanta. Already, Ivan III had been in London to speak with officials there about a London–Atlanta route. The French-owned Michelin Tire Company recently had made a $200 million investment in a plant in South Carolina; Maynard Jr. and Ivan III hoped to bring the same sort of development to Atlanta.

This was the first real opportunity for the Allens and Jacksons to get to know one another, though their schedule was tight: a series of meetings and appearances in just seventy-two hours.

As director of the city's Bureau of Cultural and International Affairs, Michael Lomax accompanied the couples. He noticed the peculiar relationship between them. "It was a strange trip," Lomax says, "because obviously there was tension in Maynard's marriage and Margaret [Allen] was the southern lady and so she was going to smile and be gracious always. . . . Bunnie hated politics. She was not a happy camper; we were always worried about her being pissed off or not doing something. She was tough to manage."

Bunnie and Margaret walked through an outdoor flea market in Paris, then visited the Hermès factory where fine scarfs and pocketbooks were made. To Bunnie, the Allens were "just political people. I didn't know them at all." Her conversations with Margaret barely scratched the surface. "We only talked about babies and schools," Bunnie remembers.

Michael Lomax also detected an uneasiness in the dialogue between the two Atlanta civic leaders. "There was tension between Maynard and Ivan because there was still some sense that Ivan might challenge him at some point politically. I think in the black community we knew that there would be a Great White Hope who would try to come back and take the city over again. And if not Ivan Allen III, who?"

Close friends of Ivan Jr. often asked about his son's political aspirations. The former mayor talked with his son about City Hall and his message was plain: "There is no way to defeat the black vote. I don't care how liberal or well respected or what name you carry, it's not going to get you in office. No white man is going to run [and win] against the black ticket."

Ivan III agreed with this assessment. During 1975, he told a chamber colleague, "We're going to see black mayors for the next fifty years in Atlanta. [But] we've got somebody [now] who can do the job. Let's rally around Maynard. If we're going to build this city, we've got to help him."

In Paris, Allen and Jackson met with high-level public officials, including the French secretary of transportation, the directors of the rapid transit and airport authorities and American ambassador Kenneth Rush. Ivan III was astonished by the mayor's energy and his ability to turn his intensity on and off. "Maynard would say he wanted to meet at 5:30 for a briefing for our 7:30 breakfast," Ivan III says. "We'd get in cars to go across Paris and Maynard would put his head back on the seat and sleep. I couldn't do that." Maynard Jr. admired Ivan III for his dependability and optimism. "He was always punctual, always positive." At functions, Maynard Jr. spoke often of his parents' marriage in France. He had lost the fluency in French that Renie had helped him achieve as a boy, but in speeches still was able to quote French writer Albert Camus.

Despite their optimism, the mayor and Ivan III were unconvincing in their presentations to the airlines. "We bragged that Hartsfield [airport] was an international gateway," Ivan III recalls, with a hint of laughter. "There was only one flight a week to Mexico City on Eastern."

At Orly airport, French officials remembered how another Ivan Allen had paid a somber visit in 1962 after the Air France tragedy. "There was a real sensitivity about that," Ivan III says. He sensed that French officials were honored to have the former mayor's son in their midst. During the trip, a floral gift was made to the American Cathedral in Paris in memory of Atlantans who had perished in that crash.

On April 4, Jackson and Allen addressed the prestigious French Manufacturers Association at the Centre Français du Commerce Extérieur. Ivan III spoke first, his theme, "Atlanta As Commercial Center." Maynard Jr. spoke of "Atlanta and the New South." Ivan III had taken public speaking lessons. He spoke capably but with little flair. He used few personal anecdotes and usually seemed in a hurry to finish. His voice was more cosmopolitan than his father's. His years at Princeton, and overseas, while in the navy, had diluted the unmistakable sound of the Old South that was evident in his father's speech. When Maynard Jr. spoke, he commanded instant attention. He told French businessmen that 480 of the top 500 American corporations had offices in Atlanta. "The gates of Atlanta are open wide. The doors to our hearts are also open wide. We invite you to join in the adventure of building the New South," he said. "We invite you to become a part of the most successful city in America—Atlanta." He concluded by delivering a few words in French.

"Maynard was sort of a really dramatic individual for them, as the first black mayor of any southern city," Ivan III says. "His press had preceded him."

Lomax recalls, "Maynard was at his absolute best on that trip. It was Maynard in his element. No mayor of a small southern city ever got the attention he got."

The differences in style between Maynard Jr. and Ivan III were obvious. "Ivan was not a scintillating speaker, but Ivan was to the manor born," Lomax says. "Ivan was as comfortable amongst the French power structure and elite as Maynard was shining among them. . . . They had met Ivan Allens before, [but] they had never met or seen a Maynard Jackson."

The Jackson-Allen relationship was mutually respectful, although during the trip they shared no personal breakthrough; a closer friendship did not develop. "Ivan III was a little stiff for me," Maynard Jr. says. "I get close with people who want to let their hair down. He and I had a business friendship . . . it was not a buddy thing."

Lomax saw another dimension to the relationship. "Maynard," he says, "is an extraordinarily guarded individual. He gives up very little of himself and is very protective, very careful."

Besides, there were political ramifications to this relationship. "I don't think Maynard said anything to Ivan that could, in any way, come back to haunt him," Lomax says.

Typical of the fact they came from parallel societies in Atlanta, Jackson and Allen had a couple dozen chances to talk intimately during this trip, but never did.

# CHAPTER 26

Maynard Jr. had been a smoker for years, though few knew it. In times of stress, which now seemed to be every waking hour, the mayor turned to cigarettes.

Once, while sitting with press aide JacLyn Morris in his black Lincoln en route to Hartsfield airport, the mayor smoked as they discussed his upcoming appearances. Morris was an enthusiastic, diminutive white woman, barely five feet tall, who playfully fancied her high heels as "my corrective shoes." She joined the mayor's staff soon after Pearl Lomax had left, beginning what would become a revolving door of Jackson press aides. The pattern was always the same—each new press aide arrived with enthusiasm, proud to be a part of the Jackson urban idealism, only to wear out from carrying bad news to the mayor from the newspapers, and vice versa.

Only recently a friend of Morris's had stopped at a downtown traffic light and tossed out a cigarette. Suddenly, in a nearby car, a window opened and there sat the mayor of Atlanta, a stickler for litter, frowning. The mayor's glare prompted Morris's friend to get out of her car and pick up the cigarette. She drove away, embarrassed, and without comment.

Now, as Maynard Jr. finished his cigarette, he lowered the back window and flicked it outside, somewhere along Interstate 75.

"I can't believe you just did that," Morris told him. "You, 'The King of Anti-Littering.'"

The mayor shrugged.

"We're past the city limits," he said.

Then he went back to studying his notes.

Maynard Jackson believed in testing limits. More than merely his nature, it was his purpose. Because he was the South's first black mayor, his every comment was significant, his every action *history-making*. As mayor, he won many battles, personal and political, large and small, through sheer resolve. He proved innovative on several fronts. He championed the neighborhood movement, creating planning units that gave representation to a previously marginal group. Borrowing from his own upbringing, he breathed life into the arts in Atlanta, even creating a Bureau of Cultural Affairs. He formed the Atlanta Economic Development Corporation, to bring much-needed private funds into the public sphere. He hired more blacks and women to city government than any Atlanta mayor ever had. He pursued affirmative action programs with such vigor and aggressiveness that some of his black friends became fearful of a white backlash and urged him to slow his pace. Criticism from white business leaders was muted in part by the adverse affect white flight was having on their investments in downtown; to criticize the mayor was to give white in-town residents one more reason to leave. Rarely were the mayor's causes, or tastes, in doubt. He redecorated his outer office at City Hall in an African motif with hide-bound chairs and prints of jungle scenes, and this, too, made a statement.

To his staff, Maynard Jr. was a visionary who seemed to produce a thousand ideas per minute in meetings, some grand and dreamy. Frequently, he had little understanding of how to execute his ideas, though aides rarely challenged him. "Maynard did not encourage [staffers] to say, 'Wait a minute. Do you realize this [idea] is going to take ten staff people twenty-four hours a day for seven days to do half of what you want to do?'" one aide recalls. To his staff, he spoke often of his fervent desire to aid Atlanta's poor, in particular, poverty-stricken blacks. By eradicating police brutality and creating jobs (thousands at the airport alone) he began to make inroads.

As competition for power raged among blacks, and hostility emanated from whites, City Hall during these years was a solitary vessel riding stormy seas, its passengers uncomfortable in tight quarters. From the beginning, Reggie Eaves and David Franklin were less than compatible. Eaves played a mean old-style politics he had brought from Boston. He luxuriated in the role of superchief. He had his own driver and bodyguard. He wore two guns, one under his shoulder, the other at his ankle. His popularity among blacks prompted whispers of a future career in elective politics.

Franklin was a creative, if undisciplined, political strategist, who, though not a City Hall staffer, sought to maneuver white and black power brokers in the city as pawns and rooks in his own chess game. He flaunted his victories and rubbed his opponents' noses in their defeats. Often he was portrayed as a shadowy figure who pulled the strings at City Hall, a portrayal he did little to discourage. Most of the mayor's staff was unclear about the role of the mayor's close friend and former law partner. They knew only that Franklin was a deal-maker who had the mayor's ear at all times.

As Franklin saw it, he was a mayoral advisor without title who "had a wider breadth of experience than the other advisors." He had enormous respect for Maynard Jr., knew his strengths and weaknesses intimately, and intervened in city affairs only when he thought he could help. In 1974, Franklin had explained his decision to return to Atlanta from Washington. "I knew Maynard was going to run for Mayor, and that we were going to open up this city." His perception of his own role seemed clear—Maynard Jr. runs for office and then *we* govern. Though Bunnie had her doubts about Franklin—"I used to say to Maynard, 'You can't trust him.' And Maynard used to get mad at me," she says—close friends understood that the mayor trusted him, unequivocally. Maynard Jr. trusted Franklin despite his penchant for making controversy. In October 1975, a white architect charged Franklin with threatening to cancel the city's airport contract if his firm did not hire a minority joint-venture partner. Franklin denied the charge and a federal grand jury investigation found little to support it. In truth, city politics was only Franklin's hobby; entertainment management was his career.

Franklin had supported Lee Brown for superchief in 1974, and by the spring of 1975 his mistrust of Eaves was so severe he mailed a letter to himself, predicting, he recalls, "I would be stopped one night by police and they would claim they found drugs in my car. And I predicted it would be orchestrated by Reggie Eaves." Franklin feared a setup that people might be inclined to believe. ("I'm an entertainment lawyer and manager and what do people in entertainment do? *They do drugs, right?*" Franklin says decades later.) He placed his postmarked letter in a safe-deposit box at the Trust Company, "as my safety valve." His concern proved unwarranted.

Tiring from the bickering, Maynard Jr. called Eaves and Franklin into his office. "I'm not going to tolerate this," he told them. "Cut it out!" In uncharted political waters, Maynard Jr. needed harmony within his staff. "There had been no other black mayor of a southern city," Bunnie says. "Where did [Maynard] go to for advice?" He had plenty of friends, but no mentors. "Lonely" is how he would remember his emotions at the time, "very lonely." Maynard Jr. answered only to himself and to the people he thought he was representing.

He governed, like his grandfather before him, by force of personality, cognizant of the historic fact, as he later wrote, that "among the greatest contributions I can make to our just cause is to show Atlanta and the world that this diverse city can be governed fairly and effectively by a black mayor." He demanded total adherence to his policies from City Council members. "If they ever disagreed with him, they were off his list," chief aide Jule Sugarman recalls. "He didn't want anything to do with them, or even to communicate with them." George Berry, a favorite among white businessmen who would replace Sugarman in 1976, remembers. "You'd go into Maynard's office and he'd puff himself up and make a long speech. Just the two of us would be in there. Somebody would ask me, 'What's Maynard Jackson really like?' I would say, 'Same as he is when he gives a speech.' I think he makes speeches to himself." Berry noticed the curious manner in which Maynard Jr. verbally worked out his problems. The more he talked about a problem, the clearer it became in his mind. As a result, when a group of Boy Scouts arrived for a photograph with the mayor, he soon was lecturing them about the intimate details of a garbage workers' strike.

Maynard Jr. was careful about the image he projected. He dressed impeccably, wearing expensive, broad-cut size 52-long suits, silver cuff links and crisp white shirts with collars starched so heavily they seemed ready to fly away. His diction was no small problem for speechwriters. Split infinitives were his pet peeve, though every scripted word was vulnerable to his red marker. Before one speechwriter left the mayor's staff, he made certain to present Maynard Jr. with a new pen and a brief message, "To the Best Editor I Have Ever Had." The mayor returned his note, corrected, to read, "To the Best Editor I *Ever* Have Had."

The mayor understood that the mechanics and the perceptions of race were important. When he hired press aide JacLyn Morris, he told her to study the cadence and syntax of black ministers. She spent several Sundays listening to Daddy King preach at Ebenezer; occasionally she dined at Paschal's restaurant, the old haunt of the civil rights movement. Interviewing John Head, a black reporter for *The Atlanta Journal* for the job of press secretary, Maynard Jr. asked, "Do you believe interracial marriage is a political statement?" The question surprised Head, who stammered over his answer at first, before his response crystallized: yes, Head replied, some whites consider interracial marriage a social taboo and some blacks consider it a betrayal of their own race. "Maynard was always looking for some indication that you understood that everything was political," says Head, who got the job. He adds, "Maynard's very demanding. You have to sublimate yourself to him and realize that anything you say or do reflects on him."

In June 1975, assessing his first five hundred days in office, Maynard Jr. said, "There is a peculiar anxiety which probably nobody was prepared to deal with, black or white. That's the anxiety which must attach to a white community which for the first time is a minority community." Blacks, he said, had been accustomed not only to being the minority, but a subjugated minority. "Whites on the other hand, although not an oppressed minority, are numerically the minority. They are not accustomed to dealing with that psychological fact.

"We have before us a challenge to have success in an area of concern—the racial area—where the nation as a whole has flunked. So the issue is, can Atlanta succeed where America has failed?"

That summer, Atlanta chamber president Ivan Allen III urged white Atlantans to accept black political power. "It will do no good to wait for a white knight on a silver charger to rescue us from reality," he said. "The challenge, indeed the absolute necessity, will be for us to establish better communications and to obtain more, not less, input into the decision-making process as it now exists.

"To those who would sit and carp and complain because things aren't as they were, I say that things will never be as they were for change is constant."

Bob Woodruff was in his eighty-sixth year. His hearing was virtually gone, his mood often restless and foul. Yet his resilience proved astounding, for he would live an additional decade. He spent much of his time with Martha Ellis, his late wife's widowed niece; some thought they would marry, though they never did.

As Woodruff's circle of friends shrank during these years, the Allens drew closer to him. They cherished his friendship and revered his patriarchal role. He appreciated their company and the fact that their families (Woodruff, Richardson, Inman and Allen) had been intertwined for several generations. To show their mutual affection, they exchanged small gifts often: Woodruff gave Ivan Jr. and Louise Baccarat ruby glasses; they gave him a humidor full of Dunhill Montecruz cigars. Ivan III paid occasional visits to Woodruff's estate to discuss his latest ventures at the chamber. Once, Ivan III and Margaret had Woodruff for dinner at their home where Amanda played "Send in the Clowns" on the piano, much to Woodruff's delight.

In the fall of 1975, Ivan Jr. made his fifteenth consecutive trip to Ichauway. To him, Woodruff now seemed a forlorn figure as he was changed into his nightgown by his black servants, then sat in a chair in his room, alone, a cigar in his mouth.

Inman Allen, the former mayor's second son, recalls an older generation of Atlanta men, sitting with Woodruff at the dining table in the Big House at Ichauway, trying to lift his spirits.

"Eh, Boss, what did Pepsi-Cola do today?" one asked.

"Down half a point," Woodruff said, chewing on his cigar.

The men chuckled.

"Boss, what did Co' Cola do today?"

"Up half a point," Woodruff reported. A small round of cheers.

The fact that Woodruff was in decline did not keep Augustus "Billy" Sterne, the Trust Company banker, from asking him in February 1975 to "re-enter the scene" in hopes that Woodruff's valued counsel might jump-start Atlanta's languishing business engine one more time. But Joe Jones, Woodruff's long-term personal secretary, cautioned Woodruff. "There's no way for you to 're-enter the scene.' In what way would you become involved?" he asked. Jones's message represented a stark jolt of reality, but Woodruff made an address to the Commerce Club directors, anyway, with little effect.

Woodruff's value to the city now lay elsewhere. Indeed, like a philanthropic fountain, Bob Woodruff continued to bestow enormous financial gifts upon Atlanta. He had given $8 million for the construction of the memorial arts center, $9 million to the city to purchase acreage for Center City Park, $1 million to the Martin Luther King, Jr., Memorial to purchase a park across from Ebenezer Baptist Church on Auburn Avenue and $36 million to various educational institutions in the white and black communities. In a fond letter, Louise told Woodruff that his impact on Atlanta culture was comparable to "what the de Medici family did for Florence." Louise was emerging as a force in Atlanta philanthropy in her own right, becoming one of its most formidable fund-raisers. Frequently, she turned to Woodruff for help. Louise had elevated to prominence the Atlanta Historical Society, initially by persuading its board to spend $500,000 in 1967 to purchase her late uncle Edward Inman's breathtaking home, the Swan House, and the twenty-two acres of pristine woodland surrounding it (four of twelve board members voted against the purchase and at least one resigned in protest). During the late 1970s, when it came time for the Historical Society to purchase several nearby homes along Buckhead's exclusive West Paces Ferry Boulevard, Louise got help from Woodruff. He pitched in about $400,000 for each of the homes. Laura Smith, Louise's longtime friend, says, "Louise can just persuade you to do anything. Whatever Louise wants, Louise gets. . . . [Woodruff] would give her anything she'd ask for. And she asked for plenty."

As mayor, Maynard Jr. made certain to stay in touch with Woodruff. Though he never was invited to Woodruff's home, he visited his office at the Coca-Cola Company on occasion to report on the latest developments in the city. Once, Woodruff even posed with Jackson for a picture that appeared in the *Journal*, a shocking event, not only because most whites in the business community were avoiding the mayor at the time but because Bob Woodruff almost never posed for pictures. (The photograph prompted a letter from Woodruff's cousin Mrs. Willaford Leach of Palm Beach, Florida. "What would mother and Aunt Emie say if they could see Atlanta's negro mayor sitting beside you?" she wrote, adding, "Guess I was born too soon!")

During each of his visits to Woodruff's office, Maynard Jackson made certain to ask, "Is there anything I can do for you?"

"No, you're doing a good job," Woodruff told him each time. "Keep it up. We appreciate you."

Once, though, Joe Jones pulled aside the mayor in the hallway outside of Woodruff's office. "I just thought I would mention to you that out at the Chastain Park ballfield there is a concession stand that has only Pepsi-Cola signs on it."

"Is Mr. Woodruff concerned about it?" Jackson asked.

"Oh, no, no, no," Jones said, instantly, and unconvincingly. "He wouldn't be concerned about it. But he has noticed it. Now, nobody is asking you to do anything—I want to stress to you that, *Nobody is asking you to do anything!* But I just wanted you to be aware that it's there."

"You're doing a fine job," Jones said, before turning and walking away.

Maynard Jr. drove directly to Chastain Park, a lovely wooded public park in northwest Atlanta. There, he spotted the sign: "It was on a raggedy little bitty concession stand about as big as an outhouse."

He approached the concession stand. "Let me have a Coke," he said.

"I don't sell Coke," the vendor told him.

"You're kidding," Maynard Jr. said. "This is Coca-Colaville. What do you mean you don't sell Coke?" The vendor explained that a Coca-Cola salesman had angered him years earlier, and he had responded by changing to Pepsi. The mayor reminded the vendor about all of the fine things that Coca-Cola, and Bob Woodruff, had done for Atlanta over the years.

"I never ever threatened him, never tried to make him do anything at all," Maynard Jr. says. In time, though, Coca-Cola signs appeared on the concession stand at Chastain Park, next to the Pepsi signs, which was satisfactory to the mayor.

*"So what does the man who has everything want?"* Maynard Jackson asked himself during a period of multiple civic crises.

*"A Coca-Cola sign on a raggedy little shack in Chastain Park."*

Some white businessmen, he discovered, were easier to please than others.

In August 1975, Maynard Jr. met with the interracial Action Forum in the offices of the Trust Company and said, defiantly, "I'm the mayor of

this city and we will have joint ventures on the airport project. Period."
One white businessman in the boardroom that day recalls how "Billy
Sterne [of the Trust Company] took it very nicely, kind of manipulated it
and nursed it so that everybody in the room took a deep breath and said,
'Well, this is going to be a way of life.' "

"I would have thought the heavens were falling down," Maynard Jr.
would say. "We were threatened with litigation six, seven times a day."

Compliance also was a problem. In September, the mayor threatened
to fire a white contractor hired by the city to perform architectural
design of the airport because the firm had not designated a minority
partner. That same month, two of Jackson's former campaign supporters,
Fleetwood Dunston and Richard Mosley, landed a portion of a $900,000
airport cleaning contract, after they had formed a minority company,
without a license or employees, solely for the purpose of entering into a
joint venture. The controversy ran on for weeks before Maynard Jr.
denounced the Dunston-Mosley firm as an "embarrassment" to his
administration and to the integrity of the joint-venture concept.

Joint ventures with blacks infuriated white contractors, particularly in
areas where blacks had little experience. "The toughest field was in
architecture," Sugarman recalls. "We basically argued that [white architectural contractors] should align with a [black] firm that didn't have
experience and teach them."

The confusion caused lengthy delays and placed the construction of
the 104-gate midfield terminal behind schedule. Even Ivan Allen III,
among the mayor's most reliable liaisons to the white business community, said in September, "If the mayor would spend as much time on getting the doggone thing built as he has insisting on black involvement, it
would work out much better." The degree of concern among white business leaders that fall was evident in a confidential letter to City Council
president Wyche Fowler from Dan Sweat, of Central Atlanta Progress,
an organization of downtown business interests. Sweat wrote:

> The biggest enemy we face in Atlanta now is fear of the uncertain eco-
> nomic future. Fear of blacks of whites and whites of blacks. Fear of the
> white business community being ripped-off by Jackson actions.... Fear of
> the blacks that if they don't get theirs now while they control the reins of
> Government that actions by the State, et al., might take it away from
> them.... We need to reorganize Atlanta into a real city, which means
> annexation or consolidation or something.

When Atlanta voters rejected three of four issues in a bond referendum December 9, 1975, approving only a new downtown library, it

amounted to a decisive rejection of Maynard Jackson. Blacks held the majority of the vote for the first time, yet whites turned out in large numbers to deal the mayor a defeat that was every bit as stinging as the referendum defeat suffered by Ivan Allen, Jr., at the outset of his mayoralty. In January 1976, white leaders at the Commerce Club, hoping to circumvent the black mayor, reported to Bob Woodruff their failed attempt to get rid of superchief Reggie Eaves and their inability to induce the state legislature to create a committee to study plans to consolidate the City of Atlanta and Fulton County governments.

In his State of the City address of January 5, 1976, Maynard Jr. said of joint venture, "We must make basic changes in how the historically unfair system works in order to be sure that 'lowest and best' is achieved in an open and competitive bidding process.

"I think 'competition' is a key word in any discussion of these complex questions," he said. "Just being black is not enough to win any city contract but neither shall it ever again be a reason for exclusion of any city contract. I am committed to excellence and efficiency and neither of these is deleted or diluted through a fair, equitable, legal process of open competition. In other words, it does not cost more and take longer just because one of the participating firms is black."

In March 1976, after protracted negotiations, the airlines announced plans to start construction of the airport terminal by year's end. Maynard Jackson, with his towering commitment to bring blacks into the city's economic mainstream, had prevailed. City contracts awarded to minorities in Atlanta during 1976 would reach 24.9 percent. By 1978, that number would grow to 38.6 percent. Years later, Maynard Jackson would boast, "We built the Atlanta airport, biggest terminal building complex in the world, ahead of schedule and within budget—and simultaneously rewrote the books on affirmative action." He also would crow that, under his watch, affirmative action in Atlanta produced about twenty-five new black millionaires, most of them at the airport.

In April 1976, Jimmy Carter's presidential campaign staff went into damage control. Aides frantically sought help from influential black leaders across the nation to counteract a slip Carter had made in South Bend, Indiana, where he used the phrase "ethnic purity" to explain his opposition to federal efforts to artificially alter the character of neighborhoods. His opponents, including Cong. Morris Udall of Arizona, used the remark to paint Carter as a prejudiced southerner.

Carter's staff already had been discussing a public endorsement with Maynard Jackson. Hoping to use his own name as leverage, Jackson, in a private meeting with Carter months earlier, had asked him if, as president, he would appoint blacks to the federal judiciary and create stronger affirmative action, equal opportunity and urban programs. Carter had refused to commit, but agreed to give consideration to each. Now, in desperate need of public support from black leaders, Carter's aides were infuriated when Maynard Jr. continued to hold out, demanding an explanation of Carter's misstep. Carter appeared at a rally in Atlanta on April 13 surrounded by a group of local black leaders, including Jesse Hill, Benjamin Mays and Daddy King ("I have a forgiving heart, so I'm with you all the way."), but Maynard Jr. failed to show. "I think they thought I was some kind of prima donna who had an exaggerated notion of the value of my endorsement," Maynard Jr. says. "Frankly, I wasn't thinking as much about Jimmy Carter as I was thinking about me. What would my defense be to people who trusted me if I asked them to vote for somebody who had not explained to me what this thing meant?" Not until nine days later, by which time he had extracted a sufficient explanation from the candidate's campaign staff, did he endorse Carter. Forty years after the Grand had traveled to the North to speak to blacks on behalf of Franklin Roosevelt, Maynard Jr., on April 22, announced plans to stump for Carter in Pennsylvania and Maryland in time for the Democratic primaries. Years later, Carter would say that Maynard Jr. was "very influential, and let the Yankees know that I was acceptable as a potential president even though I was from the Deep South." At Baltimore's Union Baptist Church on May 14, Maynard Jr. responded to the concern expressed by a group of twenty black leaders, saying, "As a fifth-generation Georgian and a black man and the first black mayor of Atlanta, I can say I know Jimmy Carter. He's not the kind of man you just described. He is a progressive man."

In truth, Maynard Jr. had shared few private moments with Carter. Jack Watson, Jr., an Atlanta attorney who later became Carter's White House chief of staff, recalls that Jackson's support during the campaign "was more political than personal," and that Carter felt more comfortable with another black politician from Atlanta, Andrew Young. Following his election in November, Carter brought a cadre of Atlantans to Washington to work in his administration, including Young and Jule Sugarman from the mayor's staff.

One high-ranking Carter administration official says that, in holding back his endorsement, Maynard Jr. "wanted a contract. Maynard's a dealmaker. He's very political." Years later, Carter, who cut no deal with Jackson for his endorsement, would say, "Maynard obviously has an ego."

Despite his Georgia connection, Maynard Jackson, among big-city mayors, did not enjoy a preferred status at the White House during the next four years.

In early April 1976, Tom Hamall of the Atlanta chamber had approached Joel Goldberg of Rich's with an idea. "Nobody in this white community has ever had Maynard to their home," Hamall said. Then he suggested that Goldberg, as the new president of the Atlanta chamber, ought to do it, as a show of good faith.

When Bunnie arrived that night at Goldberg's home in Buckhead, she came alone, driving her own car. The mayor arrived minutes later in the Lincoln driven by a city detective. Several other couples also attended. Goldberg sat next to Bunnie during dinner and listened as she bemoaned her plight as the mayor's wife. "She said she hardly ever saw him and that she had to go to a lot of functions by herself," Goldberg says.

Several days later, Goldberg read the one-sentence news release from City Hall and, upon reflection, understood the separate cars:

*"Mayor and Mrs. Maynard Jackson have agreed mutually to an amicable separation in anticipation of divorce."*

Maynard Jr. filed for divorce in July in Fulton County Superior Court, maintaining that the ten-year marriage was "irretrievably broken." Bill Hartsfield had waited until he left office before seeking his divorce. But Maynard Jackson could not wait. Consequently, each detail of the divorce agreement was spelled out in the local papers. The mayor had agreed to pay a combined $2,000 per month, both in child support ($250 per month for each of the three children until their eighteenth birthday) and alimony ($1,250 per month). Beth, his adopted daughter from Bunnie's first marriage, was seventeen, Brooke eight and Buzzy five. Bunnie would continue to live with the children in the home on Oakcrest Drive. The mayor moved into an apartment on North Avenue in midtown, near the Fox Theatre. Jule Sugarman visited him there on occasion and decided it was "an ordinary apartment that looked like it had rented furniture in it."

Once a child prodigy, Maynard Jr. had difficulty accepting failure. Though he understood his role as a political symbol to blacks, in trying to fulfill that role his marriage had withered and died. It was small solace that his father, who was his hero, had been divorced prior to meeting Renie Dobbs. (In fact, of Rev. Maynard Jackson's six children, all except Jeanne would divorce at least once.) Beth and Brooke felt the tension between the mayor and their mother in the months and years that followed the divorce. Troubling times were ahead, too, for the mayor's namesake son, Buzzy. "I think where everything went kind of awry for him," Brooke says of her brother, Buzzy, "was when my parents got divorced."

More than ever, in the spring of 1976, Maynard Jackson seemed to be fighting the fight, alone.

His popularity among poor blacks soared. With his imposing strength and style, and his intellectual grasp of his role as a great equalizer for social and economic justice, Maynard Jr. gave a sense of what was possible.

That summer, he defended a recently adopted resolution to require city police and fire personnel to live inside the city limits. A survey indicated that nearly three of every four city firefighters and police lived outside the city. Once again, whites criticized him for being a racist, though he pointed out that the resolution would force more whites, not blacks, to live in the city. He also pointed out that no one had charged Philadelphia mayor Frank Rizzo, Chicago's Richard Daley or New Orleans's Moon Landrieu with being racist even though their cities had the same residency requirement. "I am dedicated to ending this flight from the city," Maynard Jr. wrote in a letter to the editor of the *Constitution*. "I submit one of the best ways to do that is to stop using City tax money to subsidize that flight." The *Journal* criticized his position: "If Atlanta were a palisaded fort that opened her gates in the morning and closed them at night there might be some justification for such a narrow view. . . . To erect artificial barriers for questionable political motives is to do a disservice to Atlanta."

When Andrew Young accepted the position of ambassador to the United Nations and left for Washington in January 1977, Maynard Jr. gave serious consideration to running for Young's vacant Fifth District seat. He consulted with more than a dozen black officeholders, mayors and congressmen. Their response was nearly unanimous: "Run for Congress. Get out of that mayor's job as soon as you can. It's a dead-end job." Only one, Mayor Richard Hatcher of Gary, took the opposing position. He told Maynard Jr. to remain as Atlanta's mayor and to seek another term. "If you leave," Hatcher said, "they are going to have another white mayor." Maynard Jr. knew that if he chose to run for Congress, almost certainly Wyche Fowler, the white City Council president, would win election as mayor. "I will do whatever you don't do," Fowler told Maynard Jr. "It's your call." Maynard Jr. never was enamored of Congress, or of the notion of becoming one in a membership of 435. His ego required more prominence—the U.S. Senate, for instance.

He knew his reelection as Atlanta's mayor in 1977 virtually was assured since no viable opponent was on the horizon. Hatcher had made a compelling argument. So as Wyche Fowler chased, and captured, Young's congressional seat, Maynard Jackson began planning for 1977, and four more years.

\*          \*          \*

What many white Atlantans failed to understand was that their mayor did not pursue blindly, or kowtow to, black interests, or that the same resolve that enabled him to survive criticism from whites also enabled him to withstand black backlash.

The memo from Emma Darnell arrived on the mayor's desk December 8, 1976. As the mayor's administrative services commissioner, Darnell had become Jackson's battering ram on affirmative action, and an admired figure in black Atlanta. A graduate of Howard Law School, Darnell monitored city contracts to make certain white contractors complied with joint venture requirements. In absorbing criticism from white developers, she deflected some of it from the mayor. "Doctrinaire and intimidating" is how Sugarman describes Darnell. "She was intimidating to the mayor, too, though he didn't stay intimidated." As she was willing to stand her ground against white contractors, Darnell was willing to issue challenges at City Hall. In her memo to the mayor, she charged Arthur Cummings, Jr., the director of purchasing and real estate, with "incompetence" and "insubordination" and alleged that he had referred to her in a staff meeting as " 'this woman'—who thinks she is 'queen mother' of all blacks." Darnell called for Cummings's resignation or firing.

She inflamed the situation further on December 17 when she filed sex and race discrimination charges against the city and the mayor with the federal Equal Employment Opportunity Commission (EEOC). She alleged she did not have the same authority over her subordinates (namely, Arthur Cummings) that male commissioners had over theirs. Proud of his record in hiring and promoting women, the mayor was livid.

Darnell was among the highest-ranking women in city government, and fearless enough so that when David Franklin approached her once and said, blithely, "Emma Lee, we were just thinking about you the other day and saying, 'Now what would be the office that we're going to run you for?' " she replied, "David, until you get your name on a ballot and somebody votes for you I don't care what *you* think."

Devoted in her task and headstrong in her style, Darnell told white contractors hoping to land city contracts, "If you want to do business with us I've got to see who you're hiring. Are you hiring minorities?" She recalls, "That was what blew people's minds."

It didn't help matters that her department often required months to approve contract compliance.

Dissension in the ranks was the last thing Maynard Jackson needed with an election year at hand. Because of Darnell's personality, however, he knew the tempest could not be settled quietly.

George Berry, the mayor's chief administrative aide, prepared a confidential "Mayor's Decision Request" form on January 31, 1977. In it, Berry outlined three possible courses of action, and the likely effects of each: 1. to fire Darnell ("Will be a major event of your first term. Negative impact on city, you and Commissioner. . . . Will, if successful, establish you as a strong leader."); 2. to suspend Darnell ("Will not result in Council Trial. May be interpreted as a 'cop out.' "); or 3. to attempt a compromise that would seem conciliatory to the public ("You would come off as 'backing down' from challenge to your authority. But, if successful, could spare you and city from divisiveness of public controversy.").

Berry recommended option 3, a compromise; short of that, he believed the mayor should take option 2 and suspend Darnell.

Maynard Jackson chose option 1. He would assert his power and fire Darnell, fully cognizant of her many supporters in black Atlanta. "A regrettable decision," he wrote on Berry's form sheet. In a letter dated February 10, Maynard Jr. notified Darnell of her firing, citing her performance as "inept," "negligent" and "insufficient."

Berry's assessment proved prescient: Darnell became a major event of Jackson's term. She appealed her firing and began a highly publicized hearing before the City Council. With pressures rising in the black community, and with mayoral aides testifying before the council about Darnell's professional deficiencies, her case weakened until finally she submitted her resignation during an afternoon recess on the third day. She did so only after the mayor agreed to retract his criticism of her job performance and to give her severance pay.

Maynard Jr. issued a statement at a press conference on February 25, saying that Darnell had reaffirmed "that the conduct of this administration always has been and continues to be one of high integrity." He also emphasized that Cummings had been cleared of all allegations. The mayor reasserted his complete confidence in his purchasing director. "I also would like to emphasize strongly that at no time did I consider or concede to the reinstatement of Ms. Darnell," Maynard Jr. said.

His point was plain: Darnell's surrender had been unconditional and his victory complete.

Hearing the mayor's words, an enraged Darnell threatened to rescind her resignation. In order to soothe her, a deal was struck: a mayoral spokesman announced that the mayor's words of praise for Cummings were his own, "and not those of Emma Darnell."

In April 1977, more than eleven hundred city employees, primarily sanitation workers, went on strike after the mayor refused to grant a fifty-cents-per-hour pay increase. As vice mayor, Maynard Jr. once had

defied Sam Massell by announcing support for striking sanitation workers. But now, as mayor, he contended city funds were not available to
meet workers' demands. Most of the disgruntled workers were low-paid
blacks, a segment of the community that had supported Maynard Jr. with
unswerving devotion in the past. Trash services in the city stalled for a
week, and attacks on the mayor by striking black workers intensified.
But the mayor outmaneuvered the American Federation of State,
County and Municipal Employees (AFSCME), firing nine hundred of
the striking workers and then hiring back enough to restore service to
near normal standards. Even Daddy King stood by his side, spurning
sanitation workers, saying, "If you do everything you can and don't get
satisfaction, then fire the hell out of them." Maynard Jr. crushed the
month-long strike, a move that, for the moment, endeared him to the
white downtown businessmen.

The mayor first saw Valerie Richardson on August 26, 1976. They met at
the New York City apartment of singer Roberta Flack, a mutual friend
who also happened to be one of David Franklin's clients. Flack hosted a
Sunday brunch to honor record producer Quincy Jones and the mayor.
    His divorce had been final for only three days. At thirty-eight, May-
nard Jr. had no plans to remarry any time soon—"I had planned to kind
of *be out there*, right?"—but he was struck by Richardson's statuesque
beauty. The third of eight children of a Richmond, Virginia, sanitation
worker and a domestic, Richardson had become the first in her family to
attend college, at Virginia Commonwealth University. She later earned
her master's degree in marketing and industrial relations from Wharton,
and served as an account executive for Grey Advertising. At twenty-
seven, she was eleven years younger than the mayor. She had been
impressed by him five years earlier, after reading an *Ebony* magazine
profile. Having rejected two marriage proposals already, she read of
Atlanta's mayor and thought, "Now that's the type of man I want to
marry." But the article said Maynard Jackson was married, and that he
had three kids, so Valerie thought, "All the good ones are taken."
    Their relationship blossomed over the ensuing months. The mayor
sent flowers and poetry—poetry he not only wrote, but recited. "And he
recited it by memory," Valerie says. "No man had ever recited poetry to
me by memory." He was so discreet about the relationship, many staffers
were unaware of it. (When rumors of marriage began, even his mother
asked a mayoral aide to inquire of her son, using secret code, "Is it 'V'?")
Staffers did notice the mayor's devotion to a diet, which trimmed seventy-five pounds from his massive frame. For the first time in his life,

Maynard Jackson's body took on the look of an athlete's. His facial features assumed a new tautness. Somehow his eyes seemed greener. He let his hair grow into a short, modified afro. Suddenly, people couldn't help but notice how strikingly handsome he was. In September 1977, he was named among Atlanta's ten most eligible bachelors by local newspapers, along with Falcons quarterback Steve Bartkowski and Cong. Wyche Fowler, though the papers noted Maynard Jr. kept a bodyguard at all times, "so an intimate evening with a woman may not be just the two of them."

Maynard Jr. started his march toward a second term. A survey conducted in June 1977, four months before the election, posed several hypothetical races. Maynard Jr. won each by a large margin, except for two. In a head-to-head contest with former governor Carl Sanders, now an attorney in Atlanta, Sanders led 39 percent to Jackson's 32, with 29 percent undecided.

The poll also indicated that Ivan Allen III, in a two-man race against Jackson, ran nearly even.

But the mayor had little to worry about as neither Sanders nor Ivan III intended to run. However, as the summer unfolded, Emma Darnell announced her candidacy. So did Harold Dye, a conservative white businessman who had run for mayor unsuccessfully once before. Milton Farris, the alderman Maynard Jr. had defeated in the 1969 vice mayor's race, also entered the race.

Maynard Jr. had broad grassroots support in the black community, though he also had his detractors. Black leadership in the city was undergoing another generational change. The Auburn Avenue businessmen and preachers long familiar to the white business elites, such as Jesse Hill and the Rev. William Holmes Borders, were being displaced by young black businessmen and an array of black politicians, including upstart state legislators from the sit-in days such as Rep. Julian Bond and Rep. Ben Brown and old-line traditionalists such as Rep. Grace Hamilton. Greater stakes caused more infighting among black economic and political leaders, though the consensus was that Maynard Jr., symbolic as the first black mayor, should be reelected.

Sensing the inevitability of Jackson's reelection, white business leaders turned out for him, even hosting a $50 per plate fund-raising dinner in June.

Ivan Jr. and Ivan III were among those in the Jackson camp. The former mayor said anyone who challenged Maynard Jr. "would just get clobbered." At sixty-six, Ivan Jr. spoke warmly of Maynard Jackson not because of friendship but because of a more formal mayoral kinship.

"Maynard is the best man to be mayor. He has proven that," he told the *Constitution*. "He has made efforts to overcome the racism [charge] that was leveled at him by some people, and he has been able to meld black and white people into government. . . . His personal integrity has just been excellent; he's entitled to re-election." Sam Massell, the only other living former mayor of Atlanta, attacked Jackson's performance. He suggested that Atlanta's lack of leadership could stall the city's ascent and turn it into another Birmingham. Massell said, "Every index [in Atlanta] shows deterioration," and pointed to vacant office space downtown as one example.

But Ivan Jr. looked to a more intangible index. "The biggest international issue is racism. And there is no place in the world where the minority race has shown as great an improvement as in Atlanta." Some of that improvement he attributed to Maynard Jackson.

For his own part, Maynard Jr. treated every campaign as if he were running against a Talmadge. On the campaign trail, both Dye and Farris said the city was on the decline. They called for a return to calmer, safer days, code words for a white government. Darnell contended that the mayor had failed to help the city's poor. She called her former boss "a black elitist" and insisted his affirmative action success had declined since her departure. Privately, Maynard Jr. vowed to keep Darnell below 5 percent in the election.

When four black Atlanta police officers came to City Hall on August 4, two months before the 1977 elections, and met secretly with the mayor's two top aides, George Berry and Gerri Elder, their arrival seemed ominous. They said a cheating scandal had occurred on promotional examinations in the police department in 1975. They said superchief Reggie Eaves not only knew about it but was responsible for distributing the examination to black officers before the test was given. Though two years had passed since the incident occurred, these black policemen insisted they had come forward not to affect the election but because they believed the public needed to know. Years later, Berry says, "As chief administrative officer of the city, every day of your life you have a parade of people alleging everything under the sun. You learn not to overreact. And policemen, by their nature, were always making allegations."

When first alerted to the charges, Maynard Jr. replied, "Let the law department investigate it." The story became a full-fledged public controversy, though, when the four officers took out sworn affidavits alleging Eaves's involvement. Had the mayor faced a more credible challenger in the 1977 election, this scandal might have undone him. But five days before the election, he released an eighty-three-page report made by the city attorney. The report concluded that while cheating did occur, Eaves had nothing to do with it.

On election night, Maynard Jr. stood in the Colony Square Hotel with Valerie, whom he introduced as "my very close friend." They reveled in his landslide victory. He won 63 percent of the vote, the highest percentage by an Atlanta mayor since Ivan Allen, Jr., took 70 percent against Muggsy Smith in 1965. Harold Dye, a distant runner-up, captured 17 percent and Farris was next with 14 percent. Maynard Jr. succeeded in his private vow by holding the fourth-place Darnell to just 4 percent. The *Constitution* suggested that the 44 percent voter turnout represented a "turned-off feeling" to the candidates among many Atlanta voters; the lack of a real challenge to Maynard Jr. undoubtedly affected the turnout, as well.

Maynard Jr. drew at least 15 percent of the vote in many conservative white districts in northwest Atlanta and as much as 33 percent among more liberal white districts in northeast Atlanta. These numbers certainly could not be construed as widespread acceptance of the mayor by whites. But, given the tumultuous nature of his first term, these numbers did represent the possibility for a new beginning.

Three days later, Maynard Jr. married Valerie Richardson in Richmond. They honeymooned in France, first in Paris, then in Toulouse, where they visited the aged Marcus Primault, once his mother's professor. The mayor sat at the same piano in Toulouse where his father had played for Renie on their wedding night. He played for Valerie with tears in his eyes. "I played a few jazz progressions, nice and mellow chord progressions," he recalls. "It was a very important moment." Adds Valerie, "Maynard idealizes the love affair his parents had. Both of us are strong romanticists."

They returned for a wedding reception in Atlanta, hosted by David and Shirley Franklin. Maynard Jr. stood next to Shirley in the receiving line for nearly two hours, an experience that seemed not only excessive to her, but exhausting, particularly since she was pregnant. The mayor had asked her to introduce him to each person so that he would not have an embarrassing lapse and forget a name. He even asked her to introduce him to family members. *"Maynard Jackson, I'd like you to meet your mother, Irene Jackson."* "It was part of his formality," Shirley Franklin says. "I didn't realize that Maynard Jackson needed that prop. I saw that as a prop."

His second inaugural, on January 3, 1978, was a smaller affair than his first, scaled down in extravagance and in historic symbolism. In his address, Maynard Jr. said Atlantans in 1974 had had to make a decision:

"Would our city languish in the past, or would we realize we cannot eat magnolias?

"We had to decide whether to sink with the negativism of incoherent ideas whose time had passed," the mayor said, "or to swim as one together with the rising tide of our favored future."

His address was filled with themes about race. To Maynard Jr., one of the more optimistic notes of the evening was that nearly half of the audience was white.

He spoke of the need to alleviate problems such as unemployment, crime, racism and inadequate housing.

He didn't mention Reggie Eaves. Yet soon he would recognize that his superchief was a problem requiring immediate attention.

To many blacks, Reggie Eaves was a hero. His role as the South's first black big-city police chief prompted a few photographers to follow him around the city so they could take his picture with black citizens. They charged nine dollars for a single print. Eaves's smiling likeness began to appear above mantels in homes across black Atlanta. Once, Eaves stopped at the Bankhead Courts housing project in northwest Atlanta and black residents began to chant "Superchief! Superchief!" Reporter Chet Fuller of *The Atlanta Journal* remembered, "Reggie was eating it up. He loved it." In April 1977, Spelman College trustees were held captive on campus for twenty-six hours by a group of students and faculty (including a particularly vocal English professor named Millicent Dobbs Jordan, the mayor's aunt). They wanted a black woman president of the school. Eaves arrived on the scene and sauntered in with the black soul singer James Brown. Reporting on the scene, Fuller said to himself, "Man, there's the superchief *and the Godfather of Soul!*"

This popularity satisfied Reggie Eaves's ego and stoked his ambition. His driver and bodyguard were among the team of fourteen assigned to the Executive Protection Force of the Atlanta Bureau of Police. The force protected the mayor and the superchief at a combined cost to Atlanta taxpayers of $200,000 a year in salaries. By comparison, New York mayor Abraham Beame and his police chief had a team of twelve assigned to protect them in 1976. Eaves defended the size of the protection force, saying, "I'm loved by a lot of folk but I get a lot of bad innuendos coming out about me. Every time there is a negative story about me, we get an increased number of threats." He reminded: *"It just takes one nut."*

He was glib, had an impressive presence and soon created his own political base among blacks. Yet he treated the mayor with enormous deference at all times. He called him "Boss" and willingly receded in his presence in public. During the 1973 mayor's race, Eaves had stood so close to Maynard Jackson that David Franklin likened his role to a Jackson bodyguard.

But now in January 1978, three and a half years after Eaves had been named Atlanta's superchief, Maynard Jr. started his second term with a police cheating scandal that wouldn't go away. The city attorney's report had left unanswered too many questions about Eaves's role in the controversy. So the mayor appointed two respected local attorneys—Felker Ward, Jr., and Randolph Thrower, one black, the other white, one a retired lieutenant colonel, the other a respected Republican leader—to conduct an independent investigation. Their report, released February 20, accused Eaves of having "expressly authorized" the cheating and also of having nullified the reliability of a lie detector test by holding his breath. Twenty-three officers, twenty-two of them black, were implicated in the scandal. "The final decision in this case," Ward and Thrower wrote, "should clearly be that of the mayor."

To whites, Eaves was proof that a black man was incapable of directing the Atlanta police force without the use of duplicity or reverse discrimination. The Ward-Thrower report suggested Eaves ought to be fired. Whites waited for the deed to be done.

Twenty-six death threats were made against the mayor during the fortnight that followed; three arrests were made. Adding to the mayor's stress was the news that his forty-two-year-old sister, Jeanne, had died in her sleep in Nigeria. A teacher for twenty-two years, Jeanne had suffered from a congenital heart defect.

Maynard Jr. knew that crime statistics indicated Eaves was having a positive impact. He understood that white Atlanta policemen no longer were carrying "drop weapons"—weapons dropped in the hands of a black victim they had killed wrongly. He also knew that Eaves had many black supporters who were touting the fact that the number of black deaths in the city had decreased under his watch. "Maynard kept picking up from poor black people who would tell him, 'I feel safer in the streets. My children are safer,'" David Franklin remembers. Maynard Jr. continued to make public statements of confidence in his superchief.

Privately he had decided Eaves had to leave. Though not convinced Eaves had authorized cheating, he believed that once Eaves had learned of the scandal, he not only had failed to respond decisively, he hadn't responded at all.

He did not want to fire Eaves. To fire him would be to give rise to the possibility of another public appeal, and trial, before the City Council. He wanted a resignation that would allow his old Morehouse friend to save his dignity, and to prevent another publicity nightmare like Emma Darnell.

On Tuesday, March 7, the mayor hoped to engineer Eaves's removal. Maynard Jr. was scheduled to appear on live television at 7:30 that night. At seven o'clock, he was meeting with black leaders in the office of councilman Marvin Arrington. There, Daddy King was among those who told the mayor he ought to retain Eaves. Eaves participated in this meeting, agonizing until he could bear the pressure no longer; he left. "Didn't you do [the cheating]?" the mayor asked him, afterward. "No, Maynard," Eaves said, "you know I didn't."

When the mayor went on TV that night, he thought he had an agreement with Eaves. The superchief would appear with him, the mayor would praise him in broad terms, and then Eaves would resign.

At City Hall, none of the staffers knew of any deal between the mayor and superchief. Administrative aide George Berry had written two statements for the mayor, one "Fire Reggie" and the other "Keep Reggie." Maynard Jr. began by reading from the first statement.

"He's gonna fire him!" Berry exclaimed as he, and other aides crowded around a television set at City Hall.

But then something remarkable occurred. "Maynard switched over to the second paragraph of the 'Keep Him' statement," Berry recalls. He was baffled.

Standing alone in the light, Maynard Jr. spoke for forty minutes in a rambling discourse. He sounded like a lawyer muddling through the issues with legal jargon. "They saw it based on the standard of proof called 'Preponderance of the Evidence,' " he said of the Ward-Thrower report. "It is our collective opinion that a higher standard should be used when you're talking about a dischargeable offense with a member of the Cabinet."

On and on he spoke, without announcing his decision. It almost seemed as if he was stalling—and he was.

Eaves, who later denied that he had agreed with Maynard Jr. to resign that night, never showed up. "I felt like a fool," Maynard Jr. recalls. "I'm on live TV and it's like trying to do a tap dance until the main act comes on." The mayor looked ill at ease, uncertain, stumped, even timid. He had slept only three hours the night before. It was a rare show of weakness, his most indecisive public moment as mayor. He felt as if his loyalty had been treated like taffy, twisted and abused. "It was a reflection of my immaturity," Maynard Jr. says, retrospectively. "I found out something about Reggie that day. . . . He was selfish and it was all about him."

Finally, the mayor realized, Eaves was not going to show up. "His conduct causes me grave and deep concern," he told his television audience. His compromise decision that night was to name his former chief of staff, Calvin Carter, as interim head of the police bureau, replacing Eaves. A retired air force officer serving as the city's deputy commissioner of aviation, Carter stood off-camera during the announcement, until Maynard Jr. called for him. When Carter appeared next to the mayor, George Berry thought that Carter "looked like he'd been hit in the face with a wet rag."

Years later Maynard Jr. recalls how Eaves had made a grand statement upon his appointment to the mayor's cabinet in 1974. "The Boston pol, so to speak," Maynard Jr. remembers, "said, 'Mister Mayor, all of us ought to give you our undated resignation right now. We owe that to you. There must never come a time when you decide that one of us needs to go that that should not happen instantly.'" Maynard Jr. adds: "When his time came it was like he had never said a word."

When Eaves's letter of resignation finally arrived at City Hall it was dated March 8, the day after the television debacle. At a press conference March 10, Maynard Jr. announced Eaves's removal and said the superchief had caused "severe damage to the integrity of this administration and the good name of our city." David Franklin believed the mayor had been too loyal to Eaves. "Most folks thought that [loyalty] was Maynard's weakness," Franklin says. "I did, too." Some already had reached the same conclusion about the mayor's devotion to Franklin.

Three weeks after Eaves's resignation, Lee Brown was confirmed as Atlanta's new superchief.

At the close of 1978, as construction and joint venture proceeded on schedule at the airport and Jesse Hill finished his term as the first black president of the Atlanta Chamber of Commerce, Maynard Jackson met with bankers and civic leaders at the Trust Company. For several years, he had been urging local banks to name blacks and women as board directors, without success. Now, he threatened to remove the city's funds from the previously established annual rotation among local banks. The mayor became even more Machiavellian in response to the bankers' repeated question: "Where else you gonna put the money?"

He told them, "In Birmingham."

*In Birmingham!*

This was Maynard Jackson at his crusader best. With two words, he silenced the room. (Later, one local banker would suggest to the mayor that qualified blacks were difficult to find and that serving on bank boards was unimportant, anyway. "Well, why don't you let one of us make the sacrifice to serve on your board," Maynard Jr. replied in a soft, patronizing way, "even though it is not a significant responsibility?") The position of the bankers at the Trust Company meeting infuriated the mayor. "They were looking at me like I was the bad guy," Maynard Jr. recalls. "And I'm trying to eliminate injustice." During the meeting a few bankers threatened to withdraw support from the mayor. "If people felt that what they wanted to do was to punish Atlanta," Maynard Jr. says, "because they refused to comply with the policy that was right and just and fair and legal—because they were racist in their opinions—then there was nothing I could do about that." In short order, blacks and women began to appear as bank directors in Atlanta.

By the summer, Mayor Maynard Jackson had gained a semblance of tranquillity. But then came a grisly discovery. The bodies of two black boys were found on a vacant lot on Niskey Lake Road.

# Chapter 27

→←

Beneath a brilliant autumn sun, the mayor's car sped down the interstate toward the housing projects. *Dear God, Maynard Jackson thought, when will this end?* His director of communications, Angelo Fuster, had just telephoned with more bad news. Like the mayor, a minister's son, Fuster had fled his native Cuba in 1961 as Castro was rising to power. As a staffer, he won Jackson's trust almost at once, but lately Fuster's kind face hardened each time he brought into the mayor's office a report that another body of a black child had been found.

It became a ghoulish ritual: the aide standing before the mayor, stone-faced, uncertain how to say what needed to be said.

*"Oh, no! Not another one,"* the mayor would say, cringing, even before Fuster had spoken a word.

Fuster had been listening to the police radio in his car on the command post frequency, he told Maynard Jr., and heard the report that an explosion had ripped through a day-care center at Bowen Homes in northwest Atlanta. He drove directly to the scene.

Four more black children were dead, he reported. So was an adult teacher. Never mind that it didn't fit the pattern of previous killings. Black residents said this was the killer at work. "You better come over here," Fuster advised.

It was October 13, 1980, and the loveliness of autumn in Atlanta was displayed in an array of orange and yellow hues. Maynard Jackson was presiding over a city that was on the brink of terror. In the preceding eleven months, eight Atlanta children had been found slain, most of them asphyxiated or strangled; six others were reported missing. Since all of these children were black, as well as poor, black Atlanta felt an overwhelming sense of victimization and suspicion, unlike anything since the days that followed the 1906 race riot. Once again, black Atlantans believed that black life was cheap and didn't matter.

That children were being killed only increased the urgency. That these were children of poverty emphasized Atlanta's increasingly large black underclass. The 1980 U.S. Census showed that Atlanta, with 27 percent of its population living in poverty, had a higher percentage of poor than any American city except Newark. Poor blacks in Atlanta looked to their city's first black mayor for sustenance.

The Atlanta police bureau now was directed by two black men, Reggie Eaves's successor, the methodical public safety commissioner, Lee Brown, and his chief of police, George Napper, former classmates in the School of Criminology at the University of California at Berkeley. In August, Brown had announced that law enforcement specialists suspected a pattern in the killings and were conducting the investigation as if the deaths of the children were related.

A test of police work, the investigation also became a test of Maynard Jackson. During past problems with police, he had received broad support from blacks. But now, as months passed without an arrest, in what became known as Atlanta's Missing & Murdered case, and as mothers of victims formed a vocal support group, Maynard Jr. became the object of contempt and ridicule from blacks, particularly those of the underclass. *If white kids were dying you would've solved it already, wouldn't you, mayor?* It was a rare moment when Atlanta's poor blacks turned against him. For the moment, Maynard Jr. no longer was a symbol of racial progress, but a symbol of authority—authority that was failing to protect black children. One victim's mother, Camille Bell, repeatedly called the mayor "the fat boy."

"Why don't you stop lying to these people, George Napper, and tell them the truth?" a black man had said at the Wheat Street Baptist Church on July 24 at a meeting to discuss the crisis. "If Maynard Jackson was white, we'd all be the first to cry racism about the way these murders of black children have been investigated. If it weren't for the mothers of these children nothing would have happened." Napper had kept a stiff upper lip. "I am not here to argue," he replied. "I'm here to reaffirm the commitment of the Atlanta police department."

The killings stirred a complex mix of emotions in the black community. If this was the work of a serial killer, Maynard Jr. knew, "most black people could not believe that somebody black would do this." The mayor, initially, shared in this belief. "There was no history of a black serial killer," he says. "Everybody assumed right off the bat that it had to be somebody white." Over the months, however, as no new leads developed, the mayor, following the cues of task force investigators, changed his view. "I came to believe it had to be somebody black—or a white person who was made to look like he, or she, was black. You didn't have white people riding around and going into black communities and, if you did, somebody saw them and remembered them." The terror of the murders was increasingly complicated by the psychological trauma that the killer might lurk within the black community. Most blacks refused to accept even the possibility. On the streets, black children began to refer to the killer as the Man, ironically, a term often applied to police.

The mayor stepped up his presence in the black community. "My job," as he saw it, "was to keep the city together, and to keep it positive." He went into the streets. He attended three churches every Sunday. Buzzy was nearing his tenth birthday, about the age of the victims, which made the tragedy both real and personal to the mayor. For weeks Maynard Jr. had declined interviews with the national television networks, fearing it would generate a nationwide sensationalism of the child murders, which would hurt Atlanta's image across the nation. When he finally relented, his first interview, with the black CBS reporter Ed Bradley, was conducted at a local park where Buzzy was playing in a Little League baseball game. It was a poignant moment, revealing the mayor's compassion and eloquence.

Week after week, the network news programs were filled with images of small black bodies being removed from the rivers and streams of Atlanta, or plucked from the city's grassy hillsides, or of Chief Napper serving, much as the Western Union man had during World War II, as the messenger of another death in the family. White downtown business leaders drew closer to Maynard Jackson during the crisis than at any other time during his mayoralty. More than ever, they celebrated his eloquence. A shared purpose brought a mutual appreciation. Central Atlanta Progress, the collection of downtown business interests, raised money to build a replacement day-care center at Bowen Homes. At the Atlanta Chamber of Commerce came the realization that the negative publicity being generated by the murders was harming commerce. "Businesses we might have been able to interest in [moving to] sites within the city were still interested in Atlanta, but now in the metropolitan area, maybe in Cobb County," Tom Hamall, the chamber's executive director, recalls. The chamber and Coca-Cola joined to produce an advertising motto designed to boost spirits: "Let's Keep Pulling Together, Atlanta!"

The helplessness was untenable to Maynard Jr. In black Atlanta, he continued to sell optimism and the city's better qualities, "not asking," as he would say, "but reassuring."

"Stay calm!"

"Let's work through this! But also let's look out. Take care of the children."

*"Protect the kids!"*

At a community meeting at the Civic Center, where the lofty ideals of his administration were first enunciated at his inaugural nearly seven years before, Maynard Jr. told the audience to "spread the gospel of caution to all families in Atlanta."

From the moment he arrived at Bowen Homes, the mayor not only saw the grief and terror etched on the faces of the several hundred residents who milled about, but also heard the shrill rise in their voices: *"It was the Klan! It was the Klan! IT WAS THE KLAN!"*

From every indication, the explosion had not been the work of the Klan, but rather an accident caused by a faulty boiler. As the four young victims, pairs of two- and three-year-olds, were pulled from the wreckage, Hyde Post of the *Journal* was struck by how small the bodies were. Throughout Bowen Homes, rumors spread that three whites had been seen running from the facility moments before the explosion. Another rumor suggested that several whites, in a pickup with a Confederate flag, had been seen driving away. Maynard Jr., in his impeccably tailored suit, picked up a megaphone and moved to the center of the housing project, which had been built in 1964, during the Allen administration, and had been named for the black United Methodist bishop, J. W. E. Bowen. (Maynard Jr. had lived with Bowen's widow in 1964, after he had graduated law school, and studied on her back porch for the state bar examination.)

"There's no evidence that it was anything other than an accident," the mayor assured the residents. Later in the week, investigators concluded that the boiler had received little maintenance during the preceding eighteen months and that a safety device had been improperly wired. But residents of Bowen Homes jeered the mayor. "I caution you and I plead with you," he said. "Please do not, do not engage in spreading rumors if you do not know them to be true." At a community meeting that night at the Greater Fairhill Baptist Church, members of the black community refused to believe Lee Brown when he said there were no signs of foul play in the explosion. So enraged was this group that Hosea Williams asked reporters to leave the meeting, then led a twelve-mile march to City Hall, in part to defuse the seething anger.

Maynard Jr. visited the families of many of the victims. Usually the media trucks were waiting for him when he arrived. The mayor's staff began to play a game of hide-and-seek with the media, hoping to slide through unnoticed. Typically, the mayor arrived in an unmarked car, but given his size, he was hard to miss. He didn't want to transform these visits into media events. Fuster agonized over the misguided local reporters who thought the mayor's primary concern in the case related directly to the impact it might have on his political future. Fuster knew Maynard Jr. intimately and had witnessed how each death was "like telling him another person had died in his family." A number of the mayor's personal visits to Bowen Homes went unnoticed by the press.

On October 18, a biracial search party numbering three hundred swept through the woods of Dixie Hills in a hunt for more clues or perhaps even bodies. In the underbrush, a thirteen-year-old discovered a small skull and a clump of brunette hair tied together with a plastic barrette. Later, these were identified as the remains of seven-year-old LaTonya Wilson, who had been reported missing.

A numbness settled across black Atlanta. At all hours of the night and morning, black parents called George Napper's home to notify the chief that their child had not yet arrived at school, or had failed to return home. They supplied evidence for Napper to trace. Fifteen minutes after the first panicked call, the same parents sheepishly told him that their child had just returned home, or had just shown up at school, and to disregard their previous call. Napper's number was unlisted, but every black family in the city seemed to know it.

Searching for something dramatic that might help to break the baffling case, Maynard Jr., on October 22, sat behind a table on which he had stacked $100,000 in small bills. The reward money was the former encyclopedia salesman's idea. He had asked the First National Bank to provide the cash, in one-, five-, and ten-dollar bills, as an incentive for anyone who had information about the killings to come forward.

It created one of the most lasting images of modern Atlanta: the sad yet steely expression of the city's first black mayor, flanked by two Atlanta policemen (one white, one black) as he sat behind the money. "It was unfortunate that we had to get to that point," Napper says years later. "But we had to do anything that was humanly possible."

By now, Maynard Jackson had developed a proprietary sense of city government. If he could not serve again as mayor—the charter specified a two-term limit—then he would determine who would. During the fall of 1980 he heard the first rumblings that the city's white business elites aimed to engineer a Great White Hope as candidate in the 1981 mayor's race. To Maynard Jr., City Hall was a beachhead that Atlanta's blacks had claimed only after generations of struggle. The gains that had been made, inch by grudging inch, could not be lost now. He was convinced that the continuation of his Atlanta revolution, namely the ripening of black political power, was important not only to Atlanta but also to urban politics across America. Besides, if the first black mayor of Atlanta did not beget a second black mayor, then what would that say about the performance and popularity of the first?

The white business representatives who had met with him most frequently—the chamber's Hamall and Dan Sweat of Central Atlanta Progress—were exhausted from the experience. Several times the mayor and Sweat had gone months without talking to each other, so dramatic were their confrontations. To Hamall, the idea of a new mayor brought "a sense of relief."

One group of conservative white businessmen, led by Dillard Munford, creator of Majik Markets, asked Cong. Wyche Fowler to run for mayor in 1981 and offered $300,000 to back his campaign. Fowler wasn't interested. Local developer Tom Cousins and Sweat flew to Washington to ask Jack Watson, Jr., Jimmy Carter's chief of staff, to make a run at City Hall. Watson told them he had his sights set on the Georgia governor's mansion. (His bid, in 1982, failed.) The Munford group even approached Joel Goldberg, the chairman of Rich's, to test his interest; Goldberg, never a politician, declined.

Many whites, including Ivan Allen III, believed the numbers wouldn't allow for a white Atlanta mayor. Sidney Marcus did not agree. A veteran state legislator, Marcus already had decided to enter the race. In part because he was Jewish and had been Sam Massell's college roommate, Marcus was not the choice of the downtown business leaders, though, by default, eventually he was given their public, and financial, backing.

Behind the scenes, Maynard Jr. went to work. His analysis was simple: "It is going to require someone with instant credibility and instant clout and instant name recognition to win the mayor's seat." Reggie Eaves, by then a Fulton County commissioner, was making motions as if he planned to run. Though Eaves had name recognition, he lacked credibility and clout. As Maynard Jr. saw it, only one name fit the bill: Andy Young.

In black Atlanta, virtually no one called him Andrew, the more formal name by which people in Washington had known him. Andy Young was a dentist's son, raised in predominantly Irish and Italian middle-class neighborhoods in New Orleans, a race-conscious society where, though light-complected, Young says, "I was considered too black to succeed." An ordained minister, Young had shown resiliency and an ability to reinvent himself during the past two decades in and around Atlanta. Already he had had a handful of different careers of astonishing fullness. He had been among Martin Luther King's lieutenants during the civil rights movement, often acting as a bridge to white communities. He later served as a U.S. congressman from the Fifth District in Atlanta and then as Jimmy Carter's ambassador to the United Nations. "There was just so much that happened as a result of the civil rights network," Young recalls. "Jimmy Carter asked me to go to the U.N. not because I was so bright but because I was associated with Martin Luther King and he felt that would give human rights some credibility." In August 1979, Young resigned from the U.N. in the wake of an international controversy stemming from his unauthorized meeting with a member of the Palestine Liberation Organization at the New York apartment of a Kuwaiti diplomat. Secretary of State Cyrus Vance publicly reprimanded Young for having violated U.S. Middle East policy, which prohibited direct contacts with the PLO. Now, Young was back in Atlanta, developing his own firm called Young Ideas. It was not unusual to see him driving down Cascade Road on the west side or waiting patiently for his plane at Hartsfield Atlanta International Airport. Young was a familiar figure—even something of a legend—and he was available to run for mayor.

Maynard Jr. believed his job as mayor could be filled only by a black man of enormous stature. He organized a series of dinners to entice Young. Months later, he stood on Auburn Avenue, near the resting place of Martin Luther King, Jr., and urged Jesse Hill, the black political power broker and now chairman of Atlanta Life, to support Young's mayoral bid.

"I don't think that's the way to go," Hill told him. It was almost a re-creation of 1973 when Hill first had told Maynard Jr. he didn't believe the time right for a black mayor. Years later, Maynard Jr. says, "I almost fainted when Jesse responded. . . . He felt we should have a white mayor this time around."

During the fall of 1980, when Young accepted an invitation from Maynard Jr. and activist Susie LaBord of the Grady Homes Tenant Association to meet with black community leaders at the Omni Hotel, the idea of running for mayor had not yet occurred to him. But then: "Maynard spelled out the scenario where the white community had decided that they can't have another black mayor," Young says. "The talk of that meeting was that there was $2 million the business community had put up for anybody white." Young wasn't certain which white businessmen put up the money (the $2 million figure was a paranoid rumor), though he concluded "it was just about all of them." As ever, Maynard Jr. made his case convincingly. He said that local white businessmen had decided that, with the expected victory of Ronald Reagan in the upcoming presidential election, federal funds to cities would dry up and private investors would not invest in a city run by blacks. "They were absolutely convinced," Young says, "that Atlanta was on the verge of becoming a Newark or a Gary. Some of the business community were relocating not only to the suburbs, but talking about going to Dallas."

When LaBord, a fiery public housing leader who had worked in Young's previous campaigns, said at the Omni Hotel that night, "*Andy, when you came here you wadn't nothin'. We made you somebody. You've got to run for mayor!,"* Young agreed to reinvent himself once more, this time as a candidate in the 1981 Atlanta mayor's race. In time, Young urged that the Missing & Murdered case should not become a campaign issue.

If Young's decision pleased Maynard Jr., it had a decidedly different effect on many white business leaders. Bob Holder, an important player in the ranks of the Chamber of Commerce, recalls how news of Young's intentions to run for mayor sent "Atlanta business into total ballistic gridlock. Everybody went crazy because here was this guy who had started in with Yasir Arafat and he's going to come in here."

Ivan Jr. and Ivan III were among the few downtown businessmen to support Young's candidacy, though theirs, typically, was a quiet support. Ivan Jr. had admired Young since they had negotiated Atlanta's firemen's strike in 1966. Ivan III was transfixed by Young's stump speeches about transforming Atlanta into a legitimate player in the international business markets. "Ivan thought Andy Young hung the moon," Margaret Allen says. Trusting his skills as an ambassador, Young said at the time, "I got Birmingham black and white folk together. I got black and white folk together in Rhodesia and I'm not worried about Atlanta."

But when Young announced his candidacy, at least one member of the white business community declared it was "just the most awful thing that ever happened in the history of the world." Bob Holder intended those words to be taken literally.

His anger unmasked, Maynard Jr. struck a nerve. "Lindbergh was one child," he said in a press conference on November 5, "and we're talking about 15 here."

His point could not be missed: federal agents had rushed into action in 1932 when the infant son of famed aviator Charles Lindbergh had been kidnapped: was the race of the children keeping federal agencies from helping in Atlanta?

Maynard Jr. wanted plenty from Washington. He wanted funds to finance the widening investigation. He wanted a commitment of FBI agents to the case. He had spoken four times to the office of FBI director William Webster. Each time Webster had refused to commit. After his press conference, the mayor sent telegrams to Atlanta's congressional delegation, and to President Carter, maintaining that the FBI's refusal to assert jurisdiction over the Missing & Murdered case was "unjustified, discriminatory against Atlanta and reprehensible in light of the crisis." He telephoned Jack Watson, chief of staff at the White House, to complain. The next day, the FBI announced a decision to take a "quantum leap" in assisting the Atlanta case.

The Missing & Murdered crisis became for Maynard Jackson what the Iranian hostage dilemma had been for Jimmy Carter. It cast gloom, doubt and a sense of fragility over his administration. His frustrations were building. "The issue dominated everything—overwhelmed everything," Maynard Jr. says. His management style, concerning the day-to-day affairs of the city, became, "Hit a lick here, hit a lick there! You are running the city with your left hand and trying to cope with a city that is frantic, almost to the point of hysteria, with your right hand."

By February 1981 the case began to create an evil sort of circus atmosphere in Atlanta. A psychic arrived from New Jersey, claiming mystical powers that would solve the case. A dog trainer with two German Shepherds came from Philadelphia to search fields. Five nationally acclaimed homicide investigators arrived, then left, befuddled. The Guardian Angels came from New York City to restore order to the streets. At the Techwood Homes housing project, residents, acting as vigilantes, carried baseball bats and called themselves "The Hank Aaron Crime Stoppers." Symbolic green ribbons appeared all over town. The actor Burt Reynolds offered $10,000 in reward money. Sammy Davis, Jr., and Frank Sinatra performed in concert at the Civic Center, adding another $148,000 to the reward kitty. The former heavyweight champion, Muhammad Ali, in town for a benefit, phoned Maynard Jr. after midnight to announce his intention to add to the reward money ("You can't even buy a Rolls-Royce for that much money," Ali said); his pledge was $400,000.

Maynard Jr. paid frequent visits to the task force headquarters on West Peachtree Street. Internal fighting, disorganization and turf wars raged there. Bodies had been found in several jurisdictions; too many law enforcement agencies were involved. Besides city police, there were police from several counties, the FBI and the Georgia Bureau of Investigation. Each organization wanted credit. Sharing information became a problem. Overtime man hours stretched into the tens of thousands. A telephone hotline brought strange tips and suggestions. One caller recommended dressing midgets as children, believing that once midgets were captured they would stand a better chance than children of defending themselves against the killer.

Leads were few. Victims were last spotted at Church's Fried Chicken, a bus stop, a mall, a gun shop. Rumors about the Klan continued.

Before the mayor left City Hall to visit another grieving black family, he called Lee Brown. "Lee," he would say, groping for answers, "what can we do? Should we call in somebody else?"

Brown was a professional, a methodical worker whom the mayor held in high esteem. Trouble was, Brown tended to be tight-lipped about the investigation, even with the mayor. "Maynard had to ask the exact right question," Fuster says. "He would say, 'Lee, do we have any suspects?' And Lee would say to the mayor, 'At this time we do not have anybody we define as a suspect.' The question Maynard was asking was, 'Do we have any leads?' It was like pulling teeth." To circumvent Brown, Fuster used other police department sources to get information.

In his seventh State of the City address, delivered on February 2, 1981, Maynard Jr. said, solemnly, "We cry for, and we cry with, the 17 families. . . . But we must do more than that. We must exercise great care and great caution with our children and we must encircle our children with love and with our caring as we have never done before." He called for the City Council to hire an additional 160 policemen by the end of the year. He also criticized those who would criticize the task force, including Reggie Eaves, who had his eyes on the 1981 mayor's race. "There are those few critics without credibility who perch like vultures in the trees of our tragedy and try to inflict and then infect a sore of public doubt about the extraordinary, highly professional, praise-worthy efforts of our police and their leadership," Maynard Jr. said. "We reject those self-interested mistaken persons, their devious reasons and their falsehoods."

Rhetoric alone would not solve the mystery. Because the killing pace was quickening, law enforcement officials wondered if the killer was losing control. On March 8, the body of thirteen-year-old Curtis Walker, missing for two weeks, was pulled from the South River: death by asphyxiation, the method used to kill nine of the twenty victims. That day, Maynard Jr. and a detective appeared at the Bowen Homes apartment of Catherine Leach, Walker's mother. "Sit down," the mayor began, softly. This routine became harder for him each time. "I'm sorry, but that was Curtis's body they pulled out of the South River." Catherine Leach's eyes grew wide. She let out a hysterical scream, then ran out her front door. Her sister later identified the boy's body and told Leach, "Cat, half his face was torn out." Ten years later, Leach yet associated the mayor with the child murders. She would say, "I never did like Maynard Jackson."

In some way, every Atlantan was drawn into the case. Margaret Allen volunteered in one search. "We were over in south Atlanta beating around in a field," she says. Meanwhile, a twenty-nine-year-old police recruit named Dobbs Jordan joined the task force team. One of Bob and Millie Dobbs Jordan's twin sons, and a cousin to the mayor, "Buddy" Jor-

dan, as he was known to the family, had graduated from Howard Law
School in 1978 but had failed several attempts to pass the bar exam in
Georgia. A soft-spoken, handsome man, he joined the Atlanta police
force "as a Walter Mitty experience," and soon found himself walking
the Zone 2 beat along Auburn Avenue, the boulevard his grandfather
had helped make famous. With a profound sadness, Dobbs Jordan noted
the deterioration of Auburn, the boarded-up cafes, the winos wandering
at night. Since legally sanctioned segregation had ended more than a
quarter century before, the black community had dispersed, the middle
class moving to the open spaces in the suburbs, leaving Sweet Auburn as
a decaying memorial to a bygone era. "The street had died," he says.
Late in the spring of 1981, the traditional practice of placing police
recruits with an experienced officer was abandoned. "Who can swim?" a
police official asked the academy class of 1981. Dobbs Jordan raised a
hand. Soon, he was on a two- or four-man raft each night, patrolling the
cool, dark Chattahoochee River. He wore infrared goggles, which drew
on available light. It was at once eerie and oddly peaceful.

The death toll reached twenty-six on April 28. The body of twenty-
one-year-old Jimmy Payne was lifted from the Chattahoochee. During a
month-long period, he was one of five victims, all in their twenties,
placed on the Missing & Murdered list. The black writer James Baldwin
would write, "The state of Georgia had never before exhibited so intense
an interest in Black life or Black death."

The critical break in the investigation occurred at three o'clock on the
morning of May 22. Police recruit Bob Campbell, standing in the darkness beneath the Jackson Parkway Bridge in west Atlanta, alongside the
Chattahoochee River, said, excitedly, into his walkie-talkie, "I just heard
a loud splash!" Campbell shone his flashlight into the rippling waters. A
1970 Chevrolet station wagon was crossing the Jackson Parkway above
him. In a moment, the car returned across the bridge and a member of
the stakeout team pulled it over more than a mile down the road. Two
days later the body of Nathaniel Cater washed up more than a mile
downstream, close to the spot where the body of Payne had been found
a month earlier. The driver of the Chevy was named Wayne Williams.

The surveillance of Wayne Williams, a twenty-three-year-old black
freelance photographer, began immediately. On the night of June 3, and
through the following morning, law enforcement officials interrogated
him for twelve hours. Afterward, Williams told the press, "They were
mostly just saying, 'Well, you killed so and so, why did you do it, why
don't you quit lying to us, why don't you just come and admit it to us?' "
Within days, law enforcement agents entered the west Atlanta house

where Williams lived with his parents. They seized a yellow blanket, carpet sweepings, a purple robe and dog hairs. Members of the press camped outside the house. Williams astounded law enforcement officials later that day by holding his own press conference and handing out copies of his résumé. Later the newspapers discovered that much of the information in his résumé was embellished or falsified. A week later, Williams went out for an evening drive, aware he was being followed by police officers. He led them on a tour that ended when he stopped in front of Lee Brown's house. Williams was pulled over and cited with a series of traffic violations, including reckless driving.

When Williams emerged as the lead suspect, two of the most surprised Atlantans were Andy Young and Maynard Jackson. As a congressman, Young once had sworn in Williams as student body president of the Anderson Park Elementary School. Williams later started a radio station in the basement of his parents' house. In the midst of a congressional race, Young was cornered by Williams, and several of his friends, and brought into the Williamses' basement for an interview. "They had a card table and they did a very good interview," Young says. "They had questions written out and they were good questions." That night, Young returned to his home and told his wife, "Jean, these were some of the most impressive twelve- and thirteen-year-old kids I've ever met." When Maynard Jr. first heard the suspect's name, he thought, *"I remember this kid!"* The mayor knew that Williams's father, Homer, was a photographer and former schoolteacher familiar to virtually everyone in black Atlanta. As an honor student at Frederick Douglass High, Wayne Williams once had approached Jackson's law firm. "When he was fifteen years old, he came in," Maynard Jr. recalls, "precocious, clean-cut, bright, and wanted to get a license for a neighborhood radio station."

Years later, Maynard Jr. shook his head. "Something happened to him, no one knows for sure. But here's this bright kid who did not go to college, fell into a kind of netherworld, a strange world, with a preoccupation with police."

On Father's Day, June 21, 1981, law enforcement agents arrested Wayne Williams. They charged him with the murders of Jimmy Payne and Nathaniel Cater. His trial was set to begin after Christmas.

It was only a parade, and a small parade at that. The Tri-Cities of Hapeville, East Point and College Park, located near the airport, invited the mayor to make an appearance. He would sit in a fire truck and wave to people along the route. It would be easy political pickings, low-stress and good public relations. In the summer of 1981, when he sorely needed such a moment, Maynard Jr. heartily agreed to the appearance. After the fire truck delivered him to the town square for a picnic, he worked the crowd, shaking hands, slapping backs, a mayor if there ever was one.

An elderly white woman approached him and said, "Aren't you John Wesley Dobbs's grandson?"

The mayor raised an eyebrow. The Grand had been dead for twenty years. Besides, not often did elderly white women make inquiries about him.

"Yes, ma'am, I am."

"Well, my husband worked on his crew for many years."

Maynard Jr. was dumbstruck. The woman spoke of her late husband's fondness for John Wesley Dobbs, and the years he spent riding the rails with him as a government postal clerk. She even confirmed one of the mayor's favorite tales, "the story of this [white] ringleader trying to throw Grandpa off the train," and the fearless way Dobbs had stood up to the white man.

The conversation seemed an epiphany to the mayor, a moment that reminded him of who he was, and how much he had to be proud of. His style and bravado, and his actions as a modern-day race man, were traceable to the man born in the shadows of Reconstruction alongside Kennesaw Mountain.

On October 27, 1981, Andy Young and Sidney Marcus met in a runoff election for Maynard Jackson's job. The mayor's support of Young was vocal and constant. Only two percentage points had separated Young and Marcus in the primary; Eaves, proving his enduring popularity among blacks, polled 16 percent but finished a distant third.

Maynard Jr. heard a few of Marcus's black supporters spreading falsehoods about Young. Something had to be done, he decided, to make certain that black Atlantans understood the necessity for a Young victory.

In his most heavy-handed, racially inflammatory speech as mayor, in which he gave advance notice (and printed copies) to the press, Maynard Jr. told a predominantly black audience at the Butler Street YMCA on October 14 that any black supporting Marcus was a victim of self-hatred. He likened their condition to that of the freed slaves who, following the issuance of Lincoln's Emancipation Proclamation, asked to be returned to their masters. "We are beginning to see shuffling and grinning around the camp of our opponent by a few of our [black former] allies in the struggle," he said, a reference to a group that included state Rep. Douglas Dean and Charles Black, an activist during the 1960s serving as the highest-ranking black aide on Marcus's campaign staff. "These surfacing Negro voices we are hearing from our own community are the voices of the new selfishites . . . which are rooted in a shameful part of American history that has forced some Afro-Americans into the corner of racism [which] creates an anger and self-hatred that are awesome in their destructive power.

"Some slick-talking Negroes are also trying to justify their relationship to the Reagan administration," he continued. "We see them jockeying for positions closest to the Reagan table so that when Reagan is reminded to throw them a scrap, they will be able to grin and catch it."

Sitting in folding chairs around tables in the YMCA lunchroom, blacks in the audience applauded loudly and often.

"I'm not advocating a vote for Andy Young because he's black," Maynard Jr. said. "I'm advocating a vote for Andy Young because he's better. There is nothing wrong with some Negroes supporting Sam Massell's closest friend and advisor, Sidney Marcus. But there is something wrong with those Negroes justifying themselves by saying Andy Young is not qualified."

Created for an effect, the speech was every bit as caustic in its racial imagery as Massell's "Atlanta's Too Young To Die" campaign of 1973, as much a power play as Mayor Ivan Allen's call for Massell to withdraw from the 1969 mayor's race because of alleged malfeasance. The speech received wide notice across the nation. Local newspapers blasted the mayor for its divisive tone. "Does Mayor Jackson want to say that white Atlantans supporting Andrew Young are filled with 'self-hatred,' " one local columnist wondered. Wrote *The Atlanta Journal:* "If a white person made those comments about blacks, the uproar would be unimaginable." Marcus expressed incredulity, saying, "I was absolutely shocked that he would take eight years of pulling this community together . . . and destroy it in 10 minutes." Young, who believed that Marcus "would not [as mayor] have repudiated in any way" Jackson's policies, distanced himself from the speech, though not fully from Maynard Jackson, saying only that his style was "completely different" than Jackson's.

Years later, Maynard Jr. proudly referred to this speech as "a calculated move that worked." He said he expected the local newspapers to lash out against him. "[But] I knew where the vote was, and I knew that the [black] vote was asleep and had to be awakened," he says. Select black leaders "were not just supporting Sidney, they were maliciously out trying to destroy Andrew Young with a pack of lies and that's what I was attacking. And the only reason I called them 'grinning, shuffling Negroes' was that I couldn't think of anything better to call them. I despise people like that. They might as well go and spit on King's grave." More than defending Young in the speech, Maynard Jr. seemed to be defending himself and his administrative policies such as joint venture ("Some people will never, ever forgive me for that. That's their problem, not mine," he said at the time). At the same time, he rebutted the implication that a black mayor was incapable of governing.

Two weeks later, Young was elected mayor of Atlanta, capturing 55 percent of the vote. Voting in the runoff followed sharply along racial lines. Young won just 10 percent of the white vote, Marcus 11 percent of the black vote. If it had any effect at all, Jackson's speech had served only to reinforce racial polarization.

For one more time as mayor, Maynard Jr. had played the aggressor's role, and at considerable personal risk. He cared deeply about preserving the political power of Atlanta's black elite. Had Andy Young been defeated in the runoff, "it would have said that the black community had not learned anything about politics," recalls Michael Lomax, the Jackson protégé and Fulton County commissioner, "and that wasn't the case. This was a very sophisticated black community."

Standing by Young's side on election night, along with veterans from the civil rights movement such as the Rev. Jesse Jackson, the Rev. Ralph D. Abernathy, C. T. Vivian and John Lewis, was Maynard Jackson. His future remained uncertain, but his legacy was intact.

That a new day was about to begin in Atlanta became clear two days later. Young invited more than sixty of the city's downtown business elite to lunch at the World Trade Club atop the downtown Merchandise Mart. The mayor-elect said, "I know that none of you voted for me. I know that you all did everything that you could to try to defeat me." The businessmen might have expected a speech of anger. But Andy Young said, "That's over now. I can't do what I need to do without you. I need your help."

A moment of silence became a sigh of relief. Businessman Bob Holder recalls, "It was one of the most spectacular performances I have ever seen by a guy who turned out to be the best friend a business community has ever had."

At his inaugural on January 5, 1982, Young called for a closer working relationship between City Hall and the business community. "And I'll never forget Mayor Ivan Allen's advice that you can't run the city without the newspapers," Young said. In his twenty-minute address, he invoked Allen's name three times, Jackson's twice. His address amounted to a peace offering.

"Atlanta is not now rising from the ashes," Young told a crowd of more than eight thousand at the Omni. "It is rocketing into orbit from a solid foundation built by three great mayors—Ivan Allen, Sam Massell and Maynard Jackson."

During his final day as mayor, Maynard Jr. flew to Augusta where his former Morehouse College classmate Edward McIntyre was inaugurated as the city's first black mayor. He and McIntyre had pledged the Alpha Phi Alpha fraternity where their fraternity big brother was Reggie Eaves. Always quick to cite his own accomplishments, Maynard Jr. pointed out to a reporter that day that during his administration the percentage of city contracts won by minority firms had been raised from less than 1 percent to 25 percent. In a wave of nostalgia, he seemed struck by the circular nature of life. "As of now, I'm saying goodbye," he told the reporter as he left City Hall, "and I'm walking out forever." But, cryptically, he added, "At least for now."

The trial lasted nine weeks. Journalists came from as far away as India. FBI profilers had encouraged prosecutors to keep Wayne Williams on the witness stand as long as possible in the belief his temper inevitably would emerge. After testimony from nearly two hundred witnesses spanning thirty-five days, the defendant took the stand. Jack Mallard, an assistant district attorney in Fulton County known as a tough cross-examiner, exposed Williams's inner fury his second day on the stand. "You wanted the real Wayne Williams," the defendant said, defiantly, for all jurors to hear, "you got him, right here." At another moment, Williams said to Mallard, "You haven't got no proof that I did anything. All you trying to do is come up with some suppositions."

In what would become a landmark case for the use of microscopic fiber evidence, three experts had testified that more than seven hundred fibers and dog hairs had been recovered from the bodies of eleven victims. These fibers, they maintained, linked them to Williams's environment. In closing arguments, jurors heard prosecutors liken Williams to Adolf Hitler and Attila the Hun, while a defense attorney compared him with the dreamer Martin Luther King, Jr.

The jury used eleven hours of deliberation to convict Williams of the murders of Nathaniel Cater and Jimmy Payne. Immediately, he was sentenced to consecutive life prison terms. Days later, the cases of twenty-two others on the Missing & Murdered list were linked to Williams and summarily closed, which enraged some of the victims' parents and gave fodder to skeptics suggesting a cover-up. "I never agreed with the idea of closing the rest of the cases," Maynard Jr. says, "although when they made the decision I encouraged people to go along with it and understand it." Years later, Andy Young likened Wayne Williams to Nathan Leopold and Richard Loeb, two college graduates and sons of prominent Chicago businessmen, who in 1924 pleaded guilty to the kidnapping and murder of a fourteen-year-old boy. "[They] decided to commit the perfect crime [and] really thought themselves so much better than anybody else, they thought they could get away with it," Young says. "There's something of that in Wayne Williams." Maynard Jr. adds, "There's no doubt in my mind that [Williams] is the guy for the two convictions. He lied on the witness stand. They caught him in lies."

Fittingly, the most explosive crisis in the modern history of Atlanta ended concurrently with Maynard Jackson's departure from City Hall.

To white business leaders, the emergence of Andy Young seemed like a spoonful of honey following Maynard Jackson's vinegar. Maynard Jr. was an intimidator, Young a facilitator; typically, the former strove for surrender, the latter reconciliation. "I think Maynard's size intimidates people, same thing with Jesse Jackson," Young says. "One of the advantages Martin Luther King [Jr.] had—and one that I have—is that we are basically small, normal size. If I walk into the room nobody is on the defensive because I'm five foot nine. When Maynard walks into the room there is a physical factor there." With his style and history, and his most remarkable international Rolodex file, Young was well suited for the role of healer and for bringing new international development to Atlanta, a combination that restored communications between City Hall and downtown business and led the city to new levels of growth and, astonishingly, to the 1996 Olympics.

Maynard Jr. paid a personal price for his political and racial convictions. If he were to be embraced by local white leaders, battle scars first would have to heal. He hoped to land a job with a top Atlanta law firm in 1982, working municipal finance, presumably in the role of "rainmaker"—using his prominence to bring to the firm deals that would make money fall from the sky like rain. But the top municipal finance firms in town would have nothing to do with him. Finally, in September 1982, he accepted a position as partner with Chapman & Cutler, an old-line Chicago law firm. He earned roughly $300,000 per year, and set up a new Atlanta office, ironically in the same space in the Grant Building once occupied by Bill Hartsfield.

He traveled weekly to the firm's Chicago headquarters. During one visit in December 1982, Maynard Jr. sat in the living room of the Rev. Jesse Jackson and listened as the leader of Operation Breadbasket tried to convince him to run for president in 1984. Deep inside, Maynard Jr. always had wanted to be president. It was not the object of his ambition, he would say years later, merely his "preference." Saying that black Americans had been snubbed by Republicans and taken for granted by

Democrats, Jesse Jackson told the former Atlanta mayor that he had the necessary qualifications—"inside government credentials, outside credibility and [an ability to] articulate a broad range of issues." Though Maynard Jackson had not marched in the streets with Martin Luther King, Jr., Jesse Jackson believed "he was clearly identified with those of us who had done that." But Maynard Jr. didn't think the time was right. Besides, he had a family to support. Jesse Jackson would run for president instead in 1984, a historic campaign that galvanized the black vote and transformed him into a powerful symbol within the Democratic party. Years later, Maynard Jr. had regrets. "That was the time when I should have run [for president]," he would say. "I wish I had."

In Atlanta in December 1982, nobody was talking about a Maynard Jackson presidential run. That Atlanta's top law firms in municipal finance had offered perfunctory courtesy and small talk, but no job, was the former mayor's payback—for Reggie Eaves and Emma Darnell, for joint-venture projects and for eight years of racial rhetoric. "I was blamed for affirmative action," Maynard Jr. says. It was a lesson he would not forget.

# PART VII

# OLYMPIC CITY

"It is a land of the Mercedes and the mall, of the hungry and the homeless. . . . If New York is the Big Apple and New Orleans the Big Easy, Atlanta is the Big Hustle."
—*The Wall Street Journal,* 1988

# CHAPTER 28

➤⬅

By his own admission, Andy Young had been associated with a few crackpot ideas over the years. An idealist, Young was a sucker for big dreams, a quality burnished by his years with Martin Luther King, Jr. As a nineteen-year-old senior at Howard University in 1951, his big dream was to qualify for the 1952 U.S. Olympic team. Without training and with a borrowed pair of shoes that year, he ran the 220-yard dash in 21.4 seconds. kicking up cinders and setting a track record at the Quantico marine base. If that hadn't stirred his Olympic hopes then what surely had was the enduring recollection of climbing three flights of stairs as a four-year-old to sit with his father in the segregated balcony of the Orpheum Theater in New Orleans to watch the Movietone News as Jesse Owens won four gold medals in the 1936 Olympics in Berlin, shattering Hitler's premise of Aryan supremacy. Subsequent track meets proved Young didn't have speed enough to qualify for the Olympics. But his aspiration took different shape in the spring of 1987 when a local lawyer sat in his office and said he wanted to bring the 1996 Olympics to Atlanta. The lawyer's name was Billy Payne.

Payne was the type of visitor Young's staff most feared, a man with a big idea and a commitment so total he had quit his job and spent his savings to pursue it. Just thirty-nine, Payne was a former all-star football player at the University of Georgia, a compulsive Type-A personality who, Young quickly deduced, was politically naive. On a list of Atlanta's influential leaders in the spring of 1987, Billy Payne wouldn't have made the Top 1,000.

For fifteen minutes Payne outlined his idea. Across the desk, Young seemed preoccupied. Payne could feel the mayor's eyes looking past him. Bad enough Young had arrived late, now his aides paraded in and out of the office, handing him papers and phone messages.

Payne figured if anyone would be enthusiastic about the Olympics it would be the economics-oriented, international-minded Andy Young. Payne said the 1996 Olympics would have a financial impact of more than $3.5 billion. He feared that Young might perceive his Olympics quest as just another workaday idea, not unlike trying to land a Super

Bowl or big dental convention. In Payne's mind, the Olympics could change Atlanta forever.

Atlanta had become a star of the Sunbelt during the 1980s, booming during the Reagan years, its metropolitan population rising 32 percent, to nearly three million. Most of this growth was white-collar in the suburbs, consistent with a nationwide trend. With continuing white flight, the city's 1985 population was two-thirds black, and public school enrollment was 94 percent black. Young was serving his second term (he would leave office in January 1990) and during that time—even as his administration directed more than 35 percent of all city contracts to firms owned by blacks and women—the disparity between rich and poor in Atlanta was growing, as it was across America during the Reagan revolution.

Atlanta's growth had traced north along a ridge once marked as a trail by Creek Indians, with Peachtree Street as its winding spine: hotels and retail strips connected to a growing forest of skyscrapers seemingly designed by market need rather than careful planning. The preservation movement in the city largely had failed, though the Flat Iron Building (1897) and the Candler (1906) were among the few impressive structures still standing. John Portman's celebrated invention of the hotel atrium in the Regency in 1967 had given way to his exterior glass elevators at the Peachtree Plaza in 1976 and then his fifty-three-story atrium inside the Marquis Marriott. Downtown had seemingly been designed for conventioneers.

Yet by the middle 1980s, "Atlanta" meant not the city but the eighteen-county metropolitan area. Cobb and Gwinnett counties, touching Atlanta's north side, were among the nation's fastest growing. Big money fueled these booming areas: metropolitan Atlanta featured the nation's top-selling Volvo dealer, the nation's second most prolific BMW dealer and its eighth-largest Porsche dealer. The Cable News Network, founded by sportsman Ted Turner, a native South Carolinian whose family had made its money in the billboard business, began to draw global attention to Atlanta. The city was scheduled to host the 1988 Democratic National Convention. Its office building boom continued, recklessly at times, raising new skylines in midtown and also in predominantly white Buckhead, where Sam Massell, as president of the Buckhead Coalition, became known as "Mayor."

Even the death of ninety-five-year-old Bob Woodruff in March 1985 hadn't slowed Atlanta's momentum. Through his philanthropy, the Boss had made certain of that. In his lifetime, he had given away more than $350 million to benefit education, the arts and medicine, and the vast majority was given to black and white institutions in Atlanta. Woodruff had guarded his gift-giving anonymity so closely that upon creating his own foundation in 1937, he had named it the "Trebor"—Robert spelled backward. In 1980, he gave $105 million to Emory University from the Emily & Ernest Woodruff Foundation, which effectively dissolved with the gift, four decades after he had persuaded his parents to create it. That gift put the Boss in the *Guinness Book of World Records* for the largest single gift ever made to an educational institution. His imprint was spread across the city, though only in his final years had Woodruff allowed his name to grace libraries, centers and parks. His last public appearance, September 8, 1983, was at the unveiling of a seven-and-a-half-foot statue of his likeness at the Woodruff Arts Center. At ninety-three, he sat in his black Lincoln that day, holding a cigar and greeting friends. Bolstered by the astonishing growth of Coca-Cola stock, his foundation's assets would reach nearly $2 billion a decade after his death. With old friends and associates as its trustees (Ivan Allen, Jr., among them), the foundation remained, like the man for whom it was named, the guiding white conscience of Atlanta.

If Bob Woodruff had been the city's most aggressive salesman, Andy Young was its most passionate. As mayor, Young's most persistent pitch was for international investment. Japanese, Swiss and German investors responded with a rush to Atlanta. By 1990, Young had met nearly two hundred international delegations and traveled to Switzerland, the Soviet Union, France, Jamaica and Japan. Once, he even suggested privatizing Hartsfield International Airport, including selling as much as 25 percent of the stock to foreign investors and placing management in the hands of a private Georgia-based board. But, as he says, "The state legislature freaked out. They said, 'Andy Young wants to sell the airport to the Japanese.'" That big idea never materialized.

Young's critics pointed out that the mayor virtually neglected Atlanta's poor. "Jobs," Young said, defensively, "that's the way you feed the hungry." So he used his reputation and contacts, enhanced by his tenure as ambassador to the United Nations, to bring jobs to Atlanta through international investment. He was engrossed with the big-picture view of Atlanta, a macromanager who delegated authority freely, too freely, many believed; often he left the day-to-day management of the city to his staff.

During their meeting, Payne assured Young the 1996 Olympics wouldn't cost Atlanta's taxpayers a dime. He reminded the mayor of how Los Angeles, as host of the 1984 Olympics, had secured enough private-sector financing to finish with a surplus. Young listened impassively to Payne and to attorney Horace Sibley, who had arranged the meeting.

Not until Payne mentioned the children of Atlanta, and the way the Olympics would energize and unify them, did he sense Andy Young's true interest. All at once the mayor perked up. "There was a major transformation in him," Payne recalls. In truth, Young was interested from Payne's first word. He had been told of Payne's recent history: that he had suffered a heart attack in his thirties and, while working for his church during his recovery, came up with the Olympic idea. "To me," Young would say, "that's the way God works."

"What can I do to help?" Young asked, finally.

Payne had won his most necessary ally.

When the mayor later told his chief administrative officer, Shirley Franklin, that he was going to help Payne bring the Olympics to Atlanta, she and fellow staffer Gene Duffy laughed. "And we laughed for a week," says Franklin, who had first entered local politics, with husband David, with Maynard Jr. "We thought it was the most foolish thing we had ever heard."

Even as City Hall and the Atlanta Chamber of Commerce boasted that Atlanta was an international place, few residents actually believed it.

Besides, too often Shirley Franklin had had to defend herself against the charge that she, not the globetrotting Young, ran the city. Mayor Shirley, some called her. Franklin listed for the mayor ten reasons why a pursuit of the Olympics was impractical. She reminded him of the hundreds of millions of dollars Montreal had lost from hosting the 1976 Olympics. As she read her list of ongoing projects, she noticed a look in Young's eyes, the can-do look he flashed when deciding to rebuild Underground Atlanta, an entertainment–retail sales complex in downtown. Young believed both whites and blacks would frequent it, revitalizing the central city.

Ten reasons, Franklin gave him, slow and deliberate. But Andy Young looked her squarely in the eyes. "You do all of those things," Young said, "and I'll go get the Olympics."

And he was serious.

A couple of times during the late 1980s former mayor Maynard Jackson searched for his family past in Cobb County. He spoke at a black church, and later handled a case at the county courthouse in Marietta. Both times he searched for blacks named Dobbs who could help him connect with his heritage. "I would see black people walking down the road," he recalls, "and I would ask them, 'Do you know any Dobbs family here?' " He had little success in the search.

As a bond attorney for Chapman & Cutler, Maynard Jr. prospered as never before. With Valerie and their two young daughters, he had moved to an exclusive area in northwest Atlanta, into a fifteen-room, multilevel French Provincial home valued at $600,000. Set on a cul-de-sac off West Pace's Ferry Road in Buckhead, the home was a few blocks from the governor's mansion and a half mile from the Allen estate on Northside Drive. Most blacks in the area were yardmen, maids and butlers.

In an Atlanta society preoccupied with race, his move to an elegant white neighborhood did not go unnoticed. "It was an unusual thing to do," Ivan Allen, Jr., would say. "Maynard didn't consult anyone that I know about it." Andy Young recalls, "I thought it was a bad move but only because he was paying more for less." In matters of the heart—namely, where people live and where they pray—Atlanta remained sharply segregated. "But when you're segregated in a $300,000 house, what the hell!" Young says, focusing on black advancement. "Particularly if that $300,000 house would cost $700,000 on the north side."

By any standard, Maynard Jr. had a lifestyle of comfort. He often rode about town in a chauffeured black Lincoln Continental. Valerie had carved her niche as a supporter of the arts and host of a public affairs talk show on public television. Daughters Valerie Amanda and Alexandra were in public schools.

Two decades had passed since his challenge of Sen. Herman Talmadge. However prosperous and comfortable, he missed politics. He missed the policy-making power it provided and, more than he was willing to admit, the spotlight it shone on him. To Maynard Jackson, politics was like oxygen. He needed it to survive.

Just as Bill Hartsfield had had difficulty accepting the idea of Atlanta making progress during the 1960s without him, so did Maynard Jackson during the 1980s. But Hartsfield was past seventy when he had retired from politics. Maynard Jr. left City Hall at forty-three.

By February 1987, Maynard Jr. was telling *The Atlanta Journal* that he was considering either another run at City Hall in 1989 or a statewide position. Ironically, some of Jackson's old nemeses in Atlanta were suggesting that his aggressive micromanagement was just what the city needed to replace the peripatetic Young. Only recently Maynard Jr. had been placed on the fifty-member board of directors of Central Atlanta Progress, the downtown business establishment, and CAP president Dan Sweat joked, "We heard he was going to run for mayor and it's time we had one of our own in City Hall."

Michael Lomax was not laughing. Once a Jackson aide and, since 1981, chairman of the Fulton County Commission, Lomax had decided to enter the 1989 Atlanta mayor's race. His time, he thought, had come.

An urbane star of Atlanta politics named by *Time* magazine in 1981 as one of America's five up-and-coming young black leaders, Lomax knew the last thing he needed was competition from Maynard Jackson. Lomax had even discussed his candidacy with Jackson more than a year before and, at the time, the former mayor had offered his support.

So when Lomax heard whispers about Jackson's possible candidacy, he met with him late on a Saturday morning in Jackson's office.

Again bloated to more than three hundred pounds, Maynard Jr. reached into his office refrigerator filled with sandwiches. "Ham and cheese?" he asked Lomax, an associate professor of English at Spelman College. Maynard Jr. admitted he was leaning toward another run. He told Lomax that his intention was not to challenge him. He simply felt compelled to respond to a calling to public service. "And," Lomax understood, reading between the lines of Jackson's monologue, "Maynard didn't want me in his midst."

"You will lose," Maynard Jr. warned, "and it will ruin your political career."

"You're making a mistake," Lomax replied.

Lomax resented Jackson's decision. He also resented his tone. "I was pissed off," he recalls. He felt betrayed.

He told Maynard Jr. the mayor's office would not satisfy him any longer, that he had outgrown it. "Maynard, I think the race for you is lieutenant governor," he said. He pointed out that the lieutenant governor's position in Georgia was part-time, which would allow Maynard Jr. to practice law and to serve simultaneously, a prospect he believed would serve both Jackson's ego and handsome lifestyle. Lomax also appealed to Jackson's fondness for making history. He told him that, as the first black lieutenant governor in the modern Deep South, he again would become a historic pioneer. Furthermore, he said, black politicians had made inroads outside of Georgia and "being mayor of Atlanta is overshadowed by being governor of Virginia and is overshadowed by being mayor of New York."

But Maynard Jr. had made up his mind. And no protégé of his was about to change it.

Embittered by the experience, Lomax determined not to back down. For a black politician in Atlanta it was a move of uncommon boldness and moxie. Besides, Lomax and his strategists believed that if he could capture 75 percent of the white vote, he would need only about 35 percent of the black vote to defeat Jackson. Mathematics told Michael Lomax victory was possible. His better judgment told him that only a fool would try.

\*            \*            \*

For fifteen months, Billy Payne had canvassed the business community of Atlanta in search of funds. The usual response: "Great idea. *But we don't think you can win.*" Since 1971, dating to the Massell administration, boosters had proclaimed Atlanta "the world's next great international city." Indeed, for nearly a century, men of business had emerged to lead Atlanta to greater stature. In the nineteenth century, the cotton broker Samuel Inman, Louise Allen's great-uncle, single-handedly saved the 1895 Cotton States Exposition. Just when the sheriff was ready to padlock the gates of the exposition, due to unpaid bills, Inman produced $50,000 of his own money, with the caveat that the city had to raise a matching $50,000. This kept alive an event that crowned Atlanta the premier New South city in the eyes of the nation. It was nearly a century later when Payne stepped into a similar role. In April 1988, the United States Olympic Committee (USOC) designated Atlanta, over Minneapolis, as its city for the 1996 Olympics. Only then did the business community think of Payne as anything other then a noble fool obsessed with an unlikely dream.

Atlanta became one of six cities competing for the Olympics; the others were Athens, Greece; Melbourne, Australia; Toronto, Canada; Manchester, England; and Belgrade, Yugoslavia. Athens was considered the favorite since the 1996 Games would represent the centennial anniversary of the modern Olympics, which had started in Athens.

Now, armed with the USOC bid, Payne told the Atlanta Chamber of Commerce he needed more than $5 million to produce a viable final bid. In the summer of 1988, the chamber cautiously agreed to raise that money. Both Payne and businessman Bob Holder, president of the chamber and chairman of the advisory board of the Atlanta Olympic Committee, asked Ivan Allen III to chair the chamber's fund-raising drive.

Big money was needed—and fast. Few Atlantans wielded the fund-raising influence of Ivan III, a civic booster with a history of raising big money. He had produced millions for the Jimmy Carter Presidential Library in Atlanta in the early 1980s. In 1983, he had co-chaired with Coca-Cola chairman Roberto Goizueta a fund-raising drive for Morehouse College that effectively had transformed the appearance of the school's campus. Regardless of the cause, Ivan III knew only one way to make his pitch: he was blunt, direct and certain to cast a warm glow on Atlanta. He was not often turned down by any big corporation. "What I wanted was the absolute sure-fire deal," Holder says, "and that was Ivan. When Ivan told you that he would head a fund drive, or for that matter, anything else, you could put it in the bank. It was going to happen."

But Ivan III hesitated. "I've got to do a little homework on the thing," he told Holder, "to be sure." Typically, he conferred with Atlanta's business elite, Goizueta and construction executive Larry Gellerstedt, Jr., among them, recalls Margaret Allen, "before he would undertake something that he would consider 'off the wall.'"

Approaching his fiftieth birthday, Ivan III was at the apex of his powers during the summer of 1988. The Ivan Allen Company had concluded its most profitable year, with $116 million in revenues, $20 million more than the previous high set in 1987—and more than $100 million higher than the earnings of 1971, the year he had assumed the company's presidency. The remarkable revenues of 1988 were a result of RJR Nabisco moving to Atlanta and requesting massive and expensive supplies for its new corporate offices. ("They were spending so much money right and left," Inman Allen, a member of the Ivan Allen Company's board of directors, recalls, "and they just said, 'Furnish them. We want the best you've got, the best money can buy.'") Ivan III hoped to expand even further that year and asked Inman, who owned a series of small companies, to join him full-time at the family firm. Their discussions stalled. "I was focusing on the equity side, my brother on the responsibility, job function side and we never could get in sync," Inman says. The personalities of the two brothers were not at all alike. "Ivan is a control person. He'll listen to an argument up to a point, but then he's going to make a decision. I would characterize myself as a consensus-builder," Inman says. "I will just beat an issue to death and . . . I'll make other people stay after it." Inman turned down his brother's offer. Working together, he says, "would have been a disaster."

Despite his grinding pace, Ivan III agreed to assume command of the chamber's Olympics fund-raising campaign. His task was to ask the fifteen largest corporations in Atlanta, including Delta Airlines, BellSouth, Georgia Power and the local banks, to give nearly $300,000 apiece, and they had to give it not over a four- or five-year period but within eighteen months.

"I'll do it," Ivan III told Holder, "with the understanding that what we're going to tell people is that this will do it. We won't ask them for any more." Holder agreed.

Payne watched in awe as Ivan III worked on the "lead gifts campaign," which comprised about 80 percent of the funds sought. Ivan III called Payne to report each success. "Because of who he was, not because this idea was yet embraced," Payne says, "Ivan was able, in an absolutely record amount of time—and it was measured in number of days, it was that quick—to essentially assure us that we would have the money available."

Later, Payne realized he needed an additional $1.25 million for visuals and other bid materials. Holder approached Ivan III once more. He held Ivan III in great esteem. In 1987, Holder had conferred with him prior to assuming the presidency of the Atlanta chamber and later would solicit advice on running a family business. (Holder's two sons had joined him at the Holder Corporation.) Holder even played in the Tuesday night tennis game with Ivan III and other business leaders at the home of Frank Carter, former Atlanta chamber president who lived next door to the Allen estate.

When Holder asked him about raising the additional funds for the Olympics, Ivan III declined. "Remember," he said, "my deal was that this was going to be all." "And Ivan stuck to that," Holder recalls. "He was a tough, exacting, demanding kind of guy who did everything he said he would and expected you to do the same."

Eventually the additional funds were raised, the Atlanta Olympic movement advanced to the next stage, and Ivan III, his fund-raising work fully unrecognized by the public, returned to the pressures of his family business.

When Maynard Jr. returned to the campaign trail in the winter of 1989, the old political fires returned to him. The city's black voters again responded as if he were their magical Pied Piper. His slogan was "Action Jackson" and his speeches were highly charged. Where Andy Young's speeches had come off as private sessions with a pastor, each of Maynard Jackson's speeches resounded with Sermon on the Mount rhetoric. To one skeptical observer, it was as if "the next thing Maynard was going to do was turn a couple loaves into feeding the multitudes."

Maynard Jr. announced his candidacy on February 16 from the steps of City Hall, as if back home. Full of confidence, he made appearances throughout the day. He stopped at Paschal's restaurant to meet with black leaders; at Inman Park to meet with neighborhood activists; at a black Methodist church to meet with hundreds of supporters, and at a cafe in Buckhead to meet with 250 white business leaders. That night at a party at the CNN Center, more than two thousand attended. By night's end, Jackson staffers believed their candidate had slapped every back in the building. In May 1988 a newspaper series had revealed dramatically how whites in Atlanta had received five times as many home loans from local banks and savings and loans during the 1980s as blacks of the same income. On the campaign trail, Maynard Jr. responded to such inequities. He spoke of forging new economic development on the south side, creating more affordable housing, raising to new heights the battle against drugs and crime in the city, constructing a second airport, extending MARTA rail lines and fighting construction of a proposed east Atlanta parkway in the name of neighborhood preservation.

Michael Lomax never had a chance. He had announced his candidacy on New Year's Day, 1989, standing on an outdoor basketball court at the Carver Homes housing project. Lomax vowed that day to base his campaign among the city's poor, a promise that lost much of its impact when a group of protesters, holding anti-Lomax placards, marched in silence during his announcement, contending that his promise was little more than a campaign ploy.

Lomax had failed to consider that, besides running against Maynard Jr., he was running against a mythology. Because of October 16, 1973, the night Maynard Jr. became the South's first black big-city mayor, many black Atlantans forever would cherish him as a political pioneer. That Maynard Jr. had made a priority of affirmative-action programs during his eight years as mayor had only strengthened this special bond.

Though black Atlanta was not monolithic in political thought, it was, as Lomax soon discovered, virtually monolithic on certain issues—and Jackson's candidacy was one such issue. Blacks represented 61 percent of the vote in 1989 and, though some young black professionals and old guard traditionalists viewed him as high-minded and heavy-handed, Maynard Jr. seemed invulnerable.

Even the white newspapers responded to his political reemergence in 1989 with a confidence that had not existed during his first two terms. Some of this support stemmed from the realization that Atlanta, after sixteen years of black rule and affirmative action, had continued to grow. Years later, Lomax would attribute the white media response to Maynard Jr. to a collective "accumulated guilt." "They were going out of their way," Lomax says, "not to do to him what they had done [before]."

A newspaper poll conducted five months before the October 3 election gave Maynard Jr. better than a two-to-one lead. Lomax strategists hoped to cut into Jackson's advantage by convincing voters that Jackson's return to City Hall was designed to serve his ego and not his constituency. Lomax attacked Maynard Jr. from all angles. He criticized him for his poor management of crime during his first administration. He also criticized Jackson for having moved to a house in Buckhead, suggesting this was a prime example of the former mayor's insensitivity to the black working class.

Years later, Maynard Jr. would say a primary reason he had moved to Buckhead was to place his daughters in superior public schools. "Number one, I didn't leave the city," Maynard Jr. says. "Number two, it doesn't matter where I live, my commitment remains strong." In 1979, during his second term, Maynard Jr. had moved his family into a black district in southwest Atlanta, "to help the neighborhood revitalize," even though he could not seek a third term. He moved his family to Buckhead after the 1984 birth of Alexandra. "That's one of the prices you pay for living in Buckhead if you're an African-American," Maynard Jr. says. "The irony is that you can live in southwest Atlanta and still not do one one-hundredth of what I've done for the city of Atlanta. *Sacrifice nothing, do nothing for black people, but hide behind the symbol of living in the 'black community.'* No matter where I live I'm the same person. People know where I stand." The futility of Lomax's attack on this issue was reflected in a newspaper poll in April in which only 12 percent of a racially mixed pool of Atlantans said they would be less likely to vote for Maynard Jr. due to his move.

It would become the most expensive campaign in the history of Atlanta politics. Both candidates raised, and spent, in excess of $1 million. It was a mean and spiteful race, each candidate accusing the other of being an out-of-touch black elitist. In late July, Lomax began a three-week television blitz that again hammered Jackson's record in fighting crime. Unwittingly, the ads translated a stereotyped image—whites complaining that black politicians were soft on crime—and created a small backlash against Lomax. After the blitz, Lomax's polls showed he was still twenty points behind.

His campaign nearly out of money, Lomax was told that an additional $1 million was needed for the final eight weeks. His finance chairmen said those funds could not be raised, that confidence in the campaign was gone. "The first million hadn't produced anything but an increase— for Maynard," one Lomax staffer bemoaned. Maynard Jr., meanwhile, continued to lobby white business leaders, once his harshest critics. He assured them that eight years as a bond attorney had matured him and made clear the importance of relationships and negotiation.

On August 8, yielding to harsh realities, Lomax withdrew from the race.

Jackson's electoral invulnerability in Atlanta never was clearer. Though Hosea Williams subsequently entered the race, Maynard Jr. won nearly 80 percent of the vote. "Ladies and gentlemen," he said at his victory party, "the future of Atlanta begins tonight." So inevitable was his victory, voter turnout reached only 35 percent. On election night, a bitter Hosea Williams said, "Unfortunately, whites still prefer an Oreo over a black person and blacks are trying to turn white."

\*       \*       \*

Now, Maynard Jr. joined an Olympics movement already in full throttle. Several days after his election, he traveled with Payne to the Caribbean Olympics Association meeting in Cuba. Andy Young already was planning his 1990 gubernatorial run and Payne had worried about losing him as an Olympics spokesman. The Cuba trip allowed Payne his first extended conversation with Maynard Jr. Together, they visited with Fidel Castro. An avid baseball fan, Castro mentioned Atlanta's Braves and even Ponce de Leon Park, where the minor league Crackers had played. "I was shocked with his level of familiarity with Atlanta," Payne says. Maynard Jr. invited Castro to the 1996 Olympics, as if Atlanta had already captured the bid, saying with grandeur, "I think it would be good for the hemisphere." To Payne, the mayor-elect's performance with Castro was remarkable and reassuring. "We never really lost Andy and we added Maynard to the stretch drive," Payne says. "Between Andy Young and Maynard Jackson you've got two of the world's great communicators."

Maynard Jr. filled his transition team with white businessmen. Among the group was Inman Allen, assigned to a committee on infrastructure. Not a fervent supporter of Maynard Jr., Inman was among those recognizing that the former mayor could not be beaten. "The whites had been disfranchised from City Hall and this [support] was just to say, 'Let's build some bridges,'" Inman says. He made a small contribution to the Jackson campaign and, as a result, someone arranged breakfast with Maynard Jr.

"You know I support you primarily because I can't support Michael Lomax," Inman told Maynard Jr. bluntly. "And there are only two of you." He recalls the mayor-elect's response: "Thank you for your support." ("*What do politicians say?*" Inman says, with a shrug.)

Inman Allen's committee filed a distressing report about Atlanta's infrastructure. "We knew that the bridges were crumbling," he says. His committee positioned its report so that the infrastructure would become a high priority for the incoming administration. But an outside consulting firm, owned by Jackson's friend and former City Hall aide Arthur Cummings (and paid $70,000 for its work during the transition), placed infrastructure "pretty damn low," Inman says.

Inman was disgusted by what he saw during his several months on the transition team. Not only crumbling bridges and sewers, but what he perceived as cronyism.

Like many white businessmen in Atlanta, he wondered if Maynard Jackson had changed even a little bit.

Ivan Allen IV was twenty-six years old in 1990 when he decided for the first time to read the book about the life of his great-grandfather, the

Senator. Ivan IV had joined the Ivan Allen Company three years earlier and thought "it was time to get a perspective." After all, he says, "We pride ourselves on being a family business."

Like his father, Ivan IV had gone north to college, to Bucknell University in Lewisburg, Pennsylvania, where he played soccer and graduated in 1986 with a degree in economics and political science. He took a year off to go to South America and Mexico, where he fulfilled a dream by attending the World Cup soccer tournament. Then he came home to the Ivan Allen Company. The decision was his own. Ivan IV did not seriously consider any other career. He began in the company's warehouse and worked his way up. Around the office he was discreet about his name. Colleagues noticed how in large meetings he was the only employee in the room not wearing a name tag.

He was born in the summer of 1964, when his grandfather was mayor, only a month before Lester Maddox and his customers chased three blacks from the Pickrick with a pistol and pick handles. From an early age, Ivan IV knew his name was locally famous. He retained only one memory of the Senator: posing for a portrait of the four Ivans taken at 2600 Peachtree Road in 1967, the year before the Senator died and the year Ivan IV turned three.

Over time he understood his name was double-edged. In business, it "opens doors. You receive an audience when you may not necessarily deserve one." He adds, "The burden is that you always walk in the spotlight, unfortunately."

The spotlight had its privileges. As he child he remembered Bob Woodruff stopping by the house for dinner: "He's the only person I've ever seen smoke a cigar in our house." Years later, he and his father, Ivan III, hunted quail with former president Jimmy Carter, who called him "Cuatro," the Spanish word for four. Carter admired his shooting eye, saying, "Cuatro performed superbly." Humbly, Ivan IV says, "Well, I'm shooting with people who are twenty or thirty years my elder. They were a little bit slower than I was." Growing up, Ivan IV also shared the pleasures of golf with his grandfather, the ex-mayor. Together, they played the exclusive Peachtree Golf Club. "He was a little intimidating back then," Ivan IV says. "He would always advise you on what you were doing wrong."

Ivan IV was living in an apartment near Peachtree Road when the postman delivered a book of personal checks. Trouble was, the checks didn't fit into his mail slot, so the postman dropped them into an open bin for bulk mail. The checks were stolen.

If Ivan Allen IV ever doubted the prominence of his name in Atlanta, this experience erased all doubt.

A grocery store merchant realized that a young black man at his front counter was attempting to cash a check under the name Ivan Allen.

The merchant slipped away from the register and called the police. The man was arrested, almost at once.

It was early afternoon, June 18, 1990. At the corner of Peachtree Street and Martin Luther King, Jr., Boulevard, a Fulton County deputy sheriff watched Maynard "Buzzy" Jackson III, stirred by an argument over a can of Mace, lift his girlfriend and throw her to the pavement. She was sprayed in the face with Mace during the scuffle and later treated for minor cuts and bruises. The nineteen-year-old namesake son of the mayor of Atlanta was charged with simple battery and detained at the Atlanta Pretrial Detention Center on a $1,050 bond.

The headline in the *Constitution* the next morning read, "Mayor's Son in Hot Water Again."

The questions for Mayor Maynard Jackson at his weekly press conference were direct.

*"Are you going to pay the bond for Buzzy?"*

"No!" the mayor said, sharply.

*"Will you explain why?"*

"No!"

From his first term, Maynard Jr. had been convinced the newspapers were out to get him. He believed the media did not understand him, or the political process, that they picked their points to criticize and then drove a tractor-trailer through them. Much of the criticism was racially motivated, he believed. Now, they were after his family. *What did Buzzy have to do with city business?* For the incident at Five Points, Buzzy was sentenced to forty-five days in jail. Already, Maynard Jr. had released a statement, terming the arrest a "painful experience for me, my family and Buzzy's mother. It is intensely personal and I will not comment on it except to reaffirm our position that Buzzy must bear the consequences of his own actions." To his closest friends, the mayor spoke of a need for "tough love" with Buzzy.

Only five months earlier, at his inaugural, the mayor had beamed while gazing at the five children from his two marriages. With the wave of his meaty hand, he had announced, "These are my chillens." A week later, Buzzy was charged with possession of less than an ounce of marijuana after being involved in a car accident in Buckhead. He pleaded no contest to the drug charge and paid a fine of $150, plus $60 for the traffic violation.

On the day of that mishap, Brooke Jackson had taken a call at home from a music school in Boston—her brother, Buzzy, had been accepted to study there as a jazz drummer. But Brooke recalls her father, reacting harshly to Buzzy's scrape with police, telling him, "There's no way I'm sending you to school up there."

Four weeks later, on February 7, Buzzy nearly ran an unmarked police car off the road. The fine this time was $100, for driving without a license and making improper lane changes.

The mayor's older daughters never had experienced such troubles. Beth had graduated from Georgia State University in Atlanta in 1986 with a degree in marketing. "I was always very conscious never to do anything that would embarrass my dad," she says. "My dad was always really patient with me, with the mistakes I made." She had married Howie Hodges, a former Morehouse Man who reminded her of her father, and no one was happier about their union than the mayor. At the age of nine, Brooke had decided she wanted to become a hotel developer—"I wanted to be the black female John Portman," a reference to Atlanta's leading downtown developer. The day her father dropped her at Cornell University in New York, where she planned to specialize in hotel and restaurant administration, he became emotional about saying goodbye. "He cried," Brooke says, tears forming in her own eyes at the mere memory. Brooke spent a year and a half at Cornell ("Stats and microeconomics kicked me in the butt"), then finished at Spelman, with a degree in psychology. Her father's contacts helped her to land her first jobs. "He is a great parent," she says.

Like his sisters, Buzzy had been raised in Bunnie's home, apart from his father. Buzzy attended several high schools, including Frederick Douglass and North Atlanta. Maynard Jr. arranged for him to attend the prestigious McCallie prep school in Chattanooga. But Bunnie says Buzzy was expelled from McCallie "because he did everything he could to get put out. Taking somebody's homework and copying it, that's the last thing I can recall that he did. Taking somebody's hat. You know, little stuff like that."

Over the years Maynard Jr. had attended counseling with his son, but Buzzy stopped showing up at their sessions. "He has reacted in ways that were anti-social," Maynard Jr. says. As a father, he loved Buzzy unconditionally and refused to abandon him. John Wesley Dobbs, the mayor thought, "would have been less tolerant" with a son such as Buzzy. "I can't help you if you don't want to help yourself" is what Maynard Jr. believes the Grand would have said to Buzzy. The mayor took tough stands himself. Fed up with Buzzy's antics on one occasion, he drove Buzzy to the Salvation Army in Atlanta and left him at the curb, bags at his feet. In that instance, as in many others, Buzzy "was saved by a woman," Maynard Jr. says. "These women are crazy about Buzzy and he's always been able to find somebody who would take him in and take care of him."

Approaching his twentieth birthday, Buzzy was diagnosed with attention deficit disorder (ADD), an affliction that produces, among other symptoms, an inability to sustain concentration. "He had been using marijuana and he had been in and out of a drug treatment place and finally one of the counselors said, 'There's something wrong with him,'" Bunnie says. "And I said, 'I've been saying that for years, but everybody thought I was a doting mother and that I was making excuses for him, but I know something is wrong with this child. Things do not connect right.'" She adds, "He is a case study of ADD. You sit down with Buzzy for one hour, you walk out of this room convinced that's what he has. He can't focus on things."

Buzzy Jackson is a handsome young man, tall and broad-shouldered. He looks like his father. "A good heart, but a short temper," Brooke says. Says Beth, "Buzzy wants to please Daddy, he just doesn't want to go to Morehouse and be Phi Beta Kappa." On those rare occasions that Buzzy showed up at City Hall, one mayoral aide remembers, "you knew either that he was high or in trouble." Inside the mayor's office no family picture was more prominent than Buzzy's. Yet among the staff it was understood that Buzzy inevitably created embarrassing situations for the mayor.

As a teenager, Buzzy went through a period in which he did not use his given name, Maynard. "I was not happy about it," the mayor recalls. "But intellectually I could understand what turned out to be a burden on him." To become a drummer was Buzzy's ambition. Bunnie had married a third time, to Ray Ransom, a musician with Brick, whose blend of soul gained popularity during the 1970s. Ransom helped to teach Buzzy how to play the drums. "My father hated the idea of number one, my mother marrying a musician," Brooke says, "and number two, that Buzzy wanted to do [the drums]." Yet Maynard Jr. never insisted that Buzzy become a doctor, lawyer or even a mayor. "Just be what you want to be," he advised, "and be the best at it!"

As a politician who had lived on the public stage, and *for the public stage,* no two subjects caused Maynard Jr. to draw a veil of privacy faster, and more completely, than his father's death and his young son's life. Only with family members could he discuss Buzzy freely. "He has talked to all of us about it," Sandra, the mayor's sister, says. "He has wept over it. He has agonized over it."

Brooke adds, "My father is a real big dreamer and I'm sure that he had a lot of dreams for Buzzy that just went berserk. My dad was crushed. . . . I think that's been one of the low points of his life."

"He wanted his son," Bunnie says, "to be another him." She adds, "When Buzzy was born Maynard was the vice mayor. [Buzzy] has never known his father to be anything but a mayor or vice mayor. He's never had a relationship with a father. He's had a relationship with a mayor."

The mayor's abrupt refusal to discuss Buzzy during his June 21, 1990, press conference appeared on television news that night. By the time he returned home at the end of his long day, he was enervated by the experience.

As he walked toward his garage he spotted an oversized envelope that had been left near the door. He opened it. Inside was a supportive note from the former mayor of Atlanta, Ivan Allen, Jr.

It surprised him. Though they lived within a half mile, the two mayors interacted rarely, except to exchange pleasantries at an occasional civic event. Maynard Jr. had visited the Allen estate several times during his first term, once to ask Allen to lead a fund-raising committee for the downtown library.

Ivan Jr. had seen Jackson's press conference on TV. He felt sorry for him, as a former mayor and as a father. He scribbled a short, sympathetic note ("I thought he needed a little booster," Ivan Jr. recalls) and then placed an extra tie he had saved from Christmas inside the envelope. When he and Louise went out for ice cream later that night, they stopped first at the Jackson house. Ivan Jr. rang the bell. No one appeared at the door so he left his envelope by the garage.

When Maynard Jr. saw the tie, he shook his head. Then he smiled for the first time all day.

*September 18, 1990.* The eighty-six members of the International Olympics Committee marched into the ballroom at the New Takanawa Prince Hotel in Tokyo. They moved to seats on a stage in a room filled with chandeliers, journalists from across the world and the kind of civic expectations that can be produced only by spending millions of dollars. Suddenly, Billy Payne leaned over to Maynard Jackson and whispered into his ear: "We're in the finals." Then Payne whispered the same message to Andy Young. Payne had worked with a passion and fury for three years and now, on a starry night in Japan, one of his IOC sources had flashed him a signal upon entering the ballroom: "You're in the final two." Payne's immediate assumption was that Melbourne, Toronto, Belgrade and Manchester had been eliminated and that Atlanta and Athens had reached the final round.

Together, Payne, Young and Jackson made a dazzling interracial portrait and they knew it. In fact, they had played this image to the hilt in the final days of the bid process. Racial harmony had been one of the prevailing themes—that Atlanta was a city which had traversed time and misunderstanding, from the Civil War through civil rights, from the Confederacy to the Rev. Martin Luther King, Jr., to attain international renown. The members of the Atlanta bid team had boasted of Coca-Cola, a trademark known to every continent, and of Ted Turner's Cable News Network, which made Atlanta a center in the global village. They had boasted of the 53,000 hotel rooms in the city and of the world-class Hartsfield Atlanta International Airport, all proof, they proclaimed, of the city's readiness to host the world. The engineers at Georgia Tech had produced a remarkable computerized rendition of the proposed Olympic Village. A limited-edition series of books about Atlanta's history, produced at great expense, accompanied the bid and put a shine on every aspect of the city (though one transposed photograph erroneously turned the legendary golfer Bob Jones into a left-hander).

Harmony between the races, a concept that fit snugly within the Olympic spirit, was Atlanta's most carefully sculpted image. "We can set an example. People in South Africa can say, 'Well, I'll be damned, it really does work,'" Payne says of the city's Olympics pitch. "'Here is a city that despite its past, despite racial issues that paralyzed us for so many years, has basically now established that people can work together.' The world, in my estimation, has never received a major dose of that message."

Early in the bid process, Payne learned that most IOC members knew little about Atlanta or the American South; in fact, many confused Atlanta with Atlantic City, New Jersey. One African IOC member had arrived in Atlanta and said he had expected to see farmlands between the airport and downtown.

The one image of Atlanta that was known to virtually all IOC members was Margaret Mitchell's *Gone With the Wind.* "They'd all read it," Payne says. "No question." As an ode to the majesty of the Old South and slavery, though, Mitchell's classic concerned some members of Atlanta's bid team, who feared it might present a politically incorrect image. The fear was strong enough that Payne removed a clip from Selznick's *Gone With the Wind* film that had been included in Atlanta's final video presentation. "While we had not encountered any negativism about it," Payne says, "when you get to the end of the road in Olympic bids, the last thing you want to do is take a risk. And so we made a decision to pull it. . . . If that could have, potentially, negatively affected one out of one hundred, why take the risk?"

To Maynard Jr., the days in Tokyo before the final announcement had seemed like a political convention, particularly with last-minute lobbying and buttonholing of IOC members. "We were lobby lizards," Maynard Jr. says. Sparing no expense, the Atlantans had rented a house in downtown Tokyo—they called it "The Atlanta House"—where they entertained IOC members over breakfast, lunch and dinner. Maynard Jr. used his favorite adage about his home city, telling IOC members, "There are only two kinds of people in our country: those who live in Atlanta and those who want to." While several of the mayor of Athens's staffers became embroiled in a shoving match during those days in Tokyo, the gracious mayor of Atlanta served as vivid proof that blacks had emerged in Atlanta, Ga., U.S.A., Capital of the New South.

"I am Maynard Jackson, mayor of the city of Atlanta," he said in a brief speech that was part of Atlanta's last presentation in Tokyo. "I am here to say that Atlanta is ready . . . Atlanta is ready to welcome the world . . . Atlanta stands before the world a miracle modern city rebuilt from the rubble of war. With the Phoenix as our official symbol, we are a city risen from the nineteenth-century ashes of a tragic, earth-scorching conflict as old as the earth is old and as new as today's headlines." Then, speaking in French, the mayor said, "Peace, justice, tolerance, human rights, new moral values, understanding between people of different races and cultures. Atlanta . . . is the embodiment of the Olympic ideal. "(Later, Payne would marvel at Jackson's French, which he had rehearsed for the occasion: "His accent is good—real good.") Andy Young closed the Atlanta presentation with a moving address as the Atlanta Olympic theme song built to a crescendo. "It was just like in the Baptist church," Maynard Jr. says, "when they begin to bring the organ under the preacher." When the Atlantans left the room, Maynard Jackson saw some IOC members crying, so moving was Young's delivery.

Finally, at ten minutes before nine P.M. in Tokyo, the Spaniard Juan Antonio Samaranch, president of the IOC, walked to the lectern. In his thick accent, Samaranch said, "The International Olympic Committee has awarded the 1996 Olympic Games to the city of At . . ." The pause was only a microsecond, but it seemed ten minutes long to Maynard Jackson. *Would he say "Atlanta" or "Athens"?* "Our hearts were in our throats," he recalls.

And then Samaranch dragged out the final syllables: "lahn-ta!"

Jackson, Payne and Young embraced. From the Greek gallery came cries of "Coca-Cola! Coca-Cola!" suggesting the soft drink company had bought the Games for its headquarters city. But Maynard Jr. heard none of that. Resounding blasts of cannons, that's what he heard in his mind.

At least that was the only way he could describe it. "The thing you'd worked for, dreamed about, prayed over, kept the faith for, stayed positive about—came through!" he recalls. "You're surrounded by the lights, the tension, by the pressure and the expectation. And all of a sudden it happens! *It's like an atomic bomb going off—in a positive way!*" Later the Atlantans learned that Athens had led Atlanta after the first round of voting, 23–19. Then, Belgrade, Manchester and Melbourne were eliminated. In the fourth round, Toronto, with 22 votes, was eliminated. Atlanta swept most of Toronto's votes so that, in the final round, Atlanta defeated Athens, 51–35. Andy Young had been the central figure in Atlanta's bid. His days at the United Nations had helped him establish relations with the nations of the world and now the IOC's African members, 11 percent of the total, were swayed to Atlanta's side, as were voters from the Arab nations (who gratefully remembered Young's controversial contact with the PLO) and South and Central America. Years later, Young, recalling his U.N. years, says, "Everything I said that seemed to be controversial here [in the United States], everybody around the world knew was true. It did nothing but build up my credibility all over the world. Atlanta is cashing in on that."

Maynard Jr. and Georgia governor Joe Frank Harris signed the official documents in the ballroom. Maynard Jr. put his hands to his head in disbelief and said a prayer: "Thank you, God. Thank you, Jesus." And then he told the world's media: "The city of Atlanta deserves this!"

Atlanta had craved such a validation for 126 years, from the moment Sherman's embers had cooled. What began as a matter of physical necessity—growth, in every index—had become a way of life in the city. Payne's pursuit of the Olympics seemed a logical extension of Atlanta's pursuit of growth beyond invulnerability. Never too fatigued to give its sales pitch one more time, Atlanta had longed for an announcement of its own arrival.

Halfway across the world it was not yet eight A.M. in Atlanta. Ivan Allen III was driving to work when he heard the announcement that Atlanta had won the 1996 Games. Margaret was taking her daily walk with her dogs in the meadow on the Allen estate. She had her pocket radio tuned to a newsmagazine program when the Olympics announcement broke in. Alone in the meadow, Margaret, in an uncommon departure from her southern lady propriety, shouted, "YEESSSSS!"

Ivan Jr. learned of the IOC announcement watching his bedroom television set, just as he had learned of the shooting of the Rev. Martin Luther King, Jr., twenty-two years before. The seventy-nine-year-old former mayor felt a degree of self-satisfaction. "I was thrilled to death," he says. "It was another star in our belt." On TV, the former mayor, transfixed, watched two thousand Atlantans who had gathered at Underground Atlanta to see the announcement on oversized TV screens. Their celebration was raucous. Balloons rose and confetti fell from storetops. The former mayor heard someone on TV predict the 1996 Olympics would become the most important event in Atlanta since the Cotton States Exposition of 1895, where Booker T. Washington had delivered his Atlanta Compromise. The Senator had attended that Exposition as a nineteen-year-old typewriter salesman.

Ivan Jr. played his daily round later that day at the Peachtree Golf Club, which he had helped to found more than forty years earlier with a group that included Bob Jones. The stately clubhouse, built in antebellum times by slaves using handmade bricks, once had been a plantation Big House. Sherman had occupied it one night during his siege of Atlanta. Now, in the fall of 1990, the club's exclusive membership still had not been penetrated by a black or Jew, a battle Ivan Jr. wasn't willing to fight. ("I'm a tired old warrior," he says.)

On the day of the Olympics announcement, Peachtree Golf Club members were buzzing over the news. Ivan Allen Jr. told some of his oldest and dearest friends the very thing that Maynard Jackson was saying halfway across the globe: "The city of Atlanta deserves this."

# CHAPTER 29

The gun was a Smith & Wesson, .32-caliber magnum, one of many purchases Ivan Allen III had made in recent years for the family farm in Heard County. Single-handedly, Ivan III had brought the farm back to life. He had restored the stables and returned horses to them. He had fixed the interior of the house on Redland Road and made certain of the upkeep of the more than 2,300 acres. He and Margaret often entertained small groups of friends at the farm on weekends. They fished in the lake, which he kept stocked, and walked the fields for hours at a time. After dinner they gathered near the living room fireplace and talked about politics or the children. Margaret always thought her husband a farmer at heart.

The house at the farm had the look and feel of a sportsman's retreat, warm, rustic and comfortable. Fishing rods were locked in place against the wall, inside the front door leading to a spacious living room. On the back porch several high-backed rockers faced west, offering a magnificent view of the rolling fields.

Ivan III stored the shells in an open closet in his bedroom, along with his hunting wardrobe. The bedroom was small, barely big enough for twin beds side by side. The wood used to panel the walls came from an old barn on the grounds. A few hardback books, one by George Will on baseball and another by Charles Kurault on travel, stood between bookends on the nightstand between the beds. When Ivan III came to the farm alone, his favorite bird dog, Dede, usually slept on the bed next to him.

He had purchased the gun for Margaret. She took long walks across the farm with her German shepherds and occasionally wild dogs appeared from out of the brush, frightening her. She had wanted a noise-maker to chase them off.

But when she heard the .32 fired, it made her quiver. Margaret told her husband, "That's too noisy for me."

In the spring of 1992, Ivan III was a middle-aged man and leading civic pillar of Atlanta—the quintessential "Hail Fellow, Well Met"—whose lifetime formula for success in business suddenly seemed in question. For the first time since the Depression, the annual revenues of the Ivan

Allen Company had declined for three consecutive years, falling from the peak of $116 million in 1988 to $89 million in 1991. Superstores and chains such as Office Depot and Office Max had undercut the Ivan Allen Company's prices and threatened its client relationships. The office supplies industry was in a period of dramatic consolidation. Rumors that the Ivan Allen Company was about to be sold were plentiful. "For the first time in my life," Ivan III told Margaret, "I feel like I don't have the answers."

He had responded to the challenge in the only way he knew—by working harder and longer. Out the winding driveway at the Allen estate he drove each morning at 6:30 and back he came after dusk, then out again to a civic meeting. By seven o'clock on most mornings, he was at his desk in the office, his shirtsleeves already rolled up. The company's troubles became his own. "I can't hide behind something," he told a colleague, "like the chairman of IBM can. No one knows who the chairman of IBM is." Everyone knew Ivan Allen III ran the Ivan Allen Company. Privately, he worried about his son, Ivan IV, and how the name might someday cause him to face similar burdens and expectations.

The effects of mounting pressures were visible on Ivan III: his weight had swelled to more than two hundred pounds. "If Ivan doesn't look out, he's going to look like his grandfather [the Senator]," Bill Pressly, former headmaster at Westminster and mentor to Ivan III, told his wife. Ivan III attacked his weight with typical intensity, at times starving himself and at others exercising to exhaustion. He was fifty-three but looked older.

He revealed his deepest thoughts rarely. Always, he put up an optimistic front, full of the pep and spark that distinguished his grandfather. He was not religious. One morning, while jogging along Northside Drive with his close friend, orthopedist Dr. E. Ladd Jones, Ivan III passed the Rev. Frank Harrington. With all best intentions, Ivan III asked the minister, "Why don't you come jog with us next Sunday morning at eighty-thirty or nine o'clock?" Reverend Harrington raised a brow. *"Ivan, I think I've got something to do at that hour."* Later, Jones said, "Ivan, do you know what you just said?" Only then realizing his blunder, Ivan III said, "Oh, no!" He said it with a smile.

He was having trouble sleeping. Even though his house on the Allen family estate was surrounded by trees and gorgeous greenery—the view from his living room, with its vaulted ceiling and large glass back window, offered an exquisite view of nature—he felt somehow hemmed in, not only in his home city but in his home. "He could never really relax here," Margaret says.

The family farm restored his vitality and optimism. It was one of the great joys in his life. He had other more personal joys. Amanda, his only daughter, was engaged to a young man he adored, Knox Thompson, with a summer wedding date already set. He also thrived on his excursions with Ladd Jones. Margaret and Ivan III had traveled frequently over the years with Ladd and Rosie Jones. Some of the moments Ivan III most treasured occurred while fishing with Jones. Sometimes they fished in Georgia, other times in the Carolinas or the Bahamas. During one trip, Ivan III located a waterfall near Lake Toxaway, North Carolina ("See, Jonesy, I told you I could find it!"), but later, as he waded through the waters, he took a step and suddenly was submerged, his hat floating. Together, the two men laughed like schoolboys. Jones sensed that Ivan III cherished one particular aspect of their friendship—rarely, if ever, did Jones ask him about business or civic responsibilities in Atlanta.

In March 1992, Ivan III did something totally out of character and contrary to his family's traditions. He called into his office Marie Dodd, longtime vice president of advertising at the Ivan Allen Company, and told her to resign from some of her civic commitments. He said he would do the same. "We're spending too much time in the community," he said, "and not enough in the company." On March 30, Dodd sent him a memo, attaching her letters of resignation from the boards of the Atlanta Historical Society, the American Red Cross, the Georgia Conservancy, Leadership Atlanta and the Georgia Tech Advisory Board.

Ivan III attempted to reduce his commitments but discovered the task more difficult than anticipated. Mayor Maynard Jackson asked him to become a member of the MARTA board. Days later, the mayor still hadn't heard from him, so he telephoned. Only then did Ivan III say that he needed to spend more time at the company and therefore could not accept his offer. "Obviously, I had to respect that," Maynard Jr. says. "I understood." In recent years, Ivan III also had turned down a trustee role at Princeton University and the presidencies of the Atlanta Rotary Club and Westminster.

Some Atlantans, however, were unwilling to allow him to say no. In late April, Ivan III phoned in his resignation from the executive and development committees of the Woodruff Arts Center, one of his favorite causes. He agreed not to resign, though, from the center's board of directors. "I would not have accepted that," Charles Glassick, president of the Woodruff board, recalls. "Ivan Allen was a key cog in our wheel here. We needed him." About a week later, Ivan III called the former gubernatorial candidate Howard "Bo" Callaway to tender his resignation from the Ida Cason Callaway Foundation. "We'll give you a leave of absence," Callaway said. "But Ivan, *we won't let you resign.*"

The harder he struggled to extricate himself from civic chores, the deeper Ivan III seemed to fall into them. He was the president-elect of the downtown Commerce Club and chairman of the aviation committee for the Atlanta chamber. He had agreed to help raise funds for former president Jimmy Carter's new war against poverty in the city, the Atlanta Project. Andy Young had convinced him to chair a local fund-raising campaign for the United Negro College Fund. For a man who planned to give up his civic responsibilities, he carried an enormous load.

In early May, he told his father of his plans to draw back from the civic scene in Atlanta and to rededicate himself to the family company. The eighty-one-year-old former mayor said it was probably a good idea. He hoped these changes would ease his son's pressures.

On May 15, 1992, a Friday, Marie Dodd sat in Ivan III's office. He seemed in an unusually reflective mood. "Marie," he said, "am I too tough on the people here?" Dodd and Ivan III had worked together for more than thirty years at the Ivan Allen Company. Both were high achievers, aggressive. At times, they seemed in competition with each other. Now, Dodd smiled. "Ivan, you're always too tough," she said. "We'd be suspicious if things lightened up."

That night, at another fund-raising celebration, Bill Pressly spoke briefly with Ivan III. The conversation baffled the retired headmaster. Driving home, Pressly told his wife, "I just tried to talk to Ivan and I got the strangest sensation *that he wasn't there.*"

The next day, May 16, a Saturday, Inman and Tricia's daughter, Louise, graduated from Westminster, and the entire Allen family attended the ceremony. James Laney, president of Emory University, delivered the graduation address and cited the names of some of Atlanta's most responsible leaders and families—the Woodruffs and *the Allens,* among them. Listening to Laney, Ivan Jr. felt enormous pride. He hoped Ivan III accepted much of Laney's praise as his own.

That afternoon, after the ceremony, Ivan III left for the farm. He had asked his father and his friend from boyhood, Mason Lowance, to join him; both had other plans. Lowance, now a college professor in Amherst, Massachusetts, had been honored by Westminster that day with a Distinguished Alumni Award. Walking to his car with Lowance, Ivan III smiled at his friend. "I'm mighty proud of you, Mason," he said. They shook hands and agreed to meet the following night for dinner with their wives and Tread and Winifred Davis—the old Westminster Gang.

At that moment, Ivan III needed the farm. He was scheduled to spend Monday and Tuesday with Jimmy Carter. Together, they would meet with corporate chiefs in Atlanta and try to raise funds for the Atlanta Project. It was, Ivan III thought, a noble cause. Like so many others.

*          *          *

*Sunday, May 17, 1992.* Margaret hadn't heard from her husband all day. That was unlike the well-regimented Ivan. She had phoned the farm but received no answer. She was beginning to worry. The Sunday dinner hour came and then it went. Something was wrong.

Finally, she and Ivan IV got into the car and drove to the farm, a distance of seventy miles. Seventy miles is a long time to submerge dark thoughts. She had one fleeting intuition, dark and terrible, that Ivan III was dead. But then, chilling as it was, it passed. She tried to remain optimistic. Maybe he was out in the fields, walking, and had lost track of the time.

Ivan IV entered the house at the farm and found his father's body on the floor near the front bedroom, facedown and covered with blood. By his side was the Smith & Wesson handgun.

Paramedics rushed to the farm. They were unable to detect a pulse. One man later described the scene as "gruesome." Typically, Ivan III carried a large sum of cash, for business reasons. Sheriffs later found his money on the counter, undisturbed.

At 9:05 P.M. that night, Ivan III was pronounced dead at the West Georgia Medical Center. No autopsy was performed. "The situation didn't warrant it," Larry Hooks, Heard County coroner, would say. The cause of death, Hooks said, was self-evident. On the incident report filed at 9:44 P.M., the officer from the Heard County Sheriff's Department wrote, *"Self-Inflicted Gunshot Wound."*

It was not yet five o'clock in the morning on Monday when Marie Dodd heard her telephone ring. She picked up the receiver.

"Marie," she heard a familiar voice say.

"Yes," she answered, rousing herself from a deep sleep.

"I have very bad news. I need your help. Ivan is dead."

Not yet fully awake, Dodd thought she heard Ivan III telling her that his father was dead. *But wait a minute. He didn't say "Daddy." Ivan always calls his father Daddy.*

Then she knew. "I'll be right there," she told Ivan Allen, Jr.

She arrived at the Allen estate at about 5:30. The front door was unlocked. When she appeared in the dining room, Ivan IV fell into her arms, sobbing. Both Ivan Jr. and Louise struggled to control their emotions; Margaret fought back tears.

Dodd embraced the former mayor. "I want you to take care of things, Marie," Ivan Jr. told her. "Somebody needs to talk to the cemetery."

For the next forty-eight hours, Marie Dodd operated on instinct. In the predawn hours Monday, she drove downtown, to the Ivan Allen

Company offices, to prepare an obituary, a news release for local television stations and to make arrangements with Patterson's funeral home and Westview Cemetery. Nearly a quarter century before, Dodd had performed the same functions for the funeral of the Senator. Ironically, Dodd had been making periodic updates on the death notice of Ivan Jr., contacting writers on the obituary desk of the local newspapers. It never occurred to her that she would write an obituary for Ivan III. Forever modest, Ivan III kept only a one-page résumé. He had accomplished many good deeds in his life, most of them unheralded. Piecing together his career achievements as best she could, Dodd wrote the obituary and the news release, then brought them back to the Allen estate for the family's approval. Margaret decided that a graveside service would be held for her husband the next day. Now, as in 1968 when the Senator died, Dodd wrote the notice for employees that the Ivan Allen Company offices would close on Tuesday—the day of his burial. The Ivan Allen Company presses were used to print the programs for the service. Once the ink dried, company employees folded them by hand.

Margaret had taken her telephone off the hook early that morning. She put the receiver back in place about 7:30 A.M. and within seconds the phone rang. It was Jimmy Carter. He had just heard the news on National Public Radio. In another hour or so, Carter and Ivan III were to begin their fund-raising meetings for the Atlanta Project.

"Is it true, Margaret?" Carter asked. Margaret replied, "Jimmy, it's a tragedy for all of us."

The phone rang again. It was Maynard Jackson. A couple weeks earlier he had seen Ivan III in a frozen yogurt store in Buckhead. Both had professed to be on diets. "I won't tell if you won't tell," Maynard Jr. had told him, with a mischievous grin. Ivan III smiled and replied, "Okay, we'll both get no sugar and no fat." "That's a deal," Jackson said. It was the last time the mayor ever saw him. On the phone with Margaret, Maynard Jackson said, "I just heard the news. I'm very sorry . . ."

The velvet glove of Old Atlanta wrapped around the Allens that morning. Friends came to spend a few moments with Margaret, Ivan Jr. and Louise. A white-gloved City of Atlanta policeman turned away reporters who attempted to enter the long, winding driveway on Northside Drive.

Those who visited the family later would recall the matriarchal strength and stoicism of Louise. But in the old mayor they saw frailty, confusion and sadness beyond measure. On this day, Ivan Jr. wanted to hear good things about his son. When businessman Bob Holder told him, "There wouldn't be any Olympics in Atlanta if it weren't for Ivan," the old mayor smiled, as if given sustenance.

"Where did I go wrong?" Ivan Jr. asked his closest friends. Bill Pressly answered, "You didn't go wrong. You were as fine a parent as I've ever known." But even Pressly had a difficult time accepting the suicide of Ivan III, for it seemed an irrational act committed by a supremely rational man. Months later, Pressly would suggest to Ivan Jr. and Louise that maybe Ivan III had put the gun to his head, merely contemplating suicide without meaning to pull the trigger. No, the parents said, as if the moment had crystallized in their mind, when he pulled the trigger he was no longer Ivan III.

By 10:30 Tuesday morning, small clusters of mourners began to gather for the service at Westview Cemetery. The heat and humidity made the mid-May day feel like the typical August inferno in Atlanta. Standing in the shade of the scattered oaks, maples and dogwoods, the mourners whispered and waited.

Marie Dodd had handled every detail. She had driven behind the hearse en route to Westview. She had arranged for the installation of a broad green canopy next to the open grave, to shield the family and elderly friends from the intense sun.

Margaret did not want a cortege through town, as the Senator had had for his funeral, and so the cars arrived independently, yet in a steady stream. The crowd swelled. Estimates ranged from 750 to more than 1,000. One official at Westview told Dodd that this was the largest grave-side service the cemetery had ever had. "How they ever got to Westview!" Ivan Jr., the old mayor, said months later. "Most people don't know where Westview is anymore." Laura Maddox Smith, the longtime family friend, says, "I never saw anything like it. . . . Not only the people, I mean, the blacks."

Old Atlanta attended in force to bury one of its own. The black community was well represented: Donald Hollowell, the noted civil rights lawyer; Andy Young; Hugh Gloster, the former Morehouse president. Soon, Jimmy Carter appeared over a rise. A black limousine pulled next to the canopy, and out stepped Louise and Ivan Jr. Margaret and her children appeared next. With her, Margaret brought Dede, Ivan III's bird dog.

The service began at high noon, the sun blistering, and ended about thirty minutes later. The sense of shock that suicide produces was apparent in the crowd. The mourners' expressions ranged from impassive to nearly bloodless. A black minister wailed, "Jesus, Loves Me," and his voice, deep and textured, carried across the open field. The two remaining Allen brothers, Inman and Beaumont, spoke a few words while standing before their brother's casket, their voices choking with emotion. "Trying to explain Ivan's death to our children has been hard," Beaumont said. "Five-year-old Beau wants to know how Uncle Ivan died. Nine-year-old Sarah wants to know why. It's hard to help children understand something when you don't understand it yourself." Inman said of his late brother, "His commitment to us, family and friends, his city, it was absolute and it was total. His commitment, if you will, his love, caused my brother to lose his balance, and that's what I hold on to because it's the only thing I have." Jimmy Carter, in his eulogy, described Ivan III as "the essence of the Southern gentleman" and "the heart of Atlanta."

Standing a few feet from the canopy, Mayor Maynard Jackson, in a dark blue suit, used a program to shield his eyes from the sun. Beads of perspiration rolled down his cheek and the back of his neck. His respect for Ivan III dated to those difficult days of affirmative action in the 1970s. "He was somebody I could count on," Maynard Jr. recalls.

For Ivan Jr., this was the most difficult moment in his eighty-one years of privileged living. The King funeral and the riot in Summerhill were business. His son's suicide produced a personal pain that pierced to his core. One family friend suggested that, prior to the suicide, the most fretful crisis the mayor's children had ever known was the day Inman had broken off a wedding engagement. The mayor's old friend Gene Patterson, retired and living in Florida, sent a note of condolence, calling attention to a beautiful and enduring image a minister had spoken at the American Cathedral in Paris in 1962, after the plane crash at Orly: "Life is eternal and love is immortal and the horizon is only the limit of our sight."

In his light-toned summer suit, Ivan Jr. sat next to Louise. She was the stronger of the two, her chin tilted slightly upward, her eyes shielded by her broad-brimmed summer hat. The former mayor slumped in his folding chair and stared at his shoes. When a minister spoke of Ivan III as a devoted son, the old mayor nodded his head and tears formed in his eyes. He would say, "That's the only time I lost my poise."

In his mind, Ivan Jr. was trying to find his way back to the moment when the troubles began for his son. "I flounder terribly," he says. "I start trying to find things to direct me. All you do is run yourself down a blind alley. And yet I don't know which way to go." He thought about his son as never before. "He liked to [hunt] at such a pace that I sometimes wondered whether there was any relaxation. You can't have but two days to do it and you've got to leave home at five in the morning to be down there in time for breakfast at 7:30 so you can kick off with the gang. Then you hunt for a day and a half and you've got to rush back to Atlanta that night to be at some meeting." Thinking of his late son, he shook his head and said, "I don't think I had to work as hard as Ivan had to work—or elected to work. He had a very strong drive to do whatever he needed to do. To build that business. To be the top civic leader in the city."

When the service ended, Ivan Jr. stopped in front of his son's casket. He placed his right hand on it, then ran his fingers across its smooth surface. His knees buckled. Louise took him by the elbow. Gently, she pulled him away.

Marie Dodd surprised herself by how completely she had been able to hold back her emotions. She had made it on Diet Cokes and sense of duty. That night, Dodd returned home, put on a caftan, poured herself a stiff scotch, then retired to her back porch to read *The New Yorker* magazine. In it, she saw a cartoon of a cemetery, with a bubble coming out of one grave, saying, "Say, this isn't so bad." That was all it took. Alone on her porch, she wept.

Privately, friends said Ivan Allen, Jr., never again would be the same. He had lost more than his son. He had lost his hope. The old mayor who once had saved Atlanta from itself felt as if he had failed to save his son from himself. Within a month, doctors attached a pacemaker to the old mayor's heart because it had developed an erratic beat.

In the months that followed, he brooded. Louise became busier than ever with her work at the Atlanta History Center. "I have been able to accept Ivan's death," she would say, "better than Ivan has." She worried that her husband would never get over it.

"If you had set out to damage Ivan Allen, Jr., in the most heinous way possible," a family friend said later, "this is what you would have done."

Not long after the funeral the old mayor began to tell close friends that he had done an enormous disservice to his son by naming him Ivan Allen III. "I think Daddy [the Senator] demanded the name as soon as he heard Louise was pregnant," he would say. "I don't think we even considered another name."

In an interview conducted the year before his death, Ivan III was asked about his famous name. "I really don't want to talk about that," he said. His reason: "Because I never have."

*"What did Ivan mean by that?"* the old mayor asked when his son's response was related to him months after the funeral.

Searching for his own answers, Ivan Jr. came to believe that the city—and its people—had refused to let his son escape its clutches. "We were absolutely controlled by Atlanta. We were an old family, right on through Ivan, that was built around Atlanta," Ivan Jr. would say. But then the old mayor's instincts reminded him to boast of Atlanta, not criticize it. "Well, you know, I, our sense of egotism enjoyed doing those kinds of things." It was too complicated for logic.

As the old mayor walked from his son's casket, arm in arm with Louise, some of his friends wondered if the real cause of death was Atlanta.

When Amanda Allen walked down the aisle in marriage the following month, her uncle Inman and her brother, Ivan IV, took the place of her father as her escorts. Her emotions were deeply conflicted. "It was the happiest thing in my life," she would say of the wedding, "and the saddest thing in my life."

Loo-key, is what Ivan III liked to call his daughter, or sometimes Petroosh-key, silly names made up by a doting father. "Ivan absolutely thought Amanda walked on water," a family friend would say. When Amanda was a child, Ivan III often rose at five A.M. to take her to ride her horses. Sometimes he picked her up from soccer practice at dusk. On Saturday mornings, he liked to make her pancakes. As an adult, Amanda Allen hunted and fished with him. One of her happiest memories was of standing with her father in a swamp and bringing down a mallard with one shot. She would remember it not because of her marksmanship but because her father was there to see it.

Amanda was twenty-six years old and along with her fiancé, Knox Thompson, decided to proceed with the wedding but scale back its size. Instead of a reception for 400 at the Piedmont Driving Club, they invited about 150 family and friends to gather at Margaret's house on Northside Drive.

Amanda and Knox had met while students at the University of Richmond. They had been dating six years when Knox invited himself to dinner at Ivan III and Margaret's. Wearing a suit and tie, he intended to ask their permission to marry Amanda. He was certain they knew his purpose. But when Ivan III came home from work that night, he said to Knox, grand as can be, "What are you doing here? Where's Amanda?" Sitting nervously at the dinner table, Knox's throat became drier and drier. Finally, he asked. Ivan III and Margaret congratulated him. Not until a week later, Thanksgiving 1991, did Knox bend to one knee, alongside the lake at the Allen farm in Franklin, to formally ask Amanda to marry him. Ivan III rode up on horseback moments later. Amanda told her father the news and noticed "a little tiny trickle" in his eye. "I'm sure it was a tear of happiness," she says.

They were married at First Presbyterian Church, where her parents and grandparents had been married. For the ceremony, the Rev. George Wirth prepared an eloquent tribute to Ivan III and as he read it Amanda stared at the altar. "It was very hard to focus on the vows," Knox says, "knowing that that was coming."

To Margaret, the wedding seemed a much-needed burst of joy. But when she saw a videotape of the service much later, she decided never again to look at it. "Mister Allen," Margaret says of the former mayor, "just looked so sad."

The suicide made front-page news in Atlanta. The newspapers referred to the Allens as an Atlanta "dynasty" and the *Constitution* printed an old picture of the Senator, Ivan Jr., Ivan III and Inman alongside the family swimming pool. In Atlanta, the Allen suicide resonated with profound force, much like the poet Edward Arlington Robinson's dark and evocative *Richard Cory*, about the inexplicable demise of a man "richer than a king— And admirably schooled in every grace" who, on one calm night, "Went home and put a bullet through his head."

Ivan III left no suicide note. As with any unexplained suicide, rumors moved through the Atlanta aristocracy and business community. Inside the city's old social and business clubs conversation ignited about the haunting ironies between the suicide of Ivan III and the novel *Peachtree Road*, written in 1988, four years earlier, by a local novelist, Anne Rivers Siddons. A former *Atlanta* magazine writer, Siddons wrote in *Peachtree Road* of an aristocratic former Atlanta mayor who once stood atop a car during a riot, a thinly veiled version of Ivan Allen, Jr., she named Ben Cameron. In Siddons's novel, Cameron's namesake son, Ben Jr., commits suicide, using a handgun, after his wife learns of his involvement in a homosexual relationship. When Siddons heard that Ivan III had killed himself, and with a gun, she felt the blood drain from her face. A radio station had called to tell her and, noting the irony of her novel, asked for comment. *God Almighty,* Siddons thought, *what do you think I have to say? It's appalling, I hate it and I wouldn't add to the mayor's pain for anything.* She had barely known Ivan III, having met him only once or twice in passing. She greatly admired his father, though. The old mayor had even attended a local party when *Peachtree Road* was released, much to Siddons's surprise. "Mr. Mayor," she said, noting his outstretched hand, "I hope there's not a subpoena in that hand." Ivan Jr. had smiled, then complimented her book, saying, "You really caught the times." But he said he wanted to correct a few inaccuracies. "For one thing," he began, "it wasn't a 'Five-Point Plan' I had as mayor, it was a 'Six-Point Plan.'" That was all he ever said to Siddons about her book.

Siddons felt "almost guilty" about having written about suicide. "I could easily see why Ben Jr. had done it. I mean, I knew why he had done it. I had set that situation up. I had no idea why Ivan III did it." To her, "it just seemed that it was hard to be a son of those [privileged Atlanta] houses because if you didn't want to walk that particular road, there wasn't much outlet for you. You just stuck around and tried it or you left." *Peachtree Road,* Siddons says, "was a book about being broken by a small world as well as shaken by it."

Many wondered if the burden of his locally famous name, and the sheer weight of its attendant business and civic responsibilities, finally crumbled upon Ivan III. "I don't think he knew how many people compared him with his father and put him above," Hugh Gloster says. As Morehouse president in 1983, Gloster had awarded Ivan III an honorary degree, as he had for Ivan Jr. seven years earlier, and felt compelled to say to Ivan III, "You have followed in the footsteps of your distinguished father. . . . You have indeed done 'as your great progenitors have done/And by your virtues (proved) yourself their son.' "

The Allen suicide was particularly troubling to Larry Gellerstedt III. Like Ivan III, Gellerstedt's father and grandfather once served as president of the Atlanta chamber and now he, too, was establishing himself in Atlanta civic leadership. Only thirty-six, Gellerstedt looked to Ivan III as a civic role model and as a man carrying an impressive family mantle. He spoke with Ivan III about it. "I came away thinking, 'Well, when I get to the mid-forties or early fifties, I'll be done with this issue,' " Gellerstedt says.

"I think the thing that Ivan and I have had a hard time dealing with at times is, 'Am I walking down a path because it's what I love or [am I] walking down a path because it's what I feel like I should do?' And you get to where you don't know those feelings very well. And Ivan was such a perfectionist that I got a feeling that somewhere . . . I just don't think he could deal with a shortcoming in his own mind.

"When I would get down about, 'How am I supposed to expand this [construction] business and go to all of these black-tie balls and serve on all of these boards, how can I get all of that done?' I would always sort of say, 'Well, Ivan got it done.'

"And that," Gellerstedt says, "would be my light at the end of the tunnel."

Jimmy Carter did not forget his friend. In the autumn of 1993, the former president dedicated the Ivan Allen III Pavilion at the Carter Center. It was a symbolic gift to his hunting companion, not only for having helped to raise the initial $28 million that built the Carter Center in 1986 but also for his years of friendship. The $7 million pavilion featured a chandelier-lit interfaith chapel with a floor-to-ceiling glass wall, as well as a panoramic view of downtown Atlanta. The five circular buildings of the Carter Center and Presidential Library are set between two small lakes and a Japanese garden on a historic hillside where, on July 22, 1864, General Sherman maintained a command post and waited to learn if General McPherson had repulsed an assault by Confederates.

Yet, if this pavilion would stand firmly as the legacy of Ivan III, then the night of February 16, 1994, revealed a sadder and deeper truth. On that night, more than four hundred local and state politicians attended the Carter Center's annual Salute to Public Service inside the Ivan Allen III Pavilion.

Pierre Howard, the youthful lieutenant governor of Georgia, told the audience, "I can think of no better place to salute public servants than this building, which was named for one of Atlanta's mayors."

When Margaret heard Howard's misstatement the lump in her throat could have choked her. She hadn't planned to attend, but Ivan Jr. and Louise had urged her to join them. Now she felt angry, embarrassed and hollow. *Hadn't Jimmy Carter just mentioned to the audience that Ivan had been his close friend? How could Pierre Howard get it wrong?*

"I was ready to leave," Margaret says. "I wanted to slip out."

But she did not. Instead, she did the appropriate thing, as the Allens of Atlanta always have done. She followed the crowd, and two musicians playing bagpipes, through the winding corridors to a reception in the lobby of the Carter Museum. There, Pierre Howard approached her. "I wanted so badly to say something," Margaret says. But she did not. Instead, she did the appropriate thing. She smiled. Jimmy Carter had not missed the lieutenant governor's blunder. That night he patted Ivan Jr. on the shoulder, smiled and said, "Well, they gave you credit for the building."

Margaret felt a deep hurt for her husband. She thought to herself, "This was what Ivan wrestled with all of his life."

# Chapter 30

Maynard Jackson had been back in office only a few months in 1990 when he told a friend, "This was a mistake. I never should have run again."

Either he had outgrown City Hall or it, with its emphasis on administrative skills rather than pioneering social vision, had outgrown him. He was fifty-two years old, and his zest for the job had faded with his youth. He proved unable to recapture the drama and spirit of 1974 when he had been a trailblazer for his race and for the New South. Atlanta's City Hall had seemed a shining opportunity then, an extension of the civil rights movement and a stepping-stone to the U.S. Senate and then—who knew? Maybe something fantastic. Maynard Jr. had the skills and ambition. Would the mood of America allow a black man to make an even bigger political breakthrough?

But now in 1990, he, like so many other mayors across the nation, felt the intractability of the urban crisis—AIDS, crack cocaine, homelessness— a web of problems beyond the solution of any mayor. Funds from Washington had dried up during the Reagan-Bush years. The nation stumbled into an economic recession. Eastern Air Lines, with its regional hub in Atlanta, folded, leaving a huge vacancy at Hartsfield Atlanta International Airport. Rich's department store closed its flagship downtown store, something the late Dick Rich had vowed, in a different era, never would happen. With Rich's departure, Atlanta seemed to have lost a piece of its soul. Criticism of the mayor by advocacy groups and the newspapers was unyielding. The bickering and backbiting of city councilmen, a small irritant to Maynard Jr. in 1974, now became a colossal problem, though one of his floor leaders, City Councilman Bill Campbell, would say that the mayor lost only one vote in the four-year term (when the council overrode his veto of a Piedmont Park sewer treatment bill). Jackson's relationship with council president Marvin Arrington was in tatters. Once Jackson's floor leader in the council, Arrington had lost his faith in the mayor when he failed to endorse his 1980 candidacy for council president against Michael Lomax. "[Maynard Jr.] was an opportunist," Arrington decided. "He had used me and I said, 'Never again!'" Arrington provided a compelling counterpoint to Maynard Jr. Son of an Atlanta domestic and a truck driver who "won the street lottery when he was twenty-eight," Arrington was dark-skinned, bow-legged (justification for his childhood nickname: "Bo") and often spoke in the black idiom, which, he said, he learned while living on Neal Street in west Atlanta. He graduated from Clark College and later was among the first blacks to graduate from the Emory University Law School. He viewed Maynard Jackson's family with near awe: "His mother probably had a Ph.D., man, when people couldn't even pronounce Ph.D. . . . All of his aunties were Spelman graduates. . . . And his grandfather was like Ralph McGill. I mean, when you talk about John Wesley Dobbs, man, they used to call him the mayor of Auburn Avenue!" As a politician, though, Arrington viewed himself as a street populist, and more in touch with Atlanta's working-class blacks than Maynard Jackson. Friends often told him to remain on good terms with Maynard Jr., as a matter of political expedience, but Arrington replied, "I don't need Maynard Jackson socially, financially or politically."

In addition to having to absorb all of those headaches, Maynard Jr., as mayor, was giving up several hundred thousand dollars a year in bond attorney's income. He understood sacrifice in the name of public service, but this time sacrifice seemed illogical, even ridiculous. There were few rewards.

No one questioned why he had returned to politics but no one really understood why he had chosen to return to City Hall. For the love of Atlanta, is the way Maynard Jr. had explained it, and to finish his agenda from his first two terms.

But there was a harsher reality: the enduring racial intolerance in Georgia. If Atlanta's City Hall had seemed a stepping-stone in 1974, now it was the only stone for Maynard Jackson. As a black politician in Georgia, he had nowhere else to turn, save perhaps for the U.S. House of Representatives, a place that never had stirred his passions. He demanded stage front, center, and in the U.S. House he wouldn't get it.

In autumn 1990, Andy Young's attempt to join Douglas Wilder of Virginia as the only black governors in the South met a crushing defeat. Lt. Gov. Zell Miller won more than 80 percent of the white vote outside of the metropolitan Atlanta area, annihilating Young in the Democratic gubernatorial primary. The magnitude of Young's defeat stung Maynard Jr. "Here's a man who had been ambassador to the United Nations, a U.S. congressman and mayor of the city of Atlanta," Maynard Jr. says. The message was clear. A black man, even one with national and international political experience, could not be elected to statewide office in Georgia. At least not yet. "We live, as Americans, in a circumscribed way," Maynard Jr. says, "knowing that the American Dream is not a reality for us yet. . . . It's a fundamental unfairness that because I am an African-American I've got to figure that I cannot win a [statewide] campaign even though I think that I've got equal or superior qualifications to serve the people."

Atlanta's mayoralty seemed the only viable role and this bothered Maynard Jr. more than he would admit in public. As his own career stalled, he watched other blacks, in other states, advance to more prestigious positions: Dinkins as mayor of New York City, Wilder as governor of Virginia, Colin Powell as chairman of the Joint Chiefs of Staff and, another Georgian, Clarence Thomas as U.S. Supreme Court Justice.

The novelty of the black big-city mayor in America was gone. A full generation had passed since Cleveland's Carl Stokes had been elected as the nation's first. Despite all the others who had followed, the hopes among big-city blacks for an urban revival in America, which had accompanied the rise of black mayors, had been dashed long before. This experience was much the same as any political group new to power: struggling first as novices and then, over time, becoming a part of a process that is, by nature, slow-moving and at times suffocating.

In Atlanta, the cachet accompanying the title of mayor diminished daily. In 1990, the commission chairmen of Fulton, Cobb and DeKalb counties each had larger constituencies than Maynard Jackson. Even Gwinnett County to the north, with only seventy thousand residents in 1970, threatened to overtake the declining population of the city of Atlanta.

By 1990, the mayor of Atlanta controlled the reins of perception of the city, but little else.

The mayor's idiosyncracies and old habits returned to City Hall. Deb Speights, Jackson's director of communications, became so exasperated with the mayor's penned corrections of speeches that she told him, finally, "You need to get stock in Bic!" Maynard Jr. sometimes cruised the city in his Lincoln Town Car, Bill Hartsfield–like, on nights and weekends. At seven o'clock on one Sunday morning, using his car phone, he dialed his appointments secretary, Pat Allen, and received her answering machine. "Pat, Maynard Jackson. 23rd February, Sunday," he began, with a precision that tended to make his staffers mimic him when he wasn't around. "Remember we promised Jimmy Carter we'd try to keep the sidewalks near the Carter Center in pretty good shape? Have public works go out and check the area again." He still telephoned members of his staff at all hours of the night, sometimes five or six times. Yet if his formal and precise nature often seemed a parody of an old-school British barrister, he could still engender the old loyalty. When the mayor's staff and department heads gathered for a weekend retreat in mid-term, sitting around a table in bluejeans and sneakers, Chief of Staff Arthur Cummings asked, "Why are you here?" The mayor was not present at the time, but each response was a variation of, "I'm here because of Maynard Jackson." "He makes you loyal to him," one staffer would say. "You really want to die for the guy. You really want to jump on the grenade."

Not only was Maynard Jr. confronting the American urban dilemma, but also his own legend. In a sense, he was fighting the Selznick syndrome. Once producer David O. Selznick had finished *Gone With the Wind*, he recognized that regardless of his achievements during the remainder of his career (and his film *Rebecca* won an Academy Award for Best Picture the next year, in 1940) he would always be remembered only for *Gone With the Wind*. "That makes me furious," Selznick once said. "Anything else, no matter what we'll ever make, will always seem insignificant after that." Maynard Jr. would say of his own legacy, "I can see that my full name will be Maynard Jackson First Black Mayor Of Atlanta, Georgia." That rankled him. He thought it racist and wholly unfair because it cheated him of his accomplishments in office, including his affirmative action programs, airport construction, neighborhood planning, cultural affairs, the end to police brutality and his role as the first modern manager under the city's new charter. He did not want it forgotten that these accomplishments were made despite a more openly hostile opposition than any Atlanta mayor ever had faced.

He believed, naively, that he could administer his way into an even broader legacy during a third term. Almost certainly, though, that term will serve only as a historical footnote to his political odyssey. His third administration lacked continuity and vision. Maynard Jr. needed fourteen months to get his cabinet into place. During his first two years alone, he named three separate chiefs of staff and three executive officers. His incessant demands wore out his own people. His frustrations swept through his staff. To those who had served him during the 1970s, the frustration stemmed from their inability to reproduce the major achievements of the first terms.

"One of Maynard's frustrations is [that] he'd be a great charismatic leader of a movement," Andy Young says. "It's just awkward trying to combine this with administrating a city."

The coming 1996 Olympics allowed Atlanta a sense of purpose and forward motion. Maynard Jr. would boast, "I was the only mayor who went all over the world consistently in support of our search for the Olympics, the only one of the bid mayors who showed up everywhere." Nevertheless, Billy Payne and Andy Young led Atlanta's Olympics movement. They, not the mayor, managed the city's preparations for the Games.

When Jimmy Carter met with Maynard Jr. at City Hall in 1991 to discuss the Atlanta Project, a program that would battle the 27 percent poverty rate in the city, the mayor listened intently. "You know, Mr. President," he said, "what you've just described to me is the honest answer to my prayers. These things that you might accomplish in the Atlanta Project are those that have frustrated me and everyone else." The former president announced the formation of the Atlanta Project in October 1991 and Maynard Jr. offered to help in every possible way. "He basically gave me a blank check, anything I ever need," Carter says.

And so the two movements of paramount importance to Atlanta—the Olympics and the Atlanta Project, each filled with idealism and potential to effect social change in the city—functioned beyond the control of the mayor. His problems were compounded in March 1992 when Ira Jackson resigned as Atlanta's aviation commissioner, only seventeen months after his appointment. An old political friend of the mayor's, Ira Jackson faced federal corruption charges stemming from allegations that he had pocketed more than $900,000 from airport concessionaires. His resignation cast a pall over City Hall for two years.

"Am I happy being mayor? Some days, yes. Some days it's a struggle," Maynard Jr. told the *Journal-Constitution* in January 1992, the midpoint of his four-year term. "It's much tougher this time around."

He still possessed that remarkable outsized quality. He could fill up a room, not only figuratively but literally, with his voice, his laugh and his intellect. He had mastered the mayoral look and sound. Not since Bill Hartsfield—a politician who had been described a thousand different ways but who chose to chisel only one into his tombstone ("Mayor")—had Atlanta had a municipal leader who seemed to merge with his office, becoming one. His national reputation remained impressive. With the presidential election of 1992 on the horizon, *Jet* magazine named Atlanta's mayor as the man most often talked about among black leaders as a vice presidential candidate. A columnist for *The Boston Globe* went one step further, suggesting that Maynard Jackson was a possible Democratic presidential candidate.

By the time former Arkansas governor Bill Clinton moved into the front-runner position for the Democratic presidential nomination, Maynard Jr. already was a vocal supporter. On February 27, 1992, four days before the Georgia primary, Maynard Jr. was at the airport to greet Clinton. "I believe in your qualities," the broadly smiling mayor told Clinton in a speech that figured to help the candidate with the black vote in Georgia, "and I believe in your character."

Maynard Jr. understood political gamesmanship. That summer, as

Clinton swept toward the Democratic nomination, *The Washington Post* reported that Jackson was on a short list of twelve being considered as Clinton's running mate. "Complete speculation," Maynard Jr. called it at the time, though he knew exactly what it was. The news leak was a payback for lending his support to Clinton in Georgia. ("Never in my wildest dreams have I ever thought that they seriously considered anybody black, frankly, for that position," Maynard Jr. says.) As it happened, U.S. senator Albert Gore of Tennessee, ultimately Clinton's running mate, wasn't even on that twelve-name list.

The proud fathers of the city, black and white, thought it could never happen in Atlanta. Yet hundreds of young blacks shattered storefront windows, looted downtown stores and brutalized solitary whites near the Henry Grady statue on Marietta Street. The riot was contrary to the harmonious image long espoused and fiercely protected.

For several hours on April 30, 1992, downtown Atlanta belonged to the mobs. It was the inverted image of September 1906, this time young blacks venting their rage by beating any white person in sight.

Their wrath had been stirred by a jury verdict handed down in California, clearing four police officers of brutality charges in the beating of a black motorist named Rodney King. An amateur photographer's videotape of the beating, shown on nationwide television for months, had elevated the expectations among blacks for a prompt conviction. Soon after the acquittal, blacks across the nation poured into the streets.

In Atlanta, nearly one thousand Atlanta University Center students, and other young blacks living in housing projects near the campuses, marched in protest to the State Capitol that Thursday afternoon. About a hundred black youths then walked across the street to Atlanta's City Hall. Police reports at the time, monitored by the mayor's staff, indicated an increasingly unruly crowd. Already, rocks and bricks had been thrown through windows at the nearby legislative office building. Fearing for his safety, the mayor's aides advised him not to meet the crowd.

The black youths formed around the mayor on the City Hall steps, squeezing him in the center. "What happened is wrong," Maynard Jr. said of the verdict, "[but] we have to condemn it in the right way." He passed out a statement, which he had written, deploring the verdict but calling for a rational form of protest. Several young blacks shouted down the mayor. A few others balled up his prepared statement and threw it at him. Because the mayor's aides had failed to produce a megaphone, much of what he said was not heard. Most of the youths had no intention of listening, anyway. Maynard Jr. sensed that a few ringleaders were bent on violence. He offered to march with them, back to the AUC, or to bring a few leaders inside, to begin a dialogue.

"I understand what you are feeling," he told them. But several in the group shouted at him and thrust their fingers into his face. The mayor even tried one of John Wesley Dobbs's favored credos, recommending that the best way to fight injustice was with "Books, Ballots and Bucks." They only jeered louder.

To these black youths, some born after the mayor's historic political victory of 1973, Maynard Jackson represented nothing but the system they were protesting, the system that had allowed for black mayors but not for an eradication of social injustice. To them, the Rodney King verdict proved the system's failure and that Atlanta was little more than a wax museum of the civil rights movement. The old veterans of the movement had lost touch, they believed, and spent too much time drawing attention to themselves. About 100,000 black Atlantans lived in poverty, many in the shadows of Morehouse and Spelman colleges. The Martin Luther King, Jr. Center for Non-Violent Social Change on Auburn Avenue attracted three million visitors annually, but achieved virtually nothing for Atlanta's urban poor. Ironically, to the black youths gathered before him, Maynard Jackson was the opposition, just as Mayor Ivan Allen, Jr., had been the opposition in Summerhill in September 1966.

Some of the demonstrators moved away, and headed toward Underground Atlanta, still furious. The mayor called out to them that no violence would be tolerated. Undeterred, the mob shattered windows and turned over pushcarts in a rampage through the shopping and entertainment complex. White customers dove beneath tables. Later, the black youths broke glass cases and ransacked displays at Macy's on Peachtree Street. Several downtown stores owned by Koreans were vandalized. One young white man, wearing shorts and a T-shirt, was sprawled across the pavement on Broad Street, unconscious, bleeding from his head. A black youth stood over him, holding a sign that read "Justice 4 Rodney."

Maynard Jr. returned to his office, shellshocked, and, according to aide Angelo Fuster, "more than surprised by the vehemence and the anger that he felt, and that was directed at him." The mayor had walked, face first, into the cold reality of changed times.

Later that afternoon, as the dinner hour approached, National Guardsmen and Fulton County police in riot gear flooded Atlanta's downtown streets. Meanwhile, the mayor spoke to several hundred students at Clark-Atlanta University, at the invitation of school administrators who thought he could defuse their pent-up anger. His visit was a disaster. Students shouted and cursed, blaming him for intimidating tactics used by the Atlanta police force. Again, the mayor's statements were balled up and thrown at him. Maynard Jr. waited for the school administrators who had invited him to step forward and defend him. That support never came. "What they did was set me up as the sacrificial lamb and I just stood there and took it," Maynard Jr. says.

A few students suggested that the black mayor had forgotten his roots. "People like Maynard Jackson don't know where we're coming from," one Morehouse student said. "Maynard Jackson lives in Buckhead. *What does he know about the brothers in the street?*" Maynard Jr. held his ground until, finally, he could take no more, and walked out of the auditorium. "If we can't talk," he told the hostile students, "then there's no reason for me to be here."

"I lost respect for two or three friends that night," Maynard Jr. says. "[The experience] said to me that a few black academic leaders at Clark . . . had no balls."

By day's end more than three hundred arrests had been made and the mayor had called for a nighttime curfew, clearing the streets. Coca-Cola Company chairman Roberto Goizueta, reacting now as Bob Woodruff had reacted at the time of the King funeral in 1968, sent a fax to Maynard Jr. "Do what you need to do to increase security for the safety of all Atlanta's citizens and know that The Coca-Cola Co. will take the lead in making sure that the city's added costs are covered."

In the darkness, Maynard Jr. cruised the city's streets, searching for hot spots that needed cooling. He seemed omnipresent, appearing on local television, the national networks, CNN. His voice, firm and eloquent, was heard over the radio, too. "We will not tolerate lawlessness in any form," he said, repeatedly. The next afternoon, a Friday, after Rodney King and President George Bush had made televised pleas for a restoration of peace across America, Atlanta police used tear gas to disperse several hundred AUC students who intended to march, their crowd control tactics prompting a controversy.

Some city leaders met at an interracial Action Forum meeting several days later. They bared their souls about racial tensions and misunderstandings in Atlanta. A white businessman said his wife recently had gotten out of her car to mail a letter in a shopping center and two black youths had jumped into her car, trying to steal it; unable to start the engine, though, the youths ran off. A black attorney, meanwhile, said he had stopped in north Georgia to purchase gas only to be harassed by white state troopers.

In a press conference, Maynard Jr. said, "We've got to manage the issue of race and recognize that only by having a strategy, a plan are we going to make the kind of advancements that we need to make." As president of the National Conference of Democratic Mayors, he participated with other big-city mayors in a "Save Our Cities: Save Our Children" march in Washington, D.C. The purpose was to warn George Bush and Congress of the despair of American cities. Maynard Jr. likened the march to "taking a two-by-four to get their attention."

Maynard Jackson's greatest secret wish was to become the world's leading operatic tenor. "Oh, man!" he says, dreamily. "Just the power of the aria. The power of the music. *The power of the voice!* The message you can send!"

He thrived on being the center of attention and on August 9, 1992, he had that opportunity in the rarest of settings. Standing on a stage in the middle of a stadium at the closing ceremonies of the 25th Olympiad in Barcelona, Spain, Maynard Jr. received the official Olympics flag from IOC president Juan Antonio Samaranch and Barcelona mayor Pasqual Maragall. "In accordance with our tradition," Samaranch said, "I call upon the youth of the world to assemble four years from now in 1996 in Atlanta, United States of America."

Maynard Jr. had graduated from Morehouse College in 1956, but had been too overcome with emotion that day to enjoy the moment. But now, as he held the staff of the Olympic flag with one hand and waved to the capacity crowd with the other, he determined that "I was going to savor the moment, that I was going to consciously record what was going on, to remember that for the future.

"I've got enough ham in me," he admits, "to appreciate standing in front of three billion people."

Holding the Olympics flag on center stage, he seemed once again the black political phoenix risen in the New South—a role he knew and played so handsomely.

Such moments were few for Maynard Jr. Two weeks after Barcelona, his annual physical detected unusually high blood pressure. Doctors later determined that the three-hundred-pound mayor needed heart bypass surgery.

At fifty-four, Maynard Jr. suddenly considered his own mortality as never before. His father had died at fifty-nine, and though he says, "I'm not fixated on that," he made the connection in his mind. After receiving his medical report, the mayor wasted little time. On September 2, bypass surgery was performed at St. Joseph's Hospital. Doctors told him he needed to change his diet and to trim a hundred pounds. "You wake up in the hospital with these tubes coming out of your gut," Maynard Jr. says, "and that will change your life, I guarantee it."

He could not lay motionless during his recovery at home. Gov. Zell Miller had called for changing Georgia's state flag, removing the Confederate battle markings placed on it by state legislators in 1956 as a show of resistance to desegregation. In 1992, rural whites wanted to retain the flag's design while blacks, virtually across the board, wanted it replaced. During his recuperation, Maynard Jr. wrote lofty position papers on the issue that he would term "Letters from My Kitchen Table." "The Georgia flag reeks with racism," he wrote, his penmanship virtually unchanged since his college days and his tone as powerful as John Wesley Dobbs's ever was. He wrote:

It drips with demagoguery. It was born in bigotry and persists in prejudice. Here is a negative flag, saturated with symbols of the slavemasters' acts of genocide, the holocaust of tens of millions of Africans and slaves, the only slavery in history to say that the slave was not human, castration, perpetual bondage, the accepted infidelity of the married slavemaster with his helpless women and children slaves, rape, murder and economic exploitation. Cotton was king and the king was corrupt. That is the "legacy" of the Old South; that is the "Southern heritage" some Georgians now seek to protect by insisting on keeping this Georgia flag, this negative symbol of a Confederate army that fought to keep things as they were, to "defend the Southern way of life."

Most Atlantans expected Maynard Jr. to seek, and win, a fourth term in 1993, then to revel in the glory of the 1996 Olympics. Yet, in the wake of his surgery, he began to reevaluate his life. Valerie did not want her husband to run again, not in the face of relentless criticism, though she did not want to become the sole reason for his withdrawal. In truth, far more than Valerie's wishes weighed on the mayor's mind. "I got tired of giving up $500,000 a year to earn $100,000 a year [as mayor] and getting beat up for sacrificing my family, myself, my income, my health and everything," Maynard Jr. says. He believed that constant criticism and scrutiny "is making anybody with two cents of a brain avoid running for office, except those whose dedication overcomes their probable good judgment."

Personal sacrifices had also taken a toll on him. Once again Buzzy was in trouble. In July 1992, police were called to an apartment he shared with his girlfriend to break up a fight. His girlfriend was thirty-two, a decade older, and she told police that Buzzy had choked, pinched, punched, kicked and pushed her during an argument that had started when he demanded her jewelry. When police arrived, Buzzy ran and scaled a fence to get away. "I neglected my family," Maynard Jr. would say retrospectively, citing the personal sacrifice he had made during a political career that spanned a quarter century. "I neglected two families to tell you the truth."

On April 23, 1993, the mayor attended a testimonial dinner inducting Ivan Allen, Jr., into the Georgia State University Business Hall of Fame. Before nearly four hundred guests in a hotel ballroom, Maynard Jr. said, "Tonight we honor a man on whose shoulders we all stand."

More personally, he added, "I'm wearing a tie tonight that I once found in my garage. It was Scotch-taped to the door. It said, 'This is just for you, Maynard. Ivan Allen, Jr.' " He did not mention that Ivan Allen had given him the tie that day to console him for Buzzy's troubles. He did say, "I want you to know, Mr. Mayor, that I was deeply touched. I've always appreciated that. And I've always appreciated your leadership."

Maynard Jr. proclaimed Ivan Allen, Jr. Day in Atlanta, and the old former mayor, standing by his side at the lectern, playfully slapped him on the shoulder. "It's good to know that I am still Ivan Allen and not just Louise Allen's husband," Ivan Jr. deadpanned, drawing loud laughter. Ivan Jr. appeared stoop-shouldered and shook slightly as he spoke for only a few minutes.

Before the crowd, Maynard Jackson said to Ivan Jr., "Atlanta is much better, and richer, Mr. Mayor, because of you. Let there be no misunderstanding that you paved the way for better relations between the races. . . . And that, may I say, helped us win the Olympics."

In some ways, Maynard Jackson was still an encyclopedia salesman. His last sale was his best sale and his biggest sale was his next sale. Now, he was predicting an imminent development boom in the predominantly black section of south Atlanta. "When the big Mo' [momentum] starts on the south side, it's going to overtake Buckhead, in the sense of the revitalization of it," he said in 1992. To speed the process, he considered lobbying for the city to build a mayor's mansion, similar to the governor's mansion in Buckhead, except that he wanted to locate it on the south side.

In his State of the City address on January 4, 1993, Maynard Jr. sang the praises of his own administration (though he remained in a small minority in this regard) and spoke of an urgent need to unify all Atlantans in time for the 1996 Olympics. He showed off a glowing twenty-eight-page report on the city, as well as a videotape that celebrated the city's newest slogan ("Atlanta: Home of the American Dream"), then contended Atlanta was better housed and better educated under his watch. Crime in the city, he said, had decreased by 12 percent since 1990. "Atlanta is in better shape than probably any city in this country," he said. But, he added, "As long as somebody's still groveling in a garbage can and trying to find food, I'm not going to be satisfied." Having reached the twenty-fifth anniversary of his 1968 entrance into politics, Maynard Jr. closed by paraphrasing Abraham Lincoln, warning, "We cannot afford to be a house divided."

What the mayor had neglected to mention was that he also had promised to hire six hundred additional police officers by 1993, but as he spoke, the Atlanta force had ninety-two *fewer* officers. His administration also was falling short in its promise to construct 3,500 single-room occupancy units for the homeless by January 1994; as of January 1993 fewer than six hundred units had been completed. One local columnist, noting the three-year malaise of the Jackson administration, suggested, "So little has been done that many believe Mr. Jackson is fed up with it and dying for a job in the Clinton administration."

Maynard Jr. had spoken about cabinet positions in December with his old friend Vernon Jordan, chairman of President-elect Bill Clinton's transition team. The mayor had told Jordan he was not interested in joining the cabinet, in large part because he could not afford it financially. "My interest," Maynard Jr. recalls, "was in doing something from the outside. If they had a commission for me to chair, something like that." But as rumors circulated in Atlanta that he was being considered as a possible secretary of transportation, and that the Clinton team had conducted background checks on him in Atlanta, the mayor did little to disavow it. "I enjoy the rumor-mongering," he told the *Constitution*.

He had other plans. When he looked at Vernon Jordan, his former colleague in the David T. Howard High School band, Maynard Jr. liked what he saw: a rain-making attorney in Washington for Akin, Gump, Strauss, Hauer & Feld, the prestigious law firm with close connections to the Democratic National Party; its senior partner, Bob Strauss, was a former party chairman. Jordan had emerged as a consummate Washington insider and was said to be earning seven figures annually. Much of that income came from his membership on corporate boards. The irony was that Jordan once had considered running for office in Atlanta but chose instead to move north to work for the United Negro College Fund and the National Urban League. Not only did Jordan ride the corporate gravy train of the 1980s to wealth, he had faced little criticism along the way. To Maynard Jr., who had absorbed the daily shellacking common to big-city mayors, Jordan's wealth, gilded lifestyle and political stature held great appeal.

After open-heart surgery, though, the mayor's physical strength was slow to return. His complexion took on a gray, pasty tone and, to some aides, he seemed perpetually tired. In the spring, Maynard Jr. told his sister Sandra he had decided not to seek reelection. "If I ran again and won," he told her, "I'd be coming out of office at sixty. There are things I want to do before I get too old."

On June 3, five months before the 1993 mayor's race, a survey by the *Constitution* showed that Jackson's public approval rating was 70 percent. Roughly half of whites and three-fourths of blacks polled said they approved of the way he handled his job. So vast was Maynard Jackson's popularity in the black community that his reelection, should he decide to run, was virtually assured.

Yet the rumors of his impending withdrawal soon spread. By early summer Olympics chief Billy Payne and a select group of white businessmen urged him to run again, hoping for continuity at City Hall through the Olympics. "Don't walk out on what is going to be one of the greatest moments of your life," Payne told Maynard Jr. in a meeting on June 8.

His mind was made up. He called a press conference for the next day, June 9, at 5:30 P.M., in time for the six P.M. local news shows. The drama of his announcement was lost when that afternoon's *Atlanta Journal* headline shouted, "Jackson Won't Seek Re-Election." Maynard Jr. was livid when he saw the headline, for he thought he had struck a deal with the *Journal* to hold off until at least five o'clock—one more example of the local newspaper wronging him, he thought. To the very end, he did not want to be upstaged. En route to City Hall, reporter Lyle Harris of the *Constitution* rode with the mayor in the back seat of his Lincoln Town Car, chronicling the mayor's day of decision. Harris handed the mayor a copy of the *Journal* and asked him to sign it for posterity. "I still don't know what I'm going to do," the mayor insisted. Then he signed it, "Maynard, Who?"

Twenty minutes before the press conference he called members of his staff and family to meet inside the City Hall conference room. He dashed out several times to accept phone calls from the governor and others whom he had tried to notify, personally, before he made his public announcement. Surrounded by family members, including several Dobbs cousins and sisters Sandra, Carol Ann and Connie, Maynard Jr. explained his decision. It wasn't only health and money; he was just tired of it all. He said he would not mention the last reason in his press conference. "I think Maynard realized," one staffer recalls, "that it was a pain in the ass being mayor."

His cousins Bill Clement, Jr., and Juliet Blackburn Beamon were reminded of the Grand's description of his own style of oratory. The Grand had started his speeches slowly, then built to a crescendo, finishing in a cloud of dust. Noting that Maynard Jr. was about to announce his political retirement when his public approval rating was 70 percent, Clement and Beamon recited in the conference room:

> *Start low, Go slow;*
> *Strike fire, Move higher,*
> *And then Sit Down in a Storm!*

In his announcement, Maynard Jr. again praised the performance of his administration, then said, "Atlanta will get to its mountaintop . . . and I plan to be there with you. . . . Regrettably, however, I must continue to serve Atlanta in a different way. For necessary, unavoidable and compelling personal reasons and views, I must decline to seek another term as mayor of Atlanta.

"I have wrestled with this decision more than any other decision in my life. This has been a gut-wrenching process. But I am satisfied that I have made a, regrettably, necessary decision.

"I love you, Atlanta!" Maynard Jackson said.

And from the balcony a woman chimed, "And we love you!" When he was finished, Maynard Jr. embraced Valerie and daughters Valerie Amanda and Alexandra.

He had come into office in 1973 riding a tide of black political power; now that tide seemed to be receding. Los Angeles mayor Tom Bradley and Detroit's Coleman Young also had entered office in 1973, then served for two decades unbroken and they, too, announced in 1993 that they would not seek another term. Among the reasons they cited were age (both were seventy-five), poor health and deep frustrations. The nation's three most populous cities, New York, Los Angeles and Chicago, where black mayors once had served, had now elected whites.

Maynard Jr. had seven months remaining in his term. The corruption trial of Aviation Commissioner Ira Jackson loomed. Several times more the mayor's staff would bungle. In September, an obscure travel magazine named Hartsfield Atlanta International Airport the fourth best airport in the world, and the best in North America, and the mayor's office celebrated with a three-day party at the airport. "The airport was Maynard's baby," a staffer recalls. "Maynard wanted everything big about the airport." The soiree, attended largely by politicians, cost taxpayers $1 million. Later, the mayor maintained that he had been told the party was to be funded privately. He called for an audit, disciplined some low-level government officials when the results were announced, but then, fearing lawsuits, reversed himself, and reinstated them. "BestFest," as the party was known, became a public relations nightmare.

Meanwhile, in August, the mayor's chief of staff, Gerri Elder, spent $45,000 to purchase lavish furniture for the mayor's office, including a "racetrack" oval desk, even though only five months remained in the Jackson administration. When news of the purchase became known, there followed a public outcry over perceived excess.

Jackson's staff negotiated a $14,000 reduction with the furniture supplier, which trimmed the mayor's level of embarrassment only marginally. The furniture supplier, agreeing to swallow all profits in the deal for the sake of goodwill with the city, was the Ivan Allen Company.

*"I will repay you in full one of these days in the not-too-distant future,"* Maynard Jackson had written John Wesley Dobbs in 1956. Grandpa Dobbs had sent him a small amount of money, to help him at Boston University. In return, the Grand had demanded from his first grandson only fidelity: fidelity to self, fidelity to family, fidelity to race and fidelity to truth. Maynard Jackson, Jr., loved the old man. John Wesley Dobbs could be raw, blustery and demanding, but he had always been there for him and for the entire family. When the Rev. Maynard Jackson had died, Dobbs had stepped in to play the role of surrogate hero to his grandson.

A bone-chilling wind swept through the corner of Peachtree and Houston streets where, on January 10, 1994, members of the Dobbs family and several dozen Prince Hall Masons, in full regalia, gathered. In one of his final acts as mayor of Atlanta, Maynard Jackson had helped to pass legislation that changed the name of Houston Street to John Wesley Dobbs Avenue. This was the final payback thirty-eight years later. Though the spirit of the Grand lived one block south, on Sweet Auburn, his family empire had been based on Houston Street for fifty-two years.

In her fur coat and stylish pink hat, Renie, now eighty-five, sat with sisters Willie and Josie. Later they would report the event to the absent June and Geekie, the latter of whom was retired and dividing her year, with Bengt, between homes in Stockholm and Washington, D.C. (Millie, the third oldest daughter, had died at seventy-nine of Alzheimer's disease in 1991.) A handful of the Grand's twenty grandchildren and thirty-four great-grandchildren also attended. One grandson, Bill Clement, Jr., said, "Some people would be embarrassed to have their name on a street. Not John Wesley Dobbs. He had a real zest and zeal. He didn't have a small ego. He would've been shaking everybody's hand, calling them by their first name." Buzzy Jackson was there, too. Soon, he would be off to Los Angeles to study music. "I believe God has a plan for this boy," his father, Maynard Jr., would say much later. "He's been climbing up the rough side of a mountain, as they say, and he's got to get there in a different way than

I got there." Now, Maynard Jr. began to call his son Maynard. "Buzzy is a boy's name," he says, "and Maynard's a man's name. I prefer Maynard."

During a brief ceremony, Neal McQueen, grand master of the Georgia jurisdiction of Prince Hall Masons, said, "Thirty-three years later, I'm still introduced as one of John Wesley Dobbs's boys." Mayor Bill Campbell, who with Jackson's support had swamped Michael Lomax in the 1993 mayor's race, told the lunchtime gathering of about sixty that the Dobbses were "the first family of Georgia." When Renie smiled and told Campbell, "I'm as happy as an angel entering Heaven," Campbell supplied an old local joke: "Remember, to get to Heaven you have to change planes in Atlanta first."

Maynard Jackson was now a businessman. He had received job offers from several local law firms, a marked change from the first time he left City Hall, but he had accepted none of them. Instead, he had decided to build his own firm, Jackson Securities, Inc. Earlier on this morning, he had testified in the Ira Jackson trial. Though Maynard Jr. was not implicated, the airport concessions scandal caused him great sadness. In recent years some of his old political friends, who had helped him rise to local power, had exceeded the limits of propriety and, in some cases, the law. In 1988, Fulton County Commissioners Chuck Williams and Reggie Eaves had been convicted on extortion charges as part of an FBI undercover sting. Eaves had accepted $35,000 in return for votes on zoning matters. Several years earlier, David Franklin had been disbarred in Washington, D.C., for unethical and financial misconduct in a real estate deal in Georgia that he had handled for a Kuwaiti business. Now, in 1994, Ira Jackson, for two decades an Atlanta city councilman, was about to be convicted on federal corruption charges.

Maynard Jr. stood at the microphone, a sharp wind blowing. Near this spot, more than a half century before, the *Gone With the Wind* premiere had been held at the Loew's Grand theater. One block north, Irene Dobbs, with Geekie and June, had waited for Clark Gable. Now, the theater itself was gone with the wind, replaced by the gleaming salmon-toned Georgia-Pacific skyscraper.

"It's a great occasion," Maynard Jr. began, bundled against the cold. "I remember Grandpa Dobbs talking about how you take Auburn Avenue—*'Allll the Waaay to Peach-treee!'*"

But his smile quickly faded. "I also want to remind everybody," he said with a wave toward the adjacent Candler Building where the Georgia state flag, carrying the Confederate battle markings, stiffened in the breeze, "that behind us waves a flag that offended John Wesley Dobbs."

Soon, a string was pulled, the new street sign was unveiled and, just like that, Atlantans could take John Wesley Dobbs Avenue all the way to Peachtree.

Several weeks later a friend saw Maynard Jr. in his car. The former mayor rolled down his window and smiled. Then, paraphrasing an old family friend, Maynard Jackson, Jr., having fulfilled his obligation to race and family, shouted, playfully, "Free at Last, Free at Last, Thank God, Almighty, I'm Free at Last!"

# Epilogue

### ALLEN

Ivan III had been dead for less than a month when the old mayor asked the second son, Inman, "Do you want to take over responsibility for the company?"

Inman's response was immediate. "No," he said.

Introspective by nature, Inman realized that, at fifty-one, he was now the first son and that the responsibility of carrying the family mantle suddenly was his. The notion left him disoriented at first, as if the sun had begun to rise in the west. It was what he always had wanted, yet it also was what had crushed his older brother.

H. Inman Allen's very name connoted big money, cotton and two Old Atlanta, and east Tennessee, family dynasties. He bore his father's courtly grace, his mother's stoicism and a certain affinity for life's finer things that he had developed on his own. He moved through the Piedmont Driving Club with a natural ease and grace that concealed a fighter's harder edge. As Driving Club president, he and his cohorts would conspire to carry the elite century-old Atlanta social club into modern times by accepting its first black member in 1994, a move that was decades overdue but would make him unpopular with elder members nonetheless.

Growing up, Inman had understood that Ivan III would carry the family name and, one day, the family business and family legacy of civic leadership in Atlanta as well. Whereas Ivan III had responsibility, "I had the freedom," Inman says. In 1967, at the age of twenty-six, *Town & Country* magazine had named Inman one of America's twenty-five most eligible bachelors, a list that included names of prestigious American families such as Rockefeller, Romney and Revson.

At Chapel Hill, he had been a Morehead scholar and student body president. He had waited until he was thirty to marry. When he finally did marry, it was to a woman from Charleston, South Carolina, not Atlanta. Later, he formed his own firm in Atlanta, the Inman Company, buying and selling small businesses.

He considered himself the family rebel, straying from the accepted line his older brother had drawn (though never too far). In 1972, he and Tricia had moved into a small farmhouse that had its own spring well instead of building on the Allen family estate. But their farmhouse was located on Northside Drive, only a half mile from his parents. When Tricia delivered their third daughter in 1980, the lack of space in their home forced them to set up the baby's nursery inside a closet, and Inman and Tricia decided to move back to the family estate. There, they built a home on the opposite side of his parents', across from Ivan III and Margaret. Later, Inman would confess to a profound emotional attachment to the family's land, with its wildlife and natural energy, its meadow and the role it had played in his upbringing and in his children's. "It's a cohesive force that's within you," he says. "You can go away from it [but] the pull is always there."

The solitary gunshot in Heard County suggested to some that the Allen dynasty in Atlanta had ended or, at the very least, dislocated, after nearly a century of unbroken civic service. Yet families, like cities, are self-perpetuating, driven by powerful forces, some of them subtle and internal.

A year after Ivan III's suicide, the Allens met at Margaret's house to discuss selling the ninety-four-year-old family business. Once it would have been an unthinkable idea. Thirty years earlier the mayor had taken an offer to buy the Ivan Allen Company to the Senator. "Well, son, why do you want to sell?" the Senator had asked. "Daddy, we don't know if the next generation can run the company," Ivan Jr. said. The Senator had smiled. "If they can't run it, let it go broke." But now that Ivan III was gone, selling seemed the prudent thing. Besides, the family was told the Ivan Allen Company could bring about $90 million on the market. Everyone in the family agreed it was time. "A no-brainer," Inman called it.

But over the next year, two suitors, offering between $50 million and $60 million, came and went. By spring 1994, when a third suitor, a Dutch company, approached with a similar bid, the Allens had grown weary of the process. In the two years without Ivan III, the company's revenues had risen slightly. Inman, who, while declining to join the company full-time had agreed to become chairman of its newly formalized executive committee, worried about the sale and became more involved in negotiations. He decided his father was too old to study the massive documents involved in the transaction and Ivan IV too young and inexperienced. Inman challenged the family's investment advisor and Tread Davis, the Allens' close friend and family counsel.

"This is a bad decision for the family to make," Inman told his father.

"Are you willing to come in and run the company?" the old mayor asked him again. Inman said he was not, though had his father worded the question differently—"*Will you run the company, Inman?*"—he would have done it. This was more than simple semantics. "I wanted very much for the family to say, 'We want you to hold on to this business and we want you to be the leader for us,'" Inman says. But no one said it quite that way.

News of the impending sale broke over the Dow Jones wire on August 24, 1994, before the family had had time to tell the company's 650 employees. Livid, and playing his role as family rebel, Inman listened to a ninety-minute presentation on the planned sale in a subsequent company board meeting. Advisors said the sales price was roughly $55 million. Inman seethed. The price, he thought, was less than full-market value. Worse, the process infuriated him. "This is so much bullshit," he thought.

Finally, the old mayor turned to his son. "Inman," Ivan Allen, Jr., chairman of the board, said, "how do you feel about this?"

That clinched it. This time, the question had been worded right. The old mayor already knew how his son felt. Now, he wanted the other board members to hear it, too. Inman heard the call of the first son. "I don't think we ought to sell," he said. "Period. And I'm going to vote against it." A voice vote was called. Every board member voted to sell, except Inman Allen. Despite the only negative vote by a board member in the history of the Ivan Allen Company, the sale would go on.

Days later, when more than seventy company stockholders gathered to ratify the sale, details had not been finalized. The meeting was postponed for several days.

That night Inman walked next door to his parents' house. He found them in their bedroom, watching television.

He sat on the edge of the bed. "Daddy," he said, "I will take responsibility for the company if we don't sell it."

"You're telling me you're willing to take responsibility for running the Ivan Allen Company?"

"Yes, sir."

"Okay," the old mayor said, apparently satisfied, "we won't sell it."

The announcement was made the next day, September 14: the sale was off. Inman would assume the company's daily command while maintaining the title of chairman of the executive committee. "I'm living much easier," the old mayor said, adding, "Inman will be a great success. He should have been here years ago." Someday, the old mayor said, he hoped that thirty-year-old Ivan IV would lead the company, too.

It had cost $378,000 in legal/advisory fees to decide not to sell the Ivan Allen Company. That was the price of Inman Allen's personal journey. "Part of it was a business decision," he says, "[but] it was kind of like protecting your own."

Initially, Inman determined not to take his brother's old office, next to his father's, at the Ivan Allen Company. He said it was too dark and dreary, and besides, "I'm not going to have my father walk by my office every day and make a judgment as to whether I'm doing it the way Ivan did or not." But when he arrived at the company in January 1995, two and a half years after the suicide, he moved into his brother's old office, after all. I went to see him there. His plan was to install new furniture, custom-made for efficiency, and to remove a wooden desk and replace it with a small table and chairs for meetings. Methodically, Inman planned to transform Ivan III's rigid office lines into smoother, more accessible curves. "A new participative environment," Inman calls it, "the way it's moving within the workplace." His brother's death had left him angry and grieving. He read a couple of books about how to survive suicide. He needed the space of two and half years to become clearheaded. By then comfortable with the legacies of both his brother and father, and proud to carry a name "rich in history and tradition and accomplishment," Inman at last could sit in the chief's chair and say, "I came here for the right reasons."

Even the Senator cheered, to hear Ivan Jr. tell it. On the day these matters of the future were decided, the old mayor leaned back in his office chair, directly under a formal portrait done in 1942 with Ivan Jr. and Ivan III (at age four) alongside the Senator.

At that happy moment, the painting fell from the wall. It caromed off the old mayor's head and for a moment or two pinned him in his chair. Even as he extricated himself, Ivan Jr. had to smile. He reckoned the ruckus was the Senator's doing.

## DOBBS

"Take me there," Maynard Jackson said. He wanted to see the graves of his antebellum ancestors. So on a Saturday afternoon in a liquor store near the Marietta town square, he sipped a Coca-Cola and waited with anticipation. His arrival had stirred the store's owners. They rushed to greet him and insisted his drink was free. Two customers, black men in soiled worker's clothes, introduced themselves. "Whatchaknow," Maynard Jr. said, extending his hand.

There, by a liquor store refrigerator filled with beer, I told the former mayor of a white ancestor, his great-great-grandfather Dr. John Miller McAfee. I showed him various historical documents—including his great-grandmother Nannie's 1937 death certificate. She died the year before his birth. The certificate cited the maiden name of Nannie's slave mother as "McAfee." I reminded him of the Dobbs oral tradition about the patrician slavemaster, a physician in Woodstock of Scottish descent, who was Nannie's biological father. Maynard Jr. was familiar with that history. He read with interest the 1860 Georgia Slave Schedule from Woodstock and the list of McAfee's eighty-seven nameless slaves, inventoried only by gender, color (black or mulatto) and estimated age. He read the inventory of the McAfee estate, which included chandeliers and looking glasses, and the loyalty oath McAfee had signed after the Civil War, asserting his fidelity to the United States and that his slaves had been emancipated. I informed him that McAfee was a Georgia senator who had participated in the 1843 vote in Milledgeville that changed the name of Terminus to Marthasville—the city that one day became Atlanta. "Incredible," Maynard Jr. said, examining the documents. Then he asked, in a halfhearted way, "How did he vote?" The vote was unanimous.

Behind him, across Powder Springs Road, the Marietta City Cemetery sat on a lovely hillside with a separate Confederate section. Inside the old main gate, beneath a gleaming white monument standing nearly fifteen feet, among the tallest on the grounds, Dr. John Miller McAfee is buried.

When Maynard Jr. heard of McAfee's grave, he started to rise from his chair in the liquor store. But he stopped and said, "No. That man was a part of the millions who owned black people and raped them."

Two weeks later, he changed his mind. He would visit the grave, after all. Because he had forgotten the location of the John McAfee monument, he walked the hillside, searching. An hour passed. Then he noticed on the cemetery hillside a silver and blue pickup truck. It had dark-tinted windows. Through an open window he could see two white men. His instincts took over. "The Klan checking me out," he thought. The white men in the pickup never did so much as call out to him. They might have recognized the former mayor or perhaps they were looking at something totally unrelated to him. But Maynard Jr. felt their stares. He left the cemetery shortly thereafter. He never found the McAfee monument. "The McAfees are not my relatives," he would say much later. "I mean, I don't see it that way, though the truth is, there is a direct blood connection." He said he would visit the McAfee monument another day.

At the liquor store now, two black youths peeked inside the front door. "It is too Maynard Jackson!" insisted one carrying a basketball.

"Unh-uh," said his friend. He looked at the former mayor. "You ain't Maynard Jackson, are you?"

Maynard Jr. leaned forward and pointed to the boy with the basketball. "You, come here." He reached into his front right pocket and pulled out a wad of bills, as the Grand used to do. "Give me your hand," he told the youth. The boy held out his open palm and Maynard Jr. slapped a one-dollar bill into it.

"That," he said, "is for being right."

One dollar richer, the youth ran outside, flashing the bill in his friend's face, and Maynard Jackson threw back his head and laughed a good hard laugh.

About three miles up the road was a different, more obscure graveyard. To reach the Noonday Baptist Church Extension Cemetery, we drove past fast-food restaurants and furniture stores along the main road, turned onto White Circle Road and followed its winding course past a field filled with power lines.

If you didn't know where it was, you might never find it. The church up on a nearby hill still buries its members here, but has virtually abandoned the oldest section. That section has become an overgrown forest, weeds and seedlings allowed to grow in every direction. Some of the seedlings have grown in surprising places, and slinky vines crawl between them, green and moist. Here, the freedmen of Cobb County lie, disrupted occasionally by a distant train whistle or rumble of a truck on the main road or the raucous clamor raised by mischievous white teenagers who take moonlit rides on motorcycles and topple tombstones along the way.

It was a spring afternoon in Kennesaw and the sunlight fell like arrows through the scrub pines and dogwoods of the old part of the cemetery. A cool breeze rustled new dogwood leaves. Maynard Jackson moved slowly, twigs snapping beneath his feet.

With his right hand, he drew back a prickly vine, then stepped through its space. The old gray tombstones were set in clusters. Each ten yards he walked took the former mayor back in time ten years. Deep in the woods the stones predated the turn of the century. All about him were the remains of former Georgia slaves who had watched General Sherman and his bluecoats march through Marietta toward Atlanta.

"My God!" Maynard Jackson said.

He wore silver cuff links, a tie knotted as small as a marble, a freshly pressed white shirt with a starched collar. A gold pen was clipped to his breast pocket. He looked impressive, like a mayor, and though he said he would not seek public office again, he also said he would not rule out a political miracle.

Deep in the graveyard, Maynard Jr. spotted the tombstones of his slave ancestors. He gasped and placed his left hand over his mouth. He held his hand in that position for some time.

In a few moments, he stood over a small, rectangular stone embedded in the red earth. Bending, he swept dirt and debris from the stone marking the resting place of a delicate octoroon slave fathered by a white man. The former mayor read aloud:

*"Judie Dobbs. Died August 21, 1925. Age Over 90 Years. Tho' lost to Sight to Memory Dear."*

He expressed sadness. "They didn't even know how old she was." His mother had told him stories of having held Judie's hand and now he imagined Judie's thin fingers in his own massive hand.

His eyes tightened at the corners as he read from the adjacent upright tombstone:

*"Wesley Dobbs. Died February 5, 1897. Aged 78 Years."*

He began to notice small details. The stones of Wesley and Judie Dobbs faced opposite directions. Then he pointed to the distance from Wesley Dobbs's headstone to a small white footstone that read, "W.D." He said, "I'm six foot two. He must have been six foot six, at least. Maybe seven feet."

Dogwood trees had grown from the graves, one sprouting from the area of Judie Dobbs's throat, another from Wesley Dobbs's knees. Maynard Jackson stood in the shade of those trees and said, "Here lies a man who under American law was not a full human being. Only a slave."

He shook his head, awed by the sight. "I'm struck by the peacefulness of this place.

"So this was their land.

*"These trees knew them!"*

In Wesley and Judie Dobbs's time, Atlanta had seemed a faraway place, roughly four hours by horse. Now, the city's metropolitan sprawl reached out to touch these Dobbses, and even beyond, to the exurb of Cherokee County, former home of Dr. John Miller McAfee.

By coming to the grave of Josiah Dobbs's most valuable field hand, Maynard Jr. had come to a place that represented the blood of his family and provided proof of ancestors lost to time. He thought to touch the stone, but drew back his hand, disturbed for a moment by the reminder of slavery and its consequences still today. Then he touched a corner of the smooth granite with his fingertips, grazing it, as if to be certain it was real.

He had come a distance to this graveyard, a distance measured in generations. The first black mayor of Atlanta had come to the grave of an $800 slave who had been his great-great-grandfather. Bending to the stone, Maynard Jr. touched it again, this time moving his fingers across the cuttings that spelled out the name *Wesley Dobbs*. Below the name he felt the words there. *Died February 5, 1897.* Then he laid both hands atop the stone.

# SOURCE NOTES

CHAPTER 1

21. Record for: Kate Bowie: Depositors in Freedmen's Savings & Trust Company, Georgia, 1870–74. Georgia Department of Archives and History. Microfilm Drawer 159, Box 59. Depositor No. 34. Created for freed slaves, the bank's Atlanta branch had 4,518 depositors.

23. Robert Allen, was nearly sixty: Family genealogy pamphlet entitled *Data of the Allen Family*, pp. 9–10. This family history, which was prepared by an unknown author in 1920 for Ivan Allen, Sr., traces the Allens from Somerset County, England, and describes their migration to Pennsylvania and Rhode Island. Robert Allen is said to have been born in 1725 near Providence, Rhode Island. Personal files of Ivan Allen, Jr. (Author discovered this pamphlet in 1994 after three years of concentrated work on the Allen family genealogy. It has been used only to supplement author's own antebellum research.)

23. Lick Creek was near the salt licks: Richard Harrison Doughty, *Greeneville: One Hundred Year Portrait, 1775–1875* (Kingsport, Tenn.: Kingsport Press, 1975), p. 3.

24. He sent Isaac and James to the nearby Tusculum Academy: Enrollment Records of Tusculum College, Greeneville, Tenn., 1837–40. The records indicate that tuition and books were paid for Isaac and James Allen during these years. See: "Sam Doak Account Book, 1835–53," Tusculum College Library.

24. his slaves fired the bricks: Interview with Dr. Keith Harrison. Harrison purchased the home, near the Asheville Highway, in 1977 and lived in it for eighteen years.

24. "Sam Alens coat $4.66": Andrew Johnson's tailor shop logbook, June 1832, Andrew Johnson National Historic Site, Greeneville, Tenn. (The original tailor shop records are located at the Henry Huntington Library, Pasadena, Calif.)

24. no contest to a charge: *State v. Daniel Allen*, Greene County Circuit Court grand jury hearing, June 18, 1838. Charged with assaulting Samuel Smith with a stone, Allen paid the fine on October 12, 1838. Filed, by date, in Greene County Circuit Court.

24. Charged with obstruction: *The State, Jacob Dyche, plaintiff, v. Daniel Allen, defendant*, Greene County Circuit Court, June 15, 1843.

24. he planted orchards: "Data of the Allen Family," p. 11.

24. Cain broke into a storehouse: *Henry Farnsworth and Frances Farnsworth v. Samuel Allen, James Allen, Robert Allen, Polly Leming et al.* Filed in Greene County Chancery Court September 4, 1848. From Sam Allen's sworn testimony given January 5, 1849. File Box No. 52 in Greene County courthouse, Greeneville, Tenn.

25. Kennedy warned Sam Allen: *Ibid.*

25. in another decade he owned nineteen slaves: 1840 Slave Schedule for the state of Tennessee, Greene County. McClung Collection, Lawson McGhee Library, Knoxville Tenn.

25. they sent for the family physician: Unpublished Diary of Dr. Joseph Bell. Personal collection of Mrs. Evelyn Bell Carter, Greeneville, Tenn. Mrs. Carter is a great-great-granddaughter of Dr. Bell. Among the diary's entries: November 18, 1845: "To Daniel Allen, called by Daniel Jr. Visit to black woman; Examination for Vaganarium; Anodyne with directions." A more complicated visit to Daniel Allen's occurred on May 18, 1855: "A visit to black boy at night extracting 15 pieces of fractured cranium from the right superior lobe of the brain and scraping the wound, medicine and so forth. His injury resulted from a Negro man striking this one with a hoe. The intention must have been to kill. After extracting and scraping the skull the boy got much better."

25. troublesome slave on the adjacent: Interview with Goldene F. Burgner. Mrs. Burgner is a noted Greene County historian.

25. "A good slave would cost $500": Interview with T. Elmer Cox. Cox also is a Greene County historian.

25. Allen dispatched a local man: *Henry Farnsworth and Frances Farnsworth v. Samuel Allen et al.* See Sam Allen deposition.
26. "The Negro is the same as land": *Henry Farnsworth & Wife v. Samuel Allen & Others.* Filed with Tennessee Supreme Court in Knoxville, Tenn., September 9, 1850. The entire contents of the suit from Greene County Chancery Court are included. This quote was cited in the deposition of John Leming given February 23, 1849. The existing files from this case, including depositions, are more complete in Knoxville than at the Greene County courthouse in Greeneville, Tenn.
26. Allen would file suit: *Ibid.*
26. he rode on to Louisville, his anger rising: *Ibid.* As part of his response to this lawsuit, Sam Allen drew up for the court a list of his expenses on his chase of Cain.
26. Nig, which he would leave: Last Will & Testament of Samuel Allen, December 2, 1851, Greene County Court Minute Book, 1859–64. Sam Allen's will was settled February 6, 1860.
26. bounty hunter, David E. Gibson, he paid $90: *Henry Farnsworth and Frances Farnsworth v. Samuel Allen et al.* See Sam Allen deposition.
27. "Generally speaking, slaves are treated": J. Winston Coleman, Jr., "Lexington's Slave Dealers and Their Southern Trade," *Filson Club Quarterly* (January 1938). See also: Levi Coffin, *Reminiscences of Levi Coffin, the Reputed President of the Underground Railroad* (Cincinnati: Western Tract Society, 1876).
27. Sam Allen received $900. *Henry Farnsworth and Frances Farnsworth v. Samuel Allen et al.*
27. was too weak to write: *Martha Allen v. Reuben Allen,* filed in Supreme Court of Errors and Appeals of Tennessee, April 8, 1812; previously tried in lower court, Greene County Chancery Court. The text of this case, which found in favor of Martha Allen, widow of Robert, thereby establishing the legality of Robert Allen's will, was included as part of *Henry Farnsworth & Wife v. Samuel Allen & Others,* filed with Tennessee Supreme Court in Knoxville, Tenn., September 9, 1850.
27. he was enraged by its contents. *Ibid.*
28. before his senile mother's death: *Henry Farnsworth and Frances Farnsworth v. Samuel Allen & Others.* In Sam Allen's deposition of September 17, 1849, the aged Martha Allen is described as "child-like" in her ways.
28. willing to sell the ten slaves: *Ibid.*
29. Sam Allen bought back three: *Ibid.* The details concerning the sale of the slaves was recounted in Greene County Chancery Court, November 12, 1849.
29. saw water pour from the saturated boxes: Interview with Wayne Conduff. Conduff, who lives in Greene County, was told this story by his father, who witnessed the removal of the Allen caskets.
29. Allen often loaned one of his male slaves: Goldene F. Burgner interview.
30. Isaac pleaded guilty: *The State v. Isaac A. Allen,* Greene County Circuit Court, June 12, 1845.
30. Bell attempted to "electrify" him: Unpublished Diary of Dr. Joseph Bell.
30. His nine children gathered at his old: Greene County Court Minutes, Book 25, p. 405. Daniel Allen died intestate and his estate was recorded as settled on January 6, 1862.
30. James took seven of his father's slaves: *Ibid.*
30. black woman Sarah and her mulatto infant: 1870 Census for Tennessee. Sarah and her child were still living in Isaac Allen's home in 1870, five years after the Civil War.
30. Isaac moved into the old Daniel Allen home: Greene County Chancery Court, January 31, 1863, Warranty Deed Book No. 33, pp. 316–29.
30. His eyes were a magnetic blue: This description is drawn from the family genealogy pamphlet, Data of the Allen Family, pp. 12–13
30. Earnest developed an appreciation for riding: Eleanor Williams, *Ivan Allen: A Resourceful Citizen* (Atlanta: Ivan Allen-Marshall Company, 1950), p. 254.

## CHAPTER 2

31. riding horseback across: Interview with Imogene McAfee Buder. A great-niece of Dr. McAfee's, Mrs. Buder is a McAfee family genealogist.
31. He lived on a seven-hundred-acre plantation: 1850 Census for Georgia, Cherokee County, Woodstock District. Georgia Department of Archives and History, Drawer 331, Box 36.
31. an additional four hundred acres: Last Will & Testament of John M. McAfee, July 14, 1854,

recommitted April 19, 1864, Cherokee County Ordinary Estate Records, Wills, Volume C, 1866–1921. GDA&H, Microfilm Drawer 13, Box 17, pp. 10–13.

31. a fanciful array: Inventory & Appraisement of John M. McAfee Estate, Cherokee County, Ga., Inventories & Appraisement, Volume C, 1854–1924, Cherokee County courthouse in Canton, Ga. Also: GDA&H, Microfilm Drawer 165, Box 39, pp. 445–49.

31. member of the Noonday Baptist Church: Proceedings of Noonday Baptist Church, Cobb County, Ga. GDA&H, Microfilm Drawer 197, Box 74. From p. 54, July 1845 term, Josiah Dobbs and his wife, Elizabeth, were received as members. In the June 1849 church conference, p. 67, Josiah Dobbs is named as a member of a five-man committee to construct a fence around the churchyard.

32. McAfee purchased three hoes: Bill of Articles Sold from the Estate of Josiah Dobbs, November 6, 1851. Registered with ordinary of Cobb County, Ga., July 22, 1832. GDA&H, Cobb County Probate Court, Misc. Estate Records, 1837–77, Box Location 1657–16, Box 1, Folder 89, Record Group 133.

32. "WESLEY, a negro man": Inventory/Appraisement Josiah Dobbs estate, August 12, 1851, also registered with ordinary of Cobb County with Bill of Articles Sold. *Ibid.*

32. "the suspicion that a Nat Turner": Leon Litwack, *Been in the Storm So Long: The Aftermath of Slavery* (New York: Alfred A. Knopf, 1979), pp. 62–63.

33. "To George Washington": James E. Dorsey, *The History of Hall County, Georgia, Vol. 1* (Gainesville, Ga.: Magnolia Press, 1991), pp. 50–53.

33. applied in 1834 to build a toll bridge: *Acts of the General Assembly of the State of Georgia, 1834* (Milledgeville, Ga.: P.L. & B.H. Robinson, Printers, 1835), pp. 47–48. Later sold to the Holcombe family, Holcombe Bridge Road is now a main thoroughfare. Two slate-rock columns of the former McAfee bridge remain in the waters of the Chattahoochee, near Spalding Drive. About three-quarters of a mile beyond, the former plantation home of Robert McAfee's daughter Myra and her husband, Jackson Greggory, also remains.

33. prohibited slaves from preaching: *Acts of the General Assembly of the State of Georgia, 1833.* (Milledgeville, Ga.: Polhill & Fort, Printers, 1834), p. 227.

33. forbade any person of color from compounding: *Acts of the General Assembly of the State of Georgia, 1835* (Milledgeville, Ga.: John A. Cuthbert, Printer, 1836), pp. 268–69.

33. "The danger of conflict": Alexis de Tocqueville, *Democracy in America, Vol. 1* (New York: Vintage, 1945), pp. 391–92. The work of Tocqueville, who arrived in America in 1831, was first published in 1835.

33. "The more the utility": *Ibid.*, p. 395.

33. "The perpetuity": *Journal of the House of Representatives of the State of Georgia, 1835* (Milledgeville, Ga.: State Authority of Georgia, 1836), pp. 465–67.

34. city's annual Christmas ball: *The Southern Recorder,* Milledgeville, Ga., December 16, 1836. GDA&H, Microfilm Drawer 185, Box 57.

34. "the apathy of Georgia": Franklin M. Garrett, *Atlanta and Environs: A Chronicle of Its People and Events, Vol. 1* (New York: Lewis Historical Publishing Company, 1954), pp. 143–44.

34. McAfee of Hall County favored the rail line: *Journal of the House of Representatives of the State of Georgia, 1836* (Milledgeville, Ga.: State Authority of Georgia, 1837), pp. 237–39.

34. McAfee was among a group: *Ibid.*, pp. 245–47. McAfee was joined by thirty-two other representatives in this vote taken December 9, 1836. But 107 opposed tabling the bill.

34. Representative McAfee and his Hall County: *Ibid.*, pp. 256–57. The bill passed by a 100–54 vote.

35. appointed Dr. John Miller McAfee as cashier: Andrew W. Cain, *History of Lumpkin County for the First Hundred Years, 1832–1932* (Spartanburg, S.C.: The Reprint Company, 1978), p. 76.

35. some of whom paid him in gold: Imogene McAfee Buder interview.

35. the first excursion from Terminus: Garrett, *Atlanta and Environs*, pp. 184–85.

35. honor their great advocate: William Statford Irvine, "Governor Lumpkin and Marthasville," *Atlanta Historical Bulletin* (Vol. II, September 1937), pp. 46–66. Lumpkin described the changing of the name Marthasville in a letter to his daughter, Martha, dated October 25, 1853.

35. "The Senate took up": *Journal of the Senate of the State of Georgia, 1843* (Milledgeville, Ga.: State Authority of Georgia, 1844), p. 343.

35. he stepped off the train: Garrett, *Atlanta and Environs*, p. 219.

36. "Atlanta, the terminus": *Ibid.*, p. 225. See also: *Hanleiter's Atlanta City Directory,' 1871*, p. 33. Richard Peters recalled Thomson's letter to him, quoting it verbatim, in a letter he wrote to W. R. Hanleiter dated May 9, 1871. Hanleiter published the annual directory of the city. See also: Darlene R. Roth, "Metropolitan Frontiers: Atlanta, 1835–2000," *Atlanta History* (Vol. 37, Fall

1993), p. 27. Roth details another version of how Atlanta was named: an abbreviation of Martha Lumpkin's middle name—"Atalanta," for the goddess of speed in Greek mythology. Though Roth notes that Martha Lumpkin Compton once was honored by mayoral proclamation as the person for whom Atlanta twice was named, she suggests this story was perhaps "somewhat apocryphal."

36. "You may always remember": Irvine, "Governor Lumpkin and Marthasville," p. 49.
36. records were burned by federal soldiers: Sarah Blackwell Gober Temple, *The First Hundred Years: A Short History of Cobb County in Georgia* (Athens, Ga.: Agee Publishers, 1935), p. vi.
36. "She was as white": Interview with Josephine Dobbs Clement.
36. "that looked like Whistler's Mother": Interview with Willie Dobbs Blackburn.
36. Occasionally she beat: Interview with June Dobbs Butts.
37. she would have fourteen children: Interviews with several Dobbs family members, including Willie Dobbs Blackburn. The 1870 Census in Cobb County lists Wesley and Judie Dobbs as living with the following children: "William, 20, Mary, 18, Martha, 16, Ann, 14, Elbert, 10, Meariah, six and George, six months." Apart from Jesse Dobbs, born in 1874, author has been unable to identify the other children. Some might have died in infancy. See also: 1870 Census, Cobb County, Ga., Gritter District. GDA&H, Microfilm Drawer 332, Box 56, p. 325.
37. "Come here, sister": Letter to the author by Muriel Gassett James, September 17, 1992. Her reflections of Judie Dobbs were "told to me by my grandfather, Jesse L. Dobbs, and my mother, Isabel Gassett."
37. "Name of Father": Death certificate of Judie Dobbs, filed August 24, 1925. Georgia Department of Human Services, Vital Records Services, Atlanta, Ga. George Dobbs recorded his mother's name as "Julia Dobbs."
37. "He was the most trusty": *John M. McAfee v. John W. Lewis, Western & Atlantic Railroad,* Fulton County Superior Court, filed March 15, 1859. Deposition of George W. Lee, Atlanta train master, taken April 2, 1860. This was filed as part of a case heard by Georgia Supreme Court (*John W. Lewis, plaintiff in error, v. McAfee, defendant in error*), 3rd District, March term, 1861, and affirmed April 13, 1861. GDA&H, Record Group 92, Box 45, Case No. A-3641, Box Location 107–11.
37. leaped from the steps: *Ibid.*
38. amputated one leg: *Ibid.* From deposition of Dr. Willis F. Westmoreland, taken March 30, 1860. Dr. Westmoreland was the physician who treated the slave Peter after the accident.
38. "The rule of law": *Ibid.* Ruling of Supreme Court of Georgia.
38 . "In 1850, there were in the United States": Carl Sandburg, *Abraham Lincoln: The Prairie and the War Years* (New York: Harcourt, Brace & Company, 1925), p. 134.
39. "A house divided against itself": *Ibid.,* pp. 137–38. See also: Harold Holzer, editor, *The Lincoln-Douglas Debates* (New York: HarperCollins, 1993), pp. 64–68. In a subsequent debate with Stephen Douglas at Ottawa, Ill., on August 21, 1858, Lincoln elaborated on his House Divided speech.
39. not only was her master: Among the McAfee brothers of antebellum days, fathering children by slaves apparently was not an uncommon experience. Gail McAfee Hughes of Stone Mountain, Ga., said that her great-grandfather Bob McAfee also fathered a mulatto son named Oscar McAfee. Mrs. Hughes said she was told by her late aunt Irene McAfee that "everybody knew whose son Oscar McAfee was. Aunt Irene told me that Oscar was not allowed to work [on the farm because of his privileged status]. All he did was sit on the fence and open the gate." Mrs. Hughes said Oscar McAfee is buried in an unmarked grave at the Noonday Baptist Cemetery in Kennesaw, in a black section, across a dirt road from the grave of Eliza McAfee, Bob's wife. (Bob McAfee is buried somewhere outside of Georgia, she said.) It is also possible that another brother, William McAfee of Lee County in south Georgia, fathered a mulatto son, named Claiborne McAfee. According to court documents, Claiborne, a mulatto, lived in William McAfee's home in the spring of 1865, about the time the Civil War was ending, a living arrangement that often reflected a blood connection. Claiborne testified on William McAfee's behalf in a case in which William McAfee was being sued for selling a slave woman in 1862 who died of illness three months later. After a mistrial, a Lee County jury (*Mulkey v. McAfee,* 40-Ga.-115) found against William McAfee; the Georgia Supreme Court in its 1869 term (*McAfee v. Mulkey*) affirmed the decision.

The 1860 Census of Woodstock, Ga., indicates that another doctor, S. S. Smithwick, twenty-seven, was living near, or perhaps even on Dr. John M. McAfee's land in Woodstock. But Smithwick disappears from all future Georgia census records; neither is he listed among registers of Georgia doctors who served in the Confederacy. The oral history of the black

Dobbses makes no mention of Smithwick. Though his occupation, age and proximity to the McAfee plantation make him worthy of careful study in the matter of paternity, his presence is made more uncertain by the appearance of an S. W. Smithwick, twenty-one, in the 1870 Census, also in Cherokee County. In 1859, "S. W. Smithwick"—not S. S.—was licensed as a physician in Cherokee County, according to the Board of Physicians, Registry of Applicants (1826–81). Subsequent Census records suggest that S. W. Smithwick was born in 1847, meaning that in 1859 he would have been twelve years old, too young to gain a medical license. Though census-takers were renowned for their misspellings, almost certainly S. W. was not mistakenly identified as S. S. Smithwick. S. W. was a farmer who was cited as illiterate by one census-taker; he reappears in the Censuses of 1880 and 1900 as a farmer in Cherokee County. S. S. was said to be Georgia-born, while S. W. was born in South Carolina. Also, Smithwick (pronounced Smith-*ick*) is not a Scottish name but an English name that dates to the seventeenth century and the town of Smithwick in Sussex. For references to the Smithwick name, see: P. H. Reaney, *The Origin of English Surnames: Surnames from Lost or Unidentified Places* (London: Routledge & Kegan Paul, 1967), p. 48.

39. treated her with devotion: June Dobbs Butts, Willie Dobbs Blackburn and Mattiwilda Dobbs Janzon interviews.
39. "a Madagascar type": Interview with Mattiwilda Dobbs Janzon.

## CHAPTER 3

40. Georgia Railroad arrived at 5:53: Franklin M. Garrett, *Atlanta and Environs: A Chronicle of Its People and Events, Vol. 1* (New York: Lewis Historical Publishing Company, 1954), pp. 482–84.
40. slaves ranged as high as 40 percent: James M. Russell, *Atlanta 1847–1890: City Building in the Old South and the New* (Baton Rouge, La.: Louisiana State University Press, 1988), pp. 70–71.
40. SLAVE AUCTION ROOMS: Capt. David P. Conyngham, *Sherman's March Through the South* (New York: Sheldon and Company, 1865), pp. 223–24.
40. "We will teach Mr. Lincoln": Atlanta City Council Minutes. Mayor Whitaker's letter is recorded, in full, on April 24, 1861. Atlanta History Center.
41. Bartow Yankee Killers: Lillian Henderson, compiled by, *Roster of Confederate Soldiers of Georgia, 1861–65, Vol. 1–5* (Hapeville, Ga.: Longino & Porter, 1955–58).
41. "die a glorious death": Louise Biles Hill, *Joseph Brown and the Confederacy* (Chapel Hill, N.C.: University of North Carolina Press, 1939), pp. 73–74.
41. buying spree that soon put: *John Pogue v. Isaac A. Allen & Lemuel White*, Greene County Chancery Court Minute Book, November 9, 1865, pp. 402–3. After eight months in business, Isaac Allen was indebted to the firm $8,523.45, and Pogue owed $2,653.30; in addition the firm owed to others about $3,000. The partnership dissolved; a new one formed immediately (without Pogue) and was known as Allen & White.
41. son of the late Josiah Dobbs: Individual Confederate service records of Asa A., Thomas J., Nathaniel J. and William B. Dobbs. Georgia Department of Archives and History. Asa mustered into the 18th Regiment Georgia Volunteers, G Company; Nathaniel, on July 9, 1861, joined the Georgia 14th Infantry, K Company; Thomas, on March 4, 1862, joined the 41st Georgia Infantry, B Company; and William B., on April 28, 1862, joined the Phillips Legion.
41. fasting and prayer in the city: Atlanta City Council Minutes, resolution passed on June 7, 1861. AHC.
41. City Council members gathered: *Ibid.*, August 11, 1861.
41. Greeneville Convention of June 1861: Richard Doughty, *Greeneville: One Hundred Year Portrait, 1785–1885* (Kingsport, Tenn.: Kingsport Press, 1975), pp. 206–9, 328–32.
42. "The little batch of disaffected traitors": *Ibid.*, p. 328. For more on the Greeneville Convention see also: Oliver P. Temple, *East Tennessee and the Civil War* (Cincinnati: R. Clarke Company, 1899).
42. $750 in Confederate notes: War Department Records of Confederate Records. National Archives, Washington, D.C., Record Group 109, Box 14, Roll 12 (microfilmed as M346), "Confederate Citizens & Business Firms." Allen was paid on May 26 by Confederate captain and quartermaster H. G. Robertson.
42. At Spartanburg, South Carolina: *Ibid.* This transaction occurred on September 29, 1863.
42. "services as agent": *Ibid.* Isaac Allen was paid $60 for fifteen days' work in Bristol on November 30, 1863. See also: Box 15, RG109, Records for James Allen. Isaac's brother James sold

animals and foodstuff to the Confederacy on a more frequent basis; at least eighteen different entries are cited in CSA quartermaster records.

42. he saw a freshly dug grave: Interview with Sue Frick Saunders. Ms. Saunders is a niece to Ivan Allen, Sr.

42. had died during the night: *Ibid.* See also: Family Bible of Laura Haygood Allen. In this Old and New Testament Bible, purchased in November 1873, Laura H. Allen recorded the death of her daughter Margaret Luana as September 8, 1863. The Bible is in the possession of Mrs. Helen Britton, Greeneville, Tenn.

43. Earnest Allen was only fourteen: Roster of Confederate 12th Cavalry Battalion, B Company. Tennessee State Library and Archives, McGhee Library, McClung Collection, Knoxville, Tenn. Earnest Allen's solitary muster card is filed in the roster of the 12th.

43. "Come boys, if you want": Doughty, *Greeneville,* p. 213. Announcement first appeared in *The Tri-Weekly Banner,* July 25, 1862.

43. "to be shot to death by musketry": Records of the Confederate Adjutant and Inspector General's Office, General Orders, No. 68, May 27, 1863. National Archives, Washington, D.C. Arnold was found guilty of violating the Ninth Article of War, which stipulated that striking, or drawing a weapon, against a superior officer shall be capitally punished. Arnold was captured by Union forces in Bristol, Va., on December 14, 1864 (National Archives, RG109, Entry 133, Manuscript No. 3045) and subsequently paroled. He returned to the CSA army and was killed on March 28, 1865.

43. James Allen was killed: Roster of Confederate 12th Cavalry Battalion. Unlike his cousin Earnest, James Allen left an extensive record of his Confederate service. On March 24, 1863, with the 12th Cavalry serving as an escort to Major General McCown, James Allen was hospitalized, with an unknown ailment, in Shelbyville, Tenn. He was killed in action at Chickamauga on September 19, 1863.

44. "by fours in almost endless stream": H. G. Robertson, *A Small Boy's Recollections of the Civil War* (Greeneville, Tenn.: Self-Published, 1931), pp. 51–52.

44. "the uniforms showed wear and tear": *Ibid.,* p. 53.

44. "Now what has secession done?": Unpublished Diary of Dr. Joseph Bell, September 2, 1863. The diary is in the possession of Mrs. Evelyn Bell Carter of Greeneville, Tenn. She is a great-great-granddaughter of Dr. Bell.

44. three weeks recuperating at Chimborazo Hospital: Confederate service record of William B. Dobbs, a private in Phillips Legion, M Company. GDA&H, Microfilm Drawer 258, Box 44. He was injured at Antietam on September 17, 1862, and furloughed to Cobb County from Chimborazo Hospital on October 18. See also: Application for indigent pension Mary A. Dobbs, Confederate widow. GDA&H, Microfilm Drawer 272, Box 19. William Dobbs suffered from chronic diarrhea until his death in 1887 and, according to one testimonial in the application, he had "expected it to cause his death one day." His widow, Mary Dobbs, received her pension on September 21, 1900.

44. October and December 1868 in Richmond: Confederate service record of Nathaniel J. Dobbs of the Georgia 14th Infantry, K Company. GDA&H, Microfilm Drawer 255, Box 11. He rose to the rank of second sergeant on October 20, 1861. He was killed in the Battle of Chancellorsville on May 3, 1863. For reference to death, see: "Georgia Confederate Pensions and Records Department. Records of the Soldier Roster Commission, 14th Regiment Georgia Volunteers, Infantry." GDA&H, Record Group 58, Subgroup 2, Series 2, Box 37.

44. "Cease firing": Ernest B. Furgurson, *Chancellorsville 1863* (New York: Alfred A. Knopf, 1992), p. 202. For more on General Lee's reaction to Jackson's death, see: Douglas Southall Freeman, *R. E. Lee: A Biography* (New York: Charles Scribner's Sons, 1935), pp. 1–2.

45. "the shrieks and groans": *Ibid.,* p. 212. The diary of George W. Hall, who, like Nathaniel Dobbs, was a member of the 14th Georgia Infantry, is held at the Hargrett Rare Book and Manuscript Library, University of Georgia, Athens, Ga.

45. "I will not take up arms": Confederate service record of Thomas J. Dobbs, first lieutenant of 41st Georgia Infantry, B Company. GDA&H, Microfilm Drawer 257, Box 9. He was captured on July 4, 1863, at Vicksburg.

45. two frying pans: *Ibid.* He signed the receipt of this requisition order in Decatur, Ga., on September 25, 1863. On October 10, 1864, he was reported as a member of Hood's Army of Tennessee.

45. At Cold Harbor, Asa Dobbs: Confederate service record of Asa A. Dobbs, private in 18th Georgia Regiment, Infantry. GDA&H, Microfilm Drawer 252, Box 54. Also: Application for indigent pension as former Confederate soldier of Georgia filed by Asa A. Dobbs on March 31,

1899, in Bartow County. (GDA&H, Microfilm Drawer 271, Roll 14.) In his pension application of 1899 he maintained that he was a sixty-six-year-old butcher in Cartersville, Ga. Among his ailments he claimed to be "ruptured on the left side," in addition to suffering from dyspepsia and heart palpitation. Though a pension official wrote in July 1899 that it was "unclear that applicant is unable to earn a support for himself," apparently he was granted his pension.

46. even though his fifty men were armed: Albert Castel, *Decision in the West: The Atlanta Campaign of 1864* (Lawrence, Kansas: University Press of Kansas, 1992), pp. 27–28.

46. Davis felt the aristocratic Virginian: *Ibid.*, pp. 29–31.

46. reaffirm the terms of his will: Cherokee County, Ga., Ordinary Estate Records, Wills, Vol. C, 1866–1921, Cherokee County courthouse in Canton, Ga. Also: GDA&H, Microfilm Drawer 13, Box 17, pp. 10–13. Because the witnesses to the signing of his will in 1854 had either moved away, died or "become blind," Dr. McAfee reaffirmed his will, with his younger brother Lemuel as one of the four witnesses.

46. "Whereas the Lincoln government": Atlanta City Council Minutes, June 1, 1864. AHC.

46. "we were scuffling for food": Interview with Jesse L. Dobbs. A first cousin of John Wesley Dobbs, though thirty years younger, he was born on the farm in Kennesaw in 1912.

47. hastened south from Woodstock: Inventory and Appraisement of John M. McAfee Estate, Cherokee County, Ga., Vol. C, 1854–1924, Cherokee County courthouse, Canton, Ga. McAfee's removal from Woodstock during the summer of 1864 is suggested by the inventory of his estate, which lists all solvent notes due him. Three are dated by him in May 1864, the last on May 29. The next is dated October 1865, by which time the Civil War already was over.

47. "It must have cost the citizens": *New York Tribune*, July 16, 1864, datelined Marietta. See also: Sarah Blackwell Gober Temple, *The First Hundred Years: A Short History of Cobb County in Georgia* (Athens, Ga.: Agee Publishers, 1935), p. 323.

47. Eliza, had hidden the family silver: Interview with Imogene McAfee Buder. Mrs. Buder is the granddaughter of Eliza and Bob McAfee.

47. "The whole country is one vast fort": Telegraph from Gen. William T. Sherman to Henry Halleck in Washington, June 23, 1864. In: William Tecumseh Sherman, *Memoirs of General William T. Sherman, Vol. 2* (New York: Da Capo, 1984; reprint of 1875 edition), pp. 59–60.

47. "I need not call your attention": Letter from Gov. Joseph Brown to President Jefferson Davis, June 28, 1864. In Joseph E. Johnston, *Military Operations, Directed During the Late War Between the States* (New York: D. Appleton and Company, 1874), p. 360.

48. "As you have failed to arrest": *Ibid.*, pp. 348–49. See also: John B. Hood, *Advance and Retreat: Personal Experiences in the United States and Confederate States Armies* (Philadelphia: Burk & M'Fetridge, 1880), pp. 126–27.

48. a four-and-a-half-inch stump: Castel, *Decision in the West*, pp. 58–61.

48. "One thing is certain": Telegraph from William T. Sherman to Henry Halleck, August 7, 1864. In Sherman, *Memoirs, Vol. 2*, p. 101.

48. Hood's soldiers were recent additions: Confederate service record of Lemuel McAfee, private, 4th Georgia Regiment Infantry, Reserves. GDA&H, Microfilm Drawer 255, Box 9. After Jefferson Davis called in February for the enlistment of all southern men between forty-five and fifty years old, Lemuel McAfee mustered into the Confederacy at Atlanta on May 10 to enlist in the CSA, L. A. McAfee enlisted in Atlanta on May 10. He was with General Hood in Atlanta on September 1.

49. Sherman wondered if a battle: Sherman, *Memoirs, Vol. 2*, p. 108.

49. "Atlanta is at the centre": *New York Times*, September 5, 1864.

49. "I became a hero myself": Letter from Ellen Ewing Sherman to her husband, William T. Sherman, September 4, 1864. In Anna McAllister, *Ellen Ewing, Wife of General Sherman* (New York: Benzinger Brothers, 1936), pp. 288–89.

49. "famous in the annals of war": Letter from Abraham Lincoln to William T. Sherman, September 8, 1864. In Sherman, *Memoirs, Vol. 2*, p. 110.

49. "Lord, massa, is dat": Castel, *Decision in the West*, p. 548.

49. 446 families, totaling 1,565 people: Garrett, *Atlanta and Environs, Vol. 1*, p. 642.

49. "You might as well appeal": Letter from Gen. William T. Sherman to Mayor James Calhoun, and others, September 12, 1864. In Sherman, *Memoirs, Vol. 2*, pp. 125–26.

50. "transcends, in studied and ingenious cruelty": Letter from Gen. John Bell Hood to Gen. William T. Sherman, September 9, 1864. *Ibid.*, p. 119.

50. "We will fight you to the death!": Letter from Gen. John Bell Hood to Gen. William T. Sherman, September 12, 1864. *Ibid.*, pp. 123–24.

50. 200,000 would be needed: Sherman, *Memoirs, Vol. 1*, pp. 203–18.
50. "I would destroy every mill": *Ibid., Vol. 2*, pp. 128–29.
50. "The Chinese once believed": *Milledgeville Federal Union*, 1854. In Russell, *Atlanta 1847–1890*, p. 1.
50. "We have been fighting Atlanta": Henry Hitchcock, *Marching with Sherman* (New Haven, Conn.: Yale University Press, 1927), p. 58.
51. The Georgia Railroad depot had been leveled: Sherman, *Memoirs, Vol. 2*, pp. 117–18.
51. "John Brown's body lies": *Ibid.*
51. "We turned our horses' heads": *Ibid.*
51. a carriage through the front gates: This story, told by Minnie McAfee Dobbs Banks to her descendants, was cited by several members of the Dobbs family in interviews, including June Dobbs Butts and Willie Dobbs Blackburn.
52. "Why didn't you make a break": June Dobbs Butts interview.
52. "Applicant admits": Application for amnesty by John M. McAfee, Cherokee County, Ga., "Case files of Applications from former Confederates for Presidential Pardons," Records of the Adjutant General's Office, 1780s–1917, Record Group 94. National Archives and Records Administration-Southeast Region, East Point, Ga., Microfilm Publication M1003, Reel 21, pp. 165–69. McAfee's application was forwarded from Augusta to the U.S. attorney general in Washington on October 16, 1865.
52. Isaac Allen gave to her their father's home: *James Allen v. Isaac A. Allen, Lemuel White, Almagro Noell, Margaret Noell et al.*, Greene County Chancery Court, November 10, 1865. A number of suits were filed against Isaac Allen after the war. This suit, which amounts to intrafamily financial accountability, shows that Isaac Allen accepted $2,000 in Confederate treasury notes from his brother James in 1863 and that he gave up his father's home on the river to his sister, Margaret Noell.
52. sought collection in May 1866 on a $250 note: *Nicholas W. Earnest, exec. of Peter Earnest, dec'd v. Isaac A. Allen and Robert Allen*, Greene County Chancery Court, May 8, 1866.
52. Moses labored for nine years: Interview with Goldene F. Burgner.
52. Earnest Allen paid $3,000, deeding: R. G. Dun & Co. credit report from Whitfield County, Ga. "D. E. Allen," August 6, 1875, report. R. G. Dun & Co. Collection, Baker Library, Harvard University Graduate School of Business Administration, Department of Special Collections.
53. "too much indulgence": *Ibid.* R. G. Dun & Co. report on "J. M Lowry & Co.," April 1, 1875.
53. "in our opinion, is honest": *Ibid.* "D. E. Allen" report, August 6, 1875.
53. "very questionable. Their failure": *Ibid.* "J. M. Lowry & Co." report, November 19, 1875.
53. the planter's power would begin to shift: C. Vann Woodward, *Origins of the New South, 1877–1913* (Baton Rouge, La.: Louisiana State University Press, 1951), pp. 140–41.
53. 150 stores were back in operation: Russell, *Atlanta, 1847–1890*, p. 119.
53. values in the city in 1870 were triple: Howard N. Rabinowitz, *The First New South, 1865–1920* (Arlington Heights, Ill.: Harlan Davidson, 1992), pp. 52–53.
53. promising to build, free of charge: *Ibid.* See also: *Southern Recorder*, Milledgeville, Ga., March 3, 1868.
53. "The people are not such a set of asses": *Southern Recorder*, Milledgeville, Ga., March 3, 1868.
53. "Atlanta may have the penitentiary": *Ibid.*, June 23, 1868.
53. "the spirit of oppression": Report from C. C. Sibley, director of the Freedmen's Bureau in Georgia, to O. O. Howard in Washington, November 1867. GDA&H, U.S. Bureau of Refugees, Freedmen and Abandoned Lands, Records of the Assistant Commissioner for the State of Georgia, Microfilm Drawer 159, Box 61.
53. two freedmen were tied and whipped: *Ibid.*
53. Wesley Dobbs needed to borrow $75: *Wesley Dobbs to Anderson Bros.*, April 24, 1895, Cobb County Superior Court, Promiscuous Records, Book H, p. 170.
54. Wesley Dobbs signed his name: Georgia Executive Department Reconstruction Registration Oath Book, 1867, Cobb County, Senate District 35, July 29, 1867, Book 2, p. 404. Oath listed on p. 436. Signature and oath of Thomas J. Dobbs is in the same book, p. 423. GDA&H, Microfilm Drawer 296, Box 67.
54. "Ring the fire bells!": *Atlanta Constitution*,* January 30, 1879.

*The *Atlanta Constitution* (founded 1868) and the *Atlanta Journal* (founded 1883) merged in 1950, maintaining separate news staffs but publishing a joint Sunday edition. In 1982, their news staffs merged; the papers retained independence only on their editorial pages.

54. "Young man, when I got to Atlanta": William S. Ellis, "Pacesetter City of the South," *National Geographic*, February 1969, p. 248. This story had been told by Howell to Ralph McGill, who was quoted in his retelling.

54. die with the name of Jesus: Obituary of Isaac A. Allen, Big Springs Baptist Church of Mosheim, Tenn., report of April 1885. The church records are in the possession of James A. Butler of Mosheim, Tenn.

54. "Few Tennesseans were better acquainted": *Greeneville Herald*, November 27, 1884.

54. a mowing machine, two wagons: Greene County Court, Book 31, 1884–86, pp. 92, 353. Also: Estate Settlements, Box 97-98, 1871–98, Greeneville, Tenn.

55. in a pine box and carried it back: Sue Frick Saunders interview. See also: *Tennessee Mortality Schedules, 1880* (Nashville: Bryon Sistler & Associates, 1984), p. 4. Sistler's book indicates that Ernest Allen died of dyspepsia, a digestive disorder.

55. Ivan while reading a Russian novel: Interview with Ivan Allen, Jr.

CHAPTER 4

57. If Atlanta could suck: Interview with Franklin M. Garrett. Garrett is Atlanta's historian in residence at the Atlanta History Center.

59. "From the ashes": Joel Chandler Harris, editor, *Life of Henry W. Grady Including His Writings and Speeches* (New York: Haskell House, 1972), pp. 83–93. Grady delivered the speech December 21, 1886.

59. "wouldn't sell them the boxwood": *Atlanta Constitution*, September 14, 1961.

59. shot dead on the Confederate retreat: Susan Harris Allen application to join the United Daughters of the Confederacy, Bryan Thomas branch in Dalton, Ga., Whitfield-Murray Counties Historical Society. Though the application was undated, this UDC branch was formed in 1898. See also: Whitfield County History Commission, *Official History of Whitfield County, Georgia* (Dalton, Ga.: A. J. Showalter Company, 1936), pp. 147–48.

59. "He said that was too visionary": Eleanor Williams, *Ivan Allen: A Resourceful Citizen* (Atlanta: Ivan Allen-Marshall Company, 1950), p. 249. This is quoted from a speech given by Allen in May 1944 to the Dalton, Ga., high school graduating class.

60. Exposition lasted about one hundred days: Walter G. Cooper, *The Cotton States and International Exposition and South, Illustrated, Including the Official History of the Exposition* (Atlanta: Illustrator Company, 1896).

60. "How many states grow cotton?": Franklin M. Garrett, *Atlanta and Environs: A Chronicle of Its People and Events, Vol. 2* (New York: Lewis Historical Publishing Company, 1954), p. 319.

61. Washington was the sort of black spokesman: Louis R. Harlan, *Booker T. Washington: The Making of a Black Leader, 1856–1901* (New York: Oxford University Press, 1972, pp. 204–5.

61. "We have with us today": *Atlanta Constitution*, September 19, 1895.

61. "a Negro Moses stood": *New York World*, September 9, 1895. See also: Booker T. Washington, *Up from Slavery: An Autobiography* (New York: Doubleday, Page & Company, 1924), pp. 238–41.

61. "As we have proved our loyalty": *Ibid*. Washington published the entire text of his speech in his autobiography.

61. "That man's speech": *Ibid.*, p. 239. Howell also wrote to the *New York World* on September 19, 1895, suggesting Washington's speech was a "full vindication" of Grady's New South vision.

61. "his effort was most happy": *Atlanta Constitution*, September 19, 1895.

62. "What God hath separated": Harris, ed. *Life of Grady*, pp. 94–121. Grady delivered this speech, "The South and Her Problems," at the State Fair in Dallas, Tex., on October 26, 1887.

62. Allen began at a salary of $40: Williams, *Ivan Allen*, p. 3.

62. "The Cow Coroner": *Ibid.*, p. 2.

62. Ivan Allen's address was 6 West Ellis Street: *Atlanta City Directory* (Atlanta: Mutual Publishing Company, 1899).

62. In June 1897: Remarks by John Wesley Dobbs at public hearing of the Metropolitan Planning Commission, Atlanta, Ga., June 3, 1952. John Wesley Dobbs Papers, Amistad Research Center, New Orleans, La., Box 3, Folder 17. In his remarks, Dobbs said he arrived in Atlanta in June 1897, also that he first passed through the city in 1891 "when the old artesian well stood at Five Points."

63. "It wasn't always like this!": Interview with Bill Clement, Jr.
63. "I'd rather face the judge": Letter from Josephine Dobbs Clement to her son, Bill, Jr., May 13, 1963. JWD Papers, ARC, Box 5, Folder 20.
63. ran barefoot in the fields: *Atlanta Daily World*, February 18, 1974. This article about Dobbs was written by John Calhoun, a black city councilman in Atlanta, as part of a series on black leaders of Atlanta entitled "Atlanta: A Cradle of Black Leadership in America." Calhoun knew Dobbs personally.
63. Dobbs ate the lining inside: Several Dobbs family members recalled this story during interviews, including Willie Dobbs Blackburn and Sandra Irene Jackson Baraniuk.
63. only fourteen years old in 1876 when she: Dobbs family record album. JWD Papers, ARC, Box 4, Folder 2. Dobbs recorded dates of births, deaths and marriages in the family.
63. she left for Savannah: Interview with Mattiwilda Dobbs Janzon.
63. Will Dobbs went in a different direction: Interviews with Mozelle Murphy and Ernestine McDaniel. They are the granddaughters of Will Dobbs from his second marriage, to Leila Roberts of Cobb County. Will Dobbs had two daughters by his second wife, Leila and Bertha. Though no records exist, Murphy and McDaniel, daughters of Bertha Dobbs Pate, were told that their grandfather Will Dobbs died during the 1890s as a result of an accident stemming from his work as a laborer on the railroad.
64. made their clothes by hand: Letter to the author, concerning family memories, by Muriel Gassett James, September 17, 1992. Many of her stories she learned from her grandfather Jesse L. Dobbs, son of Judie and Wesley.
64. visiting once or twice a year: Cited in "I Saw the Stars," a fourteen-page description of childhood memories by John Wesley Dobbs. Though undated, it was likely written in 1939, or soon after. Dobbs presented this material in a speech to the Prince Hall Masonic chapter in Cobb County, Ga. Personal Papers of Paul E. X. Brown, Atlanta, Ga.
64. Dobbs cried each time she departed: *Ibid.*
64. When she offered him a job: *Ibid.*
64. He delivered *The Savannah Evening Press: Ibid.*
64. "Then I would pay one dollar": *Ibid.*
64. changed its name to Atlanta Baptist College: Willard Range, *The Rise and Progress of Negro Colleges in Georgia, 1865–1949* (Athens, Ga.: University of Georgia Press, 1951), pp. 24–26, 224–25. See also: Benjamin Brawley, *History of Morehouse College* (Atlanta: Morehouse College, 1917). Brawley was dean of Morehouse College.
64. skulls were said to have been dug up: Edward A. Jones, *A Candle in the Dark: A History of Morehouse College* (Valley Forge, Pa.: Judson Press, 1967), p. 50.
65. "If these studies have educational value": Brawley, *History of Morehouse*, p. 67.
65. A colored aristocracy arose: August Meier and David L. Lewis, "History of the Negro Upper Class in Atlanta, Georgia, 1890–1958," *Journal of Negro Education* (Vol. 28, 1959), pp. 128–39.
65. Dobbs worked barefoot: Dobbs, "I Saw the Stars."
65. Rev. E. J. Fisher of the Mount Olive Baptist Church: *Ibid.*
65. He opened the store at six: *Ibid.*
65. "they'd liiiiiiiiiine up": Several family members recalled this story in interviews, including Robert Jordan, Jr., Maynard Jackson, Jr., and Josephine Dobbs Clement.
65. a boardinghouse at 226 East Ellis Street: U.S. Census, 1900, Atlanta, Ga., p. 184.
65. Allen lived in a boardinghouse: *Ibid.*

CHAPTER 5

67. Shall we permit ourselves: William J. Sayward, "Important Steps for Atlanta's Future Progress," *The City Builder* (Vol. 3, May 1918), p. 13.
67. I grew up in Plains: Interview with Jimmy Carter.
69. when Minnie Dobbs again took sick: John Wesley Dobbs, "I Saw the Stars." Personal papers of Paul E. X. Brown, Atlanta, Ga.
69. salary of $800 per year: A. L. Glenn, Sr., *History of the National Alliance of Postal Employees, 1913–1956* (Washington, D.C.: NAPE, 1956), pp. 161–71. Dobbs's $800 salary also is cited in U.S. Postal Records, National Archives, Washington, D.C.
69. government-issue Colt revolver: Government service record of John Wesley Dobbs, United States Office of Personnel Management, St. Louis, Mo. Personnel records indicate that in

1923 Dobbs's Colt revolver was stolen from a postal car locker in Nashville. He was fined $14.50, which he protested in a letter. "I have always been very careful with anything belonging to the government and entrusted to my keeping," Dobbs wrote. The fine was upheld.

69. a long brass chain with keys: Glenn, *History of the National Alliance of Postal Employees*, p. 16.

69. "Great God A'mighty!": Interview with Josephine Dobbs Clement.

70. "the Black World beyond the Veil": William E. B. Du Bois, *The Souls of Black Folk* (New York: Avon, 1965), p. 265. This book was first published in 1903.

70. Du Bois was fully ignored by white Atlanta: David Levering Lewis, *W. E. B. Du Bois: Biography of a Race, 1868–1919* (New York: John Macrae/Henry Holt, 1993), p. 344.

70. ambitious dark-skinned man married: Stephen Birmingham, *Certain People: America's Black Elite* (New York: Little, Brown, 1977), pp. 36–37.

71. "Dear Irene, I hope you": Letter from John Wesley Dobbs to Irene Thompson, April 1905. John Wesley Dobbs Papers, Amistad Research Center, New Orleans, La., Box 1. See folders marked: "Correspondence-Personal—1905-1958."

71. fired if his noun and verb: Interview with Andrew Young.

72. "When you can get the best types": Unpublished speech of former President Theodore Roosevelt at First Congregational Church, October 8, 1910. Rev. Henry Hugh Proctor Papers, ARC.

72. honeymoon in Kennesaw: Interview with Mattiwilda Dobbs Janzon.

72. waved a lantern or lit a match: Written recollections of childhood in Kennesaw by Isabel Dobbs Gassett. Though the paper is undated, Mrs. Gassett, who died in 1986, is believed to have written this reflection during the early 1980s. Personal papers of her daughter, Muriel Gassett James, Sacramento, Calif.

72. A wooden bucket and gourd hung: *Ibid.*

72. racial conflict brewed in Atlanta: Dewey W. Grantham, Jr., *Hoke Smith and the Politics of the New South* (Baton Rouge, La.: Louisiana State University Press, 1958), p. 114.

73. "appears to be unable to understand": *Atlanta Journal*, November 5, 1905.

73. "What does Civilization owe": C. Vann Woodward, *Tom Watson: Agrarian Rebel* (New York: Oxford University Press, 1938), p. 380. Watson published this quote in an attack on Booker T. Washington in June 1905.

73. "It matters not": *Atlanta Independent*, June 6, 1906.

73. *"Bold Negro Kisses": Atlanta Evening News*, September 22, 1906.

73. "With his yellow lips": *Ibid.*, September 21, 1906.

74. beaten to death with fists: Walter White, *A Man Called White: The Autobiography of Walter White* (New York: Viking Press, 1948), pp. 9–10.

74. "There goes another nigger!": Charles Crowe, "Racial Massacre in Atlanta, September 22, 1906," *Journal of Negro History* (Vol. 54, 1969), pp. 150–73. Crowe synthesizes the disparate reports of the riot. See also: Charles Crowe, "Racial Violence and Social Reform—Origins of the Atlanta Riot of 1906," *Journal of Negro History* (Vol. 53, July 1969), pp. 234–56.

74. "The honor of Atlanta": *Atlanta Evening News*, September 23, 1906.

74. faced the fire hoses: Crowe, "Racial Massacre," pp. 156–57.

74. "fought like a wildcat": *Ibid.*, p. 162.

75. "A mob of poor white crackers": *Atlanta Independent*, September 29, 1906.

75. "Some times I doubt": Letter from Adrienne McNeil Herndon to Booker T. Washington, February 12, 1907. In Louis R. Harlan and Raymond W. Smock, editors, *The Booker T. Washington Papers, Vol. 9: 1906–8* (Urbana, Ill.: University of Illinois Press, 1980), pp. 216–17.

75. "No sight has ever been so sweet": Darden Asbury Pyron, *Southern Daughter: The Life of Margaret Mitchell* (New York: Oxford University Press, 1991), pp. 40–41.

75. sat on the steps of South Hall: Lewis, *W. E. B. Du Bois*, pp. 333–35.

75. "Son, don't shoot until": White, *A Man Called White*, p. 11.

75. "I knew then who I was.": *Ibid.*

76. gripping his Colt revolver: Interview with Irene (Renie) Dobbs Jackson.

76. more than three thousand white families: *Atlanta Georgian*, September 24, 1906.

76. More than one thousand blacks: Crowe, "Racial Massacre," p. 166.

76. plummeted to $4.75: Herndon Barbershop Records, 1906–1910. See records for Monday, September 24, 1906. Alonzo Herndon Home and Museum Archives, Atlanta, Ga., Record Storage Boxes 1, 2.

76. "at the mourner's bench": Letter from Booker T. Washington to Wallace Buttrick, September 30, 1906. In Harlan and Smock, eds., *The Booker T. Washington Papers, Vol. 9: 1906–8*, pp. 78–79.

76. memories in Atlanta: Scott Ellsworth, *Death in a Promised Land: The Tulsa Riot of 1921* (Baton Rouge, La.: Louisiana State University Press, 1982), pp. 98–107. Ellsworth writes of the notion of "the segregation of memory."

76. If white families: David F. Godshalk, "Silence and Memory in Local History: The Struggle over the Meaning of the Atlanta Race Riot, 1906–1959." Oral paper delivered at the 1994 Annual Meeting of the Organization of American Historians, Atlanta, Ga. Characteristically, the Allens have retained no oral history of this defining event in the city.

76. "There has been no more hopeful": Ray Stannard Baker, "Following the Color Line—A Race Riot, and After," *American Magazine* (Vol. 63, April 1907), pp. 563–79.

77. "Suppose, accidentally": *Atlanta Independent*, October 6, 1906.

77. "the proud Caucasian": *Ibid.*, October 20, 1906.

77. "What is the ultimate end?": *Atlanta Evening News*, September 24, 1906, p. 43.

77. "Dobbs kept guns and bullets": Irene Dobbs Jackson interview.

77. unable to pronounce Wilda: Interview with Mattiwilda Dobbs Janzon.

77. "People are all saying": Irene Dobbs Jackson interview.

78. "We kept thinking": Letter from John Wesley Dobbs to Harry Williamson, February 3, 1933. Schomburg Center for Research in Black Culture, New York Public Library, Harry A. Williamson Papers, Masonic Correspondence: Georgia-Missouri: Georgia, 1922–1949, Box 5, Folder 1 (Microfilm reel 2).

78. "Remember," Dobbs often said: Irene Dobbs Jackson interview.

78. Steinechen he paid $2,767: Fulton County Tax Records, Deed Book 398, p. 39. On June 7, 1909, John Wesley Dobbs bought 400 Houston Street, making a $200 down payment. His monthly mortgage was $18.

78. liken the home to a New York museum: Irene Dobbs Jackson interview.

79. "He was the king": *Ibid.*

79. he nor his wife worked: Mattiwilda Dobbs Janzon interview.

79. never were his daughters to sit: Interview with June Dobbs Butts.

79. Statue of Liberty, they climbed every: Ernest Dunbar, "Seven Dobbs Against the Odds," *Look*, December 2, 1969, pp. 27–33. A profile of the six Dobbs daughters and the influence of their late father.

79. "Oh, Wes, don't talk about that": Josephine Dobbs Clement interview.

79. refusing to enter a room: *Ibid.*

80. "If you took a very refined": Interview with Carol Jackson Miller.

80. A co-owner of two barbershops: Josephine Dobbs Clement interview. For dates of births and marriages in the Thompson family, see: "Family Record Album." John Wesley Dobbs Papers, Amistad Research Center, New Orleans, La., Box 4, Folder 2. J. W. Dobbs listed dates in this brief family history.

80. "You've got to fix the fish": Interview with Muriel Gassett James. This story was related to her by her mother, Isabel Dobbs Gassett.

80. "We're just like": Interview with Constance Jackson Carter.

80. "My Darling Boy": John Wesley Dobbs Masonic Papers, Prince Hall Masonic Temple, Atlanta, Ga. This letter was among some of Dobbs's miscellaneous papers in file cabinets in the grand master's office on Auburn Avenue.

81. "They'll push me off": Josephine Dobbs Clement interview.

81. increased under Republican administrations: Glenn, *History of the National Alliance of Postal Employees*, p. 15.

81. plagued with bickering over small matters: *Ibid*, p. 17.

81. "Colored men are put on daily duty": *Atlanta Independent*, October 6, 1906.

81. Dobbs became one of its more vocal members: Glenn, *History of the National Alliance of Postal Employees*, p. 51. Dobbs is identified as a leader of NAPE from 1917 to 1922, at which point he devoted more of his time to his Masonic duties. On July 10, 1918, NAPE held its national convention in Atlanta at the First Congregational Church. Dobbs delivered the welcome address on behalf of the Atlanta branch of NAPE.

82. "J. W. Dobbs 400 Houston St.": John Wesley Dobbs Masonic Papers, Prince Hall Masonic Temple, Atlanta, Ga. This notebook was among some of Dobbs's miscellaneous papers in file cabinets in the grand master's office on Auburn Avenue.

83. "How can I support my family?": "My Letter," a 1,250-word essay by Isabel Dobbs Gassett. Personal papers of her daughter, Muriel Gassett James, Sacramento, Calif.

83. he carried a small woven basket: *Ibid.* Mrs. Gassett later professed thanks to her cousin John

Wesley Dobbs for enabling her to gain a superior education in Atlanta. She later attended Atlanta University and the Reid Business School in west Atlanta, where she learned to type. She worked as a secretary for twenty-four years for the Cannolene Company in Atlanta. Living in Sacramento, Calif., during the 1960s, she worked in the legislative unit of the governor's office under Edmund "Pat" Brown and Ronald Reagan. These descriptions of the Kennesaw farm are drawn largely from her written reflections.

84. "Why is my grandma so white?": Irene Dobbs Jackson interview.
84. "There was a whole lot of stuff": *Ibid.*
84. "Teach me": *Ibid.*
85. "Here I am! Come to me!": Interview with Willie Dobbs Blackburn.
85. never had seen her wearing: *Ibid.*
85. twenty stately mansions: *Atlanta Journal* and *Atlanta Constitution*, May 22, 1917.
85. Dobbs rushed for home: Willie Dobbs Blackburn interview.
85. fire was part of a German conspiracy: *Atlanta Constitution*, May 22, 1917. The rumor was fueled by the fact that four other fires broke out across Atlanta that day, including one at the Candler warehouse.
85. he took out the hoses: Willie Dobbs Blackburn interview.
85. in excess of $5 million: Franklin M. Garrett, *Atlanta and Environs: A Chronicle of Its People and Events, Vol. 2* (New York: Lewis Historical Publishing Company, 1954), p. 704.

CHAPTER 6

86. Several hundred guests sat: *Atlanta Constitution*, October 25, 1907.
86. "Mr. Allen is socially well-liked": *Ibid.*
86. a black midwife named Bertha Lewis: Interview with Ivan Allen, Jr.
87. "Your Son, Grand-Son": Western Union Telegram from Ivan Allen, Sr., to his mother, Susie Allen, May 11, 1912. Ivan Allen, Sr., Papers, Atlanta History Center, Box 1, Folder 4.
87. he sent a self-addressed: *Atlanta Constitution*, September 19, 1961. Milton L. Fleetwood Column reprinted from *The Cartersville Daily Tribune*.
87. "General Johnston was the one": *Dalton* (Ga.) *Citizen*, November 2, 1912.
87. Twelve southern crosses of honor: *Ibid.*
87. "It's the fellow with four": Sinclair Lewis, *Babbitt* (New York: Harcourt Brace Jovanovich, 1922), p. 149.
87. "Here's the new generation": *Ibid.*, p. 151.
87. "The more I gave to altruistic work": *The Story of Georgia. Biographical Volume* (New York: American Historical Society, 1938), pp. 508–10.
88. "Atlanta Daily News": Recorded Minutes of the Atlanta Chamber of Commerce Meeting, March 5, 1901, Atlanta Chamber of Commerce Minutes Book, 1901, Atlanta chamber files.
88. Atlanta was the second most populous city: 1910 U.S. Census.
88. Atlanta became the South's first city of national import: Charles Paul Garofalo, "Business Ideas in Atlanta, 1916–1935" (Ph.D. diss. Emory University, Department of History, 1972), pp. 74–75.
88. His chin had a determined: *Atlanta Journal*, December 21, 1913.
88. "Biff! Biff! Biff!": *Ibid.*
89. "Sentiment, everywhere": *Ibid.*, February 22, 1912.
89. "Tersely expressed, I might say": Ivan Allen, "Atlanta, the Center of the Automobile Business of the Southeastern States," *City Builder* (Atlanta Chamber of Commerce), March 10, 1917, pp. 26–27.
89. "The Convention City of Dixie Land": *Atlanta Journal* and *Atlanta Constitution*, January 26, 1916.
89. $4 million in convention business: Eleanor Williams, *Ivan Allen: A Resourceful Citizen* (Atlanta: Ivan Allen-Marshall Company, 1950), p. 67.
89. "Beautiful, hustling, sunny Atlanta": *Industrial Index*, September 24, 1913. Ivan Allen, Sr., Papers, AHC, Box 1, Folder 5.
89. in case the mob rushing: Ivan Allen, Jr., interview.
89. "Here's the secret": *Atlanta Journal*, December 21, 1913.
89. "The Value of Organized Effort": *Ibid.*, November 14, 1913.
90. "If Atlanta elects Allen": *Dalton* (Ga.) *Citizen*, December 18, 1913.

90. "the embodiment of 'The Atlanta Spirit' ": *Atlanta Journal*, December 21, 1913.
90. a descendant of Josiah Dobbs's brother Elijah: Interview with Raymond Guffin. A leading genealogist of the Dobbs family, Guffin believes that Elijah Dobbs, who lived near Villa Rica, Ga., about forty miles west of Atlanta, was a brother to David, Asa and Josiah Dobbs.
90. "More smokestacks for Atlanta": *City Builder*, February 1918, p. 7.
90. "the guests at the German Barracks": *Ibid*.
90. "Let us fly both the flag": *Ibid*.
90. "is the love of home": *Atlanta Journal*, December 1, 1913.
90. whom he sometimes called Reno: Ivan Allen, Jr., interview.
91. "How do you find business?" Williams, *A Resourceful Citizen*, p. xi.
91. "An Atlanta man feels": *Atlanta Commercial and Industrial Bulletin*, February 1914, p. 3. The entire text of Allen's address at the Atlanta Convention Bureau Annual Meeting and Dinner on January 27, 1914, is published in this edition. Ivan Allen, Sr., Papers, AHC, Box 1, Folder 5.
91. "If you should walk up to": Williams, *A Resourceful Citizen*, pp. 120–21. This tribute to Allen was given by Thomas R. Jones of Dalton, Ga., in 1916.
91. He was typical of the chamber presidents: Garofalo, "Business Ideas in Atlanta," pp. 22–37. Garofalo's dissertation offers a detailed breakdown of the traits and ideologies of the men who served as president of the Atlanta Chamber of Commerce during these two decades.
91. Kriegshaber was denied membership: *Ibid*.
91. two chamber officials solicited the support: Recorded Minutes of the Atlanta Chamber of Commerce Meeting, February 7, 1917, Atlanta Chamber of Commerce Minutes Book, 1917, Atlanta chamber files.
92. But white citizens in the Sixth Ward: *Ibid.*, March 6 and 12, 1917.
92. "But Daddy didn't use the word": Ivan Allen, Jr., interview.
92. "Could it be true that": *City Builder*, May 1924.
92. "in a hundred other ways": *Atlanta Journal*, May 22, 1917.
92. nearly $50,000 was raised: *Ibid*.
92. Allen repeated each one aloud: Recorded Minutes of the Atlanta Chamber of Commerce Meeting, May 22, 1917, Atlanta Chamber of Commerce Minutes Book, 1917, Atlanta chamber files.
93. Ivan E. Allen announced plans: *Atlanta Constitution*, May 24, 1917.
93. "for all time the embarrassing": *Ibid.*, May 23, 1917.
93. "In a very few weeks": *Ibid.*, May 22, 1917.
93. a loft in the Georgia Savings Bank: Kenneth T. Jackson, *The Ku Klux Klan in the City, 1915–1930* (New York: Oxford University Press, 1967), p. 31.
93. "the autocratic Chamber of Commerce": *Ibid.*, p. 37.
94. to win the 1924 Dixie League title: *Ibid*.
94. "As a native Georgian": *Atlanta Constitution*, July 19, 1918.
94. At eleven o'clock, he telephoned Irene: Williams, *A Resourceful Citizen*, p. 150.
94. his own bills introduced by legislators: *Ibid.*, pp. 152–53.
94. "If Macon is anxious": *Atlanta Georgian*, June 29, 1919.
95. "That was the first time": Ivan Allen, Jr., interview.
95. "You've got to be kidding, Ivan": *Ibid*.
95. "Life couldn't have been": *Ibid*.
95. Alvie Mobley, made potted ham sandwiches: Ivan Allen, Jr., transcript for Paul Hemphill, 1971.
96. "I'd just like to say this": Williams, *A Resourceful Citizen*, p. 45.
96. Monk, Prince, Dan and Rabbit: Franklin M. Garrett, *Atlanta and Environs: A Chronicle of Its People and Events, Vol. 2* (New York: Lewis Historical Publishing Company, 1954), p. 829.
96. "character, energy and ability": Recorded Minutes of the Trust Company of Georgia Board of Directors Meeting, October 1968. A tribute to Ivan Allen, Sr., it was signed by Directors John A. Sibley, George S. Craft and Augustus H. (Billy) Sterne. Files of the Commerce Club, Atlanta, Ga.
97. to a Cadillac: Ivan Allen, Jr., interview.
97. cracked into the Social Cities Register: Garofalo, "Business Ideas in Atlanta," pp. 34–35.
97. Will Allen, left his job: Interview with Juanita Renner. Ms. Renner is a cousin of the Allens, descended from Isaac Allen's second marriage, to Laura Haygood. She lives in south Florida and befriended Will Allen during his years in Fort Lauderdale.
97. "Are you geared": *Report of the Forward Atlanta Commission, 1926–29* (Atlanta: Atlanta Cham-

ber of Commerce, 1929). A complete report of the marketing strategy of the four-year advertising program.

98. "the men in commerce": Ivan Allen, *Atlanta from the Ashes* (Atlanta: Ruralist Press, 1928), p. 5.
98. he knew of his explosive temper: Ivan Allen, Jr., interview.
98. "Ivan, the Bad Man": Interview with Laura Maddox Smith.
98. "I thought it was worth": Ivan Allen, Jr., with Paul Hemphill, *Mayor: Notes on the Sixties* (New York: Simon & Schuster, 1971), pp. 23–24.
99. to allow Georgia a place to develop: Robert B. Wallace, Jr., *Dress Her in White and Gold: A Biography of Georgia Tech* (Atlanta: Georgia Tech Foundation, 1963), pp. 2–4.
99. "I gotta Eugene Dog": William Anderson, *The Wild Man from Sugar Creek: The Political Career of Eugene Talmadge* (Baton Rouge, La.: Louisiana State University Press, 1975), p. 78.
99. "The poor dirt farmer": *Ibid.*, p. vii.
99. repay the state more than $16,000: *Ibid.*, pp. 58–60.
100. "Tell us about it, Gene": *Ibid.*, p. 74.
100. "You farmers haven't had": *Ibid.*, p. 78.
100. "*Dear Ivan: For many years*": Letter from Ivan Allen, Sr., to Ivan Allen, Jr., June 9, 1933. Personal papers of Ivan Allen, Jr.
100. before Franklin Roosevelt: Ivan Allen, Jr., interview.
101. buying small companies, or assuming control: Frederick Allen, *Secret Formula. How Brilliant Marketing and Relentless Salesmanship Made Coca-Cola the Best-Known Product in the World* (New York: HarperBusiness, 1994), p. 92.
101. "Damn it, boy": *Ibid.*, p. 144.
102. "Ivan, I want you to buy": Ivan Allen, Jr., interview. This scene is drawn from his firsthand recollection.
102. "Every time we moved": Harold H. Martin, *Three Strong Pillars: The Story of Trust Company of Georgia* (Atlanta: Trust Company of Georgia, 1974), p. 30.
102. advanced Atlanta's city government $800,000: Garrett, *Atlanta and Environs, Vol. 2*, p. 916.
102. "I thought I might just as well": Ivan Allen, Jr., interview.
102. the Senator sold some of his Coca-Cola stock: *Ibid.* These stock figures are derived from year-by-year changes in Coca-Cola Company stock, supplied by the Coca-Cola Company. The November 13, 1935, date of purchase of Coca-Cola stock by the Senator is drawn from a stock portfolio of Ivan Allen, Sr., dated January 1, 1938, and titled "Schedule of Stocks Foreign and Domestic Corporations." Personal papers of Ivan Allen, Jr.
103. while in Atlanta he met Josephine: Interview with Louise Allen.
103. A train, chartered for the occasion: *Atlanta Constitution*, September 3, 1981.
103. headmistress once took her class: Louise Allen interview.
103. before Queen Mary and Edward: *Atlanta Journal-Constitution*, April 18, 1993.
104. "It was life's darkest moment.": Louise Allen interview.
104. "You could feed six people": *Ibid.*
104. Louise earned about $35 a month: Ivan Allen, Jr., interview.
104. "More people here than I thought": Laura Maddox Smith interview
104. descendant Wash Collier: Ivan Allen, Jr., interview.
104. "a marriage marked by impressive": *Atlanta Journal*, January 1, 1936.
104. "She was the widow": *Dalton* (Ga.) *Citizen*, April 2, 1936.
104. "It was interesting to hear": *Ibid.*, March 12, 1936.
105. "It was hot as Hades that day": Louise Allen interview.
105. "*From aristocrats descended*": Poem read at the funeral of Susie Harris Allen. Private Scrapbooks of Ivan Allen, Sr., stored at the Ivan Allen Company executive offices, Atlanta, Ga.
105. "We thought it a clever idea": Ivan Allen, Jr., interview.
105. the Senator swore it had influenced: Letter from Ivan Allen, Sr., to Mildred Seydell, *Atlanta Georgian* columnist, August 22, 1938. Mildred Seydell Papers, Emory University, Woodruff Library, Department of Special Collections, Atlanta, Ga., Box 13, Folder 3. In his letter, Ivan Sr. wrote, "There's a healing for jingling nerves and tired minds under The Tree . . . and the silent stars like flickering candle flames in the heavens. . . ."
105. Welch was paid $6 per week: Ivan Allen, Jr., transcript for Paul Hemphill, 1971.
105. the Senator insisted that she would deliver: Ivan Allen, Jr., interview.
105. Now, she would earn $7 per week.: Ivan Allen, Jr., transcript for Paul Hemphill, 1971.

CHAPTER 7

106. "My Dear Sir,": Letter from twelve white clerks on the Nashville & Atlanta, RPO to Paul Henderson, Second Assistant U.S. Postmaster General, October 25, 1924. United States Office of Personnel Management, St. Louis, Mo., Federal employment records of J. W. Dobbs, 1903–35.

106. "A number of the clerks dislike Dobbs personally": Letter from Harry J. Graves, Chief Clerk, District 1, to Frank Shumate, Post Office Inspector, December 9, 1924. *Ibid.*

107. "Dobbs is a negro.": Report of Inspector Frank Shumate, December 10, 1924. *Ibid.*

107. "to uplift the employees": Letter from S. A. Cisler, General Superintendent, RMS, to M. Donaldson, Deputy Second Assistant, July 12, 1934. *Ibid.*

107. "Don't fight with the white children!": Interview with Willie Dobbs Blackburn.

107. "Your mama tells me": Interview with Irene (Renie) Dobbs Jackson.

108. "my uncle George": *Ibid.*

108. "Humph! Who got the other two?: Ernest Dunbar, "Seven Dobbs Against the Odds," *Look,* December 2, 1969, pp. 27–33.

108. play Jessie Herndon's piano: Irene Dobbs Jackson interview.

108. "Norris had a reputation": *Ibid.*

108. "moralistic jewels": Interview with June Dobbs Butts.

108. "lives in that big mansion": Irene Dobbs Jackson interview.

109. "Look at them": *Ibid.*

109. "I just bathed": June Dobbs Butts, "Goodbye, Mama. Be Home When I Get There," *Sage* (Vol. 4, Fall 1987), pp. 45–48.

109. "Go 'round the corner": Interview with Willie Dobbs Blackburn.

109. Brown-Hayes department store: *Ibid.*

109. beneath her rocking chair: Interview with Muriel Gassett James.

109. "Write 'em just like I say it.": June Dobbs Butts and Willie Dobbs Blackburn interviews.

110. "Read me Taz-zuhn": *Ibid.*

110. "Mama came back": Interview with Mattiwilda Dobbs Janzon.

110. "Don't you whistle at them!": *Ibid.*

110. "Mr. Milton, I have six daughters": Interview with Bill Clement, Sr.

110. "She wore black taffeta": Irene Dobbs Jackson interview.

110. "Mother Banks was a stately woman.": Interview with Eulabel Riley Hocker. A long-term member of Liberty Baptist Church, Mrs. Hocker, as a child, stopped at Minnie Dobbs Banks's home and was given sandwiches and candy. "She loved children," she recalls.

110. "God's been good to me!": June Dobbs Butts interview.

110. "Minnie Millie Minerva": *Ibid.*

111. Morehouse was founded as a seminary: Willard Range, *The Rise and Progress of Negro Colleges in Georgia, 1865–1949* (Athens, Ga.: University of Georgia Press, 1951), pp. 24–26, 224–25. See also: Benjamin Brawley, *History of Morehouse College* (Atlanta: Morehouse College, 1917).

111. Rockefeller visited in 1884: Brawley, *History of Morehouse College*; Range, *The Rise and Progress of Negro Colleges,* pp. 49–53, 226–27.

111. "Harlem: The Center of Race Consciousness": Dunbar, "Seven Dobbs," pp. 27–33.

111. art teacher Rose Standish: Clifford M. Kuhn, Harlan E. Joye and E. Bernard West, *Living Atlanta: An Oral History of the City, 1914–1948* (Athens, Ga.: University of Georgia Press, Athens, 1990), p. 153. The authors interviewed the late Millicent Dobbs Jordan; this information is derived from that interview.

111. "We had gotten to the point": Irene Dobbs Jackson interview.

111. "You have got to leave Georgia": *Ibid.*

112. "a funny little fat guy": Stephen Papich, *Remembering Josephine* (Indianapolis: Bobbs-Merrill, 1976), pp. 65–66.

112. "The French loved black people!": Irene Dobbs Jackson interview.

112. a $1,200 one-year scholarship: Letter from John Wesley Dobbs to Harry A. Williamson, February 3, 1933. Harry A. Williamson Papers, Masonic Correspondence: Georgia-Missouri: Georgia, 1922–49, Box 5, Folder 1 (Microfilm reel 2). Schomburg Center for Research in Black Culture, New York Public Library, Manuscript Archives and Rare Book Division.

112. "Honey, I got carried away": Irene Dobbs Jackson interview.

112. modeled once for Hart Schaffner: Interview with Maynard Jackson, Jr.

112. the African Import Company in Liberia: 68th Anniversary Program of New Hope Baptist

Church in Dallas, Tex., 1941. The program features biographical material on its young minister, the Rev. Maynard Jackson, Sr. Personal papers of Irene Jackson Baraniuk.

112. A member of Atlanta University's charter class: Solomon T. Clanton, *Fifty Years Afield: A Biographical Brochure of Alexander Stephens Jackson by a Friend* (Dallas: Dallas Express Publishing, 1993). This is an account of the Rev. A. S. Jackson's adult life. Jackson's first wife, who gave birth to six children (three died in infancy) died in December 1891. He remarried, to Odalie Morse in New Orleans in June 1893. The mother of Maynard Jackson, Sr., she was a child of freeborn parents and graduated from Leland University in New Orleans.

113. "legalized humiliation": Peter W. Agnew, "Making Dallas Moral: Two Baptist Pastors," *Heritage News* (Vol. 12, Summer 1987), pp. 19–25.

113. leaving the United States for Brazil: Alexander Stephens Jackson, *The Rebirth of Negro Ideals* (Nashville: National Baptist Publishing Board, 1920).

113. "What do people look like in Africa?": Mattiwilda Dobbs Janzon interview.

113. "I wish you could stay here": Irene Dobbs Jackson interview.

113. the inn had fourteen rooms: Interview with Sandra Irene Jackson Baraniuk.

113. "I want you to marry me": Irene Dobbs Jackson interview.

114. "The white man is not gonna do": Maynard Jackson, Jr., interview.

114. it turned out to be morning sickness: Sandra Irene Jackson Baraniuk interview.

114. "Give me your hand, Maynard": Irene Dobbs Jackson interview.

115. "When Your Hair Has Turned to Silver": Mattiwilda Dobbs Janzon interview.

115. "I feel that I am": Letter from John Wesley Dobbs to Harry A. Williamson, February 3, 1933. Harry A. Williamson Papers, Box 5, Folder 1 (Microfilm reel 2), SC.

115. The Prince Hall fraternity flourished: William A. Muraskin, *Middle Class Blacks in a White Society: Prince Hall Freemasonry in America* (Berkeley, Calif.: University of California Press, 1975), p. 37.

116. drop from 24,000 to about 2,500: *Ibid.*, pp. 29–30.

116. "Of this much I am certain": Report of the Masonic Relief Association by John Wesley Dobbs at Grand Lodge in Americus, Ga., June 14–15, 1932. Harry A. Williamson Papers, Box 15, Folder 9 (Microfilm reel 7), SC.

116. "floated upward into the moist air": Butts, "Goodbye, Mama," pp. 45–48.

116. "farms could be owned": Muraskin, *Middle Class Blacks*, p. 141.

117. "Go about it in a true": Proclamation by Georgia Grand Master John Wesley Dobbs, June 27, 1932. Harry A. Williamson Papers. Box 15, Folder 9 (Microfilm reel 7), SC.

117. "Georgia was bone dry": Interview with J. Earl Acey.

117. City statutes prohibited interracial marriages.: Edward Rudolph Rodriguez, "A Study of the Discrimination in Race and Color Current in the City of Atlanta" (MA thesis, Atlanta University, Department of Sociology, June 1934). Rodriguez's paper paints a compelling portrait of segregated Atlanta of the 1930s.

118. "A clear, whiter skin": *Atlanta Daily World*, November 15, 1934.

118. "a strange animal who will lick": *Ibid.*, February 2, 1934.

118. gone into receivership: Letter from John Wesley Dobbs to Harry A. Williamson, December 19, 1932. Harry A. Williamson Papers, Box 5, Folder 1 (Microfilm reel 2), SC.

118. "Just last week fourteen banks": Address of Grand Master John Wesley Dobbs, Special Communication, Macon, Ga., January 28, 1933. Harry A. Williamson Papers, Box 15, Folder 9 (Microfilm reel 7), SC.

118. Dobbs brought two white lawyers: *Ibid.*

119. the Grand fell asleep at the wheel: Letter from John Wesley Dobbs to Harry A. Williamson, February 3, 1933. Harry A. Williamson Papers, Box 5, Folder 1 (Microfilm reel 2), SC.

119. "I have always believed": *Ibid.*

119. "Geekie, June, get down": Butts, "Goodbye, Mama," pp. 45–48.

119. six thousand Masons had responded: Address of Grand Master John Wesley Dobbs at Annual Grand Communication, June 13–14, 1933, Americus, Ga. Harry A. Williamson Papers, Box 15, Folder 9 (Microfilm reel 7), SC.

119. "very unbecoming to the dignity": *Ibid.*

120. Dobbs had received forty demerits: Efficiency Record of John W. Dobbs, RPC, Nashville & Atlanta, RPO. From July 1, 1933, to June 30, 1934. U.S. Office of Personnel Management, Records of J. W. Dobbs.

120. "He ought to be retired": Letter from Cong. Malcolm C. Tarver (D-Ga.) to Harllee Branch, Second Assistant U.S. Postmaster General, June 6, 1934. *Ibid.*

120. "Clerk Dobbs is not popular": Report of J. B. Hemperley, Chief Clerk, District 1, on "John W. Dobbs: Reported Holding Outside Position," July 5, 1934. *Ibid.*
120. "This man, I know": Letter from Shepard Bryan to Harllee Branch, June 26, 1934, *Ibid.*
120. "While these children": Letter from John Wesley Dobbs to J. B. Hemperley, Chief Clerk, June 25, 1934. *Ibid.*
121. He had accumulated a $500 debt: *Ibid.*
121. special English tonic: Grace Tully, *F.D.R.: My Boss* (New York: Charles Scribner's Sons, 1949), p. 111.
121. placing a bowl over his head: *Ibid.*
121. Clark-Morehouse football game: *Atlanta Daily World*, November 18, 1934.
121. passed over for clerk-in-charge positions: Memorandum from Harllee Branch, Second Assistant U.S. Postmaster General to Marvin McIntyre, Assistant Secretary to the President, March 5, 1935. Franklin D. Roosevelt Library, Hyde Park, N.Y., Official File 19, Box 9, "P. Office Dept., Misc. 1935."
121. "Will you speak to Harllee Branch": Memorandum from President Franklin D. Roosevelt to Marvin McIntyre, February 19, 1935. *Ibid.*
121. "I am sure that if Mr. Dobbs": Letter from Harllee Branch to Marvin McIntyre, March 5, 1935. *Ibid.*
122. retirement fund would be depleted: Memorandum from S. A. Cisler, Postal General Superintendent, March 20, 1935. U.S. Office of Personnel Management, St. Louis, Mo., Records of J. W. Dobbs.
122. "If there is anything you can do": Letter from John Wesley Dobbs to I. H. McDuffie, Valet to the President, March 30, 1935. *Ibid.*
122. "Will there be any way": Letter from I. H. McDuffie, Valet to the President, to James B. Farley, U.S. Postmaster General, May 10, 1935. *Ibid.*
122. "I will look into this": Letter from James B. Farley, U.S. Postmaster General, to I. H. McDuffie, Valet to the President, May 15, 1935. *Ibid.*
122. His annuity of $1,158 commenced: Memorandum from S. A. Cisler, Postal General Superintendent, July 8, 1935. *Ibid.* Officially, Dobbs was granted his annuity on June 24, 1935, but it was retroactive to June 1, 1936. (In postal records, Dobbs's retirement request is Claim No. R-72891.)
122. "I'd like to meet this grand master"· Bill Clement, Sr., interview. Dobbs related this story to Clement, his son-in-law.
122. served a day in the navy brig: Tully, *F.D.R.*, p. 111.
122. Roosevelt even met with Napoleon Hall: *Atlanta Constitution*, December 3, 1934.
122. five-minute session lasted forty-five: Bill Clement, Sr., interview.
123. placed four-leaf clovers in the cornerstone: Mattiwilda Dobbs Janzon interview.
123. J. W. Dobbs as city attorney: *Atlanta Daily World*, December 2, 1935.
124. *"Sweet Auburn! loveliest village"*: Oliver Goldsmith, *Poems, Plays and Essays* (New York: Turner & Hayden, 1848), pp. 25–36.
124. "Our Buckle of Defense!": J. W. Dobbs's speech to Georgia Voters League in Atlanta, October 26, 1957. John Wesley Dobbs Papers, Amistad Research Center, Box 3, Folder 5.
124. "He'd come in from": Interview with the Rev. William Holmes Borders.
124. "what Joe said": Interview with Josephine Dobbs Clement.
124. "90,000 mixed Americans": *Atlanta Daily World*, JWD Papers, ARC, Box 7, Folder 5. This undated story in the *Atlanta Daily World* likely was written years after the fight.
125. when New York congressman Adam Clayton Powell: June Dobbs Butts interview.
125. "There's Duke Ellington on the radio.": Mattiwilda Dobbs Janzon and Josephine Dobbs Clement interviews.
125. black coat and trousers with hickory stripes": *Atlanta Daily World*, February 13, 1936.
125. "We have a city among ourselves": *Ibid.*
126. gifted in law, though not in organizing: Mary G. Rolinson, "Community and Leadership in the Atlanta NAACP, 1916–1936: The Struggles of the First Twenty Years" (unpublished graduate seminar essay, Georgia State University, Department of History, June 1995).
126. discourage awarding a prestigious NAACP medal: Letter from Josephine Dibble Murphy, head of the Women's Auxiliary of the Atlanta NAACP branch, to NAACP secretary Walter White, May 31, 1934. Papers of the NAACP, Part 12: Selected Branch Files, 1913–39, Series A: The South. Microfilm Reel 10, File Folder Frame No. 00421, Emory University, Woodruff Library.
126. "So many people are disgusted": Letter from Helen White Martin to Walter White, March 19, 1934. *Ibid.* File Folder Frame No. 00303–304.

126. "A rejuvenation is needed immediately.": *Atlanta Daily World*, July 29, 1934. This column was sent by Josephine Dibble Murphy to NAACP secretary Walter White in New York to show the growing disenchantment with A. T. Walden in the Atlanta NAACP branch. See also: Papers of the NAACP, Part 12: Selected Branch Files, 1913–39, Series A: The South, Microfilm Reel 10, File Folder Frame No. 00432–434, EU.

126. "was responsible for establishing": Letter from Forrester B. Washington, just-resigned president of the Atlanta NAACP branch, to Walter White, NAACP secretary, January 21, 1939. *Ibid.*, Microfilm Reel 11, File Folder Frame No. 0057.

127. "notice upon the white people": Letter from T. K. Gibson, Vice President of the Atlanta NAACP branch, to James Weldon Johnson, Field Secretary, NAACP, March 7, 1919. *Ibid.* Microfilm Reel 9, File Folder Frame No. 00739.

127. registered blacks to 5,905: *Atlanta Constitution*, March 9, 1921.

127. Minnie Banks in death merited front-page: *Atlanta Daily World*, May 27, 1937.

127. "startled the hell out of me": June Dobbs Butts interview.

128. "If I can't see my mother in heaven": *Ibid.*

128. "Editor M. H. Jackson and Irene Dobbs Jackson": *Dallas Express*, March 26, 1938.

128. new Hudson seal fur coat: Sandra Irene Jackson Baraniuk interview.

128. Spelman College "Fright Night": *Ibid.*

128. took twelve-year-old Hubert: Maynard Jackson, Jr., interview.


CHAPTER 8

129. Irene Dobbs waited: Interviews with Mattiwilda Dobbs Janzon and June Dobbs Butts. At the time of the premiere, Geekie was fourteen years old, June eleven.

129. more than 300,000 people: *Atlanta Constitution*, December 15, 1939; *Atlanta Journal*, December 14–15, 1939.

129. "My novel is the story": Transcript of Margaret Mitchell interview by Medora Perkerson of *The Atlanta Journal* on WSB radio, July 3, 1936. *Gone With the Wind* Collection, Atlanta History Center, Box 1, Folder 2.

129. "pointed of chin": Margaret Mitchell, *Gone With the Wind* (New York: Macmillan, 1936), p. 5.

129. "she could never long endure": *Ibid.*, p. 8.

129. "That woman has written it": Interview with Irene (Renie) Dobbs Jackson. Her father, John Wesley Dobbs, made this comment to her.

130. refused to let her daughters see *Camille:* Mattiwilda Dobbs Janzon interview.

130. written to law school deans: Harold H. Martin, *William Berry Hartsfield: Mayor of Atlanta* (Athens, Ga.: University of Georgia Press, 1978), p. 9.

130. sent a box of home-grown magnolia blossoms: Letter from Mayor William B. Hartsfield to David O. Selznick, July 24, 1939. William B. Hartsfield Papers, Emory University, Woodruff Library, Department of Special Collections, Sub-Series III, Box 18, Folder 1.

130. instructing its New York editors: Letter from Mayor William B. Hartsfield to *Life* magazine, October 23, 1939. *Ibid.*

130. to find the hoop skirts and pantalets: "G With the W," *Time*, December 25, 1929, p. 30.

131. Lana Turner, Bette Davis or Katharine Hepburn: Rudy Behlmer, editor, *Memo from David O. Selznick* (New York: Viking, 1972), pp. 137–38, 170–75.

131. United Daughters of the Confederacy to protest: Darden Asbury Pyron, *Southern Daughter: The Life of Margaret Mitchell* (New York: Oxford University Press, 1991), pp. 474–75.

131. "The little lady": Letter from Bing Crosby to David O. Selznick, January 15, 1937. In Carlton Jackson, *Hattie: The Life of Hattie McDaniel* (Lanham, Md.: Madison Books, 1990), pp. 35–36.

131. "Dear Bing: Thanks": Letter from David O. Selznick to Bing Crosby, January 19, 1937. *Ibid.*, p. 36.

131. "We are only motion-picture people": Letter from David O. Selznick to Katherine Brown, November 28, 1939. In Behlmer, *Memo from David O. Selznick*, pp. 234–35.

131. A band played "Dixie": *Atlanta Constitution*, December 15, 1939; *Atlanta Journal*, December 14–15, 1939.

131. "an expression of mingled incredulity": Wilbur G. Kurtz, Jr., " 'Gone With the Wind' Premiere, Diary of Wilbur Kurtz, Jr.," *Atlanta Historical Bulletin*, September 1961, pp. 16–17.

131. Gable and Lombard nothing more than a blur: Mattiwilda Dobbs Janzon and June Dobbs Butts interviews.

131. luminaries sitting in car 21: *Atlanta Constitution*, December 14, 1939.
132. chaired the league's patrons committee: Interview with Louise Allen.
132. ball began when forty-eight Junior Leaguers: Junior League *Gone With the Wind* World Premiere Program, December 15, 1939. *Gone With the Wind* Collection, AHC, Box 1, Folder 36.
132. Louise, and her close friends: *Ibid.*
132. Gable graciously stood and bowed: *Atlanta Constitution*, December 15, 1939.
132. the Robert Woodruffs, the Robert F. Maddoxes: *Ibid.*, December 14, 1939.
132. Black butlers and chauffeurs: *Atlanta Journal*, December 15, 1939.
132. Irene Allen wore a red velvet: *Atlanta Constitution*, December 15, 1939.
132. "Social brilliance without compare": *Atlanta Journal*, December 15, 1939.
132. pressed Selznick to remove the word "nigger": Jackson, *Hattie*, pp. 41–42.
132. Selznick's screenwriters read Du Bois's: Letter from Walter White to David O. Selznick, June 28, 1938. In *Ibid.*, p. 42.
133. "I think these are no times": Letter from David O. Selznick to Jock Whitney, February 10, 1939. In Ronald Haver, *David O. Selznick's Hollywood* (New York: Alfred A. Knopf, 1980), pp. 250–51.
133. But his advisors warned against it: Jackson, *Hattie*, p. 47.
133. "that gripping story of the Old South": *Atlanta Daily World*, December 14, 1939.
133. future references to "Negro": Harold H. Martin, *Ralph McGill, Reporter* (Boston: Atlantic Monthly Press, 1973), p. 82.
133. "Next time I see you": William Anderson, *The Wild Man from Sugar Creek: The Political Career of Eugene Talmadge* (Baton Rouge, La.: Louisiana State University Press, 1975), pp. 160–61.
133. "stop giving the opportunity": *Atlanta Daily World*, December 31, 1939.
133. I. P. Reynolds, complained: *Ibid.*, December 18, 1939.
134. Vivien Leigh brought two colored maids: *Ibid.*, December 14, 1939.
134. "Dressed as did those carriage drivers": *Ibid.*
134. "Over the doorway of the Nation's": John Wesley Dobbs's address for *Wings Over Jordan* national radio program, Cleveland, Ohio, January 1, 1939. John Wesley Dobbs Papers, Amistad Research Center, New Orleans, La., Box 3, Folder 1.
134. "The nation has gone simply ga-ga": Letter from Alice V. Harper, Secretary to the Director of *Wings Over Jordan*, to John Wesley Dobbs, January 6, 1939. *Ibid.*
134. a fifth-grade class at the age of twenty-one: Martin Luther King, Sr., with Clayton Riley, *Daddy King: An Autobiography* (New York: William Morrow, 1980), pp. 17–18.
134. "I ain't gonna plow": *Atlanta Daily World*, November 8, 1938. See also Clayborn Carson, senior editor, *The Papers of Martin Luther King, Jr., Vol. 1: Called to Serve, January 1929–June 1951* (Berkeley, Calif.: University of California Press, 1992), pp. 32–33. See also: Martin Luther King, Jr., *Stride Toward Freedom* (New York: Harper & Brothers, 1958), p. 19.
134. "I Want Jesus to Walk": *Atlanta Daily World*, December 15, 1939.
135. "It is unconscionable": June Dobbs Butts interview. She heard her father make this comment.
135. Atlanta Baptist Ministers Union concurred: *Atlanta Daily World*, December 20, 1939. The Big Bethel AME choir also performed during the *Gone With the Wind* festival, at the premiere.
135. for a two-hour tour of Atlanta: *Atlanta Constitution*, December 16, 1939.
135. "so complimentary of Atlanta": Louise Allen interview.
135. descended from a Methodist minister: Pyron, *Southern Daughter*, p. 13.
135. her uncle, Frank Rice: *Ibid.*, p. 186.
136. "I'd never have guessed": *Atlanta Journal*, July 1, 1936.
136. held her liquor admirably: Pyron, *Southern Daughter*, p. 203.
136. suffer a bout of hiccoughs: Marianne Walker, *Margaret Mitchell and John Marsh: The Love Story Behind Gone With the Wind* (Atlanta: Peachtree Publishers, 1993), pp. 115–23.
136. "Cavalry knees had the tendency": Transcript of Mitchell interview by Perkerson, *Gone With the Wind* Collection. AHC, Box 1, Folder 2.
136. "had ever undressed and nursed": Pyron, *Southern Daughter*, p. 111.
136. much as *Uncle Tom's Cabin*: Letter from Margaret Mitchell to Susan Myrick, April 17, 1939. In Susan Myrick, *White Columns in Hollywood: Reports from the GWTW Sets* (Macon, Ga.: Mercer University Press, 1982), p. 214. Myrick, from Macon, served as a specialist in southern dialect on the set of *Gone With the Wind*.
136. "I do not need to tell you": *Ibid.*, pp. 214–15.
136. she quietly made private contributions: *Atlanta Constitution*, March 29, 1995.

137. cast a glow seen sixty-five miles away: *Atlanta Journal*, December 16, 1939.
137. wearing a gold lamé gown: *Ibid.*
137. in the front right section: Louise Allen interview.
137. "The war looked just like that": *Atlanta Constitution*, December 16, 1939.
137. "They were blond": Interview with Edward Smith.
137. "They were drinking booze": Interview with Laura Maddox Smith.
137. The Loew's Grand erupted with applause: Interview with Morris Siegel. Siegel, a native Atlantan who for decades was a noted sportswriter in Washington, D.C., attended the Atlanta premiere.
138. "It's a great story.": Interview with Ivan Allen, Jr.
138. "Why was Scarlett any type": June Dobbs Butts interview.
138. "We didn't have any love": *Ibid.*
138. "The Old South's heart beats": *Atlanta Journal*, December 17, 1939.
138. to draft a certificate of distinguished: Recorded Minutes of the Atlanta Chamber of Commerce Meeting of December 27, 1939, Files of the Atlanta chamber. Ivan Allen, Sr., served on the chamber's planning committee for the *Gone With the Wind* celebration, along with James Robinson, president of the First National Bank, and Jesse Draper, president of the Draper-Owens real estate and insurance company.
138. "We ran it immediately": Letter from Carole Lombard Gable to Mayor William B. Hartsfield, April 3, 1940. William B. Hartsfield Papers, Emory University, Sub-Series III, Box 18, Folder 2.
138. "She has set herself a hard mark": *New York Times Book Review*, July 5, 1936.
138. "I hope I never write": *Memphis Commercial-Appeal*, July 9, 1936. See: *Gone With the Wind* collection, AHC, Box 2, Folder 29.
139. Gravitt served ten months and twenty days: Interview with Hugh Gravitt. The author conducted this interview in July 1991 for a story that appeared in *The Atlanta Journal-Constitution*, August 11, 1991. It was the only interview Hugh Gravitt gave during his lifetime. Gravitt died of cancer in April 1994. See: *Atlanta Constitution*, April 22, 1994.
139. "Are you the one": *Ibid.*
139. ask to be shown Scarlett O'Hara's gravesite: Interview with E. Allen Myers, Jr. Myers is the sexton of the historic Oakland Cemetery in Atlanta.

CHAPTER 9

141. Sir: There is a stretch: Herbert Aptheker, editor, *The Correspondence of W. E. B. Du Bois. Vol. 2. Selections, 1934–1944*. (Amherst, Mass.: University of Massachusetts Press, 1976), pp. 249–95. Du Bois was teaching at Atlanta University at the time he wrote this letter.
143. "That man's family.": Interview with Mattiwilda Dobbs Janzon. Her father related this story to her. The scene occurred about 1940.
144. "He's one of the few drivers": *Atlanta Daily World*, undated. John Wesley Dobbs Papers, Amistad Research Center, New Orleans, La., Box 7.
144. When Phinazee turned seventeen: *The Dobbs Family Newsletter*, June 1991. JWD Papers, ARC, Box 5, Folder 8. In this newsletter, written by Willie Dobbs Blackburn, Phinazee's death in Durham, N.C., on June 1, 1991, is recorded, along with a brief personal history. Phinazee was sent by Dobbs to Tuskegee, where he earned a bachelor's degree. He is described in the newsletter as "driver, loyal companion and support" to Grand Master Dobbs. In her remarks at the memorial service, Josephine Dobbs Clement said of Phinazee, "Mama and Daddy relied on Joe's good judgment, impeccable character, loyalty and reliability—and Joe never let them down." After Dobbs's death in 1961, Phinazee married Annette Hodge of the Atlanta School of Social Work, and moved to Durham.
144. black cat was the most valuable: Interview with Bill Clement, Jr. A grandson of Dobbs's, Clement recalls playing this car game often with the Grand during his childhood.
144. "This is the white man's way": Interview with June Dobbs Butts.
145. "Send me off a telegram": Interview with Josephine Dobbs Clement.
145. "Stop and see Mr. Dudley": Interview with William Clement, Sr.
145. They drew cold, angry stares: June Dobbs Butts interview.
145. "You never saw such": Mattiwilda Dobbs Janzon interview.
146. "We need to stick with the blue-eyed boy": Interview with Andrew Young. In 1955, Young heard Dobbs deliver a speech in south Georgia in which he used this expression.

146. Dobbs had driven with him: *Atlanta Daily World*, February 17, 1974. In a two-part series about Dobbs, his friend John H. Calhoun notes that Dobbs "loved to tell" about his travels with Myrdal. A staunch Republican, Calhoun later was elected to the Atlanta City Council.

146. "the Negro problem in America": Gunnar Myrdal with assistance of Richard Sterner and Arnold Rose, *An American Dilemma. The Negro Problem and Modern Democracy, Vol. 1* (New York: Harper & Brothers, 1944), p. xix.

146. liaisons, or "plenipotentiaries": *Ibid, Vol. 2*, pp. 724–25.

146. halving the term of office: Herbert Jenkins, *Keeping the Peace: A Police Chief Looks at His Job* (New York: Harper & Row, 1970), p. 10.

147. "Annie Mae" or "Emma Lou": Transcript of interview with O. R. "Robert" McKibbens for Clifford M. Kuhn, Harlon E. Joye and E. Bernard West, *Living Atlanta: An Oral History of the City, 1914–1948* (Athens, Ga.: University of Georgia Press, 1990). Living Atlanta Series, AHC, Box 38, Folder 15. McKibbens was one of Atlanta's first black policemen, hired in 1948.

147. "I am just plain tired": Jenkins, *Keeping the Peace*, p. 25.

147. The group facing Hartsfield: Transcript of interview with the Rev. William Holmes Borders for Kuhn *et al., Living Atlanta.* Living Atlanta Series, AHC, Box 35, Folder 16.

147. "We'll get colored policemen": *Ibid.*

147. "Books, Ballots and Bucks": Interview with Maynard Jackson, Jr.

147. "Think about it for a minute": *Atlanta Daily World*, April 7, 1940. JWD Papers, ARC, Box 7, Folder 4.

148. "Do you know those books over there": Kuhn *et al., Living Atlanta*, pp. 347–48.

148. should pay $300 to two young: *Ibid.*

149. "If you have 10,000 registered voters": Transcript of interview with Clarence Bacote for Kuhn *et al., Living Atlanta.* Living Atlanta Series, AHC, Box 35, Folder 6.

149. "A. T. Walden's right-hand man": Interview with Cornelius A. Scott.

149. drove to a polling place: Transcript of interview with Clarence Bacote for Kuhn *et al., Living Atlanta.* Living Atlanta Series, AHC, Box 35, Folder 6.

149. "Your name's not on there": *Ibid.*

150. "The Democratic primary passed": *Atlanta Journal*, July 5, 1944.

150. the 6,876 blacks registered: Lorraine Nelson Spritzer, *The Belle of Ashby Street: Helen Douglas Mankin and Georgia Politics* (Athens, Ga.: University of Georgia Press, 1982), p. 70.

150. Dobbs, Walden, Scott: *Atlanta Daily World*, February 12, 1946.

150. "The election depends": Transcript of interview with Clarence Bacote for Kuhn *et al., Living Atlanta.* Living Atlanta Series, AHC, Box 35, Folder 6.

150. Mankin won 963 of the 1,038: Spritzer, *The Belle of Ashby Street*, pp. 72–73.

150. "Negroes contributed the margin": *Atlanta Constitution*, February 27, 1946.

151. "The Belle of Ashby Street": Spritzer, *The Belle of Ashby Street*, p. 74.

151. "Bacote, just let Dobbs talk.": Transcript of interview with John H. Calhoun for Kuhn *et al., Living Atlanta.* Living Atlanta Series, AHC, Box 35, Folder 23.

151. goal was to register 25,000 blacks: *Atlanta Daily World*, March 13, 1946.

151. organized workers by census tracts: Interview with Robert Thompson.

152. "He could read the writing": *Ibid.*

152. voted to donate $50: *Atlanta Daily World*, March 21, 1946.

152. "We need better school facilities": *Ibid.*, March 29, 1946.

152. Dobbs spent the next two days touring: *Ibid.*, March 31, 1946.

152. violated the constitutional rights of blacks: *Atlanta Constitution*, April 2, 1946.

152. "our southern traditions and heritage": *Atlanta Daily World*, April 2, 1946. This article reports the reaction of the *Statesman*.

152. "The courts have spoken": *Ibid.*, April 6, 1946.

152. nearly 18,000 blacks: C. A. Bacote, "The Negro in Atlanta Politics," *Phylon* (Vol. 16, No. 4, Fourth Quarter, 1955), p. 348.

152. "Negroes now will rapidly": *Atlanta Daily World*, April 2, 1946.

153. "that woman from the wicked city." Spritzer, *The Belle of Ashby Street*, p. 85.

153. whether they had an "ascertainable": *Ibid.*, p. 95.

153. "I believe in treating the Negro right": *Atlanta Constitution*, June 5, 1946.

153. sharing in the joy of VE Day: Interviews with Maynard Jackson, Jr., Josephine Dobbs Clement and Mattiwilda Dobbs Janzon.

154. put out her cigarette and gargled: Bill Clement, Sr., interview.

154. "Then he'd point his finger": *Ibid.*

154. "Bill, I know exactly": *Ibid.*
154. "We are conscious": Maynard H. Jackson, Sr., "As One Morehouse Man to Another," a brief writing about his alma mater. Personal correspondence of the Rev. Maynard H. Jackson, pastor, Friendship Baptist Church. Personal papers of Maynard Jackson, Jr. Though undated, this letter was written in the period 1945–52.
155. Jackson often carried a medallion: Maynard Jackson, Jr., interview.
155. "would be a timely and democratic": *Dallas Express*, April 1, 1944.
155. "Is this where that nigger": Interviews with Irene Dobbs Jackson and Maynard Jackson, Jr.
155. each holding a hunting rifle: This scene is drawn from interviews with Irene Dobbs Jackson, Sandra Irene Jackson Baraniuk, Maynard Jackson, Jr., and Odellus Chambers. The Jacksons took their children that night to Chambers's home.
155. Jackson captured only 2,783 votes: *Dallas Morning News* and *Dallas Times Herald*, April 5, 1944. Both papers gave front-page coverage to the defeat of the black minister in the Dallas school board race.
156. lying beneath the covers: Maynard Jackson, Jr., interview.
156. Friendship had promised him: Sandra Irene Jackson Baraniuk interview.
156. a train engineer recognized him: Sixtieth Anniversary Program, 1882–1942, of the Rev. Edward R. Carter at Friendship Baptist Church, April 19, 1942. E. R. Carter Collection, Auburn Avenue Research Center, Box 1, Folder 9.
156. "Can this be the little boy": *Ibid.*
157. Jackmont he called it: Maynard Jackson, Jr., interview.
157. white family gave them lemonade: *Ibid.*
157. "Daddy, I didn't know": Sandra Irene Jackson Baraniuk interview.
157. "How do you ever get over": Maynard Jackson, Jr., interview.
158. "trained down": *Ibid.*
158. Greeks sometimes mistook him: Irene Dobbs Jackson interview.
158. "This is for older people": *Ibid.*
158. "No, what was your name really": Maynard Jackson, Jr., interview.
158. "They'd send me in": *Ibid.*
158. "But Dr. Jordan, how do you know": Interview with Julia Jordan. Mrs. Jordan is the widow of Dr. James Jordan of Dallas. She related this story, which, she says, her husband often told.
159. "What do you mean": Maynard Jackson, Jr., interview.
159. Each car had its headlights turned on: This scene is drawn from interviews with Irene Dobbs Jackson, Sandra Irene Jackson Baraniuk, Carol Ann Jackson Miller and Maynard Jackson, Jr.
160. the Kings had been stuffing their pockets: June Dobbs Butts and Mattiwilda Dobbs Janzon interviews.
160. "Which one of them has": June Dobbs Butts interview.
160. "M.L. and I got to know": *Ibid.*
160. "M.L. says he wants": Irene Dobbs Jackson interview.
160. heard their grandmother rave: *Ibid.*
160. In 1941, the Kings had moved: Clayborne Carson, senior editor, *The Papers of Martin Luther King, Jr., Vol. 1: Called to Serve, June 1929–June 1951* (Berkeley, Calif.: University of California Press, 1992), p. 82.
161. refused to remove his shoes: Interviews with Port Scott and J. Earl Acey. Scott and Acey became ranking officers of the Georgia Prince Hall Masons; Dobbs related this story to them.
161. "Reverend King is a stubborn old man.": Port Scott interview.
161. "All of a sudden Mrs. Lewis": June Dobbs Butts interview.
161. "Young man, you're gonna deliver.": *Ibid.*
161. "We know of no other instance": "The Six Dobbs Sisters—Now All Spelman Graduates," *Spelman Messenger* (Vol. 64–65, August 1948), p. 17.
161. "An elderly Negro couple sat": *Atlanta Journal*, June 7, 1948.
162. gunned down in a shootout: Jenkins, *Keeping the Peace*, p. 3.
162. "your ID card, the badge of honor": *Ibid.*, p. 4.
162. Sweet Auburn and Vine: Transcript of interview with Ernest Lyons for Kuhn *et al., Living Atlanta*. Living Atlanta Series, AHC, Box 38, Folder 11.
163. "I am a mayor for all": Harold H. Martin, *William Berry Hartsfield: Mayor of Atlanta* (Athens, Ga.: University of Georgia Press, 1978), p. 100.
163. signaling to the doorman: Transcript of interview with Clarence Bacote for Kuhn *et al., Living Atlanta*. Living Atlanta Series, AHC, Box 35, Folder 6.

163. "Are we going to have Negro police": Ernest Lyons interview.
163. more than four hundred blacks stood outside: *Atlanta Journal*, April 4, 1948.
163. "You are more than just policemen.": *Atlanta Daily World*, April 4, 1948.
164. "Lord, I want to give": *Ibid.*
164. "I felt almost like a god": Interview with Ernest Lyons.
164. "Nigger police!": *Ibid.*
164. "Great God a'mighty!": Maynard Jackson, Jr., interview.

## CHAPTER 10

165. He did not kiss: Interviews with Louise Allen and Ivan Allen, Jr.
165. Walter Hill, J. P. Allen: Eleanor Williams, *Ivan Allen: A Resourceful Citizen* (Atlanta: Ivan Allen-Marshall Company, 1950), p. 255.
165. the Senator was posing for students: Interview with Ivan Allen III.
165. "They were all perfectly awful": Louise Allen interview.
165. "I think he had a very fine ego": *Ibid.*
165. "I want you three fellows": Letter from Ivan Allen, Sr., to Mayor Bill Hartsfield, February 28, 1945. William B. Hartsfield Papers, Emory University, Robert W. Woodruff Library, Department of Special Collections, Box 3, Folder 16.
166. *"Daddy looks like"*: Ivan Allen, Jr., interview.
166. "actually ruined Ivan": Louise Allen interview.
166. "He was always very patient": Ivan Allen, Jr., interview.
166. *"To the Greatest Dad"*: Undated Father's Day card from Ivan Allen, Jr., to his father. Personal Scrapbook of Ivan Allen, Sr., in possession of Ivan Allen, Jr.
166. "Ivan was always very responsive": Louise Allen interview.
166. The Senator and Ivan Jr. took the train: Ivan Allen, Jr., interview.
166. FDR later appointed him: Williams, *A Resourceful Citizen*, pp. 178–79.
167. "My company pays taxes": Charlie Brown as told to James C. Bryant, *Charlie Brown Remembers Atlanta: Memoirs of a Public Man* (Columbia, S.C.: R. L. Bryan Company, 1982), p. 182.
167. he was grooming his son: Ivan Allen, Jr., interview.
167. Each Christmas eve: Interview with H. Inman Allen.
167. given him a memorable gift: Franklin M. Garrett, *Atlanta and Environs: A Chronicle of Its People and Events, Vol. 2* (New York: Lewis Historical Publishing Company, 1954), pp. 488–89.
167. "Dearie" and "Big Papa": H. Inman Allen interview. This description of Craigellachie also was drawn, in part, from "The Family Christmas Eve Dinner at Craigellachie," a three-page recollection of childhood by John W. Grant III, written on December 24, 1989. Private files of H. Inman Allen.
167. a black butler with a large bucket: H. Inman Allen, interview.
168. Ivan Jr. had worn his honorary uniform: Ivan Allen, Jr., interview.
168. "The better element": William Anderson, *The Wild Man from Sugar Creek: The Political Career of Eugene Talmadge* (Baton Rouge, La: Louisiana State University Press, 1975), p. 206.
168. "The next president we have": *Ibid.*, p. 111.
168. "bums and loafers": Lorraine Nelson Spritzer, *The Belle of Ashby Street: Helen Douglas Mankin and Georgia Politics* (Athens, Ga.: University of Georgia Press, 1982), pp. 52–53.
169. Stacking the state board of regents: *Atlanta Journal*, October 14, 1941.
169. "I love the University of Georgia.": Calvin McLeod Logue, *Eugene Talmadge: Rhetoric and Response* (New York: Greenwood Press, 1989), pp. 274–78.
169. The conference conducted an investigation: *Atlanta Journal*, October 14, 1941.
169. "If foreign elements": *Ibid.*
169. "To Hell With Talmadge": *Ibid.*, October 15, 1941.
169. "Here in the heart of Dixie": Anderson, *The Wild Man from Sugar Creek*, p. 204.
170. he spent nights at home: Ivan Allen, Jr., interview.
170. He served as Georgia's sugar administrator: Williams, *A Resourceful Citizen*, pp. 222–23.
170. Arnall effected the transfer: Ivan Allen, Jr., interview.
170. "They were having considerable trouble": *Ibid.*
170. "I've learned first-hand": *Atlanta Constitution*, August 21, 1945.
171. "I think one of the most outstanding": Katherine Barnwell, "A Close Look at Atlanta's Next Mayor," *Atlanta Journal Sunday Magazine*, December 31, 1961.

171. He purchased surplus merchandise: Ivan Allen, Jr., transcript for Paul Hemphill, 1971.

171. "You could sell it": *Ibid.*

171. it had more than two hundred employees: Williams, *A Resourceful Citizen*, p. 29.

171. "An office outfitter needs": *Ibid.*, p. 30.

171. he bequeathed his half of the company: Ivan Allen, Jr., interview.

172. "We've been here almost": Interview with Mason Lowance, Jr. In the summer of 1960, Lowance, a boyhood and college friend of Ivan III's, paid a visit to the Ivan Allen Company, in part to show his friend a new camera he had purchased. Ivan Allen, Sr., gave Lowance a tour of the building, including the basement, where he posed for a picture with John Henry Hector.

172. in his will would leave him $1,000: Second Codicil to the Last Will and Testament of Ivan Earnest Allen, Sr., February 24, 1964, p. 3. Fulton County Probate Court.

172. Their names were Booker and John: Interview with Charles Dannals, Jr.

172. they would start at dawn: Ivan Allen, Jr., interview.

173. "Booker could knock the tar": Charles Dannals, Jr., interview.

173. once had won the Atlanta Amateur: *Ibid.*

173. "They were very humble darkies": *Ibid.*

173. "It was just a way of life": Ivan Allen, Jr., interview.

173. invited his "colored friends": Anderson, *The Wild Man from Sugar Creek*, p. 226.

173. He based his claim upon a provision: *Atlanta Journal*, December 22, 1946.

174. Carmichael 669 votes: Numan V. Bartley, *The Creation of Modern Georgia* (Athens, Ga.: University of Georgia Press, 1983), pp. 187–90.

174. "If I couldn't keep Papa": John Egerton, *Speak Now Against the Day: The Generation Before the Civil Rights Movement in the South* (New York Alfred A. Knopf, 1994), p. 387.

174. "Tell 'em, Herman!": *Atlanta Journal* and *Atlanta Constitution*, January 15–16, 1947. The scene of Talmadge's late-night arrival at the governor's office is drawn largely from the coverage in these newspapers. See also: Egerton, *Speak Now Against the Day*, pp. 87–89.

174. "I know you're happy": *Atlanta Journal*, January 15, 1947.

175. "He is no longer governor": *Ibid.*

175. Arnall's only response was to set up: *Ibid.*, January 16, 1947.

175. "It appeared impossible that 34 citizens": *Ibid.*, March 2, 1947.

175. Georgia Supreme Court declared: *Ibid.*, March 19, 1947.

175. "it was the cheapest": Ivan Allen, Jr., interview.

176. the Community Chest paid the $500 national: Ivan Allen, Jr., with Paul Hemphill, *Mayor: Notes on the Sixties* (New York: Simon & Schuster, 1971), p. 12.

176. Blacks were expected to contribute about $30,000: *Atlanta Daily World*, September 18, 1949.

176. "see Negroes advancing": Transcript of interview with Lorimer D. Milton for Clifford M. Kuhn, Harlon E. Joye and E. Bernard West, *Living Atlanta: An Oral History of the City, 1914–1948* (Athens, Ga: University of Georgia Press, 1990). Living Atlanta Series, Atlanta History Center, Box 38, Folder 15.

176. "We'd like for you and Mr. Taber": Ivan Allen, Jr., interview. See also: Allen with Hemphill, *Mayor*, pp. 12–13.

177. He saw Clark Howell, Jr.: Allen with Hemphill, *Mayor*, p. 13.

177. "They quibbled over the decision": Ivan Allen, Jr., interview.

177. "Ivan, let me have": Allen with Hemphill, *Mayor*, p. 13.

177. "My generation has failed": *Ibid.*

178. they felt the eyes of the five hundred blacks: Ivan Allen, Jr., interview. Also: *Atlanta Daily World*, October 14 and 16, 1949. *The Daily World* gave prominent coverage to the Community Chest meeting in these two issues.

178. "Just acceptable": Ivan Allen, Jr., transcript for Paul Hemphill, 1971.

178. Announcements of every small pledge: Allen with Hemphill, *Mayor*, pp. 14–15.

178. "A good beginning": *Atlanta Daily World*, October 16, 1949.

178. *"So this must be what it is like"*: Ivan Allen, Jr., transcript for Paul Hemphill, 1971.

178. "You're going to have to be careful": Allen with Hemphill, *Mayor*, p. 15.

178. "Lawd, God, chillun": *Ibid.*, p. 16.

179. wrote a check for $500: Ivan Allen, Jr., interview.

179. never spoke with her, or saw her, again: *Ibid.*

CHAPTER 11

180. study of Atlanta's community "power structure": Floyd Hunter, *Community Power Structure: A Study of Decision Makers* (Chapel Hill, N.C.: University of North Carolina Press, 1953).
180. "I find that it will be necessary": Memo from Floyd Hunter to Dr. Gordon W. Blackwell, November 27, 1950. Floyd Hunter Papers, Emory University, Robert W. Woodruff Library, Department of Special Collections, Box 16, Folder 5.
180. Hartsfield once bet him: *Atlanta Constitution,* October 7, 1977.
180. *"In Memphis it is Beale Street":* Eulogy by Rev. William Holmes Borders, September 2, 1961. Reel audiotape of John Wesley Dobbs funeral, John Wesley Dobbs Papers, Amistad Research Center, New Orleans, La., Box 11 (oversize folder). Borders cites Dobbs's favorite refrain.
181. he stopped at the *Daily World:* Interview with George Coleman. Coleman was a reporter and editor at the *Atlanta Daily World.*
181. "THESE ARE MY GRANDSONS!": Interview with Bob Jordan, Jr.
181. "Grandpa, why do you argue": *Ibid.*
181. "John Brown went to the gallows": Interview with the Rev. Otis Moss, Jr. As a student at Morehouse, Moss heard Dobbs deliver a speech about John Brown.
181. "I sat in that car, freezing": Interview with Paul E. X. Brown.
182. criticize him for mispronouncing words: *Ibid.*
182. parking spaces reserved for local: Interview with Charlie Brown. A longtime Atlanta politician, Brown recalls seeing Dobbs's parking space at the game.
182. "It wasn't always this way": Interview with Bill Clement, Jr.
183. "Jack. Don't stand so close": Roger Kahn, *The Boys of Summer* (New York: Harper & Row, 1971), p. 325. See also: Jackie Robinson as told to Alfred Duckett, *I Never Had It Made* (New York: G. P. Putnam's Sons, 1972), pp. 92–93.
183. "Outer Senegambia": Interview with Morris Siegel. In 1948–49, Paul E. X. Brown, Dobbs's Masonic secretary at the time, was hired as a commentator for the Black Crackers on WEAS. During his first radio broadcast, Brown often referred to the Black Crackers as "the Crackers." Each time a white program director nudged his shoulder. Finally, as Brown ignored him, the program director passed notes to him. "BLACK Crackers!!" one read. And another: "BLACK CRACKERS!!!!!!!" Eventually, Brown corrected his terminology that day.
183. placed bets on obscure details: Interviews with Ernie Harwell, Furman Bisher and Morris Siegel. Harwell was a White Crackers broadcaster, Bisher and Siegel sportswriters.
183. put a Coca-Cola stand among blacks: Coverage of the three-game series in the *Atlanta Daily World, Atlanta Journal* and *Atlanta Constitution,* April 9–11, 1949.
183. "Atlanta double-crossed them": *Atlanta Journal,* April 9, 1949.
183. "unsung heroes who have stood": *Atlanta Daily World,* April 10, 1949.
183. "Atlanta and all Georgia": *Ibid.,* April 14, 1949.
184. The ANVL would hold: C. A. Bacote, "The Negro in Atlanta Politics," *Phylon* (Vol. 16, Fourth Quarter, 1955), pp. 348–49.
184. "my Daddy saw me": Speech by Mayor Ivan Allen, Jr., honoring Austin T. Walden for career service at the Butler Street YMCA, February 4, 1964. Records of the administration of Mayor Ivan Allen, Jr., City of Atlanta, Department of Records Management, Series 89-TR-261, Box 2.
184. his parents sent him to school: *Ibid.*
184. "Negroes don't want any special privileges": *Atlanta Daily World,* September 1, 1949.
184. "Anything I tell you here": *Ibid.*
185. "even if we have to construct": *Ibid.,* September 3, 1949.
185. "And we'll do it again": *Ibid.*
185. "Brown is too bleary": *Ibid.*
185. "You have risen superbly": Letter from John Wesley Dobbs to Mayor William B. Hartsfield, September 3, 1949. William B. Hartsfield Papers, Emory University, Box 9, Folder 2.
185. "Mr. Todd was merely trying": Letter from Mayor William B. Hartsfield to John Wesley Dobbs, September 6, 1949. *Ibid.*
185. "the fair haired boy of Dobbs": *Atlanta Constitution,* September 4, 1949.
185. "the candidate for mayor backed by Dobbs": *Ibid.*
186. 102 votes more than 51 percent: *Ibid.,* September 9, 1949.
186. "The greatest policeman": *Ibid.,* December 9, 1949.
186. "I'm glad to see the city": *Atlanta Journal,* June 11, 1951.

187. "The 'captive' officials had to grin": Herman E. Talmadge, *You and Segregation* (Birmingham, Ala.: Vulcan Press, 1955), p. 23.
187. He protested that iron bars: *Atlanta Daily World*, August 12, 1952.
187. the Grand shocked the ANVL: *Ibid.*, May 8, 1953.
187. "It was a fact that we got": *Ibid.*
187. "It is a good idea": *Ibid.*
187. "We have always maintained": *Ibid.*, May 10, 1953.
188. She drew up a list of fifty-four black leaders: Harold H. Martin, *William Berry Hartsfield: Mayor of Atlanta* (Athens, Ga.: University of Georgia Press, 1978), pp. 100–101.
188. a "powerful political machine": *Atlanta Constitution*, May 14, 1953.
188. "The Negro voters consider": *Atlanta Daily World*, May 15, 1953.
188. "Having a wonderful time": Postcard from Mayor William B. Hartsfield to John Wesley Dobbs, November 1955. JWD Papers, ARC, Box 1, Folder 10.
188. "My name is John Wesley Dobbs": Remarks of John Wesley Dobbs at the public hearing of the Metropolitan Atlanta Planning Commission, Atlanta Civic Auditorium, June 3, 1952. JWD Papers, ARC, Box 3, Folder 17. Quotations from this speech are drawn from this source.
191. "climaxed an attack": *Atlanta Constitution*, June 4, 1952.

CHAPTER 12

192. They placed two solenoid switches: Deposition of Julius Edward Smith, March 9, 1953, *Julius Edward Smith v. Maynard H. Jackson*, Fulton County Superior Court Records, Case No. A-31985.
192. It had a fold-up seat: Interview with Carol Jackson Miller.
192. landed about twenty feet away: *Atlanta Daily World*, July 23, 1952.
192. *"Oh, my God!":* Carol Jackson Miller interview.
192. After initial treatment, he was transferred: *Atlanta Daily World*, July 23, 1952.
193. allergic reaction to penicillin: Smith deposition, *Smith v. Jackson.*
193. "That was going to take my Daddy's": Carol Jackson Miller interview.
193. "Last thing I remember": Interview with Constance Jackson Carter.
193. "very nasty": *Ibid.*
193. "That policeman is only thirty-three years old": Interview with Sandra Irene Jackson Baraniuk.
193. "Patrolman Collides With Auto": *Atlanta Daily World*, July 23, 1952.
193. The two men had discussed: Interview with George Coleman.
194. "Maynard H. Johnson, 54, Negro": *Atlanta Constitution*, July 23, 1952.
194. sought from the black pastor $100,000: *Smith v. Jackson*, Fulton County Superior Court Records, Book 1648, p. 264.
194. "Glad to see you again": *Atlanta Daily World*, September 2, 1952.
194. made speeches to the Republican Credentials Committee: Interview with Elbert P. Tuttle.
195. "If I had gone into the ministry": Sandra Irene Jackson Baraniuk interview.
195. He had taken out an $8,000 loan: Loan statement with Atlanta Federal Savings & Loan Association, November 29, 1946. Correspondence of Rev. Maynard Jackson of Friendship Baptist Church (1945–53). Papers are in the possession of Maynard Jackson, Jr.
195. convincing doctors and nurses: Interview with Lucia Bacote.
195. "I don't see why": Interview with Murray Branch.
195. "Often you have to serve": Letter from Rev. Maynard H. Jackson to A. Maceo Smith, April 28, 1952. A. Maceo Smith Papers, African-American Museum, Dallas, Tex.
196. "If you can't say": Sandra Irene Jackson Baraniuk interview.
196. "put on a moan or a whoop": Murray Branch interview.
196. "Come get Reverend Jackson": Carol Jackson Miller interview.
196. nearly sixty miles per hour: *Smith v. Jackson*, Fulton County Superior Court Record Book 1648, p. 278, defendant's response, filed September 27, 1952.
196. "Was the Cadillac moving": Smith deposition, *Smith v. Jackson.*
197. "a special hinged elbow": Interview with Maynard Jackson, Jr.
197. "rise to the crown": "What We Seek to Achieve at Morehouse College." Written by the faculty and published by the school, this booklet was among the papers of Rev. Maynard Jackson during his years at Friendship Baptist Church, 1945–53. In the possession of Maynard Jackson, Jr.

197. "sadness at seeing": Maynard Jackson, Jr., interview.
197. *"Come here, Buzzy."*: Interview with Irene (Renie) Dobbs Jackson.
197. "As we got older": Interview with Bob Jordan, Jr.
198. "The way that boy talks": Irene Dobbs Jackson interview.
198. the ministry also appealed to him: Maynard Jackson, Jr., interview.
198. *"I sing because I'm happy"*: "His Eye Is on the Sparrow," *The New Baptist Hymnal* (Nashville, Tenn.: National Baptist Publishing Board, August 1984), pp. 204–5.
198. "My father had a mellifluous": Maynard Jackson, Jr., interview.
198. "a dreamer": *Ibid.*
198. "It was like": *Ibid.*
199. "Carol Ann, do you remember?": Carol Jackson Miller interview.
199. "this tendency to be preoccupied": Maynard Jackson, Jr., interview.
199. "Maynard, come on, sweetheart": Carol Jackson Miller and Maynard Jackson, Jr., interviews.
200. "What's wrong with Rev. Jackson?": Carol Jackson Miller interview.
200. "He was never as strong": Maynard Jackson, Jr., interview.
200. "This Thing Called Happiness": *Atlanta Daily World*, February 21, 1953.
200. "Life goes on": Constance Jackson Carter interview.
200. "I thought my father had gone away": Carol Jackson Miller interview.
201. his hair, only flecked with gray: *Ibid.*
201. "Anything that he may have": Constance Jackson Carter interview.
201. "I kind of went around" Maynard Jackson, Jr., interview.
201. "atypical pneumonia": Death certificate of Rev. Maynard H. Jackson, June 27, 1953, Texas Department of Health, Bureau of Vital Statistics, State File No. 34660.
201. "conscientious leader": *Atlanta Daily World*, July 1, 1953.
201. death notice at the bottom: *Atlanta Journal*, June 28, 1953.
201. *"BAPTIST*—was my father": From the poem "To My Dele," by Jeanne Jackson Oladele, as recited in a funeral tribute to her by Oladejo O. Okediji, University of Lagos, March 11, 1978. Private papers of Sandra Irene Jackson Baraniuk.
201. reached an out-of-court settlement: *Smith v. Jackson,* Fulton County Superior Court, December 11, 1953, Case No. A31985, Book 1683, p. 262. The court docket did not stipulate the amount of the settlement paid to Julius Smith.
202. "In a school zone": Maynard Jackson, Jr., interview.
202. hoping to hear his voice: Interview with Irene (Renie) Dobbs Jackson.
202. "You girls go in there": Sandra Irene Jackson Baraniuk interview.
202. "What if he tries to kiss Mama?": *Ibid.*
202. "It never dawned": Irene Dobbs Jackson interview.
202. "I told Paul how much Daddy": Maynard Jackson, Jr., interview.
203. "A young male has a problem": Irene Dobbs Jackson interview.
203. "His death was the biggest blow": Maynard Jackson, Jr., interview.

CHAPTER 13

204. Each morning his black chauffeur: Interview with Vernon Jordan.
204. had underlined Washington's phrase: *Ibid.*
204. "You got no business": *Ibid.*
204. "Vernon, what are you doing": *Ibid.*
205. "And it has air-conditioning": Interview with Ivan Allen, Jr.
206. "His social habits": *Atlanta Constitution*, June 18, 1951.
207. "Why, Bill, what in hell": Interview with Herman Talmadge.
207. "Jim Gillis fired Hartsfield's mistress once": *Ibid.*
207. "went to the coffee shop": Interview with James Mackay.
207. *"So you're the sonovabitch"*: Ibid.
207. "pale tea": Interview with Eugene Patterson. McGill made this comment to Patterson.
208. "was like the roar of the ocean": Interview with June Dobbs Butts.
208. "would attempt to make": Interview with Ralph McGill, Jr.
208. he slammed on the brakes: Interview with Cecil Alexander. Alexander sat in the front seat as Hartsfield was driving that day.

208. "Hartsfield was somewhat like Lyndon Johnson": Herman Talmadge interview. As mayor, Bill Hartsfield reacted to the growing number of Atlantans who were leaving the city for the developing suburbs by pushing through the Plan of Improvement in 1951–52. Not only did the plan more than triple Atlanta's acreage, to 127 square miles from 37, it added more than 100,000 residents to the city in the process. What most pleased Hartsfield about this increase was that the majority of these new Atlantans were white, which, Hartsfield believed, would provide the antidote, at least temporarily, to the specter of black political domination in his city.

208. "Hartsfield might not be": Interview with Celestine Sibley. Grace Hamilton made this comment to Ms. Sibley, a popular features columnist for the *Atlanta Constitution.*

208. on Saturday nights: Interview with Aubrey Morris.

209. He began his climb: Floyd Hunter, *Community Power Structure: A Study of Decision Makers* (Chapel Hill, N.C.: University of North Carolina Press, 1953). Hunter's study of "Regional City" was a thinly veiled portrait of Atlanta. Though Hunter used fictitious names for civic leaders in his book, their real names are cited in his private collection of papers. Among white leaders were some prominent Old Atlanta names, such as Candler, Haverty, Maddox and Howell, in addition to Hartsfield and Woodruff. At forty-two, Ivan Allen, Jr., was the youngest named to the list. Among the black leaders on Hunter's list were L. D. Milton, A. T. Walden, Norris Herndon, Benjamin Mays, C. A. Scott and John Wesley Dobbs. See: Floyd Hunter Papers, Emory University, Robert W. Woodruff Library, Special Collections Department.

209. Having inherited Charles Marshall's half: Ivan Allen, Jr., interview.

209. "With a Woman in mind!": *Life*, April 10, 1950, p. 1.

209. "sounds like your": *Life*, June 12, 1950, p. 55.

209. "Now, they have all of the advantages": *Atlanta Journal Sunday Magazine*, May 14, 1950.

210. Irene Allen controlled the kitchen: Interview with Windsor Jordan. Jordan's mother, Mary Jordan, was a noted black caterer in Atlanta for a half century. Windsor is the younger brother of Vernon Jordan.

210. "It is a city of cool nights": Ivan Allen, Sr., *The Atlanta Spirit: Altitude + Attitude* (Atlanta: Ivan Allen Company, 1948), pp. 6, 25.

210. "You don't move Henry Grady": Ivan Allen, Jr., interview.

211. "he has sounded like a potential": *Atlanta Journal*, July 12, 1953.

211. Ivan Jr. proposed an industrial development program: *Ibid.*

211. "learn to respect the traditional rights": *Ibid.*

212. "In the field of public education": *Atlanta Constitution*, May 18, 1954.

212. "has reduced our Constitution": *Ibid.*

212. Attorney General Eugene Cook insisted: *Ibid.*

212. "We should add trained psychologists": *Atlanta Journal*, May 19, 1954.

212. "We expect to continue": *Atlanta Constitution*, May 18, 1954.

212. "Instead of benefitting": *Savannah Morning News*, May 18, 1954.

212. "Georgia and the South today": *Macon Telegraph*, May 18, 1954.

212. "The decision—however much": *Atlanta Constitution*, May 18, 1954.

212. "The meddlers, demagogues, race-baiters": *Ibid.*

213. "The decision is even more far-reaching": The statement written by Ivan Allen, Jr., though not published by any media outlet in Atlanta, was recited by him as part of his tape-recorded reflections for writer Paul Hemphill, 1971.

213. "Granddaddy was always talking about the business.": Interview with Ivan Allen III.

213. a 1956 two-door Ford Fairlane: Interview with H. Inman Allen.

214. "We had a sense that Atlanta was a place": Interview with F. Tradewell (Tread) Davis, Jr.

214. "And we were constantly driving that home": Interview with Bill Pressly.

214. Louise supplied hamburgers: Interview with Mason Lowance, Jr.

214. they shared chili dogs at The Varsity: Interview with Margaret Poer Allen.

214. "I thought they would get a better education": Bill Pressly interview.

214. Of the thirty-nine boys in the class: *Ibid.*

215. known as the Whig-Cliosophic Club": Mason Lowance, Jr., interview.

215. "The fundamental question remains": *Atlanta Constitution*, January 31, 1956.

215. "null and void": *Atlanta Journal*, February 6, 1956.

215. delaying tactics in the courts: *Atlanta Constitution*, October 4, 1954.

215. "sounds like a good idea on the surface": *Atlanta Journal*, June 25, 1956.

216. His support for Talmadge reflected not: Ivan Allen, Jr., interview.

216. discovered that the NAACP's southern: Internal memorandum of the Georgia Bureau of

Investigation, November 28, 1956. Marvin Griffin Papers, Bainbridge College, Bainbridge, Ga. (filed by date).

216. a group of black ministers: Harold H. Martin, *William Berry Hartsfield, Mayor of Atlanta* (Athens, Ga.: University of Georgia Press, 1978), pp. 118–19.

217. Hartsfield had offered to send city limousines: James W. English, *Handyman of the Lord: The Life and Ministry of the Reverend William Holmes Borders* (New York: Meredith Press, 1967), p. 92.

217. "Mr. Hartsfield has been in office so long": *Atlanta Journal,* May 7, 1957, p. 28.

217. "I will never sell my birthright": *Ibid.,* October 11, 1957.

217. Hartsfield took all but 353: *Ibid.,* December 5, 1957.

217. urged Griffin to institute a one-cent: Ivan Allen, Jr., interview. Allen spoke of this letter several times during a series of interviews conducted over four years. During the 1961 Atlanta mayor's race, candidate Muggsy Smith made several references to a letter written by Allen to Gov. Marvin Griffin, to show Atlanta's black voters how Allen once had espoused segregationist views; Smith contended that Allen had wanted to relocate blacks in specific parts of Georgia; Smith never made mention of Allen's plan to relocate blacks to Africa, which suggests that he was referring to a different letter.

217. "must have rewritten that thing": *Ibid.*

218. "The race issue is chaos erected into a system": *Ibid.*

218. formation of a relocation commission: Gilbert C. Fite, *Richard B. Russell, Jr.: Senator from Georgia* (Athens, Ga.: University of Georgia Press, 1991), pp. 244–45.

218. "If [Griffin] wanted to resolve": Ivan Allen, Jr., interview.

218. hired a press agent and set out: *Atlanta Journal Sunday Magazine,* February 16, 1958.

218. "Born rich, fingerbowl background.": Herman Talmadge interview.

218. "Frankly, I knew Ivan was ambitious": Interview with S. Ernest Vandiver.

219. "Do you go to church?": Interview with Gerald (Jerry) Horton.

219. "As my son's speechwriter": *Ibid.*

219. "Jerry, do you know any homosexuals?": *Ibid.*

219. "Segregation is our way of life": *Atlanta Constitution,* July 10, 1957.

219. "Deathly dull": Gerald Horton interview.

220. "The only way Ivan can beat Ernie": This comment by Talmadge was heard by an interview subject, who requested anonymity. When asked by the author if he had made the comment, Herman Talmadge laughed. "Probably did," he said.

220. television cameras beamed: Taylor Branch, *Parting the Waters: America in the King Years, 1954–63* (New York: Simon & Schuster, 1988), pp. 222–24.

220. "no stone unturned": *Atlanta Journal,* September 27, 1957.

220. "Time and understanding, which have stood": *Atlanta Constitution,* September 27, 1957.

221. Roger Lawson compared Eisenhower: *Atlanta Journal,* September 27, 1957.

221. "even if it means ultimately the abandonment": *Ibid.*

221. Ulysses S. Grant and Dwight D. Eisenhower: *Ibid.,* October 1, 1957.

221. "I'm proud of the fact": *Ibid.,* September 23, 1957.

221. "must be presented to the nation": *Atlanta Constitution,* October 8, 1957.

221. "We are going to act with honor": Text for a tentative nine-page speech for Ivan Allen, Jr., written in November 1957 by speechwriter Gerald (Jerry) Horton. Both Allen and Horton said the speech was never given. The heading of the speech reads, "Notes for a tentative speech to follow up the Bremen segregation speech—Jerry." Private files of Ivan Allen, Jr.

222. "We approach our task": *Atlanta Constitution,* November 3, 1957.

222. "consistent with Christian truth": Harold H. Martin, *Atlanta and Environs: A Chronicle of Its People and Events, Vol. 3, Years of Change and Challenge, 1940–1976* (Athens, Ga.: University of Georgia Press, 1987), pp. 271–74. See also: *Atlanta Constitution,* November 4, 1957.

222. "No matter how clear and unequivocal": *Atlanta Journal Sunday Magazine,* February 16, 1958.

222. "I'll try to get Ernie": Herman Talmadge and S. Ernest Vandiver interviews.

222. "As a businessman I have analyzed": *Atlanta Constitution,* December 18, 1957.

222. "This, we submit, is the most original": *Ibid.*

222. "Making a decision promptly": *Atlanta Journal Sunday Magazine,* February 16, 1958.

223. "No, Not One!": S. Ernest Vandiver interview.

223. federal district court advised that *Calhoun v. Latimer:* Paul E. Mertz, " 'Mind Changing Time All Over Georgia': HOPE, Inc. and School Desegregation, 1958–1961," *Georgia Historical Quarterly* (Spring 1993), pp. 43–44.

223. more than 1,800 applicants were turned away: Bill Pressly interview.
223. "We supported you in the campaign": S. Ernest Vandiver interview. See also: Clifford M. Kuhn, "There's a Footnote to History!: Memory and the History of Martin Luther King's October 1960 Arrest and Its Aftermath." Paper delivered at the 1994 Annual Meeting of the Organization of American Historians, Atlanta, Ga.
223. "I was shocked": *Ibid.*
223. he once dispatched a state trooper: Herman Talmadge interview.
223. "I don't guess anybody shouted it": *Ibid.*
223. population grew by an astonishing 40 percent: *Chicago Tribune Sunday Magazine*, August 21, 1966.
223. "We roll out a red carpet": *Newsweek*, October 19, 1959, pp. 94–98.
224. Nikita Khrushchev received a Rebel: *Ibid.* In Atlanta, "M Day" was celebrated on October 10, 1959.
224. "the nerve center of the New South": *Ibid.*
224. Borders called for more black involvement: Cecil Alexander interview.
224. they ought to appreciate all: Ivan Allen, Jr., transcript for Paul Hemphill, 1971.
224. "Don't worry, we'll take care": Cecil Alexander interview.
224. "They were doing": Interview with the Rev. William Holmes Borders.
224. "It had dash!": *Ibid.*
224. "Did anything rub off?": Ivan Allen, Jr., with Paul Hemphill, *Mayor: Notes on the Sixties* (New York: Simon & Schuster, 1971), p. 102.

CHAPTER 14

225. "I want to buy some perfume": Interview with Carol Jackson Miller.
225. "I think that the decision": Letter from John Wesley Dobbs to Rev. Roy D. McClain, pastor, First Baptist Church, June 26, 1956. John Wesley Dobbs Papers, Amistad Research Center, New Orleans, La., Box 1, Folder 3.
226. "Sometimes, the darkness": Speech by John Wesley Dobbs to the Georgia Voters League in Macon, Ga., October 27, 1956. JWD Papers, ARC, Box 3, Folder 4. The Georgia Voters League was formed as part of a series of black voter registration leagues in several southern states. As a founder of the umbrella organization, Rev. Maynard Jackson asked John Wesley Dobbs to serve as president of the Georgia league.
226. he heard a knock: Interviews with a handful of Dobbs family members, including Mattiwilda Dobbs Janzon, Josephine Dobbs Clement, Irene Dobbs Jackson. John Wesley Dobbs told this story often to his family.
226. The Grand wrote his response: Letter from John Wesley Dobbs to his daughter Irene Dobbs Jackson, September 20, 1956. JWD Papers, ARC, Box 1, Folder 11. In his letter, Dobbs described the experience, including his dealings with Miller County lodge members and the Associated Press reporter.
226. 10,000 residents, including 2,686 blacks: *Ibid.*
227. He phoned Herbert Jenkins: In the sole discrepancy in the retelling of this incident by Dobbs family members, several remembered John Wesley Dobbs saying that he phoned the Fulton County sheriff, though others recall him saying he called Herbert Jenkins. It is more likely he phoned Jenkins, with whom he had developed a cordial rapport.
227. the Grand chose for his lawyer Hoke Smith, Jr.: John Wesley Dobbs letter to Irene Dobbs Jackson, September 20, 1956. JWD Papers, ARC, Box 1, Folder 11.
227. "a terrible political experience": *Ibid.*
227. "Good thing I did": *Ibid.*
227. "I do not have in my possession": *Atlanta Constitution*, September 20, 1956.
227. "honest, fair handling": *Ibid.*
228. "Hoke didn't outmaneuver anybody": Interview with Peter Zeck Geer, Jr.
228. "I don't want that experience again": John Wesley Dobbs letter to Irene Dobbs Jackson, September 20, 1956. JWD Papers, ARC, Box 1, Folder 11.
228. "At my funeral I want 20 grands": *Atlanta Daily World*, April 25, 1952.
228. hair cut short and with a blue rinse: Carol Jackson Miller interview.
229. "Would you buy that house": Interview with Mattiwilda Dobbs Janzon.
229. for a good afternoon cry: Carol Jackson Miller interview.

230. Suicide entered Renie's thoughts: *Ibid.* Not until decades later did Renie make this admission in a conversation with daughter Carol Ann.

230. "Why did you let Buzzy": Interview with Irene (Renie) Dobbs Jackson.

230. Renie hired a private tutor: Carol Jackson Miller interview.

231. a Basque woman, Madame Aillagon: *Ibid.*

231. "It is impossible to talk": Letter from Irene Dobbs Jackson to Rev. Martin Luther King, Jr., pastor, Dexter Avenue Baptist Church, Montgomery, Ala., May 21, 1957. Martin Luther King, Jr. Papers, 1954–68, Boston University, Mugar Library, Department of Special Collections, Box 25.

231. he paid for the installation: Interview with Constance Jackson Carter.

231. "My dear ones": Letter from John Wesley Dobbs to Dobbs family members, July 2, 1958. JWD Papers. ARC, Box 2, Folder 1.

231. "I know there's something": Clotye Murdock, " 'My Daughter Married a White Man'—J. Wesley Dobbs. Father Tells How He Felt About Opera Singer Mattiwilda's marriage to Spaniard," *Ebony,* January 1954.

232. "She's going to faint!": *Ibid.*

232. "Take her to New York": Harold Preece, "Mattiwilda Dobbs: Atlanta's Queen of Opera," *Sepia,* June 1958, p. 46. Mattiwilda Dobbs Papers, Robert W. Woodruff Library, Special Collections, Atlanta University, Folder 1. (This collection is made up predominantly of newspaper clippings and reviews.)

232. "He pushed me into": Mattiwilda Dobbs Janzon interview.

233. She learned of her victory: *Sepia,* June 1958, p. 48.

233. mailed copies of Geekie's letters: Mattiwilda Dobbs Janzon interview.

233. Their first trip overseas: Address by Georgia Grand Master John Wesley Dobbs of Georgia Jurisdiction, Prince Hall Masons, at the 83rd Annual Grand Communication, Savannah, Ga., June 10, 1952. Private Collection of Georgia Prince Hall Masons, Auburn Avenue, Atlanta, Ga.

233. "I am not the same man": *Ibid.*

233. "I'm coming home to America": *Atlanta Daily World,* May 20, 1952.

233. "very leetle Engleesh": *Ebony,* January 1954.

233. Dobbs noticed Geekie and Luis: *Ibid.*

234. "I wanted Mattiwilda to be sure": *Ibid.*

234. "You really hurt the boy": *Ibid.*

234. "They didn't make any big hullabaloo": Mattiwilda Dobbs Janzon interview.

234. "Many Negroes, particularly those": *Ebony,* January 1954.

235. "I positively did not attempt": Letter from John Wesley Dobbs to Clotye Murdock, Associate Editor of *Ebony,* December 16, 1953. JWD Papers, ARC, Box 1, Folder 2.

235. "Thank God for those nine": Address by Grand Master John Wesley Dobbs at 85th Annual Grand Lodge Communications at Augusta, Ga., June 8, 1954. Private Collection of Georgia Prince Hall Masons, Auburn Avenue, Atlanta, Ga.

235. king presented her with Sweden's: *Sepia,* June 1958, p. 50.

235. *Mademoiselle* named her: *Atlanta Daily World,* December 24, 1954.

236. "Miss Dobbs is easy to describe": *Sacramento* (Calif.) *Bee,* March 4, 1955. JWD Papers, ARC, Box 6, Folder 3.

236. U.S. senator James O. Eastland: *New York Times,* September 13, 1955.

236. "We feel that she should": Letter from John Wesley Dobbs to James Dombrowski, Secretary of the Southern Educational Fund, September 23, 1955. JWD Papers, ARC, Box 1, Folder 2.

236. "I do not need to tell you": Letter from John Wesley Dobbs to Leonard W. Hall, Chairman of the Republican National Committee, February 13, 1954. *Ibid.*

236. Rich's where she bought a new $165 gown: Letter from Mattiwilda Dobbs to her sister Irene Dobbs Jackson and children, October 27, 1956. *Ibid.*, Folder 12.

236. "Believe me": Letter from John Wesley Dobbs to his daughter Irene Dobbs Jackson and children, October 26, 1956. *Ibid.*

237. "I wore out my tux": Letter from Maynard Jackson, Jr., to his grandfather John Wesley Dobbs, November 1, 1956. *Ibid.*

237. "I want him to be there": Letter from John Wesley Dobbs to his daughter Irene Dobbs Jackson and her children, November 4, 1956. *Ibid.*

237. "Her body was tense": *New York Daily News,* November 10, 1956. Mattiwilda Dobbs Papers, Atlanta University, Woodruff Library, Department of Special Collections, Folder 4.

237. "The NAACP might consider Verdi": *Amsterdam News,* November 17, 1956. *Ibid.*

238. "It was nice to know": Letter from Mattiwilda Dobbs to her parents, Irene and John Wesley Dobbs, January 21, 1957. JWD Papers, ARC, Box 1, Folder 11.
238. "I have no one to spend": Letter from Mattiwilda Dobbs to her sister Irene Dobbs Jackson, July 6, 1956. *Ibid.*, Box 2, Folder 8.
238. he feared his wife's heart: Mattiwilda Dobbs Janzon interview.
238. "Janzon is the second white": *Atlanta Constitution*, December 24, 1957.
238. "He was a personality": Irene Dobbs Jackson interview.
238. In ballroom dancing: Interview with Constance Jackson Carter.
239. "Do we have any dish powder?": Interview with Maynard Jackson, Jr.
239. "The Garbage Disposal": Interview with Sandra Irene Jackson Baraniuk.
239. "I was in the stands": *Atlanta Constitution*, August 29, 1975.
239. "If you didn't bring": Maynard Jackson, Jr., interview.
239. "I grew up in a family": *Ibid.*
240. "It was like the second Emancipation.": *Ibid.*
240. "Some of us came straight": Interview with the Rev. Otis Moss, Jr.
240. "I have concluded that I am": Letter from Maynard Jackson, Jr., to his mother, Irene Dobbs Jackson, August 18, 1954. JWD Papers, ARC, Box 1, Folder 10.
240. "I had no intention": Letter from Maynard Jackson, Jr., to his grandfather John Wesley Dobbs, September 5, 1956. *Ibid.*, Folder 11.
240. "I may be out of line": Letter from Maynard Jackson, Jr., to his grandfather John Wesley Dobbs, November 26, 1956. *Ibid.*, Folder 12.
241. "You knew from the start": Letter from John Wesley Dobbs to his grandson Maynard Jackson, Jr., November 30, 1956. *Ibid.*
241. "Tell [Carol, his sister] there are": Letter from Maynard Jackson, Jr., to his mother, Irene Dobbs Jackson, December 5, 1957. *Ibid.*, Folder 14.
241. "Seemingly he did not know": Letter from John Wesley Dobbs to Thurgood Marshall of the NAACP, May 22, 1958. *Ibid.*, Folder 16.
241. "When I think of your dear": Letter from John Wesley Dobbs to James M. Nabrit, Dean of Howard University Law School, May 22, 1958. *Ibid.*
242. "I'm rather glad": Letter from Maynard Jackson, Jr., to his grandfather John Wesley Dobbs, June 18 1958. *Ibid.*, Box 2, Folder 1.
242. "Mother, I think of Clayton": Letter from Maynard Jackson, Jr., to his mother, Irene Dobbs Jackson, and his siblings Jeanne, Carol, Connie and Paul, November 15, 1958. *Ibid.*
242. "I saw 'The Second Agony' ": Letter from Maynard Jackson, Jr., to his grandfather John Wesley Dobbs, February 28, 1959. *Ibid.*, Folder 2.
242. He made more than $20,000: Maynard Jackson, Jr., interview.
242. "My desires are simple": Letter from Maynard Jackson, Jr., to his mother, Irene Dobbs Jackson, August 26, 1959. JWD Papers, ARC, Box 2, Folder 2.
242. "I am behind in three": Letter from Maynard Jackson, Jr., to his mother, Irene Dobbs Jackson, October 21, 1959. *Ibid.*, Folder 3.
242. "had best keep this continent": Letter from Maynard Jackson, Jr., to his mother, Irene Dobbs Jackson, February 6, 1960. *Ibid.*, Folder 4.
243. enter the law school of North Carolina Central: Maynard Jackson, Jr., interview. His mother, Dr. Irene Jackson, had preceded him to the school, becoming chair of the Foreign Languages Department.
243. Jewish fraternities at the University of Connecticut: Letter from Maynard Jackson, Jr., to his mother, Irene Dobbs Jackson, November 9, 1959. JWD Papers, ARC, Box 2, Folder 3.
243. "I've had it!": *Ibid.*
243. "not the closest of friends": *Ibid.*
244. "There is no doubt": Letter from John Wesley Dobbs to his daughter Irene Dobbs Jackson and her children, January 12, 1957. *Ibid.*, Box 1, Folder 13.
244. "I was certainly happy.": Letter from John Wesley Dobbs to Rev. Martin Luther King, Jr., February 15, 1957. Private Collection of Georgia Prince Hall Masons, Auburn Avenue, Atlanta, Ga.
244. "We don't want that": *Atlanta Journal*, June 19, 1956. Dobbs made this comment at the meeting of the NAACP Atlanta branch on June 18, 1956, at the Friendship Baptist Church.
245. "I moved over with them": Letter from John Wesley Dobbs to his daughter Renie Dobbs Jackson and her children, March 1957. JWD Papers, ARC, Box 1, Folder 13.
245. he gave five shares: Letter from John Wesley Dobbs to his daughter Irene Dobbs Jackson and granddaughters Carol Ann and Connie Jackson, May 9, 1958. *Ibid.*, Folder 16.

245. "I'm also grateful to God": *Ibid.*
245. "It is the crop of things sown": *Atlanta Constitution,* October 13, 1958. See also: Janice Roth-schild Blumberg, *One Voice: Rabbi Jacob M. Rothschild and the Troubled South* (Macon, Ga.: Mercer University Press, 1985), pp. 79–96.
245. Hartsfield would gloat in telling: Memorandum from Helen Bullard to Mayor-elect Ivan Allen, Jr., December 19, 1961. Records of the Administration of Mayor Ivan Allen, Jr., City of Atlanta, Department of Records Management, Atlanta, Ga., Series 90-TR-321, Box 1. Bullard, a political advisor to Hartsfield and Allen, attended Hartsfield's speech at the Public Relations Society of America and recounted Hartsfield's claim to Allen.
245. "The real disease is deeper seated": Speech entitled "Leadership and Its Responsibility," by John Wesley Dobbs in New Haven, Conn., July 12, 1958. JWD Papers, ARC, Box 3, Folder 10.
246. A 1952 Grand Lodge resolution: Resolution to honor Grand Master John Wesley Dobbs for twenty years of service at Grand Lodge, June 12, 1952, Savannah, Ga. Private papers of Paul E. X. Brown, Atlanta, Ga.
246. Dobbs paid more than $15,000: Letter from John Wesley Dobbs to Grand Master John Louis, Jr., of Louisiana, January 16, 1959. JWD Papers, ARC, Box 1, Folder 6. In the letter, Dobbs maintains that he paid $15,097.95 to the federal government (interest and penalties) for the years 1951, 1952 and 1953, and that he settled with the state for $1,830.30.
246. "Psst! Come with me!": Maynard Jackson, Jr., interview.
246. Miami, Charlotte, Louisville: *Atlanta Journal,* May 24, 1959.
247. "I want to become a member here": Irene Dobbs Jackson interview.
247. holding secret discussions: *Atlanta Journal,* May 24, 1959.
247. indicated that few blacks had used: *Ibid.*
247. "does not represent the thinking": *Ibid.,* May 25, 1959.
247. "A public library is a symbol": *Ibid.*
247. "the first card issued to a Negro": *Ibid.*
248. "Doncha know Niggers": Constance Jackson Carter interview.
248. "It is just like somebody giving": Irene Dobbs Jackson interview.

CHAPTER 15

249. "Atlanta has given the South": Bill Ryan, commentator, NBC News as reprinted in the *Atlanta Constitution,* August 31, 1961.
249. "Atlanta was no different": Interview with Jamil Abdullah al Amin (né H. Rap Brown, black militant).
251. "AN APPEAL FOR HUMAN RIGHTS": *Atlanta Daily World, Atlanta Constitution* and *Atlanta Journal,* March 9, 1960.
251. sat at the whites-only lunch counter: Taylor Branch, *Parting the Waters. America in the King Years, 1954–63* (New York: Simon & Schuster, 1988), pp. 270–71.
251. "Wherever M. L. King, Jr., has been": *Atlanta Daily World,* December 2, 1959.
251. "those guys hit the ceiling": Interview with Paul Delaney.
252. "Mr. Mays wants to see you": Interview with Lonnie C. King.
252. "scared us to death, man": *Ibid.*
252. "We are not going to tell you": *Atlanta Journal* and *Constitution Magazine,* August 15, 1965, p. 38. In an article about Atlanta University, Clement gave his version of the meeting.
253. "Gene, you better come in here": Interview with Eugene Patterson.
253. "A left-wing statement": *Atlanta Journal,* March 9, 1960.
253. "He can walk, instead of march": *Ibid.*
253. "Constructive. It must be admitted": *Ibid.*
254. "I grew up with these people": Branch, *Parting the Waters,* pp. 266–68.
254. "Now I've got to help him": *Ibid.*
254. "They didn't have to say it": Interview with Andrew Young.
254. nearly two hundred black students staged: *Atlanta Journal, Atlanta Daily World* and *Atlanta Constitution,* March 15–16, 1960.
254. "Since the students had so intelligently": *Atlanta Daily World,* March 16, 1960.
255. "bi-racial conferences in every city": *New York Times,* March 17, 1960.
255. "He was a hometown boy": Howell Raines, *My Soul Is Rested: Movement Days in the Deep South Remembered* (New York: G. P. Putnam's Sons, 1977), pp. 85, 102.

255. Their destination was the State Capitol: Lonnie C. King interview. See also: *Atlanta Constitution*, *Atlanta Journal* and *Atlanta Daily World*, May 17–18, 1960.
255. "I'm turning you": *Atlanta Constitution*, May 18, 1960.
255. "You have been an inspiration to": *Ibid*.
256. "just as much a segregationist": Interview with S. Ernest Vandiver.
256. Ivan Allen, Jr., read the chamber's official: Recorded Minutes of the Atlanta Chamber of Commerce Meeting of March 22, 1960, files of the Atlanta Chamber, Atlanta, Ga.
256. "This is no popularity contest": *Atlanta Journal*, *Atlanta Constitution* and *Atlanta Daily World*, March 24, 1960.
256. "I'd rather die fighting": Testimony by Jack Dorsey, March 23, 1960, Sibley Commission Hearings Transcript, p. 154. John Sibley Papers, Emory University, Robert W. Woodruff Library, Department of Special Collections, Box 3.
257. "I mention this because": Testimony by John Wesley Dobbs, March 23, 1960, Sibley Commission Hearings Transcript, pp. 168–70. Sibley Collection, Box 3.
257. "A hatred for discrimination": *Atlanta Daily World*, March 24, 1960.
257. Only Ivan Allen, Jr., and Mills B. Lane: Ivan Allen, Jr., with Paul Hemphill, *Mayor: Notes on the Sixties* (New York: Simon & Schuster, 1971), pp. 34–35.
258. "It fell my task": Lonnie C. King interview.
258. "The minute I got into it": Interview with Ivan Allen, Jr.
258. transforming Rich's into an all-white store: Ivan Allen, Jr., transcript for Paul Hemphill, 1971.
258. There, amidst a crowd: *Atlanta Journal*, October 10, 1960.
259. "We were exponents": Lonnie C. King interview.
259. "They had difficulty getting anybody": Ivan Allen, Jr., interview.
260. "I will serve": *Ibid*.
260. Rich, a chamber stalwart: Raines, *My Soul Is Rested*, p. 90.
260. "I don't feel that I did anything": *Atlanta Constitution*, October 20, 1960.
260. packing a toothbrush and a bar of soap: Interview with Herschelle Sullivan Challenor.
260. phone messages, books, a checkerboard: Branch, *Parting the Waters*, p. 352.
260. Hartsfield called a meeting with sixty: *Atlanta Daily World*, October 23, 1960.
261. Hartsfield was empowered to release: Branch, *Parting the Waters*, p. 354.
261. "the best meeting we've ever had": *Atlanta Daily World*, October 23, 1960.
261. Wofford phoned Atlanta attorney Morris Abram: Branch, *Parting the Waters*, p. 353. The scene of the conversations with Wofford and Abram is drawn primarily from Branch's version. See also: Morris Abram, *The Day Is Short: An Autobiography* (New York: Harcourt Brace Jovanovich, 1982).
262. "Now, I know that I ran": Branch, *Parting the Waters*, p. 355.
262. "The Senator is hopeful": *Ibid.*, p. 355.
262. "But M.L., *we need you!*": Lonnie C. King interview.
262. Mitchell would call for a fountain: Interview with Dan Sweat. Sweat worked at the time for DeKalb County Commissioner Charles Emmerich.
262. More than two hundred supporters of Rev. King: *Atlanta Constitution*, October 26, 1960.
262. "Dobbs was not only a solid": Interview with Donald Hollowell.
263. "He wanted me to know": *New York Times*, October 27, 1960.
263. "Val, this is gon' have": Raines, *My Soul Is Rested*, p. 95.
263. Daddy King immediately switched: *Atlanta Constitution*, October 28, 1960.
263. "'No Comment' Nixon Versus": Raines, *My Soul Is Rested*, p. 95. See also: Cliff Kuhn, "There's a Footnote to History!: Memory and the History of Martin Luther King's October 1960 Arrest and Its Aftermath." Paper delivered at the 1994 Annual Meeting of the Organization of American Historians, Atlanta, Ga.
263. black voters provided the margin: Theodore H. White, *The Making of the President* (New York: Atheneum, 1960), pp. 363–64.
263. "They tell me that everybody": Donald Hollowell interview. See also: David Levering Lewis, *King: A Biography* (Urbana, Ill.: University of Illinois Press, 1978), pp. 127–28.
263. "I don't know any way to pay": Letter from the Rev. Martin Luther King, Jr., to John Wesley Dobbs, December 1, 1960. Martin Luther King, Jr., Papers, Boston University, Special Collections Department, Mugar Library, Boston, Mass., Box 23A, Folder D.
263. "My life has been made better": Letter from John Wesley Dobbs to the Rev. Martin Luther King, Jr., December 15, 1960. *Ibid*.
264. "If I had been militant": This quote was cited by Atlanta mayor Ivan Allen, Jr., in a testimonial

for Walden on February 24, 1964. Records of the Mayoral Administration of Ivan Allen, Jr., City of Atlanta, Records Management Division, Series 89-TR-261, Box 2.

264. "May I use the rest room?": Ivan Allen, Jr., interview.

265. Ivan Allen, Jr., with a single red rose: Interview with Jenelsie Walden Holloway.

265. "Come over here": Ivan Allen, Jr., interview.

265. These businessmen, Ivan Jr. believed": Allen with Hemphill, *Mayor,* p. 38.

265. "You boys have got to handle this.": *Ibid.* Also: Ivan Allen Jr., interview.

265. "You want a downtown club?": Ivan Allen, Jr., interview.

265. "It was rather lavish quarters": *Ibid.*

266. "It takes a few decades": Eugene Patterson interview.

266. students turned to Walden and discovered: Raines, *My Soul Is Rested,* pp. 86–87.

266. "Every one of them": Ivan Allen, Jr., interview.

266. "You get that goddamned Nigger out": Interview with Joel Goldberg.

267. "It was a nervous tic, okay": Lonnie C. King interview.

267. "very much a white southerner": Herschelle Sullivan Challenor interview.

267. "We have come a long distance.": Interview with Rev. Otis Moss, Jr.

267. "He had more guts than any of them": Ivan Allen, Jr., interview.

267. "I'll never yield": Eugene Patterson interview.

267. "Open the goddamned stores": Ivan Allen, Jr., interview.

267. "BOY, I'M TIRED OF YOU!": Lonnie C. King interview.

267. "He was obviously a traditional man": Herschelle Sullivan Challenor interview.

267. "I think he's right": Lonnie C. King interview.

268. "I've been segregated all of my life": *Ibid.*

268. Ivan Jr. made the announcement: *Atlanta Journal,* March 7, 1961.

268. over his car radio: Lonnie C. King interview.

268. "Every effort will be made to eliminate": *Atlanta Constitution,* March 8, 1961.

268. "We feel that the fine relationship": *Atlanta Journal,* March 7, 1961.

268. "Mr. Allen, you are creating": Lonnie C. King interview.

269. *"You're giving it away to the Niggers.":* Ivan Allen, Jr., interview.

269. "There's certain things the majority": *Ibid.*

269. "To call this businessman ambitious": *Atlanta Constitution,* March 9, 1961.

269. platoon leader during World War II: Eugene Patterson interview.

269. "Before you had the guts": *Ibid.*

270. A group of Black Muslims circulated: Lionel Newsom and William Gorden, "A Stormy Rally in Atlanta," *Today's Speech* (Vol. 11, April 1963), pp. 18–21.

270. "You'll have to take my word for it": *Ibid.*

270. "By your saying I've sold out": Branch, *Parting the Waters,* p. 396.

270. "I don't see how in the name of heaven": Newsom and Gorden, "A Stormy Rally in Atlanta, " pp. 18–21.

270. *"The whole thing is going to blow up":* Allen with Hemphill, *Mayor,* p. 41.

270. "his eyes were a little glassy": Lonnie C. King interview.

271. "I'm surprised at you.": Newsom and Gorden, "A Stormy Rally in Atlanta," pp. 18–21.

271. "If this contract is broken": Allen with Hemphill, *Mayor,* p. 42.

271. "Little Jesus": *Ibid.*

271. "What do you think?": *Ibid.,* p. 110.

272. "Give me the scoop": Dan Sweat interview.

272. Plans and Procedures Committee presented "control programs.": Confidential Minutes of the Atlanta Chamber of Commerce Meetings. John Calhoun Papers, Woodruff Library, Special Collections Division, Atlanta University. (This collection, made up of more than a dozen boxes of materials, was not indexed at the time of author's research.) The planning process for desegregation of Atlanta's lunch counters is discussed in minutes from meetings of March 16, March 22 and May 18, 1961.

272. a white merchant asked if light-skinned blacks: Lonnie C. King interview.

273. "one of the most descript people": Interview with James Mackay.

273. changing from one taxi to another: *Ibid.*

273. "could not have happened if the government": Letter from Helen Bullard to Be Haas, November 15, 1967. Helen Bullard Papers, Emory University, Robert W. Woodruff Library, Department of Special Collections, Box 18.

273. managed 165 state and local campaigns: *Ibid.*

273. "If anything good spills over": Raines, *My Soul Is Rested*, p. 410.
273. "Helen, I want to run": Ivan Allen, Jr., interview. Also: Interview with Raleigh Bryans. Bryans was told about this exchange by Bullard.
274. *"The Boss thinks it's time"*: Eugene Patterson interview.
274. "Mr. Hartsfield, I wonder": Allen with Hemphill, *Mayor*, pp. 48–49. Also: Ivan Allen, Jr., interview.
274. "Helen, do you think people": Interview with Sam Massell. Bullard related this anecdote to Massell.
274. "I've had this job for 23 years": Allen with Hemphill, *Mayor*, p. 49.
275. "MAYOR BOWS OUT": *Atlanta Journal*, June 7, 1961.
275. "Hartsfield Calls It Quits": *Atlanta Constitution*, June 8, 1961.
275. "peaceful racial calm": *Atlanta Journal*, June 26, 1961.
275. "My son is going to make": Interviews with Paul E. X. Brown and George Coleman.
275. "Say Negro, Ah-vin": Ivan Allen, Jr., interview.

CHAPTER 16

276. "Look, I'm going to sign this": Interview with Maynard Jackson, Jr.
276. *"Gifts count for nothing"*: Ella Wheeler Wilcox, "Will." In *Maurine and Other Poems* (Chicago: W. B. Conkey Company, 1888), p. 144.
277. "[Attucks] made the down payment": Address by John Wesley Dobbs at Boston Common before black Shriners, August 16, 1960. John Wesley Dobbs Papers, Amistad Research Center, New Orleans, La., Box 3, Folder 11.
277. "Grandpa was beginning to lose": Maynard Jackson, Jr., interview.
277. "When you get ready to march": Interview with Rev. Otis Moss, Jr.
277. His mind retained its clarity: The description of Dobbs's physical decline is drawn from interviews with many family members.
277. "It was depressing for us": Interview with Bill Clement, Jr.
278. closed out his account, paying $159.88: Letter from John Wesley Dobbs to Rich's, September 16, 1961. Richard Rich Papers, Emory University, Robert W. Woodruff Library, Department of Special Collections, Box 37, Folder 2.
278. "my Conscience and Self-Respect": *Ibid.*
278. "So far as we are aware": Letter from Frank Neely of Rich's to John Wesley Dobbs, September 21, 1961. *Ibid.*
279. "He preached the gospel on Sunday": Rev. Otis Moss, Jr., interview.
279. "Wear Old Clothes With New Dignity": *The Torch: Morehouse College Yearbook, 1960–61.* The description of Dobbs on the picket line is drawn from the picture in *The Torch* as well as from interviews with those on the picket line with him.
279. Borders had called for the old guard: Interviews with Lonnie C. King and the Rev. Otis Moss, Jr.
279. "He walked that day": Rev. Otis Moss, Jr., interview. The dialogue between John Wesley Dobbs and John Calhoun is drawn from Reverend Moss, who heard the conversation.
279. "Look at that jaw set.": Maynard Jackson, Jr., interview.
280. John Wesley Dobbs was for Brown: 1961 Notes of George Goodwin. A former Pulitzer Prize–winning reporter for the *Atlanta Journal*, Goodwin retained his notebooks from his work that spring when he surveyed the political leanings of black Atlanta for the First National Bank. According to one of his notes, Rev. Martin Luther King, Jr., told him, "Dobbs is for Charlie Brown." Private Papers of George Goodwin.
280. "There have been some questions about Allen": *Ibid.*
280. Their plane had landed in a rainstorm: Letter from John Wesley Dobbs to his wife, Irene T. Dobbs, May 7, 1960. JWD Papers, ARC, Box 2, Folder 4.
280. To remove the swelling: Letter from John Wesley Dobbs to friends and family, May 16, 1960. *Ibid.*
280. "My Dear Babe": Letter from John Wesley Dobbs to his wife, Irene T. Dobbs, from Rochester, Minn., May 7, 1960. *Ibid.*
280. "They know about 70 different kinds": Letter from John Wesley Dobbs to his daughter Willie and her husband, Ben Blackburn, May 11, 1960. *Ibid.*
281. "I heard you last night": Interview with Willie Dobbs Blackburn.
281. "Everybody participated.": Bill Clement, Jr., interview.

281. "I guess they looked at me": Interview with Carol Jackson Miller.
281. "You know we've got five hundred": Interview with Eugene Patterson.
282. frequently sent a cook: Interview with B. B. Beamon.
282. His plan was to write the history: *Atlanta Daily World*, September 3, 1961.
282. "Now, Maynard, I am calling this to your attention": Letter from John Wesley Dobbs to Maynard Jackson, Jr., July 31, 1961. JWD Papers, ARC, Box 2, Folder 5.
283. She had him transferred at once: Willie Dobbs Blackburn interview.
283. At 8:45 that morning: *Atlanta Journal*, August 30, 1961.
283. "Stop the presses!": *Atlanta Constitution*, August 31, 1961.
283. "I strongly urge the officials": *New York Times*, August 31, 1961.
283. "There's something wrong here.": Eugene Patterson interview.
283. "Atlanta Integration Is Peaceful": *New York Times*, August 31, 1961.
283. "Negro Students Make Historic Move": *Atlanta Journal*, August 30, 1961.
283. "Grand Master Dobbs passed": Western Union Telegram sent by X. L. Neal, Deputy Grand Master of Georgia, August 30, 1961. JWD Papers, ARC, Box 5, Folder 10.
283. The first person from outside: Willie Dobbs Blackburn interview. Mrs. Blackburn remembers greeting Ivan Allen, Jr., at 540 on that day.
284. did not even recall making the visit: Interview with Ivan Allen, Jr. Allen's campaign advisor, Helen Bullard, knew many people in black Atlanta, including John Wesley Dobbs. Though Allen did not recall making the visit, he said, "I'm sure that Helen Bullard would have sent me out there the first thing."
284. "I hold not the slightest ill feeling": Funeral request by John Wesley Dobbs, November 5, 1958. JWD Papers, ARC, Box 4, Folder 9.
284. "A people recently escaping from subjugation": Tribute to John Wesley Dobbs by Rev. Homer McEwen of First Congregational Church, September 2, 1961. Reel audiotape of John Wesley Dobbs's funeral. JWD Papers, ARC, Box 11 (oversize folder).
285. "Martin talked about him": Interview with Coretta Scott King.
285. "We thank thee for his love": The Lord's Prayer by Rev. Martin Luther King, Jr., September 2, 1961. Reel audiotape of Dobbs's funeral. JWD Papers, ARC, Box 11 (oversize folder).
285. signed his name on the back of the envelope: Interview with the Rev. William Holmes Borders.
285. "compassionate in love": Eulogy by the Rev. William Holmes Borders, September 9, 1961. Reel audiotape of Dobbs's funeral. JWD Papers, ARC, Box 11 (oversize folder).
286. "I didn't know my father": Interview with Josephine Dobbs Clement.

## CHAPTER 17

287. "Mister Maddox, let you": *Atlanta Journal*, June 27, 1961.
287. "When have you heard": *Ibid.*, June 26, 1961.
287. "You represent a group": *Atlanta Constitution*, June 27, 1961.
287. "You're the silk-stocking": Interview with Lester Maddox.
287. "We are teaching love": *Atlanta Constitution*, June 27, 1961.
288. "Had he not stopped when": News release by Lester Maddox, July 5, 1961. Private papers of Ivan Allen, Jr.
288. "I couldn't get into the Capital City Club": Lester Maddox interview.
289. old guard on Auburn Avenue: Interview with Cecil Alexander. Bullard spoke at length about her concerns with Alexander during August 1961.
289. For the primary alone, he spent $175,000: Interview with Ivan Allen, Jr.
289. "We decided that as long": *Ibid.*
290. the four hundred employees of his company: Ivan Allen, Jr., with Paul Hemphill, *Mayor: Notes on the Sixties* (New York: Simon & Schuster, 1970), p. 49.
290. "Shoot, I'm no silk-stockinged boy": *Atlanta Journal*, July 13, 1961.
290. "We are making twice as many": Confidential campaign memorandum from Ivan Allen, Jr., July 13, 1961. Robert W. Woodruff Papers, Emory University, Robert W. Woodruff Library, Department of Special Collections, Document Case 8, Folder 8, "Ivan Allen, Jr., Correspondence, 1959–64."
290. "political opportunist": *Atlanta Constitution*, July 29, 1961.
291. "[Allen] laced into his enemies": *Ibid.*

291. Hartsfield had told Smith he could not support him: Interview with Scott Smith. Muggsy Smith related his conversation with Hartsfield to his son, Scott, years later.

291. his father viewed the mayor as Judas: *Ibid.*

291. "I'm perfectly willing to acknowledge": *Atlanta Journal*, August 1, 1961.

291. *"Since I achieved a social conscience":* Ibid.

291. "No one ever knew his real convictions.": *Ibid.*, September 1, 1961.

292. 1,600 blacks showed up: Allen with Hemphill, *Mayor*, pp. 57–58.

292. "Mister Allen, don't worry": Reese Cleghorn, "Allen of Atlanta Collides with Black Power and White Racism," *New York Times Sunday Magazine*, October 15, 1966, p. 140.

292. "We were not sold on somebody": Interview with Paul E. X. Brown.

292. "Cecil, I'm concerned": Cecil Alexander interview.

293. there had been a gentlemen's agreement: Allen with Hemphill, *Mayor*, p. 55.

293. "has dinner nearly every night": *Atlanta Journal*, July 30, 1961.

293. surprised to be served from a sterling: Ivan Allen, Jr., interview.

293. "Yeah. We know that you've": *Ibid.*

293. "Mr. Patterson, I have just had the damndest": Interview with Eugene Patterson.

293. "Mr. Milton introduced and endorsed me": Confidential campaign memorandum from Ivan Allen, Jr., August 3, 1961. RWW Papers, EU, Document Case 8, Folder 8, "Ivan Allen, Jr., Correspondence, 1959–64."

294. "I've got the courage": *Atlanta Journal*, August 4, 1961.

294. "I can't understand how Mr. Allen": *Ibid.*

294. Ivan Jr. assumed they came from Maddox supporters: Ivan Allen, Jr., interview.

294. "They were the meanest people": *Ibid.*

294. stuffing envelopes and answering telephones: Interview with H. Inman Allen.

294. Allens hired two police detectives: Interview with George Royal.

295. Ivan Jr. would win about 40 percent: Interview with Joe Heyman.

295. "Mr. Allen will keep us in the main stream": *Atlanta Journal*, August 18, 1961.

295. "We knew what Ivan's record was": Interview with Donald Hollowell.

295. "Some of these votes and influence": *Atlanta Daily World*, September 9, 1961.

295. "raving candidate who recognizes": *Ibid.*

296. "for his comprehensive grasp": *Ibid.*, September 10, 1961.

296. "They want Ivan to run for mayor": Interview with Laura Maddox Smith.

296. "I'll be glad to go with you": Ivan Allen, Jr., interview. Also Ivan Allen, Jr., transcript for Hemphill, 1971. The scene from the rally is drawn from these sources as well as from interviews with Louise Allen and Raleigh Bryans.

297. She rose and greeted him warmly: Interview with Raleigh Bryans.

297. "If Ivan didn't already have every": *Ibid.*

297. "I could have stayed there": *Atlanta Constitution*, September 14, 1961.

297. "Got any money left over?": Allen with Hemphill, *Mayor*, p. 60.

298. he made small bets: Ivan Allen, Jr., interview.

298. "It is customary, if not trite": *Atlanta Journal*, September 20, 1961.

298. "we will provide for the Negro": *Atlanta Daily World*, September 20, 1961.

298. "I am absolutely opposed to integration": *Atlanta Journal*, September 21, 1961.

298. "This talk is dangerous": *Atlanta Daily World*, September 20, 1961.

298. "a turncoat segregationist": *Atlanta Journal*, September 20, 1961.

298. "I don't say that Ivan Allen": *Ibid.*, September 21, 1961.

299. "The white people of Atlanta.": *Ibid.*

299. "This is what Atlanta can expect": *Ibid.*

299. "I shouldn't be telling": Cecil Alexander interview.

299. "You have done more harm": *Atlanta Constitution*, September 22, 1961.

299. "He's not worried": WSB Television Collection, University of Georgia, Instructional Resources Center, Reel 1565.

299. "It is to be remembered": *Augusta* (Ga.) *Herald*, September 20, 1961.

300. "Lookee! Lookee!": *New Yorker*, December 31, 1973, p. 32.

300. "This victory shows Atlanta": *Atlanta Constitution*, September 23, 1961.

300. "Daddy, where are you?": *Atlanta Journal*, September 23, 1961.

301. "Buy property on Peachtree Street": Interview with Sam Massell.

301. Ivan Jr. stood in the corner of a field: Ivan Allen, Jr., interview.

301. "where the deer sleep": *Wall Street Journal*, January 9, 1981.

301. sing spirituals to Woodruff and his guests: Frederick Allen, *Secret Formula: How Brilliant Marketing and Relentless Salesmanship Made Coca-Cola the Best-Known Product in the World* (New York: HarperBusiness, 1994), pp. 281–82.

301. "Mornin', suh.": *Ibid.*, p. 279. Also: Interview with James Sibley.

301. "You had to be pretty good": *Wall Street Journal*, January 9, 1981.

302. "I killed the limit": Ivan Allen, Jr., interview.


CHAPTER 18

303. "a new generation of Americans": *Atlanta Journal*, January 21, 1961.

303. "We are a legend that has become real": Inaugural Address by Mayor Ivan Allen, Jr., January 2, 1962. Personal files of Ivan Allen, Jr.

303. ordered the removal of all signs: Ivan Allen, Jr., with Paul Hemphill, *Mayor: Notes on the Sixties* (New York: Simon & Schuster, 1971), p. 84.

304. "By the time I got into": Interview with Ivan Allen, Jr.

304. purchased $8.55 cents worth: Records of First Congregational Church of Atlanta, Ga., 1924. Georgia Department of Archives and History, Atlanta, Ga., Microfilm Drawer 188, Box 65, covering the following years: 1867–82, 1912–23 and 1924–30.

304. "The crispest gentleman": Interview with Morris Abram.

304. written the names of preferred candidates: Letter from Helen Bullard to Be Haas, November 15, 1967. Helen Bullard Papers, Emory University, Robert W. Woodruff Library, Department of Special Collections, Box 18. In the letter, Bullard describes what prompted her to become a political strategist.

304. "Helen Bullard is the only person": *Ibid.* Bullard cited Allen's quote in this letter.

305. "It might be a good idea": Confidential memorandum from Helen Bullard to Mayor-elect Ivan Allen, Jr., November 16, 1961. Records of the Mayoral Administration of Ivan Allen, Jr., City of Atlanta, Records Management Division, 90-TR-Box 1.

305. "I think we might gently": *Ibid.*, January 9, 1962.

305. "You need to go": Ivan Allen, Jr., interview.

305. to the Caribbean and Great Britain: Interview with Mattiwilda Dobbs Janzon.

305. There to greet her was Sam Massell: *Atlanta Daily World*, January 31, 1962.

306. "She won the hearts": *Atlanta Constitution*, February 1, 1962.

306. *"Daddy would have been so proud"*: Mattiwilda Dobbs Janzon interview.

306. "It was a very moving experience for me.": *Ibid.*

306. "You have brought great honor": *Atlanta Constitution*, February 1, 1962.

306. "My heart is so full": *Atlanta Journal*, February 2, 1962.


CHAPTER 19

307. increasing by thirty thousand a year: *Time*, August 17, 1962, p. 20.

307. "The gracious belle": *Ibid.*

307. attempts to raise cattle: Interview with Ivan Allen, Jr.

307. Louise called from Atlanta: *Ibid.*

307. *"What if Lester Maddox"*: Ivan Allen, Jr., with Paul Hemphill, *Mayor: Notes on the Sixties* (New York: Simon & Schuster, 1971), p. 77.

308. "I know them all": *Atlanta Constitution*, June 5, 1962.

308. run off the eleven-thousand-foot runway: *Ibid.*

308. He saw a pastel dress: Allen with Hemphill, *Mayor*, p. 78.

308. "I rode my Indian bicycle": Ivan Allen, Jr., interview.

308. "He had absolute and complete": Interview with Aubrey Morris.

308. "Life is eternal": Interview with Eugene Patterson.

308. "Have just read with grief and horror": Telegram from Vivien Leigh to Mayor Ivan Allen, Jr., June 1962. Records of the Mayoral Administration of Ivan Allen, Jr., City of Atlanta, Records Management Division, Box 90-TR-321.

308. "It is indeed a rarity": Letter from Roby Robinson III to Mayor Ivan Allen, Jr., June 1962. *Ibid.*

308. "I'm so happy!": Eugene Patterson interview.

309. Hartsfield was placed on retainer: Harold H. Martin, *William Berry Hartsfield: Mayor of*

*Atlanta* (Athens, Ga.: University of Georgia Press, 1978), pp. 163–64. According to Martin, Woodruff also put other less-affluent friends into these stock syndicates. When the stock price rose, Woodruff sold it and divided the profits among Hartsfield and the others. Woodruff took back only his initial investment, to be reinvested.

309. "ROAD CLOSED.": *Atlanta Constitution*, December 19, 1962.
309. "It was in Berlin": Inaugural address of Mayor Ivan Allen, Jr., January 2, 1962. Private papers of Ivan Allen, Jr.
309. "We must let Mayor Allen know": *Atlanta Constitution*, December 19, 1962.
309. "These are the darkest days": *Ibid.*
309. The median income of a black family: Report of the National Advisory Commission on Civil Disorders (New York: Bantam, 1968), pp. 52–53.
310. realtors pointed at homes: *Atlanta Constitution*, January 13, 1963.
310. A decade earlier, Hartsfield had faced: *Ibid.*, January 8, 1963.
310. "I saw it as a happy compromise": Allen with Hemphill, *Mayor*, pp. 71–72.
311. "This action will focus the eyes": Letter from Ralph Moore to Mayor Ivan Allen, Jr., December 22, 1962. Records of the Mayoral Administration of Ivan Allen, Jr., City of Atlanta, Records Management Division, Box-TR-321.
311. "an artificial, unnatural condition": *Ibid.*
311. "A charitable view": *Atlanta Constitution*, December 22, 1962.
311. "The mayor, who is quite properly": *Ibid.*, December 29, 1962.
311. thrown into a nearby creek: *Atlanta Journal*, February 25, 1963.
311. "The concept of political equality": *New York Times*, March 19, 1963.
312. gave the city until March 4: *Atlanta Daily World*, *Atlanta Constitution* and *Atlanta Journal*, March 2–3, 1963.
312. "The real problem is that of an inadequacy": *Atlanta Daily World*, March 3, 1963.
312. thirty white residents of Utoy–Peyton Forest: *Atlanta Constitution*, March 27, 1963.
312. *"We are in the deepest depths"*: Telegram from Jack Adair and Lee Talley to Mayor Ivan Allen, Jr., March 10, 1963. Robert W. Woodruff Papers, Emory University, Robert W. Woodruff Library, Department of Special Collections, Document Case 8, Folder 8, "Ivan Allen, Jr., Correspondence, 1959–64."
312. "for a sober assessment": *New York Times*, March 1, 1963.
312. "the basic reason is because": *Ibid.*
313. "maintain the city's healthy climate": *Atlanta Journal*, May 30, 1963.
313. "The principal motivation": Allen with Hemphill, *Mayor*, pp. 106–7.
313. Atlanta was nineteenth, Birmingham forty-eighth: 1960 U.S. Census.
314. "Mrs. Herndon, do you have a problem?": Allen with Hemphill, *Mayor*, pp. 85–87. Also: Ivan Allen, Jr., interview.
314. "You're a bunch of damned fools": *Ibid.*
315. "We are confronted primarily": *New York Times*, June 12, 1963.
315. "Should Eugene Talmadge be reelected": Morris. B. Abram, *The Day Is Short: An Autobiography* (New York: Harcourt Brace Jovanovich, 1982), pp. 51–52.
316. "I don't know a single important official": Allen with Hemphill, *Mayor*, pp. 104–6. Also: Interviews with Morris Abram and Ivan Allen, Jr.
316. "You know the dilemma I'm in": *Ibid.*
317. "You're right, your testimony alone": *Ibid.*
317. "I was reluctant to go": Ivan Allen, Jr., interview.
317. named Margaret Mitchell godmother: Interview with Annesley Howland; she is the late Bill Howland's daughter.
317. "the right of a chimpanzee to vote": Letter from Robert W. Woodruff to Ralph Hayes, November 22, 1960. John Sibley Papers, Emory University, Robert W. Woodruff Library, Department of Special Collections, Box 1.
318. "I know it's going to be an unpopular": Allen with Hemphill, *Mayor*, p. 108.
318. a public relations agency to keep his name *out*: *Wall Street Journal*, January 9, 1981.
318. The Boss always enjoyed a good dirty joke: Ivan Allen, Jr., interview.
318. "Mr. Woodruff always stood with me": *Ibid.*
318. "He avoids dreary characters": *Atlanta Journal*, March 8, 1985.
318. "[Woodruff] liked the kind of fellow": Interview with Joseph Jones.
318. "As far as I was concerned": Ivan Allen, Jr., interview.
318. "You'll have a hard time living": Allen with Hemphill, *Mayor*, p. 109.

319. "This is the kind of leadership": Interview with Leroy Johnson. Also: Interviews with Jesse Hill and Ivan Allen, Jr.
319. "Are you sure you're going": Interview with Margaret Shannon.
319. "I figured he was playing domestic politics": Interview with Herman Talmadge.
320. "a soft, almost apologetic Southern tone": Alistair Cooke in unspecified newspaper, July 28, 1963. Records of the Mayoral Administration of Ivan Allen, Jr., City of Atlanta, Records Management Division, Box 90-TR-321.
320. "It is true that Atlanta has achieved": Testimony of Mayor Ivan Allen, Jr., of Atlanta, July 26, 1963. *Hearings Before the Committee on Commerce, United States Senate, Eighty-Eighth Congress on S. 1732* (Washington, D.C.: U.S. Government Printing Office, 1963), pp. 861–83. All of Allen's testimony is drawn from this source.
320. "To liberty and enfranchisement": Raymond B. Nixon, *Henry W. Grady: Spokesman of the New South* (New York: Alfred A. Knopf, 1943), pp. 340–50. Grady's entire address, "The New South," delivered to the New England Society of New York in December 1886, is printed in the appendix.
321. "Let me say that I am humbled": Testimony of Mayor Ivan Allen, Jr., of Atlanta, July 26, 1963. *Hearings Before the Committee on Commerce, United States Senate*, p. 867.
321. "I couldn't cope with him legally": Ivan Allen, Jr., interview.
321. "I observe from what you say": *Hearings Before the Committee on Commerce, United States Senate*, pp. 867–77.
322. "One thing about it was": Ivan Allen, Jr., interview.
322. "We got under his skin pretty bad": *Ibid.*
323. "Mr. Patterson, I want you to know": Eugene Patterson interview.
323. a brass band and a thousand people: Nixon, *Henry W. Grady*, p. 248.
323. "I think you better come down here": Interview with Be Haas.
323. "We are grateful, indeed": *Rome* (Ga.) *News-Tribune*, July 31, 1963.
323. "I have often wondered how Benedict Arnold": Postcard sent anonymously to Mayor Ivan Allen, Jr., July 1963. Records of the Mayoral Administration of Ivan Allen, Jr., City of Atlanta, Records Management Division, Box 90-TR-321.
323. "Dear Mr. Allen": *Ibid.*
323. "How much Nigger blood": *Ibid.*
323. "On rare occasions the oratorical fog": *New York Times*, July 28, 1963.
323. "You made a number of very effective points": Letter from President John F. Kennedy to Mayor Ivan Allen, Jr., of Atlanta, July 26, 1963. Personal papers of Ivan Allen, Jr.
324. "put the cork in the bottle": *Atlanta Constitution*, July 31, 1963.
324. "We praise the mayor's presentation": *Atlanta Constitution*, July 27, 1963.
324. "Mayor Allen has ignored the myths": *Atlanta Daily World*, July 28, 1963.
324. "Two years from now things": Letter from Ralph McGill to Ivan Allen, Jr., July 30, 1963. Records of the Mayoral Administration of Ivan Allen, Jr., City of Atlanta, Records Management Division, Box 90-TR-321.
324. "In the scheme of time": Letter from Helen Bullard to Ivan Allen, Jr., July 29, 1963. *Ibid.*
324. "progressive moderate": Memo from secretary Ann Moses to Ivan Allen, Jr., *Ibid.* Though undated, Moses wrote this memo soon after Allen's testimony in Washington on July 26, 1963, warning, "The national press has a good horse in you and might just try to ride you to death." She feared the press would try to make the mayor appear out of step with his city and region.
324. "That was the end of the rope": Ivan Allen, Jr., interview.

CHAPTER 20

325. "What are you so nervous about?": Interview with Ivan Allen, Jr.
325. employees were not to ride: Interview with Marie Dodd.
326. "Bob, you look so good.": Ivan Allen, Jr., interview.
326. Virginia ham, broccoli: Mary A. Jordan Catering Service date book, March 1963, including assorted menus. Personal papers of Windsor Jordan.
326. They played gin rummy: Marie Dodd interview.
326. "This is for your boys": Interview with George Royal.
326. "Daddy, are you having": Ivan Allen, Jr., interview.
327. "Sometimes I think people": Interview with Louise Allen.

327. "I was born with money": *Atlanta Constitution,* January 6, 1969.
327. "much to my chagrin": Ivan Allen, Jr., interview.
328. the company owned more than eleven thousand shares: *Ivan Allen Company v. United States.* Decision rendered by the United States Supreme Court on June 26, 1975. The Internal Revenue Service determined that securities classed as a corporation's earnings must be figured at net liquidation value rather than as costs, for tax purposes. The court ruled that in 1965 and 1966 the Ivan Allen Company permitted its earnings and profits to exceed its business needs, in part to avoid paying taxes, and ordered the company to pay $77,383.98 in taxes for 1965 and $73,131.87 for 1966. The company paid the taxes, then filed a claim for a refund in U.S. District Court for the Northern District of Georgia. At issue, according to documents, was Xerox Corp. stock. In June 1965 the Ivan Allen Company owned 11,140 shares of Xerox common stock with a fair market value of $1,573,525 and $30,600 in Xerox convertible debentures. In a 6–3 ruling, the Supreme Court upheld the lower court ruling with Justice Blackmun writing the majority opinion and Justice Powell filing the dissenting opinion. See also: *Atlanta Constitution,* June 27, 1975.
328. But months later a taxi pulled: Ivan Allen, Jr., interview.
328. "Like Mammy": Interview with Beaumont Allen.
328. "Look, I've got this cook": Ivan Allen, Jr., interview.
328. "Are you all right": *Ibid.*
329. The car hit the edge: *Ibid.*
329. "Mr. Allen, when did you": *Ibid.*
329. carried her purse around the house: Marie Dodd interview.
329. "Mrs. Allen did not approve": *Ibid.*
329. added a codicil that awarded $1,000: Last Will and Testament of Ivan Earnest Allen, including codicils, May 25, 1953. Codicils dated: November 11, 1959, February 24, 1964, and January 5, 1965. Fulton County Probate Court Records, Fulton County Courthouse, Atlanta, Ga.
329. *"Mare-ee, pssst! Come here":* Marie Dodd interview.
330. "People cannot devote themselves": *Life,* November 7, 1960, pp. 123–24.
330. "Our Mayor a-go-go": Reese Cleghorn, "Allen of Atlanta Collides with Black Power and White Racism," *New York Times Sunday Magazine,* October 16, 1966.
330. "The aura of power was just palpable": Interview with Anne Rivers Siddons.
330. Atlanta's 2 percent unemployment rate: Inaugural Address of Mayor Ivan Allen, Jr., January 6, 1964. Private papers of Ivan Allen, Jr.
330. The city's new airport terminal: Betsy Braden and Paul Hagan, *A Dream Takes Flight: Hartsfield Atlanta International Airport and Aviation in Atlanta* (Athens, Ga.: University of Georgia Press, 1989), pp. 137–46.
330. "We were going to absolutely solve": Interview with Larry Gellerstedt, Jr.
331. On most mornings, Ivan Jr. dropped: Beaumont Allen interview.
331. "I hate dirt": Ivan Allen, Jr., interview.
331. "One, I won't make speeches.": Ivan Allen, Jr., with Paul Hemphill, *Mayor: Notes on the Sixties* (New York: Simon & Schuster, 1971), p. 68.
331. "Please stay out.": *Atlanta Journal,* January 26, 1964.
331. *"The old K-K, she ain't what":* *Ibid.*
332. "I was never a segregationist": *Ibid.,* January 27, 1964.
332. "Man, that sure does look good.": *Ibid.*
332. "Atlanta will accept no ultimatums": *Time,* February 7, 1964.
332. "There is widespread fear": *U.S. News & World Report,* February 10, 1964.
332. "a capital letter day": Letter from Ivan Allen, Jr., to Robert W. Woodruff, February 18, 1964. Robert W. Woodruff Papers, Emory University, Robert W. Woodruff Library, Department of Special Collections, Document Case 8, Folder 8, "Ivan Allen, Jr., Correspondence, 1959–64."
332. "[Charles] would even go down to the creek": Beaumont Allen interview.
332. "I would like to talk": Ivan Allen, Jr., letter to Robert W. Woodruff, February 18, 1964. RWW Papers, EU, Document Case 8, Folder 8, "Ivan Allen, Jr., Correspondence, 1959–64."
333. "there is no alternative": *Atlanta Constitution,* July 3, 1964.
333. "Get out of here": This scene is drawn from reports in *Atlanta Journal* and *Atlanta Constitution,* July 3–4, 1964.
333. "Such conduct would create": *Atlanta Constitution,* July 8, 1964.
333. "I'm a preacher and we like chicken": *Ibid.*
334. "I'm not going to integrate": *Ibid.,* July 23, 1964.

335. "They're scraping the bottom": *Ibid.*, October 15, 1964.
335. "How can you win the Peace Prize": *Ibid.*
335. "He has displayed remarkable leadership": *Atlanta Journal,* October 14, 1964.
335. "The South one day will be grateful": *Atlanta Constitution,* October 16, 1964.
336. waged an intensive operation to discredit him: David J. Garrow, *Bearing the Cross: Martin Luther King, Jr., and the Southern Christian Leadership Conference* (New York: William Morrow, 1986), pp. 362–80. Garrow writes in great detail of the FBI's wiretaps and of the destructive effects on King.
336. "abiding faith in America": *New York Times,* December 11, 1964.
336. His family and close associates knew: Garrow, *Bearing the Cross,* pp. 365–66.
336. "King, like all frauds your end": *Ibid.,* pp. 372–73.
336. An agent told Gene Patterson that King engaged: Howell Raines, *My Soul Is Rested: Movement Days in the Deep South Remembered* (New York: G. P. Putnam's Sons, 1977), pp. 368–69.
336. "Jenkins told me there wasn't anything": Ivan Allen, Jr., interview.
336. "We feel that the city must move": Ivan Allen, Jr., transcript for Paul Hemphill, 1971.
337. "I have listened to your reasons": Allen with Hemphill, *Mayor,* p. 97.
337. "I do not understand": Letter from Archbishop Paul J. Hallinan to Rabbi Jacob Rothschild, February 5, 1965. Rabbi Jacob Rothschild Papers, Emory University, Robert W. Woodruff Library, Department of Special Collections, Box 6, Folder 6.
337. "high-level bank executive": *New York Times,* December 29, 1964.
337. "I was not the one": Raines, *My Soul Is Rested.* This Mills Lane quote is related by Helen Bullard, p. 413.
337. "hate to see my town held up": *Atlanta Constitution,* December 29, 1964.
337. "I don't agree with everything": Letter from Ralph McGill to Granger Hansell, January 6, 1965. Ralph McGill Papers, Emory University, Robert W. Woodruff Library, Department of Special Collections, Box 14, Folder 6.
338. "I have seen [King] only three times": Letter from Ralph McGill to Mrs. Horace Wright of Atlanta, January 31, 1965. *Ibid.*
338. a $430 Steuben bowl: Letter from James A. Thurston of Steuben Glass Co. in New York to Janice Rothschild, January 12, 1965. Jacob Rothschild Papers, Emory University, Box 6, Folder 6. See also: Raines, *My Soul Is Rested,* pp. 411–12.
338. "At one point Martin was so agitated": Interview with Coretta Scott King.
338. Chief Jenkins had told Daddy King: Garrow, *Bearing the Cross,* pp. 381–82.
338. "Peace with violence!": *Atlanta Constitution,* January 28, 1965.
338. "Everybody, I think, was nervous": Interview with Sam Massell.
338. "It was one of those occasions": Ivan Allen, Jr., transcript for Paul Hemphill, 1971.
339. "Don't worry about that": Allen with Hemphill, *Mayor,* p. 98.
339. "Through the years, as history": *Atlanta Constitution,* January 28, 1965.
339. "in the white South millions": *Ibid.* See also: *Time,* February 5, 1965, p. 24.
339. "the first thing Atlanta": Raines, *My Soul Is Rested,* p. 415.
339. "It was a testimonial not only": Letter from the Rev. Martin Luther King, Jr., to Rabbi Jacob Rothschild, March 8, 1965. Jacob Rothschild Papers, Emory University, Box 6, Folder 7.
339. "was remarkable even for Atlanta": *Time,* February 5, 1965, p. 24.
340. "true Time style": Letter from Archbishop Paul J. Hallinan to Rabbi Jacob Rothschild, February 5, 1965. Jacob Rothschild Papers, EU, Box 6, Folder 6.
340. The FBI preceded him: Garrow, *Bearing the Cross,* p. 382.
340. "This is a right sound editorial": Letter from Mayor Ivan Allen, Jr., to Robert W. Woodruff, February 3, 1965. RWW Papers, EU, Document Case 8, Folder 9, "Ivan Allen, Jr., Correspondence, 1965–72."
340. Department store sales rose by 11 percent: Inaugural address by Mayor Ivan Allen, Jr., January 4, 1965. Personal papers of Ivan Allen, Jr.
340. "We continue toward our destiny": *Ibid.*
340. creation of Economic Opportunity Atlanta: Clarence N. Stone, *Regime Politics: Governing Atlanta, 1946–1988* (Lawrence, Kansas: University Press of Kansas, 1989), p. 67.
341. "We built a stadium on ground": *Atlanta Constitution,* January 6, 1969. This quote was cited often through the years.
341. "stadium standing vacant will probably": Letter from Helen Bullard to a friend, November 20, 1964. Hellen Bullard Papers, Emory University, Robert W. Woodruff Library, Department of Special Collections, Box 1, Folder 2.

341. "We do not have large areas of poverty": *Atlanta Constitution,* September 3, 1965.
341. "It was as though I was carrying a Bible": Allen with Hemphill, *Mayor,* pp. 133–34. Also: Ivan Allen, Jr., interview.
341. "There aren't many people": *Ibid.*
341. Ivan Jr. visited the Senator: *Atlanta Constitution,* September 9, 1965.
342. the mayor won only 51 percent: *New York Times,* October 16, 1966.
342. "Dear Ivan Baby": *Atlanta Constitution,* September 9, 1965.
342. He received feelers for federal positions: Ivan Allen, Jr., interview. See also: *Atlanta Constitution,* January 6, 1969.
342. a pamphlet entitled, "I Cannot Take Kennedy": *Time,* September 2, 1966.
342. "Yorty was the sorriest white": Ivan Allen, Jr., interview.
342. "You are shortchanging a few": *Time,* September 2, 1966.
342. "The mayor of Los Angeles I would like": *Ibid.*
343. "I thought he was gonna blow": Interview with Dan Sweat.
343. "Most southern cities": Ivan Allen, Jr., interview.
344. The shelf was covered with dust: Interview with Aubrey Morris.
344. "How much is this thing": Dan Sweat interview.
345. words that froze this moment: Beaumont Allen interview.
345. "If trouble breaks out": Interview with Louise Allen.
345. Riots broke out in black ghettos: Fred R. Harris and Roger W. Wilkins, editors, *Quiet Riots: Race and Poverty in the United States* (New York: Pantheon, 1988), pp. 5–7.
345. "Well, tell him": Ivan Allen, Jr., interview.
345. Royal rushed into the mayor's office: George Royal interview.
346. a SNCC soundtruck circulated: *Atlanta Constitution, Atlanta Journal* and *Atlanta Daily World,* September 7, 1966. See also: *New York Times,* October 16, 1966.
346. "*What's up?*": Interview with Chet Fuller. Then a teenager, Fuller was at the Summerhill riot.
346. "tear the place up": *Atlanta Constitution,* September 7, 1966.
346. pinpointed Summerhill as the neighborhood: Stone, *Regime Politics,* p. 71.
346. crowded into 354 acres: Allen with Hemphill, *Mayor,* pp. 179–80.
346. "My God, Mr. Mayor, a riot!": George Royal and Ivan Allen, Jr., interviews.
347. "A white man put this in my belly.": Ivan Allen, Jr., interview.
347. "Give me a cigarette": Allen with Hemphill, *Mayor,* p. 188.
348. "Why are there only white people": *Atlanta Constitution,* September 7, 1966.
348. "We ain't going to no goddamned": Allen with Hemphill, *Mayor,* p. 188.
348. "You could hear his voice cracking": Chet Fuller interview.
348. "Atlanta is a Cracker town.": *Atlanta Journal,* September 7, 1966.
348. Redding, holding the mayor's belt: Interview with Morris Redding.
348. "I couldn't believe some white man": Interview with Hosea Williams.
348. "Ivan Allen was a chump, man.": Interview with Jamil Abdullah al Amin (né H. Rap Brown).
349. "If I only had my strength": *Atlanta Constitution,* September 7, 1966.
349. "For God sake's, mayor": Allen with Hemphill, *Mayor,* p. 191.
349. "If it had broken out": Ivan Allen, Jr., interview.
349. saw the mayor wore shin guards: Dan Sweat interview.
350. "I saw plenty of brutality": *Atlanta Journal,* September 7, 1966.
350. "If there is a hero on the domestic": *New York Times,* October 16, 1966.
350. "No other mayor of any city": *Atlanta Constitution,* September 8, 1966.
350. "The late Mr. Jack Spalding often": Letter from John Sibley to Mayor Ivan Allen, Jr., September 9, 1966. Records of the Mayoral Administration of Ivan Allen, Jr., City of Atlanta, Records Management Division, Series 89-TR-266, Box 7.
350. "You've given dinners": Letter from Atlantan to Mayor Ivan Allen, Jr.
350. "Dear Ivan: The next time you get": *Ibid.*
350. build sixteen thousand low- and moderate-income housing units: Stone, *Regime Politics,* p. 71.
350. "ashamed to be a Georgian": David J. Garrow, *Bearing the Cross: Martin Luther King, Jr., and the Southern Christian Leadership Conference* (New York: William Morrow, 1986), p. 532.
351. "It is deplorable that the combined": *Atlanta Constitution,* September 30, 1966.

CHAPTER 21

352. "First Kennedy": Ivan Allen, Jr., with Paul Hemphill, *Mayor: Notes on the Sixties* (New York: Simon & Schuster, 1971), pp. 195–96. Also: Interview with Ivan Allen, Jr.

352. "Coretta, Doc just got shot.": Coretta Scott King, *My Life with Martin Luther King, Jr.* (New York: Holt, Rinehart and Winston, 1969), p. 318.

352. "I'm coming over myself": *Ibid.,* p. 319.

352. "What are you going to do?": Interview with Louise Allen. See also: Allen with Hemphill, *Mayor,* pp. 196–97.

352. "tall ship on a fine day": *Atlanta Journal-Constitution,* April 18, 1993.

353. "A lot of times a woman can do better": Louise Allen interview.

353. "But adding to the honor": Allen with Hemphill, *Mayor,* p. 194.

353. "Central Time, Eastern Standard Time": Ivan Allen, Jr., interview. Also: Ivan Allen, Jr., transcript for Paul Hemphill, 1971.

353. "To my good friend, Ivan Allen, Jr.": Allen with Hemphill, *Mayor,* p. 194.

354. The convoy began for the airport: Interviews with Billye Williams Aaron, Louise Allen, George Royal and Ivan Allen, Jr.

354. He knew the media monitored: Ivan Allen, Jr., interview.

354. record 142 murders had been committed the previous year: Harold H. Martin, *Atlanta and Environs: A Chronicle of Its People and Events. Vol. 3. Years of Change and Challenge, 1940–1976* (Athens, Ga.: University of Georgia Press, 1987), p. 537.

354. Twenty-six were left dead on the streets of Newark: William Manchester, *The Glory and the Dream* (New York: Little, Brown, 1974), pp. 1078–81.

354. a black policeman had shot and wounded: *Atlanta Journal* and *Atlanta Constitution,* June 19, 1967.

354. Congress no longer could delay funding to cities: *Atlanta Constitution,* July 11, 1967.

354. Carmichael was jeopardizing the civil rights movement: *Ibid.*

354. "What white Americans have never": *Report of the National Advisory Commission on Civil Disorders* (New York: Bantam, March 1968), p. 2.

354. "Morris, for God's sake": Ivan Allen, Jr., interview.

354. Suddenly a page for Coretta King sounded: Interview with Coretta Scott King.

354. "Come on!": Coretta King, *My Life with Martin Luther King, Jr.,* pp. 318–19.

355. "I've been asked to inform you": Ivan Allen, Jr., interview.

355. "Mayor Allen, I have been instructed": Allen with Hemphill, *Mayor,* p. 200.

355. "Mrs. King, I have to inform you": *Ibid.*

355. Louise instinctively reached for a paper towel: Coretta Scott King interview.

355. then gave her the silk handkerchief: *Ibid.*

355. "Mrs. King, is it your wish": Coretta King, *My Life with Martin Luther King, Jr.,* pp. 320–21.

355. "Mommy, when is Daddy coming home?": *Ibid.,* p. 321.

355. "I ask every citizen to reject": *Atlanta Constitution,* April 5, 1968.

356. He placed all City of Atlanta policemen: Ivan Allen, Jr., interview.

356. "What does it look like down there?": Allen with Hemphill, *Mayor,* p. 203.

356. He had been trying to get through: Interview with Joseph W. Jones.

356. "I'm sorry that I have to be": Charles Elliot, *"Mr. Anonymous.": Robert W. Woodruff of Coca-Cola* (Atlanta: Cherokee Publishing Company, 1982), p. 189.

356. "I want to give you a little advice": Ivan Allen, Jr., interview.

356. "You've got to start looking ahead": Allen with Hemphill, *Mayor,* pp. 204–5.

357. "At the moment the trigger man fired": *Atlanta Constitution,* April 5, 1968.

357. "They are going to march": Interview with Eugene Patterson.

357. the mayor met with the six presidents: *Atlanta Journal,* April 5, 1968.

357. "I'm going down there.": Ivan Allen, Jr., interview.

357. "Ivan was just a gutsy little guy": Eugene Patterson interview.

357. "This is a black people's march.": *Atlanta Journal,* April 5, 1968.

357. "I'm just as sorry as you": Eugene Patterson interview.

358. a reporter from the Swedish television newsagency: Interview with Mattiwilda Dobbs.

358. The Peace Corps in Bombay: *Ibid.*

358. June, and her friend Juanita Sellers Stone: Interview with June Dobbs Butts.

358. sew veils on the black hats: *Ibid.*

358. "In Summerhill, Mechanicsville and Pittsburg": Allen with Hemphill, *Mayor,* pp. 209–10.

359. He ordered liquor stores: *Atlanta Journal,* April 8, 1968.
359. skirts down to the knees for women: *Atlanta Constitution,* June 2, 1967.
359. secured raises for Georgia's teachers: *Atlanta Journal,* December 4, 1967.
359. He rejected a request: *Atlanta Journal,* April 8, 1968.
359. "We were told that there were": Interview with Lester Maddox.
359. "If they do storm the Capitol": *Ibid.*
359. "There were three television crews": Ivan Allen, Jr., transcript for Paul Hemphill, 1971.
359. "I didn't think we oughta use our flag": Lester Maddox interview.
360. "It struck us as an affair of state": June Dobbs Butts interview.
360. crazed black woman from Georgia: David J. Garrow, *Bearing the Cross: Martin Luther King, Jr., and the Southern Christian Leadership Conference* (New York: William Morrow, 1986), pp. 109–11.
360. "Have you ever been afraid": June Dobbs Butts interview.
360. "I loved him.": *Ibid.*
360. "You better let him in!": *New York Times,* April 10, 1968. See also: Same-day coverage in *Atlanta Constitution* and *Atlanta Journal.*
360. football star Jim Brown and his girlfriend: June Dobbs Butts interview.
361. Lenox Square Mall in Buckhead was filled: *New York Times,* April 10, 1968.
361. "Coretta, she's a cool lady": Louise Allen interview.
361. "one of the darkest hours of mankind": *Atlanta Journal,* April 9, 1968.
361. "If any of you are around": *New York Times,* April 10, 1968.
361. "Play what you know": June Dobbs Butts interview.
362. About 10 percent of the marchers were white.: *New York Times,* April 10, 1968.
362. "It was one of the strangest corteges": *Ibid.*
362. marched with ten members: Interview with Beaumont Allen.
362. "that I was on the side": Allen with Hemphill, *Mayor,* p. 216.
362. "I saw George Romney and Bobby Kennedy": Lester Maddox interview.
362. "I was just reflecting on birth to death." Maynard Jackson, Jr., interview.
362. "Jesus died at 33": *New York Times,* April 10, 1968.
363. "really miraculous": *Atlanta Journal,* April 10, 1968.
363. "There was nothing to tarnish the good name": *Ibid.*
363. 41 percent of whites in the city: *Atlanta Constitution,* March 31, 1969.
363. "I want you to know": *Ibid.*
363. "This cemetery is too small": Ralph David Abernathy, *And the Walls Came Tumbling Down* (New York: Harper & Row, 1989), p. 464.
363. June saw her father's grave: June Dobbs Butts interview.
363. "M.L. was a person of transcendence": *Ibid.*

## CHAPTER 22

364. Maynard Jackson was home alone: Interview with Maynard Jackson, Jr.
364. "So my thanks to all of you": *New York Times,* June 6, 1968.
364. "to keep a people in virtual bondage": Maynard Jackson, Jr., interview.
365. agreed that she would take a maternity leave: Interview with Bunnie Jackson-Ransom.
365. "it was almost like a sign": Maynard Jackson, Jr., interview.
365. "as vicious a racist as there is": *Atlanta Constitution,* August 24, 1970.
365. "Herman Talmadge?": Maynard Jackson, Jr., interview.
365. Rich's saleswoman as "two Indians": Bunnie Jackson-Ransom interview.
365. She was a free spirit: Interviews with Meredith Ogden Conklin and Bunnie Jackson-Ransom. Conklin is the daughter of the late Leila Ogden.
366. saw tears streaking his cheek: Maynard Jackson, Jr., interview. Sullivan, from Fort Valley, Ga., was a soft-spoken man who had worked as butler and chauffeur for the Ogden family for nearly fifteen years. He wore a tie and coat inside the home, according to Conklin and Bessie Sullivan, Albert's widow.
366. "If only he had seen this now": Interviews with Bessie Sullivan and Maynard Jackson, Jr. Albert Sullivan related this exchange to his wife.
366. *"Hello, I'm Maynard Jackson, interviewing":* Maynard Jackson, Jr., interview.
367. "IS RALPH FRAY-ZUH HE-UH?": Bunnie Jackson-Ransom interview.

367. she had bathed in a tin tub: *Ibid.*
367. "not as active as I wanted": Maynard Jackson, Jr., interview.
368. "Maynard was selling encyclopedias": Interview with Lonnie C. King.
368. "I was hobbling around": Bunnie Jackson-Ransom interview.
368. "Maynard was a part of that group": *Ibid.*
368. "I almost think Maynard read things": *Ibid.*
369. "I could have had a duck.": Maynard Jackson, Jr., and Bunnie Jackson-Ransom interviews.
369. "Talmadge was the guy you'd see": Bunnie Jackson-Ransom interview.
369. "I saw him on the street": Interview with Chet Fuller.
369. "We all knew what that meant": *New York Times*, August 4, 1968.
370. "Hank Henderson, I was in college": Interview with Herman Talmadge.
370. swelled to nearly 350,000: *New York Times*, August 4, 1968.
370. "I knew that no black at that time": Herman Talmadge interview.
370. "You've messed everything up!": Maynard Jackson, Jr., interview.
370. "[There was] nothing he could mess up": Interview with Leroy Johnson.
371. "I got betrayed": Maynard Jackson, Jr., interview.
371. "What in the world are you running": Interview with Eugene Patterson.
371. Fowler had been appointed: *Atlanta Constitution*, June 5, 1968.
371. "Do you think they'll let me": Interview with Wyche Fowler.
372. used Woodruff's seats at the Kentucky Derby: Letters from Louise and Ivan Allen, Jr., to Robert W. Woodruff, May 6, 1968. Robert W. Woodruff Papers, Emory University, Robert W. Woodruff Library, Department of Special Collections, Document Case 8, Folder 9, "Ivan Allen, Jr., Correspondence, 1965–72."
372. took the Coca-Cola jet to Robert Kennedy's: Letter from Ivan Allen, Jr., to Robert W. Woodruff, June 12, 1968. *Ibid.*
372. noted Maynard Jackson's boyish good looks: Interview with Ivan Allen, Jr.
372. "How does it feel": *Atlanta Journal*, July 10, 1968.
372. "I could say it's a ball": *Ibid.*
373. "He had to protect Atlanta": Maynard Jackson, Jr., interview.
373. "He's a nice young man": *Atlanta Constitution*, July 11, 1968.
373. "He had reached his calling": Bunnie Jackson-Ransom interview.
373. "It's a scandalous situation": *Atlanta Journal*, July 3, 1968.
373. "I don't have a million dollars": *Atlanta Constitution*, July 16, 1968.
374. "To me it means the ability": *Ibid.*
374. Small Farmers Administration to provide: *Atlanta Journal*, August 4, 1968.
374. "They know what's going on": *Ibid.*, August 14, 1968.
374. "for his record, for his bigotry": Maynard Jackson, Jr., interview.
374. "Understand, I ain't never lost": *New York Times*, October 18, 1973.
374. "I was insulted at first": *Ibid.*
375. "We like some of Mr. Jackson's ideas": *Atlanta Journal*, September 6, 1968. The *Journal* reprinted *The Valdosta Times* editorial.
375. "I am not running as a Negro": *Atlanta Constitution*, June 7, 1968.
375. "Forget for a moment": *Ibid.*, June 23, 1968.
375. "Maynard Jackson is fighting the battle": *New York Times*, July 28, 1968.
375. "I am running as a citizen": *Dallas Express*, April 1, 1944.
375. "a good thing": *Atlanta Journal*, September 9, 1968.
376. "He's not a deadhead": *Ibid.*, September 10, 1968.
376. "An historic victory has been achieved": *New York Times*, September 12, 1968.
376. "All things considered": *Atlanta Constitution*, September 16, 1968.

## CHAPTER 23

377. As he "bounced out" the first ball: *Atlanta Constitution*, October 17, 1968.
377. four days earlier he had undergone: *Atlanta Journal*, October 17, 1968.
377. The mayor ran the city: Interview with Ivan Allen, Jr.
377. "one of Atlanta's most valuable citizens": *Atlanta Constitution*, October 17, 1968.
377. "dean of the city's businessmen": *Atlanta Journal*, October 17, 1968.
377. "The name Ivan Allen had meant": *Atlanta Constitution*, October 17, 1968.

377. "He outlived his generation": *Atlanta Journal*, October 17, 1968.
378. Fulton County and DeKalb County rejected: *Atlanta Constitution*, November 7, 1969. See also: Clarence N. Stone, *Regime Politics: Governing Atlanta, 1946–1988* (Lawrence, Kansas: University Press of Kansas, 1989), pp. 73–75.
379. Twenty-one thousand blighted housing units: *Atlanta Constitution*, May 24, 1968.
379. segregation in Atlanta was two and a half times more: *Ibid.*, May 28, 1968.
379. Ranked second only to New Orleans: *Atlanta Journal*, February 2, 1967.
379. Atlanta's 183 murders: *Ibid.*, December 2, 1967.
379. "reminded me of Miss Nell": Undated 1968 note from Louise Allen to Robert W. Woodruff. Robert W. Woodruff Papers, Emory University, Robert W. Woodruff Library, Department of Special Collections, Document Case 8, Folder 9, "Ivan Allen, Jr., Correspondence, 1965–72."
379. "for your confidence in Ivan": *Ibid.*
379. "WHAT'RE Y'ALL TALKING ABOUT?": Ivan Allen, Jr., interview.
380. "Mister Bob's or Mister George's?": Interview with J. M. Mulliford.
380. "I always thought Ichauway": *Ibid.*
380. "Do you have a Pepsi?": *Ibid.*
381. "Retiring, Allen Tells City Today.": *Atlanta Constitution*, January 6, 1969.
381. He told Gene Patterson, Jack Tarver: Ivan Allen, Jr., with Paul Hemphill, *Mayor: Notes on the Sixties* (New York: Simon & Schuster, 1971), p. 220.
381. "I'm anxious to have the privilege": January 6, 1969. WSB Television Collection, University of Georgia, Instructional Resources Center, Reel 1029.
381. "Our only hope is to continue to develop": *Atlanta Constitution*, January 7, 1969.
381. "Even in the face of despair": State of the City Address delivered by Mayor Ivan Allen, Jr., January 6, 1969. Private papers of Ivan Allen, Jr.
381. "In some respects we're sorry": January 6, 1969. WSB Television Collection, University of Georgia, Instructional Resources Center, Reel 1029.
382. "Spend less time trying to understand": Carl B. Stokes, *Promises of Power: A Political Autobiography* (New York: Simon & Schuster, 1973), pp. 258–60.
382. "You're sitting there with the vice president": Ivan Allen, Jr., interview.
382. "Mr. Vice President, I came to this meeting": Stokes, *Promises of Power*, p. 260.
382. "Don't tell me I don't understand": *Ibid.*
382. "I want you to know": Ivan Allen, Jr., interview.
383. "Mr. President, are you asking me": *Ibid.*
383. "There are some feelings": *Ibid.*
383. attorney Maynard Jackson was expected: *Atlanta Constitution*, January 7, 1969.
383. gathered in a Hyatt Regency suite: Interviews with Leroy Johnson and David Franklin.
383. "They recorded in black and white": *Atlanta Journal*, March 7, 1969.
384. "Maynard had not been in town long": Interview with Jesse Hill.
384. "[They believed] Atlanta was different": David Franklin interview.
385. The agreed-upon goal was to gain five more": Leroy Johnson interview.
385. "There was a feeling among blacks": *Ibid.*
385. "the single most powerful": *New York Times*, November 8, 1970.
385. smoked eight-inch-long Tabacalera cigars: *New York Times*, November 8, 1970.
386. once had attempted to court a light-skinned: Interview with Windsor Jordan, younger brother of Vernon Jordan.
386. "Now you know why": Interview with Vernon Jordan, Jr.
386. "I knew that Leroy was carrying Sam's water": David Franklin interview.
386. "They can't tell me what to do": *Ibid.*
387. "When I ran against Talmadge": *Ibid.*
387. "To allow a young boy to handle": *Atlanta Constitution*, October 2, 1969.
387. "Nobody running for the office of vice mayor": *Ibid.*
387. "People thought he was Greek": David Franklin interview.
388. "the voice of the people": *Atlanta Constitution*, October 2, 1969.
388. "If Atlanta is to grow and prosper": *Ibid.*
388. he swept past Farris by more than eight thousand votes: *Atlanta Journal*, October 8, 1969.
388. "shows that whites are willing to vote": *Ibid.*
388. "a giant-killer in Atlanta elections": *Atlanta Constitution*, October 9, 1969.
389. "Good Lord, we've got more candidates": Allen with Hemphill, *Mayor*, p. 230.
389. Howard Massell had been soliciting: *Atlanta Constitution*, October 17, 1969.

389. "the dirtiest, lowest, meanest method": *Ibid.*

390. "And don't use my desk": Interview with Sam Massell.

390. "It is my personal feeling": *Atlanta Constitution*, October 20, 1969.

390. "Anti-Semitic WASPs": *Ibid.*

390. "five angry adversaries": *Atlanta Journal*, October 20, 1969.

391. "a base power play on behalf": *Ibid.*

391. "Ivan doesn't go out of his way": Interview with Cecil Alexander.

391. "Sam was standing on a banana peel": Maynard Jackson, Jr., interview.

392. "kosher chitlins": *Ibid.*

392. "You just couldn't pull it off": *Atlanta Constitution*, October 22, 1969.

392. "It had a perfectly gorgeous long horn": Ivan Allen, Jr., interview.

392. "They hauled me seventy-five miles": *Ibid.*

393. "Our city will not be measured": *Atlanta Daily World*, January 8, 1970.

393. "For the first time since Reconstruction": *Ibid.*

393. "I can no longer hold my peace": Transcript of press conference of Vice Mayor Maynard Jackson, April 16, 1970. Records of the Mayoral Administration of Maynard H. Jackson, Jr., City of Atlanta, Records Management Division, Box 86-RS-5A.

393. "playing to the gallery": Sam Massell interview.

394. sidestep the vice mayor: *Ibid.*

394. "things ain't what they ought to be": *Atlanta Constitution*, May 14, 1970.

394. "high-handed" manner of presiding: *Ibid.*, August 25, 1970.

394. "didn't like black folks": Interview with Wade Mitchell.

394. "Now we can truly call ourselves": *Atlanta Constitution*, July 1, 1971.

394. "The word around town": Speech by Mayor Sam Massell to Hungry Supper Club at Butler Street YMCA, October 6, 1971. Central Atlanta Progress Papers, Atlanta History Center, Box 23.

395. affirmative action programs, consistent with federal guidelines: Stone, *Regime Politics*, pp. 99–100.

395. give up his demand for broad-scale forced busing: Interview with Lonnie C. King.

395. whites comprised only 23 percent: Stone, *Regime Politics*, pp. 104–6.

395. cultivated support from the city's black middle class: *Ibid.*, p. 98.


CHAPTER 24

397. After a decade of virtually: Milton Viorst, "Black Mayor, White Power Structure," *New Republic*, June 7, 1975, pp. 9–11.

399. "But 'Maynard' ": Interview with Bunnie Jackson-Ransom.

399. "He definitely wanted him": *Ibid.*

399. "We don't cut blacks' hair here": *Atlanta Journal* and *Atlanta Constitution*, March 6, 1973.

399. "I want their license!": Bunnie Jackson-Ransom interview.

399. "This is to reinforce to you": *Atlanta Constitution*, March 6, 1973.

400. another case of the dreamer dreaming: Interview with Bill Clement, Jr.

400. "Atlanta is the best city in America": Peter Ross Range, "Making It in Atlanta: Capital of Black-Is-Bountiful," *New York Times Sunday Magazine*, April 7, 1974, p. 29.

400. "This is the best place": *Ibid.*

400. he met on Saturdays: Bill Clement, Jr., interview.

401. on the strength of $40,000: Interviews with David Franklin and Bill Clement, Jr.

401. "Carl Holman once told me": David Franklin interview.

402. "[Hill] said Atlanta was not ready": Interview with Maynard Jackson, Jr.

402. "We want you to say": Bill Clement, Jr., and David Franklin interviews.

402. "there were some efforts": Interview with Jesse Hill.

402. "People were saying that Maynard": Bill Clement, Jr., interview.

402. Franklin spent more than $8,000: David Franklin interview.

402. Maynard Jr. received 45 percent: *Atlanta Constitution*, May 24, 1973.

403. "It's very clear": David Franklin interview.

403. "Who Hired Mayor Survey?": *Atlanta Journal*, March 9, 1973.

403. "But you said": Interview with Leroy Johnson.

404. local politicians across the country: *New York Times Sunday Magazine*, November 8, 1970.

404. he had earned a reported $175,000: *Ibid.*
404. had not forgotten Johnson standing: Interview with Michael Lomax.
404. "never . . . never . . . never": *Atlanta Constitution*, April 11, 1973.
404. "I haven't been Sam Massell's boy": *Ibid.*
404. "I'm one of you.": Leroy Johnson interview.
404. Maynard Jr. won 2,113: *Atlanta Journal*, April 13, 1973.
404. Maynard Jr. received 80 percent: *Atlanta Constitution*, May 24, 1973.
404. "If the election were held": *Ibid.*, May 25, 1973.
404. "We told them that in the past": Jesse Hill interview.
405. "Sam, we don't want you to run": Interview with Sam Massell.
405. *"You're doing all this stuff":* *Ibid.*
405. "I subsequently advised Charles Weltner": Letter from Ivan Allen, Jr., to Robert W. Woodruff, May 24, 1973. Robert W. Woodruff Papers, Emory University, Robert W. Woodruff Library, Department of Special Collections, Document Case 8, Folder 10, "Ivan Allen, Jr. (and family), Correspondence, 1971–85." Allen's first choices were banker Wade Mitchell and attorney Jack Watson, Jr.
405. "We only got the 'B' money from Coke.": David Franklin interview.
405. "Black people love Maynard Jackson.": *Ibid.* J. Paul Austin of Coca-Cola related this story to David Franklin in a meeting during the 1973 campaign.
405. had not been raised on the city's style: Clarence N. Stone, *Regime Politics: Governing Atlanta, 1946–1988* (Lawrence, Kansas: University Press of Kansas, 1989), p. 106.
406. "I fully intend to do everything": *Atlanta Constitution*, August 17, 1973.
406. "Bigots and fear-mongers": *Atlanta Journal*, September 10, 1973.
406. When the buses arrived each morning: Bill Clement, Jr., interview.
406. "Maynard could go on": David Franklin interview.
407. "This is the best speech": Michael Lomax interview.
407. "Maynard was the Second Coming": *Ibid.*
407. "They wanted one of their own": Interview with Wyche Fowler.
407. "They are trying to pull": *Ibid.*
408. "to break up the deal": Interview with Hosea Williams.
408. raised the total by nearly 20 percent: Sam Massell campaign literature for 1973 mayor's race. Personal papers of Sam Massell.
408. He had struck a financing deal: Sam Massell interview.
408. "There wasn't one.": *Ibid.*
408. "unholy alliance": *Atlanta Journal*, July 9, 1973.
408. "Massell-Jackson administration": *Ibid.*, August 29, 1973.
408. "We all know that Mayor Massell": *Ibid.*
409. The mayor has refused": *Ibid.*, August 1, 1973.
409. "While the mayor and vice mayor": *Ibid.*
409. feared their control would cause: Hosea Williams interview.
409. reportedly was $60,000 in debt: *Atlanta Constitution*, September 17, 1973.
409. Hill was handed the title: *Ibid.*, September 14, 1973.
409. The concert raised at least $40,000: *Ibid.*, September 17, 1973.
409. "We have in this contest two officials": *Atlanta Daily World*, September 27, 1973.
409. *Inquirer,* controlled by Jesse Hill, endorsed: Duncan R. Jamieson, "Maynard Jackson's 1973 Election as Mayor of Atlanta," *Midwest Quarterly* (Vol. 18, No. 1, Autumn 1976), pp. 7–26.
410. serve a brief prison term: *Atlanta Constitution*, October 13, 1976.
410. "It is important for us to remember": *Ibid.*, October 3, 1973.
410. "All I had to do": Wyche Fowler interview.
410. "the top people in the agency talked": Interview with Ralph McGill, Jr.
411. "Sam, if you keep doing this": Sam Massell and Ralph McGill, Jr., interviews.
411. "Fear not only hit the campaign": Ralph McGill, Jr., interview.
411. "What Has Sam Massell Done": 1973 Sam Massell mayoral campaign literature. Personal files of Sam Massell.
411. 105 black elected officials: *Atlanta Constitution*, October 17, 1973.
411. "They were real teeth-jarrers": Ralph McGill, Jr., interview.
412. he scribbled a few words: Interviews with Mark Doyle, Ralph McGill, Jr., and Bob Shira.
412. "it was not really created as a slogan": Mark Doyle interview.
412. "Mark and I were having reservations": Bob Shira interview.

412. "[The slogan] was created to say": Mark Doyle interview.
412. "The race thing scared me": Ralph McGill, Jr., interview.
412. "You wanted something really powerful": Interview with Ron Sharbo.
413. "that I can run the city": Sam Massell interview.
413. "It was very much, I would think": Ralph McGill, Jr., interview.
413. The agency placed a wind-blowing machine: *Ibid.*
413. "We were run off by the police": *Ibid.*
413. "The thought of a Maynard Jackson–Hosea Williams": *Atlanta Journal*, October 10, 1973.
413. "Did you do this ad?": Bob Shira interview.
413. "It was from Philadelphia.": *Ibid.*
413. "The man has made my campaign": Maynard Jackson, Jr., interview.
414. "I want to thank you for running": Interview with Beaumont Allen.
414. "I made such a mess": David Franklin interview.
414. "We are going into a two-week runoff": *Atlanta Constitution*, October 4, 1973.
414. "Right or wrong that's the feeling": *Ibid.*, October 8, 1973.
414. "He's running whites out of the city": *Ibid.*
414. "unite our city under the banner": *Ibid.*, October 9, 1973.
414. "But I don't think that means": *Ibid.*
415. "Wyche, seeing as how we're gonna": Wyche Fowler interview.
415. "perfectly coiffured, hair combed back": *Ibid.*
415. "All of a sudden, Hosea gets out": *Ibid.*
416. "That stuff only works": Interview with A. Reginald Eaves.
416. "We knew the race": David Franklin interview.
416. "Atlanta is indeed too young": *Atlanta Constitution*, October 11, 1973.
416. "Atlanta's Greatest Black Leader": *Atlanta Daily World*, October 11, 1973.
416. "He Loves Atlanta So Much": *Atlanta Journal*, October 15, 1973.
417. "Isn't it interesting that all": Maynard Jackson, Jr., interview.
417. "raised the question of just how much": *Atlanta Daily World*, October 9, 1973.
417. "Most white southern politicians": *Ibid.*, October 11, 1973.
418. the idea was to frighten blacks: Michael Lomax interview.
418. At Precinct 2-G: *Atlanta Journal*, October 17, 1973.
418. Black musicians played to a crowd: WSB Television Collection, University of Georgia, Instructional Resources Center, October 16, 1973, Reels 1978 and 10.
418. "I just got elected": Michael Lomax interview.
418. saw people dancing in the streets: A. Reginald Eaves interview.
419. "as one of the few times": Interview with Robert Jordan, Jr.
419. "referred to me as 'Bobby' ": *Ibid.*
419. "the crowd was so hot": Bunnie Jackson-Ransom interview.
419. "We walked out onto that stage": Michael Lomax interview.
419. "They lifted me off my feet": David Franklin interview.
419. "Very unlike Boston politics": A. Reginald Eaves interview.
419. "Maynard was it.": Bunnie Jackson-Ransom interview.
420. "My only motive was to tell": *Atlanta Constitution*, October 17, 1973.
420. "I come with my father in mind": WSB Television Collection, University of Georgia, Instructional Resources Center, October 16, 1973, Reel 10.
420. never even discussed it with Bunnie: Bunnie Jackson-Ransom interview.
420. "It is not solely the culmination": WSB Television Collection, University of Georgia, Instructional Resources Center, October 16, 1973, Reel 10.
420. "I had a hard time digesting it": Interview with Josephine Dobbs Clement.
420. "Wouldn't it have been something": Bill Clement, Jr., and Josephine Dobbs Clement interviews.
420. "We are the city whose people refuse": *Atlanta Journal*, October 17, 1973.
420. *No matter how many suns may set*: *New Yorker*, December 31, 1973, p. 39. This election night exchange is described in full.
421. "I don't hate Sam": WSB Television Collection, University of Georgia, Instructional Resources Center, October 16, 1973, Reel 10.
421. "What good will it do": Harold H. Martin, *William Berry Hartsfield: Mayor of Atlanta* (Athens, Ga.: University of Georgia Press, 1978), p. 172. See also: *Atlanta Journal*, August 14, 1964.
422. Cousins, uncles and siblings arrived: *Atlanta Journal-Constitution Sunday Magazine*, February 10, 1974.

422. "The shorter they are, the more": Letter from Mayor William B. Hartsfield to Mayor-elect Ivan Allen, Jr., November 29, 1961. Records of the Mayoral Administration of Ivan Allen, Jr., City of Atlanta, Records Management Division, Box 90-TR-321, Box 1.

422. "the Supreme Court saying, 'You don't' ": Interview with Emma I. Darnell.

422. "Maynard could turn a parking ticket": Interview with Joel Babbit. Babbit served on Jackson's staff during his third term in office, 1990–94.

422. "I don't know of anybody else": Interview with Mattiwilda Dobbs Janzon.

423. Civic Center, about 90 percent: *Atlanta Constitution* and *Atlanta Journal*, January 8, 1974.

423. Coretta Scott King appeared in a flowing: *Ibid.*

423. "There's no better time to come home": *Ibid.*

423. "Few occasions in my life": Interview with Hank Ezell.

423. felt the explosive power of their voices: Wyche Fowler interview.

423. sang a French aria: *Atlanta Journal-Constitution Sunday Magazine*, February 10, 1974.

423. Young's went on for three days: *Time*, January 14, 1974. See also: Coleman Young and Lonnie Wheeler, *Hard Stuff: The Autobiography of Coleman Young* (New York: Viking, 1994), p. 200.

423. "I was so involved and so caught up": Maynard Jackson, Jr., interview.

423. "It was, well, grandiose.": Interview with Margaret Allen.

423. "To this day, I test people": Sam Massell interview.

424. "Let's talk about": Michael Lomax interview.

424. "We will respect it and require its respect": Inaugural Address of Mayor Maynard H. Jackson, Jr., January 7, 1974. In Clayborne Carson and David J. Garrow *et al.*, editors. *The Eyes on the Prize Civil Rights Reader: Documents, Speeches and First Hand Accounts from the Black Freedom Struggle, 1954–1990* (New York: Penguin, 1991), pp. 614–18.

424. "Right on! Right on!": *Atlanta Journal*, January 8, 1974.

425. He found the quote in a monograph: Maynard Jackson, Jr., interview.

425. "That was like a signal.": *Ibid.*

425. address was interrupted by applause sixteen times: *Atlanta Constitution*, January 8, 1974.

425. "Black Atlanta's favorite son": *Atlanta Daily World*, January 10, 1974.

425. "A bore. Terrible and pompous": Sam Massell interview.

425. "This is the happiest moment": *Atlanta Constitution*, January 8, 1974.

425. offset the Jackson campaign's $30,000 debt: *Time*, January 14, 1974.

425. town centers were sprouting in Buckhead: Joel Garreau, *Edge City: Life on the New Frontier* (New York: Doubleday, 1991), pp. 143–78.

425. would rise to 66 percent in six years: 1980 U.S. Census.

425. blacks represented roughly 80 percent: Truman A. Hartshorn, *Metropolis in Georgia: Atlanta's Rise as a Major Transaction Center* (Cambridge, Mass.: Ballinger Publishing Company, 1976), pp. 50–51.

425. "Long live the King!": *Atlanta Constitution*, January 8, 1974.

## CHAPTER 25

426. Aaron had received numerous death threats: Hank Aaron and Lonnie Wheeler, *I Had a Hammer: The Hank Aaron Story* (New York: HarperCollins, 1991), pp. 241–43.

426. he wanted soul food: Interview with Bunnie Jackson-Ransom.

427. "Sammy, you can't leave now.": Interview with Maynard Jackson, Jr.

427. "It is inconceivable to me": Press release from Office of Mayor Maynard Jackson, April 12, 1974. Records of the Mayoral Administration of Maynard Jackson, Jr., City of Atlanta, Records Management Division, Box 90-TR-330, Folder 7.

427. "It's not gonna happen tonight, Boss": Interview with Ivan Allen, Jr.

427. "He literally seemed to jump seven feet": Maynard Jackson, Jr., interview.

427. proposing that the name of the Atlanta ballpark: Letter from Mayor Maynard Jackson to Stadium Authority, April 12, 1974. Records of the Mayoral Administration of Maynard Jackson, Jr., City of Atlanta, Records Management Division, Box 90-TR-330, Folder 7.

427. "Exaggerated expectations in the black community": Maynard Jackson, Jr., interview.

428. commanding as much as $2,000 per speech: *Atlanta Constitution*, March 25, 1974.

428. walked on stage during a Stevie Wonder concert: Interview with Michael Lomax.

428. *"He invited us to come to Atlanta!"*: Interview with George Berry.

428. "I felt that things": Maynard Jackson, Jr., interview.

428. "Maynard surrounded himself with people": Michael Lomax interview.
429. helped the mayor land as his chief: Interview with Jule Sugarman. In luring Sugarman to Atlanta, the Atlanta Chamber of Commerce purchased his home in New York, then resold it for Sugarman, making certain he did not lose money in the transaction.
429. "He only hires blacks and *outsiders.*": Peter K. Eisinger, *The Politics of Displacement: Racial and Ethnic Transition in Three American Cities* (New York: Academic Press, 1980), p. 106.
429. "the vapid, jejune trappings": *New York Times Sunday Magazine,* April 7, 1974.
430. "Throughout our history": News release from Atlanta City Hall, June 14, 1974. Records of the Mayoral Administration of Maynard Jackson, Jr., City of Atlanta, Records Management Division, Box 90-TR-330, Folder 6.
430. created Dobbs Associates, Inc.: Interview with Bill Clement, Jr.
430. founded *The Dobbs Family Newsletter: The Dobbs Family Newsletter* (Vol. 16, No. 1, September 1992), John Wesley Dobbs Papers, Amistad Research Center, New Orleans, La., Box 5, Folder 8. A footnote on page 1 of this newsletter dates the initial newsletter to September 1977.
430. "he was supposedly a really romantic husband": Interview with Brooke Jackson.
430. "Daddy is so intelligent, super-smart": Interview with Beth Jackson Hodges.
431. "Daddy always asks something": *Ibid.*
431. unlikely to make the change under a black mayor: Interview with Charles Wittenstein. Wittenstein was executive director of the Atlanta Charter Commission.
431. white Atlantans would define as a failure: Gary Orfield and Carole Ashkinaze, *The Closing Door: Conservative Policy and Black Opportunity* (Chicago: University of Chicago Press, 1991), p. 24.
432. "What I wanted to do was get those [white] voters": Interview with Larry Gellerstedt, Jr.
432. after receiving a recommendation: *Atlanta Journal and Constitution Magazine,* August 25, 1974.
432. reducing twenty-six departments to nine superagencies: *Atlanta Constitution,* February 5, 1974.
433. "I want [Inman] out the moment": Jule Sugarman interview.
433. "I'll leave the door cracked": Interview with A. Reginald Eaves.
433. "[Inman] was playing games with us": Jule Sugarman interview. See also reports of Inman's firing: News release from Atlanta City Hall, May 3, 1974. Records of the Mayoral Administration of Maynard Jackson, Jr., City of Atlanta, Records Management Division, Box 90-TR-330, Folder 6. Also: *Atlanta Constitution,* May 4, 1974.
433. brought twenty-five armed members: *Atlanta Journal,* May 6, 1974.
433. large numbers of black officers, enraged: Jule Sugarman interview.
434. "The best police chief Maynard ever had": Michael Lomax interview.
434. "a hit man": *Atlanta Constitution,* June 10, 1974.
434. "the most extraordinary of his career": *Ibid.*
434. "I have tried to keep my peace": *Ibid.,* June 7, 1974.
434. "I have come to believe": *Ibid.*
435. rated Atlanta as the worst city: *Ibid.,* June 19, 1974.
435. had increased by nearly 300 percent: *Charlotte Observer,* September 8, 1974.
435. "You could tell Maynard was troubled": Jule Sugarman interview.
435. "When Peachtree Creek floods": Maynard Jackson, Jr., interview.
436. "I wasn't talking to Inman": Jule Sugarman interview.
436. carrying two pistols and claiming to be: *Atlanta Journal,* July 1, 1974.
436. "How much more can a man take?": *Ibid.*
436. seen the romance of Daddy King: Interview with Irene (Renie) Dobbs Jackson.
436. "We need something from you now": *Atlanta Journal,* July 1, 1974.
436. Georgia Supreme Court ruled that Atlanta's new city charter: *Atlanta Constitution,* July 4, 1974.
436. "I've got my candidate.": A. Reginald Eaves interview.
437. "Maynard went from picking the person": Jule Sugarman interview.
437. "He called back on my fraternity stuff": A. Reginald Eaves interview.
437. "I did not appoint him because of our friendship": *Charlotte Observer,* September 8, 1974.
437. "emphasizes the shaky ground": *Atlanta Journal,* August 15, 1974.
437. "I did not want that job": A. Reginald Eaves interview.
437. "Sam, you were right!": Interview with Sam Massell.
438. letter warned that crime and racial problems: Letter from Harold Brockey to Mayor Maynard Jackson, September 16, 1974. Private files of Central Atlanta Progress, Atlanta, Ga.
438. "perceived attitude of the mayor as anti-white": *Ibid.*

438. "The dilution of this partnership": *Ibid.*
438. "I knew, but did not fully appreciate": Maynard Jackson, Jr., interview.
438. "The two times I went": Interview with Bob Holder.
438. "some Tuesday soon [Allen] may be declared": *Atlanta Constitution*, December 30, 1974.
439. Sanders said Maynard Jr. ought to stop: *Atlanta Journal*, September 25, 1974.
439. "Too many of us have been too concerned": *Ibid.*
440. The success of a black mayor, he believed: Ivan Allen, Jr., interview.
440. "Now that you have given these Niggers": *Ibid.*
440. "Every now and then": *Atlanta Constitution*, December 9, 1974.
441. "I was conscious then that Ivan Jr.": Interview with Bill Pressly.
441. In her daily calendar book: Interview with Margaret Allen.
441. "The Chamber and city government": *Atlanta Constitution*, December 5, 1974.
441. Ivan III refused to listen to racial jokes: Interview with Mason Lowance, Jr.
441. "We had a big luncheon": Interview with Ivan Allen III.
442. The majority of the Morehouse trustees were white: *Morehouse College Bulletin* (Vol. 40, No. 130, Fall 1973), p. 6.
442. "I tried to get people who were wealthy": Interview with Hugh Gloster.
442. Allens sent their son, Ivan IV: Margaret Allen interview.
442. "We were all for public education": *Ibid.*
443. "He's so big": *Atlanta Constitution*, January 22, 1975. The description of the mock fight is drawn, too, from the *Atlanta Journal*, January 22, 1975.
443. "Not since the 1930's": State of the City Address by Mayor Maynard Jackson, January 6, 1975. Records of the Mayoral Administration of Maynard Jackson, Jr., City of Atlanta, Records Management Division, Box 90-TR-330.
443. obtained one of 225: *Atlanta Constitution*, April 18, 1975.
443. "My uncle told me the people": *Ibid.*
443. "it was too much of a hassle": *Ibid.*
444. convictions for possession of drugs and illegal draft cards: *Ibid.*
444. a railroad man who married a black Jew: A. Reginald Eaves interview.
444. known to classmates as "Mister Civil Rights": *Ibid.*
444. "Reginald, don't you know me?": *Ibid.*
444. "Things will remain the same": *Atlanta Constitution*, February 21, 1978.
444. four assistant police chiefs, six majors: *Ibid.*
444. remove officers from downtown and place them: A. Reginald Eaves interview.
445. "Not one black person in this town is willing": *Ibid.*
445. "You can take this position": *Ibid.*
445. "He has abused [the mayor's] confidence": *Atlanta Constitution*, April 17, 1975.
445. They went for a drive: Interview with Pearl (Lomax) Cleage. Ms. Cleage formerly was married to Michael Lomax.
445. "For the first time in twenty-seven years": Pearl (Lomax) Cleage and A. Reginald Eaves interviews.
446. a group of black policemen blocking his path: *Ibid.*
446. "You're a helluva man": *Atlanta Constitution*, April 17, 1975.
446. supported virtually every major development: Adolph Reed, Jr., "A Critique of Neo-Progressivism in Theorizing About Local Development Policy: A Case from Atlanta." In Clarence N. Stone and Heywood T. Sanders, editors, *The Politics of Urban Development* (Lawrence, Kansas: University Press of Kansas, 1987), pp. 204–6.
446. a mayor they perceived as self-absorbed: *Ibid.*
446. "to let them know": Maynard Jackson, Jr., interview.
447. "If we do it this time": *Ibid.*
447. "Now, if anxiety attaches": "Can Atlanta Succeed Where America Has Failed? An Exclusive Interview with Mayor Maynard Jackson as He Completes His First 500 Days in Office." *Atlanta Magazine*, June 1975.
447. turning over airport management: Betsy Braden and Paul Hagan, *A Dream Takes Flight: Hartsfield Atlanta International Airport and Aviation in Atlanta* (Athens, Ga.: University of Georgia Press, 1989), pp. 181–82.
447. Lyndon Johnson signed Executive Order 11246: Nicholas Lemann, "Taking Affirmative Action Apart," *New York Times Sunday Magazine*, June 11, 1995, pp. 36–43.
447. Pete Wilson in 1971 persuaded the city council: *New York Times*, August 8, 1995.

447. he also refused to set foot inside the Piedmont Driving Club: Maynard Jackson, Jr., interview.
447. "You know, Maynard": *Ibid.*
448. "It is time to stop talking about 'we' ": *Atlanta Journal,* February 19, 1975.
448. "is too big for this city to solve": *New York Times,* March 12, 1975.
448. "Camelot has faded": *Atlanta Constitution,* March 28, 1975.
448. "I'm ready to give up": *Ibid.,* March 23, 1975.
448. "Maynard Jackson's no good.": *Ibid.*
448. "Can I deliver what I think is important?": *Atlanta Constitution,* March 30, 1975.
448. "For a nice guy with good intentions": *Economist* (London). Reprinted in *Atlanta Constitution,* April 3, 1975.
449. "nothing to fear but fear itself": *Atlanta Constitution,* April 2, 1975.
449. "I think it's a natural reaction": *Ibid.,* March 30, 1975.
449. "It was a strange trip": Michael Lomax interview.
450. "just political people": Bunnie Jackson-Ransom interview.
450. "There was tension between Maynard and Ivan": Michael Lomax interview.
450. "There is no way to defeat the black vote.": Ivan Allen, Jr., interview.
450. "We're going to see black mayors": Interview with Joel Goldberg.
450. "Maynard would say he wanted": Ivan Allen III interview.
450. "He was always punctual, always positive.": Maynard Jackson, Jr., interview.
450. able to quote Albert Camus: Interview with Michel Cornier. Cornier, the French trade commissioner and vice consul in Atlanta in 1975, made the trip to Paris with the group.
450. "We bragged that Hartsfield [airport]": Ivan Allen III interview.
450. "There was a real sensitivity": *Ibid.*
451. "Atlanta As Commercial Center": News release from Atlanta City Hall, March 28, 1975. Records of the Mayoral Administration of Maynard Jackson, Jr., City of Atlanta, Records Management Division, Box 90-TR-330.
451. "The gates of Atlanta are open wide.": *Atlanta Constitution,* April 5, 1975.
451. "Maynard was sort of a really dramatic": Ivan Allen III interview.
451. "Maynard was at his absolute best": Michael Lomax interview.
451. "Ivan was not a scintillating speaker": *Ibid.*
451. "Ivan III was a little stiff for me": Maynard Jackson, Jr., interview.
451. "Maynard is an extraordinarily guarded individual.": Michael Lomax interview.

## CHAPTER 26

452. "my corrective shoes": Interview with JacLyn Morris.
452. The mayor's glare prompted Morris's friend": *Ibid.*
452. "I can't believe you just did that": *Ibid.*
453. urged him to slow his pace: *Atlanta Constitution,* February 26, 1990.
453. Criticism from white business leaders was muted: Clarence N. Stone, *Regime Politics: Governing Atlanta, 1946–1988* (Lawrence, Kansas: University Press of Kansas, 1989), p. 91.
453. He redecorated his outer office at City Hall: *Atlanta Journal and Constitution Magazine,* November 11, 1979.
453. He wore two guns: Interview with A. Reginald Eaves.
454. "had a wider breadth of experience": Interview with David Franklin.
454. "I knew Maynard was going to run": *New York Times Sunday Magazine,* April 7, 1974.
454. "I used to say to Maynard": Interview with Bunnie Jackson-Ransom.
454. a white architect charged Franklin: *Atlanta Constitution,* October 24, 1975.
454. "I would be stopped one night by police": David Franklin interview.
454. "I'm an entertainment lawyer": *Ibid.*
454. postmarked letter in a safe-deposit box: *Ibid.*
454. "I'm not going to tolerate this": Interview with Maynard Jackson, Jr.
454. "There had been no other black mayor": Bunnie Jackson-Ransom interview.
454. "among the greatest contributions": Letter from Mayor Maynard Jackson to Rep. Hosea Williams, February 24, 1977. Records of the Mayoral Administration of Maynard Jackson, Jr., City of Atlanta, Records Management Division, Box 90-TR-331.
454. "If they ever disagreed with him": Interview with Jule Sugarman.
455. "You'd go into Maynard's office": Interview with George Berry.

455. "To the Best Editor I Have Ever Had": Interview with John Head.

455. several Sundays listening to Daddy King: JacLyn Morris interview.

455. "Do you believe interracial marriage": John Head interview.

455. "Maynard was always looking": *Ibid.*

455. "There is a peculiar anxiety": "Can Atlanta Succeed Where America Has Failed? An Exclusive Atlanta Magazine Interview with Mayor Maynard Jackson as He Completes His First 500 Days in Office," *Atlanta Magazine*, June 1975.

456. "It will do no good to wait": Ivan Allen III, undated civic speech from summer of 1975 (location unspecified). WSB Television Collection, University of Georgia, Instructional Resources Center, Reel 2183.

456. some thought they would marry: Frederick Allen, *Secret Formula: How Brilliant Marketing and Relentless Salesmanship Made Coca-Cola the Best-Known Product in the World* (New York: HarperBusiness, 1994), pp. 355–56.

456. Woodruff gave Ivan and Louise Baccarat ruby glasses: Letter from Louise Allen to Robert W. Woodruff, January 29, 1976. Robert W. Woodruff Papers, Emory University, Robert W. Woodruff Library, Department of Special Collections, Document Case 8, Folder 10, "Ivan Allen, Jr. (and family), Correspondence, 1971–85."

456. they gave him a humidor full of Dunhill: Letter from Robert W. Woodruff to Ivan Allen, Jr., December 8, 1980. *Ibid.*

456. Amanda played "Send in the Clowns": Interviews with Margaret Allen and Amanda Allen Thompson.

456. then sat in a chair in his room: Interview with Ivan Allen, Jr.

456. "Eh, Boss, what did Pepsi-Cola do today?": Interview with H. Inman Allen.

457. "re-enter the scene": Allen, *Secret Formula,* pp. 366–67.

457. "There's no way for you": *Ibid.*

457. $8 million for the construction: *Atlanta Constitution*, April 10, 1976.

457. "what the de Medici family did for Florence": Letter from Louise Allen to Robert W. Woodruff, September 4, 1975. RWW Papers, EU, Document Case 8, Folder 10, "Ivan Allen, Jr. (and family), Correspondence, 1971–85."

457. persuading its board to spend $500,000: *Atlanta Constitution*, April 18, 1993.

457. He pitched in about $400,000 for each: Interview with Bill Pressly. At the time, Pressly, retired headmaster of Westminster, served as an administrator with the Atlanta Historical Society.

457. "Louise can just persuade you": Interview with Laura Maddox Smith.

457. Woodruff even posed with Jackson: Allen, *Secret Formula,* pp. 366–67.

458. "What would mother and Aunt Emie say": Letter from Mrs. Willaford Leach to her cousin Robert W. Woodruff, July 4, 1976. RWW Papers, EU, Document Case 181, Folder 20, 1973–77. (See: "Leach Family.") See also: Allen, *Secret Formula,* pp. 366–67.

458. "Is there anything I can do": Maynard Jackson, Jr., interview.

458. "I just thought I would mention to you": *Ibid.*

458. "It was on a raggedy little bitty concession stand": *Ibid.*

458. "*So what does the man who has everything want?*": *Ibid.*

458. "I'm the mayor of this city": Interview with Joel Goldberg.

459. "Billy Sterne [of the Trust Company] took it": *Ibid.*

459. "I would have thought the heavens": Maynard Jackson, Jr., interview.

459. Fleetwood Dunston and Richard Mosley: *Atlanta Constitution*, September 22, 1975.

459. as an "embarrassment": *Atlanta Journal*, January 5, 1976.

459. "The toughest field was in architecture": Jule Sugarman interview.

459. "If the mayor would spend as much time": *Atlanta Constitution*, September 17, 1975.

459. "The biggest enemy we face in Atlanta": Letter from Dan Sweat to City Council president Wyche Fowler, September 10, 1975. Central Atlanta Progress Papers, Atlanta History Center, Folder entitled "Dan, Personal, 1975."

460. yet whites turned out in large numbers to deal: *Atlanta Constitution*, December 10, 1975.

460. failed attempt to get rid of superchief: Letter from James Sibley to Robert W. Woodruff, January 28, 1976. RWW Papers, EU, Document Case 252, Folder 7.

460. "We must make basic changes": State of the City Address by Mayor Maynard Jackson, Jr., January 5, 1976. Records of the Mayoral Administration of Maynard Jackson, Jr., City of Atlanta, Records Management Division, Box 90-TR-331.

460. City contracts awarded to minorities in Atlanta: Annual Contract Compliance Records of City of Atlanta, 1973–93, Office of the Mayor.

460. "We built the Atlanta airport": *Atlanta Constitution*, February 26, 1990.
460. produced about twenty-five new black millionaires: Maynard Jackson, Jr., interview. See also: *Christian Science Monitor*, May 29, 1987. The *Monitor* suggests that twenty-one black millionaires were made at the Atlanta airport alone. To punctuate his role in the construction of the new airport terminal, Jackson, returning from a speaking engagement in the Midwest by private plane September 21, 1980, arranged to become the first passenger to land at the just-opened terminal. His plane touched down in the darkness at 1:05 A.M.—sixty-five minutes after the terminal had opened. See also: *Atlanta Journal*, September 21, 1980; and Betsy Braden and Paul Hagan, *A Dream Takes Flight: Hartsfield Atlanta International Airport and Aviation in Atlanta* (Athens, Ga.: University of Georgia Press, 1989), p. 210.
460. he used the phrase "ethnic purity": *Atlanta Constitution*, April 9, 1976.
461. appoint blacks to the federal judiciary: Maynard Jackson, Jr., interview.
461. Carter appeared at a rally: *New York Times*, April 14, 1976.
461. "I think they thought": Maynard Jackson, Jr., interview.
461. "very influential, and let the Yankees know": Interview with Jimmy Carter.
461. "As a fifth-generation Georgian": *Atlanta Constitution*, May 15, 1976.
461. "was more political than personal": Interview with Jack Watson, Jr.
461. "Maynard obviously has an ego.": Jimmy Carter interview.
462. "Nobody in this white community": Joel Goldberg interview.
462. "She said she hardly ever saw him": *Ibid.*
462. "*Mayor and Mrs. Maynard Jackson have agreed*": News Release from Atlanta City Hall, April 14, 1976. Records of the Mayoral Administration of Maynard Jackson, Jr., City of Atlanta, Records Management Division, Box 90-TR-330.
462. agreed to pay a combined $2,000: Fulton County Superior Court Records, Civil Action File: C-21124. *Maynard Holbrook Jackson, Plaintiff v. Burnella Hayes Burke Jackson, Defendant,* July 9, 1976.
462. "an ordinary apartment that looked": Jule Sugarman interview.
462. "I think where everything went kind of awry": Interview with Brooke Jackson.
463. nearly three of every four city firefighters: *Atlanta Constitution*, June 21, 1976.
463. "I am dedicated to ending this flight": *Ibid.*
463. "If Atlanta were a palisaded fort": *Atlanta Journal*, June 3, 1976.
463. "Run for Congress.": Maynard Jackson, Jr., interview.
463. "If you leave": *Ibid.*
463. "I will do whatever you don't do": *Ibid.*
464. A graduate of Howard Law School: Interview with Emma I. Darnell.
464. "Doctrinaire and intimidating": Jule Sugarman interview.
464. "incompetence" and "insubordination": Memorandum from Emma I. Darnell, Commissioner, Department of Administrative Services, to Mayor Maynard Jackson, December 8, 1976. Records of the Mayoral Administration of Maynard Jackson, Jr., City of Atlanta, Records Management Division, Box 90-TR-331, Folder 4.
464. referred to her in a staff meeting: *Ibid.*
464. filed sex and race discrimination charges: *Atlanta Constitution*, January 13, 1977.
464. "Emma Lee, we were just thinking": Emma I. Darnell interview.
464. "If you want to do business with us": *Ibid.*
465. "Will be a major event": "Mayor's Decision Request" from George Berry, Chief Administrative Officer, to Mayor Maynard Jackson, January 31, 1977. Records of the Mayoral Administration of Maynard Jackson, Jr., City of Atlanta, Records Management Division, Box 90-TR-331, Folder 4.
465. "inept," "negligent" and "insufficient": Letter from Maynard Jackson to Emma I. Darnell, February 10, 1977. *Ibid.*
465. "that the conduct of this administration": News Release from Atlanta City Hall, February 25, 1977. *Ibid.*
465. "and not those of Emma Darnell": *Atlanta Constitution*, March 1, 1977.
466. he contended city funds were not available: *Ibid.*, April 2, 1977.
466. firing nine hundred of the striking workers: *Ibid.*, May 1 and May 27, 1977.
466. "If you do everything you can": *Ibid.*, April 5, 1977.
466. brunch to honor record producer Quincy Jones: Maynard Jackson, Jr., interview.
466. "I had planned to kind of *be out there*": *Ibid.*
466. "Now that's the type of man": Interview with Valerie Richardson Jackson.

466. "Is it 'V'?": John Head interview.
467. "So an intimate evening": *Atlanta Constitution*, September 11, 1977.
467. Sanders led 39 percent to Jackson's 32: *Ibid.*, June 25, 1977.
467. Ivan Allen III, in a two-man race against Jackson": *Ibid.*
467. hosting a $50 per plate fund-raising dinner: *Ibid.*, June 28, 1977.
467. "would just get clobbered": *Ibid.*, June 7, 1977.
468. "Maynard is the best man to be mayor.": *Ibid.*
468. "Every index [in Atlanta] shows deterioration.": *Ibid.*
468. "The biggest international issue": *Ibid.*
468. "a black elitist": *Atlanta Journal-Constitution*, September 11, 1977.
468. met secretly with the mayor's two top aides: Confidential memo from George Berry and Geraldine H. Elder to Mayor Maynard Jackson, August 15, 1977. Records of the Mayoral Administration of Maynard Jackson, Jr., City of Atlanta, Records Management Division, Box 90-TR-331, Folder 4.
468. "As chief administrative officer": George Berry interview.
468. "Let the law department": *Ibid.*
469. The report concluded that: *Atlanta Constitution*, September 29, 1977.
469. "my very close friend": *Atlanta Journal*, October 7, 1977.
469. "turned-off feeling": *Atlanta Constitution*, October 6, 1977.
469. they visited the aged Marcus Primault: Maynard Jackson, Jr., interview.
469. "I played a few jazz progressions": *Ibid.*
469. "Maynard idealizes the love affair": Valerie Richardson Jackson interview.
469. The mayor had asked her to introduce him: Interview with Shirley Franklin.
470. "Would our city languish": *Atlanta Journal*, January 4, 1978.
470. take his picture with black citizens: A. Reginald Eaves interview.
470. "Superchief! Superchief!": Interview with Chet Fuller.
470. vocal English professor named Millicent Dobbs Jordan: *Atlanta Journal*, April 23, 1976.
470. "Man, there's the superchief *and the Godfather*": Chet Fuller interview.
470. combined cost to Atlanta taxpayers of $200,000 a year: *Atlanta Constitution*, May 7, 1976.
470. New York mayor Abraham Beame: *Ibid.*
470. "I'm loved by a lot of folk but": *Ibid.*
471. likened his role to a Jackson bodyguard: David Franklin interview.
471. "expressly authorized": *Atlanta Constitution*, February 21, 1978.
471. "The final decision in this case": *Ibid.*
471. Twenty-six death threats were made: *Ibid.*, March 3, 1978.
471. policemen no longer were carrying "drop weapons": Maynard Jackson, Jr., interview.
471. "Maynard kept picking up from poor black people": David Franklin interview.
472. "Didn't you do [the cheating]?": A. Reginald Eaves interview.
472. The superchief would appear with him: Maynard Jackson, Jr., interview.
472. George Berry had written two statements: George Berry interview.
472. "He's gonna fire him!": *Ibid.*
472. "They saw it based on the standard of proof": *Atlanta Journal*, March 8, 1978.
472. "I felt like a fool": Maynard Jackson, Jr., interview.
472. "It was a reflection of my immaturity": *Ibid.*
472. "His conduct causes me grave": *Atlanta Journal*, March 8, 1978.
473. "looked like he'd been hit": George Berry interview.
473. "The Boston pol, so to speak": Maynard Jackson, Jr., interview.
473. "severe damage to the integrity": *Atlanta Journal-Constitution*, March 11, 1978.
473. "Most folks thought that [loyalty]": David Franklin interview.
473. "Where else you gonna put": Maynard Jackson, Jr., interview.
474. "Well, why don't you let": *Ibid.*

CHAPTER 27

475. *"Oh, no!"*: Interview with Angelo Fuster.
475. "You better come over here": *Ibid.*
475. 27 percent of its population living in poverty: Clarence N. Stone, *Regime Politics: Governing Atlanta, 1946–1988* (Lawrence, Kan.: University Press of Kansas, 1989), pp. 247–50.

476. "the fat boy": James Baldwin, *The Evidence of Things Not Seen* (New York: Holt, Rinehart & Winston, 1985), p. 55.
476. "Why don't you stop lying": *Atlanta Constitution*, July 24, 1980.
476. "most black people could not believe": Interview with Maynard Jackson, Jr.
476. "I came to believe it had to be somebody black": *Ibid.*
477. children began to refer to the killer as the Man: Jerry Adler and Vern E. Smith, "The Terror in Atlanta," *Newsweek*, March 2, 1981, p. 37.
477. "My job": Maynard Jackson, Jr., interview.
477. with the black CBS reporter Ed Bradley: Angelo Fuster interview.
477. raised money to build a replacement day-care center: *Atlanta Constitution*, August 11, 1987.
477. "Businesses we might have been able": Interview with Tom Hamall.
477. "not asking, but reassuring": Maynard Jackson, Jr., interview.
478. "spread the gospel of caution": *Atlanta Journal*, September 10, 1980.
478. *"It was the Klan!"*: Maynard Jackson, Jr., and Angelo Fuster interviews.
478. was struck by how small the bodies: Interview with Hyde Post.
478. several whites, in a pickup with a Confederate flag: Angelo Fuster interview.
478. Maynard Jr. had lived with Bowen's widow: Maynard Jackson, Jr., interview.
478. "There's no evidence that it was anything": *Atlanta Journal*, October 13, 1980.
478. boiler had received little maintenance: *Atlanta Journal*, October 19, 1980.
478. "I caution you and I plead": *Ibid.*, October 13, 1980.
478. refused to believe Lee Brown: *Ibid.*, October 14, 1980.
478. "like telling him another person had died": Angelo Fuster interview.
479. discovered a small skull and a clump: *Atlanta Journal*, October 19, 1980.
479. black parents called George Napper's home: Interview with George Napper.
479. asked the First National Bank to provide: *Atlanta Journal*, October 22, 1980.
479. "It was unfortunate that we had": George Napper interview.
479. heard the first rumblings that the city's white: Maynard Jackson, Jr., interview.
480. the mayor and Sweat had gone months: Interview with Dan Sweat.
480. "a sense of relief": Tom Hamall interview.
480. offered $300,000 to back his campaign: Interview with Wyche Fowler.
480. Tom Cousins and Sweat flew to Washington: Interview with Jack Watson, Jr.
480. "It is going to require someone": Maynard Jackson, Jr., interview.
480. "I was considered too black to succeed.": Interview with Andrew Young.
480. "There was just so much that happened.": *Ibid.*
481. "I don't think that's the way to go.": Maynard Jackson, Jr., interview.
481. "Maynard spelled out the scenario": Andrew Young interview.
481. "They were absolutely convinced": *Ibid.*
481. *"Andy, when you came here"*: *Ibid.*
482. "Atlanta business into total ballistic gridlock": Interview with Bob Holder.
482. "Ivan thought Andy Young": Interview with Margaret Allen.
482. "I got Birmingham black and white": *Atlanta Constitution*, October 14, 1981.
482. "just the most awful thing": Bob Holder interview.
482. "Lindbergh was one child": *Atlanta Constitution*, November 6, 1980.
482. "unjustified, discriminatory against Atlanta": *Atlanta Journal*, November 7, 1980.
483. "quantum leap": *Ibid.*
483. "The issue dominated everything": Maynard Jackson, Jr., interview.
483. acclaimed homicide investigators arrived: *Atlanta Journal*, November 25, 1980.
483. The Guardian Angels arrived from New York City: *Atlanta Constitution*, March 8, 1981.
483. "The Hank Aaron Crime Stoppers": *Atlanta Journal*, March 17, 1981.
483. Sammy Davis, Jr., and Frank Sinatra performed: *Ibid.*, March 10, 1981.
483. "You can't even buy a Rolls-Royce": *Atlanta Constitution*, May 9, 1981.
483. Maynard Jr. paid frequent visits: Maynard Jackson, Jr., interview.
483. recommended dressing midgets as children: *Atlanta Journal-Constitution*, June 16, 1992.
483. "Lee, what can we do?": Angelo Fuster interview.
484. "Maynard had to ask the exact right question": *Ibid.*
484. "We cry for, and we cry with": *Atlanta Constitution*, February 3, 1981.
484. "There are those few critics": *Ibid.*
484. officials wondered if the killer was losing control: *Atlanta Constitution*, February 25, 1981.
484. "Sit down": *Atlanta Journal-Constitution*, June 1, 1992.

484. "I never did like Maynard Jackson.": Author interview with Catherine Leach as research for a story that appeared in the *Atlanta Journal-Constitution*, June 16, 1992.
484. "We were over in south Atlanta": Margaret Allen interview.
485. "as a Walter Mitty experience": Interview with Dobbs "Buddy" Jordan.
485. "Who can swim?": *Ibid.*
485. He wore infrared goggles: *Ibid.*
485. "The state of Georgia had never before": Baldwin, *The Evidence of Things Not Seen*, p. 58.
485. "I just heard a loud splash!": *Atlanta Journal-Constitution*, June 16, 1992.
485. Nathaniel Cater washed up more than a mile: *Atlanta Constitution*, May 26, 1981.
485. "They were mostly just saying": *Atlanta Journal*, June 4, 1981.
486. They seized a yellow blanket: *Atlanta Constitution*, June 5, 1981.
486. he stopped in front of Lee Brown's house: *Atlanta Journal*, June 11, 1981.
486. had sworn in Williams: Andrew Young interview.
486. "They had a card table": *Ibid.*
486. "When he was fifteen": Maynard Jackson, Jr., interview.
486. "Something happened to him": *Ibid.*
487. "Aren't you John Wesley Dobbs's grandson?": *Ibid.*
487. "the story of this [white] ringleader": *Ibid.*
487. "We are beginning to see shuffling": *Atlanta Constitution*, October 15, 1981.
488. "Does Mayor Jackson want to say": *Ibid.*, October 16, 1981.
488. "If a white person made those comments": *Atlanta Journal*, October 15, 1981.
488. "I was absolutely shocked": *Atlanta Constitution*, October 16, 1981.
488. "would not [as mayor] have repudiated": Andrew Young interview.
488. "a calculated move that worked": Maynard Jackson, Jr., interview.
489. "Some people will never, ever forgive me": *Atlanta Constitution*, October 15, 1981.
489. Young won just 10 percent of the white vote": *Atlanta Journal*, October 28, 1981.
489. "it would have said that the black community": Interview with Michael Lomax.
489. "I know none of you voted for me.": Bob Holder interview.
489. "It was one of the most spectacular": *Ibid.*
489. "And I'll never forget Mayor Ivan Allen's": *Atlanta Constitution*, January 5, 1982.
489. "Atlanta is not now rising": *Ibid.*
490. "As of now, I'm saying goodbye": *Ibid.*
490. "You wanted the real Wayne Williams": *Atlanta Journal*, February 24, 1982.
490. prosecutors liken Williams to Adolf Hitler: *Atlanta Constitution*, February 27, 1982.
490. "I never agreed with the idea": Maynard Jackson, Jr., interview.
491. "[They] decided to commit the perfect crime": Andrew Young interview.
491. "There's no doubt in my mind": Maynard Jackson, Jr., interview.
491. "I think Maynard's size": Andrew Young interview.
491. he accepted a position as partner with Chapman and Cutler: News release, August 25, 1982. Central Atlanta Progress Papers, Atlanta History Center, Box 15, Folder entitled "Maynard Jackson, 1981."
491. same space in the Grant Building: Maynard Jackson, Jr., interview.
491. sat in the living room of the Rev. Jesse Jackson: *Ibid.*
492. "inside government credentials": Interview with Rev. Jesse Jackson.
492. "That was the time when I should have run": Maynard Jackson, Jr., interview.
492. "I was blamed for affirmative action": *Ibid.*

CHAPTER 28

493. "It is a land of the Mercedes": *Wall Street Journal*, February 20, 1988.
495. qualify for the 1952 U.S. Olympic team: Interview with Andrew Young.
495. setting a track record at the Quantico marine base: *Ibid.*
495. watch the Movietone News as Jesse Owens: Andrew Young, *A Way Out of No Way: The Spiritual Memoirs of Andrew Young* (Nashville: Thomas Nelson, 1994), pp. 145–46.
495. Young seemed preoccupied: Interview with Billy Payne.
496. population rising 32 percent: U.S. Census 1980 and 1990. The Atlanta metropolitan area grew from 2.23 million in 1980 to 2.96 million in 1990.
496. 1985 population was two-thirds black: *New York Times*, May 6, 1985.

496. 35 percent of all city contracts: Nehl Horton, *The Young Years: A Report on the Administration of the Honorable Andrew Young, Mayor of the City of Atlanta, 1982–1989* (Atlanta: City of Atlanta, December 1989), pp. 117–22. In 1982, Young changed the Minority Business Enterprise (MBE) program begun by Jackson to the Minority and Female Business Enterprise (MFBE). In 1985, he increased the city's MFBE goal from 25 percent to 35 percent, which placed Atlanta's affirmative action goal among the nation's highest. On March 2, 1989, the Georgia Supreme Court, in *American Sub-contractors Association, Georgia Chapter v. City of Atlanta*, struck down the city's MFBE ordinance, citing insufficient evidence of discrimination in past city contracting to justify the program. (Five weeks earlier, the U.S. Supreme Court, in *J. A. Croson Co. v. City of Richmond, Va.*, had ruled that Richmond's 30 percent minority business set-aside was unconstitutional.) The author of this administrative report, Nehl Horton, served as director of legislative affairs under Young. Figures for the Contract Compliance office of the city of Atlanta show that 36 percent of contracts awarded in 1986, 1987 and 1988 went to minority and female-owned businesses.
496. nation's top-selling Volvo dealer: *Wall Street Journal*, February 29, 1988.
497. Young had met nearly two hundred international: Horton, *The Young Years*, pp. 107–12. See also: *Atlanta Journal-Constitution*, December 31, 1989.
497. 25 percent of the stock to foreign investors: Andrew Young interview.
497. "The state legislature freaked out.": *Ibid.*
497. "Jobs, that's the way you feed the hungry.": *Atlanta Journal-Constitution*, December 31, 1989.
498. "There was a major transformation": Billy Payne interview.
498. "To me, that's the way God works.": Andrew Young interview.
498. "And we laughed for a week": Interview with Shirley Franklin.
498. "You do all those things.": *Ibid.*
498. "I would see black people walking": Interview with Maynard Jackson, Jr.
499. fifteen-room, multilevel French Provincial: *Atlanta Constitution*, September 24, 1989.
499. "It was an unusual thing to do": Interview with Ivan Allen, Jr.
499. "I thought it was a bad move": Andrew Young interview.
499. "But when you're segregated": *Ibid.*
499. in a chauffeured black Lincoln Continental: *Atlanta Constitution*, September 24, 1989.
499. "We heard he was going to run": *Atlanta Journal*, February 27, 1987.
500. "Ham and cheese?": Interview with Michael Lomax.
500. "being mayor of Atlanta is overshadowed": *Ibid.* On November 7, 1989, Douglas Wilder and David Dinkins became the first blacks ever elected to those positions.
500. would need only about 35 percent of the black vote: *Atlanta Constitution*, March 19, 1989.
501. "Great idea.": Billy Payne interview.
501. "What I wanted was the absolute sure-fire deal": Interview with Bob Holder.
502. "before he would undertake something": Interview with Margaret Allen.
502. with $116 million in revenues: Records of the Ivan Allen Company. "Ivan Allen Company Sales," a year-by-year accounting of revenues, 1960–94. Personal files of Ivan Allen, Jr.
502. "They were spending so much money": Interview with H. Inman Allen.
502. "I was focusing on the equity side": *Ibid.*
502. "I'll do it, with the understanding": Bob Holder interview.
502. "Because of who he was": Billy Payne interview.
503. "Remember, my deal was that": Bob Holder interview.
503. He stopped at Paschal's restaurant: *Atlanta Constitution*, February 17, 1989.
503. received five times as many home loans: *Atlanta Journal-Constitution*, May 1, 1988. A four-part series entitled "The Color of Money" earned reporter Bill Dedman a Pulitzer Prize.
504. protesters, holding anti-Lomax placards: *Atlanta Constitution*, January 2, 1989.
504. "They were going out of their way.": Interview with Michael Lomax.
504. "Number one, I didn't leave the city": Maynard Jackson, Jr., interview.
505. "to help the neighborhood revitalize": *Ibid.*
505. "That's one of the prices you pay": *Ibid.*
505. only 12 percent of a racially mixed pool: *Atlanta Constitution*, March 19, 1989.
505. the ads translated a stereotyped image: *Ibid.*, August 9, 1989.
505. "Ladies and gentlemen, the future of Atlanta": *Ibid.*, October 4, 1989.
505. "Unfortunately, whites still prefer": *Ibid.*
506. "I was shocked with his level": Maynard Jackson, Jr., interview.
506. "I think it would be good": *Ibid.*
506. "We never really lost Andy": Billy Payne interview.

506. "The whites had been disfranchised": H. Inman Allen interview.
506. "We knew that the bridges": *Ibid.*
506. Arthur Cummings and paid $70,000: Richard Shumate, "Maynard, The Sequel," *Atlanta,* December 1991, pp. 56–59, 120–26.
507. "We pride ourselves": Interview with Ivan Allen IV.
507. "opens doors. You receive an audience": *Ibid.*
507. "Cuatro performed superbly": Interview with Jimmy Carter.
507. "Well, I'm shooting with people": Ivan Allen IV interview.
508. a young black man at his front counter: *Ibid.*
508. lift his girlfriend and throw her: *Atlanta Constitution,* June 19, 1990.
508. "Mayor's Son in Hot Water Again.": *Ibid.*
508. *"Are you going to pay"*: *Ibid.,* June 22, 1990.
508. "painful experience for me": *Ibid.*
508. "These are my chillens": *Ibid.,* January 30, 1990.
508. Buzzy, had been accepted to study there: Interview with Brooke Jackson.
509. "There's no way I'm sending you": *Ibid.*
509. Buzzy nearly ran an unmarked police car: *Atlanta Constitution,* June 22, 1990.
509. "I was always very conscious": Interview with Beth Jackson Hodges.
509. "I wanted to be the black female John Portman": Brooke Jackson interview.
509. "He cried": *Ibid.*
509. "But it never occurred to me": Maynard Jackson, Jr., interview.
509. "because he did everything he could": Interview with Bunnie Jackson-Ransom.
509. "He has reacted in ways that were anti-social": Maynard Jackson, Jr., interview.
510. "would have been less tolerant": *Ibid.*
510. drove Buzzy to the Salvation Army: *Ibid.*
510. "was saved by a woman": *Ibid.*
510. "He had been using marijuana": Bunnie Jackson-Ransom interview.
510. "A good heart, but a short temper": Brooke Jackson interview.
510. "Buzzy wants to please Daddy": Beth Jackson Hodges interview.
510. "I was not happy about it": Maynard Jackson, Jr., interview.
510. "My father hated the idea": Brooke Jackson interview.
510. "Just be what you want to be": Maynard Jackson, Jr., interview.
511. "He has talked to all of us": Interview with Sandra Irene Jackson Baraniuk.
511. "My father is a real big dreamer": Brooke Jackson interview.
511. "He wanted his son": Bunnie Jackson-Ransom interview.
511. As he walked toward his garage: Maynard Jackson, Jr., interview.
511. "I thought he needed a little booster": Ivan Allen, Jr., interview.
511. "We're in the finals.": Maynard Jackson, Jr., interview.
512. "We can set an example.": Billy Payne interview.
512. had expected to see farmlands: *Ibid.*
512. "While we had not encountered any negativism": *Ibid.*
513. "We were lobby lizards": Maynard Jackson, Jr., interview.
513. the Atlantans had rented a house: Bob Holder interview.
513. "I am Maynard Jackson, mayor": Speech by Mayor Maynard Jackson, Jr., delivered at final bid presentation to IOC in Tokyo, September 8, 1990. Personal files of Maynard Jackson, Jr.
513. "His accent is good": Billy Payne interview.
513. "It was just like in the Baptist church": Maynard Jackson, Jr., interview.
513. Maynard Jackson saw some IOC members crying: *Ibid.*
513. "The International Olympic Committee has": *Atlanta Journal,* September 18, 1990.
513. "Our hearts were in our throats": Maynard Jackson, Jr., interview.
514. "Coca-Cola!": *Atlanta Journal,* September 19, 1990. Also in an interview with Bert Roughton.
514. "The thing you'd worked for": *Ibid.*
514. Atlanta swept most of Toronto's votes: *Atlanta Journal,* September 18, 1990.
514. "Everything I said that seemed": Andrew Young interview.
514. "Thank you, God.": Maynard Jackson, Jr., interview.
514. Ivan Allen III was driving to work: Margaret Allen interview.
514. "YEESSSSS!": *Ibid.*
515. "I was thrilled to death": Ivan Allen, Jr., interview.
515. "The city of Atlanta deserves this.": *Ibid.*

CHAPTER 29

516. restored the stables and returned horses: Interview with Ivan Allen, Jr.
516. a farmer at heart: Interview with Margaret Allen.
516. wild dogs appeared from out of the brush: *Ibid.*
517. "For the first time in my life": *Ibid.*
517. he drove each morning at 6:30: Ivan Allen, Jr., interview.
517. "I can't hide behind something.": Interview with Marie Dodd.
517. "If Ivan doesn't look out": Interview with Bill Pressly.
517. "Why don't you come jog with us": Interview with Dr. E. Ladd Jones.
517. "He could never really relax here": Margaret Allen interview.
518. "See, Jonesy, I told you": Dr. E. Ladd Jones interview.
518. "We're spending too much time": Marie Dodd interview.
518. resignation from the boards: Memorandum from Marie Dodd to Ivan Allen III, March 30, 1992. Private files of Marie Dodd.
518. "Obviously, I had to respect that": Interview with Maynard Jackson, Jr.
518. turned down a trustee role at Princeton: Margaret Allen interview.
518. "I would not have accepted that": Interview with Charles Glassick.
518. "We'll give you a leave of absence": Interview with Howard "Bo" Callaway.
519. Andy Young had convinced him to chair: Interview with Andrew Young.
519. he told his father of his plans: Ivan Allen, Jr., interview.
519. "Marie, am I too tough": Marie Dodd interview.
519. "I just tried to talk to Ivan": Bill Pressly interview.
519. cited the names of some of Atlanta's: Ivan Allen, Jr., interview.
519. "I'm mighty proud of you, Mason": Mason Lowance, Jr., letter to the author, February 18, 1994. Lowance responded in writing to a series of questions posed by the author.
519. Together, they would meet with corporate chiefs: Interview with Jimmy Carter.
520. dark and terrible, that Ivan III was dead: Margaret Allen interview.
520. By his side was the Smith & Wesson: Incident Report, May 17, 1992, Heard County Sheriff's Department, Franklin, Ga.
520. Ivan III was pronounced dead: *Ibid.*
520. "The situation didn't warrant it": Interview with Larry Hooks.
520. *"Self-Inflicted Gunshot Wound."* Incident Report, May 17, 1992, Heard County Sheriff's Department, Franklin, Ga.
520. "I have very bad news.": Marie Dodd interview.
520. Ivan IV fell into her arms, sobbing: *Ibid.*
521. It never occurred to her: *Ibid.*
521. once the ink dried, company employees folded them: *Ibid.*
521. taken her telephone off the hook early: Margaret Allen interview.
521. Just heard the news on National Public Radio: Jimmy Carter interview.
521. "Is it true, Margaret?": Margaret Allen interview.
521. "I won't tell if you won't tell": Maynard Jackson, Jr., interview.
521. A white-gloved City of Atlanta policeman: *Atlanta Constitution,* May 19, 1992.
521. "There wouldn't be any Olympics": Interview with Bob Holder.
522. "Where did I go wrong?": Bill Pressly interview.
522. when he pulled the trigger he was no longer Ivan III: *Ibid.*
522. Margaret did not want a cortege: Marie Dodd interview.
522. "How they ever got to Westview!": Ivan Allen, Jr., interview.
522. "I never saw anything like it": Interview with Laura Maddox Smith.
523. "Trying to explain Ivan's death": Audiotape of Beaumont Allen graveside tribute, May 19, 1992. Personal files of Margaret Allen.
523. "His commitment to us": Audiotape of H. Inman Allen graveside tribute, May 19, 1992. *Ibid.*
523. "the essence of the Southern gentleman": Audiotape of Jimmy Carter eulogy at graveside service. *Ibid.*
523. "He was somebody I could count on": Maynard Jackson, Jr., interview.
523. "Life is eternal and love is immortal": Interview with Eugene Patterson.
523. "That's the only time I lost": Ivan Allen, Jr., interview.
523. "I flounder terribly": *Ibid.*
524. "Say, this isn't so bad.": *New Yorker,* May 25, 1992.

524. Alone on her porch, she wept.: Marie Dodd interview.
524. "I have been able to accept Ivan's death": Interview with Louise Allen.
524. "I think Daddy [the Senator] demanded": Ivan Allen, Jr., interview.
524. "I really don't want to talk about that": Interview with Ivan Allen III.
524. "We were absolutely controlled by Atlanta.": Ivan Allen, Jr., interview.
525. "It was the happiest thing in my life": Interview with Amanda Allen Thompson.
525. Loo-key, is what Ivan III: *Ibid.*
525. "What are you doing here?": Interview with Knox Thompson.
525. did Knox bend to one knee: *Ibid.*
525. "a little tiny trickle": Amanda Allen Thompson interview.
526. "It was very hard to focus": Knox Thompson interview.
526. "just looked so sad": Margaret Allen interview.
526. "richer than a king": Edward Arlington Robinson, "Richard Cory." In Ralph L. Woods, editor, *A Treasury of the Familiar* (New York: Macmillan, 1955), pp. 222–23.
526. Ivan III left no suicide note.: Margaret Allen and Ivan Allen, Jr., interviews.
526. Ben, Jr., commits suicide: Anne Rivers Siddons, *Peachtree Road* (New York: Harper & Row, 1988), p. 474.
526. *God Almighty,* Siddons thought: Interview with Anne Rivers Siddons.
526. "Mr. Mayor, I hope there's not a subpoena": *Ibid.*
527. "I don't think he knew how many people": Interview with Hugh Gloster.
527. "You have followed in these footsteps": Citation to Ivan Allen III by Hugh Gloster, President of Morehouse College, Presentation of Honorary Degree of Doctor of Laws, May 22, 1983. Personal files of Hugh Gloster.
527. "I came away thinking": Interview with Larry Gellerstedt III.
528. The $7 million pavilion featured: *Atlanta Constitution,* October 21, 1993.
528. "I can think of no better place": Tape recording of speech delivered by Lt. Gov. Pierre Howard of Georgia at Carter Center's annual Salute to Public Service, February 16, 1994. Private files of Elizabeth Kurylo, *Atlanta Constitution* reporter, who attended the event.
528. "I was ready to leave": Margaret Allen interview.
528. "Well, they gave you credit for the building.": *Ibid.* Margaret Allen heard Carter's remark.
528. "This was what Ivan": *Ibid.*

CHAPTER 30

529. lost only one vote in the four-year term: Interview with Bill Campbell.
529. "[Maynard Jr.] was an opportunist": Interview with Marvin Arrington.
530. "won the street lottery": *Ibid.*
530. "His mother probably had a Ph.D.": *Ibid.*
530. Miller won more than 80 percent of the white: *Atlanta Constitution,* August 9, 1990.
530. "Here's a man who had been ambassador": Interview with Maynard Jackson, Jr.
531. "You need to get stock in Bic!": Interview with Deb Speights.
531. "Pat, Maynard Jackson, 23rd February, Sunday": Maynard Jackson, Jr., interview. On this morning, Jackson gave a car tour of Atlanta to the author.
532. "Why are you here?": Interview with Joel Babbit.
532. "That makes me furious": Ronald Bowers, *The Selznick Players* (New York: A. S. Barnes, 1976), p. 15.
532. "I can see that my full name": Maynard Jackson, Jr., interview.
532. named three separate chiefs of staff: *Atlanta Constitution,* January 15, 1992.
532. "One of Maynard's frustrations": Interview with Andrew Young.
532. "I was the only mayor who went all over": Maynard Jackson, Jr., interview.
533. "You know, Mr. President": Interview with Jimmy Carter.
533. "He basically gave me a blank check": *Ibid.*
533. "Am I happy being mayor?": *Atlanta Constitution,* January 15, 1992.
533. A columnist for *The Boston Globe: Ibid.* The story by *Globe* columnist Robert Jordan was referred to in this story in the *Atlanta Constitution.*
533. "I believe in your qualities": *Atlanta Constitution,* February 28, 1992.
534. Jackson was on a short list of twelve: *Washington Post,* June 22, 1992.
534. "Complete speculation": *Atlanta Constitution,* June 23, 1992.

534. "Never in my wildest dreams": Maynard Jackson, Jr., interview.
534. nearly one thousand Atlanta University Center students: *Atlanta Constitution*, May 1, 1992.
534. indicated an increasingly unruly crowd: Interview with Angelo Fuster.
534. the mayor's aides advised him not to meet: Deb Speights interview.
534. "What happened is wrong": Angelo Fuster interview.
534. Most of the youths had no intention of listening: Maynard Jackson, Jr., Angelo Fuster and Deb Speights interviews.
535. shattered windows and turned over pushcarts: *Atlanta Constitution*, May 1, 1992.
535. "Justice 4 Rodney": *Ibid.*
535. "more than surprised by the vehemence": Angelo Fuster interview.
536. mayor's statements were balled up and thrown: Deb Speights interview.
536. "What they did was set me up": Maynard Jackson, Jr., interview.
536. "People like Maynard Jackson don't know": *Atlanta Constitution*, May 2, 1992.
536. "If we can't talk": Maynard Jackson, Jr., interview.
536. "I lost respect": *Ibid.*
536. more than three hundred arrests had been made: *Atlanta Constitution*, May 1, 1992.
536. "Do what you need to do": *Ibid.*, May 24, 1992.
536. "We will not tolerate lawlessness": Angelo Fuster and Maynard Jackson, Jr., interviews.
536. A white businessman said his wife: Interview with Bob Holder.
536. harassed by white state troopers: *Ibid.*
536. "We've got to manage the issue of race": *Atlanta Constitution*, May 6, 1992.
537. "taking a two-by-four to get their attention": *Ibid.*, May 17, 1992.
537. "Oh, man!": Maynard Jackson, Jr., interview.
537. "In accordance with our tradition": *Atlanta Constitution*, August 10, 1992.
537. "I was going to savor the moment": Maynard Jackson, Jr., interview.
537. "I'm not fixated on that": *Ibid.*
537. "You wake up in the hospital": *Ibid.*
538. "The Georgia flag reeks with racism": "Letters from My Kitchen Table," written by Mayor Maynard Jackson, Jr., September 15, 1992. Personal files of Joel Babbit, former City Hall staffer.
538. "I got tired of giving up $500,000": Maynard Jackson, Jr., interview.
538. "is making anybody with two cents": *Ibid.*
538. Buzzy had choked, pinched: *Atlanta Constitution*, July 23, 1992.
538. "I neglected my family": Maynard Jackson, Jr., interview.
539. "Tonight we honor a man": Maynard Jackson, Jr., speech at testimonial for former Mayor Ivan Allen, Jr., by Georgia State University, April 23, 1993. The author attended the testimonial.
539. "It's good to know that I am still Ivan Allen": Ivan Allen, Jr., speech at testimonial in his honor by Georgia State University, April 23, 1993.
539. "When the big Mo'": Maynard Jackson, Jr., interview.
539. considered lobbying for the city to build: *Ibid.*
539. "Atlanta is in better shape": State of the City Address, Mayor Maynard H. Jackson, Jr., January 4, 1993. Files of City of Atlanta Mayor's Office, City Hall, Atlanta, Ga.
540. the Atlanta force had ninety-two *fewer* officers: *Atlanta Constitution*, January 10, 1993.
540. fewer than six hundred units had been completed: *Ibid.*
540. "So little has been done": *Atlanta Journal*, December 8, 1992.
540. "My interest was in doing": Maynard Jackson, Jr., interview.
540. "I enjoy the rumor-mongering": *Atlanta Constitution*, December 9, 1992.
541. "If I ran again and won": Interview with Sandra Irene Jackson Baraniuk.
541. Jackson's public approval rating was 70 percent: *Atlanta Journal-Constitution*, June 3, 1993.
541. "Don't walk out on what is going to be": Interview with Billy Payne.
541. he signed it, "Maynard, Who": Interview with Lyle Harris.
541. He dashed out several times to accept phone calls: Sandra Irene Jackson Baraniuk interview.
542. Clement and Beamon recited: Bill Clement, Jr., interview.
542. "Atlanta will get to its mountaintop": Announcement by Mayor Maynard Jackson, Jr., that he would not seek a fourth term, June 9, 1993. The author attended the announcement.
542. where black mayors once had served: *Time*, "Bright City Lights," November 1, 1993.
542. cost taxpayers $1 million: *Atlanta Journal-Constitution*, September 30, 1994.
543. staff negotiated a $14,000 reduction: *Atlanta Constitution*, August 11, 1993.
543. "*I will repay you in full*": Letter from Maynard Jackson, Jr., to John Wesley Dobbs, October 21, 1956. John Wesley Dobbs Papers, Amistad Research Center, New Orleans, La., Box 1, Folder 12.

543. "Some people would be embarrassed": Bill Clement, Jr., interview.
543. "I believe God has a plan for this boy": Maynard Jackson, Jr., interview.
544. "Thirty-three years later": Speech at dedication of John Wesley Dobbs Avenue by Neal McQueen, Grand Master of the Georgia jurisdiction of Prince Hall Masons, January 10, 1994. The author attended the ceremony.
544. He had received job offers from several: Maynard Jackson, Jr., interview.
544. Eaves had accepted $35,000: *Atlanta Constitution*, May 3, 1988.
544. Franklin had been disbarred: *Ibid.*, May 28, 1986.
544. "It's a great occasion": Speech by former Mayor Maynard Jackson, Jr., at the dedication of John Wesley Dobbs Avenue, January 10, 1994.
545. "Free at Last, Free at Last": Interview with Windsor Jordan. Jordan witnessed this scene.

EPILOGUE

547. "Do you want to take over": Interview with H. Inman Allen.
547. by accepting its first black member in 1994: *Atlanta Constitution*, November 19, 1994.
547. "I had the freedom": H. Inman Allen interview.
547. one of America's twenty-five most eligible bachelors: *Town & Country*, June 1967, pp. 92–93.
548. set up the baby's nursery inside a closet: H. Inman Allen interview.
548. "It's a cohesive force": *Ibid.*
548. "Well, son, why do you want to sell?": Interview with Ivan Allen, Jr.
548. his father was too old to study: H. Inman Allen interview.
548. "This is a bad decision": *Ibid.*
549. "I wanted very much for the family to say": *Ibid.*
549. News of the impending sale broke: *Atlanta Constitution*, August 25, 1995.
549. "This is so much bullshit": H. Inman Allen interview.
549. Every board member voted to sell: *Ibid.*
549. "Daddy, I will take": H. Inman Allen and Ivan Allen, Jr., interviews.
549. "I'm living much easier": *Atlanta Constitution*, September 15, 1994.
549. cost $378,000 in legal/advisory fees: H. Inman Allen interview.
550. "Part of it was a business decision": *Ibid.*
550. "I'm not going to have my father walk": *Ibid.*
550. He read a couple books about how to survive suicide: *Ibid.*
550. It caromed off the old mayor's head: Ivan Allen, Jr., interview.
550. "Take me there": Visits to Marietta City Cemetery and the Noonday Baptist Church Extension Cemetery with Maynard Jackson, Jr., April 23, 1994. The author accompanied Maynard Jr. on the visit. The scenes are drawn from that visit.
551. "No. That man was a part of the millions": Interview with Maynard Jackson, Jr.
551. Then he noticed on the cemetery hillside: Maynard Jackson, Jr., interview. The author did not accompany Jackson on this separate trip to the Marietta cemetery.
551. "The Klan checking me out": *Ibid.*
551. "The McAfees are not my relatives": *Ibid.*
551. "It is too Maynard Jackson!": Scene at liquor store witnessed by the author, April 23, 1994.
553. "They didn't even know how old she": Maynard Jackson, Jr., interview at the Noonday Baptist Church Extension Cemetery.
553. disturbed for a moment by the reminder of slavery: Maynard Jackson, Jr., interview.

# AUTHOR'S NOTE

I moved to Atlanta in 1988 and almost at once felt the profound resonance of race. Turning to volumes of local history, I found pieces of the city and its racial past scattered about—bits on the white side here, bits on the black side there. I wanted a more complete picture.

Early in 1991, I determined to write about Atlanta's racial conscience. My initial idea was to write about Peachtree and Sweet Auburn as symbols to southern dreamers, white and black. To humanize these famous boulevards, to give them flesh and bone, I decided to tell Atlanta's racial history through families. Families, with the passing of traditions and core beliefs across the generations, are the foundation of any city. Like cities, families grow organically over time.

The Allens and the Dobbses are Old Atlanta families. They arrived in Atlanta in the 1890s, which, it has been said, is the local equivalent of arriving on the *Mayflower*. Further, both families have been involved in virtually every critical political decision made in Atlanta during the past half century, a period when the city came of age.

At the start of this project, I knew only of the popular legend of Mayor Ivan Allen, Jr. It seemed outsized, yet no more outsized than the man who tapped me on the shoulder at an Atlanta hotel in 1989, and, with splendid eye contact and handshaking precision, announced, *"I'm May-nard Jackson. I'm running for mayor . . ."* Then, he moved artfully to the next person. I had seen the Ivan Allen Company delivery trucks moving through downtown and once, while visiting the Commerce Club, saw a bust of Ivan Allen, Sr., in "The Allen Room." I'm not certain where I first heard the name John Wesley Dobbs; most likely it came up during my work as a city reporter for *The Atlanta Constitution*. Yet I soon discovered that Dobbs's legend still sheds sparks. Anyone who remembers the Grand—and that includes virtually every native black Atlantan older than fifty—remembers him vividly, usually for his oratory. Early in my research, I read William A. Muraskin's *Middle Class Blacks in a White Society: Prince Hall Freemasonry in America*. Muraskin wrote of Dobbs as a Masonic king, noting how in 1956 the Committee on the Grand Master's Address at the annual Grand Lodge of the Georgia jurisdiction had described him as "a unique combination of aristocracy and democracy." Buried in a Muraskin footnote on page 272 I read: "A biography of Dobbs would be exceptionally rewarding."

Once my idea for this book crystallized in the summer of 1991, I sought out Maynard Jackson, Jr., and Ivan Allen, Jr., and their families. It took some time for the families to grasp my intentions. Neither envisioned their clan as significant in the grand scheme of Atlanta. "Why us?" one Dobbs family member asked. Said Ivan Jr.: "We're not very interesting." The two families were protective of their good name. Early on, one Dobbs member told me, "I've been told not to speak with you until it's been cleared by *the Atlanta office.*" I assumed that meant the mayor. In time, though, both families opened up and allowed me inside, a privilege I did not take lightly. Because of the cooperation of the Allens and the Dobbses, this is a more candid and complete book.

A product of nearly five years of work, this book is a hybrid history-journalism. These two practices are not so different, after all. "The first rough draft of history" is how Phil Graham, *The Washington Post* publisher, once described journalism, and his description seems apt.

In synthesizing the written and spoken words, I have relied heavily on volumes of primary materials, including manuscript collections, private letters and diaries, government files, court records, newspapers and periodicals, in addition to hundreds of personal interviews. Most interview subjects were gracious with their time and many consented to several interview sessions. The average interview lasted roughly two hours. Nearly all were tape-recorded and then transcribed. Only a small percentage of interviews were conducted by telephone, a less personal and therefore less desirable form.

In a project such as this, the historian becomes much like a detective, searching for clues, some recent and others from the distant past. "Writing a book is an adventure" goes the famous saying by Winston Churchill. "To begin with, it is a toy and an amusement. Then it becomes a mistress, then it becomes a tyrant. The last phase is that just as you are about to be reconciled to your servitude, you kill the monster, and fling him to the public."

Early on, when this book still seemed an amusement (though a passionate amusement, at that), I tracked the freed slave Judie Dobbs through census records that began in 1870 when blacks in the South first were recognized fully as citizens. The revered grandmother of the Grand, Judie Dobbs was only a name to me then. But in 1992, when I secured a photo of her from a descendant, Jesse L. Dobbs, who had one stored in his attic in Cleveland, Ohio, Judie Dobbs became a name *and a face*. Later, I interviewed Irene Dobbs Jackson, her great-granddaughter. She remembered Judie Dobbs vividly, the way she appeared, the way she cooked, the way she sewed. Irene Jackson even recalled how she had tried to teach Judie Dobbs to read and write. She said Grandma Dobbs sounded like a cracker. I asked, "Mrs. Jackson, could you speak to me as Grandma Dobbs spoke to you?" When she did, Judie Dobbs, believed to have been born in 1824, became a name, a face *and a voice*. Historically, she had come alive.

Interviews were an essential source of information. Many of the anecdotes in this book occurred during the families' private moments, moments beyond the scope of written documentation. By nature, oral history is imperfect. As Josephine Dobbs Clement said, "We organize our memories around feelings, not facts."

Yet to discount the importance of oral history would be to rob history of much of its richness and luster. Even the most celebrated public figures spend more time off the public stage than on it; in many respects, what we, as humans, do in private moments, among family and friends, is more telling about our character than what we do when the public spotlight turns on.

Every scene in this book is drawn either from firsthand sources or, in some instances (particularly those involving John Wesley Dobbs and Ivan Allen, Sr., in the late nineteenth and early twentieth century), from someone who was told about the scene by a participant. In the latter instances, I have been scrupulous in sorting out the variables, seeking corroboration when possible.

# BIBLIOGRAPHY

## MANUSCRIPTS AND PERSONAL PAPERS

*Amistad Research Center, New Orleans, Louisiana*—John Wesley Dobbs, Rev. Henry Hugh Proctor
*Atlanta History Center*—Ivan Allen, Sr., Atlanta Braves, Atlanta City Council Minutes, 1848–94, Central Atlanta Progress, *Gone With the Wind*, Grace Towns Hamilton, Help Our Public Education (HOPE), Herbert T. Jenkins, *Living Atlanta*, Long-Rucker-Aiken Family, Sam Massell, Jr., Austin T. Walden
*Atlanta University, Robert W. Woodruff Library, Department of Special Collections*—Atlanta's Missing & Murdered Children Collection, Clarence A. Bacote, John A. Calhoun, Commission on Interracial Cooperation, Mattiwilda Dobbs, First Congregational Church, John and Lugenia Burns Hope, Benjamin E. Mays, Southern Regional Council, 1944–68, Student Non-Violent Coordinating Committee, 1959–72
*Bainbridge College, Bainbridge, Georgia*—Marvin Griffin
*Emory University, Robert W. Woodruff Library, Department of Special Collections, Atlanta, Georgia*—Morris B. Abram, Helen Bullard, Asa Griggs Candler, Henry Woodfin Grady, Joel Chandler Harris, William Berry Hartsfield, Floyd Hunter, Robert James Lowry, Ralph Emerson McGill, James A. Mackay, Robert Foster Maddox, Margaret Mitchell, Richard H. Rich, Samuel P. Richards, Jacob M. Rothschild, Mildred Seydell, John Adams Sibley, Robert Winship Woodruff, *Civil War Era*: Lewis H. Andrews, Samuel Bachtel, Nellie Peters Black, Calhoun Family, W. R. Montgomery, Dr. Samuel Hollingsworth Stout
*Georgia Department of Archives and History, Atlanta, Georgia*—First Congregational Church, Noonday Baptist Church, Cobb County, Ga., Western & Atlantic Railroad Correspondence, Executive Department, 1824–26, 1835–39
*Harvard University, Baker Library, Cambridge, Massachusetts*—R. G. Dun & Co.
*Franklin D. Roosevelt Presidential Library, Hyde Park, New York*—President's Official Files (Post Office Department, 1935)
*Schomburg Center for Research in Black Culture, New York Public Library, New York, New York*—Harry A. Williamson (Prince Hall Masonry)
*University of Georgia, Richard B. Russell Library, Athens, Georgia*—Lester G. Maddox, Hoke Smith, S. Ernest Vandiver
*Whitfield-Murray Historical Society, Dalton, Georgia*—United Daughters of the Confederacy (Local Chapter)

## BOOKS

Aaron, Hank, with Lonnie Wheeler. *I Had a Hammer: The Hank Aaron Story*. New York: HarperCollins, 1991.
Abernathy, Ralph David. *And the Walls Came Tumbling Down*. New York: Harper & Row, 1989.
Abram, Morris B. *The Day Is Short: An Autobiography*. New York: Harcourt Brace Jovanovich, 1982.
Adams, Myron Whitlock. *A History of Atlanta University*. Atlanta: Atlanta University Press, 1930.
Alexander, Charles C. *Ty Cobb*. New York: Oxford University Press, 1984.
Alexander, Theodore Martin (T. M.). *Beyond the Timberline: The Trials and Triumphs of a Black Entrepreneur*. Edgewood, Md.: M. E. Duncan & Company, 1992.
Allen, Frederick. *Secret Formula: How Brilliant Marketing and Relentless Salesmanship Made Coca-Cola the Best-Known Product in the World*. New York: HarperBusiness, 1994.
Allen, Ivan, Jr., with Paul Hemphill. *Mayor: Notes on the Sixties*. New York: Simon & Schuster, 1971.

Allen, Ivan, Sr. *Atlanta from the Ashes*. Atlanta: Ruralist Press, 1928.

———. *The Atlanta Spirit: Altitude + Attitude*. Atlanta: Ivan Allen Company, 1948.

———. *Rotary in Atlanta: The First Twenty-Five Years*. Atlanta: Darby Printing Company, 1956.

Anderson, William. *The Wild Man from Sugar Creek: The Political Career of Eugene Talmadge*. Baton Rouge, La.: Louisiana State University Press, 1975.

Aptheker, Herbert, editor. *The Correspondence of W. E. B. Du Bois*. Amherst, Mass.: University of Massachusetts Press, 1973–78.

Bacote, Clarence A. *The Story of Atlanta University: A Century of Service, 1865–1965*. Atlanta: Atlanta University Press, 1969.

Baldwin, James. *The Evidence of Things Not Seen*. New York: Holt, Rinehart & Winston, 1985.

Barnett, George D. *Heritage and Hope: A Sesquicentennial History of Noonday Baptist Church, Marietta, Georgia*. Marietta, Ga.: Noonday Baptist Church, 1985.

Bartley, Numan V. *The Creation of Modern Georgia*. Athens, Ga.: University of Georgia Press, 1983.

Behlmer, Rudy, editor. *Memo from David O. Selznick*. New York: Viking, 1972.

Birmingham, Stephen. *Certain People: America's Black Elite*. New York: Little, Brown, 1977.

Bisher, Furman. *Miracle in Atlanta: The Atlanta Braves Story*. Cleveland: World Publishing Company, 1966.

Blumberg, Janice Rothschild. *One Voice: Rabbi Jacob M. Rothschild and the Troubled South*. Macon, Ga.: Mercer University Press, 1985.

Bonner, James C. *Milledgeville: Georgia's Antebellum Capital*. Athens, Ga.: University of Georgia Press, 1978.

Borders, William Holmes. *45th Pastoral Anniversary: Rev. William Holmes Borders, 1937–1982, Wheat Street Baptist Church, Atlanta, Ga.* Atlanta: Josten's American Yearbook Company, 1982.

Bowden, Haygood S. *Two Hundred Years of Education: Bicentennial, 1733–1933, Savannah, Chatham County, Georgia*. Richmond, Va.: Press of the Dietz Printing Co., 1932.

Bowers, Ronald. *The Selznick Players*. New York: A. S. Barnes, 1976.

Bowles, Billy, and Remer Tyson. *They Love a Man in the Country: Saints and Sinners in the South*. Atlanta: Peachtree Publishers, 1989.

Braden, Betsy, and Paul Hagan. *A Dream Takes Flight: Hartsfield Atlanta International Airport and Aviation in Atlanta*. Athens, Ga.: University of Georgia Press, 1989.

Branch, Taylor. *Parting the Waters: America in the King Years, 1954–63*. New York: Simon & Schuster, 1988.

Brawley, Benjamin. *History of Morehouse College*. Atlanta: Morehouse College, 1917.

Brown, Charlie, as told to James C. Bryant. *Charlie Brown Remembers Atlanta: Memoirs of a Public Man*. Columbia, S.C.: R. L. Bryan Company, 1982.

Bryant, James C. *Capital City Club: The First One Hundred Years, 1883–1993*. Atlanta: Capital City Club, 1993.

Burgner, Goldene Fillers. *Chancery Court Minutes Greene County, Tennessee, November 1825–January 1831*. Easley, S.C.: Southern Historical Press, 1987.

Cain, Andrew W. *History of Lumpkin County for the First Hundred Years, 1832–1932*. Spartanburg, S.C.: Reprint Company, 1978.

Calloway, William L. *The "Sweet Auburn Avenue" Business History, 1900–1988*. Atlanta: Central Atlanta Progress, 1988.

Candler, Charles Howard. *Asa Griggs Candler*. Atlanta: Emory University Press, 1950.

Carson, Clayborne, senior editor. *The Papers of Martin Luther King, Jr. Vol. 1: Called to Serve, January 1929–June 1951*. Berkeley, Calif.: University of California Press, 1992.

Carson, Clayborne, and David J. Garrow et al., editors. *The Eyes on the Prize Civil Rights Reader: Documents, Speeches and First Hand Accounts from the Black Freedom Struggle, 1954–1990*. New York: Penguin, 1991.

Carter, Edward R. *The Black Side: A Partial History of the Business, Religious and Educational Side of the Negro in Atlanta*. Freeport, N.Y.: Books for Libraries Press, 1971. (This is a reprint of the 1894 edition.)

Cash, W. J. *The Mind of the South*. New York: Alfred A. Knopf, 1941.

Castel, Albert. *Decision in the West: The Atlanta Campaign of 1864*. Lawrence, Kan.: University Press of Kansas, 1992.

Clanton, Solomon T. *Fifty Years Afield: A Biographical Brochure of Alexander Stephens Jackson by a Friend*. Dallas: Dallas Express Publishing, 1923.

Clayton, Xernona. *I've Been Marching All the Time: An Autobiography*. Atlanta: Longstreet Press, 1991.

Cobb, Thomas R. R. *A Digest of the Statute Laws of the State of Georgia in Force Prior to the Session of the General Assembly of 1851*. Athens, Ga.: Christy, Kelsea & Burke, 1851.

Coffin, Levi. *Reminiscences of Levi Coffin, the Reputed President of the Underground Railroad*. Cincinnati: Western Tract Society, 1876.

Conyngham, Capt. David P. *Sherman's March Through the South*. New York: Sheldon and Company, 1865.

Cooper, Walter G. *The Cotton States and International Exposition and South, Illustrated, Including the Official History of the Exposition*. Atlanta: Illustrator Company, 1896.

———. *Official History of Fulton County*. Atlanta: Walter W. Brown Publishing Company, 1934.

Daniel, Frank, editor. *Addresses and Public Papers of Carl Edward Sanders, Governor of Georgia, 1963–67*. Atlanta: Georgia Department of Archives and History, 1968.

David, Harry. *A History of Freemasonry Among Negroes in America*. U.S.: United Supreme Council, Ancient and Accepted Scottish Rite of Freemasonry, Northern Jurisdiction, 1946.

Davis, Harold E. *Henry Grady's New South: Atlanta, a Brave and Beautiful City*. Tuscaloosa, Ala.: University of Alabama Press, 1990.

Davis, William C. *Jefferson Davis: The Man and His Hour*. New York: HarperCollins, 1991.

Dennett, John Richard. *The South As It Is, 1865–1866*. New York: Viking, 1965.

Donald, David Herbert. *Lincoln*. New York: Simon & Schuster, 1995.

Dorsey, James E. *The History of Hall County, Georgia. Vol. 1*. Gainesville, Ga.: Magnolia Press, 1991.

Doughty, Richard Harrison. *Greeneville: One Hundred Year Portrait, 1775–1875*. Greeneville, Tenn.: Kingsport Press, 1975.

Dowdey, Clifford, editor, and Louis H. Manarin, assistant editor. *The Wartime Papers of R. E. Lee*. New York: Bramhall House, 1961.

Drago, Edmund L. *Black Politicians and Reconstruction in Georgia: A Splendid Failure*. Athens, Ga.: University of Georgia Press, 1992.

Du Bois, William E. B. *The Souls of Black Folk*. New York: Avon, 1965.

Dykeman, Wilma. *The French Broad*. Knoxville, Tenn.: University of Tennessee Press, 1955.

Dykeman, Wilma, and James Stokely. *Seeds of Southern Change: The Life of Will Alexander*. Chicago: University of Chicago Press, 1962.

Edge, Sarah Simms. *Joel Hurt and the Development of Atlanta*. Atlanta: Atlanta Historical Society, 1955.

Egerton, John. *Speak Now Against the Day: The Generation Before the Civil Rights Movement in the South*. New York: Alfred A. Knopf, 1994.

Ehle, John. *Trail of Tears: The Rise and Fall of the Cherokee Nation*. New York: Anchor, 1988.

Eisinger, Peter K. *The Politics of Displacement: Racial and Ethnic Transition in Three American Cities*. New York: Academic Press, 1980.

Elliott, Charles. *"Mr. Anonymous": Robert W. Woodruff of Coca-Cola*. Atlanta: Cherokee Publishing Company, 1982.

Ellsworth, Scott. *Death in a Promised Land: The Tulsa Riot of 1921*. Baton Rouge, La.: Louisiana State University Press, 1982.

English, James. *Handyman of the Lord: The Life and Ministry of the Reverend William Holmes Borders*. New York: Meredith Press, 1967.

Fellman, Michael. *Citizen Sherman: A Life of William Tecumseh Sherman*. New York: Random House, 1995.

Fite, Gilbert C. *Richard B. Russell, Jr.: Senator from Georgia*. Athens, Ga.: University of Georgia Press, 1991.

Freeman, Douglas Southall. *R. E. Lee. A Biography*. New York: Charles Scribner's Sons, 1935.

Furgurson, Ernest B. *Chancellorsville 1863*. New York: Alfred A. Knopf, 1992.

Garreau, Joel. *Edge City: Life on the New Frontier*. New York: Doubleday, 1991.

Garrett, Franklin M. *Atlanta and Environs: A Chronicle of Its People and Events. Vols. 1 and 2*. New York: Lewis Historical Publishing Company, 1954.

Garrow, David J. *Bearing the Cross: Martin Luther King, Jr., and the Southern Christian Leadership Conference*. New York: William Morrow, 1986.

Genovese, Eugene D. *Roll, Jordan, Roll: The World the Slaves Made*. New York: Pantheon, 1974.

Gibson, John M. *Those 163 Days: A Southern Account of Sherman's March from Atlanta to Raleigh*. New York: Coward-McCann, 1961.

Glenn, A. L., Sr. *History of the National Alliance of Postal Employees, 1913–1956*. Washington, D.C.: NAPE, 1956.

Goldsmith, Oliver. *Poems, Plays and Essays*. New York: Turner & Hayden, 1848.

Goodwin, Doris Kearns. *No Ordinary Time: Franklin and Eleanor Roosevelt: The Home Front in World War II*. New York: Simon & Schuster, 1994.
Grant, Donald L. *The Way It Was in the South: The Black Experience in Georgia*. New York: Birch Lane Press, 1993.
Grantham, Dewey W., Jr. *Hoke Smith and the Politics of the New South*. Baton Rouge, La.: Louisiana State University Press, 1958.
Hacker, Andrew. *Two Nations: Black and White, Separate, Hostile, Unequal*. New York: Charles Scribner's Sons, 1992.
Hahn, Stephen. *The Root of Southern Populism, Yeoman Farmers and the Transformation of the Georgia Upcountry, 1850–1890*. New York: Oxford University Press, 1983.
Harlan, Louis R., *Booker T. Washington: The Making of a Black Leader, 1856–1901*. New York: Oxford University Press, 1972.
Harlan, Louis R., and Raymond W. Smock, editors. *The Booker T. Washington Papers*. Vols. 1–10. Urbana, Ill.: University of Illinois Press, 1980.
Harris, Fred R., and Roger W. Wilkins, editors. *Quiet Riots: Race and Poverty in the United States*. New York: Pantheon, 1988.
Harris, Joel Chandler, editor. *Life of Henry Grady Including His Writings and Speeches*. New York: Haskell House, 1972.
Hartshorn, Truman A. *Metropolis in Georgia: Atlanta's Rise as a Major Transaction Center*. Cambridge, Mass.: Ballinger Publishing Company, 1976.
Haver, Ronald. *David O. Selznick's Hollywood*. New York: Alfred A. Knopf, 1980.
Henderson, Alexa Benson. *Atlanta Life Insurance Company: Guardian of Black Economic Dignity*. Tuscaloosa, Ala.: University of Alabama Press, 1990.
Henderson, Lillian, compiled by. *Roster of Confederate Soldiers of Georgia, 1861–65*. Vols. 1–5. Hapeville, Ga.: Longino & Porter, 1955–58.
Hill, Louise Biles. *Joseph Brown and the Confederacy*. Chapel Hill, N.C.: University of North Carolina Press, 1939.
Hitchcock, Henry. *Marching with Sherman*. New Haven, Conn.: Yale University Press, 1927.
Holzer, Harold, editor. *The Lincoln-Douglas Debates*. New York: HarperCollins, 1993.
Hood, John. B. *Advance and Retreat: Personal Experiences in the United States and Confederate States Armies*. Philadelphia: Burk & M'Fetridge, 1880.
Howard, Oliver Otis. *Autobiography of Oliver Otis Howard, Major General United States Army*. Vol. 2. New York: Baker & Taylor, 1907.
Howe, M. A. De Wolfe, editor. *Home Letters of General Sherman*. New York: Charles Scribner's Sons, 1909.
Hunter, Floyd. *Community Power Structure: A Study of Decision Makers*. Chapel Hill, N.C.: University of North Carolina Press, 1953.
———. *Community Power Succession: Atlanta's Policy-Makers Revisited*. Chapel Hill, N.C.: University of North Carolina Press, 1980.
Hurok, S., in collaboration with Ruth Goode. *Impresario: A Memoir by S. Hurok*. Westport, Conn.: Greenwood Press, 1946.
Jackson, Alexander Stephens. *The Rebirth of Negro Ideals*. Nashville: National Baptist Publishing Board, 1920.
Jackson, Carlton. *Hattie: The Life of Hattie McDaniel*. Lanham, Md.: Madison Books, 1990.
Jackson, Kenneth T. *The Ku Klux Klan in the City, 1915–1930*. New York: Oxford University Press, 1967.
Jenkins, Herbert. *Keeping the Peace: A Police Chief Looks at His Job*. New York: Harper & Row, 1970.
Jennings, M. Kent. *Community Influentials: The Elites of Atlanta*. New York: Free Press of Glencoe, 1964.
Johnson, Michael P., and James L. Roark. *Black Masters: A Free Family of Color in the Old South*. New York: W. W. Norton, 1984.
Johnston, Joseph E. *Narrative of Military Operations, Directed During the Late War Between the States*. New York: D. Appleton and Company, 1874.
Jones, Edward A. *A Candle in the Dark: A History of Morehouse College*. Valley Forge, Pa.: Judson Press, 1967.
Kahn, Roger. *The Boys of Summer*. New York: Harper & Row, 1971.
King, Coretta Scott. *My Life with Martin Luther King, Jr.* New York: Holt, Rinehart, & Winston, 1969.
King, Martin Luther, Jr. *Stride Toward Freedom*. New York: Harper & Brothers, 1958.
King, Martin Luther, Sr., with Clayton Riley. *Daddy King: An Autobiography*. New York: William Morrow, 1980.

Kuhn, Clifford M., Harlan E. Joye, and E. Bernard West. *Living Atlanta: An Oral History of the City, 1914–1948.* Athens, Ga.: University of Georgia Press, 1990.

Lemann, Nicholas. *The Promised Land: The Great Black Migration and How It Changed America.* New York: Alfred A. Knopf, 1991.

Levine, Lawrence W. *Black Culture and Black Consciousness: Afro-American Folk Thought From Slavery To Freedom.* New York: Oxford University Press, 1977.

Lewis, David Levering. *King: A Biography.* Urbana, Ill.: University of Illinois Press, 1978.

———. *W. E. B. Du Bois: Biography of a Race, 1868–1919.* New York: John Macrae/Henry Holt, 1993.

Lewis, Sinclair. *Babbitt.* New York: Harcourt Brace Jovanovich, 1922.

Litwack, Leon F. *Been in the Storm So Long: The Aftermath of Slavery.* New York: Alfred A. Knopf, 1979.

Logue, Calvin McLeod. *Eugene Talmadge: Rhetoric and Response.* New York: Greenwood Press, 1989.

Manchester, William. *The Glory and the Dream.* New York: Little, Brown, 1974.

Mantius, Peter. *Shell Game: A True Story of Banking, Spies, Lies, Politics and the Arming of Saddam Hussein.* New York: St. Martin's, 1995.

Marszalek, John F. *Sherman: A Soldier's Passion for Order.* New York: Free Press, 1993.

Martin, Harold H. *Atlanta and Environs: A Chronicle of Its People and Events. Vol. 3. Years of Change and Challenge, 1940–1976.* Athens, Ga.: University of Georgia Press, 1987.

———. *Ralph McGill, Reporter.* Boston: Atlantic Monthly Press, 1973.

———. *Three Strong Pillars: The Story of Trust Company of Georgia.* Atlanta: Trust Company of Georgia, 1974.

———. *William Berry Hartsfield: Mayor of Atlanta.* Athens, Ga.: University of Georgia Press, 1978.

Martin, Thomas H. *Atlanta and Its Builders: A Comprehensive History of the Gate City of the South.* Atlanta: Century Memorial Publishing Company, 1902.

Mason, Herman "Skip," Jr. *Going Against the Wind: A Pictorial History of African-Americans in Atlanta.* Marietta, Ga.: Longstreet Press, 1992.

Mays, Benjamin Elijah. *Born to Rebel: An Autobiography.* Athens, Ga.: University of Georgia Press, 1987.

———. *Lord, the People Have Driven Me On.* New York: Vantage, 1981.

McAllister, Anna. *Ellen Ewing, Wife of General Sherman.* New York: Benzinger Brothers, 1936.

McCullough, David. *Truman.* New York: Simon & Schuster, 1992.

McGill, Ralph. *The Fleas Come with the Dog.* New York: Abingdon Press, 1954.

Mitchell, Margaret. *Gone With the Wind.* New York: Macmillan, 1936.

Muraskin, William A. *Middle-Class Blacks in a White Society: Prince Hall Freemasonry in America.* Berkeley, Calif.: University of California Press, 1975.

Myrdal, Gunnar, with assistance from Richard Sterner and Arnold Rose. *An American Dilemma: The Negro Problem and Modern Democracy. Vols. 1 and 2.* New York: Harper & Brother, 1944.

Myrick, Susan. *White Columns in Hollywood: Reports from the GWTW Sets.* Macon, Ga.: Mercer University Press, 1982.

Nichols, George Ward. *The Story of the Great March from the Diary of a Staff Officer.* New York: Harper & Brothers, 1866.

Nixon, Raymond B. *Henry W. Grady: Spokesman of the New South.* New York: Alfred A. Knopf, 1943.

Orfield, Gary, and Carole Ashkinaze. *The Closing Door: Conservative Policy and Black Opportunity.* Chicago: University of Chicago Press, 1991.

Papich, Stephen. *Remembering Josephine.* Indianapolis: Bobbs-Merrill, 1976.

Pendergrast, Mark. *For God, Country and Coca-Cola: The Unauthorized History of the Great American Soft Drink and the Company That Makes It.* New York: Charles Scribner's Sons, 1993.

Pyron, Darden Asbury. *Southern Daughter: The Life of Margaret Mitchell.* New York: Oxford University Press, 1991.

Rabinowitz, Howard N. *The First New South, 1865–1920.* Arlington Heights, Ill.: Harlan Davidson, 1992.

Raines, Howell. *My Soul Is Rested: Movement Days in the Deep South Remembered.* New York: G. P. Putnam's Sons, 1977.

Range, Willard. *The Rise and Progress of Negro Colleges in Georgia, 1865–1949.* Athens, Ga.: University of Georgia Press, 1951.

Reaney, P. H. *The Origin of English Surnames: Surnames from Lost or Unidentified Places.* London: Routledge & Kegan Paul, 1967.

Reeves, Richard. *President Kennedy: Profile of Power.* New York: Simon & Schuster, 1993.

Robertson, H. G. *A Small Boy's Recollections of the Civil War.* Greeneville, Tenn.: Self-Published, 1931.

Robinson, Jackie, as told to Alfred Duckett. *I Never Had It Made.* New York: G. P. Putnam's Sons, 1972.

Rothschild, Janice O. *As But a Day: The First Hundred Years, 1867–1967*. Atlanta: Hebrew Benevolent Congregation, 1967.

Russell, James Michael. *Atlanta 1847–1890: City Building in the Old South and the New*. Baton Rouge, La.: Louisiana State University Press, 1988.

Russell, William Howard. *My Diary North and South*. New York: Harper & Row, 1865.

Sandburg, Carl. *Abraham Lincoln: The Prairie Years and the War Years*. New York: Harcourt, Brace & Company, 1925.

Shavin, Norman. *Days in the Life of Atlanta*. Atlanta: Capricorn, 1987.

Sherman, William Tecumseh. *Memoirs of General William T. Sherman*. New York: Da Capo, 1984; reprint of 1875 edition.

Sibley, Celestine. *Dear Store: An Affectionate Portrait of Rich's*. Garden City, N.Y.: Doubleday, 1967.

———. *Peachtree Street, USA*. Atlanta: Peachtree Publishers, 1986.

Siddons, Anne Rivers. *Downtown*. New York: HarperCollins, 1994.

———. *Peachtree Road*. New York: Harper & Row, 1988.

Siebert, Wilbur H. *The Underground Railroad from Slavery to Freedom*. New York: Macmillan, 1898.

Silberman, Charles. *Crisis in Black and White*. New York: Random House, 1964.

Smith, John Robert. *The Church That Stayed: The Life and Times of Central Presbyterian Church in the Heart of Atlanta, 1858–1978*. Atlanta: Historical Society, 1979.

Spritzer, Lorraine Nelson. *The Belle of Ashby Street: Helen Douglas Mankin and Georgia Politics*. Athens, Ga.: University of Georgia Press, 1982.

Stokes, Carl B. *Promises of Power: A Political Autobiography*. New York: Simon & Schuster, 1973.

Stone, Clarence N. *Regime Politics: Governing Atlanta, 1946–1988*. Lawrence, Kan.: University Press of Kansas, 1989.

Stone, Clarence N., and Heywood T. Sanders, editors. *The Politics of Urban Development*. Lawrence, Kan.: University Press of Kansas, 1987.

Talmadge, Herman E. *You and Segregation*. Birmingham, Ala.: Vulcan Press, 1955.

Tate, James H. *Keeper of the Flame: The Story of Atlanta Gas Light Company, 1856–1985*. Atlanta: Atlanta Gas Light Company, 1985.

Temple, Oliver P. *East Tennessee and the Civil War*. Cincinnati: R. Clarke Company, 1899.

Temple, Sarah Blackwell Gober. *The First Hundred Years: A Short History of Cobb County in Georgia*. Athens, Ga.: Agee Publishers, 1935.

Thomas, Edison H. *John Hunt Morgan and His Raiders*. Lexington, Ky.: University Press of Kentucky, 1975.

Thomas, Lately. *The First President Johnson: The Three Lives of the Seventeenth President of the United States of America*. New York: William Morrow, 1968.

Tocqueville, Alexis de. *Democracy in America. Vols. 1 and 2*. New York: Vintage, 1945.

Torrance, Ridgely. *The Story of John Hope*. New York: Macmillan, 1948.

Trefousse, Hans. L. *Andrew Johnson: A Biography*. New York: W. W. Norton, 1989.

Trillin, Calvin. *An Education in Georgia*. New York: Viking, 1964.

Tully, Grace. *F.D.R.: My Boss*. New York: Charles Scribner's Sons, 1949.

Tushnet, Mark V. *The American Law of Slavery, 1810–1860: Considerations of Humanity and Interest*. Princeton, N.J.: Princeton University Press, 1981.

Walker, Edward R. III. *Walking with the Walkers*. Johnson City, Tenn.: OverMountain Press, 1981.

Walker, Marianne. *Margaret Mitchell and John Marsh: The Love Story Behind Gone With the Wind*. Atlanta: Peachtree Publishers, 1993.

Wallace, Robert B., Jr. *Dress Her in White and Gold: A Biography of Georgia Tech*. Atlanta: Georgia Tech Foundation, 1963.

Washington, Booker T. *Up from Slavery: An Autobiography*. New York: Doubleday, Page & Company, 1924.

Wells, Della Wagner. *The First Hundred Years: A Centennial History of King & Spalding*. Atlanta: King & Spalding, 1985.

White, Theodore H. *The Making of the President*. New York: Atheneum, 1960.

White, Walter. *A Man Called White: The Autobiography of Walter White*. New York: Viking, 1948.

Wilcox, Ella Wheeler. *Maurine and Other Poems*. Chicago: W. B. Conkey Company, 1888.

Williams, Eleanor. *Ivan Allen: A Resourceful Citizen*. Atlanta: Ivan Allen-Marshall Company, 1950.

Williams, Loretta J. *Black Freemasonry and Middle-Class Realities*. Columbia, Mo.: University of Missouri Press, 1980.

Wills, Garry. *Lincoln at Gettysburg: The Words That Remade America*. New York: Simon & Schuster, 1992.

Winston, Robert W. *Andrew Johnson: Plebeian and Patriot*. New York: Henry Holt, 1928.
Woods, Richard L., editor. *A Treasury of the Familiar*. New York: Macmillan, 1955.
Woodward, C. Vann. *Origins of the New South, 1877–1913*. Baton Rouge, La.: Louisiana State University Press, 1951.
———. *The Strange Career of Jim Crow*. New York: Oxford University Press, 1955.
———. *Tom Watson: Agrarian Rebel*. New York: Oxford University Press, 1938.
Woodward, C. Vann, and Elizabeth Muhlenfeld. *The Private Mary Chesnutt: Unpublished Civil War Diaries*. New York: Oxford University Press, 1984.
Wright, John S. *Lincoln and the Politics of Slavery*. Reno, Nev.: University of Nevada Press, 1970.
Young, Coleman, and Lonnie Wheeler. *Hard Stuff: The Autobiography of Coleman Young*. New York: Viking, 1994.
Young, Andrew. *A Way Out of No Way: The Spiritual Memoirs of Andrew Young*. Nashville: Thomas Nelson, 1994.


OFFICIAL AND SEMI-OFFICIAL PUBLICATIONS

*Acts of the General Assembly of the State of Georgia, 1833*. Milledgeville, Ga.: Polhill & Fort, Printers, 1834.
*Acts of the General Assembly of the State of Georgia, 1834*. Milledgeville, Ga.: P. L. & B. H. Robinson, Printers, 1835.
*Acts of the General Assembly of the State of Georgia, 1835*. Milledgeville, Ga.: John A. Cuthbert, Printer, 1836.
*Hanleiter's Atlanta City Directory*. Atlanta: Cornelius R. Hanleiter, 1871.
*Hearings Before the Committee on Commerce, United States Senate, Eighty-Eighth Congress on S. 1732*. Washington D.C.: U.S. Government Printing Office, 1963.
*Journal of the House of Representatives of the State of Georgia, 1835*. Milledgeville, Ga.: State Authority of Georgia, 1836.
*Journal of the House of Representatives of the State of Georgia, 1836*. Milledgeville, Ga.: State Authority of Georgia, 1837.
*Journal of the Senate of the State of Georgia, 1843*. Milledgeville, Ga.: State Authority of Georgia, 1844.
*The New Baptist Hymnal*. Nashville: National Baptist Publishing Board, August 1984.
*Official History of Whitfield County, Georgia*. Dalton, Ga.: A. J. Showalter Company, 1936.
*The 120th Anniversary Celebration of Zion Baptist Church*. Marietta, Ga.: Zion Baptist Church, 1986.
*Report of the Forward Atlanta Commission: Being a Detailed Statement of the Administration of the Forward Atlanta Fund for the Years 1926, 1927, 1928, 1929*. Atlanta: The Commission, 1929.
*Report of the National Advisory Commission on Civil Disorders*. New York: Bantam, March 1968.
*The Story of Georgia: Biographical Volume*. New York: American Historical Society, 1938.
*Supplemental Studies for the National Advisory Commission on Civil Disorders*. New York: Frederick A. Praeger, July 1968.
*Tennessee Mortality Schedules, 1880*. Nashville: Byron Sistler & Associates, 1984.
*Timber Ridge Church: A Two Hundred Year Heritage of Presbyterian Faith, 1786–1986*. (Written by church members.) Greeneville, Tenn.: East Tennessee Printing Company, 1986.
*The Torch: Morehouse College Class Yearbook, 1960–61*. Atlanta: Morehouse College, 1961.
*The Young Years: A Report on the Administration of the Honorable Andrew Young, Mayor of the City of Atlanta, 1982–1989*. (Written by Nehl Horton, director of legislative affairs under Young.) Atlanta: City of Atlanta, December 1989.


GOVERNMENT AND ORGANIZATION STUDIES

Atlanta Community Improvement Program. "Equal Opportunity in Housing, Community Improvement Program, City of Atlanta, Georgia: Supplementary Report on Negro Housing Needs and Resources." Atlanta: Candeub, Fleissig & Associates/Atlanta Community Improvement Program, 1967.
———. "Relocation Study Supplement: Atlanta Community Improvement Program. Report Sections Three and Four." Atlanta: Eric Hill Associates/Atlanta Community Improvement Program, 1967.

Atlanta Metropolitan Planning Commission. "Up Ahead: A Regional Land Use Plan for Metropolitan Atlanta, February 1952." Atlanta: The Commission, 1952.

Atlanta Model Cities Program. "Atlanta Model Cities: Final Evaluation Report. Fourth Action Year, January–December 1973. Prepared by Research and Evaluation Division, Atlanta Model Cities Program." Atlanta: The Program, 1974.

Atlanta Urban League. "A Report of the Housing Activities of the Atlanta Urban League, November 28, 1952." Atlanta: Atlanta Urban League, 1952.

City of Atlanta. "City Charter. City of Atlanta." Approved by the General Assembly and signed by the governor, March 1973. Atlanta: City of Atlanta, 1973.

Lochner, H. W., and Company. "Highway and Transportation Plan for Atlanta, Georgia. Prepared for the State Highway Department of Georgia and the Public Roads Administration, Federal Works Agency." Chicago: H. W Lochner and Company and De Leuw, Cather & Company, 1946.

Research Atlanta. "Urban Redevelopment in Atlanta." Atlanta: Research Atlanta, 1979.

Southern Regional Council. "Housing for Negroes in Atlanta, Georgia." Atlanta: Southern Regional Council, 1959.

The Southern Center for Studies in Public Policy at Clark-Atlanta University. "The Status of Black Atlanta 1994." Atlanta: Clark-Atlanta University, 1994.

### DISSERTATIONS, THESES AND ORAL PAPERS

Autrey, William Robert. "The Negro Press: Southern Style Militancy: *The Atlanta Independent* and *The Savannah Tribune*, 1904–1928." M.A. thesis, Atlanta University, 1963.

Garofalo, Charles Paul. "Business Ideas in Atlanta, 1916–1935." Ph.D. diss., Emory University, 1972.

Godshalk, David F. "Silence and Memory in Local History: The Struggle over the Meaning of the Atlanta Race Riot, 1906–1959." Paper delivered at the 1994 annual meeting of the Organization of American Historians, Atlanta, Ga.

Kuhn, Clifford M. "There's a Footnote to History!: Memory and the History of Martin Luther King's October 1960 Arrest and Its Aftermath." Paper delivered at the 1994 annual meeting of the Organization of American Historians, Atlanta, Ga.

Lawrence, Charles Radford, Jr. "The Social Background of Negro Junior High School Pupils, Atlanta, Georgia." M.A. thesis, Atlanta University, 1938.

Page, Eugene Turner, Jr. "Race Distinctions in the Acts of the Georgia Assembly, 1765–1939." M.A. thesis, Atlanta University, 1941.

Pryor, Carranza M. "Contrast in Capital Leadership: Relative Industrial Changes Between Birmingham, Ala., and Atlanta, Ga.: 1920–1970." B.A. essay, Harvard College, 1991.

Roberts, Sylvester. "A Demographic Analysis of the Negro Population of Atlanta: 1940–1960." M.A. thesis, Atlanta University, 1961.

Rodriguez, Edward Rudolph. "A Study of the Discrimination in Race and Color Current in the City of Atlanta." M.A. thesis, Atlanta University, 1934.

Rolinson, Mary G. "Community and Leadership in the Atlanta NAACP, 1916–1936: The Struggles of the First Twenty Years." Unpublished graduate seminar essay, Georgia State University, June 1995.

Slade, Dorothy. "The Evolution of Negro Areas in the City of Atlanta." M.A. thesis, Atlanta University, 1946.

Tagger, Barbara A. "The Atlanta Race Riot of 1906 and the Black Community." M.A. thesis, Atlanta University, 1984.

### NEWSPAPERS

*Amsterdam News, Atlanta Business Chronicle, Atlanta Constitution, Atlanta Daily World, Atlanta Evening News, Atlanta Georgian, Atlanta Independent, Atlanta Intelligencer, Atlanta Inquirer, Atlanta Journal, Atlanta Voice, Augusta Herald, Boston Globe, Bremen* (Ga.) *Gateway, Cartersville* (Ga.) *Daily Tribune, Charlotte Observer, Christian Science Monitor, Dallas Express, Dallas Morning News, Dallas Times Herald, Dalton* (Ga.) *Citizen, Economist* (London), *Greeneville* (Tenn.) *Herald, Los Angeles Times, Macon Telegraph, Memphis Commercial-Appeal, New York Daily News, New York Times, Pittsburgh* (Pa.) *Courier, Rome* (Ga. ) *News-Tribune,*

*Sacramento* (Calif.) *Bee, Savannah Morning News, Savannah Tribune, Southern Recorder* (Milledgeville, Ga.), *Valdosta* (Ga.) *Times, Wall Street Journal*

## MAGAZINES

*Atlanta, Atlanta Journal Sunday Magazine, Business Atlanta, Chicago Tribune Sunday Magazine, City Builder, Ebony, Esquire, Forbes, Jet, Life, Look, Mademoiselle, National Geographic, Newsweek, New Yorker, New York Times Sunday Magazine, Sage, Saturday Evening Post, Sepia, Time, Town & Country, U.S. News & World Report*

## ACADEMIC AND LITERARY JOURNALS

*American Magazine, Atlanta Historical Bulletin, AtlantaHistory, Filson Club Quarterly, Georgia Historical Quarterly, Heritage News, Journal of Negro Education, Journal of Negro History, Midwest Quarterly, Morehouse College Bulletin, Phylon, Spelman Messenger, Today's Speech, Whitfield-Murray Historical Society Quarterly*

## INTERVIEWS

The transcripts of several previously recorded interviews are cited in the Notes. In the *Living Atlanta* collection at the Atlanta History Center, transcripts of sessions with the Rev. William Holmes Borders, O. R. "Robert" McKibbens, Clayton R. Yates and John Calhoun were particularly illuminating. Also, Ivan Allen, Jr., in 1971, tape-recorded, then transcribed, his reflections on his mayoral years for his book with writer Paul Hemphill, *Mayor: Notes on the Sixties.* Allen taped his thoughts, then gave the transcript to Hemphill, who then sculpted a narrative. Much of the material in the transcript was not included in their book. Both Allen and Hemphill graciously permitted the author access to their transcript.

All of the following interviews were conducted by the author between summer 1991 and fall 1995.

### *Dobbs*

Sandra (Irene) Jackson Baraniuk: July 14, 1991; June 11, 1993; August 26, 1993
Willie Dobbs Blackburn: September 12, 1992
June Dobbs Butts: August 26, 1991; November 24, 1991
Constance (Connie) Jackson Carter: December 5, 1992
Bill Clement, Jr.: June 8, 1992; June 9, 1993; January 10, 1994; December 6, 1994
Bill Clement, Sr.: December 29, 1994
Josephine (Josie) Dobbs Clement: October 19, 1991; August 26, 1993.
Jesse (J.L.) Dobbs: October 26, 1991; July 1, 1992
Beth Jackson Hodges: June 19, 1995
Brooke Jackson: April 5, 1995
Irene (Renie) Dobbs Jackson: July 27, 1991; July 29, 1992; March 11, 1993; May 2, 1993; March 13, 1994
Maynard H. Jackson, Jr.: September 9, 1991; February 2, 1992; April 24, 1994; May 25, 1994; November 29, 1994; August 12, 1995
Bunnie Jackson-Ransom: August 9, 1994
Muriel Gassett James: December 24, 1992; May 21, 1994
Mattiwilda (Geekie) Dobbs Janzon: November 27, 1991; December 30, 1991; November 11, 1992
Dobbs Jordan: January 25, 1993
Robert (Bobby) Jordan, Jr.: August 20, 1993
Ernestine McDaniel: September 11, 1992
Carol Jackson Miller: June 21, 1992; July 29, 1992; April 24, 1995
Mozelle Murphy: September 11, 1992
Marian Robinson: October 26, 1991; July 1, 1992

*Allen*

Beaumont Allen: September 23, 1991
H. Inman Allen: November 20, 1991; September 10, 1992; February 22, 1994; November 3, 1994; August 2, 1995
Ivan Allen, Jr.: July 18, 1991; November 12, 1991; February 12, 1992; April 7, 1992; July 17, 1992; September 3, 1992; September 23, 1992; October 27, 1992; February 3, 1993; April 16, 1993; September 9, 1993; March 15, 1994; May 23, 1994; July 28, 1994; September 8, 1994; December 20, 1994
Ivan Allen III: November 6, 1991
Ivan Allen IV: March 22, 1993
Jimmy Allen (Greeneville, Tenn.): May 24, 1993
Louise Allen: October 28, 1991; November 29, 1993
Margaret P. Allen: September 20, 1993; August 24, 1994
Juanita Renner: May 20, 1993
Sue Frick Saunders: April 28, 1993
Amanda Allen Thompson: December 14, 1994
Knox Thompson: December 14, 1994

*Others*

Billye Aaron: January 5, 1993
Morris Abram: July 22, 1993
J. Earl Acey: July 10, 1991
Cecil Alexander: June 6, 1994; June 14, 1994; September 24, 1994
T. M. Alexander, Sr.: June 30, 1992
Jamil Abdullah al Amin (né H. Rap Brown): July 22, 1992
Rosalie Andrews (Marietta, Ga.): June 12, 1992; June 18, 1993
Bonneau Ansley: December 9, 1993
Marvin Arrington: June 22, 1995
Clara Axam: July 13, 1995
Joel Babbit: February 27, 1994
Lucia Bacote: August 19, 1993
Brenda Banks: April 14, 1993
B. B. Beamon: September 10, 1993
Francis Bennett: June 3, 1992
George Berry: October 30, 1992
Milton Bevington: August 7, 1992
Furman Bisher: October 29, 1992
Merle Black: September 19, 1994
Nancy C. Bland: December 9, 1993
Julian Bond: January 20, 1992
Rev. William H. Borders: August 8, 1991
Rev. Ellis Bostick: April 3, 1993
Rev. Murray Branch: January 7, 1993
Helen Britton (Greeneville, Tenn.): August 25, 1992
Charlie Brown: July 9, 1992
Paul E. X. Brown: August 29, 1993; September 15, 1993
Raleigh Bryans: February 23, 1994
Imogene McAfee Buder: February 20, 1993; July 15, 1993
Dan Burgner (Greeneville, Tenn.): May 23, 1993
Goldene F. Burgner (Greeneville, Tenn.): May 22, 1993
Howard "Bo" Callaway: November 23, 1993
W. L. Calloway: June 23, 1992
Bill Campbell: August 7, 1995
Former President Jimmy Carter: March 18, 1993
Herschelle Sullivan Challenor: January 19, 1994
Odellus Chambers (Dallas, Tex.): October 24, 1993

Pearl (Lomax) Cleage: July 13, 1995
Reese Cleghorn: February 24, 1994
George Coleman: September 9, 1993
Wayne Conduff (Greeneville, Tenn.): August 25, 1992
Meredith Conklin: September 10, 1993
Michel Cornier: January 7, 1994
Virginia Allen Cotter: December 24, 1991
T. Elmer Cox (Greeneville, Tenn.): May 17, 1993
Tim Crimmons: October 1, 1992
Charles Dannals, Jr.: August 10, 1993
Emma Darnell: September 29, 1994
F. Tradewell (Tread) Davis, Jr.: November 2, 1993
Willie (Flash) Davis: June 6, 1995
Paul Delaney: March 23, 1995
Marie Dodd: September 28, 1994; November 3, 1994
Richard Doughty (Greeneville, Tenn.): August 25, 1992
Mark Doyle: September 7, 1994
Elizabeth Drinkard (Woodstock, Ga.): June 15, 1993
Wilma Dykeman (Newport, Tenn.): January 14, 1993
A. Reginald Eaves: November 11, 1994
Rev. Clinton Edwards (Kennesaw, Ga.): June 6, 1993
Leon Eplan: February 10, 1994
Hank Ezell: December 1, 1992
Wyche Fowler: August 15, 1994
William Fowlkes: June 4, 1992; June 28, 1992
David Franklin: September 14, 1994; October 24, 1994
Shirley Franklin: July 21, 1993
Chet Fuller: August 12, 1993; February 16, 1994
Angelo Fuster: April 13, 1993
Franklin M. Garrett: January 10, 1994
Peter Zeck Geer, Jr.: September 19, 1995
Larry Gellerstedt, Jr.: March 29, 1993
Larry Gellerstedt III: September 28, 1992
Eugene Genovese: July 20, 1993
Ben S. Gilmer: May 27, 1994
Charles Glassick: November 23, 1993
Jack Glenn: June 1, 1992; December 17, 1994
Hugh Gloster: September 29, 1992
Nick Gold: January 10, 1994
Joel Goldberg: September 29, 1994
George Goodwin: February 28, 1992
Sarah Gordon: March 8, 1993
Paula Granger: February 9, 1994
Hugh Gravitt: July 24, 1991
Montie Gregg (Johnson City, Tenn.): July 19, 1993
Denmark Groover: January 20, 1994
Raymond Guffin: May 7, 1992
Beverly Guy-Sheftall: April 2, 1993
Be Haas: September 26, 1994
Tom Hamall: October 27, 1994
Lyle Harris: June 9, 1993
Dr. Keith Harrison (Greeneville, Tenn.): August 24, 1992
Ernie Harwell: September 11, 1992
John Head: February 2, 1994; May 17, 1994
Jacob R. Henderson: September 16, 1993
Freddie Henderson: September 16, 1993
Joe Heyman: June 3, 1994
Alma Hill: January 15, 1993
Jesse Hill: February 17, 1994

George Hirthler: April 12, 1993
Eulabel Riley Hocker: March 8, 1993
Bob Holder: March 2, 1993
Jenelsie Holloway: November 19, 1993
Donald Hollowell: July 6, 1992; June 1, 1994
Bob Holmes: June 20, 1995
Larry Hooks: July 25, 1994
Gerald T. Horton: June 15, 1994
Annesley Howland: July 13, 1994
Dr. W. Slocum Howland: July 13, 1994
Gail McAfee Hughes: July 8, 1993
Juanita Hughes (Woodstock, Ga.): June 15, 1993
Alfred Jackson (Marietta, Ga.): June 12, 1992; June 15, 1992; October 1, 1992
Helen (Mrs. Graham) Jackson: August 17, 1993
Rev. Jesse Jackson: May 22, 1995
Harry Jacobs: August 8, 1994
Leroy Johnson: August 9, 1991; September 12, 1994
Boisfeuillet Jones: February 10, 1993
Dr. E. Ladd Jones: October 5, 1993
Joseph W. Jones: February 8, 1993; September 23, 1994
Julia Jordan (Dallas, Tex.): October 4, 1993
Vernon E. Jordan, Jr.: November 23, 1992
Windsor Jordan: November 28, 1992; February 16, 1994; September 8, 1994
Dennis Kelly (Kennesaw, Ga.): July 16, 1993
Coretta Scott King: July 22, 1991
Lonnie King: December 29, 1993; May 21, 1994
Helen Noel Krebs (Greeneville, Tenn.): May 24, 1993
U.S. Cong. John Lewis: December 8, 1993
Hamilton Lokey: November 7, 1992
Michael Lomax: January 28, 1993; September 22, 1994; November 2, 1994
Mason Lowance, Jr.: October 24, 1993
Susan Lowance: October 24, 1993
Rev. Joseph Lowery: June 10, 1992
Charles Lunsford: April 5, 1993
Ernest Lyons: December 5, 1991
James Mackay: July 21, 1993; August 17, 1994
Jan Maddox (Greeneville, Tenn.): August 24, 1992
Lester Maddox: June 9, 1992
Fred Mapp: January 7, 1993
Sam Massell: September 10, 1991; August 18, 1994
Lyn May: May 29, 1992; August 12, 1993
Ralph McGill, Jr.: February 10, 1994
Neal McQueen: April 1, 1993
Pete McTier: January 28, 1993; February 15, 1993
Carol Merritt: March 9, 1993
Kenneth E. Minton: October 5, 1994
Wade Mitchell: July 18, 1994
Aubrey Morris: August 12, 1992
JacLyn Morris: May 17, 1994
Rev. Otis Moss, Jr.: November 4, 1993; February 10, 1994
J. M. Mulliford: August 24, 1994
William Muraskin: April 20, 1993
E. Allen Myers, Jr.: July 23, 1991
George Napper: November 2, 1994
Dorothy Neal: March 8, 1993
Peter Noel (Greeneville, Tenn.): May 24, 1993
Alf Nucifora: February 17, 1994
James Paschal: May 8, 1992
James (AlleyPat) Patrick: April 26, 1993

Eugene Patterson: July 25, 1991; August 24, 1993; June 2, 1994
Billy Payne: February 9, 1993; August 12, 1993
Ralph Phinney (Greeneville, Tenn.): May 24, 1993
Hyde Post: November 3, 1994
William (Bill) Pressly: November 18, 1993
Curt Ratledge: February 6, 1993
Morris Redding: June 23, 1993
Kevin Ross: December 9, 1993
Bert Roughton, Jr.: March 28, 1995
George Royal: April 8, 1992
Ron Scharbo: August 8, 1994
Cornelius (C. A.) Scott: April 23, 1993
Port Scott: July 10, 1991
Portia Scott: April 23, 1993
Tom Scott (Kennesaw, Ga.): April 9, 1992
Margaret Shannon: February 24, 1994
Mark Sherman: July 1, 1992
Bob Shira: August 7, 1994
Rev. Fred Shuttlesworth: May 6, 1993
Celestine Sibley: August 25, 1993; January 14, 1994
James Sibley: February 4, 1993
Anne Rivers Siddons: May 4, 1995
Morris Siegel: November 23, 1993
Claude Sitton: April 23, 1993
Edward Smith: April 23, 1993
Mrs. Fannie Smith (Dallas, Tex.): October 5, 1993
Howell E. Smith: June 3, 1994
Laura Maddox Smith: April 23, 1993
Scott Smith: October 27, 1993
Hughes Spalding, Jr.: February 2, 1993
Jack Spalding: November 5, 1992
Deb Speights: March 11, 1994
Jule Sugarman: October 13, 1994
Bessie Sullivan: September 10, 1993
Dan Sweat, Jr.: September 23, 1991; August 9, 1994
Herman Talmadge: December 3, 1992; August 18, 1994
Robert E. Thomas: August 19, 1993
Robert Thompson: August 24, 1993; June 16, 1994
Beverly Trader: June 13, 1992
Judge Elbert P. Tuttle: September 1, 1992
S. Ernest Vandiver: July 7, 1994
Jack Watson, Jr.: October 7, 1994
Dana F. White: September 14, 1993
Hosea Williams: September 2, 1993; November 16, 1994
James Williams: February 2, 1993
Charles Wittenstein: July 13, 1995
Harold Wooley (Kennesaw, Ga.): June 7, 1995
Andrew Young: May 8, 1992; July 24, 1995

# Acknowledgments

"What's on your mind?" Receiving my phone calls at any hour of the day or night, Goldene Fillers Burgner never failed to get right to the point with me. An eighty-five-year-old genealogist and local historian living on a 207-acre east Tennessee farm worked by her son, Mrs. Burgner is one of Greene County's most precious natural resources. She is a griot, of sorts, a walking archive with more knowledge of local families in her head than in any ten books of history. She had been studying for thirty years the genealogies of the Allens and other families along the Nolichucky when I first met her in 1991. One of my greatest discoveries, she became my Jane Marple, a historical detective. Her family, the Fillerses, has been in Greene County for nearly two hundred years. "Ol' Jacob Fillers," she would say, "came here from Pennsylvania in 17-and-98." Her family has owned and operated the old Daniel Allen grist and saw mills for decades. Kind and generous, Mrs. Burgner showed me the old Allen lands by the river. She took me into the musty Greeneville courthouse where she is a legend. With me, she read 150-year-old depositions page by page, hour after hour, day after day. She found diaries and church records that no one else could find. She even showed me the spot where James Allen (Daniel's son, "Devil Jim" to Mrs. Burgner) was said to have been shot by an angry neighbor as he forded the 'Chucky. "The bullet hit him in the butt," she says, laughing, "or at least that's the story that's come down." A pro in her business, she became a shoulder for me to lean on, the voice on the other end of what seemed ten thousand phone calls, a trusted friend. During my visits, she even gave me the bed in the room upstairs. I am forever indebted to her.

I am also indebted to a group of librarians and archivists who, like Mrs. Burgner, started out as strangers but soon became, through kindness and professionalism, much like friendly colleagues. I am especially indebted to the following (some of whom have changed positions): Dale Couch and Susan Watts at the Georgia Department of Archives and History; Brenda Banks at Spelman College; Priscilla Pomazal, Sara Saunders, Ted Ryan and Helen Matthews at the Atlanta History Center; Wilson Flemister, the late Dovie Patrick, Minnie Clayton and Elaine Williams at Atlanta University's Woodruff Library; Rebecca Hankins, Frederick Stielow and Clifton Johnson at the Amistad Research Center in New Orleans, La.; Carole Merritt at the Alonzo Herndon Home in Atlanta; W. Marvin Dulaney at the African-American Museum in Dallas, Tex. (now director of the Avery Research Center for African-American History and Culture in Charleston, S.C.); Kathy Knox, Ellen Nemhauser, Linda Matthews and Beverly Allen at Emory University's Woodruff Library in Atlanta; Charlie Niles at the Martin Luther King, Jr. Papers at Boston University's Mugar Library; Mike Musick at the National Archives and Records Administration in Washington, D.C.; Polly Boggess and Marcelle White at the Whitfield-Murray Historical Society in Dalton, Ga.; John Stephens, Jr., at the Instructional Resources Center at the University of Georgia in Athens, Ga.; Wayne Moore at the Tennessee State Library and Archives in Nashville, Tenn.; Marcel David of the Cobb Landmarks and Historical Society in Marietta, Ga.; M. C. Wayman, National Personnel Records Center in St. Louis, Mo.; Joseph R. Brown and Deloise Matthews at the City of Atlanta's Division of Archives and Records Management; Gayle P. Peters at the National Archives-Southeast Region in East Point, Ga.; Sharon E. Robinson of the Auburn Avenue Research Library in Atlanta, Ga.; the late Wayne Dobson at the Tusculum College Library in Greeneville, Tenn.; Dennis Kelly at the Kennesaw Mountain Park National Historic site; and Tom Frieling at the Bainbridge College Library in Bainbridge, Ga.

I received research assistance from select sources, including Christine Jacobson in Atlanta, Rebecca McLennan in New York, Melinda Heyn in White House, Tenn., and Marie Varrelman Melchiori in Washington. Transcription of my tape-recorded interviews was conducted early on by Anita Portwood and Gigi and Angie Whitlow. In 1994, Agnes F. Stanley took over. Agnes never missed a word—or a deadline.

No writer has ever received more support from an employer than I have received from my editors at *The Atlanta Journal-Constitution:* Ron Martin, John Walter, Mike King and Paul Shea. Other

AJC colleagues also helped me during the past five years: Celestine Sibley, Mike Luckovich, Chet Fuller, Derrick Henry, Don Melvin, Bert Roughton, John Head, Alma Hill, Steve Sternberg, John Glenn, Christina Cheakalos, Peter Mantius, Joey Ivansco, Mark Sherman, Elizabeth Kurylo, Maria Saporta, Michelle Hiskey, Kay Powell, Jim Wooton, Jeff Dickerson, Glenn Hannagan, Rhonda Cook, Dan Hulburt and Doug Blackmon.

From a panel of readers, I gained invaluable criticisms and suggestions. Hyde Post of *The Atlanta Journal-Constitution* and Walter Bode in New York helped take me through the early drafts. In the final drafts, I received intensive critiques from the following: David J. Garrow, Pulitzer Prize–winning biographer of *Bearing the Cross: Martin Luther King, Jr., and the Southern Christian Leadership Conference*; my colleague, Cynthia Tucker, editorial page editor of *The Atlanta Constitution*; Dana F. White of Emory University, who has written extensively on Atlanta and is among the foremost custodians of city history; Clifford M. Kuhn of Georgia State University, a wizard of oral history and co-author (with Harlan E. Joye and E. Bernard West) of *Living Atlanta: An Oral History of the City, 1914–1948*. Several others read select portions of my manuscript in the final stages: James L. Roark of Emory University, co-author (with Michael P. Johnson) of *Black Masters: A Free Family of Color in the Old South*, read the antebellum chapters; Albert Castel, a Michigander and author of the seamless *Decision in the West: The Atlanta Campaign of 1864*, read the Civil War chapter; John Head, former press secretary to Maynard Jackson and now a colleague on the *Atlanta Constitution* editorial board, read the chapters on the 1970s; and Bob Holmes, a Georgia state legislator from Atlanta for the past two decades, and director of the Center for Studies in Public Policy at Clark-Atlanta University, which produces an annual study of black Atlanta, read the chapters on modern Atlanta, 1973 to present.

Dave Kindred should be mentioned among these readers since he did put his pen marks on more than thirteen hundred manuscript pages. Yet Kindred, who is one of the finest newspapermen of our time, did much more than that. For many years he has been my friend, colleague and mentor. His innate sensitivity and grasp of the human condition (precisely what you'd expect from a man named *Kindred*) has made me a better thinker and this a better book. Along with my former Berkeley history professors, Larry Levine and Leon Litwack, Kindred has helped me grasp how events and personalities of the past continue to influence us in profound ways.

Lisa Drew, my editor at Scribner, was a terrific advocate of this book and a soothing voice on the telephone. She also paid a visit to Atlanta to see, quite literally, where Peachtree meets Sweet Auburn. Lisa has edited many fine books, Alex Haley's *Roots*, among them. When people speak of a Midwesterner's native warmth they mean Wisconsin Lisa. Her assistants, Kate Boyle and then Marysue Rucci, also were joys to work with.

My literary agent David Black first said, "How 'bout a book about Atlanta?" To use the old coach's saying, David is young, hungry and lean, the prototype literary agent for the twenty-first century. With his prodding and cajoling, he is a writer's consummate ally. His colleagues at the David Black Literary Agency, Susan Raihofer and Lev Fruchter, were invaluable assets throughout this project.

And, lastly, in a book about family, I thank my own, the people who have shaped me and continue to shape me. My memory goes two generations back, to Abe Katz, a grandfather who owned the Tip Top Toy Store on Spring Street in Ossining, N.Y., and to Phil Pomerantz, a grandfather who celebrated his bar mitzvah in 1912 on the boat from Russia. During this project, their children—Mom and Dad—gave me the fax machine, the laptop computer and the copier, thereby stealing from me every possible excuse for procrastination. My brothers, Greg and Glenn, called often for updates; Glenn also provided a fine critique as a reader.

Carrie Schwab Pomerantz, my wife and soulmate, not only read the manuscript but lived it day by day, a task more difficult than the writing. At home she was the ballast in our ship. As for Ross and Win, our precious mates on board, I shall borrow (with apologies) from the Grand: "Great God, A'mighty! Just look at those boys!!!!" Already I have begun to share with them pieces from our family history—the toy store on Spring Street and the hopeful Russian boy on the boat bound for the New World.

# Index

✦